Romans

BHGNT

Baylor Handbook on the Greek New Testament
Lidija Novakovic
General Editor

ROMANS

A Handbook on the Greek Text

Stanley E. Porter
David I. Yoon

BAYLOR UNIVERSITY PRESS

Book design by Baylor University Press
Book typeset by Scribe Inc.
Series cover design by Pamela Poll

The Library of Congress has cataloged this book under paperback ISBN 978-1-932792-61-4.
Library of Congress Control Number: 2023939797

CONTENTS

SERIES INTRODUCTION

The Baylor Handbook on the Greek New Testament (BHGNT) is designed to guide new readers and seasoned scholars alike through the intricacies of the Greek text. Each handbook provides a verse-by-verse treatment of the biblical text. Unlike traditional commentaries, however, the BHGNT makes no attempt to expound on the theological meaning or significance of the document under consideration. Instead, the handbooks serve as supplements to commentary proper. Readers of traditional commentaries are sometimes dismayed by the fact that even those that are labeled "exegetical" or "critical" frequently have little to say about the mechanics of the Greek text, and all too often completely ignore the more perplexing grammatical issues. In contrast, the BHGNT offers an accessible and comprehensive, though not exhaustive, treatment of the Greek New Testament, with particular attention given to the grammar of the text. In order to make the handbooks more user-friendly, authors have only selectively interacted with secondary literature. Where there is significant debate on an issue, the handbooks provide a representative sample of scholars espousing each position; when authors adopt a less known stance on the text, they generally list any other scholars who have embraced that position.

The BHGNT, however, is more than a reliable guide to the Greek text of the New Testament. Each author brings unique strengths to the task of preparing the handbook, such as textual criticism, lexical semantics, discourse analysis, or other areas. As a result, students and scholars alike will at times be introduced to ways of looking at the Greek language that they have not encountered before. This feature makes the handbooks valuable not only for intermediate and advanced Greek courses, but also for students and scholars who no longer have the luxury of increasing their Greek proficiency within a classroom context. While handbook authors do not consider modern linguistic theory to be a panacea for all questions exegetical, the BHGNT does aim both to help move linguistic insights into the mainstream of New Testament reference works and, at the same time, to help weed out some of the myths about the Greek language that continue to appear in both scholarly and popular treatments of the New Testament.

Using the Baylor Handbook on the Greek New Testament

Each handbook consists of the following features. The introduction draws readers' attention to some of the distinctive characteristics of the New Testament document under consideration and treats some of the broader issues relating to the text as a whole in a more thorough fashion. In the handbook proper, the biblical text is divided into sections, each of which is introduced with a translation that illustrates how the insights gleaned from the analysis that follows may be expressed in modern English. Following the translation is the heart of the handbook, an extensive analysis of the Greek text. Here, the Greek text of each verse is followed by comments on grammatical, lexical, and text-critical issues. Every verb is parsed for the sake of pedagogical expediency, but nouns are parsed only when the form is unusual or requires additional explanation. Handbook authors may also make use of other features, such as passage overviews between the translation and notes.

Each page of the handbook includes a header to help readers quickly locate comments on a particular passage. Terminology used in the comments that is potentially unfamiliar is included in a glossary in the back of the handbook and/or cross-referenced with the first occurrence of the expression, where an explanation may be found. This is followed by a bibliography of works cited, providing helpful guidance in identifying resources for further research on the Greek text. Each volume concludes with a grammar index and an author index. The list of grammatical phenomena occurring in the biblical text provides a valuable resource for students of Greek wanting to study a particular construction more carefully or Greek instructors needing to develop illustrations, exercises, or exams.

The handbooks assume that users will possess a minimal level of competence with Greek morphology and syntax. Series authors generally utilize traditional labels such as those found in Daniel Wallace's *Greek Grammar Beyond the Basics*. Labels that are drawn from the broader field of modern linguistics are explained at their first occurrence and included in the glossary. Common labels that users may be unfamiliar with are also included in the glossary.

The primary exception to the broad adoption of traditional syntactic labels relates to verb tenses. Most New Testament Greek grammars describe the tense system as being formally fairly simple (only six tenses) but functionally complex. The aorist tense, it is frequently said, can function in a wide variety of ways that are associated with labels such as, "ingressive," "gnomic," "constative," "epistolary," "proleptic," and so forth. Similar functional complexity is posited for the other tenses. Positing such functions, however, typically stems not from a careful analysis of Greek syntax but rather from grappling with the challenges of translating Greek verbs into English. When we carefully examine the Greek verb tenses themselves, we find that the tense forms do not themselves denote semantic features such as ingressive, iterative, or conative; at best they may allow for ingressive, iterative, or conative translations. In addition, the tense labels have frequently led to exegetical claims that go beyond the syntax. For this reason, handbook authors do not generally utilize these labels but seek to express nuances typically associated with them in the translation.

Avoidance of traditional tense labels is based on the insights from the discussions about verbal aspect theory over the last three decades (McKay; Fanning; Porter 1989; Decker; Campbell 2008), which distinguish *Aktionsart* (kind of action) from aspect (subjective portrayal of an action). Many contributors to the BHGNT series agree with the basic premise of verbal aspect theory that tense forms do not grammaticalize time and adopt a three-aspect paradigm that differentiates between perfective aspect, imperfective aspect, and stative aspect. Some authors also concur with Stanley Porter's claim about different levels of semantic density or markedness, i.e., the concept of the perfective aspect as the least marked (background), the imperfective aspect as more marked (foreground), and the stative aspect as the most marked aspect (frontground). There is, however, still significant scholarly disagreement concerning the nature of verbal aspects and their semantic functions. Constantine Campbell, for example, identifies the Greek perfect not with stative aspect, like Porter and others, but with imperfective aspect with heightened remoteness, which he describes as a dynamic action in progress. Steve Runge (2014), conversely, challenges the foundational idea of Porter's verbal aspect theory that Greek tense forms do not have temporal references and argues for a mixed time-aspect system. In light of the ongoing debates about verbal aspect, handbook authors are encouraged to interact with these discussions and incorporate their insights in the analysis of the Greek text.

Deponency

Although series authors will vary in the theoretical approaches they bring to the text, the BHGNT has adopted the same general approach on one important issue: deponency. Traditionally, the label "deponent" has been applied to verbs with middle, passive, or middle/passive morphology that are thought to be "active" in meaning. Introductory grammars tend to put a significant number of middle verbs in the New Testament in this category, despite the fact that some of the standard reference grammars have questioned the validity of the label. Archibald Robertson (332), for example, argues that the label "should not be used at all."

In recent years, a number of scholars have taken up Robertson's quiet call to abandon this label. Carl Conrad's posts on the B-Greek Internet discussion list (beginning in 1997) and his subsequent formalization of those concerns in unpublished papers available on his website have helped flesh out the concerns raised by earlier scholars. Conrad argues that the fundamental polarity in the Greek voice system is not "active-passive" but "active-middle." He further suggests that the verbs that have been traditionally termed "deponent" are by their nature subject-focused, like the verbs that have been regarded as genuine middle.

In a recent article, Jonathan Pennington (61–64) helpfully summarizes the rationale for dispensing with the label, maintaining that widespread use of the term "deponent" stems from two key factors: (1) the tendency to attempt to analyze Greek syntax through reference to English translation—if a workable translation of a middle form appears "active" in English, we conclude that the verb must be active in meaning even though it is middle in form; and (2) the imposition of Latin categories on Greek grammar. Pennington concludes that "most if not all verbs that are considered 'deponent' are in fact truly middle in meaning" (61). The questions that have been raised regarding deponency as a syntactic category, then, are not simply issues that interest a few Greek scholars and linguists but have no bearing on how one understands the text. Rather, if these scholars are correct, the notion of deponency has, at least in some cases, effectively obscured the semantic significance of the middle voice, leading to imprecise readings of the text (see also Bakker; Taylor).

It is not only middle voice verbs, however, that are the focus of attention in this debate. Conrad, Pennington, and others also maintain that deponency is an invalid category for passive verbs that have traditionally been placed in this category. To account for putative passive deponent verbs, these scholars have turned to the evolution of voice morphology in the Greek language. They draw attention to the fact that middle morphology was being replaced by passive morphology (the -θη- morpheme) during the Koine period (see esp. Conrad, 3, 5–6; cf. Pennington, 68; Taylor, 175; Caragounis, 153). Consequently, in the Common Era we find "an increasing number of passive forms without a distinctive passive idea . . . replacing older middle forms" (Pennington, 68). This diachronic argument leads Conrad (5) to conclude that the -θη- morpheme should be treated as a middle/passive rather than a passive morpheme. Such arguments have a sound linguistic foundation and raise serious questions about the legitimacy of the notion "passive deponent."

Should, then, the label "deponent" be abandoned altogether? While more research needs to be done to account for middle/passive morphology in Koine Greek fully, the arguments, which are very briefly summarized above, are both compelling and exegetically significant. "The middle voice needs to be understood in its own status and function as indicating that the subject of a verb is the focus of the verb's action or state" (Conrad, 3; cf. Taylor, 174). Consequently, users of the BHGNT will discover that verbs that are typically labeled "deponent," including some with -θη- morphology, tend to be listed as "middle."

In recognizing that so-called deponent verbs should be viewed as true middles, users of the BHGNT should not fall into the trap of concluding that the middle form emphasizes the subject's involvement in the action of the verb. At times, the middle voice appears simply to be a morphological flag indicating that the verb is intransitive. More frequently, the middle morphology tends to be driven by the "middle" semantics of the verb itself. In other words, the middle voice is sometimes used with the verb not in order to place a focus on the subject's involvement in the action, but precisely because the sense of the lexical form itself involves subject focus.

It is the hope of Baylor University Press, the series editor, and each of the authors that these handbooks will help advance our understanding of the Greek New Testament, be used to further equip the saints for the work of ministry, and fan into flame a love for the Greek New Testament among a new generation of students and scholars.

Martin M. Culy
Founding Series Editor

Lidija Novakovic
Series Editor

PREFACE

A work like this is never the work of one or even two people, but it is always the result of the work of many people who all collaborate to make possible what one or two could not do on their own, or at least could not do as well. This handbook on Romans is just such a project. Although, at times, it seemed as if we were working alone to work through and then finish our analysis of Romans, throughout the entire process we were always working together and supported by a number of other people to ensure that we finally reached the goal. We realize that the process has taken much longer than we had initially anticipated and even latterly imagined that it would take. There were reasons for this, not least all the demands of life, academic administration, teaching, other publishing projects, editorial changes, and, of course, COVID. We offer no excuses for our delay but do offer the explanation that all these elements together conspired against our finishing this handbook in the time that we thought would be required. What we thought would be slight hindrances and annoyances became major obstructions. COVID no doubt was the most deleterious of all. We are now finishing this handbook just as COVID is receding and becoming endemic rather than pandemic. During the time that it was pandemic, our attention was often distracted by much more pressing issues—such as attempting to live our lives and navigate our various responsibilities while living with the specter of COVID. We are sure that we have not yet seen the full effects of COVID on all of us and will not see those effects for a number of years hence. Our suspicion is that COVID has had a far greater effect than anyone imagined, including for those within the academic world. Nevertheless, despite these major problems, we have now been able to finish this handbook and are able to release it for others to use.

We wish to make clear the nature of this handbook. We have noticed that the Baylor handbook series, like many book series and especially many commentary series, has developed over the years. What began as relatively straightforward and basic presentations of the interpretive data of the Greek text have more and more come to resemble full-blown commentaries, with all of the commentary apparatus. This includes not just the formal identifications for which the Baylor handbooks are known but also extended comments on various topics, including some more theological than perhaps exegetical, and citation of extensive secondary literature, much of it not very language-oriented. Perhaps this is inevitable, especially in a series that has developed over a relatively lengthy period of time and continues to develop in various ways.

As a result, we try to make clear that we have attempted to avoid commentary-like analysis and to remain faithful to the notion of a handbook such as this providing the basic analysis of the text that is required. We have referred on occasion to some standard reference tools and the occasional commentary, but we have resisted the temptation to make this into another commentary on Romans. This is and is meant to be a handbook on Romans that guides those with minimal, or even those with informed, knowledge of Greek more fully into the issues involved in the Greek text. We have attempted to present the exegetical data in a straightforward way. We have attempted to use categories that are, themselves, more minimalistic than are often found in other volumes in this series or in the field of New Testament studies itself. We intentionally do this, because we have a particular viewpoint and position on such items—one that we had agreed to at the outset of the project and have attempted to retain and incorporate as the project developed over a much longer period of time than we had originally anticipated. We have not always been successful in meeting our aspirations. We recognize that many topics demand further exposition, even if we have resisted providing that elucidation ourselves. A handbook such as this ends up demanding, with relatively little room to move, that one makes a firm exegetical decision—even if the data are ambiguous. We have therefore had to make such exegetical decisions and select appropriate kinds of wording to describe such decisions, sometimes when we thought the categories might be inadequate for the task or insufficient for understanding of the text. Nevertheless, we have attempted to fulfill all of the requirements of us and to present a useful handbook with the kind of information necessary for someone interested in working on Paul's Letter to the Romans.

One of the authors of this volume, Stanley Porter, was asked to write the handbook on Romans a number of years ago, probably because of his work in linguistics and his long-standing interest in the Letter to the Romans. We wish to thank Dr. Martin Culy for his initial invitation to become a contributor to this series. Porter still remembers the initial meeting when a group of potential contributors gathered together at an academic conference and discussed the viability and possibilities of the project. The result was enthusiasm for a project that, despite some overall parameters, also had reasonable flexibility in it that recognized that there is not just one way to describe the Greek of the New Testament, and certainly not just one way to describe the language of the book of Romans. The continued interest in Romans, whether because of the handbook or of other projects, culminated in a commentary on the book published in 2015, oriented towards a linguistic and literary analysis of Paul's letter. The comments in the volume itself presented the results in English, although the analysis was all based upon the Greek text, due to the nature of the original design of the project. Nevertheless, underneath the presentation of the English text of Romans and the descriptions of its language lay a thorough analysis of the Greek text that provided the foundation. In that sense, this commentary attempted to be a true linguistic commentary on Paul's Letter to the Romans, even if it did not display the kind of apparatus that one might expect in such a project.

The period from initial contact to finishing the commentary on Romans took much longer than originally envisioned. As a result, because of some delays in finishing the manuscript, the second author was enlisted in the project to help bring the handbook to completion. This co-author, David Yoon, had helped by proofreading and editing the Romans commentary, so he was already familiar with the perspective represented in that commentary and envisioned for the handbook. As a result, he was able to bring cohesion and coherence to the Greek analysis. In line with the commentary, this handbook not only focuses on meanings of individual words but incorporates discourse analysis (from a systemic functional linguistics framework). We believe that Greek analysis is not simply relegated to word studies, or even parsings of individual words, as valuable as these may sometimes be, but in observing how word groups, clauses, clause complexes, and other features make meaning in the text. We have attempted to instill this perspective in this handbook as well. We believe that the final product presented to our readers is a defensible explanation of the Greek text of Romans.

As a result, we wish to thank a number of people for helping to make this volume possible and for helping to ensure that it has reached fruition. We wish first to thank Marty Culy for his initial invitation and conversations regarding the handbook. We are sorry that he had to leave the project, but we realize that he has also had many other responsibilities that have demanded his attention. We still look to some of his early handbooks as models of what was envisioned in the series. We also wish to thank Marty's replacement as series editor, Dr. Lidija Novakovic, the current series editor. We realize that she was placed in a difficult situation of having to inherit a project that was not of her original imagining or devising and then seeing it through to completion, despite some cantankerous and sometimes obstinate contributors. We appreciate her Jobian patience, her helpful and detailed feedback on our manuscript, and her willingness to allow us still to flex some of our exegetical muscles in ways that were perhaps not anticipated in the series. It is evident that she took into careful consideration our analysis and offered us many helpful suggestions on our many interpretive choices of words, syntax, and grammar in this letter.

We also wish to thank Dr. Karl Armstrong, who provided an initial template to work with when we began this project. His work enabled us to have a workable platform for assembling and presenting our results. The authors wish to thank each other for their own patience and understanding regarding each other. It has not always been easy to negotiate such a project during a variety of competing factors (did we mention COVID?), but we have now at least reached the end of the journey. Stan wishes, as always but always sincerely, to thank his wife Wendy for all of her support and encouragement, during this and so many other projects. Thanks, Wend. We dedicate this volume to all those exegetes who continue to struggle with Paul's wonderful, timeless, challenging, and incredible Letter to the Romans. Even though he originally sent it to the Romans, our continued work on it has convinced us that this is a letter that was written to and for us.

ABBREVIATIONS

1st	first person
2nd	second person
3rd	third person
acc	accusative
act	active
aor	aorist
BDAG	Danker, *A Greek-English Lexicon of the New Testament*, 2000
BDF	Blass, Debrunner, Funk, *A Greek Grammar of the New Testament*
CEB	Common English Bible
ch.	chapter
cf.	compare (*confer*)
dat	dative
e.g.	for example (*exempli gratia*)
ESV	English Standard Version
fem	feminine
fut	future
gen	genitive
GNB	Good News Bible
GNT	Greek New Testament
i.e.	that is (*id est*)
impf	imperfect
impv	imperative

ind	indicative
inf	infinitive
JB	Jerusalem Bible
KJV	King James Version
LEB	The Lexham English Bible
lit.	literally
LN	Louw and Nida, *Greek-English Lexicon*
LXX	Septuagint
masc	masculine
mid	middle
n.	note
NA[28]	Nestle-Aland, *Novum Testamentum Graece*, 28th ed.
NASB	New American Standard Bible
NEB	New English Bible
NET	New English Translation Bible
neut	neuter
NIV	New International Version
NKJV	New King James Version
nom	nominative
NRSV	New Revised Standard Version
NT	New Testament
opt	optative
OT	Old Testament
pass	passive
pl	plural
plprf	pluperfect
pres	present
prf	perfect
ptc	participle
RSV	Revised Standard Version
SBLGNT	The SBL Greek New Testament
sg	singular

subj	subjunctive
THGNT	Tyndale House Greek New Testament
UBS[5]	The United Bible Societies' Greek New Testament, 5th ed.
v./vv.	verse/verses
voc	vocative

INTRODUCTION

Paul's Letter to the Romans has long been recognized as his major theological masterpiece that deserves full theological attention. Commentaries that especially deal with the theology of this important letter abound, but this handbook serves as a resource that focuses on analyzing the Greek lexicogrammar and syntax of this letter. As such, we do not aim to address the theological issues in Romans, unless they specifically involve the lexicogrammar and syntax.

Romans contains many of the elements of Greco-Roman language and culture, which are identified throughout the analysis. One of the prominent Greco-Roman dialogical techniques that Paul uses is diatribe (Stowers 1981; Song). The use of diatribe is prominent throughout the early chapters but appears in later chapters as well. Diatribe was an ancient technique associated with Socrates that utilized a question-and-answer format to lead the student through logical and illogical thought to arrive at conclusions (similar in some ways to the modern use of "rhetorical questions"). Diatribe is especially prominent in chapters 2–5 and 9–11. Paul also uses a host of conditional structures within the diatribe sections.

Our analysis of the language in Romans is based on the overall framework of Systemic Functional Linguistics (SFL), which has provided a robust theory to analyze language in its social context. The next section provides a brief overview of SFL as applied in this handbook.

Systemic Functional Linguistics and Discourse Analysis

SFL is an approach to linguistics that focuses on language as a social semiotic, that is, language is almost always a social phenomenon (Halliday 1973, 1978; 2014; Halliday and Hasan 1985). It works from the premise that language is used for social reasons. Even when a person speaks to himself/herself, he/she is speaking to an imagined, projected self. Thus, a major question that SFL seeks to understand is *what is the speaker/ writer doing*? In relation to Romans, we are interested in what Paul is *doing* in his Letter to the Romans. In SFL, there are two main functions, or *metafunctions*, of language, overarching functions that language has: ideational and interpersonal. The ideational metafunction of language reflects how language is used to represent thoughts and ideas into meaningful messages and texts. The interpersonal metafunction reflects how language is used to relate those messages to others. A third metafunction, the textual, reflects how the message is organized and structured in a meaningful way. It is primarily this textual metafunction that we are concerned with in this analysis, although ideational and interpersonal metafunctions are analyzed as well.

In this sense, SFL is an approach to discourse analysis that is concerned with meaning as being multi-faceted. Some of the elements of SFL discourse analysis that we utilize in this handbook are identified in the following sections (for more detailed descriptions of SFL discourse analysis, see Porter and O'Donnell; Yoon 2019; Westfall; Reed 1997; among others).

Verbal Aspect and Tense-Forms

Verbal aspect in Greek has been an important topic since the 1990s (cf. Porter 1989; Fanning) and continues to produce thoughtful discussion in Greek studies. It is readily established that the Greek in the New Testament (Koine Greek) is primarily aspectual and not temporal, although we recognize that some proponents of verbal aspect view temporality as a secondary feature in verbal forms. In this handbook, we utilize the term "tense-form" because there is a long history of scholarship using such labels as aorist, present, or perfect, but we also recognize that verbal aspect is the predominant category of the Koine Greek tense-form system.

We work from a tripartite aspectual framework: perfective (aorist tense-form), imperfective (present and imperfect tense-forms), and stative (perfect and pluperfect tense-forms). The perfective aspect represents the verbal process as a complete whole, undifferentiated. The imperfective aspect represents the process as in progress, regardless of how it objectively occurs. The stative aspect represents the process as a state or condition. Aspect relates to the ideational metafunction in that it depicts a process as a particular type (perfective, imperfective, or stative). The choice of aspect also relates to prominence as a textual metafunctional feature, especially in terms of grounding (background, foreground, and frontground) as described in the next section.

A distinction within the imperfective and stative aspects relates to *remoteness*. The semantic difference between the present tense-form and the imperfect tense-form, both conveying imperfective aspect, is that the imperfect tense-form contains an added category of remoteness with its ε-augment. Remoteness can be seen as a distinction between "there" [+remoteness] vs. "here" [−remoteness] (cf. Porter 1989, 207; Lyons, 819–20). Thus, while both forms depict the process as in progress, the imperfect form has an added component of "there-ness."

Prominence, Thematization, and Levels of Discourse

Prominence is a category based on the premise that there are certain parts of texts that stand out more than others and are emphasized. There are various levels at which prominence is related: word group at the lowest level (see below on levels of discourse), clause, clause-complex, and finally paragraph or discourse (see Porter 2009; Yoon 2019, 124–33).

At the word group level (which includes a head term and related modifiers of various types), prominence is determined by the ordering of words. For example, the default word order in a genitive construction would be the head term first, then genitive modifier (e.g., υἱὸς θεοῦ). However, when the order is flipped (θεοῦ υἱός), the fronted element is emphasized over the head term. We also use the label "word group" rather than the more common "phrase" in our analysis, since word group is better defined than phrase (so "prepositional word group" instead of "prepositional phrase").

At the clause level, prominence can be determined by the ordering of clause constituents, also referred to as thematization. The fronted element in the clause is emphasized in the clause; for example, accusative direct objects or prepositional word groups which are fronted are prominent in the clause. At some places, we use the term "thematized" to refer to elements in the clause which are placed in prime position and are prominent.

At the clause complex level, prominence can be determined by the ordering of the clauses. Clause complexes are defined as a grouping of related clauses, usually one primary (main) clause and the other secondary (relative, subordinate, or embedded) clauses. The default order is that primary clauses appear first, then secondary, but when that order is reversed, the fronted element (the secondary clause) is emphasized or prominent in the clause complex. Conditional constructions are an exception to this tendency. In a conditional construction (a special type of clause complex containing two clauses), the protasis usually appears before the apodosis, so when the order is reversed and the apodosis appears first, it is prominent in the clause complex.

At the paragraph or discourse level, prominence can be determined by several factors such as verbal aspect, mood forms, and other morphologically based factors. We focus on aspect in our analysis as the primary category for discourse level prominence. Drawing from the language of grounding, use of the perfective aspect is seen as background and (especially in discursive or expositional texts like Romans) reflects background material in the discourse; it is the least prominent in the discourse. Use of the imperfective aspect is seen as foreground and reflects the mainline of discourse; it is prominent in the discourse as carrying mainline material. Use of the stative aspect is seen as frontground and is the most prominent in the discourse, providing prominent material for emphasis at a discourse/paragraph level.

Cohesion

Another procedure to analyze the textual metafunction of a text is cohesion (Halliday and Hasan 1976). While prominence is interested in dissimilarity within a text, cohesion is interested in similarity. Cohesion reflects how parts of a text are connected to each other, or how textual unity is formed. There are five categories of cohesion we use in this handbook.

Reference is a type of cohesion whereby an item is used to *refer* it to something else in the text, usually anaphoric (occurring before the referent, usually more common) or cataphoric (occurring after the referent, usually rarer). Pronouns are common items used for cohesive reference.

Substitution is related to reference in that the substituting item refers to something else, but it is a substitution of one item for something else. A substantive in apposition to another is an example of cohesive substitution. Another example is when "Jesus" is later referred to as "Lord."

Ellipsis is a type of substitution by omission. It omits an element in the clause that depends on some preceding or following item. For example, when a verb is implied from the previous clause ("He went with her, and I with him"), the verb is elided in the second clause and implied from the first.

Conjunction is one of the most common ways of creating cohesion. The system of Greek conjunctions can become quite complex, with categories such as coordinating or connecting, adversative, causal, inferential, explanatory, emphatic, comparative, conditional, or temporal, among others. Conjunctions connects words, word groups, clauses, and clause-complexes.

Lexical cohesion is created by selection of vocabulary items that are similar to each other. It includes repetition of lexemes or use of synonyms (or words in the same semantic domains), antonyms, hypernyms, hyponyms, and complementary words. Lexical cohesion also has an effect of reflecting prominence for certain words which are repeated in the same co-text (see below on co-text). For example, a cluster of reconciliation words (καταλλάσσω and cognates) in Romans 5 makes it a prominent item in that section.

Syntactical Categories

The categories used in this handbook are largely based on Porter's Greek grammar (1994a). We prefer a system where a minimal number of categories is used to explain the functions of each form, while still maintaining as much continuity as we can with this handbook series. For each form, we minimalize its function to one basic, overarching function. For example, the genitive has the core function of restriction, so the function (or metafunction) of the genitive modifier restricts the head term in some way, which is further determined by its usage in context. However, we realize that the co-text modulates the restricting function of the genitive in various ways, so we use the categories in Porter (1994a). Further, we do not think that the categories of objective genitive and subjective genitive are fitting ways to describe the genitive, as objective and subjective apply verbal categories to substantives (a form of grammatical metaphor), although we recognize that substantives are related to verbal processes. However, we do note places where some may label a genitive as an objective or subjective genitive.

We also prefer using nominative of address instead of vocative in the plural, as we do not think that the so-called vocative form is a distinct category from the nominative.

Based on our view of verbal aspect, which includes aspectual vagueness for a few verbs, we replace the tense-forms of "present" and "imperfect" with "unaugmented" or "augmented" (respectively) for those aspectually vague words like εἰμί. Aspectually vague words are so called because they do not contain the full range of aspectual choices. Thus, the difference between augmented and unaugmented is simply that of remoteness and non-remoteness.

The series introduction describes deponency already, and we endorse the view that deponency is a mistaken notion. In general, voice-forms reflect causality and agency (these are synonymous in our view), which can be reflected in the following sets of binary choices. The initial choice is between direct causality (active) and indirect causality (non-active). Between the choices for indirect causality, there are two further choices: internal (middle), and external (passive). In other words, the active voice reflects direct causality, the middle voice reflects indirect and internal causality, and the passive voice reflects indirect and external causality. While active and passive voices tend to be understood fairly easily, the middle voice needs further explanation. Our view is that the middle voice indicates indirect causality/agency, in that the direct cause of the verbal process is not specified (even if there is a grammatical subject of the verb; see Mathewson). As an example in English, *the glass broke* does not specify what/who caused the glass to break—the glass probably did not cause itself to break, even if it is the grammatical subject of the clause. The middle voice is not only indirect but internal, in that the cause is associated with the subject. Again, as in the English example *the glass broke*, while the direct cause or agent is unspecified, the process of breaking is represented as internal and concerns the glass. In contrast, the passive voice version, *the glass was broken*, represents the cause or agent as external. While not every voice-form is described in detail in the handbook, those that may be significant are noted.

Further, we use the term "agent" (lowercase) for the cause (hence causality and agency are used interchangeably) instead of the SFL term Actor to refer to the *logical* subject of the process (contra grammatical subject). We, however, use the SFL term Goal (capitalized) to refer to the *logical* direct object, or the one to whom the action/process is directed. In passive voice clauses, for example, the agent is typically represented by a direct object or a prepositional word group, and the Goal is represented by the grammatical subject.

Context and Co-Text

In SFL, context is a broad umbrella term for various types of context. Co-text is used to refer to the surrounding text, before and after the text in question, whether immediate or remote. It is often simply referred to as context in biblical studies, but we prefer co-text because it more specifically identifies the type of context referred to. There is also the context of situation, which is the non-textual circumstances in which the text is found, and the context of culture, which reflects the semiotic and semantic potentiality in which the text occurs.

Outline of Romans

A. 1:1–7 Opening
B. 1:8–15 Thanksgiving
C. 1:16–11:36 Body
    1:16–17 Body Introduction and Theme
    1:18–11:32 Body Proper
        1:18–4:25 The Human Condition and Its Forensic Solution
            1:18–2:11 Human Sinfulness
                1:18–32 Condemnation of Humanity
                2:1–11 Does Anyone Escape Paul's Depiction of
                Humanity?
            2:12–3:20 The Law of God
                2:12–16 Law and Humanity
                2:17–3:8 Jewish Advantage
                3:9–20 Human Condition
            3:21–4:25 Solution to the Human Condition
                3:21–26 God's Righteousness
                3:27–31 Exclusion of Boasting
                4:1–25 Example of Abraham
        5:1–21 Climax of Paul's Argument: Reconciliation
            5:1–11 Reconciliation, God, and Humanity
            5:12–21 Christ and Adam
        6:1–7:25 The Christian Life
            6:1–7:6 Life in Christ
                6:1–14 Status in Christ
                6:15–7:6 Obligations to Christ
            7:7–25 Continuing Problem of Sin in Relation to Law
                7:7–12 Function of the Law
                7:13–25 Sin, Law, and Faith
        8:1–39 Life of the Spirit
            8:1–17 Description of Life in the Spirit
            8:18–30 Glorification and Earthly Renewal
            8:31–39 Doxology
        9:1–11:32 Important Retrogression Regarding Israel
            9:1–13 Israel in God's Economy
            9:14–29 God's Justice and Mercy
            9:30–10:21 The Destiny of Israel
            11:1–32 Israel's Final Salvation
    11:33–36 Body Closing: Doxology
D. 12:1–15:33 Parenesis
    12:1–2 Introductory Transition

A HANDBOOK ON THE GREEK TEXT OF ROMANS

Romans 1:1-7

[1]Paul, a slave of Christ Jesus, a called apostle, one who is set apart for the good news of God, [2]which he announced beforehand through his prophets in the holy Scriptures [3]concerning his son, who was born from the seed of David according to the flesh, [4]who was designated as Son of God in power on the basis of the Spirit of holiness from resurrection of the dead, Jesus Christ our Lord, [5]through whom we received grace and apostleship resulting in faithful obedience among all nations for his name, [6]among whom indeed you yourselves are called of Jesus Christ, [7]to all who are in Rome, beloved of God, called holy ones. Grace to you and peace from God our father and Lord Jesus Christ.

The first section of Paul's Letter to the Romans is the formal letter opening. The letter opening contains the indication of the sender and the recipient, and the greetings (see Exler, 23–68; Stowers 1986; Schnider and Stenger, 3–68; Adams; Tite; cf. White 1972, for examples). The standard Greco-Roman letter of the first century had the opening X (nominative) to Y (dative) and "greetings" (χαίρειν). Each of these elements could be modified for further description. In Rom 1:1–7, Paul has adapted this letter opening in several ways. These include his expansion of the designation of the sender and his change from the infinitive ("greetings") to the bipartite noun phrase ("grace and peace").

1:1 Παῦλος δοῦλος Χριστοῦ Ἰησοῦ, κλη τὰ ι ἀπόστολος ἀφωρισμένος εἰς εὐαγγέλιον θεοῦ,

Παῦλος. Nominative absolute. Paul begins the letter, as he does in all of his letters, with his Greek name, used in the nominative case as the subject of the construction, a verbless clause. "Paul" is his cognomen, but we do not know Paul's other names (his praenomen or formal name or his nomen or tribal name). We do know his supernomen or alternative name, Saul, a Jewish name he may have taken when he studied under Gamaliel in Jerusalem. Paul elaborates upon the use of his name with a series of three modifying phrases, all in the nominative case.

δοῦλος Χριστοῦ Ἰησοῦ. The first modifying phrase consisting of the noun ("slave") and the modifying genitive ("Christ Jesus").

δοῦλος. Nominative in apposition to Παῦλος.

Χριστοῦ Ἰησοῦ. Possessive genitive, modifying δοῦλος. For those who accept the categories of subjective and objective genitives, this may be seen as an objective genitive, since Jesus Christ would be the object of serving or being enslaved (see Introduction for an explanation on genitive categories). Paul's designation as slave indicates that he is totally owned by Christ Jesus. Paul alternates between "Christ Jesus" as given here and "Jesus Christ" (Ἰησοῦ Χριστοῦ). The use of "Christ" indicates more than simply a name, but an honorific, probably indicating the recognition of Jesus as Messiah (see Novenson 2010 and 2012). The word order Χριστοῦ Ἰησοῦ is found in 𝔓[10] B 81 and some versions (accepted by NA[28] and UBS[5]), while the order Ἰησοῦ Χριστοῦ is found in 𝔓[26] ℵ A G K L P Ψ 33 104 630 1175 1241 1505 1506 1739 1881 2464 *l*249 𝔐 and several versions. Despite the number of manuscripts, the better early reading is Χριστοῦ Ἰησοῦ.

κλητὸς ἀπόστολος. The second modifying phrase, consisting of the verbal adjective ("called") and the noun ("apostle"). If this word group is regarded as a single unit, it functions as the nominative in apposition to Παῦλος. ἀπόστολος indicates an emissary, here of Christ Jesus. This phrase may be interpreted as consisting of two separate appositional units ("called" and "apostle"), but the use of the adjective with the noun is more likely a single unit.

ἀφωρισμένος εἰς εὐαγγέλιον θεοῦ. The third modifying phrase, consisting of the participle with the adjunctive prepositional word group.

ἀφωρισμένος. Prf pass ptc masc nom sg ἀφορίζω (substantival). Nominative in apposition to Παῦλος. The passive voice of ἀφορίζω ("to set apart" or "to separate") indicates indirect, external causality, here not specifying Christ Jesus as the cause of this separation. The use of the perfect tense-form (stative aspect) indicates prominence of the verbal phrase in balance with the other two appositional phrases. In other words, Paul highlights himself being set apart over the other two identifications here of being a slave and an apostle. This does not necessarily mean it is more inherently important, but that this is what he highlights in this part of the letter.

εἰς εὐαγγέλιον. Purpose. εὐαγγέλιον refers to the "good news," or alternatively translated "gospel." It was used in Roman inscriptions to indicate the good news that accompanied auspicious circumstances, such as the birth of an emperor (see the Priene inscription; Ehrenberg and Jones, 81–83).

θεοῦ. Genitive of origin or source, modifying εὐαγγέλιον.

1:2 ὃ προεπηγγείλατο διὰ τῶν προφητῶν αὐτοῦ ἐν γραφαῖς ἁγίαις

ὃ. Accusative direct object of προεπηγγείλατο. The relative pronoun refers anaphorically to εὐαγγέλιον in 1:1. The relative clause hypotactically enhances description of the good news.

προεπηγγείλατο. Aor mid ind 3rd sg προεπαγγέλλω. The middle voice indicates internal, indirect causality (see Introduction). Reference to the prophets and Scriptures indicates past reference of the clause with perfective aspect of the verb. The prefixed preposition πρό indicates that the announcement occurred previously or beforehand. The verb προεπηγγείλατο is modified by three adjunctive uses of prepositional word groups in 1:2–3: διὰ τῶν προφητῶν αὐτοῦ, ἐν γραφαῖς ἁγίαις, and περὶ τοῦ υἱοῦ αὐτοῦ.

διὰ τῶν προφητῶν. Instrumental. It refers to secondary or intermediate agency—the channel through which the proclamation occurred. God is the implied ultimate source behind the speaking of the prophets. The article is used to indicate the prophets taken as a group in their entirety. This is the first of three prepositional word groups further elaborating on this announcement by God.

αὐτοῦ. Possessive genitive, modifying τῶν προφητῶν. The antecedent of the pronoun is God.

ἐν γραφαῖς ἁγίαις. Locative or possibly instrumental. The prepositional word group indicates tertiary instrumentality—not the source or the channel but the means by which the proclamation was made. This is the second of three prepositional word groups regarding God's announcement. The placement of the adjective after its head term is usual for Pauline adjectival modification. The designation of γραφαῖς as "holy" indicates that these are not merely "writings" (the noun indicates any kind of writing), but the holy writings of Israel, the Scriptures.

1:3 περὶ τοῦ υἱοῦ αὐτοῦ τοῦ γενομένου ἐκ σπέρματος Δαυὶδ κατὰ σάρκα,

περὶ τοῦ υἱοῦ. Reference (or focal). This is the third of three prepositional word groups regarding God's announcement, here regarding the
focus of the announcement. God's son (τοῦ υἱοῦ αὐτοῦ) is elaborated
by two parallel participial clauses: τοῦ γενομένου ἐκ σπέρματος Δαυὶδ
κατὰ σάρκα (1:3) and τοῦ ὁρισθέντος υἱοῦ θεοῦ ἐν δυνάμει κατὰ πνεῦμα
ἁγιωσύνης ἐξ ἀναστάσεως νεκρῶν (1:4).

αὐτοῦ. Possessive genitive, modifying τοῦ υἱοῦ.

τοῦ γενομένου. Aor mid ptc masc gen sg γίνομαι (attributive). The
articular participle modifies τοῦ υἱοῦ (second attributive position) and
is parallel with the articular participle in 1:4, τοῦ ὁρισθέντος. The verb
of being or becoming indicates here coming into human existence,
based upon the following adjunctive prepositional word groups.

ἐκ σπέρματος. Instrumental (causal, agentive). σπέρματος is singular, pointing to the son as the singular seed (cf. Rom 4:13, 16, 18; Gal
3:16, 19, 29).

Δαυὶδ. Genitive of source or origin (indeclinable proper noun),
modifying σπέρματος. David is the source or origin of the seed.

κατὰ σάρκα. Standard or basis. The fleshly world or the realm of
human existence is the basis for speaking of the son as being from the
seed of David.

1:4 τοῦ ὁρισθέντος υἱοῦ θεοῦ ἐν δυνάμει κατὰ πνεῦμα ἁγιωσύνης ἐξ
ἀναστάσεως νεκρῶν, Ἰησοῦ Χριστοῦ τοῦ κυρίου ἡμῶν,

τοῦ ὁρισθέντος. Aor pass ptc masc gen sg ὁρίζω (attributive). The
participle either modifies the head term τοῦ . . . υἱοῦ in this verse, in
which case the genitive phrase τοῦ ὁρισθέντος υἱοῦ functions as the
genitive in apposition to τοῦ υἱοῦ from v. 3 ("concerning his son . . . ,
the designated son"), or it modifies the previous τοῦ υἱοῦ in 1:3 ("concerning his son . . . who was designated . . ."). The latter is more likely,
with "son" here as the object of the designation ("designated as son").
The verb appears without the prefixed preposition ἀπό but with the article. The participial clause is parallel with the one in 1:3, functioning as
a modifier of τοῦ υἱοῦ. The passive voice of the verb does not specify
agency, although external, but the implication is that this was an action
of God even if mediated.

υἱοῦ. Predicate genitive.

θεοῦ. Possessive genitive, modifying υἱοῦ. Since the entire participial
clause serves as a modifier of "son" in 1:3, the use of the term "son of

God" appears redundant. The redundancy is alleviated by the fact that the designation is of a particular type of son. The "son of God" is characterized by the use of three prepositional word groups that are closely associated with who the son is.

ἐν δυνάμει. State or condition ("the son of God in power" or "the son of God invested with power"; cf. Cranfield, 1:62).

κατὰ πνεῦμα. Standard or basis. Here, the basis of being designated as the son of God is the "spirit of holiness."

ἁγιωσύνης. Genitive of definition, explaining πνεῦμα ("a spirit defined by holiness"), or genitive of description, modifying πνεῦμα ("a spirit characterized by holiness"). This phrase is unique to the NT. The designation πνεῦμα ἁγιωσύνης may be of a human spirit characterized by holiness that warrants elevation to sonship status (the adoptionist view; cf. Kirk, 41–42) or, more likely, a Semitically dependent paraphrase for the divine Spirit of God.

ἐξ ἀναστάσεως. Temporal (the designation as "son" in his power occurred from the time of the resurrection of the dead [the adoptionist interpretation]) or means (the designation as "son" in his power occurred by means of the resurrection of the dead). The resurrection referred to here is the resurrection of Jesus Christ.

νεκρῶν. Genitive of source or origin, modifying ἀναστάσεως. The plural of "dead" probably indicates the realm of dead people. The use of the plural modifying genitive, νεκρῶν, might imply that the resurrection of Jesus was the beginning of an entire movement called the resurrection of dead people, not just his resurrection (see 1 Corinthians 15) or that it is a resurrection of Jesus from the realm of dead people.

Ἰησοῦ Χριστοῦ. Genitive in apposition to τοῦ υἱοῦ in 1:3. In this instance the phrase "Jesus Christ" is used (rather than Christ Jesus as in 1:1). The name of the person is Jesus, and his honorific designator is Messiah.

τοῦ κυρίου. Genitive in apposition to Ἰησοῦ Χριστοῦ. This phrase probably reflects frequent translation in the Septuagint of the name of God as κύριος.

ἡμῶν. Possessive genitive, modifying τοῦ κυρίου.

1:5 δι' οὗ ἐλάβομεν χάριν καὶ ἀποστολὴν εἰς ὑπακοὴν πίστεως ἐν πᾶσιν τοῖς ἔθνεσιν ὑπὲρ τοῦ ὀνόματος αὐτοῦ,

δι' οὗ. Instrumental (secondary or intermediate agency). The antecedent of the relative pronoun is Ἰησοῦ Χριστοῦ τοῦ κυρίου ἡμῶν (1:4). This is the first of two relative prepositional clauses that hypotactically enhance description of Ἰησοῦ Χριστοῦ τοῦ κυρίου ἡμῶν (the other is in 1:6).

ἐλάβομεν. Aor act ind 1st pl λαμβάνω. Contextual indicators do not make clear whether this is past-referring or present-referring in a general sense. The verb is adjunctively modified by three prepositional word groups: εἰς ὑπακοὴν πίστεως, ἐν πᾶσιν τοῖς ἔθνεσιν, and ὑπὲρ τοῦ ὀνόματος αὐτοῦ.

χάριν καὶ ἀποστολὴν. Compound accusative direct object of ἐλάβομεν. Χάρις is regularly used in Paul to indicate God's gracious benefaction (cf. Moffatt; Breytenbach). The use may imply the Roman patronage system, in which clients were dependent upon beneficence of others (Crook). ἀποστολή indicates the call to engaging in the mission of spreading the good news.

εἰς ὑπακοὴν. Result or possibly purpose. Thus, grace and apostleship results in faithful obedience.

πίστεως. Genitive of definition or description, modifying ὑπακοὴν. "Obedience" is described as "of faith" or "faithful."

ἐν πᾶσιν τοῖς ἔθνεσιν. Distributional ("among all nations"). The adjective πᾶσιν indicates extent of distribution. The word ἔθνος indicates ethnicity, the basis for distinctions among peoples in the ancient world (as opposed to nationality).

ὑπὲρ τοῦ ὀνόματος. Beneficial.

αὐτοῦ. Possessive genitive, modifying τοῦ ὀνόματος.

1:6 ἐν οἷς ἐστε καὶ ὑμεῖς κλητοὶ Ἰησοῦ Χριστοῦ,

ἐν οἷς. Distributional ("among whom"). The antecedent of the relative pronoun is ἔθνεσιν (1:5). This is the second of two parallel prepositional relative clauses that are used hypotactically to enhance description of Ἰησοῦ Χριστοῦ τοῦ κυρίου ἡμῶν.

ἐστε. Unaugmented ind 2nd pl εἰμί. This verb is aspectually vague (see Porter 1989, 1994).

καὶ. Adverbial use of καὶ used for emphasis.

ὑμεῖς. Nominative subject of ἐστε. The use of explicit pronoun, which is not necessary with 2nd pl verb, emphasizes subject of verb.

κλητοὶ. Predicate adjective.

Ἰησοῦ Χριστοῦ. Possessive genitive, modifying κλητοὶ. See 1:1 and 1:4 regarding alternation of "Jesus Christ" and "Christ Jesus."

1:7 πᾶσιν τοῖς οὖσιν ἐν Ῥώμῃ ἀγαπητοῖς θεοῦ, κλητοῖς ἁγίοις, χάρις ὑμῖν καὶ εἰρήνη ἀπὸ θεοῦ πατρὸς ἡμῶν καὶ κυρίου Ἰησοῦ Χριστοῦ.

πᾶσιν τοῖς οὖσιν. Dative indirect object of verbless clause (typically used of the recipient of the letter). The adjective πᾶσιν appears in predicate position and functions substantivally with the following articular participle.

τοῖς οὖσιν. Ptc masc dat pl εἰμί (attributive). On the function, see above.

ἐν Ῥώμῃ. Locative. The phrase ἐν Ῥώμῃ is omitted in a few relatively insignificant manuscripts (G 1739^mg 1908^mg it^g Origen) but found in the vast majority of the others, including 𝔓^10 𝔓^26mg ℵ A B C D^abs1 K P Ψ 33 81 88 104 181 Byzantine text, most lectionaries, and many versions. Some later writers may have wished to universalize the Letter to the Romans by omitting the reference. Without the reference to Rome, the phrasing is πᾶσιν τοῖς οὖσιν ἀγαπητοῖς θεοῦ ("to all those who are beloved of God").

ἀγαπητοῖς. Dative in apposition to τοῖς οὖσιν ἐν Ῥώμῃ. The adjective ἀγαπητοῖς is here used as a substantive.

θεοῦ. Genitive of source or origin, modifying ἀγαπητοῖς. The source of "beloved" is "God." Combined with the adjective ἀγαπητοῖς, source or origin has the idea of agency with it.

κλητοῖς ἁγίοις. Dative in apposition to πᾶσιν τοῖς οὖσιν. The adjective ἁγίοις is used as a substantive. Paul describes himself as a "called apostle" in 1:1 and here his audience as "called saints."

χάρις . . . καὶ εἰρήνη. Nominative absolutes. Paul has transformed the traditional epistolary greeting from the use of the infinitive χαίρειν to a compound noun phrase common to all of his letters. Χάρις has already been used in 1:5 but is used here as part of the formal greeting. This word, often translated "grace," indicates divine beneficence, extended by God to the recipients of the letter. Εἰρήνη indicates the lack of strife with God and with fellow believers. The use of "peace" may indicate Paul's greeting combining Greek and Jewish elements, but parallel instances outside of Paul are hard to find. A better explanation is Paul's use of active (grace) and passive (peace) characteristics of the Christian life.

ὑμῖν. Dative of advantage. The pronoun refers anaphorically to the Roman Christians (πᾶσιν τοῖς οὖσιν ἐν Ῥώμῃ) to whom the letter is addressed. It is used only with the first of the two nouns in Paul's greeting, although the notion may well be extended to the second.

ἀπὸ θεοῦ . . . καὶ κυρίου. Source. The source of grace and peace is God our father and the Lord Jesus Christ, with the scope of the preposition extending over the entire compound genitive word group.

πατρὸς. Genitive in apposition to θεοῦ.
ἡμῶν. Possessive genitive, modifying πατρὸς.
Ἰησοῦ Χριστοῦ. Genitive in apposition to κυρίου (see 1:1, 6).

Romans 1:8–15

[8]First of all, I give thanks to my God through Jesus Christ concerning all of you, because your faith is proclaimed in the entire world. [9]For God, whom I worship in my spirit in the good news of his son, is my witness how unceasingly I have remembrance of you [10]always in my prayers, requesting if somehow already I can expect to have my way made by the will of God to come to you. [11]For I long to see you, so that I may share some spiritual gift with you in order for you to be strengthened, [12]that is, to be mutually encouraged with you through both your faith and mine with each other. [13]I do not want you to be ignorant, brothers [and sisters], that many times I intended to come to you, and I was hindered until now, so that I may have certain fruit among you also, just as also among the rest of the nations. [14]To both Greeks and barbarians, to both wise and ignorant, I am a debtor. [15]Thus my eagerness to proclaim good news also to you who are in Rome.

Verses 8–15 form the second major part of the Letter to the Romans, the thanksgiving (see Schubert; O'Brien; Reed 1996; Pao; Arzt-Grabner; Collins). The thanksgiving is greatly enhanced from its secular counterpart, consisting of the expansion of the transitional health wish. Whereas the health wish is a brief statement usually addressed to one of the gods to ensure the health of the author, the thanksgiving is not addressed to a local god but to the God of Israel and his son, Jesus Christ. Paul expands this section into its own part of the letter in order to emphasize his thanks to God for his recipients. Paul is more effusive in his thanks in other letters (e.g., Phil 1:3–11 or 1 Thess 1:2–10), but his thanks for the Roman Christians appears to be genuine in light of his travel plans.

1:8 Πρῶτον μὲν εὐχαριστῶ τῷ θεῷ μου διὰ Ἰησοῦ Χριστοῦ περὶ πάντων ὑμῶν ὅτι ἡ πίστις ὑμῶν καταγγέλλεται ἐν ὅλῳ τῷ κόσμῳ.

Πρῶτον. Adverbial accusative. Paul's "first" is not followed by a "second."
μὲν. Postpositive particle, often used with δέ to mark contrasting elements. There is no contrasting δέ used here, however.
εὐχαριστῶ. Pres act ind 1st sg εὐχαριστέω. The use of the present tense-form (imperfective aspect) provides the mainline in most

expositional (including epistolary) discourse. Paul does similarly in Romans, with the main verbs of the mainline of this thanksgiving being in the present tense-form/imperfective aspect (εὐχαριστῶ, ἐπιποθῶ, and θέλω). The clause πρῶτον μὲν εὐχαριστῶ indicates Paul's transition from the opening to the thanksgiving ("First of all, I give thanks"). The two transitional words are reinforced by the use of the imperfective aspect of the present tense-form of the verb to introduce the thanksgiving as a new stage in Paul's argument.

τῷ θεῷ. Dative complement of εὐχαριστέω.

μου. Possessive genitive, modifying τῷ θεῷ.

διὰ Ἰησοῦ Χριστοῦ. Instrumental (secondary or intermediate agency). This is the first of two adjunctive prepositional word groups that modify εὐχαριστέω. The object of Paul's thanks is God, but the means of his thanksgiving is Jesus Christ.

περὶ πάντων ὑμῶν. Reference (or focal). This is the second of two adjunctive prepositional word groups that modify εὐχαριστέω. It marks the focus of Paul's thanksgiving here, "all of you." The modifying adjective πάντων is used to indicate extent with ὑμῶν.

ὅτι. Introduces a causal clause, which provides the reason for Paul's thanksgiving ("I give thanks . . . because your faith is proclaimed in the whole world") or a clausal complement (indirect discourse) of εὐχαριστῶ that provides the content of Paul's thanksgiving ("I give thanks . . . that your faith is proclaimed in the whole world"). The use here is probably causal because the verb εὐχαριστέω is not usually followed by a content clause. The hypotactic use of the clause enhances Paul's words of thanks to God for the Roman Christians.

ἡ πίστις. Nominative subject of καταγγέλλεται.

ὑμῶν. Possessive genitive, modifying ἡ πίστις.

καταγγέλλεται. Pres pass ind 3rd sg καταγγέλλω. The form of the verb may be either middle (internal causality) or passive (external causality). Even though there is no expressed agent of the action, the inanimate subject indicates an implied (external) agency by an unspecified agent, presumably those who are aware of the faith of the Roman Christians.

ἐν ὅλῳ τῷ κόσμῳ. Locative. The preposition is not being used instrumentally (tertiary or instrumental agency), as the object is not an instrument. ὅλῳ stands in the predicate position even when it functions as an attribute, as here (cf. BDAG, 704.1.b.α). The hyperbolic phrase "the entire world" is used to refer to the known Roman world, or at least the known Roman world with which Paul was acquainted (as he writes from Corinth). Paul is already familiar with some Christians in Rome (see 16:3–16).

1:9 μάρτυς γάρ μού ἐστιν ὁ θεός, ᾧ λατρεύω ἐν τῷ πνεύματί μου ἐν τῷ εὐαγγελίῳ τοῦ υἱοῦ αὐτοῦ, ὡς ἀδιαλείπτως μνείαν ὑμῶν ποιοῦμαι

μάρτυς. Predicate nominative. Μάρτυς, occurring only here in Romans, is not the grammatical subject, since it does not have the article attached to it. Colwell's rule, or rather McGoughy's modified version of it, applies here. When there are two substantives with a linking verb (such as εἰμί), the subject is either (1) the demonstrative or relative pronoun, if one of them is a demonstrative or relative pronoun, (2) the one with the article, if only one is articular, or (3) the first one, if both are articular (Colwell; McGaughy; Porter 1994a, 109–10). Μάρτυς, as the predicate nominative occurring before the subject, is placed in thematic clausal position to reflect clausal prominence (emphasis).

γάρ. The postpositive conjunction γάρ is found frequently in Romans. In most instances, as here, it is inferential, that is, it leads to what can be inferred from what has been previously stated.

μού. Possessive genitive, modifying μάρτυς.

ἐστιν. Unaugmented ind 3rd sg εἰμί.

ὁ θεός. Nominative subject of ἐστιν. The article marks θεός as the grammatical subject of the clause.

ᾧ. Dative direct object of λατρεύω. The relative pronoun introduces a clause that is used hypotactically to enhance the description of God.

λατρεύω. Pres act ind 1st sg λατρεύω. The verb is adjunctively modified by two prepositional word groups, both using the same preposition ἐν. Even though the two uses seem to be similar in function, the objects of the prepositions denote two separate realms, one of personal location and the other of topical location.

ἐν τῷ πνεύματί. Locative (sphere or realm). Πνεῦμα is used of any immaterial being, here of the human spirit, as indicated by the following genitive modifier μου. Paul says here that he worships God in the realm of his spirit. The double accent on πνεύματί is the result of the following word (μου) being enclitic, so an additional accent on the ultima is placed for pronunciation purposes.

μου. Possessive genitive, modifying τῷ πνεύματί.

ἐν τῷ εὐαγγελίῳ. Locative (sphere or realm). The "good news" is the second sphere or realm where Paul worships God. Like his spirit, he indicates the realm in which he worships him, the realm of the message that originates in God's son (as opposed to other notices of good news, such as the emperor). Alternatively, the prepositional word group can function instrumentally, with the good news beings the means by which Paul worships God, although the former is more likely.

τοῦ υἱοῦ. Genitive of definition or description. The good news is further defined or described as "of his son." While some may wish to see this as an objective genitive, we do not think the categories of objective and subjective genitives accurately reflect the grammatical function of the genitive and mix verbal and nominal categories (see Introduction for an explanation on this).

αὐτοῦ. Possessive genitive, modifying τοῦ υἱοῦ. The pronominal referent is ὁ θεός.

ὡς. Particle which functions as a "marker of discourse content" after μάρτυς (BDAG, 1105.5; LN 90.21) that introduces a declarative clause. Its use is similar to ὅτι, but it places more focus on manner (Culy, Parsons, and Stigall, 212).

ἀδιαλείπτως. Adverb of manner ("unceasingly") that modifies ποιοῦμαι. The placement of the adverb up front in this clause signifies thematic prominence. Paul's emphasis in this clause and the following participial clause (v. 10) is his "constant" remembrance and prayer for the Roman Christians.

μνείαν. Accusative direct object of ποιοῦμαι. This noun is used only here in Romans, but occasionally in Paul's other letters (Eph 1:16; Phil 1:3; 1 Thess 1:2; 3:6; 2 Tim 1:3; Phlm 1:4).

ὑμῶν. Genitive of definition, delineating μνείαν as "your" or "of you."

ποιοῦμαι. Pres mid ind 1st sg ποιέω. The middle voice indicates indirect, internal causality, with Paul as the implied grammatical subject.

1:10 πάντοτε ἐπὶ τῶν προσευχῶν μου, δεόμενος εἴ πως ἤδη ποτὲ εὐοδωθήσομαι ἐν τῷ θελήματι τοῦ θεοῦ ἐλθεῖν πρὸς ὑμᾶς.

πάντοτε ἐπὶ τῶν προσευχῶν μου. It is not clear whether this word group is to be construed with ἀδιαλείπτως μνείαν ὑμῶν ποιοῦμαι (1:9) as further adjunctive modification or with the following participle δεόμενος and the conditional clause (1:10). We have interpreted the construction according to the first option because it seems to make better sense of the verse, and have placed a comma after μου (which is absent in NA[28] but included in SBLGNT) to indicate this. This makes the participle δεόμενος an adjunctive (adverbial) use of the participle in relation to the governing verb ποιοῦμαι.

πάντοτε. Adverb (temporal). It is used only here in Romans, continuing the idea of Paul's constant remembrance of the Roman Christians. The use of both ἀδιαλείπτως and πάντοτε may seem redundant, but the redundancy may be for an emphatic effect.

ἐπὶ τῶν προσευχῶν. Positional (figurative). The figurative extension of the positional function is temporal; Paul's "requesting" is during his prayers.

μου. Possessive genitive, modifying τῶν προσευχῶν.

δεόμενος. Pres mid ptc masc nom sg δέομαι (means or temporal). The participle modifies the main verb ποιοῦμαι in 1:9, showing the means of how Paul makes his remembrance of the Roman Christians (by requesting that he may succeed in coming to Rome) or indicating the time when Paul makes his remembrance of the Roman Christians (while requesting that he may succeed in coming to Rome). The verb of speaking is used to project the content of Paul's words of prayer.

εἴ. Introduces the protasis of a first-class conditional—the content of Paul's prayer.

πως. Emphatic adjunctive particle.

ἤδη. Temporal adjunctive adverb.

ποτὲ. Temporal adjunctive particle. The three adjunctive uses of particles, along with the introductory conditional conjunction, indicate the tentativeness of Paul's assertion. In fact, it is not so much an assertion as a hope (see use of the future form of the following verb). The tentativeness is marked by the thematic positioning of all three of the particles/adverbs.

εὐοδωθήσομαι. Fut pass ind 1st sg εὐοδόω. The future form indicates that Paul, as the ungrammaticalized subject of the clause, has the expectation of making his way to Rome (on the semantics of expectation with the future form, see Porter 1994a, 43–45). The passive voice indicates external causality, indicated by the following prepositional word group.

ἐν τῷ θελήματι. Instrumental, indicating tertiary or indirect causality.

τοῦ θεοῦ. Possessive genitive or genitive of source, modifying τῷ θελήματι. The will belongs to God, as the one Paul indicates as effecting the possibility of his making his way to Rome.

ἐλθεῖν. Aor act inf ἔρχομαι (result). The infinitival clause, ἐλθεῖν πρὸς ὑμᾶς, expresses the result of the main verb εὐοδωθήσομαι. Paul's expectation is for a way to be made (by God) to come to Rome.

πρὸς ὑμᾶς. Directional (movement toward).

1:11 ἐπιποθῶ γὰρ ἰδεῖν ὑμᾶς, ἵνα τι μεταδῶ χάρισμα ὑμῖν πνευματικὸν εἰς τὸ στηριχθῆναι ὑμᾶς,

ἐπιποθῶ. Pres act ind 1st sg ἐπιποθέω. Despite Paul's tentativeness regarding his making his way to Rome (see 1:10), he retains his desire to see the Roman Christians.

γὰρ. Postpositive explanatory conjunction.

ἰδεῖν. Aor act inf ὁράω (complementary). The infinitival clause, ἰδεῖν ὑμᾶς, functions as the complement or object of the clause with ἐπιποθῶ as the main verb. Paul says that he desires or longs to see the Roman Christians.

ὑμᾶς. Accusative direct object of ἰδεῖν.

ἵνα. Introduces a purpose clause. The use of the ἵνα clause indicates hypotactic enhancement of Paul's expression of desire to see the Romans. He enhances the main clause by elucidating the purpose of his desire to see them: it is so that he might share something with them. Paul's purpose is divided into two parts; the first, the ἵνα clause, is then restated with the redefining clause of 1:12.

τι . . . χάρισμα . . . πνευματικὸν. Accusative direct object of μεταδῶ. This phrase is characterized by a discontinuous structure; the indefinite pronoun τι is separated from the noun it modifies, χάρισμα, by the main verb of the clause, and the adjective πνευματικὸν is separated from the noun it modifies by the indirect object of the verb. This structure serves to place this word group in thematic position, especially its characteristic of being some kind of a gift. Χάρισμα refers to a "grace gift," that is, a gift given graciously and generously (LN 57.103). This "grace gift" is defined by means of the attributive use of the adjective πνευματικὸν. This makes the grace gift a "spiritual" one.

μεταδῶ. Aor act subj 1st sg μεταδίδωμι. Subjunctive with ἵνα. This is the first finite verb in this section that has perfective aspect (aorist tense-form), thus background (not mainline) information, but it is also in a hypotactic, subordinate clause.

ὑμῖν. Dative indirect object of μεταδῶ. This personal pronoun is placed after the noun χάρισμα and before its further adjectival modifier πνευματικὸν. The effect is to draw attention to the "grace gift" as one directed (by means of the dative case of the pronoun) to "you," the Roman Christians (see Moffatt, 106–7).

στηριχθῆναι. Aor pass inf στηρίζω. Used with εἰς τό to indicate purpose. The passive voice indicates external causality, which is not expressed here. The assumed cause of the strengthening would appear to be God, but Paul does not say that here.

ὑμᾶς. Accusative subject of the infinitive στηριχθῆναι.

1:12 τοῦτο δέ ἐστιν συμπαρακληθῆναι ἐν ὑμῖν διὰ τῆς ἐν ἀλλήλοις πίστεως ὑμῶν τε καὶ ἐμοῦ.

τοῦτο. Nominative subject of ἐστιν. The demonstrative pronoun refers cataphorically to the infinitival clause that expresses a second reason for Paul's desire to see the Roman Christians. It restates and defines further what he has already said regarding the sharing of a spiritual grace gift with them.

δέ. Adversative conjunction (mild). The postpositive conjunction indicates mild disjunction between the connective elements. Its semantic range is between καί (equal coordination) and ἀλλά (strong disjunction). Here it indicates a further clarification of the previous ἵνα clause.

ἐστιν. Unaugmented ind 3rd sg εἰμί.

συμπαρακληθῆναι. Aor pass inf συμπαρακαλέω (purpose). This infinitive is parallel to στηριχθῆναι in the previous verse. The passive voice of the verb indicates external causality, which is here not explicitly stated. The prefixed preposition συν has its local meaning to emphasize the mutuality of the action of comfort and encouragement indicated by the verb. The mutuality of the gift is emphasized throughout this section by means of (1) the use of the prefixed verb, (2) Paul's use of reciprocal language, and (3) his mention of both the Romans and himself together (see Engberg-Pedersen and Barclay on expectations of reciprocity in the ancient world).

ἐν ὑμῖν. Distributional ("among you"). The prepositional word group modifies the infinitive συμπαρακληθῆναι.

διὰ τῆς... πίστεως. Instrumental (secondary or instrumental agency).

ἐν ἀλλήλοις. Locative (sphere or realm). The phrasing here has one prepositional word group (ἐν ἀλλήλοις) placed within another prepositional word group (διὰ τῆς... πίστεως). Greek prepositional word groups usually function as adjunctive modifying units, and here the embedded one specifies the realm (among each other) in which their faith functions. In that regard, prepositional word groups function as a type of modifier, regardless of their prepositional composition. In essence, then, the "faith" being described is one that is "among one another," i.e., a "one-another faith."

ὑμῶν. Possessive genitive, modifying τῆς... πίστεως. The personal pronoun refers to the Roman Christians.

τε καὶ. Enclitic conjunction τε used with καί to form a "both and" linkage between ὑμῶν and ἐμοῦ. Paul describes this faith as belonging to both the Roman Christians and himself by means of the possessive use of two genitive pronouns connected with a "both and" construction.

ἐμοῦ. Possessive genitive, modifying τῆς... πίστεως. Paul refers to himself.

1:13 οὐ θέλω δὲ ὑμᾶς ἀγνοεῖν, ἀδελφοί, ὅτι πολλάκις προεθέμην ἐλθεῖν πρὸς ὑμᾶς, καὶ ἐκωλύθην ἄχρι τοῦ δεῦρο, ἵνα τινὰ καρπὸν σχῶ καὶ ἐν ὑμῖν καθὼς καὶ ἐν τοῖς λοιποῖς ἔθνεσιν.

οὐ θέλω . . . ὑμᾶς ἀγνοεῖν. Paul begins this verse with a disclosure formula (see Porter and Pitts 2013). A disclosure formula, like other epistolary formulas, is designed for a particular function, in this instance to draw attention to information that the recipients should take note of. Disclosure formulas consist of a number of fixed elements, even if there is some variation among them. The elements include a verb of intention and a verb of knowing (forming a catenative construction; see Porter 1989, 487–92; Porter 1994a, 197–98), as well as often negation. This phrase is also an example of a double negative (οὐ + α-prefixed verb) and an instance of litotes.

οὐ. Negative particle normally used with the indicative mood (Porter 1994a, 281, citing Moorhouse, 40).

θέλω. Pres act ind 1st sg θέλω. Verb of will or intention, the main verb in a catenative construction.

δὲ. Adversative conjunction (mild), indicating that the material here follows on from what has preceded, even if there is a shift in emphasis, here to the material that Paul wishes the Roman Christians to be reminded of.

ὑμᾶς. Accusative subject of the infinitive ἀγνοεῖν.

ἀγνοεῖν. Pres act inf ἀγνοέω (complementary). The infinitival clause is the complement of the verb of intent in the catenative construction. Together, they form a unit indicating desire or intention toward an action; here, with the negation, Paul does not want them to be ignorant or unaware of something. The emphasis of the construction is upon the verbal aspect of the complementary infinitive, here imperfective aspect.

ἀδελφοί. Nominative of address (so-called vocative). The nominative case is used for direct address in the plural (as the vocative case is a partial case, perhaps best seen as a sub-case of the nominative and not found in distinct plural forms). Paul addresses the Romans for the first time with this form of address for Christians in various churches that he uses elsewhere around 80 times (he uses the singular form also). Since the family was the most important social institution in the ancient world, including the world of the early Christians, kinship terms, even if they are fictive, are important for community formation and identity (Banks, 47–57; Aasgaard).

ὅτι. Introduces a clausal complement (indirect discourse) of ἀγνοεῖν, in which case the ὅτι clause projects the content of the disclosure formula, or a causal clause, in which case the ὅτι clause enhances the disclosure formula by providing the basis for it.

πολλάκις. Adverb (temporal), placed in thematic position in the clause. The scope of the adverb extends over this clause and the next, which are joined by conjunction καί.

προεθέμην. Aor mid ind 1st sg προτίθημι. The middle voice indicates indirect, internal causality (so "I intended") with the idea that Paul was involved in his own planning. As a so-called deponent verb, the subject is inherently involved in the act of intending or planning, so the semantics of the middle voice fits (see "Deponency" in the Series Introduction). This clause should be interpreted as indicating past time, not on the basis of the use of the aorist tense-form but on the basis of the contextual indicators, including the prefixed preposition προ-, the adverb, and Paul's statement of being hindered.

ἐλθεῖν. Aor act ind ἔρχομαι (complementary). The infinitive functions as the complement or object of προεθέμην. Paul's intention or plan was to come to Rome.

πρὸς ὑμᾶς. Directional (movement toward).

καί. Coordinating conjunction linking two elements of similar status. The conjunction καί is continuative and indicates continuity between the previous and subsequent elements. In this case, the two clauses provide the two facets of what Paul wanted the Roman Christians to know: that many times he determined to come to them and many times he was hindered from doing so.

ἐκωλύθην. Aor pass ind 1st sg κωλύω. The passive voice verb indicates external causality, which is not specified here, i.e., the agent of the verb is not explicit.

ἄχρι τοῦ δεῦρο. Temporal. This word group only appears here in the New Testament. ἄχρι is a so-called improper preposition indicating a continuous extent of time (see BDAG, 160.1; Porter 1994a, 179). Many of the so-called improper prepositions are adverbs or similar types of words. The distinction between improper and proper prepositions is merely that proper prepositions are prefixed to verb forms. They function similarly in other ways. The article τοῦ functions as a nominalizer, changing the adverb δεῦρο into the genitive object of the preposition, indicating the extent of the time as lasting until the present.

ἵνα. Introduces a purpose clause that hypotactically enhances the description of Paul's intention by indicating the purpose of his intended but hindered trip to Rome.

τινὰ καρπὸν. Accusative direct object of σχῶ. The entire noun word group is placed in thematic position.

σχῶ. Aor act subj 1st sg ἔχω. Subjunctive with ἵνα.

καὶ. Adverbial use (adjunctive), whether translated as "also" or "indeed."

ἐν ὑμῖν. Distributional ("among you").

καθὼς. Comparative conjunction with the following verbless clause.

καὶ. Adverbial use (adjunctive).

ἐν τοῖς λοιποῖς ἔθνεσιν. Distributional ("among the rest of the nations"). The sense is that Paul has previously evangelized and produced spiritual fruit among the nations or Gentiles and now wishes to do the same with those who remain, including the Roman Christians and beyond.

1:14 Ἕλλησίν τε καὶ βαρβάροις, σοφοῖς τε καὶ ἀνοήτοις ὀφειλέτης εἰμί,

Ἕλλησίν . . . βαρβάροις, σοφοῖς . . . ἀνοήτοις. Dative complements of ὀφειλέτης εἰμί. The fronting of the group of datives in this verse does not reflect the usual Greek word order (whether SVO or VSO; see Porter 1994a, 286–97), thereby thematizing them. Thus, the emphasis of this clause is "To both Greeks and barbarians, to both wise and ignorant . . ." The modern English word "barbarian" does not have the same meaning as βάρβαρος, but rather it simply refers to one who is non-Greek or one who did not participate in the Greco-Roman culture and society. Both adjectives, σοφοῖς and ἀνοήτοις, are used substantively.

τε καὶ. Enclitic particle and conjunction. This combination is rare in the NT (except in Acts). The usage is emphatic. The first occurrence of τε καὶ connects "Greeks" and "barbarians," although here it seems as if these two items are compared to one another. The second occurrence connects "wise" and "ignorant" as comparisons.

ὀφειλέτης. Predicate nominative. Paul states that he is a debtor, one who is under obligation, to all categories of people, using two extreme examples, in terms of race and ability.

εἰμί. Unaugmented ind 1st sg εἰμί. The placement of the verb at the end of the clause is infrequent.

1:15 οὕτως τὸ κατ᾽ ἐμὲ πρόθυμον καὶ ὑμῖν τοῖς ἐν Ῥώμῃ εὐαγγελίσασθαι.

οὕτως. Adverb (manner), functioning as a modifier to εὐαγγελίσασθαι. Thus, Paul seeks to preach the good news "in this way."

τὸ . . . πρόθυμον. Nominative subject of verbless clause. The neuter form of the adjective πρόθυμος is used as a substantive.

κατ᾽ ἐμὲ. Standard ("according to me," "corresponding to me," or "in reference to me"). This prepositional word group is wedged between τὸ and πρόθυμον, serving as a modifier for this noun. In other words, it is not only "the eagerness," but "the eagerness [which is] according to me (Paul)."

καί. Adverbial use (adjunctive).

ὑμῖν. Dative indirect object of εὐαγγελίσασθαι. The pronoun refers to Paul's readership in Rome.

τοῖς ἐν Ῥώμῃ. The article functions as a nominalizer, changing the prepositional word group ἐν Ῥώμῃ into the dative in apposition to ὑμῖν.

ἐν Ῥώμῃ. Locative.

εὐαγγελίσασθαι. Aor mid inf εὐαγγελίζω (epexegetical to πρόθυμον).

Romans 1:16–17

[16]For I am not ashamed of the good news, for it is the power of God for salvation to everyone who believes, to the Jew first and also to the Greek. [17]For in it, the righteousness of God is revealed from faith to faith, as it stands written: "And the righteous person by faith can expect to live."

The third major part of Romans is the body of the letter (1:16–11:36). The body of the ancient letter is the least well-defined unit (see Exler; White 1972; Martin). The body is the most flexible and fluid, formulaically at least, compared to the other parts of the ancient letter, and contains the main argument or substance of the letter. In Paul's Letter to the Romans, the body contains the theology that he wants the Romans to understand.

Verses 16–17 comprise the body introduction and the overall theme of the letter, as many commentators suggest (Porter 2015, 57–60; cf. Moo, 63–79; Fitzmyer, 253; Sumney, 5). This body introduction begins with Paul's statement of his personal confidence in the good news of Christ because it not only contains the power of God, but Paul also equates it to the power of God, for the end of saving everyone who believes, regardless of their ethnic or national identification. The major themes of Romans 1–11 are introduced here: the good news, salvation, faith/belief, righteousness, and argumentation from the Old Testament.

1:16 Οὐ γὰρ ἐπαισχύνομαι τὸ εὐαγγέλιον, δύναμις γὰρ θεοῦ ἐστιν εἰς σωτηρίαν παντὶ τῷ πιστεύοντι, Ἰουδαίῳ τε πρῶτον καὶ Ἕλληνι.

Οὐ. Negative particle normally used with indicative verbs. Here it modifies ἐπαισχύνομαι. Paul uses litotes (an understatement in the form of a negative statement) here to express his confidence in the good news of Jesus Christ: "I am not ashamed" = "I am extremely proud."

γὰρ. Postpositive explanatory conjunction that introduces the clause that explains not only what he has written already but what he is about to write, rather than introducing a reason.

ἐπαισχύνομαι. Pres mid ind 1st sg ἐπαισχύνομαι. This verb has no active voice-form (so-called deponent verb; see the Series Introduction), because the act of "being ashamed" contains inherently internal causation or direct participation (see Porter 1994a, 67–73).

τὸ εὐαγγέλιον. Accusative direct object of ἐπαισχύνομαι. This is the second of seven occurrences of this noun in Romans (1:1; 1:16; 2:16; 11:28; 15:16; 15:19; 16:25).

δύναμις. Predicate nominative. It is the predicate of ἐστιν, even though it appears before the verb, because it is anarthrous.

γὰρ. Postpositive explanatory conjunction that introduces the clause that explains why Paul is not ashamed of the good news.

θεοῦ. Genitive of source or origin, modifying δύναμις ("the power that comes from God").

ἐστιν. Unaugmented ind 3rd sg εἰμί. δύναμις θεοῦ is equated, through the 3rd sg verbal form of εἰμί, with the previously mentioned τὸ εὐαγγέλιον, which is the implied subject of the verb: the "good news" is the "power of God."

εἰς σωτηρίαν. Purpose. In this case, the purpose of the power of God (which is the good news) is salvation for all believers.

παντὶ τῷ πιστεύοντι. Dative of advantage. Salvation is the advantage for everyone who believes. The adjective παντὶ functions substantivally, as the head term of the participial phrase τῷ πιστεύοντι.

τῷ πιστεύοντι. Pres act ptc masc dat sg πιστεύω (attributive). On the function of this participle, see παντὶ τῷ πιστεύοντι above. The participle is used here to refer to those who believe (cf. BDF §413.2; Robertson, 772–73). This is the most frequent verb for "believing" in the New Testament (cf. Porter 2015, 57). The imperfective aspect of the present participle reflects Paul's depiction of believing as in progress, in comparison to a perfective aspect which would depict the believing as a complete process.

Ἰουδαίῳ . . . Ἕλληνι. Datives in apposition to παντὶ τῷ πιστεύοντι. Paul returns to this notion of "to the Jew first" extensively later in this letter (chs. 9–11).

τε . . . καὶ. Enclitic particle τε is also emphatic with καὶ, emphasizing that salvation is first to the Jew.

πρῶτον. Adverbial accusative, modifying Ἰουδαίῳ.

1:17 δικαιοσύνη γὰρ θεοῦ ἐν αὐτῷ ἀποκαλύπτεται ἐκ πίστεως εἰς πίστιν, καθὼς γέγραπται· ὁ δὲ δίκαιος ἐκ πίστεως ζήσεται.

δικαιοσύνη. Nominative subject of ἀποκαλύπτεται. This word and its cognates appear over 30 times in this letter (especially in chs. 4 and 10).

γὰρ. Postpositive explanatory conjunction that introduces the clause that explains how the power of God works for the salvation for all believers.

θεοῦ. Possessive genitive, modifying δικαιοσύνη. The meaning of the semantic relationship between δικαιοσύνη and θεοῦ has been thoroughly discussed (e.g., Käsemann 1969, 168–82, as "God's covenant-faithfulness," [177], with apocalyptic concerns; Cousar, 36–43, as "God's faithfulness and moral integrity in action" [42]; Hays, who argues for the subjective genitive based on other purported subjective genitives in context; Burk, who argues that δικαιοσύνη is a nominalization of an attribute or quality, so δικαιοσύνη θεοῦ is a metonymical idiom indicating either possessive genitive or genitive of source; Wright 2014, who in agreement with Käsemann prefers the reading of "God's own righteousness"). But viewing the genitive case as depicting restriction as its core, overarching semantic category (Porter 1994a, 92), it is best to see the genitive relationship as restricting "righteousness" to "God," and in this co-text, the relationship is modulated to refer to righteousness that belongs to God.

ἐν αὐτῷ. Locative. The pronoun refers to the previously mentioned εὐαγγέλιον (also neuter). Thus, Paul is saying that "in" the good news (which is the power of God for salvation), the righteousness of God is revealed.

ἀποκαλύπτεται. Pres pass ind 3rd sg ἀποκαλύπτω. The subject of this verb is δικαιοσύνη θεοῦ (see above), but the agent (the one doing the "revealing") is the "good news"; so in other words, the good news reveals the righteousness of God. Paul constructs the statement in the passive voice, which focuses attention on the righteousness of God.

ἐκ πίστεως. Instrumental, indicating origin or source (Porter 1994a, 155–56). The origin or source of the righteousness of God (being revealed) is faith.

εἰς πίστιν. Goal. The goal of the righteousness of God is faith.

ἐκ πίστεως εἰς πίστιν. The meaning of this phrase has been discussed extensively, with the following suggestions: (1) from OT faith to NT faith; (2) all faith inclusively; (3) from the faith of the Jews to the faith of the Gentiles; (4) from the faith of Jesus to the faith of believers; and (5) from Abraham's faith to the faith of current believers (Cranfield, 1:99; cf. Porter 2015, 58). None of these interpretative options, however, take into consideration the grammatical-syntactic functions of the prepositions. The best explanation, given the above observations on the functions of the prepositions ἐκ and εἰς, is that this word group refers to the good news being revealed by faith in its entirety, faith from start to finish (Porter 2015, 58). So "from faith to faith" (or "by faith for faith") means that faith is both the source and goal of the righteousness of God. The quotation from Hab 2:4 clarifies this when it says, "The righteous will live by faith."

καθὼς γέγραπται. Common formula for Paul ("as it is written") when quoting from the Old Testament. This is the first of many OT reference formulas in this letter (cf. Rom 2:24; 3:4, 10; 4:17; 8:36; 9:13, 33; 10:15; 11:8, 26; 15:3, 9, 21).

καθὼς. Comparitive conjunction.

γέγραπται. Prf pass ind 3rd sg γράφω. The use of the perfect tense-form of this word by Paul, when referring to the OT, is common, but nevertheless it is frontgrounded (emphatic) in this context because of its stative aspect. While the perfect tense-form has both middle and passive voice-forms as identical, the semantic difference in this case is minimal.

ὁ . . . δίκαιος. Nominative subject of ζήσεται.

δὲ. Adversative conjunction (mild). The conjunction has more semantic significance in the Habbakuk context, since here in Romans it is simply included in the quotation.

ἐκ πίστεως. Instrumental, indicating origin or source (see above).

ζήσεται. Fut mid ind 3rd sg ζάω. The future form grammaticalizes the semantic feature of expectation, so we translate it as "can expect to live." The middle voice indicates indirect, internal agency (see Introduction) and reflects discourse prominence.

Romans 1:18–23

[18]For the wrath of God is revealed from heaven against all the ungodliness and unrighteousness of people who suppress the truth by their unrighteousness. [19]Since what can be known of God is manifest to them, for God manifested it to them. [20]For his invisible qualities—from the creation of the world, understood through creation—have been clearly seen, indeed his eternal power and divine nature, so they are without excuse. [21]For although they knew God, they did not glorify [him] as God or give [him] thanks, but they were made futile in their thinking, and their senseless hearts were darkened. [22]Claiming to be wise, they were made fools, [23]and they exchanged the glory of the immortal God for the likeness of a mortal human being, and birds, and four-footed animals, and reptiles.

Romans 1:18–11:32 marks the body proper of the letter, after the introductory or thematic introduction. This section contains the content of
the letter. Whereas most ancient letters were roughly about 250 words
in length, the body of the Letter to the Romans extends to the end of
ch. 11. Whereas ancient letters usually only introduced a limited number of topics for discussion, and the organization was not structured,
Paul's letter introduces and exemplifies a number of topics, with clear
structure and arrangement.

The body proper is divided into five major units, the first one being
Rom 1:18–4:25 concerning the human condition and its forensic solution.
This section is divided into three sub-sections: 1:18–2:11; 2:12–3:20; and
3:21–4:25. The first sub-section (1:18–2:11) provides the foundation for
Paul's description of the human condition and the forensic (legal) solution to this sinfulness. His first word to humanity, found in 1:18–32, is
regarding the universal condemnation of humanity for its sinfulness. For
the sake of analysis here, this section is divided into two further sections,
1:18–23 and 1:24–32. In the first section, Paul established the basis for the
condemnation of humanity through a description of this sinfulness and
then provides the background in support of this exposition.

On the basis of this outline, Rom 1:18 marks a significant transition
point in the letter. In this verse, there is one verb at the beginning of the
clause, with one noun (subject of the verb) and numerous prepositional word groups and secondary (relative) clauses to further modify
the noun. The conjunction translated "for" introduces the entire body
proper of the letter, along with all of the sub-sections indicated above.
Because this is an expository discourse, the mainline of the discourse
is generally carried by the use of the present tense-form (imperfective
aspect), with the other tense-forms used to provide either background
(perfective aspect) or emphatic material (stative aspect) which either
provides further information or signals importance for Paul. Further
exposition is provided by non-finite forms, such as participles, infinitives, and secondary (relative) clauses.

**1:18 Ἀποκαλύπτεται γὰρ ὀργὴ θεοῦ ἀπ᾽ οὐρανοῦ ἐπὶ πᾶσαν ἀσέβειαν
καὶ ἀδικίαν ἀνθρώπων τῶν τὴν ἀλήθειαν ἐν ἀδικίᾳ κατεχόντων,**

Ἀποκαλύπτεται. Pres pass ind 3rd sg ἀποκαλύπτω. There is lexical cohesion (repetition of lexemes) and a parallel here with the previous verse (1:17). There, the "righteousness of God is revealed"
(δικαιοσύνη . . . θεοῦ . . . ἀποκαλύπτεται), whereas here, the "wrath of
God is revealed" (Ἀποκαλύπτεται . . . ὀργὴ θεοῦ); the same lexeme ἀποκαλύπτεται is used. The difference between the two, however, is that in

1:17, δικαιοσύνη θεοῦ is fronted in the clause, thus emphatic, while here, ἀποκαλύπτεται is fronted. After having stated the theme of the letter, God's righteousness revealed through the good news, which originates with and aims towards faith, Paul states the reality of the human condition, that the wrath of God is revealed.

γὰρ. Postpositive inferential conjunction. This is the fourth time in three verses that γὰρ has appeared. First, Paul explains his eagerness to preach the gospel: because of his confidence in the good news (1:16a). Second, Paul explains why he is not ashamed of the good news: because it is the power of God for salvation (1:16b). Third, he explains why the good news is the power of God: because in the good news, God's righteousness is revealed (1:17). Here, fourth, he does not explain something from the previous co-text, as much as he infers or relates God's righteousness being revealed to how God's wrath being revealed.

ὀργὴ. Nominative subject of Ἀποκαλύπτεται. While ὀργή was used to describe the wrath of the ancient Greek gods, whose anger was capricious and perhaps even arbitrary, God's wrath is not the same. God's wrath is entirely justified, as Paul explains in the rest of this section regarding the ungodliness and unrighteousness of humanity.

θεοῦ. Genitive of source or origin, modifying ὀργὴ.

ἀπ᾽ οὐρανοῦ. Locative.

ἐπὶ πᾶσαν ἀσέβειαν καὶ ἀδικίαν. Directional (movement upon). πᾶσαν is attributive, modifying ἀσέβειαν καὶ ἀδικίαν.

ἀνθρώπων. Possessive genitive, modifying ἀσέβειαν καὶ ἀδικίαν.

τῶν . . . κατεχόντων. Pres act ptc masc gen pl κατέχω (attributive). The participle modifies ἀνθρώπων (third attributive position). The participial phrase contains the object τὴν ἀλήθειαν and the prepositional word group ἐν ἀδικίᾳ embedded between the article and the participle in order to form a more cohesive word group.

τὴν ἀλήθειαν. Accusative direct object of κατεχόντων.

ἐν ἀδικίᾳ. Instrumental (manner). People supress the truth in a manner of "unrighteousness."

1:19 διότι τὸ γνωστὸν τοῦ θεοῦ φανερόν ἐστιν ἐν αὐτοῖς· ὁ θεὸς γὰρ αὐτοῖς ἐφανέρωσεν.

διότι. Causal or inferential conjunction. It introduces the cause for God's wrath.

τὸ γνωστὸν. Nominative subject of ἐστιν.

τοῦ θεοῦ. Genitive of definition, modifying τὸ γνωστὸν ("what is known" is defined in terms of "God").

φανερόν. Predicate adjective.

ἐστιν. Unaugmented ind 3rd sg εἰμί. It equates τὸ γνωστὸν τοῦ θεοῦ with φανερόν.

ἐν αὐτοῖς. Locative. The above translation supplies "to them" for smooth English purposes, but the idea is that knowledge of God is manifest *in* or *within* them.

ὁ θεὸς. Nominiative subject of ἐφανέρωσεν.

γὰρ. Postpositive explanatory conjunction that introduces a clause that explains why knowledge of God is manifest to them: because God manifested it to them.

αὐτοῖς. Dative indirect object of ἐφανέρωσεν. The placement of the pronoun before the verb, instead of after it, makes it emphatic.

ἐφανέρωσεν. Aor act ind 3rd sg φανερόω. The φαν- root (first as an adjective, here as a verb) is repeated here.

1:20 τὰ γὰρ ἀόρατα αὐτοῦ ἀπὸ κτίσεως κόσμου τοῖς ποιήμασιν νοού-μενα καθορᾶται, ἥ τε ἀΐδιος αὐτοῦ δύναμις καὶ θειότης, εἰς τὸ εἶναι αὐτοὺς ἀναπολογήτους,

τὰ . . . ἀόρατα. Nominative subject of καθορᾶται. Adjective functioning substantivally.

γὰρ. Explanatory conjunction that introduces a clause to further explain how God has manifested knowledge of himself to all of humanity.

αὐτοῦ. Possessive genitive, modifying τὰ . . . ἀόρατα.

ἀπὸ κτίσεως. Temporal. The fronting of the participial phrase is prominent at the clause level (i.e., within the embedded clause, ἀπὸ κτίσεως κόσμου τοῖς ποιήμασιν νοούμενα).

κόσμου. Genitive of definition, modifying κτίσεως (defining or restricting "creation" to "world").

τοῖς ποιήμασιν. Dative of instrument. It serves as the agent of the passive participle, νοούμενα, although the grammatical subject is unspecified. In other words, creation is the means by which God's invisible qualities are understood.

νοούμενα. Pres pass ptc neut nom pl νοέω (causal). The participle provides the reason, or cause, for why God's invisible attributes are seen clearly since the creation of the world: because they are "understood through creation."

καθορᾶται. Pres mid ind 3rd sg καθοράω. This word, containing the prefix κατ- with ὁράω, is a NT *hapax legomenon* that means "deeply seen" (Porter 2015, 65).

ἥ . . . ἀΐδιος . . . δύναμις καὶ θειότης. Nominatives in apposition to τὰ ἀόρατα αὐτοῦ. ἀΐδιος functions attributively and modifies δύναμις.

The acute accent on the article ἡ (normally unaccented) appears as a result of the subsequent enclitic particle τε.

τε. Postpositive enclitic particle. Emphatic.

αὐτοῦ. Possessive genitive, modifying δύναμις.

εἶναι. Inf εἰμί. Used with εἰς τὸ to denote result. The result of the previous statement that his invisible qualities are clearly seen is that "they are without excuse."

αὐτοὺς. Accusative subject of the infinitive εἶναι.

ἀναπολογήτους. Predicate accusative. Two prepositional prefixes, ἀνά and ἀπό, are attached to the root. The word means "without excuse."

1:21 διότι γνόντες τὸν θεὸν οὐχ ὡς θεὸν ἐδόξασαν ἢ ηὐχαρίστησαν, ἀλλ' ἐματαιώθησαν ἐν τοῖς διαλογισμοῖς αὐτῶν καὶ ἐσκοτίσθη ἡ ἀσύνετος αὐτῶν καρδία.

διότι. Causal or inferential conjunction, establishing a cause-and-effect relation. The cause is God manifesting knowledge of himself in the world and his invisible attributes being clearly seen. The effect is that they did not glorify him or give him thanks.

γνόντες. Aor act ptc masc nom pl γινώσκω (concessive). The participle functions contextually as circumstantial and modifies οὐχ . . . ἐδόξασαν. The perfective aspect depicts the process of "knowing" as an undifferentiated whole.

τὸν θεὸν. Accusative direct object of γνόντες.

οὐχ . . . ἀλλ'. A point/counterpoint set. The negative particle negates ἐδόξασαν and ηὐχαρίστησαν.

ὡς. Comparative conjunction. It functions adverbially here, modifying θεὸν.

θεὸν. Accusative direct object of ἐδόξασαν.

ἐδόξασαν. Aor act ind 3rd pl δοξάζω. Beginning with ἐδόξασαν, the rest of the section contains main verbs in the perfective aspect (aorist tense-form), which depicts the actions as background information. Up until now, the main verbs have been in the imperfective aspect (present tense-form), communicating mainline material. The rest of this section serves to provide background information for what happened when God made himself and his attributes clearly evident in the world.

ἢ. Disjunctive conjunction ("or"). It connects ἐδόξασαν and ηὐχαρίστησαν.

ηὐχαρίστησαν. Aor act ind 3rd pl εὐχαριστέω.

ἐματαιώθησαν. Aor pass ind 3rd pl ματαιόω. The passive voice-form indicates external causality, but the agent for this action is not identified. ματαιόω is a NT *hapax legomenon*.

ἐν τοῖς διαλογισμοῖς. Locative.

αὐτῶν. Possessive genitive, modifying τοῖς διαλογισμοῖς. The antecedent of this pronoun is the implied grammatical subject of ἐδόξασαν, ηὐχαρίστησαν, and ἐματαιώθησαν.

καὶ. Coordinating conjunction. It connects ἐματαιώθησαν and ἐσκοτίσθη.

ἐσκοτίσθη. Aor pass ind 3rd sg σκοτίζω. The passive voice-form indicates external causality, which is not specified here.

ἡ ἀσύνετος . . . καρδία. Nominative subject of ἐσκοτίσθη. ἀσύνετος is attributive of καρδία ("senseless heart"). The genitive plural αὐτῶν indicates that καρδία is a distributive singular that represents a group.

αὐτῶν. Possessive genitive, modifying ἡ ἀσύνετος . . . καρδία. The antecedent of the pronoun is the continuing implied subject of ἐδόξασαν, ηὐχαρίστησαν, and ἐματαιώθησαν.

1:22 φάσκοντες εἶναι σοφοὶ ἐμωράνθησαν

φάσκοντες εἶναι σοφοὶ. This secondary clause is subordinate to the main verb, ἐμωράνθησαν, providing supportive material. The fronting of the secondary clause is prominent in the clause complex (φάσκοντες εἶναι σοφοὶ ἐμωράνθησαν). In other words, their claim to be wise is emphasized.

φάσκοντες. Pres act ptc masc nom pl φάσκω (means or concessive). The participle functions as circumstantial and cataphorically modifies ἐμωράνθησαν.

εἶναι. Inf εἰμί (indirect discourse).

σοφοὶ. Predicate adjective.

ἐμωράνθησαν. Aor pass ind 3rd pl μωραίνω. This is another passive voice-form in a series of passive voice-forms in this section. As in the previous passive verbs, the agent is not specified.

1:23 καὶ ἤλλαξαν τὴν δόξαν τοῦ ἀφθάρτου θεοῦ ἐν ὁμοιώματι εἰκόνος φθαρτοῦ ἀνθρώπου καὶ πετεινῶν καὶ τετραπόδων καὶ ἑρπετῶν

καὶ. Coordinating conjunction. It connects ἐμωράνθησαν with ἤλλαξαν.

ἤλλαξαν. Aor act ind 3rd pl ἀλλάσσω.

τὴν δόξαν. Accusative direct object of ἤλλαξαν.

τοῦ ἀφθάρτου θεοῦ. Possessive genitive or genitive of source, modifying τὴν δόξαν. The primary semantic category of restriction for the genitive applies either way. The so-called alpha privative (ἀ-) in the attributive adjective ἄφθαρτος negates the root word φθαρτός.

ἐν ὁμοιώματι. Instrumental. The idiom ἀλλάσσειν/μεταλλάσειν τι ἔν τινι ("exchange something for something else"; cf. BDAG, 329.5.b) uses ἔν to express means or instrumentality (i.e., the object of the preposition is the means by which the accusative object is "replaced").

εἰκόνος. Genitive of definition, defining the "likeness" (ὁμοίωμα) as "image." The use of two synonyms, ὁμοίωμα and εἰκών, however, seems repetitive, serving as a sort of cohesive emphasis. The emphasis is that it is merely an image or likeness of mortal humanity, not even the real thing.

φθαρτοῦ ἀνθρώπου. Genitive of definition, defining the type of image to be that of mortal humanity. Repetition of the root word φθαρτός serves to compare the "immortal God" with "mortal humanity."

καὶ . . . καὶ . . . καὶ. Coordinating conjunctions, linking four paratactic genitives that qualify εἰκόνος.

πετεινῶν. Genitive of definition, further defining ὁμοιώματι εἰκόνος. The word is used only here by Paul.

τετραπόδων. Genitive of definition, further defining ὁμοιώματι εἰκόνος. The adjective τετράπους functions as substantive. The word is used only here by Paul (cf. Acts 10:12; 11:6).

ἑρπετῶν. Genitive of definition, further defining ὁμοιώματι εἰκόνος.

Romans 1:24–32

[24]Therefore, God gave them up in the lusts of their hearts to impurity for the dishonoring of their bodies among themselves, [25]who exchanged the truth of God for a lie and accepted worship and served the creature rather than the Creator, who is blessed forever. Amen. [26]Because of this God gave them over to dishonorable passions, for their females exchanged the natural (sexual) relations for unnatural ones, [27]and likewise also the males, abandoning the natural (sexual) relations for the female, were inflamed in their lust toward one another, males with males performing shameful acts and receiving in themselves the penalty for their error which was necessary. [28]And as they did not approve of having knowledge of God, God gave them over to an unapproved mind to do improper things, [29]having been filled with every kind of unrighteousness, evil, greed, wickedness, full of envy, murder, discord, deceit, malice, gossipers, [30]slanderers, haters of God, insolent, arrogant, boasters, inventors of evil, disobedient to parents, [31]senseless, faithless, heartless, ruthless. [32]Although whoever understood the righteous requirement of God, that those who practice such things are worthy of death, they not only do them but also (gladly) approve of those who practice [them].

This section is a continuation from the previous one, beginning with the inferential conjunction διό. From what has been stated already, regarding humanity's response (or lack of proper response) to God's revelation of himself to the world, Paul outlines God's counter-response: allowing humanity to fully realize their ungodliness and unrighteousness, especially in terms of improper sexual relationships and activities. In the middle of this discourse, discussing the impure and improper conduct of humanity in response to God's revelation of himself to the world, Paul breaks into a brief doxology (v. 25), recognizing how great God is.

The string of aorist tense-forms provides background material. In other words, the basis of Paul's condemnation of humanity as sinful is provided in his recounting of their sinful behavior. Humans committed a number of different types of acts that resulted in God's response to them and their condemnation.

1:24 Διὸ παρέδωκεν αὐτοὺς ὁ θεὸς ἐν ταῖς ἐπιθυμίαις τῶν καρδιῶν αὐτῶν εἰς ἀκαθαρσίαν τοῦ ἀτιμάζεσθαι τὰ σώματα αὐτῶν ἐν αὐτοῖς ·

Διὸ. Inferential conjunction. The following statements are inferences based on what has been stated already.

παρέδωκεν. Aor act ind 3rd sg παραδίδωμι. The continuation of the perfective aspect (aorist tense-form) denotes continued background information from the previous section. The active voice-form is noteworthy; God was active in his handing them over to the lusts of their hearts, and not simply a passive handing them over, especially compared to the passive voice-forms noted above in which the agent is not specified.

αὐτοὺς. Accusative direct object of παρέδωκεν.

ὁ θεὸς. Nominative subject of παρέδωκεν.

ἐν ταῖς ἐπιθυμίαις. Locative. God gave them over to the sphere of the lusts of their hearts.

τῶν καρδιῶν. Genitive or origin or source, modifying ταῖς ἐπιθυμίαις. The lust comes from their hearts.

αὐτῶν. Possessive genitive, modifying τῶν καρδιῶν.

εἰς ἀκαθαρσίαν. Result. The result of God giving them over to the lusts of their heart is impurity.

τοῦ ἀτιμάζεσθαι. Pres mid/pass inf ἀτιμάζω (result). The so-called alpha privative (ἀ-) negates the root τιμάζω. The result of their being given to lust of the hearts is their bodies being dishonored among them.

τὰ σώματα. Accusative subject of the infinitive ἀτιμάζεσθαι (if the infinitive is passive) or accusative direct object of the infinitive ἀτιμάζεσθαι (if the infinitive is middle). Although both are grammatically viable options, the former is probably preferable, since the latter would lack the grammatical subject of ἀτιμάζεσθαι.

αὐτῶν. Possessive genitive, modifying τὰ σώματα.

ἐν αὐτοῖς. Distributional ("among them").

1:25 οἵτινες μετήλλαξαν τὴν ἀλήθειαν τοῦ θεοῦ ἐν τῷ ψεύδει καὶ ἐσεβάσθησαν καὶ ἐλάτρευσαν τῇ κτίσει παρὰ τὸν κτίσαντα, ὅς ἐστιν εὐλογητὸς εἰς τοὺς αἰῶνας, ἀμήν.

οἵτινες. Nominative subject of μετήλλαξαν, ἐσεβάσθησαν, and ἐλά-τρευσαν. οἵτινες is an indefinite relative pronoun. Most English versions translate this as "they," but it has an indefinite sense of "whoever," as in "whoever this might describe."

μετήλλαξαν. Aor act ind 3rd pl μεταλλάσσω. The prepositional pre-fix μετ- is attached to ἀλλάσσω to intensify the root word.

τὴν ἀλήθειαν. Accusative direct object of μετήλλαξαν.

τοῦ θεοῦ. Possessive genitive or genitive of source or origin, modify-ing τὴν ἀλήθειαν ("the truth that belongs to God or comes from God").

ἐν τῷ ψεύδει. Instrumental (see note in 1:23 on ἐν ὁμοιώματι).

καὶ. Coordinating conjunction that paratactically connects ἐσεβάσθησαν with the main verb μετήλλαξαν.

ἐσεβάσθησαν. Aor pass ind 3rd pl σεβάζομαι. The passive voice indicates indirect causality, so "they were worshipped" or "they accepted worship." The passive voice is significant here, as most English trans-lations reflect an active voice, but the Greek form of this word as pas-sive means that they were the objects of worship. The meaning here is that they exchanged the truth of God and *received worship*, that they did not properly *give* worship (to God, to the one who properly should receive worship) but *received* it instead, presumably among themselves (cf. BDAG, 917, which says that this is the aorist passive in active sense. However, we doubt that a passive form is used in an active sense, or else the available active form would have been used). This lexeme is a *hapax legomenon* in the NT.

καὶ. Coordinating conjunction that paratactically connects ἐσεβάσθησαν and ἐλάτρευσαν.

ἐλάτρευσαν. Aor act ind 3rd pl λατρεύω.

τῇ κτίσει. Dative direct object of ἐλάτρευσαν.

παρὰ τὸν κτίσαντα. Locative. παρά generally has the meaning of "alongside" or "beside" and here metaphorically is a replacement of one over another (cf. LN 89.132; Porter 1994a, 166–67).

τὸν κτίσαντα. Aor act ptc masc acc sg κτίζω (substantival). The focus falls on the action described by the verbal part of the word.

ὅς. Nominative subject of ἐστιν. The relative pronoun refers to τὸν κτίσαντα, who is God.

ἐστιν. Unaugmented ind 3rd sg εἰμί.

εὐλογητὸς. Predicate adjective.

εἰς τοὺς αἰῶνας. Goal (temporal).

ἀμήν. Asseverative particle. It is Semitic in origin, functioning as emphatic (strong affirmation of what has been stated). In the LXX, it is occasionally used for אָמֵן (BDAG, 53; cf. Rom 9:5; 11:36; 15:33; 16:27).

1:26 Διὰ τοῦτο παρέδωκεν αὐτοὺς ὁ θεὸς εἰς πάθη ἀτιμίας, αἵ τε γὰρ θήλειαι αὐτῶν μετήλλαξαν τὴν φυσικὴν χρῆσιν εἰς τὴν παρὰ φύσιν

Διὰ τοῦτο. Causal. The combination of the two words διὰ τοῦτο signifies cause and reason. τοῦτο refers to what has just been said, exchanging the truth of God for a lie.

παρέδωκεν. Aor act ind 3rd sg παραδίδωμι. The same verb is used in 1:24 with God as the subject, as here.

αὐτοὺς. Accusative direct object of παρέδωκεν.

ὁ θεὸς. Nominative subject of παρέδωκεν.

εἰς πάθη. Locative (sphere or realm). The sphere in which God gave them over to is dishonorable passions. While the previous section (1:18–23) was on desires, this section has to do with passions, particularly sexual passions.

ἀτιμίας. Genitive of definition or description, modifying πάθη. Passions are defined or described as that of dishonor. They had dishonored their bodies with one another (1:24); so God allows that dishonor to continue by giving them over to dishonorable passions.

αἵ . . . θήλειαι. Nominative subject of μετήλλαξαν. This noun is used only here and in Gal 3:28 by Paul. It refers to the female of a species. The use of this word, along with οἱ ἄρσενες in the next verse, signifies the focus on gender in this context. In other words, these lexemes are gender focused words, used of male and female, not just of humans but also can extend to other living creatures (cf. LXX Gen 1:2; 6:19). The article is accented due to the subsequent enclitic particle τε.

τε. Enclitic conjunction and particle.

γὰρ. Postpositive conjunction that introduces a clause that explains further how God gave them over to dishonorable passions.

αὐτῶν. Partitive genitive, modifying αἵ . . . θήλειαι.

μετήλλαξαν. Aor act ind 3rd pl μεταλλάσσω. The same verb occurs in 1:25. Above, there was an "exchange" between God's truth for a lie; here, there is an "exchange" between natural relations for unnatural ones.

τὴν φυσικὴν χρῆσιν. Accusative direct object of μετήλλαξαν.

εἰς τὴν παρὰ φύσιν. Directional (movement toward). While εἰς rarely has an instrumental function, here it is similar to ἐν ὁμοιώματι in 1:23 and ἐν τῷ ψεύδει in 1:25 (see entry notes above) with μεταλλάσσω. The use of εἰς here, however, highlights the directionality of "into" or its extensive function (goal or state; cf. BDAG, 639, which notes a similar idiom).

τὴν παρὰ φύσιν. The article functions as a nominalizer, changing the prepositional word group παρὰ φύσιν into the accusative object of the preposition εἰς.

παρὰ φύσιν. Locative. In this co-text, the locative function of "alongside" represents that which is aside from the natural, i.e., the "unnatural." The modern word "para-church" illustrates this well; a para-church is one that is not a church but strives to be alongside "church."

1:27 ὁμοίως τε καὶ οἱ ἄρσενες ἀφέντες τὴν φυσικὴν χρῆσιν τῆς θηλείας ἐξεκαύθησαν ἐν τῇ ὀρέξει αὐτῶν εἰς ἀλλήλους, ἄρσενες ἐν ἄρσεσιν τὴν ἀσχημοσύνην κατεργαζόμενοι καὶ τὴν ἀντιμισθίαν ἣν ἔδει τῆς πλάνης αὐτῶν ἐν ἑαυτοῖς ἀπολαμβάνοντες.

The clause structure in this verse contains a main clause, οἱ ἄρσενες ... ἐξεκαύθησαν (ἐν τῇ ὀρέξει αὐτῶν εἰς ἀλλήλους), along with three participial clauses, one before the main clause and two after: (1) ἀφέντες τὴν φυσικὴν χρῆσιν τῆς θηλείας; (2) ἄρσενες ἐν ἄρσεσιν τὴν ἀσχημοσύνην κατεργαζόμενοι; and (3) τὴν ἀντιμισθίαν ἣν ἔδει τῆς πλάνης αὐτῶν ἐν ἑαυτοῖς ἀπολαμβάνοντες. These participial clauses are further explanations or developments of the main clause ("males were inflamed in their lusts towards each other"). The last two participial phrases have the participle at the end of the clause, signifying that the other elements are fronted and thus thematized (or emphasized). In other words, the participial phrase that occurs first is fronted and prominent in relation to the latter two participial clauses.

ὁμοίως. Adverb. It points out a similarity between the previous clause and the following clause.

τε καί. Enclitic particle and conjunction. The usage is emphatic (see 1:14). καί functions adverbially ("also").

οἱ ἄρσενες. Nominative subject of ἐξεκαύθησαν. This noun is used only here and in Gal 3:28 by Paul. It refers to the male of a species (see 1:26 on αἵ ... θήλειαι for a note on the use of gender specific words in this context).

ἀφέντες. Aor act ptc masc nom pl ἀφίημι (causal, temporal, or means). The participle functions contextually as circumstantial and modifies ἐξεκαύθησαν. This is the first of three subordinate participles which modify ἐξεκαύθησαν. The participle governs the rest of the clause τὴν φυσικὴν χρῆσιν τῆς θηλείας, which is background information.

τὴν φυσικὴν χρῆσιν. Accusative direct object of ἀφέντες (see 1:26).

τῆς θηλείας. Genitive of description, modifying τὴν φυσικὴν χρῆσιν. The natural function is further described as and restricted to "the female."

ἐξεκαύθησαν. Aor pass ind 3rd pl ἐκκαίω. An identifiable agent is not specified in the co-text for this passive voice verb. But looking back at the previous co-text, the passive voice verb simply identifies the result of a chain of events (e.g., exchanging the truth of God for a lie, being given over to their dishonorable passions, and then engaging in unnatural sexual relations). The word is a NT *hapax legomenon* but occurs 56 times in the LXX, often used of a fire burning, although it is used figuratively with emotions as well (e.g., Num 11:1; Deut 29:19; 32:22; 2 Sam 24:1; Ps 2:12; 79:5; Jer 51:6), as here.

ἐν τῇ ὀρέξει. Locative (sphere or realm). The sphere or realm where they burned is in their lust.

αὐτῶν. Possessive genitive, modifying τῇ ὀρέξει.

εἰς ἀλλήλους. Directional (movement toward).

ἄρσενες. Nominative in apposition to οἱ ἄρσενες at the beginning of this verse.

ἐν ἄρσεσιν. Accompaniment ("with males"). The use of ἐν for accompaniment (instead of σύν or μετά for example) maintains its semantic core meaning of "in" or "in the realm of." The fronting of the prepositional word group before the participle (κατεργαζόμενοι) and accusative direct object (τὴν ἀσχημοσύνην) signifies prominence at the clause level.

τὴν ἀσχημοσύνην. Accusative direct object of κατεργαζόμενοι. It is placed before the verb for prominence (although less prominent than ἐν ἄρσεσιν).

κατεργαζόμενοι. Pres mid ptc masc nom pl κατεργάζομαι (manner). The participle functions contextually as circumstantial and modifies ἐξεκαύθησαν. This is the second of three subordinate participles which modify ἐξεκαύθησαν. κατεργάζομαι is a so-called deponent verb (see "Deponency" in the Series Introduction).

καί. Coordinating conjunction that paratactically links two participial clauses.

τὴν ἀντιμισθίαν. Accusative direct object of ἀπολαμβάνοντες. Fronted for prominence and thematization.

ἥν. Accusative in attributive structure to τὴν ἀντιμισθίαν. The relative pronoun describes the penalty as being necessary. A rough wooden translation would be "the which-was-necessary penalty of their error." Most English translations supply "due" for the expression ἣν ἔδει (e.g.,

NASB, NIV, NKJV, NRSV). But it does not refer to something expected or owed (as "due" means in English) but rather something that is necessary or required.

ἔδει. Augmented act ind 3rd sg δεῖ.

τῆς πλάνης. Genitive of source, modifying τὴν ἀντιμισθίαν. The source of the penalty is their error.

αὐτῶν. Possessive genitive, modifying τῆς πλάνης.

ἐν ἑαυτοῖς. Locative.

ἀπολαμβάνοντες. Pres act ptc masc nom pl ἀπολαμβάνω (result). The participle functions contextually as circumstantial and modifies ἐξεκαύθησαν. This is the third of three subordinate participles that modify ἐξεκαύθησαν (ἀφέντες and κατεργαζόμενοι being the other two).

1:28 Καὶ καθὼς οὐκ ἐδοκίμασαν τὸν θεὸν ἔχειν ἐν ἐπιγνώσει, παρέδω-κεν αὐτοὺς ὁ θεὸς εἰς ἀδόκιμον νοῦν, ποιεῖν τὰ μὴ καθήκοντα,

Καὶ. Coordinating conjunction. It connects this clause to the previous one.

καθὼς. Comparative conjunction. The comparative conjunction is used in a causal sense here ("as" = "since"; cf. BDF §453.2 and Robertson, 968).

οὐκ. Negative particle normally used with indicative verbs. Here it negates ἐδοκίμασαν.

ἐδοκίμασαν. Aor act ind 3rd pl δοκιμάζω. The 3rd plural has been unspecified for a series of verbs in this section, but the implied subject is still humanity in general (ἀνθρωπῶν going back to 1:18).

τὸν θεὸν. Accusative direct object of the infinitive ἔχειν.

ἔχειν. Pres act inf ἔχω (complementary). The infinitive complements ἐδοκίμασαν.

ἐν ἐπιγνώσει. Locative. A literal translation might be "to have God in knowledge/recognition," but for purposes of smooth English, the translation above states "having the knowledge of God." The idea is that they did not have God *in the realm* of knowledge.

παρέδωκεν. Aor act ind 3rd sg παραδίδωμι. The same word is used in 1:26, with the same subject ("God").

αὐτοὺς. Accusative direct object of παρέδωκεν.

ὁ θεὸς. Nominative subject of παρέδωκεν.

εἰς ἀδόκιμον νοῦν. Purpose. Note the parallel root of ἐδοκίμασαν and ἀδόκιμον. Just as they did not "approve" of the knowledge of God, God in turn gave them over to an "unapproved" mind.

ποιεῖν. Pres act inf ποιέω (result). The result of God handing them over to a debased mind is "to do improper things."

τὰ ... καθήκοντα. Pres act ptc neut acc pl καθήκω (substantival). Accusative direct object of the infinitive ποιεῖν.

μὴ. Negative particle normally used with non-indicative verbs. Here it modifies the participle καθήκοντα.

1:29 πεπληρωμένους πάσῃ ἀδικίᾳ πονηρίᾳ πλεονεξίᾳ κακίᾳ, μεστοὺς φθόνου φόνου ἔριδος δόλου κακοηθείας, ψιθυριστὰς

This verse contains one participle that governs several words in the dative, followed by a string of accusative substantives (through the next two verses) to further describe humanity. Asyndeton is used in this list, not uncommon to Paul in lists (e.g., 1 Cor 13:13; Gal 5:22–23), to focus on the meanings of the words.

πεπληρωμένους. Prf pass ptc masc acc pl πληρόω (substantival). Accusative in apposition to αὐτοὺς in 1:28, further describing those whom God gave over to an unapproved mind. The stative aspect in the perfect tense-form means that they were in a state of "being filled," but it is also frontgrounded (prominent) in this co-text. The passive voice also indicates external causality, but as in the previous co-text, the agent (the one who filled them) is not specified.

πάσῃ ἀδικίᾳ πονηρίᾳ πλεονεξίᾳ κακίᾳ. Dative complements of πεπληρωμένους. The complements or objects of "being filled" are all unrighteousness, evil, greed, and wickedness. The adjective πάσῃ is attributive, modifying all of the dative words, ἀδικίᾳ, πονηρίᾳ, πλεονεξίᾳ, and κακίᾳ.

μεστοὺς. Accusative in apposition to αὐτοὺς in 1:28. The adjective has a substantival function in the clause and further defines "them" (humanity) from the previous co-text.

φθόνου φόνου ἔριδος δόλου κακοηθείας. Genitives of description, modifying μεστοὺς. These genitives further describe what they are full of.

ψιθυριστὰς. Accusative in apposition to αὐτοὺς in 1:28. This word ends the list of the "full of"s and begins a list of eight labels for the subject of Paul's discourse here.

1:30 καταλάλους θεοστυγεῖς ὑβριστὰς ὑπερηφάνους ἀλαζόνας, ἐφευρετὰς κακῶν, γονεῦσιν ἀπειθεῖς,

καταλάλους. Accusative in apposition to αὐτοὺς in 1:28. The prefix κατα- is attached to the root λαλ-, making the word mean "slander" or more literally "against-speech."

θεοστυγεῖς. Accusative in apposition to αὐτοὺς in 1:28. θεοστυγεῖς is a combination of the words θεός ("God") and στυγέω ("to abhor, hate").

ὑβριστάς. Accusative in apposition to αὐτοὺς in 1:28. Interpreters should be careful not to read the English word "hubris" into this word. "It is important to recognize in the term ὑβριστής more than merely an attitude of pride, for ὑβρίζω implies an attitude of superiority which results in mistreatment of and violent acts against others" (LN 88.132).

ὑπερηφάνους. Accusative in apposition to αὐτοὺς in 1:28. Prefix ὑπερ with the root φαίνομαι means to "show oneself above."

ἀλαζόνας. Accusative in apposition to αὐτοὺς in 1:28.

ἐφευρετάς. Accusative in apposition to αὐτοὺς in 1:28. ἐφευρετής is a NT *hapax legomenon* and also does not occur in the LXX.

κακῶν. Objective genitive, modifying ἐφευρετὰς. Evil is the object of their inventing.

γονεῦσιν. Dative complement of ἀπειθεῖς. The fronting of the dative before the head term signifies prominence (emphasis) in the word group.

ἀπειθεῖς. Accusative in apposition to αὐτοὺς in 1:28.

1:31 ἀσυνέτους ἀσυνθέτους ἀστόργους ἀνελεήμονας·

ἀσυνέτους ἀσυνθέτους ἀστόργους ἀνελεήμονας. The four substantival adjectives in this verse all begin with the so-called alpha privative (prefix ἀ-; but the last word has the prefix ἀν-), posing these ungodly/unrighteous qualities from a negative perspective (i.e., without understanding, without loyalty, without natural affection, without mercy). These are also all in the accusative, functioning appositionally (independently) as the previous accusatives.

ἀσυνέτους. Accusative in apposition to αὐτοὺς in 1:28.

ἀσυνθέτους. Accusative in apposition to αὐτοὺς in 1:28. One letter, θ, distinguishes this word from the previous one, providing a literary effect of assonance (cf. BDF §488.2).

ἀστόργους. Accusative in apposition to αὐτοὺς in 1:28.

ἀνελεήμονας. Accusative in apposition to αὐτοὺς in 1:28. Although the prefix is slightly different here than the first three, the assonance of these four words gives an effect of attention grabbing.

1:32 οἵτινες τὸ δικαίωμα τοῦ θεοῦ ἐπιγνόντες ὅτι οἱ τὰ τοιαῦτα πράσσοντες ἄξιοι θανάτου εἰσίν, οὐ μόνον αὐτὰ ποιοῦσιν ἀλλὰ καὶ συνευδοκοῦσιν τοῖς πράσσουσιν.

οἵτινες. Nominative subject of ἐπιγνόντες. Most English versions translate this indefinite relative pronoun as "they," but it has an indefinite sense of "whoever," as in "whoever this might describe."

τὸ δικαίωμα. Accusative direct object of ἐπιγνόντες. The singular depicts God's righteous requirements of God as a unified whole rather than as a number of separate requirements.

τοῦ θεοῦ. Possessive genitive, modifying τὸ δικαίωμα.

ἐπιγνόντες. Aor act ptc masc nom pl ἐπιγινώσκω (concessive). The participle functions as concessive—introducing a clause identifying a circumstance (i.e., circumstantial) which might be expected to preclude the main clause—and modifies ποιοῦσιν and συνευδοκοῦσιν at the end of the verse, providing supportive material to the two main predicates.

ὅτι. Introduces the clausal complement (indirect discourse) of ἐπιγνόντες.

οἱ . . . πράσσοντες. Pres act ptc masc nom pl πράσσω (substantival). Nominative subject of εἰσίν.

τὰ τοιαῦτα. Accusative direct object of πράσσοντες. The demonstrative adjective is placed between the article and the participle for emphasis.

ἄξιοι. Predicate adjective.

θανάτου. Genitive complement of ἄξιοι.

εἰσίν. Unaugmented ind 3rd pl εἰμί. It equates οἱ . . . πράσσοντες with ἄξιοι θανάτου.

οὐ μόνον . . . ἀλλὰ καί. A point/counterpoint set ("not only . . . but also").

αὐτά. Accusative direct object of ποιοῦσιν. The intensive pronoun functions as a personal pronoun ("them") and refers to τὰ τοιαῦτα above.

ποιοῦσιν. Pres act ind 3rd pl ποιέω. This is one of two main verbs in this sentence.

συνευδοκοῦσιν. Pres act ind 3rd pl συνευδοκέω. This is the other main verb in this sentence.

τοῖς πράσσουσιν. Pres act ptc masc dat pl πράσσω (substantival). Dative complement of συνευδοκοῦσιν (cf. BDAG, 970). πράσσω is a synonym of ποιέω, possibly used for stylistic purposes, or more likely used because πράσσω is a semantically narrower word than ποιέω, which has a broader semantic range.

Romans 2:1-11

[1]Therefore, you are without excuse, person, everyone who judges; for in the thing which you judge another, you condemn yourself, for you who judge do the same things. [2]And we know that the judgment of God is based on truth upon those who practice such things. [3]And do you think this, person who judges those who practice such things and does them, that you would escape the judgment of God? [4]Or do you look down

on the wealth of his kindness and tolerance and patience, not knowing that God's kindness brings you into repentance? [5]And according to your stubbornness and unrepentant heart, you are storing up for yourself wrath in the day of wrath and revelation of the righteous judgment of God, [6]who will repay each one according to their deeds: [7]to those who by persevering with good works seek glory and honor and immortality [he will give] eternal life, [8]but to those who out of selfish ambition also disobey the truth but are persuaded towards unrighteousness [there will be] wrath and anger. [9][There will be] suffering and distress upon every human soul who accomplishes evil, the Jew first and also the Greek. [10]But glory and honor and peace to everyone who does good, to the Jew first and also to the Greek. [11]For there is no favoritism with God.

Romans 2:1–11 is the second sub-section under Paul's exposition of human sinfulness found in Rom 1:18–2:11. In this section, Paul answers the question of whether anyone escapes his depiction of sinful humanity. In the previous section, Paul has differentiated varied dimensions of the human response to the knowledge of God that humans have been given. He has described humanity in a variety of ways, using broad and inclusive descriptions. This might raise the question of whether some humans may not fall into such a bleak characterization. Some might even deny such a characterization. In response to such objections, Paul takes up the challenge and through the use of a question-and-answer technique—note the shift to the use of the second person—directly addresses such a possible objector. In ancient literature, this would have been referred to as the use of diatribe, where the author engages in a constructed dialogue. Paul uses this approach here to extend discussion by anticipating the kinds of responses he might receive. Such a constructed dialogue makes use of parallelism and the linkage of similar words. The use of the imperfective aspect (present tense-form) continues the expositional mainline of the discourse.

2:1 Διὸ ἀναπολόγητος εἶ, ὦ ἄνθρωπε πᾶς ὁ κρίνων· ἐν ᾧ γὰρ κρίνεις τὸν ἕτερον, σεαυτὸν κατακρίνεις, τὰ γὰρ αὐτὰ πράσσεις ὁ κρίνων.

Διὸ. Inferential conjunction. As a result of all that has been said by Paul regarding the bleak human condition in the previous chapter, Paul states that no one is without excuse and that no one should judge another.

ἀναπολόγητος. Predicate adjective. Two prepositions, ἀνά and ἀπό, are attached as prefixes to the root, λογ-. This lexeme is fronted for emphasis.

εἶ. Unaugmented ind 2nd sg εἰμί. The 2nd person singular is a hypothetical conversation partner, further described by the singular ἄνθρωπε and πᾶς ὁ κρίνων in this verse.

ὤ. Interjection.

ἄνθρωπε. Nominative of address (so-called vocative).

πᾶς ὁ κρίνων. Nominative in apposition to ἄνθρωπε. πᾶς is adjectival, modifying ὁ κρίνων.

ὁ κρίνων. Pres act ptc masc nom sg κρίνω (substantival).

ἐν ᾧ. Locative.

γὰρ. Postpositive explanatory conjunction that introduces a clause that explains why the one who judges is without excuse: because the standard by which one judges is placed on him-/herself.

κρίνεις. Pres act ind 2nd sg κρίνω.

τὸν ἕτερον. Accusative direct object of κρίνεις.

σεαυτὸν. Accusative direct object of κατακρίνεις. It is placed in front of the verb for emphasis.

κατακρίνεις. Pres act ind 2nd sg κατακρίνω. The prefix κατα- intensifies the root κρίνω (so, "to judge against," or "to condemn"), which is used in the previous clause.

τὰ . . . αὐτὰ. Accusative direct object of πράσσεις. The article with the intensive pronoun αὐτὰ indicates that it functions as an identifying substantival adjective ("the same things").

γὰρ. Postpositive explanatory conjunction. This is the second occurrence of γάρ, this time introducing a clause that explains why the one who judges another ends up condemning him-/herself: because he/she does the same type of things.

πράσσεις. Pres act ind 2nd sg πράσσω.

ὁ κρίνων. Pres act ptc masc nom sg κρίνω (substantival). Nominative in apposition to the implied second-person subject of πράσσεις.

2:2 οἴδαμεν δὲ ὅτι τὸ κρίμα τοῦ θεοῦ ἐστιν κατὰ ἀλήθειαν ἐπὶ τοὺς τὰ τοιαῦτα πράσσοντας.

οἴδαμεν. Prf act ind 1st pl οἶδα. The lexeme in the perfect tense-form (stative aspect) is prominent in this co-text. It is used in reference to knowledge without reference to its attainment, as a means of forcefully introducing Paul's argument.

δὲ. Adversative conjunction (mild).

ὅτι. Introduces the clausal complement (indirect discourse) of οἴδαμεν.

τὸ κρίμα. Nominative subject of ἐστιν.

τοῦ θεοῦ. Genitive of source or origin, modifying τὸ κρίμα ("the judgment that comes from God").

ἐστιν. Unaugmented ind 3rd sg εἰμί. The verb equates τὸ κρίμα τοῦ θεοῦ and κατὰ ἀλήθειαν ἐπὶ τοὺς τὰ τοιαῦτα πράσσοντας.

κατὰ ἀλήθειαν. Standard. The standard or basis for God's judgment is "truth." The anarthrous noun signifies truth in general.

ἐπὶ τοὺς . . . πράσσοντας. Directional.

τοὺς . . . πράσσοντας. Pres act ptc masc acc pl πράσσω (substantival).

τὰ τοιαῦτα. Accusative direct object of πράσσοντας. The demonstrative adjective is placed between the article and participle for emphasis on the adjective (see οἱ τὰ τοιαῦτα πράσσοντες in 1:32).

2:3 λογίζῃ δὲ τοῦτο, ὦ ἄνθρωπε ὁ κρίνων τοὺς τὰ τοιαῦτα πράσσοντας καὶ ποιῶν αὐτά, ὅτι σὺ ἐκφεύξῃ τὸ κρίμα τοῦ θεοῦ;

λογίζῃ. Pres mid ind 2nd sg λογίζομαι. As a so-called deponent verb, λογίζομαι carries the middle voice function as indirect, internal causation; so the process of thinking involves the subject in some way, while the agent is unspecified (see "Deponency" in the Series Introduction and the Introduction).

δὲ. Adversative conjunction (mild).

τοῦτο. Accusative direct object of λογίζῃ. The content of "this" comes a bit later in the sentence after the nominal phrase, signalled by ὅτι.

ὦ. Interjection, occasionally used with a nominative of address (so-called vocative) for further emphasis on the address.

ἄνθρωπε. Nominative of address (so-called vocative). This is the same hypothetical person Paul is addressing, the person who fits the description of one who judges here.

ὁ κρίνων . . . καὶ ποιῶν. Nominatives in apposition to ἄνθρωπε. The phrase ὦ ἄνθρωπε . . . ὁ κρίνων from 2:1 is repeated here. Granville Sharp's rule applies here, as one article governs two substantives, although in participle form (see Winer, 162–63; Wallace 1983; Porter 1994a, 110–12). "The one who judges" is further described as "one who does."

ὁ κρίνων. Pres act ptc masc nom sg κρίνω (substantival). On its function in the sentence, see ὁ κρίνων . . . καὶ ποιῶν above.

ποιῶν. Pres act ptc masc nom sg ποιέω (substantival). On its function in the sentence, see ὁ κρίνων . . . καὶ ποιῶν above.

τοὺς . . . πράσσοντας. Pres act ptc masc acc pl πράσσω (substantival). Accusative direct object of κρίνων.

τὰ τοιαῦτα. Accusative direct object of πράσσοντας (see οἱ τὰ τοιαῦτα πράσσοντες in 1:32 and τοὺς τὰ τοιαῦτα πράσσοντας in 2:2).

αὐτά. Accusative direct object of ποιῶν. The intensive pronoun functions as a personal pronoun that refers back to τὰ τοιαῦτα ("them").

ὅτι. Introduces a content clause that is epexegetical to τοῦτο.

σὺ. Nominative subject of ἐκφεύξῃ. The personal pronoun refers to ἄνθρωπε (and appositions) from this co-text. The use of this pronoun is emphatic here.

ἐκφεύξῃ. Fut mid ind 2nd sg ἐκφεύγω. The prefix ἐκ- is attached to the root φεύγω (to flee), adding the meaning of ἐκ ("out of") to it.

τὸ κρίμα. Accusative direct object of ἐκφεύξῃ.

τοῦ θεοῦ. Genitive of source or origin, modifying τὸ κρίμα.

2:4 ἢ τοῦ πλούτου τῆς χρηστότητος αὐτοῦ καὶ τῆς ἀνοχῆς καὶ τῆς μακροθυμίας καταφρονεῖς, ἀγνοῶν ὅτι τὸ χρηστὸν τοῦ θεοῦ εἰς μετάνοιάν σε ἄγει;

ἢ. Disjunctive conjunction. It functions adversatively, contrasting the statements before and after it. It refers back to λογίζῃ and the content signalled by ὅτι in the previous verse and introduces another option to what was proposed in 2:3, as to what they are thinking.

τοῦ πλούτου . . . καὶ τῆς ἀνοχῆς καὶ τῆς μακροθυμίας. Genitive direct objects of καταφρονεῖς, which appears as the last element in this clause.

τῆς χρηστότητος. Genitive of description, further describing or delineating τοῦ πλούτου.

αὐτοῦ. Possessive genitive. It refers to God and modifies τῆς χρηστότητος.

καταφρονεῖς. Pres act ind 2nd sg καταφρονέω. The preposition κατά is attached as a prefix to the root φρονέω, resulting in the meaning of "thinking down on." The meaning of the word is not so much "to despise" (as in an emotion) but "to think (of something) as lowly" or even worthless.

ἀγνοῶν. Pres act ptc masc nom sg ἀγνοέω (causal). It functions co-textually as circumstantial and modifies καταφρονεῖς, providing supportive material.

ὅτι. Introduces the clausal complement (indirect discourse) of ἀγνοῶν.

τὸ χρηστὸν. Nominative subject of ἄγει. The same root appears earlier in this verse as a noun, χρηστότητος, as one of three objects of what they might look down on. Here it appears as an adjective used as a substantive, to focus on the quality of the description rather than simply identify the description itself.

τοῦ θεοῦ. Genitive of source or origin, modifying τὸ χρηστὸν.

εἰς μετάνοιάν. Purpose. The purpose of God's kindness is repentance. The preposition μετά is prefixed to the root, giving it the etymological meaning of "after thinking," but it means to have a change in orientation and direction. This is the only occurrence of this word in this letter (cf. 2 Cor 7:9–10; 2 Tim 2:25).

σε. Accusative direct object of ἄγει.
ἄγει. Pres act ind 3rd sg ἄγω.

2:5 κατὰ δὲ τὴν σκληρότητά σου καὶ ἀμετανόητον καρδίαν θησαυρίζεις σεαυτῷ ὀργὴν ἐν ἡμέρᾳ ὀργῆς καὶ ἀποκαλύψεως δικαιοκρισίας τοῦ θεοῦ

κατὰ . . . τὴν σκληρότητά . . . καὶ ἀμετανόητον καρδίαν. Standard (ground or basis for something). Here, the basis for which wrath is being stored up is "your stubbornness and unrepentant heart." The noun σκληρότητά, which has an acute accent on the antepenult, acquires an additional accent, the acute, on the ultima from the enclitic σου. The prepositional word group is fronted, making the phrase prominent or thematic in the clause.

δὲ. Adversative conjunction (mild).
σου. Possessive genitive, modifying τὴν σκληρότητά.
θησαυρίζεις. Pres act ind 2nd sg θησαυρίζω.
σεαυτῷ. Dative indirect object or dative of disadvantage of θησαυρίζεις.
ὀργὴν. Accusative direct object of θησαυρίζεις.
ἐν ἡμέρᾳ. Temporal.
ὀργῆς. Genitive of definition, modifying ἡμέρᾳ, defining "day" as "day of wrath."
καὶ. Coordinating conjunction. It connects the compound genitive modifiers.
ἀποκαλύψεως. Genitive of definition, modifying ἡμέρᾳ, further defining "day" as "day of revelation." It is parallel to ὀργῆς.
δικαιοκρισίας. Genitive of description, modifying ἀποκαλύψεως, with "revelation" being further described or circumscribed as "righteous judgment." Some may call this an objective genitive. A NT *hapax legomenon*.
τοῦ θεοῦ. Genitive of source or origin, modifying δικαιοκρισίας ("righteous judgment from God").

2:6 ὃς ἀποδώσει ἑκάστῳ κατὰ τὰ ἔργα αὐτοῦ·

ὃς. Nominative subject of ἀποδώσει. The relative pronoun refers anaphorically to τοῦ θεοῦ.
ἀποδώσει. Fut act ind 3rd sg ἀποδίδωμι. The prefix ἀπο- is attached to the root δίδωμι, providing a directional meaning to the root.
ἑκάστῳ. Dative indirect object of ἀποδώσει.

κατὰ τὰ ἔργα. Standard (ground or basis of something). The basis by which one is repaid is each person's deeds.

αὐτοῦ. Genitive of origin or source, modifying τὰ ἔργα. The pronoun refers anaphorically to ἑκάστῳ.

2:7 τοῖς μὲν καθ' ὑπομονὴν ἔργου ἀγαθοῦ δόξαν καὶ τιμὴν καὶ ἀφθαρσίαν ζητοῦσιν ζωὴν αἰώνιον,

τοῖς . . . ζητοῦσιν. Pres act ptc masc dat pl ζητέω (substantival). Dative in apposition to ἑκάστῳ in the previous verse. The article and substantive (participle) are far removed from each other in the clause, depicting the items between them as modifying this word group.

μὲν. The first element of a point/counterpoint set that correlates the clause introduced by μέν in this verse with the clause introduced by δέ in the next verse.

καθ' ὑπομονὴν. Standard (ground or basis of something). The basis of their seeking glory, honor, and immortality is persevering through good works.

ἔργου ἀγαθοῦ. Genitive of definition, modifying ὑπομονὴν. Perseverance is defined as "good works."

δόξαν καὶ τιμὴν καὶ ἀφθαρσίαν. Accusative direct objects of ζητοῦσιν.

ζωὴν αἰώνιον. Accusative direct object of ἀποδώσει from the previous verse.

2:8 τοῖς δὲ ἐξ ἐριθείας καὶ ἀπειθοῦσι τῇ ἀληθείᾳ πειθομένοις δὲ τῇ ἀδικίᾳ ὀργὴ καὶ θυμός.

τοῖς . . . ἀπειθοῦσι. Pres act ptc masc dat pl ἀπειθέω (substantival). Dative in apposition to ἑκάστῳ in 2:6. The prefix ἀ- is attached to the root for negation. The article and substantival participle are not as far removed from each other as in the previous verse, but the prepositional word group that appears between them is a modifier of it.

δὲ. Postpositive conjunction, mild disjunctive, used in coordination with μὲν in the previous verse. This signifies the second part of the contrast.

ἐξ ἐριθείας. Instrumental (cause, agent). The cause of "disobeying" is "selfish ambition."

καὶ. Adverbial use (adjunctive). It modifies ἀπειθοῦσι.

τῇ ἀληθείᾳ. Dative direct object of ἀπειθοῦσι.

πειθομένοις. Pres pass ptc masc dat pl πείθω (substantival). Dative in apposition to ἑκάστῳ (2:6), and parallel to ζητοῦσιν (2:7) and ἀπειθοῦσι

(2:8). Because there is no direct object (although grammatically τῇ ἀδι-κίᾳ can be a dative direct object), it seems that this is passive voice, not middle ("they are persuaded"), but without a specified agent.

δὲ. Conjunction, mild disjunctive. It mildly juxtaposes τοῖς . . . ἐξ ἐριθείας καὶ ἀπειθοῦσι τῇ ἀληθείᾳ with πειθομένοις . . . τῇ ἀδικίᾳ.

τῇ ἀδικίᾳ. Dative indirect object of πειθομένοις ("persuaded towards unrighteousness") or possibly dative of means/instrument ("persuaded by unrighteousness").

ὀργὴ καὶ θυμός. This phrase seems to be parallel to ζωὴν αἰώνιον in the previous verse, functioning as direct objects of ἀποδώσει in 2:6, but ὀργὴ and θυμός are in the nominative case, not the accusative. Thus, it is more likely that they are nominative absolutes in a verbless nominal clause (see Porter 1994a, 85). It likely continues to 2:9, which begins with a similar construction: two nouns in the nominative case joined by καὶ and without a finite verb attached.

2:9 θλῖψις καὶ στενοχωρία ἐπὶ πᾶσαν ψυχὴν ἀνθρώπου τοῦ κατεργα-ζομένου τὸ κακόν, Ἰουδαίου τε πρῶτον καὶ Ἕλληνος·

θλῖψις καὶ στενοχωρία. Nominative absolutes in a verbless clause. In English translations, a linking verb "to be" would be implied.

ἐπὶ πᾶσαν ψυχὴν. Directional.

ἀνθρώπου. Genitive of description, describing the type of soul ("a human soul").

τοῦ κατεργαζομένου. Pres mid ptc masc gen sg κατεργάζομαι (attributive). The articular participle modifies ἀνθρώπου (third attributive position). The middle voice conveys indirect, internal causality (see "Deponency" in the Series Introduction and Introduction).

τὸ κακόν. Accusative direct object of κατεργαζομένου.

Ἰουδαίου . . . Ἕλληνος. Genitives in apposition to ἀνθρώπου τοῦ κατεργαζομένου.

τε . . . καὶ. Enclitic particle τε is combined with adverbial καί to form a linkage between Ἰουδαίῳ and Ἕλληνι.

πρῶτον. Adverbial accusative. It modifies Ἰουδαίου.

2:10 δόξα δὲ καὶ τιμὴ καὶ εἰρήνη παντὶ τῷ ἐργαζομένῳ τὸ ἀγαθόν, Ἰου-δαίῳ τε πρῶτον καὶ Ἕλληνι·

δόξα . . . καὶ τιμὴ καὶ εἰρήνη. Nominative absolutes in a verbless clause (see 2:9 on θλῖψις καὶ στενοχωρία).

δὲ. Adversative conjunction (mild).

παντὶ τῷ ἐργαζομένῳ. Dative of advantage that is parallel to ἐπὶ πᾶσαν ψυχὴν ἀνθρώπου τοῦ κατεργαζομένου τὸ κακόν in 2:9. The adjective παντὶ functions as a substantive. See 1:16 on παντὶ τῷ πιστεύοντι.

τῷ ἐργαζομένῳ. Pres mid ptc masc dat sg ἐργάζομαι (attributive). It modifies παντὶ (third attributive position). In constructions with πᾶς and an articular participle, one is generally a substantive and the other one attributive (Culy 2004, 56; cf. BDF 413.2; Robertson, 772–73). The middle voice conveys indirect, internal causality (see Series Introduction and Introduction).

τὸ ἀγαθόν. Accusative direct object of ἐργαζομένῳ.

Ἰουδαίῳ . . . Ἕλληνι. Datives in apposition to παντὶ τῷ ἐργαζομένῳ. They are parallel to Ἰουδαίου τε πρῶτον καὶ Ἕλληνος in 2:9.

τε . . . καὶ. Enclitic particle τε is combined with adverbial καί to form a linkage between Ἰουδαίῳ and Ἕλληνι.

πρῶτον. Adverbial accusative. It modifies Ἰουδαίῳ.

2:11 οὐ γάρ ἐστιν προσωπολημψία παρὰ τῷ θεῷ.

οὐ. Negative particle normally used with indicative verbs. Here it negates ἐστιν.

γάρ. Postpositive explanatory conjunction that introduces an explanation of Ἰουδαίῳ τε πρῶτον καὶ Ἕλληνι.

ἐστιν. Unaugmented ind 3rd sg εἰμί.

προσωπολημψία. Nominative subject of ἐστιν.

παρὰ τῷ θεῷ. Locative. Favoritism is not something that is "alongside" God.

Romans 2:12–16

[12]For whoever sins without the law will also perish without the law, and all who sin within the law will through the law be judged. [13]For [it is] not the hearers of the law [who are] righteous towards God, but the doers of the law will be justified. [14]For whenever Gentiles, who do not have the law, by nature do that which is of the law, they, while not having the law, are a law to themselves. [15]They demonstrate the work of the law, written upon their hearts, as their consciences testify in confirmation and their thoughts either accusing or even defending between one another, [16]on the day when God judges people's secrets, according to my gospel through Christ Jesus.

Romans 2:12–3:20 constitutes the second sub-section of this first major part of the body proper of the Letter to the Romans (Rom 1:18–4:25).

This section is focused upon the law of God in several dimensions, indicated by its further topics of discussion. Paul has established the nature of humanity as standing condemned before God, incapable of meriting or earning salvation. He appears to have all of humanity in view, not just non-Jews. Paul now introduces the matter of God's law, something distinctive of the Jews, making clear that those disobedient to it stand condemned by it. Throughout this section, Paul continues to use his dialogical convention, including the use of parallelism, linking of words, asking of questions, and direct address. This sub-section is itself divided into three sub-sections. The first, Rom 2:12–16, is concerned with abstract notions of law and humanity. The lexeme νόμος (and cognates) is used nine times in this section, as well as nine times in the next section, creating strong lexical cohesion throughout the units.

2:12 Ὅσοι γὰρ ἀνόμως ἥμαρτον, ἀνόμως καὶ ἀπολοῦνται, καὶ ὅσοι ἐν νόμῳ ἥμαρτον, διὰ νόμου κριθήσονται·

Ὅσοι. Nominative subject of ἥμαρτον. Ὅσοι is a quantitative correlative relative pronoun.

γὰρ. Postpositive conjunction that introduces a clause that explains the previous statement that there is no favoritism with God.

ἀνόμως. Adverb (manner), modifying ἥμαρτον.

ἥμαρτον. Aor act ind 3rd pl ἁμαρτάνω. The perfective aspect (aorist tense-form) here and in the next clause signifies background information in this discourse.

ἀνόμως. Adverb (manner), modifying ἀπολοῦνται.

καὶ. Adverbial use (adjunctive). It modifies ἀπολοῦνται.

ἀπολοῦνται. Fut mid ind 3rd pl ἀπόλλυμι. The middle voice indicates indirect, internal causality (see Series Introduction and Introduction).

καὶ. Coordinating conjunction. It connects anaphoric and cataphoric clauses.

ὅσοι. Nominative subject of ἥμαρτον (see above).

ἐν νόμῳ. Locative ("within the sphere of the law").

ἥμαρτον. Aor act ind 3rd pl ἁμαρτάνω.

διὰ νόμου. Instrumental. The person is judged by means of the law.

κριθήσονται. Fut pass ind 3rd pl κρίνω. The agent is not specified here, probably to state a general fact without specification. The one who does the judging is God (cf. 2:5–6), but here it is in the passive voice to state a general fact.

2:13 οὐ γὰρ οἱ ἀκροαταὶ νόμου δίκαιοι παρὰ [τῷ] θεῷ, ἀλλ' οἱ ποιηταὶ νόμου δικαιωθήσονται.

This verse consists of two main clauses, connected together by ἀλλ'. Interestingly, the first clause is verbless, while the second clause contains a finite verb. The semantic effect of this is that in the first clause, the description of the "hearers of the law" is emphasized, while in the second, the focus is on the act of being made righteous for the "doers of the law."

οὐ ... ἀλλ'. A point/counterpoint set that contrasts the first clause with the subsequent clause.

γὰρ. Postpositive explanatory conjunction.

οἱ ἀκροαταὶ. Nominative subject of this verbless clause.

νόμου. Genitive of description or definition, modifying οἱ ἀκροαταὶ. "Hearers" is further described or circumscribed as "of the law." Some may wish to label this as an objective genitive if νόμου is seen as the direct object of the verbal form of οἱ ἀκροαταὶ (however, see the Introduction in this handbook on syntactical categories and genitives).

δίκαιοι. Predicate adjective.

παρὰ [τῷ] θεῷ. Positional (alongside), with the idea of being "alongside" as "to" or "for" here in this co-text. Most of the major manuscripts contain the dative article, but two of them (A D*) do not.

οἱ ποιηταὶ. Nominative subject of δικαιωθήσονται.

νόμου. Genitive of description or definition. "Doers" is further described or circumscribed as "of the law." Some may wish to label this as an objective genitive as above, if νόμου is seen as the direct object of the verbal form of οἱ ποιηταὶ (however, see the Introduction in this handbook on genitive categories).

δικαιωθήσονται. Fut pass ind 3rd pl κρίνω. The passive voice reflects external causality, but the agent is not specified here. The point is that they do not make themselves "just" or "righteous," but that they are made just/righteous by an outside agent, who is implied to be God.

2:14 ὅταν γὰρ ἔθνη τὰ μὴ νόμον ἔχοντα φύσει τὰ τοῦ νόμου ποιῶσιν, οὗτοι νόμον μὴ ἔχοντες ἑαυτοῖς εἰσιν νόμος·

The main and subordinate verbs in this section now switch, for the most part, to the present tense-form, depicting imperfective aspect, indicating mainline material in expositional discourse.

ὅταν. Subordinating conjunction that introduces a temporal clause, which functions not so much temporally as it presents a hypothetical situation (regardless of whether it reflects reality).

γὰρ. Postpositive explanatory conjunction. Paul further explains why doers of the law are superior to hearers of the law, including the argument from Gentiles, who are doers of the law, even though they do not consciously know the law.

ἔθνη. Nominative subject of ποιῶσιν. The anarthrous noun depicts Gentiles in general.

τὰ . . . ἔχοντα. Pres act ptc neut nom pl ἔχω (attributive). The participle modifies ἔθνη (third attributive position).

μὴ νόμον. The insertion of this phrase between the article and participle (τὰ . . . ἔχοντα) indicates that the phrase functions as a modifier of τὰ ἔχοντα.

μὴ. Negative particle normally used with non-indicative verbs. Here it negates the participle ἔχοντα.

νόμον. Accusative direct object of ἔχοντα.

φύσει. Dative of manner. The manner in which Gentiles "do" (ποιῶσιν) the things of the law is by nature or according to nature. The fronting of the dative before the predicate indicates clausal prominence.

τὰ τοῦ νόμου. The article functions as a nominalizer, changing the genitive phrase τοῦ νόμου into the accusative direct object of ποιῶσιν.

τοῦ νόμου. Genitive of definition ("the things of the law"). τὰ τοῦ νόμου is used here, instead of the more straightforward τὸν νομόν, to reflect that Gentiles do the things in relation to the law, but not the law itself.

ποιῶσιν. Pres act subj 3rd pl ποιέω. Subjunctive with ὅταν.

οὗτοι. Nominative subject of εἰσιν in this clause. There is a lack of grammatical concord in gender here (Porter 2015, 78; Robertson, 704; cf. Acts 8:10; 9:15; Rom 2:14), with the masculine plural pronoun οὗτοι anaphorically referring to the neuter plural noun ἔθνη (*constructio ad sensum*).

νόμον. Accusative direct object of ἔχοντες.

μὴ. Negative particle normally used with non-indicative verbs. Here it negates the participle ἔχοντες.

ἔχοντες. Pres act ptc masc nom pl ἔχω (temporal or concessive). The participle functions co-textually as circumstantial. The participle modifies and is subordinate to ἑαυτοῖς εἰσιν νόμος.

ἑαυτοῖς. Dative of advantage. The fronting of the dative before the predicate indicates clausal prominence.

εἰσιν. Unaugmented ind 3rd pl εἰμί.

νόμος. Predicate nominative.

2:15 οἵτινες ἐνδείκνυνται τὸ ἔργον τοῦ νόμου γραπτὸν ἐν ταῖς καρδίαις αὐτῶν, συμμαρτυρούσης αὐτῶν τῆς συνειδήσεως καὶ μεταξὺ ἀλλήλων τῶν λογισμῶν κατηγορούντων ἢ καὶ ἀπολογουμένων,

οἵτινες. Nominative subject of ἐνδείκνυνται. The indefinite relative pronoun is used here in reference to whoever fits the above description. Paul uses asyndeton (no connecting word) here in continuing his discourse from the previous verse.

ἐνδείκνυνται. Pres mid ind 3rd pl ἐνδείκνυμαι. The middle voice indicates indirect, internal causality (see "Deponency" in the Series Introduction and Introduction).

τὸ ἔργον. Accusative direct object of ἐνδείκνυνται in a double accusative object-complement construction with γραπτὸν.

τοῦ νόμου. Genitive of description, modifying τὸ ἔργον. "Work" is further circumscribed or described as "of the law."

γραπτὸν. Predicative adjective, functioning as a complement to τὸ ἔργον in a double accusative object-complement construction.

ἐν ταῖς καρδίαις. Locative.

αὐτῶν. Possessive genitive, modifying ταῖς καρδίαις.

συμμαρτυρούσης. Pres act ptc fem gen sg συμμαρτυρέω (genitive absolute, temporal). The prefix συμ- (συν) is attached to the root μαρτυρέω, making the meaning of the verb, "to testify in confirmation with."

αὐτῶν. Possessive genitive, modifying τῆς συνειδήσεως.

τῆς συνειδήσεως. Genitive subject of συμμαρτυρούσης.

καὶ. Coordinating conjunction that connects two genitive absolutes.

μεταξὺ ἀλλήλων. Relational/reciprocal ("between one another" or "among one another"). This prepositional word group (using a rare preposition) modifies τῶν λογισμῶν.

τῶν λογισμῶν. Genitive subject of κατηγορούντων and ἀπολογουμένων.

κατηγορούντων. Pres act ptc masc gen pl κατηγορέω (genitive absolute, temporal). This verb is used only here in Paul.

ἤ. Disjunctive conjunction.

καὶ. Adverbial use (adjunctive), modifying ἀπολογουμένων.

ἀπολογουμένων. Pres mid ptc masc gen pl ἀπολογέομαι (genitive absolute, temporal).

2:16 ἐν ἡμέρᾳ ὅτε κρίνει ὁ θεὸς τὰ κρυπτὰ τῶν ἀνθρώπων κατὰ τὸ εὐαγγέλιόν μου διὰ Χριστοῦ Ἰησοῦ.

ἐν ἡμέρᾳ. Temporal.

ὅτε. Introduces a temporal clause.

κρίνει. Pres act ind 3rd sg κρίνω.

ὁ θεὸς. Nominative subject of κρίνει.

τὰ κρυπτὰ. Accusative direct object of κρίνει.

τῶν ἀνθρώπων. Possessive genitive, modifying τὰ κρυπτά.

κατὰ τὸ εὐαγγέλιόν. Standard. The basis by which God judges is Paul's gospel, which he expounds in this letter. The extra accent on the ultima of εὐαγγέλιόν is a result of the following word being enclitic.

μου. Possessive genitive, modifying τὸ εὐαγγέλιόν.

διὰ Χριστοῦ Ἰησοῦ. Instrumental. It explains the means by which the good news exists (see notes at 1:1 on this title).

Romans 2:17–29

[17]But if you are called a Jew, and you rely upon the law and boast in God, [18]and you know his will and you discern what is better, being instructed from the law—[19]you have convinced yourself that you are a guide to the blind, a light to those in darkness, [20]an instructor of the unlearned, a teacher of children, having the form of the knowledge and the truth of the law—[21]therefore, do you, who teach another, not teach yourself? Do you, who proclaim not to steal, steal? [22]Do you, who say not to commit adultery, commit adultery? Do you, who detest idols, rob temples? [23]You who boast in the law, through the transgression of the law you dishonor God. [24]For "God's name, because of you, is blasphemed among the Gentiles," as it stands written. [25]For, on the one hand, circumcision profits you if you practice the law; but, on the other hand, if you are a transgressor of the law, your circumcision has become uncircumcision. [26]So if the uncircumcised person keeps the regulations of the law, will not his uncircumcision be considered as circumcision? [27]And [will not] the physically uncircumcised person who fulfills the law judge you, a transgressor of the law by the letter and circumcision? [28]For neither is one in appearance a Jew, nor [is] circumcision in appearance physically, [29]but one who is inwardly [is] a Jew, and circumcision of the heart [is] spiritual, not literal; his praise is not from people but from God.

Romans 2:17–3:8 constitutes the second sub-section within this unit. This sub-section addresses the question of whether the Jews have an advantage over Gentiles. The Jews appeared to have such an advantage because of their clear and explicit law, which they believed was given to them by God. Paul addresses such concerns by using a dialogical technique (diatribe), but he makes clear that despite their advantage, all of

humanity stands before God in the same condition. Throughout this
section there is an alternation of tense-forms used to carry the narrative
line, depending upon whether the main focus (present = imperfective
aspect) or background material (aorist = perfective aspect) is being elucidated, with the perfect tense-form (stative aspect) occasionally used
for prominence. For the sake of analysis, this section is divided into
three further sub-sections, the first of which is 2:17–29. This section
mostly consists of a conditional statement (2:17–22), with arguments
supporting it. Paul argues here that what certain Jews proclaim of themselves does not match with their behavior, and that Gentiles who do not
proclaim such things actually reflect the law better than they do.

**2:17 Εἰ δὲ σὺ Ἰουδαῖος ἐπονομάζῃ καὶ ἐπαναπαύῃ νόμῳ καὶ καυχᾶσαι
ἐν θεῷ**

Εἰ. Introduces the protasis of a first-class conditional. The protasis
extends through the end of 2:20. The apodosis appears in 2:21–22. Most
English translations include 2:23 as a part of the apodosis, but it seems
likely that this verse is a new (albeit related) statement (see below).

δὲ. Adversative conjunction (mild).

σὺ. Nominative subject of ἐπονομάζῃ (and by implication ἐπαναπαύῃ
and καυχᾶσαι) in a double nominative subject-complement construction with Ἰουδαῖος. Since the second-person subject is embedded in
these verb-forms, the use of the personal pronoun is emphatic. The singular shows that Paul is not addressing his audience as a whole (all in
Rome; 1:7) but depicts the hypothetical Jew, to whom this statement
(and following) might apply.

Ἰουδαῖος. Nominative complement to σὺ in a double nominative
subject-complement construction with σὺ (cf. Culy 2009 for this construction with passive voice verbs).

ἐπονομάζῃ. Pres pass ind 2nd sg ἐπονομάζω. The middle voice-form
is the same, but the context seems to warrant a passive sense, as there is
no direct object (accusative noun) for this verb.

καὶ . . . καὶ. Coordinating conjunctions that paratactically join the
three clauses together, with the same subject σὺ.

ἐπαναπαύῃ. Pres mid ind 2nd sg ἐπαναπαύομαι. The passive voice-
form is the same, but the passive sense does not semantically fit here.
This is a so-called deponent verb (see "Deponency" in the Series Introduction and Introduction).

νόμῳ. Dative complement of ἐπαναπαύῃ.

καυχᾶσαι. Pres mid ind 2nd sg καυχάομαι. The passive voice-form is
the same, but it would not make sense in this context. This is a so-called

deponent verb (see "Deponency" in the Series Introduction and Introduction). It also has negative connotations in the co-text (on "boasting," see Gathercole, 197–262).

ἐν θεῷ. Locative (sphere or realm). Their boasting is located "in" God.

2:18 καὶ γινώσκεις τὸ θέλημα καὶ δοκιμάζεις τὰ διαφέροντα κατηχού-μενος ἐκ τοῦ νόμου,

καὶ. Coordinating conjunction. It continues the protasis and paratactically connects the present clause to the clauses from the previous verse.

γινώσκεις. Pres act ind 2nd sg γινώσκω. The subject of this verb is still σὺ from 2:17 (the implied 2nd sg "you").

τὸ θέλημα. Accusative direct object of γινώσκεις. Some might expect to see τοῦ θεοῦ as a modifier to θέλημα—since the question might arise "the will of whom?"—but the attached article is sufficient to relate it back to "God" in the previous verse.

καὶ. Coordinating conjunction. This is the last connective conjunction that paratactically joins several independent clauses together.

δοκιμάζεις. Pres act ind 2nd sg δοκιμάζω. This is the last parallel verb (ἐπονομάζῃ, ἐπαναπαύῃ, καυχᾶσαι, γινώσκεις, and δοκιμάζεις) in this series of independent clauses paratactically connected.

τὰ διαφέροντα. Pres act ptc neut acc pl διαφέρω (substantival). Accusative direct object of δοκιμάζεις.

κατηχούμενος. Pres pass ptc masc nom sg κατηχέω (causal). The participle functions co-textually as circumstantial. Some English translations supply "because," interpreting this participle as causal (e.g., NIV, NRSV, ESV). The middle voice-form is the same, but the passive voice makes more sense ("you are taught").

ἐκ τοῦ νόμου. Instrumental. The instrument, or cause or agent, that taught them was the law.

2:19 πέποιθάς τε σεαυτὸν ὁδηγὸν εἶναι τυφλῶν, φῶς τῶν ἐν σκότει,

πέποιθάς τε σεαυτὸν ὁδηγὸν εἶναι τυφλῶν, φῶς τῶν ἐν σκότει. While this verse still continues the protasis of the conditional statement that began in Rom 2:17, there is no connective here (asyndeton). What this does is distinguish the following material from the paratactically connected clauses. In light of this, we have included em-dashes in our translation above to reflect this distinction.

πέποιθάς. Prf act ind 2nd sg πείθω. The perfect tense-form (stative aspect) is prominent in this discourse, depicting frontground material.

In the active voice, the subject ("you") is the agent, so the object ("your-self") is the Goal.

τε. Enclitic conjunction and particle. Connects the preceding and subsequent words.

σεαυτὸν. Accusative subject of the infinitive εἶναι.

ὁδηγὸν. Predicate accusative of εἶναι.

εἶναι. Inf εἰμί (indirect discourse). It modifies πέποιθάς as a subordi-nate predicate. The subject of εἶναι is the same as the implied subject of its head verb, πέποιθάς.

τυφλῶν. Genitive of definition or description, modifying ὁδηγὸν. It further describes or circumscribes the "guide" as "of the blind." Some may wish to call this an objective genitive if ὁδηγὸν were a predicate.

φῶς. Accusative in apposition to ὁδηγὸν.

τῶν ἐν σκότει. The article functions as a nominalizer, changing the prepositional word group ἐν σκότει into a genitive of definition or description, modifying φῶς. The genitive phrase retains the consistency of the predicate accusative + genitive constructions continuing in 2:20.

ἐν σκότει. Locative. The use of the preposition in a genitive con-struction (instead of φῶς σκότους, for example) emphasizes the locative sense of the preposition, that the light is in darkness, while maintaining the genitive meaning of restriction.

2:20 παιδευτὴν ἀφρόνων, διδάσκαλον νηπίων, ἔχοντα τὴν μόρφωσιν τῆς γνώσεως καὶ τῆς ἀληθείας ἐν τῷ νόμῳ·

παιδευτὴν. Predicate accusative of εἶναι from 2:19. The root is παι-δίον, which means "little or young child," with the suffix -της, which connotes agency. The meaning, thus, is "one who trains, teaches, or dis-ciplines a child" (cf. LN 33.244).

ἀφρόνων. Genitive of definition or description, modifying παιδευτὴν. It further specifies the "instructor" to be "of the unlearned." Some may wish to call this an objective genitive. The so-called alpha privative (prefix ἀ-) is attached to the root, φρονέω ("to think"). The base meaning of this lexeme, then, is "one who lacks thinking," here translated as "unlearned."

διδάσκαλον. Predicate accusative of εἶναι from 2:19.

νηπίων. Genitive of definition or description, modifying διδάσκαλον. It further describes or circumscribes the "teacher" as of "children." Some may wish to call this an objective genitive. The meaning is probably fig-urative of a baby or infant—as in "spiritual infant."

ἔχοντα. Pres act ptc masc acc sg ἔχω (attributive). It modifies ὁδηγὸν . . . τυφλῶν, παιδευτὴν ἀφρόνων, and διδάσκαλον νηπίων (fourth attributive position).

τὴν μόρφωσιν. Accusative direct object of ἔχοντα. The only other use of this lexeme in the NT is in 2 Tim 3:5.

τῆς γνώσεως. Genitive of definition or description, modifying τὴν μόρφωσιν. It further describes or circumscribes τὴν μόρφωσιν as the form of knowledge.

καὶ. Coordinating conjunction that joins τῆς γνώσεως and τῆς ἀληθείας.

τῆς ἀληθείας. Genitive of definition or description, modifying τὴν μόρφωσιν. It further describes or circumscribes τὴν μόρφωσιν as the form of truth. It is parallel to τῆς γνώσεως.

ἐν τῷ νόμῳ. Locative. The sphere of the form of the knowledge and truth is "the law."

2:21 ὁ οὖν διδάσκων ἕτερον σεαυτὸν οὐ διδάσκεις; ὁ κηρύσσων μὴ κλέπτειν κλέπτεις;

This verse and the next contain a series of four parallel (rhetorical) questions that make up the apodosis of the conditional statement that began in 2:17. All four questions begin with an article and participle construction (used substantivally), grammatically parallel to each other.

ὁ . . . διδάσκων. Pres act ptc masc nom sg διδάσκω (substantival). Nominative in apposition to the implied subject of διδάσκεις.

οὖν. Postpositive inferential conjunction. It marks the apodosis of the conditional statement that began in 2:17. It is used to draw inferences from Paul's above description of this hypothetical Jew.

ἕτερον. Accusative direct object of διδάσκων.

σεαυτὸν. Accusative direct object of διδάσκεις. Its placement in the front of the clause (σεαυτὸν οὐ διδάσκεις) shows thematization and prominence.

οὐ. Negative particle that negates διδάσκεις and indicates that Paul expects a positive answer ("yes").

διδάσκεις. Pres act ind 2nd sg διδάσκω. The 2nd person singular addresses the hypothetical Jew who fits the description laid out here.

ὁ κηρύσσων. Pres act ptc masc nom sg κηρύσσω (substantival). Nominative in apposition to the implied subject of κλέπτεις.

μὴ. Negative particle normally used with non-indicative verbs. Here it negates the infinitive κλέπτειν.

κλέπτειν. Pres act inf κλέπτω (indirect discourse).

κλέπτεις. Pres act ind 2nd sg κλέπτω. No negative particle is attached (as in the first question), so it is an open question.

2:22 ὁ λέγων μὴ μοιχεύειν μοιχεύεις; ὁ βδελυσσόμενος τὰ εἴδωλα ἱεροσυλεῖς;

ὁ λέγων. Pres act ptc masc nom sg λέγω (substantival). Nominative in apposition to the implied subject of μοιχεύεις.

μὴ. Negative particle normally used with non-indicative verbs. Here it negates the infinitive μοιχεύειν.

μοιχεύειν. Pres act inf μοιχεύω (indirect discourse).

μοιχεύεις. Pres act ind 2nd sg μοιχεύω. No negative particle is attached, so it is an open question.

ὁ βδελυσσόμενος. Pres mid ptc masc nom sg βδελύσσομαι (substantival). Nominative in apposition to the implied subject of ἱεροσυλεῖς. This is the only occurrence of this lexeme in Paul (cf. Rev 21:8, the only other occurrence in the NT).

τὰ εἴδωλα. Accusative direct object of βδελυσσόμενος.

ἱεροσυλεῖς. Pres act ind 2nd sg ἱεροσυλέω. The verb is a compound word composed of ἱερον ("temple") and συλέω ("to steal"). Unlike the previous three questions, which repeated the same lexeme for the participial substantive and the main verb, this one uses different ones, probably because the thought requires different lexemes to be used. No negative particle is attached, so it is an open question.

2:23 ὃς ἐν νόμῳ καυχᾶσαι, διὰ τῆς παραβάσεως τοῦ νόμου τὸν θεὸν ἀτιμάζεις·

Most English translations include this verse within the series of questions in 2:21–23, but GNT editions identify this verse as a separate statement, and probably rightly so. The shift in grammatical construction here (the above questions all begin with an articular participle with a corresponding finite verb) seems to be a clue that Paul has also shifts from asking questions to posing a statement here. Since the earliest manuscripts do not contain punctuation and questions are identified in Greek based on context, it seems best to interpret this verse as a statement.

ὃς. The relative pronoun introduces a relative clause (ὃς ἐν νόμῳ καυχᾶσαι) which, in its entirety, serves as the apposition to the implied subject of ἀτιμάζεις ("you"). Within its clause, ὃς functions as the nominative in apposition to the implied subject of καυχᾶσαι ("you"). It refers back to the articular participles that begin each of the previous four questions.

ἐν νόμῳ. Locative (sphere or realm). Their boasting is located in the realm of "law." The placement of the prepositional word group before the verb it modifies, καυχᾶσαι, makes it prominent.

καυχᾶσαι. Pres mid ind 2nd sg καυχάομαι. For "boasting," see Gathercole. Other occurrences of this lexeme in Romans are in 2:17; 5:2, 3, and 11.

διὰ τῆς παραβάσεως. Instrumental. The prepositional word group modifies ἀτιμάζεις.

τοῦ νόμου. Genitive of definition or description, modifying τῆς παραβάσεως. The "transgression" is further described or circumscribed as "the law." Some may wish to call this an objective genitive.

τὸν θεὸν. Accusative direct object of ἀτιμάζεις.

ἀτιμάζεις. Pres act ind 2nd sg ἀτιμάζω. The so-called alpha privative (prefix ἀ-) attached to the root word τιμάζω negates it.

2:24 τὸ γὰρ ὄνομα τοῦ θεοῦ δι᾽ ὑμᾶς βλασφημεῖται ἐν τοῖς ἔθνεσιν, καθὼς γέγραπται.

τὸ . . . ὄνομα τοῦ θεοῦ δι᾽ ὑμᾶς βλασφημεῖται ἐν τοῖς ἔθνεσιν. A quotation, minorly adapted for Paul's own context, from LXX Isa 52:5 (δι᾽ ὑμᾶς διὰ παντὸς τὸ ὄνομα μου βλασφημεῖται ἐν τοῖς ἔθνεσιν).

τὸ . . . ὄνομα. Nominative subject of βλασφημεῖται.

γὰρ. Postpositive explanatory conjunction that introduces a clause that further explains why Paul has just said that they dishonor God: because God's name is blasphemed among the Gentiles because of their behavior.

τοῦ θεοῦ. Possessive genitive, modifying τὸ . . . ὄνομα.

δι᾽ ὑμᾶς. Causal. The cause of God's name being blasphemed is ὑμᾶς. The shift to 2nd person singular here may simply be the result of quoting Isaiah.

βλασφημεῖται. Pres pass ind 3rd sg βλασφημέω. While the passive voice indicates indirect, external causality, the agent is not directly identified. The prepositional word group ἐν τοῖς ἔθνεσιν, however, indicates that the agent can be found within that sphere.

ἐν τοῖς ἔθνεσιν. Distributional ("among the Gentiles").

καθὼς γέγραπται. Paul's usual mode is to place this Scripture reference formula before the reference (cf. Rom 1:17; 3:4, 10; 4:17; 8:36; 9:13, 33; 10:15; 11:8, 26, 15:3, 9, 21; 1 Cor 1:31; 2:9; 2 Cor 8:15; 9:9), but here is the only instance in Paul where he places it after the reference, indicating the reference to Scripture as background material. In other words, by placing καθὼς γέγραπται after the reference, Paul's emphasis is on the content of the reference itself rather than on appealing to scriptural authority or source.

καθὼς. Comparative conjunction (see note on 1:17).

γέγραπται. Prf pass ind 3rd sg γράφω (see note on 1:17).

2:25 Περιτομὴ μὲν γὰρ ὠφελεῖ ἐὰν νόμον πράσσῃς· ἐὰν δὲ παραβάτης νόμου ᾖς, ἡ περιτομή σου ἀκροβυστία γέγονεν.

Περιτομὴ. Nominative subject of ὠφελεῖ. It marks the beginning of the apodosis of a third-class conditional. The fronting of the apodosis before the protasis emphasizes the apodosis in the conditional (clause-complex prominence).

μὲν . . . δὲ. A point/counterpoint set that establishes the contrast between the two conditional statements.

γὰρ. Postpositive inferential conjunction. It introduces an inference from the above statements regarding the new, but related, topic of circumcision and its potential profit or loss. In this clause, γὰρ comes third because of the postpositive μὲν, which comes second.

ὠφελεῖ. Pres act ind 3rd sg ὠφελέω.

ἐὰν. Introduces the protasis of a third-class conditional, which indicates less certainty (with the subjunctive) than the first-class conditional.

νόμον. Accusative object of πράσσῃς. The fronting of the accusative object before the predicate indicates clausal prominence.

πράσσῃς. Pres act subj 2nd sg πράσσω. Subjunctive with ἐάν. The subject of the verb ("you") is implied in the verb form. Paul switches back to 2nd person singular here, the hypothetical Jew.

ἐὰν. Introduces the protasis of a third-class conditional. This time, the order is standard: the protasis comes before the apodosis.

παραβάτης. Predicate nominative. The root is the same as παράβασις in 2:13.

νόμου. Genitive of definition or description, modifying παραβάτης. It further describes or circumscribes the "teacher" as "of children." Some may wish to call this an objective genitive.

ᾖς. Subj 2nd sg εἰμί. Subjunctive with ἐάν. The subject of the verb ("you") is implied in the verb form.

ἡ περιτομή. Nominative subject of γέγονεν. It marks the beginning of the apodosis.

σου. Possessive genitive, modifying ἡ περιτομή. The pronoun refers to the hypothetical Jew.

ἀκροβυστία. Predicate nominative.

γέγονεν. Prf act ind 3rd sg γίνομαι. The perfect tense-form depicts stative aspect and is frontgrounded in this discourse. Paul wants to especially emphasize that "your circumcision has become uncircumcision."

2:26 ἐὰν οὖν ἡ ἀκροβυστία τὰ δικαιώματα τοῦ νόμου φυλάσσῃ, οὐχ ἡ ἀκροβυστία αὐτοῦ εἰς περιτομὴν λογισθήσεται;

ἐὰν. Introduces the protasis of a third-class conditional, which communicates less certainty than a first-class conditional.

οὖν. Postpositive inferential conjunction. There is a further inference from what was just stated (or asked) regarding the value of circumcision with respect to practicing or transgressing the law.

ἡ ἀκροβυστία. Nominative subject of φυλάσσῃ. The noun "circumcision" is used here as a personification of one who is circumcised in order to highlight the act of circumcision over the person who fulfills the act.

τὰ δικαιώματα. Accusative direct object of φυλάσσῃ.

τοῦ νόμου. Genitive of definition or description, modifying τὰ δικαιώματα. It further describes or circumscribes "the regulations" as "of the law." Some may wish to call this a subjective genitive, if δικαιώματα (regulations) is seen as a verb (regulate).

φυλάσσῃ. Pres act subj 3rd sg φυλάσσω. Subjunctive with ἐάν.

οὐχ. Negative particle that negates λογισθήσεται and indicates that Paul expects a positive answer to this question. This begins the apodosis of the conditional statement.

ἡ ἀκροβυστία. Nominative subject of λογισθήσεται.

αὐτοῦ. Possessive genitive, modifying ἡ ἀκροβυστία. The masculine pronoun represents a *constructio ad sensum*, reflecting the metonymy of the first clause, where the abstract noun ἡ ἀκροβυστία refers to an uncircumcised person (BDF §282.2).

εἰς περιτομὴν. Goal or state.

λογισθήσεται. Fut pass ind 3rd sg λογίζομαι. The passive voice indicates indirect, external causality; here the agent is not specified.

2:27 καὶ κρινεῖ ἡ ἐκ φύσεως ἀκροβυστία τὸν νόμον τελοῦσα σὲ τὸν διὰ γράμματος καὶ περιτομῆς παραβάτην νόμου.

While the major GNT editions (e.g., NA²⁸, UBS⁵, and THGNT) and many English translations (e.g., NIV, ESV, and NRSV) translate this as a sentence rather than a question, the NASB and NKJV, for example, translate this verse as a question, and probably rightly so. The question is more appropriate due to the connective καί at the beginning of this verse, signifying grammatical continuity with the previous question, both referring to the same nominative subject (the uncircumcised person), and the greater co-text of rhetorical questions in this section.

καί. Coordinating conjunction. It connects the previous clause to the current one.

κρινεῖ. Fut act ind 3rd sg κρίνω.

ἡ . . . ἀκροβυστία. Nominative subject of κρινεῖ. ἡ . . . ἀκροβυστία is again a personification for the uncircumcised person.

ἐκ φύσεως. Instrumental. The prepositional word group is inserted between the article and the noun (ἀκροβυστία) to reflect its attribution of the noun more clearly.

τὸν νόμον. Accusative direct object of τελοῦσα. The fronting of the accusative direct object before the predicate indicates clausal prominence.

τελοῦσα. Pres act ptc fem nom sg τελέω (attributive or conditional). If the participle is attributive, it modifies ἀκροβυστία (most English translations), but in such a case we would expect the repetition of the article ἡ. It is therefore better to take it as an adverbial participle that "implies a condition on which the fulfillment of the idea indicated by the main verb depends" (Wallace 1996, 632).

σὲ. Accusative direct object of κρινεῖ.

τὸν . . . παραβάτην. Accusative in apposition to σὲ.

διὰ γράμματος καὶ περιτομῆς. Instrumental, expressing the means by which the addressee is considered a transgressor of the law. This prepositional word group is embedded between the article and the noun it modifies in order to reflect its attribution of the noun more clearly.

νόμου. Genitive of definition or description, modifying τὸν . . . παραβάτην. It further describes and circumscribes "transgression" as "law." Some may wish to call this an objective genitive.

2:28 οὐ γὰρ ὁ ἐν τῷ φανερῷ Ἰουδαῖός ἐστιν οὐδὲ ἡ ἐν τῷ φανερῷ ἐν σαρκὶ περιτομή,

οὐ . . . οὐδὲ. "Neither . . . nor." The two negative clauses in this verse form the first half of the οὐ . . . ἀλλ' point/counterpoint set that extends through the next verse.

γὰρ. Explanatory conjunction. Paul explains more clearly the implication from the previous rhetorical questions about the physically uncircumcised.

ὁ ἐν τῷ φανερῷ. The article functions as a nominalizer, changing the prepositional word group ἐν τῷ φανερῷ into the nominative subject of ἐστιν.

ἐν τῷ φανερῷ. Locative (within the sphere of visibility or appearance).

Ἰουδαῖός. Predicate nominative.

ἐστιν. Unaugmented ind 3rd sg εἰμί.

ἡ ἐν τῷ φανερῷ. The article functions as a nominalizer, changing the prepositional word group ἐν τῷ φανερῷ into the nominative subject of an implied ἐστιν. The nominalizing article, which is now feminine to agree with the predicate nominative περιτομή, indicates that the first prepositional word group in the clause functions as the subject.

ἐν τῷ φανερῷ. Locative (within the sphere of visibility or appearance).

ἐν σαρκὶ. Locative (within the sphere of the flesh, or "physically").

περιτομή. Predicate nominative.

2:29 ἀλλ᾽ ὁ ἐν τῷ κρυπτῷ Ἰουδαῖος, καὶ περιτομὴ καρδίας ἐν πνεύματι οὐ γράμματι, οὗ ὁ ἔπαινος οὐκ ἐξ ἀνθρώπων ἀλλ᾽ ἐκ τοῦ θεοῦ.

ἀλλ᾽. Adversative conjunction (strong) that introduces the second half of the οὐ . . . ἀλλ᾽ point/counterpoint set that began in the previous verse.

ὁ ἐν τῷ κρυπτῷ. The article functions as a nominalizer, changing the prepositional word group ἐν τῷ κρυπτῷ into the nominative subject of an implied ἐστιν.

ἐν τῷ κρυπτῷ. Locative (within the sphere of being hidden, private, secret, or inward). Although the adjective κρυπτός means "secret," it has a broader meaning of "hidden" or "unseen," i.e., "inward."

Ἰουδαῖος. Predicate nominative.

καὶ. Coordinating conjunction that joins paratactically the previous verbless clause to the following verbless clause.

περιτομὴ. Nominative subject of the verbless clause. The anarthrous noun refers to circumcision abstractly (as opposed to concretely; see Peters).

καρδίας. Genitive of definition or description, modifying περιτομὴ. The "circumcision" is further described or circumscribed by "heart." Some may wish to call this an objective genitive.

ἐν πνεύματι οὐ γράμματι. Locative (in the sphere of the spirit, i.e., spiritual, and not in the sphere of the letters, i.e., literal).

οὗ. Possessive genitive that qualifies ὁ ἔπαινος. The relative pronoun refers to ὁ ἐν τῷ κρυπτῷ.

ὁ ἔπαινος. Nominative subject of the verbless clause.

οὐκ . . . ἀλλ᾽. A point/counterpoint set that contrasts adversely ἐξ ἀνθρώπων with ἐκ τοῦ θεοῦ.

ἐξ ἀνθρώπων. Source (agentive). The origin, or source, of the praise is (not) people.

ἐκ τοῦ θεοῦ. Source (agentive). The origin, or source, of the praise is God.

Romans 3:1-8

[1]Therefore, what [is] the benefit of the Jew, or what [is] the advantage of circumcision? [2]Much in every way. First, they have been entrusted with the words of God. [3]What then? If some do not believe, their unbelief will not nullify God's faithfulness, will it? [4]Indeed not. But God must be true and every person a liar, as it stands written, "So that you might be justified in your words and will conquer when you judge." [5]But if our unrighteousness establishes God's righteousness, what shall we say? [That] God who brings wrath [is] not unrighteous, is he? I speak humanly. [6]Indeed not. Because how will God judge the world? [7]But if the truth of God, by my lie, increases in his glory, why am I still judged as a sinner? [8]And it is not the case, is it, as we have been slandered and as some say that we are to have said, that we should do evil so that good might come? Their condemnation is deserved.

Although this is a new chapter in Romans, Paul's thought continues in this second sub-section of Romans 2:17–3:8, regarding the Jewish advantage. His use of diatribe continues, as he poses questions for his line of argument, many of which expect a negative answer. There is also a liberal use of conditional statements, most of which are in the forms of questions, for Paul's argumentation here.

3:1 Τί οὖν τὸ περισσὸν τοῦ Ἰουδαίου ἢ τίς ἡ ὠφέλεια τῆς περιτομῆς;

Τί οὖν. The opening question of the verse that is syntactically parallel to the following question.

Τί. Nominative subject of a verbless clause (implied ἐστιν). The interrogative pronoun matches in gender (neuter) the noun to which it refers (τὸ περισσὸν).

οὖν. Postpositive inferential conjunction. Paul draws an inference, using the dialogical style, from what he has stated regarding being a Jew outwardly versus inwardly, and being circumcised in the flesh versus in the heart.

τὸ περισσὸν. Predicate nominative. The adjective functions as a substantive.

τοῦ Ἰουδαίου. Possessive genitive, modifying τὸ περισσὸν.

ἤ. Disjunctive conjunction ("or") that links two parallel questions.

τίς. Nominative subject of a verbless clause (implied ἐστιν). The interrogative pronoun matches in gender the noun to which it refers (ἡ ὠφέλεια).

ἡ ὠφέλεια. Predicate nominative.

τῆς περιτομῆς. Possessive genitive, modifying ἡ ὠφέλεια.

3:2 πολὺ κατὰ πάντα τρόπον. πρῶτον μὲν [γὰρ] ὅτι ἐπιστεύθησαν τὰ λόγια τοῦ θεοῦ.

πολύ. Predicate nominative of a verbless clause. The neuter form of this adjective (πολύς, πολή, πολύ) can be nominative or accusative, and Robertson, for example, considers this word an adverbial accusative (Robertson, 659). However, as the answer to the previously posed questions (3:1), "what benefit/advantage," it is likely that it modifies τὸ περισσὸν and ἡ ὠφέλεια rather than a verb in the previous verse, and thus a predicate nominative (i.e., "the benefit/advantage is much [or many]").

κατὰ πάντα τρόπον. Standard. The standard, or basis, of πολὺ ("much") is πάντα τρόπον ("every way").

πρῶτον. Adverbial accusative. Modifies the subsequent clause. Paul offers no "second," however.

μὲν. Emphatic particle. Since there is no δέ that follows (related to having no "second"), μὲν does not function as comparative or contrastive.

[γὰρ]. Postpositive explanatory conjunction. Most manuscripts do not contain this word; only 1881 does. Two other manuscripts (6 and 1739) contain πρῶτοι γάρ.

ὅτι. Introduces a content clause that is epexegetical to τὸ περισσὸν and ἡ ὠφέλεια from 3:1, explaining "the benefit of the Jew" and "the advantage of circumcision."

ἐπιστεύθησαν. Aor pass ind 3rd pl πιστεύω. Perfective aspect indicated by the aorist tense-form depicts action as a whole, so the entrusting is seen as a whole. The passive voice indicates indirect, external causality; inferred from the context, the agent is God who entrusts them. "They," implied in the third-person plural form, is a referent to the Jews and circumcision (those who have been circumcised).

τὰ λόγια. Accusative direct object of ἐπιστεύθησαν. This is the only use of this word in Paul, although cognates are used frequently. The fact that the Jews were given the words of the law that contained the legal requirements for obedience is still important, although Paul asserts they had focused on the legality of it (γράμμα) over the spirit of the law.

τοῦ θεοῦ. Genitive of source or origin, modifying τὰ λόγια.

3:3 τί γάρ; εἰ ἠπίστησάν τινες, μὴ ἡ ἀπιστία αὐτῶν τὴν πίστιν τοῦ θεοῦ καταργήσει;

τί. Nominative subject of verbless clause.

γάρ. Inferential conjunction. It introduces an inference from the previous statement regarding the Jews' advantage in their being entrusted with the words of God.

εἰ. Introduces the protasis of a first-class conditional, which is phrased as a (rhetorical) question for the sake of argument.

ἠπίστησάν. Aor act ind 3rd pl ἀπιστέω. The same verbal root from the previous verse (ἐπιστεύθησαν), with the negative prefix ἀ-, is used here in an active sense. The Jews were "entrusted" with the words of God (3:2), so what if some of them reciprocate with "distrust" (or unbelief)? In this verse, πιστ- words occur three times (four including the previous verse). The lexical cohesion formed by the repetition of πιστ-words reflects Paul's emphasis on "faith" or "trust" (or the lack thereof) as important in obedience to God's law.

τινες. Nominative subject of ἠπίστησάν.

μὴ. Negative particle that marks the beginning of the apodosis. It negates the entire clause and indicates that Paul expects a negative answer to the question. Note the translation with the tag line, "will it," indicating formulation expecting a negative answer.

ἡ ἀπιστία. Nominative subject of καταργήσει.

αὐτῶν. Possessive genitive, modifying ἡ ἀπιστία.

τὴν πίστιν. Accusative direct object of καταργήσει.

τοῦ θεοῦ. Possessive genitive, modifying τὴν πίστιν. In 3:2, it is stated that the Jews/circumcised were entrusted (by God) with the words of God. Thus, in this co-text, this πίστιν τοῦ θεοῦ is a referent to the trust of God with his words. In other words, their disbelief does not nullify his entrusting of them with his words (τὰ λόγια).

καταργήσει. Fut act ind 3rd sg καταργέω. Future form grammaticalizes the semantic feature of expectation. The prefix κατα- intensifies the root ἀργέω.

3:4 μὴ γένοιτο· γινέσθω δὲ ὁ θεὸς ἀληθής, πᾶς δὲ ἄνθρωπος ψεύστης, καθὼς γέγραπται· ὅπως ἂν δικαιωθῇς ἐν τοῖς λόγοις σου καὶ νικήσεις ἐν τῷ κρίνεσθαί σε.

μὴ γένοιτο. A frequently used emphatic negation by Paul; it occurs ten times in Romans (3:4, 6, 31; 6:2, 15; 7:7, 13; 9:14; 11:1, 11; cf. 1 Cor 6:15; Gal 2:17; 3:21; 6:14).

μὴ. Negative particle normally used with non-indicative verbs. Here it negates γένοιτο.

γένοιτο. Aor mid opt 3rd sg γίνομαι. The optative mood form depicts projection (like the subjunctive) but with an added element of contingency. This does not mean that Paul is uncertain that it should not be, but that the possibility of the action reflecting reality is further removed than the subjunctive.

γινέσθω. Pres mid impv 3rd sg γίνομαι. The imperative force of the third person is often missed, since there is no English equivalent. The third-person imperative addresses its commanding force not to the addressee but to a non-present entity. The idea is that "God must be true." The middle voice reflects indirect, internal causality.

δὲ. Adversative conjunction (mild).

ὁ θεὸς. Nominative subject of γινέσθω.

ἀληθής. Predicate adjective.

πᾶς ἄνθρωπος. Nominative subject of an implied γινέσθω, but the verb is not grammatically necessary.

δὲ. Adversative conjunction (mild).

ψεύστης. Predicate nominative.

καθὼς γέγραπται. A standard Pauline formula for introducing a scriptural quotation (see note on 1:17).

καθὼς. Comparative conjunction.

γέγραπται. Prf pass ind 3rd sg γράφω. The following, mostly reflecting the LXX, is from Ps 51:4 (LXX Ps 50:6).

ὅπως. Introduces a purpose clause and marks the beginning of the quotation.

ἄν. Conditional particle that indicates contingency.

δικαιωθῇς. Aor pass subj 2nd sg δικαιόω. Subjunctive with ἄν. The passive voice indicates indirect, external causality. The agent, however, is not specified, although it is likely God who does the justifying.

ἐν τοῖς λόγοις. Instrumental. The justifying is by means of words.

σου. Possessive genitive, modifying τοῖς λόγοις.

καὶ. Coordinating conjunction. It connects the previous and subsequent clauses.

νικήσεις. Fut act ind 2nd sg νικάω. The future form depicts action that reflects the semantic feature of expectation. So νικήσεις conveys the expectation of overcoming or conquering. Paul uses the future form of this word instead of the aorist subjunctive in the LXX, νικήσῃς, to depict the semantics of expectation rather than projection. ἄν is usually associated with the subjunctive, but it may only modify δικαιωθῇς. In other words, Paul expects God to conquer, rather than projects the possibility of God conquering.

κρίνεσθαί. Pres mid inf κρίνω. Used with ἐν τῷ to denote contemporaneous time. The middle voice reflects indirect, internal causality. This form can also be passive, which would mean that God is the one being judged. But it may be preferable to interpret this as God being the one judging and the one conquering when he judges, since the co-text discusses God not being a liar and God's words. However, the passive voice meaning can also work, as Paul can be conveying that God conquers when he is judged to be a liar. Both options can make sense in this co-text. The additional accent on the ultima is a result of the following word being enclitic (see note on πνεύματί in 1:9).

σε. Accusative subject of the infinitive κρίνεσθαί.

3:5 εἰ δὲ ἡ ἀδικία ἡμῶν θεοῦ δικαιοσύνην συνίστησιν, τί ἐροῦμεν; μὴ ἄδικος ὁ θεὸς ὁ ἐπιφέρων τὴν ὀργήν; κατὰ ἄνθρωπον λέγω.

εἰ. Introduces the protasis of a first-class conditional. The conditional statement includes a double apodosis.

δὲ. Adversative conjunction (mild).

ἡ ἀδικία. Nominative subject of συνίστησιν.

ἡμῶν. Possessive genitive, modifying ἡ ἀδικία.

θεοῦ. Possessive genitive, modifying δικαιοσύνην. Its placement before the head term (δικαιοσύνην) reflects thematization and emphasis.

δικαιοσύνην. Accusative direct object of συνίστησιν.

συνίστησιν. Pres act ind 3rd sg συνίστημι. The prefix συν- to the root ἵστημι adds the meaning of the preposition to it, having a metaphorical picture of standing with (something), to recommend, approve, demonstrate, or show.

τί ἐροῦμεν. The first of the double apodosis of the conditional statement.

τί. Accusative direct object of ἐροῦμεν.

ἐροῦμεν. Fut act ind 1st pl λέγω. The future form depicts expected action.

μὴ ἄδικος ὁ θεὸς ὁ ἐπιφέρων τὴν ὀργήν. The second of the double apodosis of the conditional statement.

μὴ. Negative particle that negates ἄδικος and indicates that Paul expects a negative answer to the question, which is a follow-up to the previous question.

ἄδικος. Predicate adjective.

ὁ θεὸς. Nominative subject of an implied ἐστιν.

ὁ ἐπιφέρων. Pres act ptc masc nom sg ἐπιφέρω (attributive). The articular participle modifies ὁ θεὸς (second attributive position).

τὴν ὀργήν. Accusative direct object of ἐπιφέρων.

κατὰ ἄνθρωπον. Standard. The standard, or basis, of which he speaks, is "human."

λέγω. Pres act ind 1st sg λέγω.

3:6 μὴ γένοιτο· ἐπεὶ πῶς κρινεῖ ὁ θεὸς τὸν κόσμον;

μὴ γένοιτο. A common emphatic negation for Paul after posing a (often rhetorical) question (see 3:4) μὴ. Negative particle normally used with non-indicative verbs. Here it negates γένοιτο.

γένοιτο. Aor mid opt 3rd sg γίνομαι.

ἐπεὶ. Causal conjunction. Assuming what Paul had just said, the cause, stated in a question form, follows.

πῶς. Interrogative particle, referring to the means for the action of judging.

κρινεῖ. Fut act ind 3rd sg κρίνω. Future form depicts semantic feature of expectation, so the idea is "expect to judge."

ὁ θεὸς. Nominative subject of κρινεῖ.

τὸν κόσμον. Accusative direct object of κρινεῖ.

3:7 εἰ δὲ ἡ ἀλήθεια τοῦ θεοῦ ἐν τῷ ἐμῷ ψεύσματι ἐπερίσσευσεν εἰς τὴν δόξαν αὐτοῦ, τί ἔτι κἀγὼ ὡς ἁμαρτωλὸς κρίνομαι;

εἰ. Introduces the protasis of a first-class conditional.

δὲ. Adversative conjunction (mild). It connects the previous clause-complex with the subsequent clause-complex.

ἡ ἀλήθεια. Nominative subject of ἐπερίσσευσεν.

τοῦ θεοῦ. Possessive genitive, modifying ἡ ἀλήθεια.

ἐν ἐμῷ ψεύσματι. Instrumental. The means by which the truth of God increases is "my lie." Note the contrasting antonyms ἀλήθεια ("truth") and ψεῦσμα ("lie").

ἐπερίσσευσεν. Aor act ind 3rd sg περισσεύω.

εἰς τὴν δόξαν. Purpose. The purpose of the truth of God increasing is his glory.

αὐτοῦ. Possessive genitive, modifying τὴν δόξαν.

τί. Adverbial accusative ("why"). The interrogative pronoun marks the beginning of the apodosis.

ἔτι. Adverb (temporal). It modifies κρίνομαι.

κἀγὼ. Formed by crasis from καί ἐγώ. In this construction, καί is adverbial (adjunctive). ἐγώ functions as a nominative subject of κρίνομαι. The presence of the first singular pronoun is emphatic.

ὡς. Comparative conjunction. The judging is compared to or likened to that of judging a sinner.

ἁμαρτωλὸς. Nominative subject in an elliptical clause (i.e., "why am I still judged as a sinner [would be judged]?" or "why am I still judged as [I am] a sinner?"). The adjective functions as a substantive.

κρίνομαι. Pres pass ind 1st sg κρίνω. External causality indicated by the use of the passive voice.

3:8 καὶ μὴ καθὼς βλασφημούμεθα καὶ καθὼς φασίν τινες ἡμᾶς λέγειν ὅτι ποιήσωμεν τὰ κακά, ἵνα ἔλθῃ τὰ ἀγαθά; ὧν τὸ κρίμα ἔνδικόν ἐστιν.

καὶ. Coordinating conjunction.

μὴ. Negative particle that negates the clause ὅτι ποιήσωμεν τὰ κακά, ἵνα ἔλθῃ τὰ ἀγαθά and introduces a question that expects a negative answer.

καθὼς. Comparative conjunction. A comparison is made with them (Paul and others he includes with him) being slandered.

βλασφημούμεθα. Pres pass ind 1st pl βλασφημέω. The passive voice reflects indirect, external causality. The agent is not specified, but the embedded subject ("we") are the recipients of the slander of others.

καὶ. Coordinating conjunction. It connects καθὼς βλασφημούμεθα with καθὼς φασίν.

καθώς. Comparative conjunction. A comparison is made with some saying things about them (again, Paul and others he includes with him).

φασίν. Pres act ind 3rd pl φημί.

τινες. Nominative subject of φασίν. The exact identity of those indicated is not clear.

ἡμᾶς. Accusative subject of the infinitive λέγειν.

λέγειν. Pres act inf λέγω (indirect discourse).

ὅτι. Introduces the clausal complement (indirect discourse) of λέγειν. Alternatively, the function can be introducing direct discourse (ὅτι-recitativum; cf. e.g., NIV, NASB, NKJV, NRSV).

ποιήσωμεν. Aor act subj 1st pl ποιέω (hortatory subjunctive).

τὰ κακά. Accusative direct object of ποιήσωμεν.

ἵνα. Introduces a result clause. While a majority of ἵνα clauses indicate purpose, there are some instances where it can indicate result (Moulton, 206–220; Porter 1994a, 235). The result of doing evil is so that it might bring good. This interpretation fits well with the rest of the clause.

ἔλθῃ. Aor act subj 3rd sg ἔρχομαι. Subjunctive with ἵνα.

τὰ ἀγαθά. Nominative subject of ἔλθῃ. τὰ ἀγαθά is a substantival adjective. Neuter plural subjects have a tendency to take singular verbs.

ὧν. Possessive genitive, modifying τὸ κρίμα. The relative pronoun refers anaphorically to τινες, those who have slandered and said wrong things about Paul and his people.

τὸ κρίμα. Nominative subject of ἐστιν.

ἔνδικόν. Predicate adjective.

ἐστιν. Unaugmented ind 3rd sg εἰμί.

Romans 3:9–20

⁹What then? Are we any better? Not entirely, for we have already alleged that both Jews and Greeks are all under sin, ¹⁰as it stands written, "There is no one righteous, not one, ¹¹there is no one who understands, there is no one who seeks out God. ¹²All have turned away, together they have become worthless; there is no one who does good, there is not even one. ¹³Their throat [is] an opened grave, they deceive with their tongues, the poison of asps [is] under their lips; ¹⁴their mouths are full of cursing and bitterness. ¹⁵Their feet [are] swift to shed blood, ¹⁶destruction and misery [are] in their ways, ¹⁷and they do not know the way of peace. ¹⁸The fear of God is not before their eyes." ¹⁹Now we know that whatever the law says, it speaks to those who are within the law, in order that every mouth might be silenced, and the whole world might become accountable to God, ²⁰because by works of the law no flesh will be justified before him, for through the law [is] the knowledge of sin.

Romans 3:9–20 is the third sub-section of the larger section of 2:12–3:20, which expounds on the law of God and humanity. This sub-section describes the general human condition, in which Paul joins the allegation against both Jew and Gentile. A large part of this sub-section contains more or less loose quotations from various parts of the OT, including Psalms and Isaiah. The dialogical interaction continues. Paul draws the previous argument to a close, after depicting the general sinfulness of humanity, including the judgmental person, and even including the Jews, despite their having God's words. Paul brings this section to a close with a summary statement brought to the reader's attention by means of the perfect tense-form (stative aspect).

3:9 Τί οὖν; προεχόμεθα; οὐ πάντως· προῃτιασάμεθα γὰρ Ἰουδαίους τε καὶ Ἕλληνας πάντας ὑφ' ἁμαρτίαν εἶναι,

Τί οὖν. The opening question of the verse that is syntactically separate from the following verb.

Τί. Nominative absolute. The nominative singular neuter and accusative singular neuter forms are identical for this interrogative pronoun, but as a single lexeme clause (plus conjunction), it may be preferable to interpret this as a nominative absolute.

οὖν. Postpositive inferential conjunction. The inference is from the advantage that Jews are supposed to have in being trusted with the words of God.

προεχόμεθα. Pres mid ind 1st pl ἡμϋέχω. A NT *hapax legomenon*. The major question here is whether προεχόμεθα is passive in voice and indicating a negative sense ("are we any worse or disadvantaged?") or middle in voice and indicating a positive sense ("are we any better or advantaged?"). The positive sense is more in keeping with Paul's line of argument. Since, his readers think, they are not general sinners or overly judgmental or self-righteous Jews, they perhaps have an advantage over others (see Porter 2015, 87–88). The middle voice indicates indirect, internal causality. The use of the single verb as a clause could indicate a response to the previous question, but it is probably used as a further question that elucidates the first.

οὐ. Negative particle that negates πάντως.

πάντως. Adverb. With οὐ, it answers the question raised by προεχόμεθα from the previous clause. The phrase οὐ πάντως is not a strong response ("definitely not") but a muted one ("not entirely").

προῃτιασάμεθα. Aor mid ind 1st pl προαιτιάομαι. The prefix προ- attached to αἰτιάομαι ("to accuse") adds the prepositional meaning to it ("to accuse beforehand"). The middle voice depicts indirect, internal causality with direct subject involvement or participation.

γὰρ. Postpositive explanatory conjunction that introduces a clause that further explains how they (Jews) are not better (than Gentiles).

Ἰουδαίους . . . Ἕλληνας. Accusative subjects of the infinitive εἶναι.

τε καὶ. Enclitic particle τε joined with conjunction καί. Emphatic. For a similar usage, see 1:14.

πάντας. Accusative in apposition to Ἰουδαίους . . . Ἕλληνας. The adjective functions as a substantive here.

ὑφ᾽ ἁμαρτίαν. Locative ("beneath sin") or subordination ("under sin"). It is the control and authority of "sin" that all are "under."

εἶναι. Inf εἰμί (indirect discourse).

3:10 καθὼς γέγραπται ὅτι οὐκ ἔστιν δίκαιος οὐδὲ εἷς,

καθὼς γέγραπται. A standard Pauline formula for introducing a scriptural quotation (see note on 1:17).

καθὼς. Comparative conjunction.

γέγραπται. Prf pass ind 3rd sg γράφω. Romans 3:10b–12 is a loose quotation from LXX Ps 13:1–3 and 53:1–3 (which have similar wording to each other).

ὅτι. Introduces the clausal complement (direct discourse) of γέγραπται.

οὐκ . . . οὐδὲ. A point/counterpoint expression, here having an intensifying effect: "not/none . . . not even" (cf. Robertson, 1164).

ἔστιν. Unaugmented ind 3rd sg εἰμί. Since the subject of ἔστιν is not expressed, this clause is best translated as an impersonal clause, "there is . . ." (see also 3:11).

δίκαιος. Predicate adjective.

εἷς. Nominative subject of an implied ἔστιν. Cardinal number.

3:11 οὐκ ἔστιν ὁ συνίων, οὐκ ἔστιν ὁ ἐκζητῶν τὸν θεόν.

οὐκ. Negative particle normally used with indicative verbs. Here it negates ἔστιν.

ἔστιν. Unaugmented ind 3rd sg εἰμί. Since the subject of ἔστιν is not expressed, this clause is best translated as an impersonal clause.

ὁ συνίων. Pres act ptc masc nom sg συνίημι (substantival). Predicate nominative.

οὐκ. Negative particle normally used with indicative verbs. Here it negates ἔστιν.

ἔστιν. Unaugmented ind 3rd sg εἰμί. Since the subject of ἔστιν is not expressed, this clause is best translated as an impersonal clause.

ὁ ἐκζητῶν. Pres act ptc masc nom sg ἐκζητέω (substantival). Predicate nominative. The prefix ἐκ- to the root ζητέω adds the prepositional meaning to it ("to seek out").

τὸν θεόν. Accusative direct object of ἐκζητῶν.

3:12 πάντες ἐξέκλιναν ἅμα ἠχρεώθησαν· οὐκ ἔστιν ὁ ποιῶν χρηστό-τητα, [οὐκ ἔστιν] ἕως ἑνός.

πάντες. Nominative subject of ἐξέκλιναν.

ἐξέκλιναν. Aor act ind 3rd pl ἐκκλίνω. The prefix ἐκ- to the root κλίνω adds the prepositional meaning to it ("to turn away or out").

ἅμα. Adverb. It modifies ἠχρεώθησαν.

ἠχρεώθησαν. Aor pass ind 3rd pl ἀχρειόω. The passive voice depicts indirect, external causality; the agent here is not specified, so the focus is on the Goal (which is the grammatical subject here), "they all" (i.e., humanity in general).

οὐκ. Negative particle normally used with indicative verbs. Here it negates ἔστιν.

ἔστιν. Unaugmented ind 3rd sg εἰμί. Since the subject of ἔστιν is not expressed, this clause is best translated as an impersonal clause.

ὁ ποιῶν. Pres act ptc masc nom sg ποιέω (substantival). Predicate nominative.

χρηστότητα. Accusative direct object of ποιῶν.

[**οὐκ ἔστιν**]. Most of the earliest manuscripts (except ‍B) contain this word group.

οὐκ. Negative particle normally used with indicative verbs. Here it negates ἔστιν.

ἔστιν. Unaugmented ind 3rd sg εἰμί. Since the subject of ἔστιν is not expressed, this clause is best translated as an impersonal clause.

ἕως ἑνός. Degree and measure, denoting the upper limit ("there is not even one"; BDAG, 424.5).

3:13 τάφος ἀνεῳγμένος ὁ λάρυγξ αὐτῶν, ταῖς γλώσσαις αὐτῶν ἐδολιοῦσαν, ἰὸς ἀσπίδων ὑπὸ τὰ χείλη αὐτῶν·

While Paul is still quoting LXX Ps 13:1–3, these words parallel with LXX Ps 5:10 (the first half of this verse) and LXX Ps 139:4 (the second half through the next verse). This verse contains three clauses: (1) a verbless clause, (2) an independent clause, and (3) another verbless clause. These grammatical constructions reflect indirect, external (passive voice) agency, direct (active voice) agency, and again indirect, external (passive voice) agency.

τάφος. Predicate nominative.

ἀνεῳγμένος. Prf pass ptc masc nom sg ἀνοίγω (attributive). The participle modifies τάφος (fourth attributive position). The stative aspect (perfect tense-form) reflects the process ("open") as a complex state of affairs and is frontgrounded (emphatic material).

ὁ λάρυγξ. Nominative subject of the verbless clause.

αὐτῶν. Possessive genitive, modifying ὁ λάρυγξ.

ταῖς γλώσσαις. Dative of means/instrument.

αὐτῶν. Possessive genitive, modifying ταῖς γλώσσαις.

ἐδολιοῦσαν. Impf act ind 3rd pl δολιόω. This is the first imperfect in the letter, thus standing out. The imperfective aspect of the imperfect tense-form reflects mainline material with remoteness (see Introduction on the imperfect tense-form and remoteness), in contrast to the use of the present tense-form. Remoteness here is probably temporal (i.e., past referring) rather than spatial.

ἰὸς. Nominative subject of the verbless clause. This anarthrous noun (to focus on its quality than its particularity) starts a new quotation from LXX Ps 139:4.

ἀσπίδων. Genitive of origin, modifying ἰὸς. The origin of "poison" is "asps."

ὑπὸ τὰ χείλη. Locative. The "poison of asps" is located "under their lips."

αὐτῶν. Possessive genitive, modifying τὰ χείλη.

3:14 ὧν τὸ στόμα ἀρᾶς καὶ πικρίας γέμει,

This verse is parallel to LXX Ps 9:28. This is a continuation (and end) of the quotation from LXX Ps 139:4.

ὧν. Possessive genitive, modifying τὸ στόμα. The relative pronoun refers anaphorically to αὐτῶν in the previous verse (i.e., humanity in general).

τὸ στόμα. Nominative subject of γέμει. The genitive plural ὧν indicates that στόμα is a distributive singular.

ἀρᾶς. Genitive object of γέμει. A NT *hapax legomenon*.

καὶ. Coordinating conjunction. It connects the compound genitive objects.

πικρίας. Genitive object of γέμει (cf. Eph 4:31).

γέμει. Pres act ind 3rd sg γέμω.

3:15 ὀξεῖς οἱ πόδες αὐτῶν ἐκχέαι αἷμα,

The section in 3:15–17 is parallel to LXX Isa 59:7–8.

ὀξεῖς. Predicate adjective.

οἱ πόδες. Nominative subject of an implied copulative. The metaphor of "feet" reflects active participation in this sort of behavior (Porter 2015, 90).

αὐτῶν. Possessive genitive, modifying οἱ πόδες.

ἐκχέαι. Aor act inf ἐκχέω (epexegetical to ὀξεῖς).

αἷμα. Accusative direct object of ἐκχέαι.

3:16 σύντριμμα καὶ ταλαιπωρία ἐν ταῖς ὁδοῖς αὐτῶν,

This verse, and the next, is a continuation of the loose quotations of LXX Ps 13:3 (cf. also LXX Isa 59:7–8).

σύντριμμα καὶ ταλαιπωρία. Compound nominative subject of the verbless clause.

ἐν ταῖς ὁδοῖς. Locative. The prepositional word group is used figuratively, referring to their lives.

αὐτῶν. Possessive genitive, modifying ταῖς ὁδοῖς.

3:17 καὶ ὁδὸν εἰρήνης οὐκ ἔγνωσαν.

καὶ. Coordinating conjunction.

ὁδὸν. Accusative direct object of ἔγνωσαν. The fronting of the direct object reflects thematization and thus is emphatic. The lack of the article refers to "way" abstractly; the way of peace has not been specified yet in this letter. The use of the same lexeme (ὁδός) in the previous verse contrasts the way of destruction and misery with the way of peace.

εἰρήνης. Genitive of definition, modifying ὁδὸν, further defining "way" with "peace."

οὐκ. Negative particle normally used with indicative verbs. Here it negates ἔγνωσαν.

ἔγνωσαν. Aor act ind 3rd pl γινώσκω. Perfective aspect depicted by the aorist tense-form views action as a complete whole; it also reflects background material in this discourse.

3:18 οὐκ ἔστιν φόβος θεοῦ ἀπέναντι τῶν ὀφθαλμῶν αὐτῶν.

This verse marks the end of the quotation from LXX Ps 13:3 that began in 3:13 (cf. also LXX Ps 35:2).

οὐκ. Negative particle normally used with indicative verbs. Here it negates ἔστιν.

ἔστιν. Unaugmented ind 3rd sg εἰμί.

φόβος. Nominative subject of ἔστιν.

θεοῦ. Genitive of description, modifying φόβος ("fear" is delineated to "God"). Some may wish to label this as an objective genitive, with God being the object of fear (but see the Introduction for our view of genitives).

ἀπέναντι τῶν ὀφθαλμῶν. Locative. ἀπέναντι is an improper preposition (cf. Porter 1994a, 179–80). Two prefixes, ἀπ- and ἐν-, are attached to the preposition ἀντι, adding their prepositional meanings to it.

αὐτῶν. Possessive genitive, modifying τῶν ὀφθαλμῶν.

3:19 οἴδαμεν δὲ ὅτι ὅσα ὁ νόμος λέγει τοῖς ἐν τῷ νόμῳ λαλεῖ, ἵνα πᾶν στόμα φραγῇ καὶ ὑπόδικος γένηται πᾶς ὁ κόσμος τῷ θεῷ·

οἴδαμεν. Prf act ind 1st pl οἶδα. The perfect tense-form (stative aspect) refers to their being in a state of knowing. This prominent use of this verb marks the summary statement that Paul introduces at the end of this section.

δὲ. Adversative conjunction (mild). It marks the transition from the OT quotations to resuming Paul's argument.

ὅτι. Introduces the clausal complement (indirect discourse) of οἴδαμεν.

ὅσα. The quantitative correlative pronoun ("as much as," "as many things as") introduces a headless relative clause (ὅσα ὁ νόμος λέγει) that functions, in its entirety, as the direct object of λαλεῖ. Within its clause, ὅσα is the accusative direct object of λέγει.

ὁ νόμος. Nominative subject of λέγει and λαλεῖ.

λέγει. Pres act ind 3rd sg λέγω.

τοῖς ἐν τῷ νόμῳ. The article functions as a nominalizer, changing the prepositional word group ἐν τῷ νόμῳ into the dative indirect object of λαλεῖ. Choice of the prepositional word group as a nominal unit focuses on the meaning of the preposition.

ἐν τῷ νόμῳ. Locative ("in the sphere of the law").

λαλεῖ. Pres act ind 3rd λαλέω.

ἵνα. Introduces a purpose clause.

πᾶν στόμα. Nominative subject of φραγῇ (cf. 3:14).

φραγῇ. Aor pass subj 3rd sg φράσσω. Subjunctive with ἵνα. The passive voice indicates external causality, without specification of the agent as God or another agent.

καὶ. Coordinating conjunction.

ὑπόδικος. Predicate adjective. A NT *hapax legomenon*.

γένηται. Aor mid subj 3rd sg γίνομαι. Subjunctive with ἵνα. Perfective aspect depicts action as a whole and reflects background material.

πᾶς ὁ κόσμος. Nominative subject of γένηται.

τῷ θεῷ. Dative complement of ὑπόδικος. ὑπόδικος τινος = "liable for a thing"; ὑπόδικος τινι = "liable to a person" (LSJ).

3:20 διότι ἐξ ἔργων νόμου οὐ δικαιωθήσεται πᾶσα σὰρξ ἐνώπιον αὐτοῦ, διὰ γὰρ νόμου ἐπίγνωσις ἁμαρτίας.

διότι. Causal conjunction. From what has been said—that all who are under the law have it speak to them in order to silence every mouth—the cause or reason is that no one is justified by works of the law.

ἐξ ἔργων. Instrumental. The means by which no one will be justified is works of the law.

νόμου. Genitive of definition or description, modifying ἔργων. It further describes or circumscribes "works" to the "law."

οὐ. Negative particle normally used with indicative verbs. Here it negates δικαιωθήσεται. However, while in the Greek text οὐ negates the verb (lit. "all flesh will not be justified"), an idiomatic English rendering requires connecting the negative particle with the subject: "no flesh will be justified."

δικαιωθήσεται. Fut pass ind 3rd sg δικαιόω. The future form depicts the semantic feature of expectation. The passive voice indicates indirect, external causality; agent is not specified.

πᾶσα σὰρξ. Nominative subject of δικαιωθήσεται. While σὰρξ is consistently translated as "flesh" in most English translations, here it refers to physical (human) beings. More specifically, it refers to any "individual in earthly existence" (Porter 2015, 91).

ἐνώπιον αὐτοῦ. Locative. ἐνώπιον is an improper preposition (cf. Porter 1994a, 179–80). The antecedent of αὐτοῦ is God.

διὰ . . . νόμου. Instrumental. Law is the means through which human beings come to know sin.

γὰρ. Postpositive explanatory conjunction. It introduces a clause that further explains the previous statement that no one will be justified before him.

ἐπίγνωσις. Nominative subject of a verbless clause.

ἁμαρτίας. Genitive of description, modifying ἐπίγνωσις. It further describes "knowledge" as "of sin." Some may wish to see this as an objective genitive.

Romans 3:21–26

[21]But now, apart from the law, the righteousness of God has been revealed, being witnessed by the law and the prophets, [22]and the righteousness of God [is] through faith in Jesus Christ for all who believe; for there is no distinction, [23]for all have sinned and lack the glory of God, [24]being justified freely by his grace through the redemption which is in Christ Jesus, [25]whom God displayed as a propitiation through faith, by his blood, as evidence of his righteousness, because of the bypass of previously committed sins, [26]in the forbearance of God, for the evidence of his righteousness, in the present time, in order that he might be righteous and making righteous the one who has faith in Jesus.

Romans 3:21–4:25 is the third (and final) sub-section of the first major section of the body proper (1:18–4:25) which we have labeled "The Human Condition and Its Forensic Solution." This third sub-section describes the solution to the Jewish dilemma and human condition that has been identified so far in this letter. Within it, there are three major points: God's righteousness (3:21–26), exclusion of boasting (3:27–31), and an argument from the example of Abraham (4:1–25). Romans 3:21–26 is the first point within the solution to the human condition, describing God's righteousness. His righteousness is not for a particular people group but applies universally to all without discrimination. The work of God's righteousness, Paul describes, is focused on the atoning sacrifice of Christ Jesus, in order that he would be both righteous and righteous-making of those who put their faith in him.

**3:21 Νυνὶ δὲ χωρὶς νόμου δικαιοσύνη θεοῦ πεφανέρωται μαρτυρου-
μένη ὑπὸ τοῦ νόμου καὶ τῶν προφητῶν,**

Νυνὶ. Adverb (temporal).
δὲ. Adversative conjunction (mild). It marks the continuation of thought, but also a slight transition to a new topic.
χωρὶς νόμου. Separation. χωρὶς is an improper preposition (cf. Porter 1994a, 179–80). Anarthrous νόμου refers to the law abstractly rather than concretely.
δικαιοσύνη. Nominative subject πεφανέρωται.
θεοῦ. Possessive genitive, modifying δικαιοσύνη. For a fuller discussion, see 1:17 on θεοῦ.
πεφανέρωται. Prf pass ind 3rd sg φανερόω. Stative aspect of the perfect tense-form reflects a complex state of affairs, so the predicate refers to a state of being revealed or manifested. It also reflects frontground material (heavy emphasis) in the discourse. The passive voice indicates indirect, external agency; the agent is not specified here, but it is probably God revealing his own righteousness.
μαρτυρουμένη. Pres pass ptc fem nom singular μαρτυρέω (concessive). The participle functions contextually as circumstantial, modifying the primary clause (containing πεφανέρωται). External agency is indicated by the prepositional word group ὑπὸ τοῦ νόμου καὶ τῶν προφητῶν.
ὑπὸ τοῦ νόμου καὶ τῶν προφητῶν. Instrumental (agency). The prepositional word group grammaticalizes primary or personal agency, here a personified law and prophets. This second use of "law" in this verse is articular and so refers concretely to the Torah (along with reference to the Prophets, it refers to the entirety of the OT).

3:22 δικαιοσύνη δὲ θεοῦ διὰ πίστεως Ἰησοῦ Χριστοῦ εἰς πάντας τοὺς πιστεύοντας. οὐ γάρ ἐστιν διαστολή,

δικαιοσύνη. Nominative subject of the verbless clause. This could also be a nominative in apposition to δικαιοσύνη in the previous verse; however, the use of δέ seems to point to this being a separate clause from the previous verse.
δὲ. Adversative conjunction (mild).
θεοῦ. Possessive genitive, modifying δικαιοσύνη. For a fuller discussion, see 1:17 on θεοῦ.
διὰ πίστεως. Instrumental. The instrument or means for the righteousness of God is faith in Jesus Christ.
πίστεως Ἰησοῦ Χριστοῦ. This word group has garnered much scholarly discussion, often called the "πίστις Χριστοῦ debate." While this is

not the place to go into extensive discussion on this topic, the major issue is whether Ἰησοῦ Χριστοῦ is a subjective genitive or an objective genitive, i.e., whether Ἰησοῦ Χριστοῦ is the subject ("Jesus Christ's faith/faithfulness") or object ("faith/faithfulness in Jesus Christ"). Neither of these is meant by the genitive. Our view is that the genitive case reflects the one broad semantic feature of restriction—the genitive case restricts or limits the head term to restrict or specify its referent—but we see the use of the genitive as having any number of different uses in discourse. The so-called subjective genitive can be explained by other functions, such as possessive, origin, or source. For instance, some might wish to view the word group ἐντολὴ θεοῦ as a subjective genitive, that "God" is one who "commands," but it may be better explained as having a possessive or source function: the commandment (keeping the noun a noun instead of making it a verb) that belongs to God or comes from God (see Porter 1994a, 92–97, describing the various functions of the genitive case). In the same way, the so-called objective genitive can be explained through other categories, such as genitive of definition or description. The word group πίστεως Ἰησοῦ Χριστοῦ restricts πίστεως to Ἰησοῦ Χριστοῦ, which functions here as definition or description, further defining or describing what kind of "faith" is being identified, i.e., faith that is related in some way or restricted to "Jesus Christ" (see next entry for more). The attempt to identify the correct category of the genitive here does not solve the issue, as seen in the number of pages spent trying to argue for a reading based on genitive categories (see Porter 1994a, 95; Porter and Pitts 2009; Porter 2015, 94; and the essays in Bird and Sprinkle for further discussion, among the many other sources on this topic. See also the next entry for more on the genitive).

Ἰησοῦ Χριστοῦ. Genitive of description, modifying πίστεως (see above entry). Faith is further described as and delineated to Jesus Christ. If we were to use the subjective/objective genitive categories, our interpretation would correspond most with the objective category, seeing that Jesus is the object of faith—but we affirm that the genitive does not connote subject/object relations. However, the reason we translate this phrase (including πίστεως) as "faith in Jesus Christ" is due to co-textual factors, including the phrase being used following the preposition διὰ restricting the meaning of πίστις to "faith" and not "faithfulness" and hence to a meaning closer to the objective genitive regarding Jesus Christ (Porter and Pitts 2009, 48–51; see 3:26, where "faith in Jesus" makes better sense). While Χριστοῦ is not a proper noun, it has come to be a title for Jesus that has become his name (see comments in 1:1).

εἰς πάντας τοὺς πιστεύοντας. Purpose. The purpose for the righteousness of God is so all could believe. The adjective πάντας functions as a substantive.

τοὺς πιστεύοντας. Pres act ptc masc acc pl πιστεύω (attributive). The participle modifies πάντας (third attributive position). The root πίστ- is repeated here to emphasize the role of faith.

οὐ. Negative particle normally used with indicative verbs. Here it negates ἐστιν.

γάρ. Postpositive explanatory conjunction.

ἐστιν. Unaugmented ind 3rd sg εἰμί. The subject of the verb is inherent in the 3rd person singular, referring to a general state.

διαστολή. Predicate nominative. This word was used to indicate an instance of dittography in scribal tendencies (Porter 2015, 94).

3:23 πάντες γὰρ ἥμαρτον καὶ ὑστεροῦνται τῆς δόξης τοῦ θεοῦ

πάντες. Nominative subject of ἥμαρτον and ὑστεροῦνται.

γὰρ. Postpositive explanatory conjunction. It introduces a clause that further explains his statement that there is no distinction.

ἥμαρτον. Aor act ind 3rd pl ἁμαρτάνω. Perfective aspect depicted by aorist tense form reflects action viewed as a whole, hence background material.

καὶ. Coordinating conjunction.

ὑστεροῦνται. Pres pass ind 3rd pl ὑστερέω. There are several observations to be made regarding this lexeme. (1) In contrast to the perfective aspect of ἥμαρτον, the imperfective aspect of this word foregrounds this process. In other words, the background is "they sinned," and "they lacked the glory of God" is brought to the foreground. This does not mean that their sinning is unimportant, but it provides the backdrop for their lacking God's glory. (2) While most English translations have "fall short" as the meaning of this word, it is more accurate here to render it as "lack (something)," based on its usage in other places, especially Paul, in its middle/passive voice-forms (see Cirafesi; Enderlein; and Porter and Cirafesi for an extended discussion of the meaning of this word). The sense of the word, generally, is to lack, to be in need (or to be wanting), to fall short, or to run out of something (cf. John 2:3, where the wine "runs out" at the wedding in Cana), but the middle/passive voice-form constrains its meaning. (3) Although the middle and passive voice-forms are identical for the present tense-form, we take this occurrence of the word to be passive. The passive voice reflects external causality/agency, which means they were in need of God's glory by some external cause or agent. This makes better sense given the previous statement about all having sinned; their sin resulted in needing or lacking God's glory. The passive voice of δικαιούμενοι in the next verse (3:24) also makes better sense of interpreting this word as a parallel passive voice instead of middle.

τῆς δόξης. Genitive object of ὑστεροῦνται (BDAG, 1044.5.b). This genitive should be distinguished from the objective genitive as the direct object of a verbal idea implicit in the head noun.

τοῦ θεοῦ. Possessive genitive, modifying τῆς δόξης.

3:24 δικαιούμενοι δωρεὰν τῇ αὐτοῦ χάριτι διὰ τῆς ἀπολυτρώσεως τῆς ἐν Χριστῷ Ἰησοῦ·

δικαιούμενοι. Pres pass ptc masc nom pl δικαιόω (result). The participle functions contextually as circumstantial, modifying the previous clause. Although the middle and passive voice-forms are identical, the passive voice (external causality) makes more sense; internal causality does not semantically fit here.

δωρεάν. Adverbial accusative, modifying δικαιούμενοι.

τῇ . . . χάριτι. Dative of instrument/means. The means by which they are justified is "his grace."

αὐτοῦ. Possessive genitive, modifying τῇ . . . χάριτι. Its position between the article and the noun is emphatic.

διὰ τῆς ἀπολυτρώσεως. Instrumental. The means by or through which they have been justified (along with the more abstract "his grace") is "the redemption in Christ Jesus." In the ancient world, ἀπολύτρωσις denotes release from slavery, or even sinfulness (Porter 2015, 95–96).

τῆς ἐν Χριστῷ Ἰησοῦ. The article functions as an adjectivizer, changing the prepositional word group ἐν Χριστῷ Ἰησοῦ into an attributive modifier of τῆς ἀπολυτρώσεως.

ἐν Χριστῷ Ἰησοῦ. Locative (sphere or realm). The redemption is in the sphere of Christ Jesus. While discussion of "in Christ" is extensive in recent literature, we caution against reading theological implications into every instance of this prepositional word group.

3:25 ὃν προέθετο ὁ θεὸς ἱλαστήριον διὰ [τῆς] πίστεως ἐν τῷ αὐτοῦ αἵματι εἰς ἔνδειξιν τῆς δικαιοσύνης αὐτοῦ διὰ τὴν πάρεσιν τῶν προγεγονότων ἁμαρτημάτων

Romans 3:25–26 forms one long relative clause identifying Christ Jesus' work of redemption. The use of a series of short prepositional word groups that parallel each other and modify the main clause (here, προέθετο ὁ θεὸς ἱλαστήριον) reflects the ancient diatribe style (see Campbell 1992).

ὅν. Accusative direct object of προέθετο in a double accusative object-complement construction with ἱλαστήριον. The relative pronoun refers back to Χριστῷ Ἰησοῦ, although the cases clearly do not match; a relative pronoun is used in a case relative to its function in the clause, not its antecedent (Porter 1994a, 132–33).

προέθετο. Aor mid ind 3rd sg προτίθημι. The prefix προ- attached to τίθημι adds the prepositional meaning to the root ("to set before," or "display"). The middle voice indicates indirect, internal causality.

ὁ θεὸς. Nominative subject of προέθετο.

ἱλαστήριον. Complement to ὅν in a double accusative object-complement construction.

διὰ [τῆς] πίστεως. Instrumental. The means by which God displayed Jesus as a propitiation is "faith." While some may view this to be Jesus' faith, it is more likely, given our discussion of πίστις Χριστοῦ above, that it is the faith of the believer that makes propitiation meaningful. Most of the early manuscripts omit the article, which reflects "faith" qualitatively rather than particularly.

ἐν τῷ . . . αἵματι. Instrumental. The instrumental function of ἐν + dative is broader than διὰ + genitive. The means of propitiation is "his blood." Additionally, it is not "faith in his blood," but "through faith, in his blood."

αὐτοῦ. Possessive genitive, modifying τῷ . . . αἵματι (see discussion in Porter 2015, 97–98, regarding whether αὐτοῦ refers to Jesus or God; it is more likely Jesus, given the co-text). Its position between the article and the noun emphasizes its modification of it.

εἰς ἔνδειξιν. Purpose. The purpose of propitiation is to provide "evidence of his righteousness."

τῆς δικαιοσύνης. Genitive of definition or description, modifying ἔνδειξιν. The "evidence" is further described or circumscribed as "his righteousness." Some may wish to call this an objective genitive, if one sees ἔνδειξις as a verbal process.

αὐτοῦ. Possessive genitive, modifying τῆς δικαιοσύνης. The personal pronoun refers to Jesus, as the unblemished, perfect, and righteous sacrifice of atonement.

διὰ τὴν πάρεσιν. Causal. This is the only occurrence of πάρεσις in Paul.

τῶν . . . ἁμαρτημάτων. Genitive of definition or description, modifying τὴν πάρεσιν. The "bypass" is described or circumscribed as "the previously committed sins." Some may wish to call this an objective genitive.

προγεγονότων. Prf act ptc neut gen pl προγίνομαι (attributive). The participle modifies τῶν . . . ἁμαρτημάτων (first attributive position). The stative aspect (perfect tense-form) reflects frontground material

and refers to being in a state of previously existent sins. The prefix προ-
attached to the root γίνομαι adds the prepositional meaning to the word
("to happen previously"). A NT *hapax legomenon*. The position of the participle between the article and the noun emphasizes its modification of it.

**3:26 ἐν τῇ ἀνοχῇ τοῦ θεοῦ, πρὸς τὴν ἔνδειξιν τῆς δικαιοσύνης αὐτοῦ
ἐν τῷ νῦν καιρῷ, εἰς τὸ εἶναι αὐτὸν δίκαιον καὶ δικαιοῦντα τὸν ἐκ
πίστεως Ἰησοῦ.**

ἐν τῇ ἀνοχῇ. Locative. The "forbearance of God" is in the sphere or
realm of "propitiation" (from 3:25).

τοῦ θεοῦ. Possessive genitive or genitive of source or origin, modifying τῇ ἀνοχῇ.

πρὸς τὴν ἔνδειξιν. Directional (movement toward). The forbearance
of God is directed towards "evidence of his righteousness." The word
group τὴν ἔνδειξιν τῆς δικαιοσύνης αὐτοῦ is repeated from 3:25 (but
there with the first article omitted).

τῆς δικαιοσύνης. Genitive of definition, modifying τὴν ἔνδειξιν
("the object of the evidence is his righteousness").

αὐτοῦ. Possessive genitive, modifying τῆς δικαιοσύνης.

ἐν τῷ νῦν καιρῷ. Temporal. The adverb νῦν has an attributive function. Its position between the article and the noun reflects strong attribution to καιρῷ.

εἶναι. Inf εἰμί. Used with εἰς τὸ to denote purpose.

αὐτὸν. Accusative subject of the infinitive εἶναι.

δίκαιον. Predicate accusative. δίκαιον is a substantival adjective.

καὶ. Coordinating conjunction. It connects the compound predicate
accusatives.

δικαιοῦντα. Pres act ptc masc acc sg δικαιόω (substantival). The participle functions in the clause as a predicate accusative.

τὸν ἐκ πίστεως. The article functions as a nominalizer, changing the
prepositional word group ἐκ πίστεως into the accusative direct object of
δικαιοῦντα.

ἐκ πίστεως. Instrumental. The means or instrument of being justified is faith in Jesus.

Ἰησοῦ. Genitive of definition or description, modifying πίστεως.
"Faith" is described or circumscribed as "of Jesus." The so-called objective
or subjective genitives are neither helpful nor legitimate categories for the
genitive (as explained in the Introduction), especially here. The subjective genitive view would interpret τὸν ἐκ πίστεως Ἰησοῦ, for example, as
"him/her [who is] of the faithfulness of Jesus" (Wright 2013, 844, suggests
"everyone who trusts in the faithfulness of Jesus," but this requires two

occurrences of the "faith/trust/faithfulness" lexeme, rather than the actual one in the verse). And the objective genitive view would interpret it, for example, as "him/her [who is] of faith in Jesus" (cf. Dunn, 1:175, "him who believes in Jesus"). Both of these statements may be generally true, but the second option makes better sense than the first in this context (who are those who are of Jesus' act of faithfulness?). The grammar of the genitive relationship alone does not indicate how "faith" is delineated as to "Jesus," so other contextual factors must be taken into consideration, including that this phrase follows the preposition ἐκ and restricts the meaning of πίστις to "faith" and not "faithfulness" and hence a meaning closer to the objective genitive regarding Jesus (Porter and Pitts 2009, 48–51; see also the discussion in 3:22 on πίστεως Ἰησοῦ Χριστοῦ).

Romans 3:27–31

27Therefore, where [is] the boast? It is excluded. By what kind of law? Of works? No, but by a law of faith. 28For we consider that a person is justified by faith apart from works of the law. 29Or [is he] God of Jews only? Is [he] not also [the God] of Gentiles? Yes, also of Gentiles, 30since God [is] one, who will justify the circumcised by faith and the uncircumcised through faith. 31Therefore, do we cancel out the law through faith? Indeed not. But we establish the law.

Romans 3:27–31 comprises the second point within the solution to the human condition: there is no room for boasting, in light of what Paul has just said regarding the universality of sin and the righteous-making work that God did in giving Jesus as an atoning sacrifice. The natural progression to Paul's argument is that human sinfulness demands a forensic solution as humans have broken God's law. Since all humans finds themselves in a similar condition, there is no room for boasting. Paul utilizes his dialogical technique throughout this section, introducing questions from his dialogue partner. The conversational partner is depicted as having hidden assumptions about the human forensic dilemma. Paul moves from specific to broad questions and encompasses the major issues discussed previously.

3:27 Ποῦ οὖν ἡ καύχησις; ἐξεκλείσθη. διὰ ποίου νόμου; τῶν ἔργων; οὐχί, ἀλλὰ διὰ νόμου πίστεως.

Ποῦ. Adverb (interrogative).
οὖν. Postpositive inferential conjunction. It introduces the inference from what Paul has said regarding righteousness and redemption.

ἡ καύχησις. Nominative absolute or nominative subject of the verbless clause (question).

ἐξεκλείσθη. Aor pass ind 3rd sg ἐκκλείω. This is a one-word clause, answering the posed question. The passive voice indicates indirect, external causality, without specifying the agent, whether God or otherwise.

διὰ ποίου νόμου. Instrumental. The means by which boasting is excluded is posed as a question, "By what kind of law?"

τῶν ἔργων. Genitive of definition, further defining νόμου as "of works."

οὐχί ἀλλά. A point/counterpoint set that contrasts (νόμου) τῶν ἔργων ("law of works") with νόμου πίστεως ("law of faith").

διὰ νόμου. Instrumental. The means by which boasting is excluded is "law of faith." διὰ νόμου parallels διὰ ποίου νόμου above.

πίστεως. Genitive of definition, further defining νόμου as "of faith."

3:28 λογιζόμεθα γὰρ δικαιοῦσθαι πίστει ἄνθρωπον χωρὶς ἔργων νόμου.

λογιζόμεθα. Pres mid ind 1st pl λογίζομαι.

γὰρ. Postpositive explanatory conjunction. It introduces a clause that explains what Paul has just said regarding excluding boasting because of the "law of faith."

δικαιοῦσθαι. Pres pass inf δικαιόω (indirect discourse).

πίστει. Dative of means/instrument. The means by which one is justified is faith. Anarthrous noun reflects the abstract notion of faith, as opposed to a concrete referent.

ἄνθρωπον. Accusative subject of the infinitive δικαιοῦσθαι.

χωρὶς ἔργων. Separation. χωρὶς is an improper preposition (cf. Porter 1994a, 179–80).

νόμου. Genitive of definition, further defining ἔργων.

3:29 ἢ Ἰουδαίων ὁ θεὸς μόνον; οὐχὶ καὶ ἐθνῶν; ναὶ καὶ ἐθνῶν,

ἢ. Disjunctive conjunction.

Ἰουδαίων. Possessive genitive, modifying ὁ θεὸς. Its placement before the head term thematizes it within the clause.

ὁ θεὸς. Nominative absolute or nominative subject of the verbless clause (question).

μόνον. Adverbial accusative.

οὐχὶ. Negative particle that negates the entire (verbless) clause καὶ ἐθνῶν and indicates that Paul expects a positive response to his question.

καὶ. Adverbial use (adjunctive), modifying ἐθνῶν.

ἐθνῶν. Possessive genitive, modifying an implied ὁ θεὸς from the previous clause. It parallels Ἰουδαίων.

ναί. Emphatic particle. It functions as affirmation.

καί. Adverbial use (adjunctive), modifying ἐθνῶν.

ἐθνῶν. Possessive genitive, modifying an implied ὁ θεὸς from the previous clause.

3:30 εἴπερ εἷς ὁ θεὸς ὃς δικαιώσει περιτομὴν ἐκ πίστεως καὶ ἀκροβυστίαν διὰ τῆς πίστεως.

εἴπερ. Introduces the protasis of a first-class conditional with the apodosis (ναὶ καὶ ἐθνῶν in 3:29) occurring before the protasis (εἴπερ εἷς ὁ θεὸς). εἴπερ is an intensive form of εἰ (Porter 1994a, 209).

εἷς. Predicate adjective. Since "God is one," Paul argues that he is the God not only of one particular people group but of the human race together as one. The fronting of εἷς before ὁ θεὸς emphasizes the "one-ness" of God.

ὁ θεὸς. Nominative subject of the verbless clause.

ὅς. Nominative subject of δικαιώσει. The relative pronoun refers anaphorically to θεός and begins the relative clause.

δικαιώσει. Fut act ind 3rd sg δικαιόω. The future form grammaticalizes the semantic feature of expectation regarding God's justifying action.

περιτομὴν. The first of two accusative direct objects of δικαιώσει. The abstract noun περιτομή ("circumcision") is a metonymy (part for the whole) that refers to the person ("a circumcised person") rather than to the condition.

ἐκ πίστεως. Instrumental. The means by which the circumcised are justified is "faith."

καί. Coordinating conjunction. It connects the two accusative objects.

ἀκροβυστίαν. The second accusative direct object of δικαιώσει. The abstract noun ἀκροβυστία ("uncircumcision") is a metonymy (part for the whole) that refers to the person ("an uncircumcised person") rather than to the condition.

διὰ τῆς πίστεως. Instrumental. The means by which the uncircumcised are justified is "faith."

ἐκ πίστεως . . . διὰ τῆς πίστεως. While the two prepositional word groups are parallel to each other, there are two marked differences: (1) the use of two different prepositions (ἐκ and διά) to reflect instrumentality, and (2) one having an article with πίστεως and the other without. The use of two different prepositions can be explained in a number of ways, but we conclude that the circumcised Jews know that the law calls them to have faith, so they are justified "by" explicit faith. The uncircumcised non-Jews, who do not know the law as the Jews do, are still justified "through" faith. The figurative movement of ἐκ is "out of," while διά depicts "through"; so the circumcised are justified from within faith (i.e., their religious heritage), so to speak, while the uncircumcised are justified from outside going through faith (see Porter 2015, 101–2 for further discussion). The first instance of the anarthrous πίστεως refers abstractly to "faith," while the second instance of the articular πίστεως refers concretely to "faith." In other words, the faith by which the circumcised Jews are justified is depicted abstractly, while the faith through which the uncircumcised non-Jews are justified is referred to concretely.

3:31 νόμον οὖν καταργοῦμεν διὰ τῆς πίστεως; μὴ γένοιτο· ἀλλὰ νόμον ἰστάνομεν.

νόμον. Accusative direct object of καταργοῦμεν. The fronting of the verb object makes it prominent in the clause.

οὖν. Postpositive inferential conjunction. The inference (in question form) follows from what Paul has just said about being justified by faith apart from works of the law.

καταργοῦμεν. Pres act ind 1st pl καταργέω. The prefix κατ- attached to the root αργέω intensifies the root meaning ("to lie down," "to do nothing"); so "to nullify" or "to cancel out."

διὰ τῆς πίστεως. Instrumental. The means by which the law is cancelled is "faith."

μὴ γένοιτο. A common emphatic negation for Paul after posing a (often rhetorical) question (see 3:4).

μὴ. Negative particle normally used with non-indicative verbs. Here it negates γένοιτο.

γένοιτο. Aor mid opt 3rd sg γίνομαι.

ἀλλὰ. Adversative conjunction (strong).

νόμον. Accusative direct object of ἰστάνομεν. The anarthrous noun refers to the law abstractly, so probably God's universal law, not the written law.

ἰστάνομεν. Pres act ind 1st pl ἵστημι (ἰστάνω; late form of ἵστημι). It is parallel to καταργοῦμεν.

Romans 4:1–25

[1]What, then, will we say that we have found with respect to Abraham, our earthly forefather? [2]For if Abraham was justified by works, he has a reason for boasting, but not before God. [3]For what does the Scripture say? "Abraham trusted in God, and it was considered to him as righteousness." [4]But to the one who works, the reward is not considered

according to grace but according to something owed. [5]But to the one who does not work but trusts in him who justifies the ungodly, his faith is considered as righteousness, [6]just as David also speaks of the blessing of the person to whom God credits righteousness apart from works: [7]"Blessed [are those] whose lawlessness is forgiven and whose sins are covered. [8]Blessed [is] the man whose sin the Lord does not consider." [9]Therefore, [is] this blessedness for the circumcised or also for the uncircumcised? For we say, "Faith was reckoned to Abraham as righteousness." [10]How was it, therefore, reckoned? Was it after he was circumcised or before? Not after he was circumcised but before. [11]And he received a sign of circumcision, a seal of the righteousness that came from faith while he was uncircumcised, so that he would be the father of all who believe through uncircumcision, so that righteousness might also be reckoned to them, [12]and the father of the circumcised to those who are not only of the circumcision but also to those who walk in the steps of the in-uncircumcision faith of our father Abraham. [13]For [it was] not through the law that the promise [was given] to Abraham or his descendants, that he would be the heir of the world, but through the righteousness of faith. [14]For if those of the law are heirs, faith stands emptied and the promise stands nullified. [15]Because the law brings wrath; but where there is no law neither [is] there transgression. [16]That is why [it is] by faith so that [it is] according to grace, that the promise is in a state of being guaranteed to all the offspring, not to those of the law only but also to those of the faith of Abraham, who is the father of us all, [17]just as it has been written: "I have placed you [as] a father of many nations," in front of God in whom he believed, the one who gives life to the dead and calls those not being as being. [18]With hope upon hope, he believed to become a father of many nations according to what had been spoken, "So will your offspring be." [19]And not being weak in faith, he considered his own body as having been already dead, being about 100 years old, and the deadness of Sarah's womb. [20]But he did not doubt the promise of God in unbelief, but was strengthened in faith, giving glory to God, [21]and being completely convinced that what he had promised he is able also to do. [22]Therefore, it was also reckoned to him as righteousness. [23]But it was not written because of him only that it was reckoned to him, [24]but also because of us, to whom it is about to be reckoned, who believe upon him who raised Jesus our Lord from the dead, [25]who was given over because of our transgressions and was raised because of our justification.

Romans 4:1–25 is the third sub-section of Romans 3:21–4:25, which outlines the solution to the human condition. In this current sub-section, after Paul has detailed God's righteousness and the exclusion of boasting based on the work of Christ in justification, Paul's third point (4:1–25) revolves around the example of Abraham, as well as David.

4:1 Τί οὖν ἐροῦμεν εὑρηκέναι Ἀβραὰμ τὸν προπάτορα ἡμῶν κατὰ σάρκα;

This verse presents some interpretive difficulty due to its grammatical construction. The two issues are whether this is one or two questions, and the grammatical function of Ἀβραάμ in the co-text (see below). There are four possibilities for interpreting (translating) this verse: (1) "What therefore will we say that Abraham our forefather according to the flesh has found?" (2) "What will we say? We have found Abraham to be our forefather according to the flesh?" (3) "What will we say? Abraham our forefather has found something according to the flesh?" Or (4) "What will we say that we have found with respect to Abraham our forefather according to the flesh?" Based on what follows in the co-text, it appears that the fourth option makes the best sense. Abraham was a well-known figure to the Jews, possibly even to Gentiles, as their forefather who was considered righteous because of his obedience to God. Paul seems to be saying that he has discovered something important about Abraham here (see Porter 2015, 103–4 for a more detailed analysis).

Τί οὖν ἐροῦμεν. A rhetorical question that has been used by Paul throughout this letter to transition to a related but new logical progression (Rom 4:1; 6:1; 7:7; 8:31; 9:14, 30).

Τί. Accusative direct object of ἐροῦμεν. The interrogative pronoun is in its usual position in an interrogative clause as the fronted element.

οὖν. Postpositive inferential conjunction. Inference is based on what has been said regarding not canceling out the Law but establishing it.

ἐροῦμεν. Fut act ind 1st pl λέγω. The future form grammaticalizes the semantic feature of expectation: "what are we expected to say?" The use of the first-person plural continues the reference to the inclusive use of "we" from the previous chapter, by which Paul identifies with his addressees.

εὑρηκέναι. Prf act inf εὑρίσκω (indirect discourse). Stative aspect reflected by perfect tense form depicts a state of finding; frontground material in the co-text.

Ἀβραάμ. Accusative of respect (cf. Porter 1994a, 90). The Semitic name is not declined in Greek. The action of "finding" is with respect to (manner) "Abraham." While an infinitive that functions as predicate takes an accusative as a subject, the infinitive here functions as introducing indirect discourse (from ἐροῦμεν), and the accusative Ἀβραάμ functions here as respect. Thus, εὑρηκέναι Ἀβραάμ can be rendered "to find with respect to Abraham."

τὸν προπάτορα. Accusative in apposition to Ἀβραάμ. A NT *hapax legomenon*.

ἡμῶν. Possessive genitive, modifying τὸν προπάτορα.

κατὰ σάρκα. Standard. The standard by which Abraham is a forefather is "flesh." Although σάρξ refers to flesh, the prepositional word group κατὰ σάρκα here could be rendered as "physically" or "earthly."

4:2 εἰ γὰρ Ἀβραὰμ ἐξ ἔργων ἐδικαιώθη, ἔχει καύχημα, ἀλλ' οὐ πρὸς θεόν.

εἰ. Introduces the protasis of a first-class conditional. After having introduced him, a majority of this chapter focuses on Abraham as an example of Paul's argument. Paul uses the first-class conditional to posit an argument for the sake of discussion.

γὰρ. Postpositive explanatory conjunction. It introduces an explanation of the answer to the previously posed question regarding Abraham.

Ἀβραάμ. Nominative subject of ἐδικαιώθη.

ἐξ ἔργων. Instrumental or causal. The instrument or cause by which Abraham was justified (or posed as being justified) is "by works." The prepositional word group is fronted, making it prominent in the clause.

ἐδικαιώθη. Aor pass ind 3rd sg δικαιόω. Passive voice indicates external agency, likely referring to God, although agency is not specified here.

ἔχει. Pres act ind 3rd sg ἔχω. The subject is implied in the third-person singular, Abraham, from the previous clause. ἔχει marks the beginning of the apodosis.

καύχημα. Accusative direct object of ἔχει.

ἀλλ'. Adversative conjunction (strong). It contrasts ἔχει καύχημα with οὐ πρὸς θεόν.

οὐ. Negative particle, negating the entire word group πρὸς θεόν.

πρὸς θεόν. Locative (motion toward). The idea of being or directed toward being "face to face" is applicable here (see Porter 1994a, 172–73).

4:3 τί γὰρ ἡ γραφὴ λέγει; ἐπίστευσεν δὲ Ἀβραὰμ τῷ θεῷ καὶ ἐλογίσθη αὐτῷ εἰς δικαιοσύνην.

τί. Accusative direct object of λέγει. As in 4:1, the fronting of this pronoun in the clause follows the usual word order in a question using an interrogative pronoun.

γὰρ. Postpositive explanatory conjunction. It introduces an explanation of the previous statement with a scriptural reference (see below).

ἡ γραφή. Nominative subject of λέγει. The articular use of the noun in this co-text specifies it as more than simply any writing, but as a specific writing of importance known by Paul's audience.

λέγει. Pres act ind 3rd sg λέγω.

ἐπίστευσεν. Aor act ind 3rd sg πιστεύω. ἐπίστευσεν marks the beginning of a quotation of LXX Gen 15:6; the only difference is Αβραμ in the LXX and Ἀβραὰμ here.

δὲ. Adversative conjunction (mild). It may just be present due to the LXX quotation, as the connective does not have a specific function in this co-text.

Ἀβραάμ. Nominative subject of ἐπίστευσεν.

τῷ θεῷ. Dative direct object of ἐπίστευσεν. The use of the dative as object signifies *relation* as the main semantic relationship between the predicate and dative.

καὶ. Coordinating conjunction. It connects the two clauses before and after it.

ἐλογίσθη. Aor pass ind 3rd sg λογίζομαι. Passive voice indicates external agency; the agent is not specifically mentioned here, but it is likely God. The grammatical subject of the verb, and the Goal, is Ἀβραάμ from the previous clause.

αὐτῷ. Dative of advantage. The personal pronoun refers anaphorically to Ἀβραάμ.

εἰς δικαιοσύνην. Goal or state. In other words, the figurative state that Abraham was considered to be in was "righteousness."

4:4 τῷ δὲ ἐργαζομένῳ ὁ μισθὸς οὐ λογίζεται κατὰ χάριν ἀλλὰ κατὰ ὀφείλημα,

τῷ . . . ἐργαζομένῳ. Pres mid ptc masc dat sg ἐργάζομαι (substantival). Dative indirect object of λογίζεται, fronted for prominence.

δὲ. Adversative conjunction (mild).

ὁ μισθὸς. Nominative subject of λογίζεται. The noun denotes here compensation with regards to work rendered. Paul here introduces an analogy by way of earthly work to explain the notion of accounting and differentiating wages earned from grace given.

οὐ . . . ἀλλὰ. A point/counterpoint set that contrasts κατὰ χάριν with κατὰ ὀφείλημα.

λογίζεται. Pres pass ind 3rd sg λογίζομαι. The passive voice indicates external causality, agent unspecified here.

κατὰ χάριν. Standard or basis. The standard or basis by which the reward is considered (or not considered in this case) is grace.

κατὰ ὀφείλημα. Standard or basis. The standard or basis by which the reward is considered is debt, "for the one who works." ὀφείλημα is used only here in Paul and one other place in the NT (Matt 6:12).

4:5 τῷ δὲ μὴ ἐργαζομένῳ πιστεύοντι δὲ ἐπὶ τὸν δικαιοῦντα τὸν ἀσεβῆ λογίζεται ἡ πίστις αὐτοῦ εἰς δικαιοσύνην·

The repetition of the words "faith/believe," "justify/righteous," and "consider" reflects lexical cohesion in this (and the previous) verse, highlighting these topics.

τῷ δὲ μὴ ἐργαζομένῳ πιστεύοντι δὲ ἐπὶ τὸν δικαιοῦντα τὸν ἀσεβῆ. This fronted clause complex should be viewed as one unit, the complement of the main clause, containing several embedded clauses within it ("but to the one who does not work but trusts in him who justifies the ungodly").

τῷ . . . ἐργαζομένῳ. Pres mid ptc masc dat sg ἐργάζομαι (substantival). Dative indirect object of λογίζεται.

δὲ. Adversative conjunction (mild). It connects, with mild contrast, the previous clause complex (4:4) with the present clause complex (4:5).

πιστεύοντι. Pres act ptc masc dat sg πιστεύω (substantival). Dative in apposition to ἐργαζομένῳ, except without an article attached to it. Granville Sharp's rule as a general principle may apply here, where one article governs two substantives for referring the second substantive to the first.

δὲ. Adversative conjunction (mild). It contrasts (mildly) ἐργαζομένῳ with πιστεύοντι.

ἐπὶ τὸν δικαιοῦντα. Locative. According to BDAG (817.2.a.δ), ἐπί + accusative is used with πιστεύω to indicate the object of belief or trust. The figurative sense of "upon" is also applicable here; i.e., the one who trusts "upon."

τὸν δικαιοῦντα. Pres act ptc masc acc sg δικαιόω (substantival).

τὸν ἀσεβῆ. Accusative direct object of δικαιοῦντα.

λογίζεται. Pres pass ind 3rd sg λογίζομαι. The repetition of λογίζεται in this and the previous verse creates lexical cohesion, reflecting that "considering" is a major concern in these two verses.

ἡ πίστις. Nominative subject of λογίζεται. The repetition of πιστεύοντι and πίστις in this discourse creates lexical cohesion, signaling that "faith" is an important topic.

αὐτοῦ. Possessive genitive, modifying ἡ πίστις.

εἰς δικαιοσύνην. Goal or state (see above in 4:3). δικαιοσύνη is repeated from above, creating lexical cohesion. Thus, for the one who trusts in him who justifies the ungodly, his trust is considered as making him justified.

4:6 καθάπερ καὶ Δαυὶδ λέγει τὸν μακαρισμὸν τοῦ ἀνθρώπου ᾧ ὁ θεὸς λογίζεται δικαιοσύνην χωρὶς ἔργων·

καθάπερ. Comparative conjunction. It compares the previous clause with the current one. This conjunction begins one comparative clause, and then a relative clause subordinate to this one begun by ᾧ.

καὶ. Adverbial use (adjunctive). It modifies the clause Δαυὶδ λέγει.

Δαυὶδ. Nominative subject of λέγει.

λέγει. Pres act ind 3rd sg λέγω.

τὸν μακαρισμὸν. Accusative direct object of λέγει.

τοῦ ἀνθρώπου. Possessive genitive, modifying τὸν μακαρισμὸν.

ᾧ. Dative indirect object of λογίζεται. The relative pronoun refers anaphorically to τοῦ ἀνθρώπου.

ὁ θεὸς. Nominative subject of λογίζεται within the relative clause begun by ᾧ.

λογίζεται. Pres mid ind 3rd sg λογίζομαι. Middle voice indicates indirect, internal causality (contrary to the view that sees such verbs as deponent; see Series Introduction). The lexical meaning of λογίζομαι inherently views the process as having internal causality.

δικαιοσύνην. Accusative direct object of λογίζεται.

χωρὶς ἔργων. Separation. χωρίς is an improper preposition (see Porter 1994a: 179–80).

4:7 μακάριοι ὧν ἀφέθησαν αἱ ἀνομίαι καὶ ὧν ἐπεκαλύφθησαν αἱ ἁμαρτίαι·

μακάριοι ὧν ἀφέθησαν αἱ ἀνομίαι καὶ ὧν ἐπεκαλύφθησαν αἱ ἁμαρτίαι. A quotation of LXX Ps 31:1. It is viewed as one main clause (begun with μακάριοι), composed of two subordinate clauses: (1) ὧν ἀφέθησαν αἱ ἀνομίαι and (2) ὧν ἐπεκαλύφθησαν αἱ ἁμαρτίαι.

μακάριοι. Nominative absolute (independent). μακάριοι is a predicative adjective.

ὧν. Possessive genitive, modifying αἱ ἀνομίαι. The relative pronoun refers anaphorically to μακάριοι.

ἀφέθησαν. Aor pass ind 3rd pl ἀφίημι. Passive voice indicates external agency, which is most likely God in this co-text.

αἱ ἀνομίαι. Nominative subject of ἀφέθησαν.

καὶ. Coordinating conjunction. It connects the two subordinate clauses before and after it.

ὧν. Possessive genitive, modifying αἱ ἁμαρτίαι. The relative pronoun refers anaphorically to μακάριοι.

ἐπεκαλύφθησαν. Aor pass ind 3rd pl ἐπικαλύπτω. Passive voice indicates external agency; the agent is most likely God.

αἱ ἁμαρτίαι. Nominative subject of ἐπεκαλύφθησαν.

4:8 μακάριος ἀνὴρ οὗ οὐ μὴ λογίσηται κύριος ἁμαρτίαν.

μακάριος ἀνὴρ οὗ οὐ μὴ λογίσηται κύριος ἁμαρτίαν. A quotation of LXX Ps 31:2a. It is likely that by citing only the first couple of verses of this Psalm, Paul is invoking the entire Psalm (see Porter 2015, 105).

μακάριος. Predicate nominative. μακάριος is a predicative adjective.

ἀνὴρ. Nominative subject of verbless clause.

οὗ. Possessive genitive, modifying ἁμαρτίαν. The relative pronoun refers anaphorically to ἀνὴρ.

οὐ μὴ. Negative particles. The use of both negative particles makes it emphatic (see Porter 1994a, 57, 283); they are used with the aorist subjunctive form. οὐ μὴ negates λογίσηται.

λογίσηται. Aor mid subj 3rd sg λογίζομαι. Used with οὐ μή to express emphatic negation. The middle voice indicates indirect, internal causality with direct subject involvement or participation. Subjunctive mood form indicates projection, so it refers to the tentativeness of the Lord's (lack of) consideration or reckoning of one's sin.

κύριος. Nominative subject of λογίσηται.

ἁμαρτίαν. Accusative direct object of λογίσηται.

4:9 Ὁ μακαρισμὸς οὖν οὗτος ἐπὶ τὴν περιτομὴν ἢ καὶ ἐπὶ τὴν ἀκροβυστίαν; λέγομεν γάρ· ἐλογίσθη τῷ Ἀβραὰμ ἡ πίστις εἰς δικαιοσύνην.

Ὁ μακαρισμὸς . . . οὗτος. Nominative subject of verbless clause. The demonstrative pronoun (οὗτος) modifies μακαρισμὸς and functions attributively. The entire word group Ὁ μακαρισμὸς . . . οὗτος refers anaphorically to τὸν μακαρισμὸν τοῦ ἀνθρώπου ᾧ ὁ θεὸς λογίζεται δικαιοσύνην χωρὶς ἔργων in v. 6, as developed in vv. 7–8.

οὖν. Postpositive inferential conjunction. It introduces inference (in the form of a question) from the previous Psalms quotation in 4:7–8.

ἐπὶ τὴν περιτομὴν. Directional (movement upon or onto).

ἢ. Disjunctive conjunction. It distinguishes ἐπὶ τὴν περιτομὴν from ἐπὶ τὴν ἀκροβυστίαν.

καὶ. Adverbial use (adjunctive). It modifies the prepositional word group ἐπὶ τὴν ἀκροβυστίαν. It functions to include the "uncircumcision" with the "circumcision" in the "blessedness."

ἐπὶ τὴν ἀκροβυστίαν. Directional (movement upon or onto) ἀκροβυστία ("uncircumcision") is a metonymy (part for the whole) for "an uncircumcised person" (see 2:26; 3:30).

λέγομεν. Pres act ind 1st pl λέγω. This is not the usual Pauline introduction of an OT quotation (γέγραπται). Instead, λέγομεν γάρ is used for possibly two reasons: (1) in order to convey that Paul joins the OT in making this claim, and (2) because the quotation is loosely rendered with a few changes in wording (Porter 2015, 105).

γάρ. Postpositive explanatory conjunction. It introduces the explanation for the implicit answer to the previous question—this blessedness is for both the circumcised and the uncircumcised.

ἐλογίσθη τῷ Ἀβραὰμ ἡ πίστις εἰς δικαιοσύνην. A loose quotation of LXX Gen 15:6 (καὶ ἐπίστευσεν Αβραμ τῷ θεῷ καὶ ἐλογίσθη αὐτῷ εἰς δικαιοσύνην).

ἐλογίσθη. Aor pass ind 3rd sg λογίζομαι. Passive voice indicates external agency. Agency is not specified directly, but as above, it is implicit that God is the one who considers, or credits, Abraham's faith as righteousness.

τῷ Ἀβραάμ. Dative indirect object of ἐλογίσθη.

ἡ πίστις. Nominative subject of ἐλογίσθη. Articular noun refers to "faith" concretely (as opposed to abstractly), namely, the faith that has been discussed so far in this letter (see Peters).

εἰς δικαιοσύνην. Goal or state. Here it refers to a state of righteousness.

4:10 πῶς οὖν ἐλογίσθη; ἐν περιτομῇ ὄντι ἢ ἐν ἀκροβυστίᾳ; οὐκ ἐν περιτομῇ ἀλλ' ἐν ἀκροβυστίᾳ·

πῶς. Adverb (interrogative). It modifies ἐλογίσθη, functioning to establish manner.

οὖν. Postpositive inferential conjunction. The inference is based on the Gen 15:6 quotation in 4:9.

ἐλογίσθη. Aor pass ind 3rd sg λογίζομαι. The subject is not identified here, but based on the previous occurrence of ἐλογίσθη, ἡ πίστις is the implied subject.

ἐν περιτομῇ. State, indicating that the faith was reckoned in a state of circumcision.

ὄντι. Ptc masc dat sg εἰμί (attributive). The use of the dative participle is to supply an adjectival participle to modify τῷ Ἀβραὰμ in v. 9 (cf. Moo, 268 n. 9; see Culy 2003, 441 for an argument against ὄντι being an adverbial participle of time).

ἤ. Disjunctive conjunction. It distinguishes ἐν περιτομῇ from ἐν ἀκροβυστίᾳ.

ἐν ἀκροβυστίᾳ. State. It refers to the state of uncircumcision and is parallel to ἐν περιτομῇ.

οὐκ . . . ἀλλ᾽. A point/counterpoint set that emphasizes the contrast between ἐν περιτομῇ and ἐν ἀκροβυστίᾳ.

ἐν περιτομῇ. State (see above).

ἐν ἀκροβυστίᾳ. State (see above).

4:11 καὶ σημεῖον ἔλαβεν περιτομῆς σφραγῖδα τῆς δικαιοσύνης τῆς πίστεως τῆς ἐν τῇ ἀκροβυστίᾳ, εἰς τὸ εἶναι αὐτὸν πατέρα πάντων τῶν πιστευόντων δι᾽ ἀκροβυστίας, εἰς τὸ λογισθῆναι [καὶ] αὐτοῖς [τὴν] δικαιοσύνην,

This verse contains one main clause (σημεῖον ἔλαβεν περιτομῆς), followed by an apposition to the subject of the main clause, followed by two subordinate clauses both beginning with purpose markers (εἰς τὸ + infinitive). Paul is saying that Abraham's faith, prior to his circumcision, was instrumental in his justification, and that circumcision was simply a sign of that faith. His faith, prior to circumcision, would make him the father of fellow uncircumcised believers (see Porter 2015, 106).

καὶ. Coordinating conjunction. It connects the previous clause complex to the current one.

σημεῖον. Accusative direct object of ἔλαβεν.

ἔλαβεν. Aor act ind 3rd sg λαμβάνω. Abraham is the implied subject from the previous co-text.

περιτομῆς. Genitive of definition or description, modifying σημεῖον. It further defines or circumscribes the "sign" as "of circumcision."

σφραγῖδα. Accusative in apposition to σημεῖον.

τῆς δικαιοσύνης. Genitive of definition or description, modifying σφραγῖδα. It further defines or circumscribes the "seal" as "of righteousness." The articular noun refers to a concrete notion of "righteousness," the righteousness that has been discussed so far in this letter, rather than referring to it abstractly.

τῆς πίστεως. Genitive of source or origin, modifying τῆς δικαιοσύνης, indicating that the source of this seal is "the faith." In other words, righteousness comes from faith.

τῆς ἐν τῇ ἀκροβυστίᾳ. The article functions as an adjectivizer, changing the prepositional word group ἐν τῇ ἀκροβυστίᾳ into an attributive modifier of τῆς πίστεως. In other words, it describes a "faith [which Abraham had] while uncircumcised."

ἐν τῇ ἀκροβυστίᾳ. State (see 4:10).

εἶναι. Inf εἰμί. Used with εἰς τό to indicate purpose. The purpose of the "seal of righteousness of faith in uncircumcision" is so that Abraham would be father to the uncircumcised.

αὐτόν. Accusative subject of the infinitive εἶναι.

πατέρα. Predicate accusative. πατέρα stands in predicate relation to αὐτόν, to which it is joined by the infinitive εἶναι.

πάντων. Possessive genitive, modifying πατέρα. πάντων is a substantival adjective.

τῶν πιστευόντων. Pres act ptc masc gen pl πιστεύω (attributive). The participle functions in attributive structure (third attributive position) with πάντων.

δι᾽ ἀκροβυστίας. Instrumental. This prepositional word group modifies τῶν πιστευόντων, depicting those who believe as doing so "through uncircumcision." Harris argues that διά overlaps with ἐν, making δι᾽ ἀκροβυστίας a stylistic variation on ἐν ἀκροβυστίᾳ (Harris 2012, 77). However, the choice of διά is not merely for stylistic purposes but to actually depict uncircumcision as the means or instrument by which they would believe. In other words, Paul is making the bold and perhaps exaggerated claim that those who believe do so by means of uncircumcision.

λογισθῆναι. Aor pass inf λογίζομαι. Used with εἰς τό to denote purpose. The purpose of the sign/seal is that they would be reckoned or considered to be righteous. The passive voice indicates external agency, implicitly God as the agent.

[καὶ]. Adverbial use (adjunctive). Most major manuscripts do not contain this καί. It is most likely an addition by a later scribe to make the point more strongly (Porter 2015, 106–7).

αὐτοῖς. Dative indirect object of λογισθῆναι.

[τὴν] δικαιοσύνην. Accusative subject of the infinitive λογισθῆναι. Most major manuscripts do not contain the article.

4:12 καὶ πατέρα περιτομῆς τοῖς οὐκ ἐκ περιτομῆς μόνον ἀλλὰ καὶ τοῖς στοιχοῦσιν τοῖς ἴχνεσιν τῆς ἐν ἀκροβυστίᾳ πίστεως τοῦ πατρὸς ἡμῶν Ἀβραάμ.

καὶ. Coordinating conjunction. It adds a second predicate to the infinitival clause εἰς τὸ εἶναι αὐτὸν in 4:11.

πατέρα. Predicate accusative. πατέρα stands in predicate relation to αὐτὸν from the previous verse, to which it is joined by the infinitive εἶναι (also in the previous verse). It is parallel to πατέρα in 4:11.

περιτομῆς. Genitive of description, modifying πατέρα. "Father" is further delineated to "circumcision." περιτομή ("circumcision") is again used as a metonymy (part for the whole) for "a circumcised person" (see 3:30; 4:9).

τοῖς . . . ἐκ περιτομῆς. The article functions as a nominalizer, changing the prepositional word group ἐκ περιτομῆς into a dative of advantage.

ἐκ περιτομῆς. Locative ("out of" or "from").

οὐκ . . . μόνον ἀλλὰ καί. A point/counterpoint set ("not only . . . but also") that corrects the the first description of Abraham's descendants (τοῖς . . . ἐκ περιτομῆς) by supplementing it by the second description his descendants (τοῖς στοιχοῦσιν τοῖς ἴχνεσιν . . . Ἀβραάμ).

τοῖς στοιχοῦσιν. Pres act ptc masc dat pl στοιχέω (substantival). The participle functions as the dative of advantage like τοῖς . . . ἐκ περιτομῆς above.

τοῖς ἴχνεσιν. Dative complement of στοιχοῦσιν. The "steps" are where the "walking" occurs.

τῆς . . . πίστεως. Genitive of definition, modifying τοῖς ἴχνεσιν, further delineating what type of "steps" they are.

ἐν ἀκροβυστίᾳ. Locative (sphere or realm). The prepositional word group, which is placed in attributive position between the article and noun, has the effect of making its modification of the noun tighter. A wooden translation would be for example "the 'in-uncircumcised' faith of our father Abraham."

τοῦ πατρός. Genitive of source of origin, modifying τῆς . . . πίστεως. The origin of this "faith" is "our father Abraham."

ἡμῶν. Possessive genitive, modifying τοῦ πατρός.

Ἀβραάμ. Genitive in apposition to τοῦ πατρός.

4:13 Οὐ γὰρ διὰ νόμου ἡ ἐπαγγελία τῷ Ἀβραὰμ ἢ τῷ σπέρματι αὐτοῦ, τὸ κληρονόμον αὐτὸν εἶναι κόσμου, ἀλλὰ διὰ δικαιοσύνης πίστεως.

Οὐ. Negative particle. It negates the prepositional word group διὰ νόμου.

γὰρ. Postpositive explanatory conjunction. It introduces the sentence that explains further the previous co-text regarding the role of circumcision in justification and faith as a sign.

διὰ νόμου. Instrumental. Fronted for prominence.

ἡ ἐπαγγελία. Nominative absolute or nominative subject of a verbless clause.

τῷ Ἀβραάμ. Dative of advantage.

ἤ. Disjunctive conjunction.

τῷ σπέρματι. Dative of advantage.

αὐτοῦ. Possessive genitive, modifying τῷ σπέρματι. The personal pronoun anaphorically refers to Ἀβραάμ.

τὸ κληρονόμον. Predicate accusative. τὸ κληρονόμον stands in predicate relation to αὐτὸν, to which it is joined by the infinitive εἶναι.

αὐτὸν. Accusative subject of the infinitive εἶναι.

εἶναι. Inf εἰμί (epexegetical to ἐπαγγελία). The infinitive explains the content of the promise.

κόσμου. Possessive genitive, modifying τὸ κληρονόμον.

ἀλλὰ. Adversative conjunction (strong). It contrasts Οὐ . . . διὰ νόμου with διὰ δικαιοσύνης πίστεως.

διὰ δικαιοσύνης. Instrumental. Fronted for prominence.

πίστεως. Genitive of origin or source modifying δικαιοσύνης. The source or origin of righteousness is faith (see 4:5).

4:14 εἰ γὰρ οἱ ἐκ νόμου κληρονόμοι, κεκένωται ἡ πίστις καὶ κατήργηται ἡ ἐπαγγελία·

εἰ. Introduces the protasis of a first-class conditional.

γὰρ. Postpositive explanatory conjunction that introduces the explanation of the basis of the promise to Abraham that continues from the previous co-text, between the law and the righteousness of faith.

οἱ ἐκ νόμου κληρονόμοι. Nominative absolute or nominative subject of a verbless clause. There are potentially two ways to interpret the function of this word group here: (1) as a nominative group that is its own clause (independent), with an embedded prepositional word group (i.e., "the of-the-law heirs"); or (2) as a substantive (οἱ ἐκ νόμου) with a predicate nominative (κληρονόμοι): "those out of the law are heirs." The second option is most likely, due to the first option being an awkward protasis of itself.

ἐκ νόμου. Locative ("out of the law" or "from the law"). The prepositional word group refers to those who belong to the law.

κεκένωται. Prf pass ind 3rd sg κενόω. κεκένωται marks the beginning of the apodosis. The stative aspect (perfect tense-form) is frontgrounded in this discourse (along with κατήργηται below). The passive voice depicts external agency, although the agent is not specified here.

ἡ πίστις. Nominative subject of κεκένωται.

καὶ. Coordinating conjunction. It connects the two clauses κεκένωται ἡ πίστις and κατήργηται ἡ ἐπαγγελία.

κατήργηται. Prf pass ind 3rd sg καταργέω. The stative aspect (perfect tense-form) is frontgrounded in this discourse (along with κεκένωται above). The passive voice indicates external agency, although the agent is not specified here.

ἡ ἐπαγγελία. Nominative subject of κατήργηται.

4:15 ὁ γὰρ νόμος ὀργὴν κατεργάζεται· οὗ δὲ οὐκ ἔστιν νόμος οὐδὲ παράβασις.

ὁ ... νόμος. Nominative subject of κατεργάζεται.

γὰρ. Postpositive explanatory conjunction. It introduces the clause that continues the line of thought from the previous apodosis that faith is empty and that the promise is null.

ὀργὴν. Accusative direct object of κατεργάζεται.

κατεργάζεται. Pres mid ind 3rd sg κατεργάζομαι. Middle voice indicates indirect, internal causality.

οὗ. Genitive relative pronoun. It functions as a marker of situation or set of circumstances (BDAG 733.2), which is posed in the rest of the relative clause.

δὲ. Adversative conjunction (mild).

οὐκ ... οὐδὲ. A point/counterpoint expression: "neither ... nor" (or here, "no law, neither transgression").

ἔστιν. Unaugmented ind 3rd sg εἰμί.

νόμος. Nominative subject of ἔστιν. The anarthrous noun reflects law in general (non-particular).

παράβασις. Nominative subject of an implied ἔστιν. The anarthrous noun reflects transgression in general (non-particular).

4:16 Διὰ τοῦτο ἐκ πίστεως, ἵνα κατὰ χάριν, εἰς τὸ εἶναι βεβαίαν τὴν ἐπαγγελίαν παντὶ τῷ σπέρματι, οὐ τῷ ἐκ τοῦ νόμου μόνον ἀλλὰ καὶ τῷ ἐκ πίστεως Ἀβραάμ, ὅς ἐστιν πατὴρ πάντων ἡμῶν,

Διὰ τοῦτο. Causal. The cause for the previous statement is explained by ἐκ πίστεως. In other words, faith nullifies the previous statements. The demonstrative pronoun is headless and refers generally to what has been stated previously.

ἐκ πίστεως. Instrumental. This prepositional word group stands on its own as an independent clause. It cataphorically modifies "promise" by ellipsis (i.e., "by faith" modifies "promise").

ἵνα. Introduces a purpose clause. The purpose of being by faith is so that it is by grace.

κατὰ χάριν. Standard or basis. The standard or basis is "grace." Like ἐκ πίστεως above, κατὰ χάριν stands as an independent clause of itself and modifies "promise."

εἶναι. Inf εἰμί. Used with εἰς τό to denote purpose. The purpose is so that the promise would be guaranteed.

βεβαίαν. Predicate adjective.

τὴν ἐπαγγελίαν. Accusative subject of the infinitive εἶναι.

παντὶ τῷ σπέρματι. Dative of advantage. The recipients of the guaranteed promise are "all of the offspring." In this construction, παντὶ is in predicate structure with τῷ σπέρματι, signifying the togetherness of the offspring, and can be translated as "all of the offspring" (see Porter 1994a, 119).

οὐ . . . μόνον ἀλλὰ καὶ. A point/counterpoint set ("not only . . . but also") that corrects the notion that the promise is guaranteed to those of the law by supplementing it by the notion that the promise is guaranteed to those of the faith of Abraham.

τῷ ἐκ τοῦ νόμου. The article functions as a nominalizer, changing the prepositional word group ἐκ τοῦ νόμου into the dative of advantage.

ἐκ τοῦ νόμου. Instrumental or causal. It is parallel to ἐκ πίστεως above.

τῷ ἐκ πίστεως. The article functions as a nominalizer, changing the prepositional word group ἐκ πίστεως into the dative of advantage.

ἐκ πίστεως. Instrumental or causal. It is parallel to the other ἐκ prepositional word groups above.

Ἀβραάμ. Genitive of source or origin, modifying πίστεως (the faith that comes from Abraham).

ὅς. Nominative subject of ἐστιν. The relative pronoun refers anaphorically to Ἀβραάμ and begins a relative clause.

ἐστιν. Unaugmented ind 3rd sg εἰμί.

πατὴρ. Predicate nominative.

πάντων. Genitive of description, modifying πατὴρ. It further describes or delineates "father" to "all of us." Some may wish to call this a genitive of relationship, but this would be a semantic category rather than a grammatical one.

ἡμῶν. Partitive genitive, modifying πάντων.

4:17 καθὼς γέγραπται ὅτι πατέρα πολλῶν ἐθνῶν τέθεικά σε, κατέναντι οὗ ἐπίστευσεν θεοῦ τοῦ ζῳοποιοῦντος τοὺς νεκροὺς καὶ καλοῦντος τὰ μὴ ὄντα ὡς ὄντα.

καθὼς γέγραπται. A standard Pauline formula for introducing a scriptural quotation (see note on 1:17).

καθὼς. Comparative conjunction. It compares what has been previously said with what has been written.

γέγραπται. Prf pass ind 3rd sg γράφω.

ὅτι. Introduces the clausal complement (direct discourse) of γέγραπται.

πατέρα. Complement to σε in a double accusative object-complement construction.

πολλῶν ἐθνῶν. Genitive of definition of description, modifying πατέρα. "Father" is further defined or circumscribed as "of many nations."

τέθεικά. Prf act ind 1st sg τίθημι. The perfect tense-form (stative aspect) depicts the process as being in a state of "placing" or "putting." Most English translations supply the gloss "made" here (e.g., NIV, NASB, NKJV, NRSV, ESV), but the idea is one of placing or putting Abraham in the position of the father of many nations. τέθεικά, which has an acute accent on the antepenult, acquired an additional accent, the acute, on the ultima from the enclitic σε.

σε. Accusative direct object of τέθεικά in a double accusative object-complement construction.

κατέναντι οὗ ἐπίστευσεν θεοῦ. An internally headed relative clause because its antecedent (θεοῦ) is incorporated into the relative clause (cf. Culy, Parsons, and Stigall, 115). When this happens, "the article going with the noun must be omitted and the noun itself then attracted to the case of the relative" (BDF §294.5). A reconstructed wording of the clause is: κατέναντι τοῦ θεοῦ ᾧ ἐπίστευσεν (BDF §294.2).

κατέναντι οὗ. Positional (opposite, in front of). κατέναντι is an improper preposition (cf. Porter 1994a, 180). The relative pronoun refers cataphorically to θεοῦ.

ἐπίστευσεν. Aor act ind 3rd sg πιστεύω. The implied subject is Abraham.

θεοῦ. Genitive direct object of ἐπίστευσεν. θεός could have been in the dative because ἐπίστευσεν takes its object in the dative, but it was attracted to the genitive case of the relative pronoun οὗ. On the absence of the article, see κατέναντι οὗ ἐπίστευσεν θεοῦ above.

τοῦ ζῳοποιοῦντος . . . καὶ καλοῦντος. Genitive in apposition to θεοῦ. Granville Sharp's rule may apply here, with one article (τοῦ) governing two substantives (ζῳοποιοῦντος and καλοῦντος) joined by καί referring to the same entity.

ζῳοποιοῦντος. Pres act ptc masc gen sg ζῳοποιέω (substantival).

καλοῦντος. Pres act ptc masc gen sg καλέω (substantival).

τοὺς νεκροὺς. Accusative direct object of ζῳοποιοῦντος.

τὰ . . . ὄντα. Ptc neut acc pl εἰμί (substantival). Accusative direct object of καλοῦντος.

μὴ. Negative particle normally used with non-indicative verbs. Here it negates the participle ὄντα.

ὡς. Comparative conjunction. Compares μὴ ὄντα with ὄντα.

ὄντα. Ptc neut acc pl εἰμί (substantival). Accusative direct object of καλοῦντος.

4:18 Ὃς παρ' ἐλπίδα ἐπ' ἐλπίδι ἐπίστευσεν εἰς τὸ γενέσθαι αὐτὸν πατέρα πολλῶν ἐθνῶν κατὰ τὸ εἰρημένον· οὕτως ἔσται τὸ σπέρμα σου,

Ὃς. Nominative subject of ἐπίστευσεν. The relative pronoun refers anaphorically to the same implied subject of ἐπίστευσεν in 4:17, Abraham.

παρ' ἐλπίδα ἐπ' ἐλπίδι. Probably a Greek idiom meaning "piling hope upon hope" (Porter 2015, 109). Against most English translations, παρά does not have a sense of "against" but "alongside," so the idiom refers to having hope upon, or alongside, hope.

ἐπίστευσεν. Aor act ind 3rd sg πιστεύω.

γενέσθαι. Aor mid inf γίνομαι. Used with εἰς τὸ to denote result. The result of Abraham's belief was becoming the father of many nations.

αὐτὸν. Accusative subject of the infinitive γενέσθαι.

πατέρα. Predicate accusative.

πολλῶν ἐθνῶν. Genitive of definition or description, modifying πατέρα. It further defines or circumscribes "father" to be "of many nations."

κατὰ τὸ εἰρημένον. Standard. The standard is "what had been spoken."

εἰρημένον. Prf mid ptc pass acc sg λέγω (substantival).

οὕτως. Predicate adverb of manner. Predicate adverbs function as predicates of equative verbs, such as εἰμί and γίνομαι (BDF §434.1).

ἔσται. Fut 3rd sg εἰμί.

τὸ σπέρμα. Nominative subject of ἔσται.

σου. Genitive of possession, modifying τὸ σπέρμα.

4:19 καὶ μὴ ἀσθενήσας τῇ πίστει κατενόησεν τὸ ἑαυτοῦ σῶμα [ἤδη] νενεκρωμένον, ἑκατονταετής που ὑπάρχων, καὶ τὴν νέκρωσιν τῆς μήτρας Σάρρας·

καὶ. Coordinating conjunction. It connects the previous clause with the current clause.

μὴ. Negative particle normally used with non-indicative verbs. Here it negates ἀσθενήσας.

ἀσθενήσας. Aor act ptc masc nom sg ἀσθενέω (manner). The participle functions contextually as circumstantial, modifying κατενόησεν.

τῇ πίστει. Dative of respect. He did not weaken with respect to "faith."

κατενόησεν. Aor act ind 3rd sg κατανοέω. Abraham is the implied subject, as maintained from the 3rd person singular verbs in the previous verse.

τὸ . . . σῶμα. Accusative direct object of κατενόησεν in a double accusative object-complement construction.

ἑαυτοῦ. Possessive genitive, modifying τὸ . . . σῶμα.

[ἤδη]. Adverb (temporal). It modifies νενεκρωμένον. The square brackets represent a textual variant, either with or without the word. The UBS committee favors retaining this reading based on the early manuscript tradition (ℵ C Dᵍʳ K P) but gives it a C rating based on internal considerations, such as a heightening of the statement of Sarah's barrenness using the adverb and unlikelihood of scribal omission the word if it was original (Metzger, 451).

νενεκρωμένον. Prf mid ptc neut acc sg νεκρόω (attributive). Complement to τὸ . . . σῶμα in a double accusative object-complement construction. The stative aspect (perfect tense-form) grammaticalizes a state or condition of being dead (i.e., in a deadened state), and even as a participle, it is marked and thus prominent in the co-text.

ἑκατονταετής. Predicate adjective (numeral).

που. Adverb (enclitic) that is used as a marker of numerical approximation ("about," "around," or "approximately").

ὑπάρχων. Pres act ptc masc nom sg ὑπάρχω (causal). The participle functions contextually as circumstantial. It modifies νενεκρωμένον.

καὶ. Coordinating conjunction. It connects τὸ ἑαυτοῦ σῶμα with τὴν νέκρωσιν τῆς μήτρας Σάρρας.

τὴν νέκρωσιν. Accusative direct object of κατενόησεν. It is parallel to τὸ . . . σῶμα.

τῆς μήτρας. Genitive of definition, modifying τὴν νέκρωσιν. It defines further the barrenness as "womb."

Σάρρας. Possessive genitive, modifying τῆς μήτρας.

4:20 εἰς δὲ τὴν ἐπαγγελίαν τοῦ θεοῦ οὐ διεκρίθη τῇ ἀπιστίᾳ ἀλλ' ἐνεδυναμώθη τῇ πίστει, δοὺς δόξαν τῷ θεῷ

εἰς . . . τὴν ἐπαγγελίαν. Goal. The fronting of this prepositional word group makes it prominent in the clause.

δὲ. Adversative conjunction (mild). It contrasts Abraham considering his own body and Sarah's barrenness with his undoubting the promises of God.

τοῦ θεοῦ. Genitive of origin or source, modifying τὴν ἐπαγγελίαν. The promise comes from God.

οὐ . . . ἀλλ'. A point/counterpoint set ("not this . . . but that") that negates the idea that Abraham doubted the promise of God and replaces it with the idea that Abraham was strengthened in faith. The use of ἀλλά instead of δὲ notes a strong contrast.

διεκρίθη. Aor mid ind 3rd sg διακρίνω. On the middle voice, see "Deponency" in the Series Introduction and Introduction.

τῇ ἀπιστίᾳ. Dative of respect or manner.

ἐνεδυναμώθη. Aor pass ind 3rd sg ἐνδυναμόω.

τῇ πίστει. Dative of respect or manner.

δούς. Aor act ptc masc nom sg δίδωμι (manner). The participle functions as circumstantial and modifies ἐνεδυναμώθη (see parallel participle πληροφορηθεὶς in 4:21).

δόξαν. Accusative direct object of δούς.

τῷ θεῷ. Dative indirect object of δούς.

4:21 καὶ πληροφορηθεὶς ὅτι ὃ ἐπήγγελται δυνατός ἐστιν καὶ ποιῆσαι.

καὶ. Coordinating conjunction. It connects δούς (4:20) with πληροφορηθεὶς.

πληροφορηθεὶς. Aor pass ptc masc nom sg πληροφορέω (manner). The participle functions as circumstantial and modifies ἐνεδυναμώθη (4:20; parallel to δούς in 4:20). In its middle and passive voice-forms (which are identical), πληροφορέω means "to be completely convinced" (cf. LN 31.45). The distinction between middle and passive voice here is insignificant (i.e., "completely convincing himself" or "being completely convinced") with agency unspecified.

ὅτι. Introduces the clausal complement (indirect discourse) of πληροφορηθεὶς.

ὃ. Accusative direct object of ἐπήγγελται. The relative pronoun does not refer to a particular item in the immediate co-text but to the content of the promise, namely that Abraham would be the father of many nations.

ἐπήγγελται. Prf mid ind 3rd sg ἐπαγγέλλομαι. This can also be interpreted as passive voice ("what was promised"). The difference between the middle and passive voices here are semantically minimal.

δυνατός. Predicate adjective.

ἐστιν. Unaugmented ind 3rd sg εἰμί.

καὶ. Adverbial use (adjunctive). It modifies ποιῆσαι.

ποιῆσαι. Aor act inf ποιέν (complementary). It complements δυνατός.

4:22 διὸ [καὶ] ἐλογίσθη αὐτῷ εἰς δικαιοσύνην.

διὸ. Inferential conjunction.

[καὶ]. Adverbial use (adjunctive). It modifies ἐλογίσθη. The square brackets represent a textual variant, with or without the word. The UBS committee gives it a C rating based on the split manuscript evidence for

and against this reading (for majuscules with: ℵ A C D¹; without: B D*
F G).

ἐλογίσθη. Aor pass ind 3rd sg λογίζομαι. Passive voice indicates
external agency, unspecified in this co-text.

αὐτῷ. Dative indirect object of ἐλογίσθη.

εἰς δικαιοσύνην. Goal.

4:23 Οὐκ ἐγράφη δὲ δι᾽ αὐτὸν μόνον ὅτι ἐλογίσθη αὐτῷ

Οὐκ . . . μόνον. The first half of the point/counterpoint set ("not
only . . . but also") that is completed in the next verse, which negates
the idea that the words ἐλογίσθη αὐτῷ were written for Abraham's sake
alone.

ἐγράφη. Aor pass ind 3rd sg γράφω. The agent and Goal of the passive voice verb are not grammatically identified in this verse, as with
usual occurrences of γέγραπται (also passive but stative aspect/perfect
tense-form). Here, the use of the perfective aspect instead of the stative
is probably due to this not being a direct scriptural quotation but a general reference to what has been stated (elucidated by ὅτι).

δὲ. Adversative conjunction (mild). It connects with previous clause.

δι᾽ αὐτὸν. Instrumental/causal. The personal pronoun refers to
Abraham.

ὅτι. Introduces the clausal complement (indirect discourse) of
ἐγράφη.

ἐλογίσθη. Aor pass ind 3rd sg λογίζομαι.

αὐτῷ. Dative indirect object of ἐλογίσθη. The personal pronoun
refers to Abraham.

4:24 ἀλλὰ καὶ δι᾽ ἡμᾶς, οἷς μέλλει λογίζεσθαι, τοῖς πιστεύουσιν ἐπὶ τὸν ἐγείραντα Ἰησοῦν τὸν κύριον ἡμῶν ἐκ νεκρῶν,

ἀλλὰ καὶ. The second half of the point/counterpoint set ("not only . . .
but also") that began in the previous verse, which supplements the idea
that the words ἐλογίσθη αὐτῷ were written for the sake of Abraham
with the idea that they were written for our sake.

δι᾽ ἡμᾶς. Instrumental/causal. The cause of what was written was not
only Abraham (4:23) but "also us."

οἷς. Dative of indirect object λογίζεσθαι. The relative pronoun refers
anaphorically to ἡμᾶς.

μέλλει. Pres act ind 3rd sg μέλλω.

λογίζεσθαι. Pres pass inf λογίζομαι (complementary). Catenative
construction with μέλλει.

τοῖς πιστεύουσιν. Pres act ptc masc dat pl πιστεύω (substantival). Dative in apposition to οἷς.

ἐπὶ τὸν ἐγείραντα. Locative (movement upon). The prepositional word group modifies πιστεύουσιν. According to BDAG (817.2.a.δ), ἐπί + accusative is used with πιστεύω to indicate the object of belief or trust. This combination occurs seven times in the NT (Matt 27:42; Acts 9:42; 11:17; 16:31; 22:19; Rom 4:5, 24). However, this is the usage of ἐπί in context as object, but it retains its grammatical function of locative (figuratively where trust or faith is placed).

τὸν ἐγείραντα. Aor act ptc masc acc sg ἐγείρω (substantival). The articular participle refers to God based on the context.

Ἰησοῦν. Accusative direct object of ἐγείραντα.

τὸν κύριον. Accusative in apposition to Ἰησοῦν.

ἡμῶν. Possessive genitive, modifying τὸν κύριον.

ἐκ νεκρῶν. Locative (movement out of/separation). The prepositional word group modifies ἐγείραντα.

4:25 ὃς παρεδόθη διὰ τὰ παραπτώματα ἡμῶν καὶ ἠγέρθη διὰ τὴν δικαίωσιν ἡμῶν.

The two clauses in this verse contain several parallels: use of a passive voice verb, prepositional word group beginning with διά, and the pronoun ἡμῶν:

παρεδόθη διὰ τὰ παραπτώματα ἡμῶν
ἠγέρθη διὰ τὴν δικαίωσιν ἡμῶν

Causality (use of διά) here, for the death and resurrection of Jesus, is both retrogressive and progressive (cf. Porter 2015, 111).

ὅς. Nominative subject of παρεδόθη and ἠγέρθη. The relative pronoun refers anaphorically to Ἰησοῦν τὸν κύριον ἡμῶν. As the subject of a passive voice verb, it is the Goal of the processes of delivering and raising; the agent is unspecified in the clause.

παρεδόθη. Aor pass ind 3rd sg παραδίδωμι. The agent is unspecified in the clause.

διὰ τὰ παραπτώματα. Causal. The reason why Jesus "was given over" was because of "our trespasses" (they caused it).

ἡμῶν. Genitive of origin or possessive genitive, modifying τὰ παραπτώματα. It refers to the transgressions that came from "us" or belong to "us."

καί. Coordinating conjunction. It connects παρεδόθη with ἠγέρθη.

ἠγέρθη. Aor pass ind 3rd sg ἐγείρω.

διὰ τὴν δικαίωσιν. Causal. The reason Jesus "was raised" was because of "our justification" (which effected or caused it, indirectly albeit).

ἡμῶν. Possessive genitive, modifying τὴν δικαίωσιν. It points to the justification that belongs to "us."

Romans 5:1–11

[1]Therefore, having been justified by faith, we should have peace with God through our Lord Jesus Christ, [2]through whom we have also obtained access by faith into this grace in which we stand. And we should boast in the hope of the glory of God. [3]But not only [this], but we should also boast in tribulations, knowing that tribulation produces perseverance, [4]and perseverance, character, and character, hope. [5]And hope does not disappoint, because the love of God is poured out in our hearts through the Holy Spirit who has been given to us. [6]For Christ still—while we were still weak—according to the appropriate time, died for the ungodly. [7]For rarely for a righteous person will someone die; for on behalf of a good person, perhaps someone is even willing to die. [8]But God demonstrates his own love for us that while we were still sinners Christ died for us. [9]Much more, therefore, having been justified now in his blood, will we be saved through him from the wrath. [10]For if, while we were enemies, we were reconciled to God through the death of his Son, much more, having been reconciled, will we be saved by his life. [11]But not only [that], but we should also boast in God through our Lord Jesus Christ, through whom we now receive reconciliation.

Romans 5:1–11 is the first of two sub-sections of the next major section of the body of the letter (5:1–21). The themes of reconciliation, God, and humanity are prominent. The beginning of this section (5:1–5) contains several parallelisms, including the subjunctives ἔχωμεν (5:1; see below on the textual variant), καυχώμεθα (5:2), and καυχώμεθα (5:3); repetition of διὰ (5:1, 2, 5); and the concluding step progression (5:4–5). These parallelisms create cohesion for this unit.

5:1 Δικαιωθέντες οὖν ἐκ πίστεως εἰρήνην ἔχωμεν πρὸς τὸν θεὸν διὰ τοῦ κυρίου ἡμῶν Ἰησοῦ Χριστοῦ

Δικαιωθέντες. Aor pass ptc masc nom pl δικαιόω (causal). The participle modifies the predicate in the clause ἔχωμεν and functions as causal to the main predicate. In this co-text, the adverbial (or adjunctive) participle in the perfective aspect (aorist) serves to summarize the central

notion of the previous section (1:18—4:25) and transitions to the main
clause (εἰρήνην ἔχωμεν πρὸς τὸν θεὸν . . .).

οὖν. Postpositive inferential conjunction. The inference is from the
previous co-text.

ἐκ πίστεως. Instrumental. The core meaning of ἐκ, movement out
of (modulated as instrumental in this co-text), is applicable here; i.e.,
justification comes out of faith.

εἰρήνην. Accusative direct object of ἔχωμεν. The fronting of the accusative direct object before the main predicate indicates emphasis, prominence at the clause level.

ἔχωμεν. Pres act subj 1st pl ἔχω. The variant reading—the subjunctive
ἔχωμεν—has stronger manuscript support (ℵ* A B* C D K L 33 81 630
1175) than the indicative ἔχομεν (ℵ¹ B² F G P Ψ 0220^vid 104 365 1241)
and is adopted in this handbook. For defense of use of the subjunctive,
see Porter (1991, 662–65; 2015, 114). The use of the subjunctive is not
strictly exhortative ("let us have peace")—as if peace was not reflective of
their reality at this point, so Paul is exhorting them to attain to that peace.
However, the subjunctive mood form indicates Paul's projection of the
next stage of his argument, that since they have been justified by faith,
they should enjoy or realize the peace that they already had (i.e., we should
enjoy or realize peace). The history of scholarship is that the subjunctive
reading was accepted until the early- to mid-twentieth century, when,
without a substantial change in external evidence, scholars understood
the subjunctive to indicate exhortation, rather than simply projection
of the next stage of the argument. Several recent commentators have
accepted the subjunctive (e.g., Jewett, 344; Hultgren, 677–80).

πρὸς τὸν θεὸν. Directional (movement toward).

διὰ τοῦ κυρίου. Instrumental. The means by which peace is had
is "through our Lord Jesus Christ." A similar expanded instrumental
phrase is used in 5:11 and 21, marking the beginning, middle, and end
of the chapter, and emphasizing the role of Jesus Christ in God's actions
toward humanity.

ἡμῶν. Possessive genitive, modifying τοῦ κυρίου.

Ἰησοῦ Χριστοῦ. Genitive in apposition to τοῦ κυρίου.

**5:2 δι' οὗ καὶ τὴν προσαγωγὴν ἐσχήκαμεν [τῇ πίστει] εἰς τὴν χάριν
ταύτην ἐν ᾗ ἑστήκαμεν καὶ καυχώμεθα ἐπ' ἐλπίδι τῆς δόξης τοῦ θεοῦ.**

δι' οὗ. Instrumental. The instrument by which we obtain our freedom is "him" (i.e., Jesus Christ). The genitive relative pronoun modifies
Ἰησοῦ Χριστοῦ (5:1), and the prepositional word group δι' οὗ is appositional to διὰ τοῦ κυρίου ἡμῶν Ἰησοῦ Χριστοῦ in the previous verse.

καί. Adverbial use (adjunctive). Modifies ἐσχήκαμεν.

τὴν προσαγωγὴν. Accusative direct object of ἐσχήκαμεν. This lexeme occurs two other times in the NT (Eph 2:18; 3:12).

ἐσχήκαμεν. Prf act ind 1st pl ἔχω. The stative aspect (perfect tense-form) describes a state of possession and is prominent in this section.

ἐσχήκαμεν . . . ἑστήκαμεν. The two words reflects assonance, a literary device used to draw attention to the assonant elements. They are both also in the stative aspect, adding to their emphasis in the co-text. The literary effect is to draw attention to the fact that they *have* (access through Christ) and *stand* (in this grace).

[τῇ πίστει]. Dative of respect. It refers to "access" with respect to "faith." The brackets reflect a textual variant, with (ℵ* C K L P Ψ 33 81 104 𝔐 lat.) or without (B D G 0220 it^{d*}) the word. The external evidence is divided, and the presence or absence has a minimal effect on the overall meaning of the text.

εἰς τὴν χάριν ταύτην. Goal. The goal of obtaining access is "this grace." The use of εἰς to modify προσαγωγὴν (Eph 2:18 has two prepositions, ἐν and πρός, while Eph 3:12 has ἐν) focuses on its basic meaning of movement into (as opposed to being in without movement, ἐν, or movement towards, πρός), i.e., access "into" this grace. The demonstrative pronoun ταύτην modifies τὴν χάριν and refers cataphorically to the grace in which they stand (ἐν ᾗ ἑστήκαμεν).

ἐν ᾗ. Locative (sphere or realm). The relative pronoun ᾗ refers to τὴν χάριν ταύτην.

ἑστήκαμεν. Prf act ind 1st pl ἵστημι. The stative aspect describes being in a state or condition of standing. Its prominence in the clause complex is reduced due to appearing in a relative clause but still prominent in the co-text.

καί. Coordinating conjunction. It connects the clause containing ἔχωμεν with the clause containing καυχώμεθα.

καυχώμεθα. Pres mid subj 1st pl καυχάομαι. While the indicative mood form is identical to the subjunctive for this word, it is preferred to interpret this as a subjunctive, parallel to ἔχωμεν (not ἑστήκαμεν; contra Wilckens, 1:288; see Porter 2015, 116). The subjunctive functions, in the same way as ἔχωμεν, as projection, not that they were not boasting already and must boast, but that boasting should result from being justified by faith. "Boasting" here does not refer to haughty bragging but to rejoicing in the hope of the glory of God.

ἐπ' ἐλπίδι. Locative (upon).

τῆς δόξης. Genitive of description, modifying ἐλπίδι. It further describes or circumscribes "hope" as "of glory." Some may wish to see this as an objective genitive.

τοῦ θεοῦ. Possessive genitive, modifying τῆς δόξης.

5:3 οὐ μόνον δέ, ἀλλὰ καὶ καυχώμεθα ἐν ταῖς θλίψεσιν, εἰδότες ὅτι ἡ θλῖψις ὑπομονὴν κατεργάζεται,

Paul builds his parallelism from peace to boasting, but boasting in tribulations, which leads to a step parallelism in 5:3–4. The step parallelism moves from tribulation through to peace, by means of perseverance and character.

οὐ μόνον ... ἀλλὰ καὶ. A point/counterpoint set ("not only ... but also"). The compound is intensive. The contrast (adversative) is between οὐ μόνον (which refers to the previous statement, καυχώμεθα ἐπ' ἐλπίδι τῆς δόξης τοῦ θεοῦ) and καυχώμεθα ἐν ταῖς θλίψεσιν.

δέ. Adversative conjunction (mild). It connects the previous clause-complex with the current one in a mild adversative relationship.

καυχώμεθα. Pres mid subj 1st pl καυχάομαι. As used above, the subjunctive functions as projection, rather than hortatory (see note in 5:2): "we should boast in tribulations." It is parallel to ἔχωμεν (5:1) and καυχώμεθα (5:2). The middle voice indicates indirect, internal causality (against the view that sees such a verb as deponent; see "Deponency" in the Series Introduction and Introduction). The same sense of boasting as rejoicing, as in 5:2, is to be interpreted here.

ἐν ταῖς θλίψεσιν. Locative (sphere or realm).

εἰδότες. Prf act ptc masc nom pl οἶδα (causal). The participle functions in the co-text as circumstantial and modifies καυχώμεθα.

ὅτι. Introduces the clausal complement (indirect discourse) of εἰδότες.

ἡ θλῖψις. Nominative subject of κατεργάζεται.

ὑπομονὴν. Accusative direct object of κατεργάζεται.

κατεργάζεται. Pres mid ind 3rd sg κατεργάζομαι.

5:4 ἡ δὲ ὑπομονὴ δοκιμήν, ἡ δὲ δοκιμὴ ἐλπίδα.

The two verbless clauses here are parallel to the previous clause with the predicate κατεργάζεται, which is implied in both clauses.

ἡ ... ὑπομονὴ. Nominative absolute or nominative subject of an implied κατεργάζεται.

δὲ. Adversative conjunction (mild).

δοκιμήν. Accusative direct object of an implied κατεργάζεται.

ἡ ... δοκιμὴ. Nominative absolute or nominative subject of an implied κατεργάζεται.

δὲ. Adversative conjunction (mild).

ἐλπίδα. Accusative direct object of an implied κατεργάζεται.

5:5 ἡ δὲ ἐλπὶς οὐ καταισχύνει, ὅτι ἡ ἀγάπη τοῦ θεοῦ ἐκκέχυται ἐν ταῖς καρδίαις ἡμῶν διὰ πνεύματος ἁγίου τοῦ δοθέντος ἡμῖν.

ἡ . . . ἐλπὶς. Nominative subject of καταισχύνει.

δὲ. Adversative conjunction (mild).

οὐ. Negative particle normally used with indicative verbs. It negates καταισχύνει.

καταισχύνει. Pres act ind 3rd sg καταισχύνω.

ὅτι. Introduces a causal clause. The reason that "hope does not disappoint" is "the love of God."

ἡ ἀγάπη. Nominative subject of ἐκκέχυται. This is the first time this word is used in this letter (cf. 5:8; 8:35, 39; 12:9; 13:10 (2x); 14:15; 15:30).

τοῦ θεοῦ. Genitive of source or origin, modifying ἡ ἀγάπη ("love that comes from God").

ἐκκέχυται. Prf pass ind 3rd sg ἐκχέω. The stative aspect (perfect tense-form) describes being in a state of being poured out and is prominent in this co-text. The passive voice indicates external causality; the Holy Spirit is the agent (through the prepositional word group διὰ πνεύματος ἁγίου).

ἐν ταῖς καρδίαις. Locative (sphere or realm).

ἡμῶν. Possessive genitive, modifying ταῖς καρδίαις.

διὰ πνεύματος ἁγίου. Instrumental. Indicates the instrument or agency by which "God's love is poured out in our hearts."

τοῦ δοθέντος. Aor pass ptc neut gen sg δίδωμι (attributive). The participle modifies πνεύματος (third attributive position).

ἡμῖν. Dative indirect object of δοθέντος.

5:6 Ἔτι γὰρ Χριστὸς ὄντων ἡμῶν ἀσθενῶν ἔτι κατὰ καιρὸν ὑπὲρ ἀσεβῶν ἀπέθανεν.

In this clause complex, the primary clause is Ἔτι γὰρ Χριστὸς . . . κατὰ καιρὸν ὑπὲρ ἀσεβῶν ἀπέθανεν and the embedded clause is ὄντων ἡμῶν ἀσθενῶν ἔτι.

Ἔτι. Adverb (temporal). A significant textual variant is between εἰς τί γὰρ or omission of the second ἔτι instead of ἔτι γὰρ . . . ἔτι. The first two readings may seem to make better sense of Paul's diatribe in this section, as well as less awkward with the repetition of ἔτι, but most of the early major manuscripts attest to the reading above (ℵ A C^vid D*). For purposes of this handbook, the majority reading is analyzed; see the discussion of this variant in Porter (1991, 666–68; 2015, 117). In this case, the adverb modifies ἀπέθανεν and the clause associated with the verb (ἔτι does not require proximity to its modifying word; cf. Luke 14:26; John 7:33; Acts 2:26; Rom 3:7; 1 Cor 12:31; Phil 1:9; Heb 7:10; 11:36).

γάρ. Postpositive explanatory conjunction that introduces the explanation of the statements made in 5:3–5.

Χριστός. Nominative subject of ἀπέθανεν.

ὄντων. Ptc masc gen pl εἰμί (genitive absolute, temporal). The participle functions as circumstantial. It provides background to the main clause (see above). As an embedded clause, it is prominent in clause structure by its placement before the main predicate (ἀπέθανεν).

ἡμῶν. Genitive subject of ὄντων.

ἀσθενῶν. Predicate genitive.

ἔτι. Adverb (temporal). It modifies ὄντων. It has the same function as the previous ἔτι (both rendered "still" here). The repetition of ἔτι is emphatic in this verse, highlighting the temporality of both clauses (i.e., we were still sinners and Christ still died for us).

κατὰ καιρὸν. Temporal. The placement of this prepositional word group before the main predicate (ἀπέθανεν) makes it prominent according to clause structure.

ὑπὲρ ἀσεβῶν. Substitutionary. The placement of this prepositional word group before the main predicate (ἀπέθανεν) makes it prominent (secondary to the previous prepositional word group) according to clause structure.

ἀπέθανεν. Aor act ind 3rd sg ἀποθνήσκω.

5:7 μόλις γὰρ ὑπὲρ δικαίου τις ἀποθανεῖται· ὑπὲρ γὰρ τοῦ ἀγαθοῦ τάχα τις καὶ τολμᾷ ἀποθανεῖν·

μόλις. Adverb (manner). It modifies ὑπὲρ δικαίου. The fronting of the adverb is prominent in the clause.

γάρ. Postpositive explanatory conjunction. The series of explanations for previous statements continues.

ὑπὲρ δικαίου. Substitutionary.

τις. Nominative subject of ἀποθανεῖται. τις is an indefinite pronoun.

ἀποθανεῖται. Fut mid ind 3rd sg ἀποθνήσκω. The future form depicts expectation.

ὑπὲρ . . . τοῦ ἀγαθοῦ. Substitutionary.

γάρ. Postpositive explanatory conjunction.

τάχα. Adverb (probability). It modifies ὑπὲρ τοῦ ἀγαθοῦ.

τις. Nominative subject of τολμᾷ.

καί. Adverbial use (adjunctive). Modifies τολμᾷ.

τολμᾷ. Pres act ind 3rd sg τολμάω.

ἀποθανεῖν. Aor act inf ἀποθνήσκω (complementary).

5:8 συνίστησιν δὲ τὴν ἑαυτοῦ ἀγάπην εἰς ἡμᾶς ὁ θεός, ὅτι ἔτι ἁμαρτω-λῶν ὄντων ἡμῶν Χριστὸς ὑπὲρ ἡμῶν ἀπέθανεν.

συνίστησιν. Pres act ind 3rd sg συνίστημι.

δὲ. Adversative conjunction (mild). It contrasts the previous statement with the following.

τὴν . . . ἀγάπην. Accusative direct object of συνίστησιν.

ἑαυτοῦ. Possessive genitive, modifying τὴν . . . ἀγάπην. ἑαυτοῦ is a reflexive pronoun.

εἰς ἡμᾶς. Directional (movement into).

ὁ θεός. Nominative subject of συνίστησιν.

ὅτι. Introduces a content clause (epexegetical to τὴν ἑαυτοῦ ἀγάπην) that further describes "his own love."

ἔτι ἁμαρτωλῶν ὄντων ἡμῶν. A restatement of the previous clause, ὄντων ἡμῶν ἀσθενῶν ἔτι (5:6), now thematizing the condition (ἔτι ἁμαρτωλῶν).

ἔτι. Adverb (temporal). It modifies ἁμαρτωλῶν ὄντων ἡμῶν.

ἁμαρτωλῶν. Predicate genitive.

ὄντων. Ptc masc gen pl εἰμί (genitive absolute, temporal).

ἡμῶν. Genitive subject of ὄντων.

Χριστὸς. Nominative subject of ἀπέθανεν.

ὑπὲρ ἡμῶν. Substitutionary. The prepositional word group fronted before the main predicate in the clause makes it prominent.

ἀπέθανεν. Aor act ind 3rd sg ἀποθνήσκω. This is the third time (5:6–8) where "death" is used, highlighting Christ's death (cf. 5:10).

5:9 πολλῷ οὖν μᾶλλον δικαιωθέντες νῦν ἐν τῷ αἵματι αὐτοῦ σωθησό-μεθα δι' αὐτοῦ ἀπὸ τῆς ὀργῆς.

πολλῷ . . . μᾶλλον. Dative of advantage + the comparative of the adverb μάλα. πολλῷ μᾶλλον is an idiom meaning "much more" or "all the more." A heightened contrast is indicated (used again in 5:10). The comparison is between Χριστὸς ὑπὲρ ἡμῶν ἀπέθανεν (5:8) and σωθησόμεθα δι' αὐτοῦ ἀπὸ τῆς ὀργῆς.

οὖν. Postpositive inferential conjunction. The inference is from the previous statement regarding Christ dying for the ungodly. Paul returns to the circumstance of justification (as in 5:1, both words represented by a participle).

δικαιωθέντες. Aor pass ptc masc nom pl δικαιόω (causal). The participle functions as circumstantial and modifies the predicate in the clause σωθησόμεθα. Passive voice indicates external causality, which is "his blood."

νῦν. Adverb (temporal). Modifies δικαιωθέντες.

ἐν τῷ αἵματι. Instrumental. The instrument (or cause) of "having been justified" is "his blood."

αὐτοῦ. Possessive genitive, modifying τῷ αἵματι.

σωθησόμεθα. Fut pass ind 1st pl σῴζω. This is the main predicate of the clause. Future form grammaticalizes the semantic feature of expectancy. The agent of the passive voice verb is identified with the prepositional word group δι' αὐτοῦ, which is Jesus.

δι' αὐτοῦ. Instrumental. The instrument that "will save" is "him" (i.e., Jesus).

ἀπὸ τῆς ὀργῆς. Locative (movement away from/separation).

5:10 εἰ γὰρ ἐχθροὶ ὄντες κατηλλάγημεν τῷ θεῷ διὰ τοῦ θανάτου τοῦ υἱοῦ αὐτοῦ, πολλῷ μᾶλλον καταλλαγέντες σωθησόμεθα ἐν τῇ ζωῇ αὐτοῦ·

εἰ. Introduces the protasis of a first-class conditional.

γὰρ. Postpositive explanatory conjunction. Paul continues the explanation of salvation in the previous verse through use of a conditional statement.

ἐχθροὶ. Predicate nominative.

ὄντες. Ptc masc nom pl εἰμί (temporal). The participle functions co-textually as circumstantial, modifying κατηλλάγημεν.

κατηλλάγημεν. Aor pass ind 1st pl καταλλάσσω (on the meaning and use of this verb, see Porter 1994b; cf. Marshall).

τῷ θεῷ. Dative of advantage.

διὰ τοῦ θανάτου. Instrumental. "The death of his Son" is the instrument by which "we have been reconciled."

τοῦ υἱοῦ. Genitive of definition or description, modifying τοῦ θανάτου. Death is further described or circumscribed as "of his Son."

αὐτοῦ. Possessive genitive, modifying τοῦ υἱοῦ. The personal pronoun refers to God.

πολλῷ μᾶλλον. Dative of advantage + the comparative of the adverb μάλα. πολλῷ μᾶλλον is an idiom meaning "much more" or "all the more" (see 5:9). The comparison is between κατηλλάγημεν . . . διὰ τοῦ θανάτου τοῦ υἱοῦ αὐτοῦ and σωθησόμεθα ἐν τῇ ζωῇ αὐτοῦ. πολλῷ μᾶλλον marks the beginning of the apodosis.

καταλλαγέντες. Aor pass ptc masc nom pl καταλλάσσω (temporal). The participle functions co-textually as circumstantial. It provides background information to the main clause σωθησόμεθα ἐν τῇ ζωῇ αὐτοῦ.

σωθησόμεθα. Fut pass ind 1st pl σῴζω. The agent of the passive voice is identified (as in the previous verse) by the prepositional word group;

in this case, ἐν τῇ ζωῇ αὐτοῦ refers to Jesus' life, which is the instrument of saving.

ἐν τῇ ζωῇ. Instrumental.

αὐτοῦ. Possessive genitive, modifying τῇ ζωῇ. The personal pronoun refers to τοῦ υἱοῦ αὐτοῦ in the protasis.

5:11 οὐ μόνον δέ, ἀλλὰ καὶ καυχώμενοι ἐν τῷ θεῷ διὰ τοῦ κυρίου ἡμῶν Ἰησοῦ Χριστοῦ δι᾽ οὗ νῦν τὴν καταλλαγὴν ἐλάβομεν.

οὐ μόνον . . . ἀλλὰ καί. A point/counterpoint set ("not only . . . but also"). The "not only" is applied by ellipsis to the previous statement about being saved by his life.

δέ. Adversative conjunction (mild).

καυχώμενοι. Pres mid ptc masc nom pl καυχάομαι (independent predicate; cf. Rom 12:9–19; 13:11; 2 Cor 6:3–10; 8:24; 9:11, 13; Eph 3:17–18; 4:2; 5:16–22; Phil 1:30; Col 2:2; 4:11; for the participle functioning as an independent predicator, see Cranfield, 1:268 n. 5; Porter 1989, 370–77; Porter 2015, 122–23). This participle is not dependent upon a finite verb in this co-text. The only possible finite verb it could modify would be ἐλάβομεν at the end of the verse, but this would make Paul's point/counterpoint statement unnecessarily redundant: verse 10 already refers to being reconciled and saved, so it would be redundant to make a counterpoint repeating that we are reconciled. The participle seems to function as a statement (in place of an indicative) here.

ἐν τῷ θεῷ. Locative (sphere or realm). The sphere or domain (figurative location) of boasting is "God."

διὰ τοῦ κυρίου. Instrumental. Similar instrumental phrase using an expanded title for Jesus Christ is found in 5:1 and 11.

ἡμῶν. Possessive genitive, modifying τοῦ κυρίου.

Ἰησοῦ Χριστοῦ. Genitive in apposition to τοῦ κυρίου.

δι᾽ οὗ. Instrumental (see 5:2). The relative pronoun οὗ anaphorically refers to τοῦ κυρίου ἡμῶν Ἰησοῦ Χριστοῦ in the previous prepositional word group.

νῦν. Adverb (temporal). It modifies ἐλάβομεν.

τὴν καταλλαγὴν. Accusative direct object of ἐλάβομεν. The fronting of the accusative direct object is prominent in the clause.

ἐλάβομεν. Aor act ind 1st pl λαμβάνω.

Romans 5:12–21

[12]On account of this, just as sin entered into the world through one person and through sin death, also in the same way death passed through

unto all people, because all sinned; [13]for until the law, sin was in the
world, but sin is not reckoned to one's account when there is no law.
[14]But death ruled from Adam until Moses, and upon those who did not
sin in the likeness of the transgression of Adam, who is a type of the
coming one. [15]But isn't the gracious gift thus indeed not like the transgression? For if by the transgression of the one many died, much more
did the grace of God and the gift by the grace of the one man Jesus
Christ abound to the many. [16]And the gift [is] not like through one
who sinned, right? For, on the one hand, the judgment [was] from one,
resulting in complete judgment, but, on the other hand, the gracious gift
[was] from many transgressions, resulting in justification. [17]For if by the
transgression of the one death ruled through the one, much more those
who receive the abundance of the grace and the gift of righteousness will
rule in life through the one, Jesus Christ. [18]Therefore then, as [it was]
through one trespass [which resulted] in condemnation for all people, in
the same way also [it was] through one righteous act [which resulted]
in righteousness of life for all people. [19]For as by the disobedience of the
one man the many were established sinners, so also by the obedience of
the one the many will be established righteous. [20]But the law fully entered
so that the transgression would increase; but where sin increased, grace
super-multiplied, [21]so that just as sin ruled in death, in the same way also
grace might rule through righteousness into eternal life through Jesus
Christ our Lord.

This is the second sub-section of 5:1–21, the second major section of the
body of the letter. Here, Paul uses the Old Testament illustrations of Christ
and Adam to make his point.

**5:12 Διὰ τοῦτο ὥσπερ δι᾽ ἑνὸς ἀνθρώπου ἡ ἁμαρτία εἰς τὸν κόσμον
εἰσῆλθεν καὶ διὰ τῆς ἁμαρτίας ὁ θάνατος, καὶ οὕτως εἰς πάντας
ἀνθρώπους ὁ θάνατος διῆλθεν, ἐφ᾽ ᾧ πάντες ἥμαρτον·**

The first clause complex here (5:12–13) is incomplete until it resumes
in 5:19 (or perhaps 5:18) (cf. Porter 2015, 124). This verse also reflects
chiastic structure and parallelism through the fronting of the prepositional word group in each clause for clausal prominence (Porter 2015,
124–25):

A—δι᾽ ἑνὸς ἀνθρώπου ἡ ἁμαρτία εἰς τὸν κόσμον εἰσῆλθεν
B—διὰ τῆς ἁμαρτίας ὁ θάνατος
B′—εἰς πάντας ἀνθρώπους ὁ θάνατος διῆλθεν
A′—ἐφ᾽ ᾧ πάντες ἥμαρτον

Διὰ τοῦτο. Causal. The demonstrative pronoun refers anaphorically to the previous statement about receiving reconciliation through Jesus Christ.

ὥσπερ. Comparative particle. The comparison resumes in 5:19.

δι᾽ ἑνὸς ἀνθρώπου. Instrumental.

ἡ ἁμαρτία. Nominative subject of εἰσῆλθεν.

εἰς τὸν κόσμον. Directional (movement into).

εἰσῆλθεν. Aor act ind 3rd sg εἰσέρχομαι.

καὶ. Coordinating conjunction. It connects δι᾽ ἑνὸς ἀνθρώπου ἡ ἁμαρτία εἰς τὸν κόσμον εἰσῆλθεν with διὰ τῆς ἁμαρτίας ὁ θάνατος.

διὰ τῆς ἁμαρτίας. Instrumental.

ὁ θάνατος. Nominative subject of an implied εἰσῆλθεν from previous clause.

καὶ. Coordinating conjunction.

οὕτως. Inferential particle. It introduces an inference from what has been stated thus far regarding sin coming into the world and through sin, death.

εἰς πάντας ἀνθρώπους. Extensive (figurative goal or state). The figurative goal of death passing through is "all people." The prepositional word group modifies διῆλθεν and is fronted for clausal prominence (or emphasis).

ὁ θάνατος. Nominative subject of διῆλθεν.

διῆλθεν. Aor act ind 3rd sg διέρχομαι. The use of διῆλθεν with εἰσῆλθεν in this immediate co-text creates cohesive ties, with the same root ἔρχομαι having two different prepositional prefixes, διά and εἴς, depicting two different directions of motion.

ἐφ᾽ ᾧ. Causal; hence the translation above as "because." It functions as compound conjunction. The relative pronoun refers to the previous statement that "death passed through unto all people." There are four main ways in which this compound conjunction is interpreted: (1) locative (e.g., "upon" or "in which"), concessive (e.g., "in as much as"), (3) resultive ("with the result that"), or (4) causal ("on account of" or "because") (see Cranfield, 1:274–81; Fitzmyer, 413–17; Porter 2015, 125). Most English translations (e.g., NIV, NRSV, NKJV, ESV, NASB) appear to interpret this compound conjunction as causal ("because"), and we agree that this is the best way to interpret its function. If locative, the verse might be translated as "death passed through unto all people, in which [i.e., in death] all sinned," which would mean that all sinned in death. If concessive, the translation might be "death passed through unto all people, in as much as all sinned," which would mean that death only came as much as people sinned. If resultive, the translation might be "death passed through unto all people, with the result that all sinned," making death the cause or reason for all sinning. However, Paul's argumentation in this verse is that (1) sin entered the world through one man (another way of stating this is that the one man caused sin to enter the world through his sin), (2) and through sin, death (another way of stating this is that sin caused death), (3) so death came to everyone. Thus, following the parallelism in this verse (see above), it is most likely that this compound conjunction is causal, that death came to everyone because all sinned.

πάντες. Nominative subject of ἥμαρτον. πάντες is a substantival adjective.

ἥμαρτον. Aor act ind 3rd pl ἁμαρτάνω.

5:13 ἄχρι γὰρ νόμου ἁμαρτία ἦν ἐν κόσμῳ, ἁμαρτία δὲ οὐκ ἐλλογεῖται μὴ ὄντος νόμου,

ἄχρι . . . νόμου. Extensive. ἄχρι ("until") is a temporal conjunction, which here serves as an improper preposition (cf. Porter 1994a, 179).

γὰρ. Postpositive explanatory conjunction.

ἁμαρτία. Nominative subject of ἦν.

ἦν. Augmented ind 3rd sg εἰμί.

ἐν κόσμῳ. Locative.

ἁμαρτία. Nominative subject of ἐλλογεῖται.

δὲ. Adversative conjunction (mild).

οὐκ. Negative particle normally used with indicative verbs. Here it negates ἐλλογεῖται.

ἐλλογεῖται. Pres pass ind 3rd sg ἐλλογέω. This lexeme is a cognate of the same word used of Abraham (λογίζομαι; throughout Romans 4), although it is not the same lexeme. While there it seems to indicate a simple accounting, here it seems to have a negative sense, where something is regarded as a demerit (Porter 2015, 126–27).

μὴ. Negative particle normally used with non-indicative verbs. Here it negates ὄντος.

ὄντος. Ptc masc gen sg εἰμί (genitive absolute, temporal; e.g., NASB, NIV, NKJV, NRSV).

νόμου. Genitive subject of ὄντος.

5:14 ἀλλὰ ἐβασίλευσεν ὁ θάνατος ἀπὸ Ἀδὰμ μέχρι Μωϋσέως καὶ ἐπὶ τοὺς μὴ ἁμαρτήσαντας ἐπὶ τῷ ὁμοιώματι τῆς παραβάσεως Ἀδὰμ ὅς ἐστιν τύπος τοῦ μέλλοντος.

ἀλλὰ. Adversative conjunction (strong).

ἐβασίλευσεν. Aor act ind 3rd sg βασιλεύω.

ὁ θάνατος. Nominative subject of ἐβασίλευσεν.

ἀπὸ Ἀδάμ. Temporal, marking the beginning of the time period.

μέχρι Μωϋσέως. Temporal, marking the end of the time period. μέχρι is an improper preposition (cf. Porter 1994a, 179).

καί. Adverbial use (ascensive). It modifies the prepositional word group ἐπὶ τοὺς μὴ ἁμαρτήσαντας.

ἐπὶ τοὺς μὴ ἁμαρτήσαντας. Directional (movement upon or onto). μὴ is the usual negative particle with non-indicative verbs.

τοὺς ... ἁμαρτήσαντας. Aor act ptc masc acc pl ἁμαρτάνω (substantival).

ἐπὶ τῷ ὁμοιώματι. Locative (upon). The figurative picture of "upon" may depict those whose sinning lies atop the likeness of Adam's sins; in other words, those whose sins piled upon the likes of Adam's sin. According to BDAG (364.6.a), this expresses the basis for a state of being. However, this is probably the contextual usage of ἐπί rather than its grammatical function. The prepositional word group modifies ἁμαρτήσαντας.

τῆς παραβάσεως. Genitive of definition or description, modifying τῷ ὁμοιώματι. It further describes or circumscribes "likeness" to "transgression."

Ἀδάμ. Genitive of source or origin, modifying τῆς παραβάσεως.

ὅς. Nominative subject of ἐστιν. Relative pronoun refers anaphorically to Ἀδάμ.

ἐστιν. Unaugmented ind 3rd sg εἰμί.

τύπος. Predicate nominative. The word here refers an "archetype," or "type," Adam as a "type" of the coming Christ (LN 58.63).

τοῦ μέλλοντος. Pres act ptc masc gen sg μέλλω (substantival). Genitive of source or origin, modifying τύπος.

5:15 Ἀλλ' οὐχ ὡς τὸ παράπτωμα, οὕτως καὶ τὸ χάρισμα · εἰ γὰρ τῷ τοῦ ἑνὸς παραπτώματι οἱ πολλοὶ ἀπέθανον, πολλῷ μᾶλλον ἡ χάρις τοῦ θεοῦ καὶ ἡ δωρεὰ ἐν χάριτι τῇ τοῦ ἑνὸς ἀνθρώπου Ἰησοῦ Χριστοῦ εἰς τοὺς πολλοὺς ἐπερίσσευσεν.

Ἀλλ' οὐχ ὡς τὸ παράπτωμα, οὕτως καὶ τὸ χάρισμα. While most Greek editions punctuate this as a sentence, it is preferable to interpret this as a question due to the negative particle at the beginning of the clause and co-textual factors, since the syntax is ambiguous (see Caragounis 1985, 132–48; Porter 1991, 673–74; Jewett, 371, 379, 381). The clause beginning 5:16 is also interpreted as a question rather than as a statement, as a parallel. The question beginning with οὐ expects a positive answer.

Ἀλλ'. Adversative conjunction (strong).

οὐχ ὡς... οὕτως καὶ. A point/counterpoint set ("not like... thus indeed") that establishes a contrast between transgression and gracious gift.

τὸ παράπτωμα. Nominative subject of verbless clause.

τὸ χάρισμα. Nominative subject of verbless clause.

εἰ. Introduces the protasis of a first-class conditional. The apodosis begins with πολλῷ μᾶλλον.

γὰρ. Postpositive explanatory conjunction. It introduces the clause that explains why the transgression is not like the gracious gift.

τῷ... παραπτώματι. Dative of agency or cause. The cause of "the many died" is "the transgression of the one."

τοῦ ἑνὸς. Genitive of source or origin, modifying τῷ... παραπτώματι. It is embedded between the dative article and its noun, indicating that the entire word group τῷ τοῦ ἑνὸς παραπτώματι is a single unit.

οἱ πολλοὶ. Nominative subject of ἀπέθανον. Substantival adjective.

ἀπέθανον. Aor act ind 3rd pl ἀποθνῄσκω.

πολλῷ μᾶλλον. Dative of advantage + the comparative of the adverb μάλα (see 5:9). It heightens the contrast that builds on the previous and marks the beginning of the apodosis.

ἡ χάρις... καὶ ἡ δωρεὰ. Compound nominative subject of ἐπερίσσευσεν. The compound nominative subject takes a singular verb probably because ἡ δωρεὰ refers to ἡ χάρις τοῦ θεοῦ.

τοῦ θεοῦ. Genitive of source or origin, modifying ἡ χάρις.

ἐν χάριτι. Instrumental. The prepositional word group modifies ἡ δωρεὰ. "The grace of the one man Jesus Christ" is the instrument by which the gift was abounding.

τῇ τοῦ ἑνὸς ἀνθρώπου. The article functions as a nominalizer, changing the genitive word group τοῦ ἑνὸς ἀνθρώπου into a dative in apposition to χάριτι. In other words, "gracious gift" is further described as "the thing that comes from one man."

τοῦ ἑνὸς ἀνθρώπου. Genitive of source or origin. The source or origin of the gracious gift is "the one man."

Ἰησοῦ Χριστοῦ. Genitive in apposition to τοῦ ἑνὸς ἀνθρώπου.

εἰς τοὺς πολλοὺς. Extensive. The figurative goal of the gift is "the many." The prepositional phrase is fronted before the main predicate, making the prepositional word group prominent.

ἐπερίσσευσεν. Aor act ind 3rd sg περισσεύω.

5:16 καὶ οὐχ ὡς δι᾽ ἑνὸς ἁμαρτήσαντος τὸ δώρημα· τὸ μὲν γὰρ κρίμα ἐξ ἑνὸς εἰς κατάκριμα, τὸ δὲ χάρισμα ἐκ πολλῶν παραπτωμάτων εἰς δικαίωμα.

καὶ οὐχ ὡς δι᾽ ἑνὸς ἁμαρτήσαντος τὸ δώρημα. While most Greek editions punctuate this to reflect a statement, it is preferable to interpret this as a question due to the negative particle at the beginning of the clause and co-textual factors, since the syntax is ambiguous. The question beginning with οὐ expects a positive answer (so the addition of "right" in the above translation reflects that expectation; see the first note in 5:15).

καὶ. Coordinating conjunction. It connects the previous clause complex to this one.

οὐχ. Negative particle. The use of οὐ at the beginning of a question reflects the expectation of a positive answer.

ὡς. Comparative conjunction. It compares δι᾽ ἑνὸς ἁμαρτήσαντος with τὸ δώρημα.

δι᾽ ἑνὸς ἁμαρτήσαντος. Instrumental. If the participle ἁμαρτήσαντος is substantival, ἑνὸς functions as an adjective. If ἑνὸς functions as a noun, the participle ἁμαρτήσαντος functions as an adjective.

ἁμαρτήσαντος. Aor act ptc masc gen sg ἁμαρτάνω (substantival or attributive).

τὸ δώρημα. Nominative subject of verbless clause (with an implied "to be" verb).

τὸ . . . κρίμα. Nominative subject of verbless clause (with an implied "to be" verb).

μὲν . . . δὲ. A point/counterpoint set that contrasts the statement in this clause with the statement in the subsequent clause.

γὰρ. Postpositive explanatory conjunction. It is used to introduce an explanation of the previous statement about the gift not being like that from which came from the one who sinned (i.e., Adam).

ἐξ ἑνὸς. Instrumental (source or origin). The source or origin of the "judgement" is the "one."

εἰς κατάκριμα. Result. The result of judgment from the one person is "complete judgment." The lexeme κατάκριμα is a prefixed form of κρίμα, signifying "complete judgment." It only occurs here, Rom 5:18; and 8:1 in the NT, although κρίμα occurs 20 times in the NT.

τὸ . . . χάρισμα. Nominative subject of verbless clause (with an implied "to be" verb).

ἐκ πολλῶν παραπτωμάτων. Locative (source or origin). The source or origin of the "gracious gift" is the "many sins."

εἰς δικαίωμα. Result. The result of the gift from many transgressions is "justification." The sense of the lexeme δικαίωμα here is not that of requirement but of result or fulfillment (Porter 2015, 127). The resultant sense is also reflected in the -μα ending of the substantive (Robertson, 151).

5:17 εἰ γὰρ τῷ τοῦ ἑνὸς παραπτώματι ὁ θάνατος ἐβασίλευσεν διὰ τοῦ ἑνός, πολλῷ μᾶλλον οἱ τὴν περισσείαν τῆς χάριτος καὶ τῆς δωρεᾶς τῆς δικαιοσύνης λαμβάνοντες ἐν ζωῇ βασιλεύσουσιν διὰ τοῦ ἑνὸς Ἰησοῦ Χριστοῦ.

εἰ. Introduces the protasis of a first-class conditional. The apodosis begins with πολλῷ μᾶλλον (see 5:15 for a similar construction).

γὰρ. Postpositive inferential conjunction. It introduces a (conditional) clause that draws an inference from the previous statement that the gracious gift was from many transgressions, resulting in justification.

τῷ ... παραπτώματι. Dative of instrument. The instrument or cause of "the many died" is "the transgression of the one."

τοῦ ἑνός. Genitive of definition or description, modifying τῷ ... παραπτώματι, circumscribing "transgression" to "the one" (some may label this as a subjective genitive, with "one man" as the subject of transgressing). It is embedded between the dative article and its noun, functioning attributively and indicating that the entire word group τῷ τοῦ ἑνὸς παραπτώματι is a single unit (see 5:15). τοῦ ἑνός refers to Adam.

ὁ θάνατος. Nominative subject of ἐβασίλευσεν.

ἐβασίλευσεν. Aor act ind 3rd sg βασιλεύω.

διὰ τοῦ ἑνός. Instrumental. τοῦ ἑνός refers to Adam as above.

πολλῷ μᾶλλον. Dative of advantage + the comparative of the adverb μάλα (see 5:9, 15). It marks the beginning of the apodosis.

οἱ ... λαμβάνοντες. Pres act ptc masc nom pl λαμβάνω (substantival). Nominative subject of βασιλεύσουσιν. The embedded word group τὴν περισσείαν τῆς χάριτος καὶ τῆς δωρεᾶς τῆς δικαιοσύνης between the nominative article and the substantival participle indicates that the entire word group οἱ τὴν περισσείαν τῆς χάριτος καὶ τῆς δωρεᾶς τῆς δικαιοσύνης λαμβάνοντες is a single unit, with the embedded word group functioning attributively.

τὴν περισσείαν. Accusative direct object of λαμβάνοντες.

τῆς χάριτος καὶ τῆς δωρεᾶς. Genitives of description, further describing, delineating, or circumscribing "abundance" with "grace" and "gift."

τῆς δικαιοσύνης. Genitive of description, modifying τῆς δωρεᾶς, further circumscribing "gift" with "righteousness."

ἐν ζωῇ. Locative (sphere or realm). The prepositional word group modifies βασιλεύσουσιν and identifies the sphere in which they will reign.

βασιλεύσουσιν. Fut act ind 3rd pl βασιλεύω.

διὰ τοῦ ἑνὸς. Instrumental. The instrument or means by which they will reign is "through the one Jesus Christ."

Ἰησοῦ Χριστοῦ. Genitive in apposition to τοῦ ἑνὸς.

5:18 Ἄρα οὖν ὡς δι᾽ ἑνὸς παραπτώματος εἰς πάντας ἀνθρώπους εἰς κατάκριμα, οὕτως καὶ δι᾽ ἑνὸς δικαιώματος εἰς πάντας ἀνθρώπους εἰς δικαίωσιν ζωῆς·

There is parallelism in this verse with the first and second clauses, both beginning with a conjunction (ὡς and οὕτως) and containing three prepositional word groups: (1) δι᾽ . . . (indicating instrument or agency), (2) εἰς . . . (indicating extent or goal), and (3) εἰς . . . (indicating result or purpose):

δι᾽ ἑνὸς παραπτώματος	εἰς πάντας ἀνθρώπους	εἰς κατάκριμα
δι᾽ ἑνὸς δικαιώματος	εἰς πάντας ἀνθρώπους	εἰς δικαίωσιν ζωῆς

Ἄρα οὖν. A combination of two inferential conjunctions. The inference is not a resumption of the comparison from 5:12 as some translations reflect (e.g., NIV, NRSV), but is an inference from and restatement of the previous verse regarding transgression of the one resulting in death (cf. Porter 2015, 128). This is the first occurrence of this combination, also found in Rom 7:3, 25; 8:12; 9:16, 18; 14:12, 19; Gal 6:10; Eph 2:19; 1 Thess 5:6; and 2 Thess 2:15. The combination emphasizes the inference (cf. Porter 1994a, 207).

ὡς . . . οὕτως καὶ. A point/counterpoint set ("as . . . so also") that establishes a comparison between the consequences of Adam's and Christ's actions.

δι᾽ ἑνὸς παραπτώματος. Instrumental.

εἰς πάντας ἀνθρώπους. Goal.

εἰς κατάκριμα. Result.

δι᾽ ἑνὸς δικαιώματος. Instrumental.

εἰς πάντας ἀνθρώπους. Goal.

εἰς δικαίωσιν. Result. The same δικ-root in nominal form appears in 5:16 as δικαίωμα, there focusing on the result of justification/

righteousness but here focusing on its abstraction (Robertson, 152).
Hence, in 5:16, δικαίωμα is translated as "justification" and here as
"righteousness."

ζωῆς. Genitive of quality or description, modifying δικαίωσιν. Life is
a further description or quality associated with righteousness.

**5:19 ὥσπερ γὰρ διὰ τῆς παρακοῆς τοῦ ἑνὸς ἀνθρώπου ἁμαρτωλοὶ
κατεστάθησαν οἱ πολλοί, οὕτως καὶ διὰ τῆς ὑπακοῆς τοῦ ἑνὸς δίκαιοι
κατασταθήσονται οἱ πολλοί.**

This verse resumes the argument of 5:12, after the intervention of
5:13–18.

Another parallelism exists here with the two clauses: (1) διὰ . . .
(indicating instrument or cause) (2) nominative complement, (3) a form
of καθίστημι, and (4) subject:

διὰ τῆς παρακοῆς τοῦ ἑνὸς ἀνθρώπου	ἁμαρτωλοὶ	κατεστάθησαν	οἱ πολλοί
διὰ τῆς ὑπακοῆς τοῦ ἑνὸς	δίκαιοι	κατασταθήσονται	οἱ πολλοί

ὥσπερ . . . οὕτως καὶ. A point/counterpoint set ("just as . . . so also")
that further develops a comparison between the consequences of Adam's
and Christ's actions. This verse restates the comparison from 5:12, with
οὕτως καὶ signifying the completion of comparison. In other words, the
comparison is introduced in 5:12 (sin came into the world through one
man and death through one man); the resumption of that comparison
begins in this verse (just as by the disobedience of one man, the many
were established sinners), with the completion of the comparison in the
second clause of this verse (so also by the obedience of the one many will
be established righteous).

γὰρ. Postpositive explanatory conjunction. It introduces a clause to
explain the previous statements in 5:13–18 but with a new set of contrasts here: one man's disobedience resulted in many becoming sinners.

διὰ τῆς παρακοῆς. Instrumental.

τοῦ ἑνὸς ἀνθρώπου. Genitive of source of origin, modifying τῆς
παρακοῆς. The source or origin of "disobedience" is "one man."

ἁμαρτωλοί. Nominative complement to οἱ πολλοί in a double nominative subject-complement construction. Some may wish to see this as a
double accusative object-complement construction passivized into a double nominative subject-complement construction, but that is a displacing

of grammatical with semantic categories (cf. Culy 2009). See directly below on use of the passive voice.

κατεστάθησαν. Aor pass ind 3rd pl καθίστημι. The lexeme has the idea of setting down or instituting (Porter 2015, 128). The passive voice indicates external causality, with the nominative subject indicating the Goal of the process.

οἱ πολλοί. Nominative subject of κατεστάθησαν in a double nominative subject-complement construction. οἱ πολλοί is a substantival adjective.

διὰ τῆς ὑπακοῆς. Instrumental.

τοῦ ἑνὸς. Genitive of source or origin, modifying τῆς ὑπακοῆς. The source or origin of "obedience" is the "one."

δίκαιοι. Nominative complement to οἱ πολλοί in a double nominative subject-complement construction (see ἁμαρτωλοὶ above).

κατασταθήσονται. Fut pass ind 3rd pl καθίστημι.

οἱ πολλοί. Nominative subject of κατασταθήσονται in a double nominative subject-complement construction. οἱ πολλοί is a substantival adjective.

5:20 νόμος δὲ παρεισῆλθεν, ἵνα πλεονάσῃ τὸ παράπτωμα· οὗ δὲ ἐπλεόνασεν ἡ ἁμαρτία, ὑπερεπερίσσευσεν ἡ χάρις,

νόμος. Nominative subject of παρεισῆλθεν.

δὲ. Adversative conjunction (mild).

παρεισῆλθεν. Aor act ind 3rd sg παρεισέρχομαι.

ἵνα. Introduces a result clause. The result of the law coming in was an increase of trespasses. While ἵνα also can also indicate purpose, this would seem to be inconsistent with Paul's statement in 6:1–2 that the law should not continue to be violated so that grace would super-multiply. Rather, the transgression increasing is the result of the law fully entering.

πλεονάσῃ. Aor act subj 3rd sg πλεονάζω. Subjunctive with ἵνα.

τὸ παράπτωμα. Nominative subject of πλεονάσῃ.

οὗ. The genitive relative pronoun sometimes serves, as it does here, as an adverb of place (cf. BDAG, 732). It anaphorically refers to the previous clause.

δὲ. Adversative conjunction (mild).

ἐπλεόνασεν. Aor act ind 3rd sg πλεονάζω.

ἡ ἁμαρτία. Nominative subject of ἐπλεόνασεν.

ὑπερεπερίσσευσεν. Aor act ind 3rd sg ὑπερπερισσεύω.

ἡ χάρις. Nominative subject of ὑπερεπερίσσευσεν.

5:21 ἵνα ὥσπερ ἐβασίλευσεν ἡ ἁμαρτία ἐν τῷ θανάτῳ, οὕτως καὶ ἡ χάρις βασιλεύσῃ διὰ δικαιοσύνης εἰς ζωὴν αἰώνιον διὰ Ἰησοῦ Χριστοῦ τοῦ κυρίου ἡμῶν.

ἵνα. Introduces a result clause. As above (5:20), while ἵνα can indicate purpose or result, it seems consistent to interpret the following clause as the result of the relationship between sin and grace, not purpose. The result of grace super-multiplying is introduced.

ὥσπερ . . . οὕτως καὶ. A point/counterpoint set ("just as . . . so also") that compares ἐβασίλευσεν ἡ ἁμαρτία ἐν τῷ θανάτῳ with ἡ χάρις βασιλεύσῃ διὰ δικαιοσύνης. This is the third comparison in this co-text (see 5:18, 19).

ἐβασίλευσεν. Aor act ind 3rd sg βασιλεύω.

ἡ ἁμαρτία. Nominative subject of ἐβασίλευσεν.

ἐν τῷ θανάτῳ. Locative (sphere or realm). The sphere or realm of sin reigning is "death."

ἡ χάρις. Nominative subject of βασιλεύσῃ.

βασιλεύσῃ. Aor act subj 3rd sg βασιλεύω. Subjunctive with ἵνα.

διὰ δικαιοσύνης. Instrumental. The means by which grace reigns is "righteousness."

εἰς ζωὴν αἰώνιον. Goal. In contrast to the use of ἐν in relation to sin reigning (signifying a locative/spherical function), the use of εἰς in relation to grace reigning signifies goal.

διὰ Ἰησοῦ Χριστοῦ. Instrumental. The means for eternal life is "Jesus Christ." The change in word order here from the usual τοῦ κυρίου ἡμῶν Ἰησοῦ Χριστοῦ (e.g., 5:1, 11) may simply be a stylistic change but more likely is a change in prominence, highlighting the person of Jesus Christ—parallel to Adam—over his title.

τοῦ κυρίου. Genitive in apposition to Ἰησοῦ Χριστοῦ.

ἡμῶν. Possessive genitive, modifying τοῦ κυρίου.

Romans 6:1–14

[1]What therefore will we say? Should we remain in sin so that grace may increase? [2]Indeed not. Whoever of us died to sin, how will we still live in it? [3]Or are you unaware that as many of us who have been baptized into Christ Jesus have been baptized into his death? [4]We were buried, therefore, with him through baptism into death, so that just as Christ was raised from the dead through the glory of the Father, in the same way, we might also walk in the newness of life. [5]For if we have been joined together in the likeness of his death, so also we will certainly be of the resurrection—[6]knowing this, that our

old person was crucified together, so that the body of sin might be rendered powerless, so that we would no longer serve sin as slaves. [7]For the one who died has been justified from sin. [8]But if we died with Christ, we believe that we also will live with him, [9]knowing that Christ, being raised from the dead, will no longer die; death no longer has lordly dominion over him. [10]For what he died for, he died to sin once for all; but what he lives for, he lives to God. [11]In the same way you also should consider yourselves dead, on the one hand, to sin, but alive, on the other hand, to God in Christ Jesus. [12]Therefore, sin must not reign in your mortal body to make you obey its passions. [13]Do not present your members to sin as weapons of unrighteousness, but present yourselves to God as if living from the dead and your members to God as weapons of righteousness. [14]For your sin will have no authority, for you are not under law but under grace.

This section (6:1–7:25) is the next (third) major section of the body of the letter. Paul outlines the Christian life here, including some imperatives resulting from what he has said thus far. The first sub-section (6:1–7:6) outlines the life in Christ that is expected.

6:1 Τί οὖν ἐροῦμεν; ἐπιμένωμεν τῇ ἁμαρτίᾳ, ἵνα ἡ χάρις πλεονάσῃ;

Τί οὖν ἐροῦμεν. A rhetorical question that has been used by Paul throughout this letter to transition to a related but new logical progression (4:1; 6:1; 7:7; 8:31; 9:14, 30).

Τί. Accusative direct object of ἐροῦμεν.

οὖν. Postpositive inferential conjunction. From what has been stated thus far, Paul poses a potential interlocutionary inference.

ἐροῦμεν. Fut act ind 1st pl λέγω.

ἐπιμένωμεν. Pres act subj 1st pl ἐπιμένω (deliberative subjunctive).

τῇ ἁμαρτίᾳ. Dative of sphere. The sphere in which they remain is "sin."

ἵνα. Introduces a purpose clause. While previous uses of ἵνα (5:20–21) seem to prefer result as the function, it could be interpreted here that the purpose of one remaining in sin is to make grace super-multiply, and not merely the result (the senses of purpose and result are too far off from each other).

ἡ χάρις. Nominative subject of πλεονάσῃ.

πλεονάσῃ. Aor act subj 3rd sg πλεονάζω. Subjunctive with ἵνα.

6:2 μὴ γένοιτο. οἵτινες ἀπεθάνομεν τῇ ἁμαρτίᾳ, πῶς ἔτι ζήσομεν ἐν αὐτῇ;

μὴ γένοιτο. A common emphatic negation for Paul after posing a question, usually rhetorical (see 3:4). Note the translation above, which better captures the semantics of the use of the optative than the usual translation ("may it never be").

μὴ. Negative particle normally used with non-indicative verbs. Here it negates γένοιτο.

γένοιτο. Aor mid opt 3rd sg γίνομαι.

οἵτινες. Nominative subject of ἀπεθάνομεν. οἵτινες is an indefinite relative pronoun.

ἀπεθάνομεν. Aor act ind 1st pl ἀποθνῄσκω.

τῇ ἁμαρτίᾳ. Dative of respect.

πῶς. Adverb (interrogative).

ἔτι. Adverb (temporal).

ζήσομεν. Fut act ind 1st pl ζάω. The future form grammaticalizes expectancy. Those who died to sin are not expected to still live in it.

ἐν αὐτῇ. Locative (sphere or realm). Personal pronoun anaphorically refers to τῇ ἁμαρτίᾳ.

6:3 ἢ ἀγνοεῖτε ὅτι, ὅσοι ἐβαπτίσθημεν εἰς Χριστὸν Ἰησοῦν, εἰς τὸν θάνατον αὐτοῦ ἐβαπτίσθημεν;

There is a micro-chiasm in this verse:

(a) ἐβαπτίσθημεν
   (b) εἰς Χριστὸν Ἰησοῦν
   (b′) εἰς τὸν θάνατον αὐτοῦ
(a′) ἐβαπτίσθημεν.

The emphasis is on the middle items (represented by the prepositional word groups); emphasis is also conveyed through lexical cohesion (repetition) of the middle items.

ἤ. Disjunctive particle. The disjunction is with the previous (rhetorical) question and what the addressees should have known.

ἀγνοεῖτε. Pres act ind 2nd pl ἀγνοέω.

ὅτι. Introduces the clausal complement (indirect discourse) of ἀγνοεῖτε.

ὅσοι. Nominative subject of ἐβαπτίσθημεν. ὅσοι is quantitative correlative relative pronoun.

ἐβαπτίσθημεν. Aor pass ind 1st pl βαπτίζω.

εἰς Χριστὸν Ἰησοῦν. Goal or state.
εἰς τὸν θάνατον. Goal or state.
αὐτοῦ. Possessive genitive, modifying τὸν θάνατον.
ἐβαπτίσθημεν. Aor pass ind 1st pl βαπτίζω.

6:4 συνετάφημεν οὖν αὐτῷ διὰ τοῦ βαπτίσματος εἰς τὸν θάνατον, ἵνα ὥσπερ ἠγέρθη Χριστὸς ἐκ νεκρῶν διὰ τῆς δόξης τοῦ πατρός, οὕτως καὶ ἡμεῖς ἐν καινότητι ζωῆς περιπατήσωμεν.

συνετάφημεν. Aor pass ind 1st pl συνθάπτω.
οὖν. Postpositive inferential conjunction. Assuming the answers to the rhetorical questions above, Paul makes an inference in the following statements.
αὐτῷ. Dative of association. The personal pronoun refers to Χριστὸν Ἰησοῦν in 6:3.
διὰ τοῦ βαπτίσματος. Instrumental. The instrument by which they were buried is baptism.
εἰς τὸν θάνατον. Goal or state.
ἵνα. Introduces a purpose clause. The purpose of being "buried with him through baptism into death" is that "we might walk in the newness of life."
ὥσπερ ... οὕτως καὶ. A point/counterpoint set ("just as ... so also") that compares ἠγέρθη Χριστὸς ἐκ νεκρῶν διὰ τῆς δόξης τοῦ πατρός with ἡμεῖς ἐν καινότητι ζωῆς περιπατήσωμεν.
ἠγέρθη. Aor pass ind 3rd sg ἐγείρω.
Χριστὸς. Nominative subject of ἠγέρθη. As the grammatical subject of a passive verb, it is the Goal of the verb.
ἐκ νεκρῶν. Locative (movement out of/separation).
διὰ τῆς δόξης. Instrumental.
τοῦ πατρός. Possessive genitive, modifying τῆς δόξης.
ἡμεῖς. Nominative subject of περιπατήσωμεν. The use of personal pronoun is emphatic.
ἐν καινότητι. Locative (sphere or realm). Placed in front of the predicate it conveys prominence through clause structure. This lexeme is only used in Paul (cf. Rom 7:6; LXX 1 Kgs 8:53; LXX Ezek 47:12).
ζωῆς. Genitive of description, modifying καινότητι. It further describes, delineates, or circumscribes "newness."
περιπατήσωμεν. Aor act subj 1st pl περιπατέω. Subjunctive with ἵνα.

6:5 εἰ γὰρ σύμφυτοι γεγόναμεν τῷ ὁμοιώματι τοῦ θανάτου αὐτοῦ, ἀλλὰ καὶ τῆς ἀναστάσεως ἐσόμεθα·

εἰ. Introduces the protasis of a first-class conditional.

γὰρ. Postpositive explanatory conjunction. It introduces a further explanation of being buried with him from 6:4.

σύμφυτοι. Predicate adjective. The lexeme comes from nature and can refer to the imagery of planting or congenitally joining to something (Dunn, 1:316; Jewett, 400; Porter 2015, 134). The prefix συν- highlights the sense of togetherness, with the implied object of togetherness being Christ.

γεγόναμεν. Prf act ind 1st pl γίνομαι. Stative aspect (perfect tense-form) of the verb of becoming depicts a state of becoming joined together.

τῷ ὁμοιώματι. Dative of sphere.

τοῦ θανάτου. Genitive of description, modifying τῷ ὁμοιώματι. It further describes or circumscribes "likeness" with "his death." Some may label this as an objective genitive.

αὐτοῦ. Possessive genitive, modifying τοῦ θανάτου.

ἀλλὰ καὶ. Adversative conjunction (strong) + adverbial use of καὶ (adjunctive). Together, they form a strong disjunctive connection that elevates the contrast and makes the following element prominent (cf. Porter 2015, 134). ἀλλὰ καὶ marks the beginning of the apodosis.

τῆς ἀναστάσεως. Possessive genitive. It is parallel to τοῦ θανάτου αὐτοῦ above, with σύμφυτοι τῷ ὁμοιώματι elided: "we will also be [united with him in the likeness] of the resurrection."

ἐσόμεθα. Fut 1st pl εἰμί. The use of εἰμί here, rather than γίνομαι as in the protasis, is notable and probably reflects use of the aspectually vague verb to state the more abstract sense of being (cf. γίνομαι above). The future form conveys the semantic feature of expectation.

6:6 τοῦτο γινώσκοντες ὅτι ὁ παλαιὸς ἡμῶν ἄνθρωπος συνεσταυρώθη, ἵνα καταργηθῇ τὸ σῶμα τῆς ἁμαρτίας, τοῦ μηκέτι δουλεύειν ἡμᾶς τῇ ἁμαρτίᾳ·

τοῦτο. Accusative direct object of γινώσκοντες.

γινώσκοντες. Pres act ptc masc nom pl γινώσκω (causal). The participle functions in the co-text as circumstantial and modifies ἐσόμεθα (6:5).

ὅτι. Introduces a nominal clause that stands in apposition to τοῦτο: "knowing this, namely, that our old person was co-crucified."

ὁ παλαιὸς . . . ἄνθρωπος. Nominative subject of συνεσταυρώθη.

ἡμῶν. Possessive genitive, modifying ὁ παλαιὸς . . . ἄνθρωπος. The "old human" belongs to "us"; i.e., "our old self."

συνεσταυρώθη. Aor pass ind 3rd sg συσταυρόω.

ἵνα. Introduces a purpose clause. The purpose of the old person being crucified is so that the body of sin is rendered powerless.

καταργηθῇ. Aor pass subj 3rd sg καταργέω. Subjunctive with ἵνα. Passive voice indicates external agency/causality; however, the agent is unspecified here.

τὸ σῶμα. Nominative subject of καταργηθῇ.

τῆς ἁμαρτίας. Genitive of description, modifying τὸ σῶμα. It further describes or circumscribes the "body" as "sin."

τοῦ . . . δουλεύειν. Pres act inf δουλεύω (purpose or result with the genitive article).

μηκέτι. Adverb (temporal). It modifies δουλεύειν.

ἡμᾶς. Accusative subject of δουλεύειν.

τῇ ἁμαρτίᾳ. Dative direct object of δουλεύειν.

6:7 ὁ γὰρ ἀποθανὼν δεδικαίωται ἀπὸ τῆς ἁμαρτίας.

ὁ . . . ἀποθανὼν. Aor act ptc masc nom sg ἀποθνῄσκω (substantival). Nominative subject of δεδικαίωται.

γὰρ. Postpositive explanatory conjunction. It introduces an explanation of the previous statement of no longer serving sin as slaves.

δεδικαίωται. Prf pass ind 3rd sg δικαιόω. The stative aspect (perfect tense-form) indicates a state of being justified. The stative aspect also depicts frontground (prominence). Most translations have the gloss "free" for this lexeme; "free" in the sense of being justified from sin.

ἀπὸ τῆς ἁμαρτίας. Locative (movement away from/separation).

6:8 εἰ δὲ ἀπεθάνομεν σὺν Χριστῷ, πιστεύομεν ὅτι καὶ συζήσομεν αὐτῷ,

Three different tense-forms are used in this verse. The aorist tense-form, reflecting perfective aspect, depicts background material; the present tense-form, reflecting imperfective aspect, depicts foreground material; the future form, reflecting a non-aspect, depicts expectancy.

εἰ. Introduces the protasis of a first-class conditional.

δὲ. Adversative conjunction (mild).

ἀπεθάνομεν. Aor act ind 1st pl ἀποθνῄσκω.

σὺν Χριστῷ. Accompaniment.

πιστεύομεν. Pres act ind 1st pl πιστεύω. The apodosis of the conditional statement begins here.

ὅτι. Introduces the clausal complement (indirect discourse) of πιστεύομεν.

καὶ. Adverbial use (adjunctive). It modifies συζήσομεν.

συζήσομεν. Fut act ind 1st pl συζάω. συζήσομεν is parallel to ἀπεθάνομεν in the protasis. It also recapitulates and counters the question posed in 6:2 (how will we still live in sin?).

αὐτῷ. Dative of association.

6:9 εἰδότες ὅτι Χριστὸς ἐγερθεὶς ἐκ νεκρῶν οὐκέτι ἀποθνῄσκει, θάνατος αὐτοῦ οὐκέτι κυριεύει.

Beginning with a participle, this entire verse is subordinate to the previous clause, which has as its main predicate πιστεύομεν (6:8).

εἰδότες. Prf act ptc masc nom pl οἶδα (causal). It modifies συζήσομεν (6:8) and functions as circumstantial in the co-text. The stative aspect (perfect tense-form) reflects a state of knowing and is prominent in the discourse.

ὅτι. Introduces the clausal complement (indirect discourse) of εἰδότες.

Χριστὸς. Nominative subject of ἀποθνῄσκει.

ἐγερθεὶς. Aor pass ptc masc nom sg ἐγείρω (causal). The participial word group ἐγερθεὶς ἐκ νεκρῶν is embedded in the primary clause Χριστὸς . . . οὐκέτι ἀποθνῄσκει.

ἐκ νεκρῶν. Locative (movement out of/separation).

οὐκέτι. Adverb (temporal). It modifies ἀποθνῄσκει.

ἀποθνῄσκει. Pres act ind 3rd sg ἀποθνῄσκω.

θάνατος. Nominative subject of κυριεύει.

αὐτοῦ. Genitive direct object of κυριεύει. The personal pronoun refers anaphorically to Χριστὸς. The object being fronted before the predicate κυριεύει makes it prominent. Alternatively, this could also be seen as a possessive genitive, modifying θάνατος, resulting in a translation such as "his death no longer reigned." Both interpretations, however, yield similar meanings.

οὐκέτι. Adverb (temporal). It modifies κυριεύει.

κυριεύει. Pres act ind 3rd sg κυριεύω.

6:10 ὃ γὰρ ἀπέθανεν, τῇ ἁμαρτίᾳ ἀπέθανεν ἐφάπαξ · ὃ δὲ ζῇ, ζῇ τῷ θεῷ.

ὃ. Accusative direct object of ἀπέθανεν. The relative pronoun does not have a direct referent in the co-text (introducing a headless relative clause; cf. 1 John 1:1; Culy 2004, 2) but refers to "what he died (for)."

Some may wish to interpret the relative pronoun as referring anaphorically to θάνατος, but the parallel relative pronoun in the next clause does not have a similar antecedent, so it seems best to interpret this as introducing a headless relative clause.

γὰρ. Postpositive explanatory conjunction. It introduces an explanation of the previous statement that death no longer reigns over Christ.

ἀπέθανεν. Aor act ind 3rd sg ἀποθνήσκω.

τῇ ἁμαρτίᾳ. Dative of respect. The prepositional word group appearing before its predicate makes it prominent in the clause.

ἀπέθανεν. Aor act ind 3rd sg ἀποθνήσκω.

ἐφάπαξ. Adverb (temporal). That Christ died "once for all" is indicated by this adverb, not by the aorist tense-form (cf. Porter 2015, 135–36).

ὅ. Accusative direct object of ζῇ. The relative pronoun does not have a direct referent in the co-text (introducing a headless relative clause; see above) but refers to "what" he lives for.

δὲ. Adversative conjunction (mild).

ζῇ. Pres act ind 3rd sg ζάω.

ζῇ. Pres act ind 3rd sg ζάω. The lexeme is repeated for emphasis.

τῷ θεῷ. Dative indirect object of ζῇ. Whatever he lives for, it is "to God."

6:11 οὕτως καὶ ὑμεῖς λογίζεσθε ἑαυτοὺς [εἶναι] νεκροὺς μὲν τῇ ἁμαρτίᾳ ζῶντας δὲ τῷ θεῷ ἐν Χριστῷ Ἰησοῦ.

οὕτως. Adverb of manner. The inference, noted by the following imperative, is from what Paul has said thus far.

καὶ. Adverbial use (adjunctive). Together with οὕτως, it means "so also" (cf. 5:15, 18, 19, 21; 6:4), signaling an inference from what was just stated.

ὑμεῖς. Nominative subject of λογίζεσθε. The presence of the personal pronoun is emphatic here.

λογίζεσθε. Pres mid impv 2nd pl λογίζομαι. The middle voice with the reflexive pronoun indicates indirect, internal causality, despite the notion of the so-called deponent verb (see "Deponency" in the Series Introduction). Although the form is the same as the indicative, the subsequent co-text (6:11–14) containing a string of imperatives probably indicates that this is an imperative as well.

ἑαυτοὺς. Accusative direct object of λογίζεσθε in a double accusative object-complement construction. ἑαυτοὺς is a reflexive pronoun.

[εἶναι]. Inf εἰμί (indirect discourse). It modifies λογίζεσθε. The earliest manuscripts (𝔓⁴⁶ᵛⁱᵈ A D*) do not contain this textual variant (although ℵ² D¹ contain it after νεκροὺς μὲν and 𝔓⁹⁴ᵛⁱᵈ ℵ* B C contain it before). It is not grammatically necessary here, but it is likely that later scribes inserted it for clarity. The meaning is not significantly affected with or without this word.

νεκρούς. The first complement to ἑαυτοὺς in a double accusative object-complement construction. It could also be taken as predicate accusative (because of εἶναι), but the meaning would be the same.

μὲν . . . δὲ. A point/counterpoint set that contrasts νεκροὺς τῇ ἁμαρτίᾳ with ζῶντας τῷ θεῷ ἐν Χριστῷ Ἰησοῦ.

τῇ ἁμαρτίᾳ. Dative of respect. It modifies νεκρούς.

ζῶντας. Pres act ptc masc acc pl ζάω (adjectival). The second complement to ἑαυτοὺς in a double accusative object-complement construction.

τῷ θεῷ. Dative of respect. It modifies ζῶντας.

ἐν Χριστῷ Ἰησοῦ. Locative (sphere or realm). While discussion of "in Christ" is extensive in recent literature, we caution against reading theological implications into every instance of this prepositional word group. Here, it refers to the sphere (realm) in which they are to consider themselves alive to God (see note on ἐν Χριστῷ Ἰησοῦ in 3:24).

6:12 Μὴ οὖν βασιλευέτω ἡ ἁμαρτία ἐν τῷ θνητῷ ὑμῶν σώματι εἰς τὸ ὑπακούειν ταῖς ἐπιθυμίαις αὐτοῦ,

Μὴ. Negative particle normally used with non-indicative verbs. Here it negates βασιλευέτω.

οὖν. Postpositive inferential conjunction. The inference is given as a result of considering oneself dead to sin and alive to God.

βασιλευέτω. Pres act impv 3rd sg βασιλεύω.

ἡ ἁμαρτία. Nominative subject of βασιλευέτω.

ἐν τῷ θνητῷ . . . σώματι. Locative. σώματι is a distributive singular.

ὑμῶν. Possessive genitive, modifying τῷ θνητῷ . . . σώματι.

ὑπακούειν. Pres act inf ὑπακούω. Used with εἰς τό to indicate purpose or result.

ταῖς ἐπιθυμίαις. Dative direct object of ὑπακούειν (see Rom 1:24; 7:7–8).

αὐτοῦ. Possessive genitive, modifying ταῖς ἐπιθυμίαις.

6:13 μηδὲ παριστάνετε τὰ μέλη ὑμῶν ὅπλα ἀδικίας τῇ ἁμαρτίᾳ, ἀλλὰ παραστήσατε ἑαυτοὺς τῷ θεῷ ὡσεὶ ἐκ νεκρῶν ζῶντας καὶ τὰ μέλη ὑμῶν ὅπλα δικαιοσύνης τῷ θεῷ.

μηδὲ . . . ἀλλὰ. A point/counterpoint set ("not this . . . but that") that replaces παριστάνετε τὰ μέλη ὑμῶν ὅπλα ἀδικίας τῇ ἁμαρτίᾳ with παραστήσατε ἑαυτοὺς τῷ θεῷ ἐκ νεκρῶν ζῶντας καὶ τὰ μέλη ὑμῶν ὅπλα δικαιοσύνης τῷ θεῷ.

παριστάνετε. Pres act impv 2nd pl παρίστημι. In contrast to the perfective aspect (aorist tense-form) of the same lexeme that follows below, the imperfective aspect (present tense-form) signifies prominence in the clause-complex. In other words, Paul places more emphasis on the prohibition than on the parallel command, although both prohibition and command are important.

τὰ μέλη. Accusative direct object of παριστάνετε in a double accusative object-complement construction.

ὑμῶν. Possessive genitive, modifying τὰ μέλη.

ὅπλα. Complement to τὰ μέλη in a double accusative object-complement construction. ὅπλα reflects militaristic imagery (sometimes translated as "weapon"; cf. Porter 2015, 137).

ἀδικίας. Genitive of description, modifying ὅπλα. It further describes or circumscribes "weapons" as "of unrighteousness."

τῇ ἁμαρτίᾳ. Dative indirect object of παριστάνετε.

παραστήσατε. Aor act impv 2nd pl παρίστημι. The perfective aspect (aorist tense-form) depicts the command as general (see above on the same lexeme).

ἑαυτοὺς. Accusative direct object of παραστήσατε in a double accusative object-complement construction.

τῷ θεῷ. Dative indirect object of παραστήσατε. It is parallel to τῇ ἁμαρτίᾳ.

ὡσεὶ. Adverb (comparative/conditional). It modifies παραστήσατε. The compound word (ὡς + εἰ) conveys the sense of "as if," having both comparative and conditional senses.

ἐκ νεκρῶν. Separation.

ζῶντας. Pres act ptc masc acc pl ζάω (substantival). Complement to ἑαυτοὺς in a double accusative object-complement construction.

καὶ. Coordinating conjunction. It connects ὡσεὶ ἐκ νεκρῶν ζῶντας with τὰ μέλη ὑμῶν ὅπλα δικαιοσύνης.

τὰ μέλη. Accusative direct object of παραστήσατε in a double accusative object-complement construction. The word group is repeated from above.

ὑμῶν. Possessive genitive, modifying τὰ μέλη.

ὅπλα. Complement to τὰ μέλη in a double accusative object-complement construction.

δικαιοσύνης. Genitive of description, modifying ὅπλα. It further describes or circumscribes "weapons" as "of righteousness." It is parallel to ἀδικίας.

τῷ θεῷ. Dative indirect object of παραστήσατε. It is parallel to τῇ ἁμαρτίᾳ and to the first occurrence of τῷ θεῷ in this verse.

6:14 ἁμαρτία γὰρ ὑμῶν οὐ κυριεύσει· οὐ γάρ ἐστε ὑπὸ νόμον ἀλλὰ ὑπὸ χάριν.

ἁμαρτία. Nominative subject of οὐ κυριεύσει.

γὰρ. Postpositive explanatory conjunction. Introduces an explanation for the previous command to present themselves as instruments of righteousness, that sin will have no authority over them if they do so.

ὑμῶν. Possessive genitive or genitive or source/origin, modifying ἁμαρτία. It can also be a genitive direct object of κυριεύσει ("over you").

οὐ. Negative particle normally used with indicative verbs. Here it negates κυριεύσει.

κυριεύσει. Fut act ind 3rd sg κυριεύω. The future form grammaticalizes the semantic feature of expectancy.

οὐ . . . ἀλλὰ. A point/counterpoint set that contrasts ὑπὸ νόμον with ὑπὸ χάριν.

γάρ. Postpositive explanation conjunction. Introduces an explanation for the previous statement that sin will have no authority.

ἐστε. Unaugmented ind 2nd pl εἰμί.

ὑπὸ νόμον. Locative ("under law").

ὑπὸ χάριν. Locative ("under grace").

Romans 6:15–23

[15]What therefore? Should we sin because we are not under law but under grace? Indeed not. [16]Do you not know that to whom you present yourselves as slaves in obedience, you are slaves to whom you obey, either of sin unto death or of obedience unto righteousness? [17]But thanks [be] to God because you were slaves of sin, but you obeyed from the heart a form of teaching unto which you were given, [18]and having been set free from sin, you were enslaved to righteousness. [19]I speak humanly because of the weakness of your flesh. For just as you presented your members as slaves to uncleanness and lawlessness unto lawlessness, thus now present your members as slaves to righteousness unto holiness. [20]For when you were slaves of sin, you were free to righteousness. [21]Therefore, what fruit were you having then, of the things which you are now ashamed? For the end of those things [is] death. [22]But now, having been freed from sin, having been enslaved to God, have your fruit leading to holiness,

and in the end, eternal life. ²³For the wages of sin [is] death, but the gift of God [is] eternal life in Christ Jesus our Lord.

This sub-section is the second within the major section (6:1–7:25) of the body. After discussing the life of one who is "in Christ," Paul continues to develop this notion by asking the rhetorical question Τί οὖν. Paul uses the diatribe (question-and-answer) technique, as he has earlier in the letter, in this sub-section.

6:15 Τί οὖν; ἁμαρτήσωμεν, ὅτι οὐκ ἐσμὲν ὑπὸ νόμον ἀλλὰ ὑπὸ χάριν; μὴ γένοιτο.

Τί. Nominative absolute. The nominative singular neuter and accusative singular neuter forms are identical for this interrogative pronoun, but as a single lexeme clause (plus conjunction), it may be preferable to interpret this as a nominative absolute (see 3:9).

οὖν. Postpositive inferential conjunction. Paul anticipates his interlocutors with this broad rhetorical question (Τί οὖν).

ἁμαρτήσωμεν. Aor act subj 1st pl ἁμαρτάνω (so-called deliberative hortatory subjunctive; see Porter 1994a, 57–58). Subjunctive reflects command function posed as a question.

ὅτι. Introduces a causal clause.

οὐκ ... ἀλλά. A point/counterpoint set that contrasts ὑπὸ νόμον with ὑπὸ χάριν.

ἐσμὲν. Unaugmented ind 1st pl εἰμί.

ὑπὸ νόμον. Locative ("under law").

ὑπὸ χάριν. Locative ("under grace").

μὴ γένοιτο. A common emphatic negation for Paul after posing a (often rhetorical) question (see 3:4).

μὴ. Negative particle normally used with non-indicative verbs. Here it negates γένοιτο.

γένοιτο. Aor mid opt 3rd sg γίνομαι.

6:16 οὐκ οἴδατε ὅτι ᾧ παριστάνετε ἑαυτοὺς δούλους εἰς ὑπακοήν, δοῦλοί ἐστε ᾧ ὑπακούετε, ἤτοι ἁμαρτίας εἰς θάνατον ἢ ὑπακοῆς εἰς δικαιοσύνην;

οὐκ. Negative particle normally used with indicative verbs. Here it negates οἴδατε.

οἴδατε. Prf act ind 2nd pl οἶδα. The stative aspect (perfect tense-form) reflects a state of knowledge and is prominent in the discourse.

ὅτι. Introduces the clausal complement (indirect discourse) of οἴδατε.

ᾧ. Dative indirect object of παριστάνετε. The relative pronoun does not have a direct referent in the co-text but functions as indefinite ("whom," i.e., whomever it might be).

παριστάνετε. Pres act ind 2nd pl παρίστημι.

ἑαυτοὺς. Accusative direct object of παριστάνετε in a double accusative object-complement construction.

δούλους. Complement to ἑαυτοὺς in a double accusative object-complement construction. The double accusative is where the quality or attribute of one accusative is given to the other; i.e., the attribute of "slave" is given to "yourselves" (Porter 1994a, 89–90).

εἰς ὑπακοήν. Goal. The goal is "obedience."

δοῦλοί. Predicate nominative.

ἐστε. Unaugmented ind 2nd pl εἰμί.

ᾧ. Dative indirect object of ὑπακούετε. The relative pronoun, as above, does not have a direct referent in the co-text but functions as indefinite ("whom," i.e., whomever it might be).

ὑπακούετε. Pres act ind 2nd pl ὑπακούω. This verb is a cognate of ὑπακοήν above.

ἤτοι . . . ἤ. Disjunctive conjunctions ("either . . . or") that establish a contrast between ἁμαρτίας εἰς θάνατον and ὑπακοῆς εἰς δικαιοσύνην.

ἁμαρτίας. Genitive of description, modifying δοῦλοί. It describes or circumscribes δοῦλοί as "of sin." Some may wish to interpret this as an objective genitive.

εἰς θάνατον. Result.

ὑπακοῆς. Genitive of description, modifying δοῦλοί. It describes or circumscribes δοῦλοί as "of obedience." Some may wish to interpret this as an objective genitive.

εἰς δικαιοσύνην. Result.

6:17 χάρις δὲ τῷ θεῷ ὅτι ἦτε δοῦλοι τῆς ἁμαρτίας ὑπηκούσατε δὲ ἐκ καρδίας εἰς ὃν παρεδόθητε τύπον διδαχῆς,

χάρις. Nominative absolute. The nominative serves as its own clause, with a prepositional word group attached to it.

δὲ. Adversative conjunction (mild).

τῷ θεῷ. Dative of recipient.

ὅτι. Introduces a causal clause. The cause for attributing thanks to God is stated.

ἦτε. Augmented ind 2nd pl εἰμί.

δοῦλοι. Predicate nominative.

τῆς ἁμαρτίας. Genitive of description, modifying δοῦλοι. It describes or circumscribes δοῦλοί as "of sin." Some may wish to interpret this as an objective genitive.

ὑπηκούσατε. Aor act ind 2nd pl ὑποκούω.

δὲ. Adversative conjunction (mild).

ἐκ καρδίας. Instrumental (agency). The instrument or agent for obeying is the heart.

εἰς ὃν. Goal. The prepositional word group εἰς ὃν introduces an internally headed relative clause because it incorporates the antecedent of the relative pronoun (τύπον διδαχῆς). When this happens, "the article going with the noun must be omitted and the noun itself then attracted to the case of the relative" (BDF §294.5). Robertson (719) suggests the following reconstruction: εἰς ὃν παρεδόθητε τύπον διδαχῆς = τῷ τύπῳ διδαχῆς εἰς ὃν παρεδόθητε.

παρεδόθητε. Aor pass ind 2nd pl παραδίδωμι.

τύπον. Direct object of ὑπηκούσατε. τύπον should have been in the dative (because ὑποκούω takes its object in the dative), but because it is incorporated into the relative clause, its case is attracted to the accusative case of the relative pronoun ὃν.

διδαχῆς. Genitive of description, modifying τύπον. It describes or circumscribes "form" as "of teaching."

6:18 ἐλευθερωθέντες δὲ ἀπὸ τῆς ἁμαρτίας ἐδουλώθητε τῇ δικαιοσύνῃ.

ἐλευθερωθέντες. Aor pass ptc masc nom pl ἐλευθερόω (temporal or causal). The perfective aspect of the participle provides background information to the main clause (ἐδουλώθητε τῇ δικαιοσύνῃ).

δὲ. Adversative conjunction (mild).

ἀπὸ τῆς ἁμαρτίας. Locative (movement away from/separation).

ἐδουλώθητε. Aor pass ind 2nd pl δουλόω.

τῇ δικαιοσύνῃ. Dative of respect.

6:19 Ἀνθρώπινον λέγω διὰ τὴν ἀσθένειαν τῆς σαρκὸς ὑμῶν. ὥσπερ γὰρ παρεστήσατε τὰ μέλη ὑμῶν δοῦλα τῇ ἀκαθαρσίᾳ καὶ τῇ ἀνομίᾳ εἰς τὴν ἀνομίαν, οὕτως νῦν παραστήσατε τὰ μέλη ὑμῶν δοῦλα τῇ δικαιοσύνῃ εἰς ἁγιασμόν.

Ἀνθρώπινον. Adverbial accusative (accusative of manner). It modifies λέγω.

λέγω. Pres act ind 1st sg λέγω.

διὰ τὴν ἀσθένειαν. Causal. The reason (cause) for why Paul speaks "humanly" is stated in the accusative object of the preposition.

τῆς σαρκὸς. Genitive of description, modifying τὴν ἀσθένειαν. It describes or circumscribes "weakness" as "of your heart."

ὑμῶν. Possessive genitive, modifying τῆς σαρκὸς.

ὥσπερ . . . οὕτως. A point/counterpoint set ("just as . . . so") that compares presenting one's members as slaves to immorality and lawlessness with presenting them as slaves to righteousness.

γὰρ. Postpositive explanatory conjunction. It introduces an explanation of Paul's speaking humanly.

παρεστήσατε. Aor act ind 2nd pl παρίστημι.

τὰ μέλη. Accusative direct object of παρεστήσατε in a double accusative object-complement construction.

ὑμῶν. Possessive genitive, modifying τὰ μέλη.

δοῦλα. Complement to τὰ μέλη in a double accusative object-complement construction.

τῇ ἀκαθαρσίᾳ. Dative indirect object of παρεστήσατε.

καὶ. Coordinating conjunction. It connects τῇ ἀκαθαρσίᾳ with τῇ ἀνομίᾳ.

τῇ ἀνομίᾳ. Dative indirect object of παρεστήσατε.

εἰς τὴν ἀνομίαν. Goal or state. Lawlessness leads to more lawlessness.

νῦν. Adverb (temporal). It modifies παραστήσατε.

παραστήσατε. Aor act impv 2nd pl παρίστημι. The same lexeme used above is here in the imperative mood-form to contrast what they once did with what they are "now" to do.

τὰ μέλη. Accusative direct object of παρεστήσατε in a double accusative object-complement construction.

ὑμῶν. Possessive genitive, modifying τὰ μέλη.

δοῦλα. Complement to τὰ μέλη in a double accusative object-complement construction.

τῇ δικαιοσύνῃ. Dative indirect object of παραστήσατε.

εἰς ἁγιασμόν. Goal. In contrast to εἰς τὴν ἀνομίαν, the new goal is εἰς ἁγιασμόν.

6:20 ὅτε γὰρ δοῦλοι ἦτε τῆς ἁμαρτίας, ἐλεύθεροι ἦτε τῇ δικαιοσύνῃ.

ὅτε. Introduces a temporal clause.

γὰρ. Postpositive explanatory conjunction. It introduces an explanation for the previous command.

δοῦλοι. Predicate nominative.

ἦτε. Augmented ind 2nd pl εἰμί.

τῆς ἁμαρτίας. Genitive of description, modifying δοῦλοι. It further describes or circumscribes "slaves" as "of sin."

ἐλεύθεροι. Predicate adjective.

ἦτε. Augmented ind 2nd pl εἰμί.

τῇ δικαιοσύνῃ. Dative of respect.

6:21 τίνα οὖν καρπὸν εἴχετε τότε; ἐφ' οἷς νῦν ἐπαισχύνεσθε, τὸ γὰρ τέλος ἐκείνων θάνατος.

τίνα οὖν καρπὸν εἴχετε τότε. NA[28] and UBS[5] have a question mark after τότε, but it makes better sense to put the question mark after ἐπαισχύνεσθε (cf. SBLGNT; NRSV; NASB, NIV, ESV, LEB).

τίνα . . . καρπὸν. Accusative direct object of εἴχετε. τίνα is an interrogative pronoun that is used adjectively to modify καρπὸν. The agricultural metaphor of "fruit" reflects the production of something that culminates in maturity. Here, this culmination results in something they were ashamed of.

οὖν. Postpositive inferential conjunction.

εἴχετε. Impf act ind 2nd pl ἔχω.

τότε. Adverb (temporal). It modifies εἴχετε.

ἐφ' οἷς. Locative. The relative pronoun is headless and refers in the co-text to whatever they might be ashamed of.

νῦν. Adverb (temporal). It modifies ἐπαισχύνεσθε.

ἐπαισχύνεσθε. Pres mid ind 2nd pl ἐπαισχύνομαι.

τὸ . . . τέλος. Nominative subject of verbless clause.

γὰρ. Postpositive explanatory conjunction. It introduces a clause to explain the previous statement of being ashamed.

ἐκείνων. Genitive of description, modifying τὸ . . . τέλος. It further describes or circumscribes "the end" with a demonstrative pronoun, which refers anaphorically to οἷς.

θάνατος. Predicate nominative.

6:22 νυνὶ δὲ ἐλευθερωθέντες ἀπὸ τῆς ἁμαρτίας δουλωθέντες δὲ τῷ θεῷ ἔχετε τὸν καρπὸν ὑμῶν εἰς ἁγιασμόν, τὸ δὲ τέλος ζωὴν αἰώνιον.

νυνὶ. Adverb (temporal). It modifies ἐλευθερωθέντες.

δὲ. Adversative conjunction (mild).

ἐλευθερωθέντες. Aor pass ptc masc nom pl ἐλευθερόω (causal). It modifies ἔχετε and functions as circumstantial in this co-text. Both participles in this verse provide background information, especially being in the perfective aspect (aorist tense-form).

ἀπὸ τῆς ἁμαρτίας. Locative (movement away from/separation).

δουλωθέντες. Aor pass ptc masc nom pl δουλόω (causal). Parallel to ἐλευθερωθέντες above.

δὲ. Adversative conjunction (mild).

τῷ θεῷ. Dative of respect. A locative sense could also apply, in light of the parallel construction between the participial clauses.

ἔχετε. Pres act impv 2nd pl ἔχω. While the indicative mood-form is identical, it is preferable to interpret this as an imperative here. Paul seems to be commanding them to have the fruit that leads to sanctification as a result of being free from sin and being slaves to God, rather than simply asserting that they have this fruit (cf. Porter 2015, 141).

τὸν καρπὸν. Accusative direct object of ἔχετε.

ὑμῶν. Possessive genitive, modifying τὸν καρπὸν.

εἰς ἁγιασμόν. Goal. The goal of having fruit is holiness.

τὸ δὲ τέλος ζωὴν αἰώνιον. This construction is not common, but it occurs two other times in the New Testament (1 Tim 1:5; 1 Pet 3:8) and once in the LXX (2 Macc 5:7). In 1 Tim 1:5, a genitive construction is attached (τὸ δὲ τέλος τῆς παραγγελίας) and means "the goal of the instruction" or the like. However, in both 1 Pet 3:8 and 2 Macc 5:7, it is used in the sense of "finally," "in the end," or "at last." Here, it probably refers to a similar phrase as "in the end."

τὸ . . . τέλος. Accusative of time.

δὲ. Adversative conjunction (mild).

ζωὴν αἰώνιον. Accusative in apposition to ἁγιασμόν. It can alternatively be appositional to καρπὸν, so that it means that the end (outcome) of the fruit is eternal life, rather than the end (outcome) of holiness. Both make sense, grammatically and theologically, but the proximity of ἁγιασμόν is preferable.

6:23 τὰ γὰρ ὀψώνια τῆς ἁμαρτίας θάνατος, τὸ δὲ χάρισμα τοῦ θεοῦ ζωὴ αἰώνιος ἐν Χριστῷ Ἰησοῦ τῷ κυρίῳ ἡμῶν.

τὰ . . . ὀψώνια. Nominative subject of verbless clause. The lexeme ὀψώνιον refers to payment or compensation and is used metaphorically here.

γὰρ. Postpositive explanatory conjunction. It introduces a clause that continues the series of explanations by Paul.

τῆς ἁμαρτίας. Genitive of description, modifying τὰ . . . ὀψώνια. It further describes or circumscribes "wages" with "of sin."

θάνατος. Predicate nominative.

τὸ . . . χάρισμα. Nominative subject of verbless clause.

δὲ. Adversative conjunction (mild).

τοῦ θεοῦ. Genitive or source or origin, modifying τὸ . . . χάρισμα.

ζωὴ αἰώνιος. Predicate nominative.

ἐν Χριστῷ Ἰησοῦ. Locative (sphere or realm); see notes on ἐν Χριστῷ Ἰησοῦ in 3:24; 6:11.

τῷ κυρίῳ. Dative in apposition to Χριστῷ Ἰησοῦ.
ἡμῶν. Possessive genitive, modifying τῷ κυρίῳ.

Romans 7:1-6

¹Or are you ignorant, brothers [and sisters], for I speak to knowers of
the law, that the law rules over a person for as long as he lives? ²For
a married woman is bound to her husband by law, but if the husband
should die, she is released from the law of her husband. ³Then, therefore,
while her husband is living, she will be called an adulteress if she should
be with another man; but if the husband should die, she is free from
the law, so that she is not an adulteress while being with another man.
⁴Therefore, my brothers [and sisters], you also died to the law through
the body of Christ, so that you might be with another one, with the one
who was raised from the dead, in order that we might produce fruit for
God. ⁵For when we were in the flesh, the sinful passions, which came
about through the law, were energized in our members in order to produce fruit for death. ⁶But now we are released from the law, having died
to the thing by which we were possessed, so that we could become slaves
in the newness of the Spirit and not in the oldness of the letter.

This second sub-section within the major section (6:1–7:25) continues
the line of argument regarding the Christian life and its relationship to
sin. Here, Paul relies on the analogy of marriage to relate the relationship of the Christian to sin and the law.

**7:1 Ἢ ἀγνοεῖτε, ἀδελφοί, γινώσκουσιν γὰρ νόμον λαλῶ, ὅτι ὁ νόμος
κυριεύει τοῦ ἀνθρώπου ἐφ᾽ ὅσον χρόνον ζῇ;**

ἤ. Disjunctive conjunction. It marks a transition from what has been
stated from being slaves of either sin or righteousness to the role of the
law in the believer's life.

ἀγνοεῖτε. Pres act ind 2nd pl ἀγνοέω. English translations (e.g.,
NASB, NIV, NKJV, NRSV) tend to reflect a negation (i.e., "not know"),
but the sense here with the use of ἀγνοέω is an active sense of being
ignorant about something (cf. 1:13). The use of a "knowledge" word,
as well as the content of this knowledge initiated by ὅτι, indicates the
disclosure formula, where Paul discloses critical information at this con-
juncture (see Porter and Pitts 2013).

ἀδελφοί. Nominative of address (so-called vocative). This is the
first time since 1:13 that Paul addresses the Romans as "brothers [and
sisters]."

γινώσκουσιν. Pres act ptc masc dat pl γινώσκω (substantival). Dative indirect object of λαλῶ. Paul's use of the imperfective aspect (present tense-form) reflects his depiction of their knowing as in progress. Paul deliberately uses a cognate of ἀγνοέω from above in participial form to make the connection that they know these things. His question of whether they know it, then, is probably meant to be rhetorical—of course they should know.

γὰρ. Postpositive explanatory conjunction that introduces an explanation of Paul's questioning of their ignorance of the law.

νόμον. Accusative direct object of γινώσκουσιν. The fact that it is anarthrous indicates that Paul refers not to a specific law (i.e., the Mosaic law or Roman law) but to "law" in general. In other words, Paul's addressees know how laws in general work.

λαλῶ. Pres act ind 1st sg λαλέω.

ὅτι. Introduces the clausal complement (indirect discourse) of ἀγνοεῖτε and marks a disclosure formula.

ὁ νόμος. Nominative subject of κυριεύει. Whereas in the previous clause νόμος was anarthrous, here it is articular, referring to the law categorically (Porter 1994a, 104–5).

κυριεύει. Pres act ind 3rd sg κυριεύω.

τοῦ ἀνθρώπου. Genitive direct object of κυριεύει.

ἐφ’ ὅσον χρόνον. Directional, in a figurative sense (lit. "upon as much time").

ζῇ. Pres act ind 3rd sg ζάω. It is a predicate within the prepositional temporal clause, ἐφ’ ὅσον χρόνον ζῇ, modifying the verb κυριεύει. The object of the prepositional word group, ἐφ’ ὅσον χρόνον, is internal to the clause construction.

7:2 ἡ γὰρ ὕπανδρος γυνὴ τῷ ζῶντι ἀνδρὶ δέδεται νόμῳ· ἐὰν δὲ ἀποθάνῃ ὁ ἀνήρ, κατήργηται ἀπὸ τοῦ νόμου τοῦ ἀνδρός.

ἡ . . . ὕπανδρος γυνή. Nominative subject of δέδεται. This is the only time this word group (ἡ ὕπανδρος γυνὴ) is used in Paul (Porter 2015, 142). ὕπανδρος is a NT *hapax legomenon*. It also occurs in Proverbs (6:24, 29) and Sirach (9:9; 41:23), and in all four occurrences is collocated with γυνὴ (three times in a genitive construction and once in an accusative construction [Prov 6:29]). Although the word is a compound of ὑπό and ἀνήρ, ὕπανδρος does not essentially mean "under a man," and it is an improper use of morphology to develop a theology of marriage based on the compound, although in the Roman culture, the *paterfamilias* was the ruling authority of the family (cf. Porter 2015, 142). The word according to its usage simply refers to a "married woman."

γὰρ. Postpositive explanatory conjunction that introduces an explanation (with example) for what Paul has just stated regarding the law being required as long as the person is living.

τῷ . . . ἀνδρὶ. Dative indirect object of δέδεται.

ζῶντι. Pres act ptc masc dat sg ζάω (attributive). The participle modifies τῷ . . . ἀνδρὶ in attributive structure (first attributive position).

δέδεται. Prf pass ind 3rd sg δέω. The use of the stative aspect indicates a state of "boundness."

νόμῳ. Dative of instrument/means or cause. The instrument or cause by which the wife is bound is the law.

ἐὰν. Introduces the protasis of a third-class conditional. With the subjunctive in the protasis this type of conditional clause reflects a general, probable condition.

δὲ. Adversative conjunction (mild). It signifies a contrast between the law being binding when a husband is alive, with the law no longer having relevance if the husband should die.

ἀποθάνῃ. Aor act subj 3rd sg ἀποθνήσκω. Subjunctive with ἐάν.

ὁ ἀνήρ. Nominative subject of ἀποθάνῃ.

κατήργηται. Prf pass ind 3rd sg καταργέω. This verb begins the apodosis of the third-class conditional clause. The voice-form could be either middle or passive, but the passive sense fits best here (external agency; probably referring to the death of her husband). The implied grammatical subject (but Goal), then, is the wife. The stative aspect reflects the process as being in a state of release or nullification.

ἀπὸ τοῦ νόμου. Locative (movement away from/separation). The prepositional word group indicates, in a figurative sense, movement away from "the law of the husband" (i.e., the law that binds the woman to her husband).

τοῦ ἀνδρός. Genitive of description, modifying τοῦ νόμου. It further describes or circumscribes the law as "of the husband."

7:3 ἄρα οὖν ζῶντος τοῦ ἀνδρὸς μοιχαλὶς χρηματίσει ἐὰν γένηται ἀνδρὶ ἑτέρῳ· ἐὰν δὲ ἀποθάνῃ ὁ ἀνήρ, ἐλευθέρα ἐστὶν ἀπὸ τοῦ νόμου, τοῦ μὴ εἶναι αὐτὴν μοιχαλίδα γενομένην ἀνδρὶ ἑτέρῳ.

ἄρα οὖν. A combination of two inferential conjunctions (see Rom 5:18). It is used to continue the implications of marriage laws.

ζῶντος. Pres act ptc masc gen sg ζάω (genitive absolute, temporal).

τοῦ ἀνδρὸς. Genitive subject of ζῶντος.

μοιχαλὶς χρηματίσει. This is the apodosis of the conditional structure. In this case, the conditional construction begins with the apodosis before the protasis, making the apodosis prominent in the clause-complex, since the default order of a conditional statement is protasis followed by apodosis (cf. Porter 2009, 73). In other words, Paul emphasizes the calling of the woman as an adulteress over the condition (if she lives with another man).

μοιχαλὶς. Nominative subject of χρηματίσει.

χρηματίσει. Fut act ind 3rd sg χρηματίζω. This is the only occurrence of this verb in Paul. This verb is in the active voice, so a wooden literal translation might be: "an adulteress makes known," "an adulteress reveals," or "an adulteress calls." The translation above ("she will be called an adulteress") renders the Greek in smoother and more natural English.

ἐὰν. Introduces the protasis of a third-class conditional (see 7:2).

γένηται. Aor mid subj 3rd sg γίνομαι. Subjunctive with ἐάν. γίνομαι is a so-called deponent verb (see "Deponency" in the Series Introduction).

ἀνδρὶ ἑτέρῳ. Dative of respect (association).

ἐὰν. Introduces the protasis of a third-class conditional. The protasis is ἐὰν ἀποθάνῃ ὁ ἀνήρ; the apodosis is ἐλευθέρα ἐστὶν ἀπὸ τοῦ νόμου. This conditional structure follows the default protasis-apodosis order.

δὲ. Adversative conjunction (mild). It contrasts the previous statement about a woman being an adulteress with the following condition of her not being an adulteress.

ἀποθάνῃ. Aor act subj 3rd sg ἀποθνήσκω. Subjunctive with ἐάν.

ὁ ἀνήρ. Nominative subject of ἀποθάνῃ.

ἐλευθέρα. Predicate adjective. Feminine gender is appropriate, given that the reference is to γυνὴ from above. ἐλευθέρα marks the beginning of the apodosis of the third-class conditional.

ἐστὶν. Unaugmented ind 3rd sg εἰμί.

ἀπὸ τοῦ νόμου. Locative (movement away from/separation; see 7:2).

τοῦ . . . εἶναι. Inf εἰμί (result). Genitive infinitival construction functions as a result clause. Genitive article is used to connect with τοῦ νόμου.

μὴ. Negative particle normally used with non-indicative verbs. Here it negates εἶναι.

αὐτὴν. Accusative subject of εἶναι.

μοιχαλίδα. Predicate accusative.

γενομένην. Aor mid ptc fem acc sg γίνομαι (concessive). The participle functions as circumstantial in this co-text.

ἀνδρὶ ἑτέρῳ. Dative of respect (association).

7:4 ὥστε, ἀδελφοί μου, καὶ ὑμεῖς ἐθανατώθητε τῷ νόμῳ διὰ τοῦ σώματος τοῦ Χριστοῦ, εἰς τὸ γενέσθαι ὑμᾶς ἑτέρῳ, τῷ ἐκ νεκρῶν ἐγερθέντι, ἵνα καρποφορήσωμεν τῷ θεῷ.

ὥστε. Introduces a result clause. As a result of Paul's analogy of marriage in relation to the efficacy of the law, he states the following.

ἀδελφοί. Nominative of address (so-called vocative). Paul has used this term only once in chs. 1–6 (1:13), but he uses it twice within the span of four verses here (7:1, 4).

μου. Possessive genitive, modifying ἀδελφοί. The use of the personal pronoun μου with ἀδελφοί grammaticalizes the close relationship he wishes to depict with them.

καὶ. Adverbial use (adjunctive). It modifies ὑμεῖς ἐθανατώθητε.

ὑμεῖς. Nominative subject of ἐθανατώθητε. The use of the personal pronoun here is emphatic.

ἐθανατώθητε. Aor pass ind 2nd pl θανατόω. ἐθανατώθητε is the main predicate of the primary clause. The passive voice indicates external causality or agency (τοῦ σώματος τοῦ Χριστοῦ).

τῷ νόμῳ. Dative of respect. They were dead with respect to the law.

διὰ τοῦ σώματος. Instrumental. It is the "body of Christ" that made them "dead to the law."

τοῦ Χριστοῦ. Possessive genitive, modifying τοῦ σώματος.

γενέσθαι. Aor mid inf γίνομαι. Used with εἰς τὸ to indicate purpose.

ὑμᾶς. Accusative subject of the infinitive γενέσθαι.

ἑτέρῳ. Dative of respect (association). The adjective functions as substantive ("another one").

τῷ . . . ἐγερθέντι. Aor pass ptc masc dat sg ἐγείρω (substantival). Dative in apposition to ἑτέρῳ. The reference is to Jesus Christ.

ἐκ νεκρῶν. Locative (movement out of/separation). As an embedded prepositional word group between the article and substantive, the prepositional word group modifies τῷ ἐγερθέντι in attributive structure (lit. "the from-the-dead raised one").

ἵνα. Introduces a purpose clause. The purpose of the Romans being with the one who was raised from the dead is stated in the following secondary clause.

καρποφορήσωμεν. Aor act subj 1st pl καρποφορέω. Subjunctive with ἵνα. For more on the meaning of this, see 7:5 on εἰς τὸ καρποφορῆσαι.

τῷ θεῷ. Dative of respect. The bearing of fruit is with respect to God.

7:5 ὅτε γὰρ ἦμεν ἐν τῇ σαρκί, τὰ παθήματα τῶν ἁμαρτιῶν τὰ διὰ
τοῦ νόμου ἐνηργεῖτο ἐν τοῖς μέλεσιν ἡμῶν, εἰς τὸ καρποφορῆσαι τῷ
θανάτῳ·

The language of σάρξ, πάθημα, ἁμαρτία, νόμος, μέλος, καρπός, and
θάνατος form a co-textual semantic domain of the human condition
(Porter 2015, 144). In other words, Paul uses these words in order to
reflect the human condition prior to justification and reconciliation.

ὅτε. Introduces a temporal clause (i.e., a prior time "in the flesh").

γὰρ. Postpositive explanatory conjunction that introduces an explanation of the previous statement.

ἦμεν. Augmented ind 1st pl εἰμί.

ἐν τῇ σαρκί. Locative (sphere or realm). The sphere that they were
in is "flesh." The NIV is known to translate σάρξ as "sinful nature" (e.g.,
Rom 7:18, 25; the latest edition, NIV 2011, has changed many instances
of "sinful nature" to "flesh" from NIV 1984, e.g., Rom 8:3, 4, 5, 8, 9),
However, σάρξ simply refers to the physical body of humans or other
creatures and can have various metaphorical uses depending on its
co-text.

τὰ παθήματα τῶν ἁμαρτιῶν τὰ διὰ τοῦ νόμου. This entire word
group forms one substantive unit, consisting of the articular head term
(τὰ παθήματα), the genitive modifier (τῶν ἁμαρτιῶν), and the modifying
articular prepositional word group (τὰ διὰ τοῦ νόμου). That this entire
substantive occurs before the predicate signifies that it is prominent
(according to clause structure prominence; Porter 2009, 71–73; Yoon
2019, 131–32).

τὰ παθήματα. Nominative subject of ἐνηργεῖτο. Neuter plural subjects typically take singular verbs.

τῶν ἁμαρτιῶν. Genitive of quality, modifying τὰ παθήματα, attributing the quality of "sin" to "passion" (i.e., sinful passions).

τὰ διὰ τοῦ νόμου. The article functions as an adjectivizer, changing
the prepositional word group διὰ τοῦ νόμου into an attributive modifier
of τὰ παθήματα.

διὰ τοῦ νόμου. Instrumental. The instrument or agent of "the passions" is identified through attribution as "the law."

ἐνηργεῖτο. Impf pass ind 3rd sg ἐνεργέω. Main predicate of the
clause. While the passive voice-form here is identical to the middle
form, it is preferable to interpret this as passive, due to the identification
of agency (διὰ τοῦ νόμου).

ἐν τοῖς μέλεσιν. Locative (sphere or realm). The sphere in which the
sinful passions were "energized" is "our members." μέλος generally refers
to a body part or a member of a whole, and in this co-text contrasts τοῦ

σώματος τοῦ Χριστοῦ (7:4) by use of hyponym (μέλος would be a hyponym of σῶμα).

ἡμῶν. Possessive genitive, modifying τοῖς μέλεσιν.

καρποφορῆσαι. Aor act inf καρποφορέω. Used with εἰς τὸ to indicate purpose. While there is a conceptual parallel with the end of the previous verse (ἵνα καρποφορήσωμεν τῷ θεῷ) here, since a form of καρποφορέω appears in both, followed by a dative of respect and preceded by a purpose statement, a significant difference is in the forms of καρποφορέω. In the previous verse, an implicit subject is identified (καρποφορήσωμεν; first-person plural, so Paul and the Romans). In this verse, καρποφορῆσαι has no explicit subject as an infinitive. The effect of this difference is that in the previous verse, the personal element is more concrete (in the use of "we"), while in this verse, Paul probably states a more general statement about bearing fruit for death, without identifying a personal element.

τῷ θανάτῳ. Dative of respect. The bearing of fruit is with respect to death.

7:6 νυνὶ δὲ κατηργήθημεν ἀπὸ τοῦ νόμου ἀποθανόντες ἐν ᾧ κατειχόμεθα, ὥστε δουλεύειν ἡμᾶς ἐν καινότητι πνεύματος καὶ οὐ παλαιότητι γράμματος.

In this verse, the language of καταργέω, νόμος, ἀποθνήσκω, δουλεύω, and καινότης constitute the semantic domain of the new condition in Christ, in contrast to the semantic domain of the human condition as reflected in 7:5. The co-text influences the domain, as is seen by the repetition of νόμος and θάνατος/ἀποθνήσκω in both domains.

νυνὶ. Adverb (temporal). It is used to contrast the previous statement (beginning with ὅτε) with the following statement, indicating the contrast between past and present.

δὲ. Adversative conjunction (mild). It is used along with νυνὶ to contrast past and present circumstances.

κατηργήθημεν. Aor pass ind 1st pl καταργέω. Passive voice indicates external agency, which is not specified in this co-text.

ἀπὸ τοῦ νόμου. Locative (movement away from/separation; see 7:2).

ἀποθανόντες. Aor act ptc masc nom pl ἀποθνήσκω (causal). The participle functions as circumstantial in the co-text, modifying κατηργήθημεν and beginning a secondary (subordinate) clause.

ἐν ᾧ. Locative (sphere or realm). The relative pronoun refers anaphorically to τοῦ νόμου. The sphere in which they died is the thing by which we were possessed, i.e., the law.

κατειχόμεθα. Impf pass ind 1st pl κατέχω. κατειχόμεθα is a finite verb within a prepositional word group.

ὥστε. Introduces a result clause. The result of being released from the law is to be enslaved in the new life in the Spirit.

δουλεύειν. Pres act inf δουλεύω. Used with ὥστε to indicate result. The infinitive functions as the main predicate in this secondary clause.

ἡμᾶς. Accusative subject of the infinitive δουλεύειν.

ἐν καινότητι . . . καὶ οὐ παλαιότητι. Locative (sphere or realm). The realm in which they are now enslaved is "the newness of the Spirit and not in the oldness of the letter."

πνεύματος. Genitive of description, modifying καινότητι. It further describes or circumscribes "newness" as "of the Spirit."

γράμματος. Genitive of description, modifying παλαιότητι. It further describes or circumscribes "oldness" as "of the letter."

Romans 7:7–12

[7]What, therefore, will we say? [Is] the law sin? Indeed not. However, I would not have known sin except through the law; for I would not have known desire if the law is not saying, "You shall not covet." [8]But sin, taking opportunity through the commandment, accomplished in me every [sort of] desire; for apart from the law, sin [is] dead. [9]And I was living apart from the law then, but when the commandment came, sin sprang to life, [10]and I died. And the commandment, which was unto life, was found to me, this one [was] unto death. [11]For sin, taking an opportunity through the commandment, led me astray and, through it, killed [me]. [12]So then, the law [is] holy, and the commandment [is] holy and righteous and good.

Romans 7:7–25 constitutes a section within Romans devoted to the continuing problem that sin poses in relation to the law. This section itself is divided into two sub-sections. The first sub-section is Rom 7:7–12, where Paul addresses the function of the law, and the second sub-section is Rom 7:13–25, where he addresses the life of the Christian who struggles with sin in light of fulfilling the law's requirements. The major grammatical question arises with the shift between Rom 7:7–12 and 7:13–25 from imperfective aspect (present) to perfective aspect (aorist) verbs (see below for discussion), a view that is usually made more complex by a temporal view of the use of the tense-forms.

7:7 Τί οὖν ἐροῦμεν; ὁ νόμος ἁμαρτία; μὴ γένοιτο· ἀλλὰ τὴν ἁμαρτίαν οὐκ ἔγνων εἰ μὴ διὰ νόμου· τήν τε γὰρ ἐπιθυμίαν οὐκ ᾔδειν εἰ μὴ ὁ νόμος ἔλεγεν· οὐκ ἐπιθυμήσεις.

From clause-structure analysis in this verse, there are three elements that are prominent: (1) Paul's denial of the law being sin (use of μὴ γένοιτο), (2) sin (fronting of τὴν ἁμαρτίαν), and (3) desire (fronting of τήν . . . ἐπιθυμίαν).

Τί οὖν ἐροῦμεν. A rhetorical question that has been used by Paul throughout this letter to transition to a related but new logical progression (Rom 4:1; 6:1; 7:7; 8:31; 9:14, 30).

Τί. Accusative direct object of ἐροῦμεν.

οὖν. Postpositive inferential conjunction. The inference is from the previous verse, where Paul contrasts the newness of the Spirit with the oldness of the letter.

ἐροῦμεν. Fut act ind 1st pl λέγω.

ὁ νόμος ἁμαρτία. This clause could very well be construed as a statement rather than a question grammatically, but the co-text (the previous question and the emphatic negation that follows) indicates that it is a question as a follow-up to the previous question. Additionally, the clause as a statement would be the opposite of Paul's point in this letter so far.

ὁ νόμος. Nominative subject of verbless clause (with an implied "is" in an English translation). The "law" here is probably a reference not specifically to the Old Testament law, although not precluding it, but a reference to divine principles, even if an example from the Old Testament law is given subsequently. Divine principles for life would certainly include the Old Testament law, but the reason for understanding this as divine principles is in light of how Paul refers to the law in this letter as something innately known (cf. 1:19).

ἁμαρτία. Predicative nominative. It is placed second in the clause in relationship with the previous nominative ὁ νόμος. Colwell's rule applies here (see comments in 1:9).

μὴ γένοιτο. A common emphatic negation for Paul after posing a question, usually rhetorical (see 3:4).

μὴ. Negative particle normally used with non-indicative verbs. Here it negates γένοιτο.

γένοιτο. Aor mid opt 3rd sg γίνομαι.

ἀλλὰ. Adversative conjunction (strong). The contrast is with the previous series of questions and statements (the point being that the law is *not* sin) and the next statement about knowing sin through the law.

τὴν ἁμαρτίαν οὐκ ἔγνων εἰ μὴ διὰ νόμου·. A second-class conditional statement, with the apodosis preceding the protasis for prominence (cf. Porter 2009, 73; Yoon 2019, 132; cf. Moo, 432–35). Another way to view this construction is to see the οὐκ . . . εἰ μὴ construction as a point/counterpoint set that counters the negated clause by introducing an exception (see Runge 2010, 83–91). In such a construction, the exceptive clause introduced by εἰ μὴ regularly comes second. Even so, the conditional sense remains here with the use of εἰ; he would not have known sin without the condition of the law's agency.

τὴν ἁμαρτίαν. Accusative direct object of ἔγνων. Its position before the predicate implies prominence. Prominence for this lexeme is reflected doubly: first in its position (with the rest of the clause) in the conditional statement, and second in its position in the clause itself.

οὐκ. Negative particle normally used with indicative verbs. Here it negates ἔγνων.

ἔγνων. Aor act ind 1st sg γινώσκω.

εἰ μὴ. A combination of the conditional conjunction and the negative particle (usually translated "except" or "if not") that introduces the protasis of a second-class conditional (the so-called contrary-to-fact conditional; it reflects the writer's belief that this conditional does not reflect reality).

διὰ νόμου. Instrumental. The law was an instrument or agent for Paul's knowing sin.

τήν τε γὰρ ἐπιθυμίαν οὐκ ᾔδειν εἰ μὴ ὁ νόμος ἔλεγεν. A second-class conditional statement, with the apodosis preceding the protasis for prominence (see τὴν ἁμαρτίαν οὐκ ἔγνων εἰ μὴ διὰ νόμου above).

τήν . . . ἐπιθυμίαν. Accusative direct object of ᾔδειν. Its position at the beginning of the apodosis of the second-class conditional clause indicates prominence. The same lexeme for "desire" is used in 1:24, where Paul refers to the "desires of the heart" to which God gave over humanity.

τε. Enclitic, emphatic conjunction.

γὰρ. Postpositive explanatory conjunction. Paul explains further what he has stated in the previous clause about knowing sin through the law by providing a specific example (Moo, 432–33).

οὐκ. Negative particle normally used with indicative verbs. Here it negates ᾔδειν.

ᾔδειν. Plprf act ind 1st sg οἶδα. By using the stative aspect here with the pluperfect tense-form, Paul states that he was in a state of being fully knowledgeable.

εἰ μὴ. A combination of the conditional conjunction and the negative particle (usually translated "except" or "if not") that introduces the protasis of a second-class conditional. This is a similar conditional construction as above.

ὁ νόμος. Nominative subject of ἔλεγεν.

ἔλεγεν. Impf act ind 3rd sg λέγω.

οὐκ. Negative particle normally used with indicative verbs. Here it negates ἐπιθυμήσεις.

ἐπιθυμήσεις. Fut act ind 2nd sg ἐπιθυμέω. οὐκ ἐπιθυμήσεις is probably a reference to Exod 20:17 and Deut 5:21.

7:8 ἀφορμὴν δὲ λαβοῦσα ἡ ἁμαρτία διὰ τῆς ἐντολῆς κατειργάσατο ἐν ἐμοὶ πᾶσαν ἐπιθυμίαν· χωρὶς γὰρ νόμου ἁμαρτία νεκρά.

ἀφορμὴν. Accusative direct object of λαβοῦσα. Its fronting in the secondary (subordinate) clause reflects its prominence in the clause.

δὲ. Adversative conjunction (mild).

λαβοῦσα. Aor act ptc fem nom sg λαμβάνω (causal). The participle functions as circumstantial, modifying κατειργάσατο.

ἡ ἁμαρτία. Nominative subject of κατειργάσατο.

διὰ τῆς ἐντολῆς. Instrumental. The prepositional word group modifies the participle λαβοῦσα rather than the main verb κατειργάσατο ("taking opportunity through the commandment").

κατειργάσατο. Aor mid ind 3rd sg κατεργάζομαι. The use of the perfective aspect reflects background and functions as supportive material to the mainline of discourse (reflected by the imperfective in expositional texts).

ἐν ἐμοὶ. Locative (sphere or realm). The sphere in which sin accomplished its work is Paul.

πᾶσαν ἐπιθυμίαν. Accusative direct object of κατειργάσατο. πᾶσαν is qualitative and designates a class ("desire of every kind"; BDAG, 784.5).

χωρὶς . . . νόμου. Separation. χωρίς is an improper preposition.

γὰρ. Postpositive explanatory conjunction. It introduces an explanation of the previous statement that the law produced (or accomplished) in Paul every sort of desire.

ἁμαρτία. Nominative subject of verbless clause ("is" might be supplied in an English translation).

νεκρά. Predicate adjective.

7:9 ἐγὼ δὲ ἔζων χωρὶς νόμου ποτέ, ἐλθούσης δὲ τῆς ἐντολῆς ἡ ἁμαρτία ἀνέζησεν,

ἐγὼ. Nominative subject of ἔζων. The use of the personal pronoun is emphatic.

δέ. Adversative conjunction (mild).

ἔζων. Impf act ind 1st sg ζάω.

χωρὶς νόμου. Separation (see 7:8).

ποτέ. Adverb (temporal). It modifies ἔζων.

ἐλθούσης. Aor act ptc fem gen sg ἔρχομαι (genitive absolute, temporal).

δέ. Adversative conjunction (mild).

τῆς ἐντολῆς. Genitive subject of ἐλθούσης.

ἡ ἁμαρτία. Nominative subject of ἀνέζησεν.

ἀνέζησεν. Aor act ind 3rd sg ἀναζάω. This lexeme occurs only here in Paul.

7:10 ἐγὼ δὲ ἀπέθανον καὶ εὑρέθη μοι ἡ ἐντολὴ ἡ εἰς ζωήν, αὕτη εἰς θάνατον·

ἐγώ. Nominative subject of ἀπέθανον. Use of the personal pronoun is emphatic.

δέ. Adversative conjunction (mild).

ἀπέθανον. Aor act ind 1st sg ἀποθνήσκω.

καί. Coordinating conjunction. It connects the two clauses before and after it.

εὑρέθη. Aor pass ind 3rd sg εὑρίσκω.

μοι. Dative of advantage.

ἡ ἐντολὴ. Nominative subject of εὑρέθη.

ἡ εἰς ζωήν. The article functions as an adjectivizer, changing the prepositional word group εἰς ζωήν into an attributive modifier of ἐντολὴ.

εἰς ζωήν. Result.

αὕτη. Nominative subject of verbless clause ("is" or "was" supplied in an English translation). Demonstrative pronoun refers anaphorically to ἡ ἐντολὴ.

εἰς θάνατον. Result. The prepositional word group is conceptually parallel to εἰς ζωήν.

7:11 ἡ γὰρ ἁμαρτία ἀφορμὴν λαβοῦσα διὰ τῆς ἐντολῆς ἐξηπάτησέν με καὶ δι' αὐτῆς ἀπέκτεινεν.

The language in this verse reflects the language in 7:8, e.g., ἀφορμὴν λαβοῦσα, διὰ τῆς ἐντολῆς, and νεκρά/ἀπέκτεινεν.

ἡ . . . ἁμαρτία. Nominative subject of ἐξηπάτησέν.

γάρ. Postpositive conjunction that signals an explanation of how the commandment (or law) resulted in death for Paul, instead of life.

ἀφορμὴν. Accusative direct object of λαβοῦσα.

λαβοῦσα. Aor act ptc fem nom sg λαμβάνω (manner). The participle functions in this co-text as circumstantial and modifies ἐξηπάτησέν.

διὰ τῆς ἐντολῆς. Instrumental. The prepositional word group modifies λαβοῦσα.

ἐξηπάτησέν. Aor act ind 3rd sg of ἐξαπατάω. The double accent on this word is the result of the following word (με) being enclitic, so an additional accent on the ultima is placed for pronunciation purposes (see note on πνεύματί in 1:9).

με. Accusative direct object of ἐξηπάτησέν.

καὶ. Coordinating conjunction. It connects the two clauses before and after it.

δι᾽ αὐτῆς. Instrumental. It is parallel to διὰ τῆς ἐντολῆς.

ἀπέκτεινεν. Aor act ind 3rd sg ἀποκτείνω. The object of the verb ("me") is implied from the co-text.

7:12 ὥστε ὁ μὲν νόμος ἅγιος καὶ ἡ ἐντολὴ ἁγία καὶ δικαία καὶ ἀγαθή.

ὥστε. Introduces a result clause. Although it may seem odd at first glance for Paul to state something positive about the law and commandment, since he has been negative about it so far, it fits perfectly well in the co-text. Paul has denied that the law is sin (7:7). He also affirms the inherent nature of the law, that it is holy, in the sense that it reflects God's divine standards for living, and the nature of the commandment, that it is holy, righteous, and good, despite the negative effect it has had on him.

ὁ . . . νόμος. Nominative subject of verbless clause. A being verb ("is") can be supplied in English translations.

μὲν. Emphatic particle, functioning as contrastive. In contrast with what he has said thus far regarding the negative effect that the law has had on him, Paul affirms the nature of the law as holy.

ἅγιος. Predicative adjective.

καὶ. Coordinating conjunction. It connects two verbless clauses.

ἡ ἐντολὴ. Nominative subject of verbless clause. ἐντολή is perhaps a metonymy (part representing a whole) for the law or all of the commandments. A being verb ("is") can be supplied in English translations.

ἁγία καὶ δικαία καὶ ἀγαθή. Three predicate adjectives linked by two coordinating conjunctions.

Romans 7:13–25

[13]Therefore, did the thing that was good in me become death? Indeed not. But [it was] sin, so that it might be revealed as sin through the thing that was good accomplishing death for me, so that sin became sinful

beyond the furthest extremes through the commandment. [14]For we know that the law is spiritual, but I am fleshly, sold under sin. [15]For what I accomplish, I do not understand; for the thing that I want, this I do not practice, but what I hate, this I do. [16]But if what I do not want, this I do, I agree with the law that [it is] good. [17]But now it is no longer I who accomplishes it but the sin dwelling in me. [18]For I know that good does not dwell in me, that is, in my flesh; for to want is present in me, but to accomplish the good [is] not. [19]For what I want I do not do, the good, but what I do not want, evil, this I accomplish. [20]But if what I do not want, this I do, no longer do I accomplish it but the sin dwelling in me. [21]I found, therefore, the law in the desire in me to do good, that evil is present with me. [22]For I greatly delight in the law of God on the basis of the inner person, [23]but I see another law in my members warring against the law of my mind and taking me captive to the law of sin which is in my members. [24]Wretched person I [am]; who will rescue me from this body of death? [25]But thanks [be] to God through Jesus Christ our Lord. Now, therefore, I myself in the mind am a slave to the law of God but in the flesh, to the law of sin.

This is the second sub-section within Rom 7:7–25. It brings the third major section of the body of the letter. It continues the argument from the previous sub-section, as well as the diatribal manner by which Paul makes his argument with his hypothetical interlocutor. The major critical issue often discussed is the shift from present to aorist tense-form verbs. This is a shift in aspect from imperfective to perfective, not a shift in time from present to past, as Greek verbs are aspectual not temporal. Some interpreters have attempted to use this shift to argue that Rom 7:13–25 refers to Paul or a generic past experience (see Seifrid, 226–37, for discussion). This is predicated upon indicative verbs indicating absolute tense. A better explanation is to understand the temporal reference of the verbs within their discourse context. For example, the interlocutor asks the logical question that follows from Paul's previous argument in Rom 7:7–12, with "Therefore, did the thing that was good in me become death?" not referring to an earlier time but to the consequence of the Christian struggle with sin.

7:13 Τὸ οὖν ἀγαθὸν ἐμοὶ ἐγένετο θάνατος; μὴ γένοιτο· ἀλλὰ ἡ ἁμαρ-τία, ἵνα φανῇ ἁμαρτία, διὰ τοῦ ἀγαθοῦ μοι κατεργαζομένη θάνατον, ἵνα γένηται καθ᾽ ὑπερβολὴν ἁμαρτωλὸς ἡ ἁμαρτία διὰ τῆς ἐντολῆς.

Τὸ . . . ἀγαθὸν. Nominative subject of ἐγένετο. This substantival adjective serves as anaphoric reference to ἡ ἐντολὴ . . . ἀγαθή, and prob-ably by implication to ὁ νόμος as well (7:12).

οὖν. Postpositive inferential conjunction. The inference to be made is from Paul's previous statement that the law is holy, and the command-ment is holy, righteous, and good.

ἐμοὶ. Dative of sphere or locative dative.

ἐγένετο. Aor mid ind 3rd sg γίνομαι.

θάνατος. Predicate nominative.

μὴ γένοιτο. A common emphatic negation for Paul after posing a question, usually rhetorical (see 3:4; 7:7).

μὴ. Negative particle normally used with non-indicative verbs. Here it negates γένοιτο.

γένοιτο. Aor mid opt 3rd sg γίνομαι.

ἀλλὰ. Adversative conjunction (strong).

ἡ ἁμαρτία. Nominative absolute or nominative subject of a verb-less and single lexeme clause. For purposes of English, this is trans-lated above as "it was sin," but it serves grammatically as subject of the implied clause from the previous co-text: ἡ ἁμαρτία [ἐμοὶ ἐγένετο θάνατος].

ἵνα. Introduces a purpose clause.

φανῇ. Aor pass subj 3rd sg φαίνω. Subjunctive with ἵνα. The passive voice-form grammaticalizes external causality, signified by the prepo-sitional word group διὰ τοῦ ἀγαθοῦ, representing the previously men-tioned commandment (or law). In other words, the good commandment is the agent by which sin is revealed.

ἁμαρτία. Nominative subject of φανῇ. As the subject of a passive verb, it is the Goal of φανῇ. Being anarthrous (as compared to the pre-vious articular use), it refers to, not a specified entity, but to sin as an abstraction.

διὰ τοῦ ἀγαθοῦ. Instrumental.

μοι. Dative of disadvantage.

κατεργαζομένη. Pres mid ptc fem nom sg κατεργάζομαι (manner). The participle functions as circumstantial and modifies φανῇ.

θάνατον. Accusative direct object of κατεργαζομένη.

ἵνα. Introduces a purpose clause.

γένηται. Aor mid subj 3rd sg γίνομαι. Subjunctive with ἵνα.

καθ' ὑπερβολὴν. Standard. The standard or basis for becoming sinful is "utterly," sin to its furthest extremes.

ἁμαρτωλός. Predicative adjective.

ἡ ἁμαρτία. Nominative subject of γένηται.

διὰ τῆς ἐντολῆς. Instrumental. The means by which sin is seen to be utterly sinful is the commandment.

7:14 Οἴδαμεν γὰρ ὅτι ὁ νόμος πνευματικός ἐστιν, ἐγὼ δὲ σάρκινός εἰμι πεπραμένος ὑπὸ τὴν ἁμαρτίαν.

Οἴδαμεν. Prf act ind 1st pl οἶδα. The stative aspect (perfect tense-form) depicts "us" as being in a state of knowing.

γὰρ. Postpositive explanatory conjunction that marks Paul's explanation that continues from the previous co-text.

ὅτι. Introduces the clausal complement (indirect discourse) of Οἴδαμεν.

ὁ νόμος. Nominative subject of ἐστιν.

πνευματικός. Predicative adjective.

ἐστιν. Unaugmented ind 3rd sg εἰμί.

ἐγώ. Nominative subject of εἰμί. Use of the personal pronoun here is emphatic.

δὲ. Adversative conjunction (mild). The contrast is between the law being spiritual and Paul being fleshly.

σάρκινός. Predicative adjective. The additional accent on the ultima is the result of the following word (εἰμι) being enclitic (see note on πνεύματί in 1:9).

εἰμι. Unaugmented ind 1st sg εἰμί.

πεπραμένος. Prf pass ptc masc nom sg πιπράσκω (predicate adjective). The participle is appositional to σάρκινός. Some may see εἰμι πεπραμένος as a periphrastic construction, but the syntax here reflects εἰμι as belonging to ἐγὼ ... σάρκινός (parallel word order to ὁ νόμος πνευματικός ἐστιν), and πεπραμένος as appositional to σάρκινός. The stative aspect depicts a state of being sold.

ὑπὸ τὴν ἁμαρτίαν. Locative ("beneath sin") or subordination ("under the power of sin").

7:15 ὃ γὰρ κατεργάζομαι οὐ γινώσκω· οὐ γὰρ ὃ θέλω τοῦτο πράσσω, ἀλλ' ὃ μισῶ τοῦτο ποιῶ.

ὃ. The relative pronoun introduces a headless relative clause (ὃ γὰρ κατεργάζομαι) that serves as direct object of γινώσκω. Fronted for prominence. Within the relative clause, ὃ is the accusative direct object of κατεργάζομαι. This relative pronoun has no anaphoric or cataphoric reference in the co-text; it is abstract (same for the remainder of this section), in the sense that there is no precise identification of what Paul does or does not do here.

γὰρ. Postpositive explanatory conjunction. It introduces an explanation of the previous statement that Paul is fleshly, sold under sin.

κατεργάζομαι. Pres mid ind 1st sg κατεργάζομαι. Finite predicate within a secondary (relative) clause.

οὐ. Negative particle normally used with indicative verbs. Here it negates γινώσκω.

γινώσκω. Pres act ind 1st sg γινώσκω.

οὐ . . . ἀλλ'. A point/counterpoint set ("not this . . . but that") that creates a strong contrast between what Paul wants to do but does not do with what Paul hates and does anyway. The negative particle does not belong to the relative clause but negates the main predicate πράσσω.

γὰρ. Postpositive explanatory conjunction. It introduces an explanation for Paul's previous statement that he does not know what he does.

ὅ. The relative pronoun introduces a headless relative clause (ὃ θέλω) which stands in apposition to τοῦτο. Within the relative clause, ὅ is the accusative direct object of θέλω. This construction (relative clause—appositional pronoun—main predicate, in whatever order) is not uncommon in the Greek NT and should be considered conventional syntax due to its frequency (cf. Runge 2010, 287–313, who would label this a "left-dislocation"). The fronting of the relative clause and use of the appositional pronoun is not simply syntactical but a semantic decision to mark the relative clause and pronominal referent for prominence.

θέλω. Pres act ind 1st sg θέλω.

τοῦτο. Accusative direct object of πράσσω. The demonstrative pronoun is appositional to the headless relative clause (ὃ θέλω). Its position before the main predicate indicates prominence.

πράσσω. Pres act ind 1st sg πράσσω.

ὅ. The relative pronoun introduces a headless relative clause (ὃ μισῶ) which is the direct object of ποιῶ and is appositional to τοῦτο. Within the relative clause, ὅ is the accusative direct object of μισῶ.

μισῶ. Pres act ind 1st sg μισέω. It is parallel (in antonymy) with θέλω in this verse.

τοῦτο. Accusative direct object of ποιῶ. The demonstrative pronoun is appositional to the headless relative clause (ὃ μισῶ). Its position before the main predicate indicates prominence.

ποιῶ. Pres act ind 1st sg ποιέω. It is noteworthy that Paul uses a synonym rather than repeat πράσσω here. The difference is more than "style." ποιέω is more semantically wide-ranging than πράσσω. The latter, as used in the New Testament, refers to the practice of something, usually accompanied by an object (in the accusative case). The former is broad and used in a number of contexts.

7:16 εἰ δὲ ὃ οὐ θέλω τοῦτο ποιῶ, σύμφημι τῷ νόμῳ ὅτι καλός.

εἰ. Introduces the protasis of a first-class conditional.

δὲ. Adversative conjunction (mild).

ὃ. The relative pronoun introduces a headless relative clause (ὃ οὐ θέλω) which stands in apposition to τοῦτο. Within the relative clause, ὃ is the accusative direct object of θέλω (see note on 7:15 of the same relative pronoun.)

οὐ. Negative particle normally used with indicative verbs. Here it negates θέλω.

θέλω. Pres act ind 1st sg θέλω.

τοῦτο. Accusative direct object of ποιῶ. The demonstrative pronoun is appositional to the headless relative clause (ὃ οὐ θέλω). Its fronting before the predicate depicts prominence.

ποιῶ. Pres act ind 1st sg ποιέω.

σύμφημι. Pres act ind 1st sg σύμφημι. A NT *hapax legomenon*. This predicate begins the apodosis.

τῷ νόμῳ. Dative of respect (association). Paul "agrees" with respect to the law.

ὅτι. Introduces the clausal complement (indirect discourse) of σύμφημι. It signals the content of what Paul agrees with.

καλός. Nominative absolute. An example of a one-word clause (cf. Rom 6:17). It cannot be a predicate adjective since no predicate is attached or elided in this co-text. It refers to the law being good. Semantically, this means that while Paul goes against the law in doing what he does not want to do, the law still stands as good (cf. Porter 2015, 149–50, for further explanation on the meaning of this).

7:17 νυνὶ δὲ οὐκέτι ἐγὼ κατεργάζομαι αὐτὸ ἀλλ᾽ ἡ οἰκοῦσα ἐν ἐμοὶ ἁμαρτία.

νυνὶ. Adverb (temporal).

δὲ. Adversative conjunction (mild).

οὐκέτι … ἀλλ᾽. A point/counterpoint set that contrasts ἐγὼ with ἡ ἁμαρτία.

ἐγὼ. Nominative subject of κατεργάζομαι. The use of pronoun here is emphatic since the subject is implied in the verb form.

κατεργάζομαι. Pres mid ind 1st sg κατεργάζομαι (cf. use of the same lexeme in 7:15 for lexical cohesion).

αὐτὸ. Accusative direct object of κατεργάζομαι. The intensive pronoun refers anaphorically to ὃ οὐ θέλω.

ἡ . . . ἁμαρτία. Nominative subject of verbless clause.

οἰκοῦσα ἐν ἐμοὶ. This embedded participial clause between the article ἡ and noun ἁμαρτία modifies the noun in a strong attributive relationship.

οἰκοῦσα. Pres act ptc fem nom sg οἰκέω (attributive). The participle modifies ἡ . . . ἁμαρτία in attributive structure (first attributive position).

ἐν ἐμοὶ. Locative (sphere or realm).

7:18 Οἶδα γὰρ ὅτι οὐκ οἰκεῖ ἐν ἐμοί, τοῦτ᾽ ἔστιν ἐν τῇ σαρκί μου, ἀγα-θόν· τὸ γὰρ θέλειν παράκειταί μοι, τὸ δὲ κατεργάζεσθαι τὸ καλὸν οὔ·

Οἶδα. Prf act ind 1st sg οἶδα. The stative aspect depicts Paul being in a state of knowing.

γὰρ. Postpositive explanatory conjunction. It introduces an explanation of Paul's previous statement that sin lives in him.

ὅτι. Introduces the clausal complement (indirect discourse) of Οἶδα. The clause is used to state the content of what Paul knows.

οὐκ. Negative particle normally used with indicative verbs. Here it negates οἰκεῖ.

οἰκεῖ. Pres act ind 3rd sg οἰκέω.

ἐν ἐμοί. Locative (sphere or realm).

τοῦτ᾽ ἔστιν ἐν τῇ σαρκί μου. This is an embedded clause within the clause οὐκ οἰκεῖ ἐν ἐμοί . . . ἀγαθόν. The pronominal reference functions as epexegetical to ἐμοί, with the rest of the embedded clause further describing ἐμοί.

τοῦτ᾽. Nominative subject of ἔστιν. The demonstrative pronoun refers anaphorically to ἐμοί.

ἔστιν. Unaugmented ind 3rd sg εἰμί.

ἐν τῇ σαρκί. Locative (sphere or realm).

μου. Possessive genitive, modifying τῇ σαρκί.

ἀγαθόν. Nominative subject of οἰκεῖ. ἀγαθόν functions as a substantival adjective.

τὸ . . . θέλειν. Pres act inf θέλω (substantival). The articular infinitive functions as the subject of παράκειταί. With the article, this lexeme functions substantively, yet retaining the verbal sense of "to will."

γὰρ. Postpositive explanatory conjunction. It introduces a clause that continues the explanation of Paul's internal and external struggles between his desire and actions.

παράκειταί. Pres mid ind 3rd sg παράκειμαι. The additional accent on the ultima is due to the following word being enclitic (see note on πνεύματί in 1:9).

μοι. Locative dative.

τὸ . . . κατεργάζεσθαι. Pres mid inf κατεργάζομαι (substantival). The articular infinitive functions as the subject of verbless clause (through grammatical cohesion, the implied verb would be πάράκειται).

δὲ. Adversative conjunction (mild).

τὸ καλὸν. Accusative direct object of κατεργάζεσθαι.

οὔ. Negative particle. It negates the implied πάράκειται. This particle is accented (when it usually is not) because it is used to mean "no" at the end of a sentence (Porter, Reed, and O'Donnell, 14 n. 12).

7:19 οὐ γὰρ ὃ θέλω ποιῶ ἀγαθόν, ἀλλὰ ὃ οὐ θέλω κακὸν τοῦτο πράσσω.

οὐ . . . ἀλλὰ. Point/counterpoint set ("not this . . . but that") that contrasts the desire to do good with the practice of doing evil. The negative particle negates the main predicate ποιῶ.

γὰρ. Postpositive explanatory conjunction. It introduces a clause that continues the explanation of Paul's internal and external struggles between his desire and actions.

ὃ θέλω. This is an embedded clause within οὐ . . . ποιῶ, functioning as a modifier of the main clause in an attributive structure.

ὃ. Accusative object of θέλω. The relative pronoun is headless (unspecified referent), although some may interpret it as a referent to τὸ καλὸν in 7:18, but this is inconsistent with previous instances of the relative pronoun in the co-text.

θέλω. Pres act ind 1st sg θέλω.

ποιῶ. Pres act ind 1st sg ποιέω.

ἀγαθόν. Accusative in apposition to ὃ θέλω. The substantival adjective elaborates ὃ θέλω.

ὃ οὐ θέλω. As a secondary (subordinate) clause appearing before the primary (main) clause, it is prominent through clause-structure.

ὃ. Accusative direct object of θέλω.

οὐ. Negative particle normally used with indicative verbs. Here it negates θέλω.

θέλω. Pres act ind 1st sg θέλω.

κακὸν. Accusative in apposition to ὃ οὐ θέλω. The substantival adjective elaborates ὃ οὐ θέλω.

τοῦτο. Accusative direct object of πράσσω (for an explanation of the synonymous use of ποιέω and πράσσω, see 7:15 on ποιῶ). It is also a cohesive reference in apposition to both ὃ οὐ θέλω and κακὸν.

πράσσω. Pres act ind 1st sg πράσσω.

7:20 εἰ δὲ ὃ οὐ θέλω [ἐγὼ] τοῦτο ποιῶ, οὐκέτι ἐγὼ κατεργάζομαι αὐτὸ ἀλλὰ ἡ οἰκοῦσα ἐν ἐμοὶ ἁμαρτία.

εἰ. Introduces the protasis of a first-class conditional.

δὲ. Adversative conjunction (mild).

ὃ. The relative pronoun introduces a headless relative clause (ὃ οὐ θέλω) which stands in apposition to τοῦτο. Within its clause, ὃ is the accusative direct object of θέλω. The fronting of the relative clause indicates clausal prominence (see note on 7:15 of the same relative pronoun).

οὐ. Negative particle normally used with indicative verbs. Here it negates θέλω.

θέλω. Pres act ind 1st sg θέλω.

[ἐγὼ]. Nominative subject of ποιῶ. The use of the personal pronoun is emphatic here. The major manuscripts that include this word include ℵ and A; the major ones that do not are B, C, D, F, and G.

τοῦτο. Accusative direct object of ποιῶ. The demonstrative pronoun refers anaphorically to ὃ οὐ θέλω.

ποιῶ. Pres act ind 1st sg ποιέω.

οὐκέτι . . . ἀλλὰ. A point/counterpoint set that contrasts ἐγὼ with ἡ οἰκοῦσα ἐν ἐμοὶ ἁμαρτία. οὐκέτι is a negative temporal adverb ("no longer") that marks the beginning of the apodosis of the conditional clause.

ἐγὼ. Nominative subject of κατεργάζομαι. The use of the personal pronoun here indicates emphasis.

κατεργάζομαι. Pres mid ind 1st sg κατεργάζομαι.

αὐτὸ. Accusative direct object of κατεργάζομαι. The intensive pronoun is a cohesive referent to ὃ οὐ θέλω.

ἡ οἰκοῦσα ἐν ἐμοὶ ἁμαρτία. This word group consists of the article (ἡ), the modifier (οἰκοῦσα ἐν ἐμοὶ), and the noun (ἁμαρτία). The participle along with the prepositional word group as a unit serves as a modifier, especially as embedded between the article and noun.

ἡ . . . ἁμαρτία. Nominative subject of verbless clause. The implied predicate would be κατεργάζομαι.

οἰκοῦσα. Pres act ptc fem nom sg οἰκέω (attributive). The participle modifies ἡ . . . ἁμαρτία in attributive structure (first attributive position).

ἐν ἐμοὶ. Locative (sphere or realm).

7:21 εὑρίσκω ἄρα τὸν νόμον, τῷ θέλοντι ἐμοὶ ποιεῖν τὸ καλόν, ὅτι ἐμοὶ τὸ κακὸν παράκειται·

εὑρίσκω. Pres act ind 1st sg εὑρίσκω.

ἄρα. Inferential conjunction. It usually occupies the first position of the clause, but here it is postpositive.

τὸν νόμον. Accusative direct object of εὑρίσκω.

τῷ θέλοντι. Pres act ptc masc dat sg θέλω (substantival). Dative of sphere or locative dative. Its head term is τὸν νόμον, so it refers to the wanting/desire in locative relation to the law. In other words, in contrast to most English translations, Paul is stating that he has found the law in his inner desire to do good, because evil is right there with him. In addition, instead of Paul using a noun here, he uses a participle in order to highlight the verbal quality of "wanting," "willing," or "desiring" (a form of grammatical metaphor in Greek, in which an entity becomes a process, and hence has the features of a process or verb). This interpretation fits well with the following verse.

ἐμοί. Dative of sphere or locative dative. It is the willing or desire "in me."

ποιεῖν. Pres act inf ποιέω (complementary). The infinitive modifies θέλοντι in a catenative structure. Although θέλοντι functions in the clause as a substantive, the semantics of the verbal element of the participle allows for it to be in a catenative construction.

τὸ καλόν. Accusative direct object of ποιεῖν. τὸ καλόν is substantival adjective.

ὅτι. Introduces a nominal clause that stands in apposition to τὸν νόμον: "I find the law in the desire in me to do good, namely, that evil is present with me." In other words, the law (or the principle) that Paul finds in himself is that when he wants to do good, evil lies close at hand (cf. NRSV).

ἐμοί. Dative of sphere or locative dative. Relates to παράκειται.

τὸ κακὸν. Nominative subject of παράκειται. τὸ κακὸν is substantival adjective.

παράκειται. Pres mid ind 3rd sg παράκειμαι.

7:22 συνήδομαι γὰρ τῷ νόμῳ τοῦ θεοῦ κατὰ τὸν ἔσω ἄνθρωπον,

συνήδομαι. Pres mid ind 1st sg συνήδομαι. A NT *hapax legomenon*.

γὰρ. Postpositive explanatory conjunction. It introduces a clause that further explains the previous statement that Paul found the law in his desire to do good.

τῷ νόμῳ. Dative complement of συνήδομαι. The object of Paul's delight is "the law of God." The "law of God" is distinguished from the Old Testament Law, in that the modifier θεοῦ defines the law as being a divine set of principles (cf. notes on 7:7).

τοῦ θεοῦ. Genitive of source or origin, modifying τῷ νόμῳ.

κατὰ τὸν ... ἄνθρωπον. Standard or basis. The standard by which Paul delights in the law of God is "the inner person."

ἔσω. Adverb (positional). Its placement between the article (τὸν) and substantive (ἄνθρωπον) reflects attribution to the substantive.

7:23 βλέπω δὲ ἕτερον νόμον ἐν τοῖς μέλεσίν μου ἀντιστρατευόμενον τῷ νόμῳ τοῦ νοός μου καὶ αἰχμαλωτίζοντά με ἐν τῷ νόμῳ τῆς ἁμαρτίας τῷ ὄντι ἐν τοῖς μέλεσίν μου.

βλέπω. Pres act ind 1st sg βλέπω.

δὲ. Adversative conjunction (mild).

ἕτερον νόμον. Accusative direct object of βλέπω.

ἐν τοῖς μέλεσίν. Locative (sphere or realm). The sphere in which he sees another law is "in my members," or in his outer person, in contrast to τὸν ἔσω ἄνθρωπον.

μου. Possessive genitive, modifying τοῖς μέλεσίν.

ἀντιστρατευόμενον. Pres mid ptc masc acc sg ἀντιστρατεύομαι (attributive). The participle modifies νόμον (fourth attributive position). ἀντιστρατεύομαι and αἰχμαλωτίζω (see below) are words reflected in the domain of Roman military, eliciting warfare metaphor here.

τῷ νόμῳ. Dative direct object of ἀντιστρατευόμενον. The object of "warring against" is "the law of my mind."

τοῦ νοός. Genitive of description, modifying τῷ νόμῳ. It further describes or circumscribes "the law" as "of my mind."

μου. Possessive genitive, modifying τοῦ νοός.

καὶ. Coordinating conjunction. It connects the two participial clauses (ἀντιστρατευόμενον and αἰχμαλωτίζοντά).

αἰχμαλωτίζοντά. Pres act ptc masc acc sg αἰχμαλωτίζω (attributive). The participle modifies νόμον (fourth attributive position). The domain of this lexeme is Roman military (see ἀντιστρατευόμενον above).

με. Accusative direct object of αἰχμαλωτίζοντά.

ἐν τῷ νόμῳ. Locative (sphere or realm). The sphere in which Paul is taken captive is "the law of sin."

τῆς ἁμαρτίας. Genitive of description, modifying τῷ νόμῳ. It further describes or circumscribes "the law" as "of sin."

τῷ ὄντι ἐν τοῖς μέλεσίν μου. This word group stands as one unit. The article τῷ modifies the participle ὄντι and the following prepositional word group to make the entire word group function as an attributive adjective modifying τῷ νόμῳ τῆς ἁμαρτίας. A rough literal translation might be "the being-in-my-members."

τῷ ὄντι. Ptc masc dat sg εἰμί (attributive). The participle modifies τῷ νόμῳ (second attributive position). The use of the εἰμί participle here highlights the "beingness" of the law of sin in his members.

ἐν τοῖς μέλεσίν. Locative (sphere or realm). The prepositional word group refers to his outer person, in contrast with his inner person.

μου. Possessive genitive, modifying τοῖς μέλεσίν.

7:24 Ταλαίπωρος ἐγὼ ἄνθρωπος· τίς με ῥύσεται ἐκ τοῦ σώματος τοῦ θανάτου τούτου;

Ταλαίπωρος ἐγὼ ἄνθρωπος. While most translations reflect Paul being exasperated or Paul highlighting his wretchedness (and perhaps use an exclamation mark), it is most likely that Paul is simply stating a logical conclusion from what he has been arguing so far in this chapter regarding the battle between the inner and outer person (cf. Porter 2015, 152). We could translate with the more matter-of-fact "I [am] a wretched person," but we try to preserve the word order: "Wretched person I [am]."

Ταλαίπωρος . . . ἄνθρωπος. Predicate nominative.

ἐγώ. Nominative subject of verbless clause. Although a sequence of three nominatives occurs here, making it difficult to interpret, ἐγώ is the subject, since the first occurring nominative is an attributive adjective, modifying ἄνθρωπος. This would make ταλαίπωρος being fronted prominent in this clause.

τίς. Nominative subject of ῥύσεται. τίς is an interrogative pronoun. The question introduced by τίς reflects Paul's dialogical style throughout this letter. There is, however, no explicit answer to the question posed.

με. Accusative direct object of ῥύσεται.

ῥύσεται. Fut mid ind 3rd sg ῥύομαι. The future form grammaticalizes the semantic feature of expectation. In other words, Paul is asking who is expected to rescue him from the body of this death.

ἐκ τοῦ σώματος . . . τούτου. Locative (movement away from/separation). Paul uses a synonym σῶμα here for μέλος (see the previous verse). The demonstrative pronoun is placed at the end of this nominal unit because it modifies the entire phrase: "this body of death."

τοῦ θανάτου. Genitive of description, modifying τοῦ σώματος . . . τούτου. Paul describes or circumscribes "this body" as "of death," as a characterization of the outer person.

7:25 χάρις δὲ τῷ θεῷ διὰ Ἰησοῦ Χριστοῦ τοῦ κυρίου ἡμῶν. Ἄρα οὖν αὐτὸς ἐγὼ τῷ μὲν νοῒ δουλεύω νόμῳ θεοῦ τῇ δὲ σαρκὶ νόμῳ ἁμαρτίας.

χάρις. Nominative absolute. See note on 6:17 for the same construction (χάρις τῷ θεῷ).

δέ. Adversative conjunction (mild).

τῷ θεῷ. Dative of recipient.

διὰ Ἰησοῦ Χριστοῦ. Instrumental. Christ is the instrument by which God is given thanks. Throughout this letter, Paul uses this (or a similar) formulaic phrasing in co-texts where significant episodes are highlighted (cf. Rom 1:4; 5:1, 11, 21; also 15:6, 30; 16:20). These co-texts in which this phrasing appears identify the work of Christ by which God accomplishes his purposes.

τοῦ κυρίου. Genitive in apposition to Ἰησοῦ Χριστοῦ.

ἡμῶν. Possessive genitive, modifying τοῦ κυρίου.

Ἄρα οὖν. A combination of two inferential conjunctions (see 5:18). The inference is not from the immediate statement of thanks to God but from the statement in the previous co-text on the inner person and outer person.

αὐτὸς ἐγώ. Nominative subject of δουλεύω. αὐτὸς is an intensive pronoun ("I myself"). Together with αὐτὸς, ἐγὼ is emphatic, which is an appropriate conclusion to Paul's discussion on his internal and external struggles.

τῷ . . . νοΐ. Dative of sphere or locative dative. The sphere of serving as slave, here, is "the mind."

μὲν . . . δὲ. A point/counterpoint set that contrasts the two clauses. On the one hand, he serves the law of God in his mind, but on the other hand, he serves the law of sin in his flesh.

δουλεύω. Pres act ind 1st sg δουλεύω.

νόμῳ. Dative direct object of δουλεύω. The object of serving as a slave is the "law of God" (cf. 7:22).

θεοῦ. Genitive of source or origin, modifying νόμῳ.

δὲ. Adversative conjunction (mild).

τῇ . . . σαρκὶ. Dative of sphere or locative dative. The sphere of serving as a slave (elliptical reference from previous clause), here, is the flesh. σάρξ is another synonym for μέρος and σῶμα in this co-text, all referring to the outer person from different perspectives.

νόμῳ. Dative direct object of an implied δουλεύω. The object of being a slave is the "law of sin." There is no specific "law" of sin (this is the only instance of this word group in the New Testament) and so refers to a general principle of sin, parallel to the divine principles of God (νόμος θεοῦ).

ἁμαρτίας. Genitive of source or origin, modifying νόμῳ, parallel to νόμῳ θεοῦ.

Romans 8:1–17

[1]Therefore, no condemnation now [exists] for those who are in Christ Jesus. [2]For the law of the Spirit of the life in Christ Jesus has freed you from the law of sin and death. [3]For the powerlessness of the law in which it was weak through the flesh, God—sending his own Son in the likeness of sinful flesh and concerning sin—condemned sin in the flesh, [4]so that the just requirement of the law may be fulfilled among us who live not according to the flesh but according to the Spirit. [5]For those who exist according to the flesh think about the [things] of the flesh, but those who are according to the Spirit, the [things] of the Spirit. [6]For the way of thinking of the flesh [is] death, but the way of thinking of the Spirit [is] life and peace. [7]Therefore, the way of thinking of the flesh [is] enmity towards God, for it is not subject to the law of God, for it is not able. [8]And those who are in the flesh are not able to please God. [9]But you are not in flesh but in Spirit, since Spirit of God abides in you. But if anyone does not have Spirit of Christ, he does not belong to him. [10]But if Christ [is] in you, the body [is] dead on account of sin, but the Spirit [is] life on account of righteousness. [11]But if the Spirit of the one who raised Jesus from the dead dwells in you, the one who raised Jesus from the dead will also bring life to your mortal bodies through his indwelling Spirit in you. [12]Then, therefore, brothers [and sisters], we are debtors, not in the flesh so as to live according to the flesh, [13]for if you live according to the flesh, you are going to die; but if by the Spirit you put to death the acts of the body, you will live. [14]For whoever is led by the Spirit of God, these are sons of God. [15]For you did not receive a spirit of slavery again into fear, but you received a spirit of adoptive sonship by which we cry, "Abba, Father." [16]The Spirit himself testifies with our spirit that we are children of God, [17]and if children, also heirs; heirs of God and co-heirs with Christ, if indeed we suffer with [him], in order that we might also be glorified with [him].

This section marks a major sectional break in the body of the letter, from the conclusion of the third major section to the fourth. The fourth major part of the body consists of Romans 8, before turning to Romans 9–11 for a retrogression on Israel. While some may wish to label this the denouement, in the sense that Paul pulls his arguments in the previous chapters together, it also contains further development of the previous arguments and implications for the Christian life. In fact, the entirety of chapter 8 is devoted to Paul's exposition of the means to live life in the Spirit. On the one hand, Paul looks back to take up a number of unresolved issues regarding the Christian life, but on the other hand, he looks forward to the next stage or step in the Christian life. Unique to this section, in comparison to previous sections, is the lack of diatribe that Paul had used to formulate his arguments, although he continues to utilize parallelism in his presentation of his arguments.

Romans 8 is divided into two major sections, 8:1–17 and 8:18–30, before Paul closes the section with a doxology in 8:31–29. This first section, 8:1–17, is concerned with describing life in the Spirit. This section directly addresses the issue raised in the previous major section of the body of the letter, 6:1–7:25, regarding the nature of the Christian life, including both its incorporation into Christ and its continuing struggles with sin, as one that is to be lived in the life of the Spirit. This section speaks of the presence of the Spirit of God or Christ as the means by which a person lives not according to the flesh. While Romans 5 (especially vv. 9–11) is likely the prominent peak of the entire letter, this section (8:1–17) can be considered a sub-peak, a lesser prominent peak but nevertheless a peak in the body of the letter (cf. Lee). The section itself can be divided into two further sections, 8:1–11 and 8:12–17, each of them marked by a strong transition to indicate the shift in the argument.

8:1 Οὐδὲν ἄρα νῦν κατάκριμα τοῖς ἐν Χριστῷ Ἰησοῦ.

Οὐδὲν . . . κατάκριμα. Nominative absolute. The negative pronoun Οὐδὲν can function pronominally or adjectivally, here adjectivally, modifying κατάκριμα (cf. Luke 4:24; John 10:41 for the negative pronoun functioning adjectivally; Porter 1994a, 138). The substantive κατάκριμα (with adjectival negation, conjunction, and adverb) forms its own clause, with English translations supplying a "to be" verb or the like (e.g., "no condemnation exists" or "there is no condemnation"). The nominative absolute is not uncommon to Paul (cf. Rom 6:17; 7:16, 25; 11:33; 2 Cor 5:17; Col 3:17) and is sometimes used to make a terse but impactful statement. This lexeme exists within the domain of legal/court language.

ἄρα. Inferential conjunction. The inference stems not only from the immediate co-text but also from the larger co-text in the previous chapter where Paul contrasts his inner self with his outer self.

νῦν. Adverb (temporal).

τοῖς ἐν Χριστῷ Ἰησοῦ. The article functions as a nominalizer, changing the prepositional word group ἐν Χριστῷ Ἰησοῦ into a dative of advantage. This substantival word group indicates that the subject that Paul addresses in the previous sections (chs. 6–7) consists of Christians.

ἐν Χριστῷ Ἰησοῦ. Locative (figurative sphere or realm). This word group has only been used three other times in the letter so far (3:24; 6:11, 23; see notes there).

8:2 ὁ γὰρ νόμος τοῦ πνεύματος τῆς ζωῆς ἐν Χριστῷ Ἰησοῦ ἠλευθέρω-σέν σε ἀπὸ τοῦ νόμου τῆς ἁμαρτίας καὶ τοῦ θανάτου.

ὁ . . . νόμος. Nominative subject of ἠλευθέρωσέν. The articular substantive picks up on the previously mentioned "law of God."

γὰρ. Postpositive conjunction that introduces the explanation, or reason, for why no condemnation exists for those in Christ Jesus.

τοῦ πνεύματος. Genitive of description, modifying ὁ . . . νόμος. It further describes or circumscribes "law" as "of the Spirit." Previously, Paul has referred to "the law of God," but here he refers to "the law of the Spirit." The former refers to the divine law or principles that God has set forth, and here it probably refers to the same, except in reference to the Holy Spirit. Paul describes the work of the Holy Spirit in this letter in various ways (cf. 1:4; 5:5; 7:6). Here, he describes the Spirit's work as life-giving in Christ Jesus (cf. Porter 2015, 157).

τῆς ζωῆς. Genitive of quality, modifying τοῦ πνεύματος. The quality of "life" is attributed to "the Spirit." Paul continues to link the Spirit with life in this section (cf. Rom 8:6, 10).

ἐν Χριστῷ Ἰησοῦ. Locative (sphere or realm; cf. 8:1). The prepositional word group likely modifies ἠλευθέρωσέν, indicating the being "set free" is in the realm of Christ Jesus. The contrast is with ἀπὸ τοῦ νόμου: they are set free, in Christ Jesus and (away) from the law. The repetition of ἐν Χριστῷ Ἰησοῦ from the previous verse serves as a cohesive device for emphasis or prominence in the discourse.

ἠλευθέρωσέν. Aor act ind 3rd sg ἐλευθερόω. The additional accent on the ultima is due to the following word being an enclitic (see note on πνεύματί in 1:9).

σε. Accusative direct object of ἠλευθέρωσέν. σε is a cohesive reference to τοῖς ἐν Χριστῷ Ἰησοῦ. He likely uses the singular personal pronoun to address those who are in Christ Jesus, rather than use the plural to include all of his readers (since some of his readers may not be in Christ Jesus). A textual variant (με) is unlikely due to the fact that Paul has transitioned from himself as the major topic of Romans 7 to "those in Christ Jesus," i.e., "you" in Romans 8.

ἀπὸ τοῦ νόμου. Locative (movement away from/separation).

τῆς ἁμαρτίας καὶ τοῦ θανάτου. Genitives of description, modifying τοῦ νόμου. They further describe or circumscribe "law" as "of sin and of death." The articular genitives connected by καὶ particularize the previously mentioned sin and death in the previous co-text.

8:3 Τὸ γὰρ ἀδύνατον τοῦ νόμου ἐν ᾧ ἠσθένει διὰ τῆς σαρκός, ὁ θεὸς τὸν ἑαυτοῦ υἱὸν πέμψας ἐν ὁμοιώματι σαρκὸς ἁμαρτίας καὶ περὶ ἁμαρτίας κατέκρινεν τὴν ἁμαρτίαν ἐν τῇ σαρκί,

Τὸ . . . ἀδύνατον. Accusative in apposition to τὴν ἁμαρτίαν ἐν τῇ σαρκί at the end of this verse. Τὸ . . . ἀδύνατον is a substantival adjective. It is fronted in the clause-complex for prominence.

γὰρ. Postpositive explanatory conjunction. It introduces an explanation of the law of sin and death mentioned in the previous verse.

τοῦ νόμου. Genitive of description, modifying Τὸ . . . ἀδύνατον. It describes or circumscribes "impossibility" as "the law." Some may wish to label this as a subjective genitive, if τὸ . . . ἀδύνατον is seen as a verbal process (cf. NASB "the Law could not do").

ἐν ᾧ. Instrumental. The dative relative pronoun refers anaphorically to Τὸ . . . ἀδύνατον.

ἠσθένει. Impf act ind 3rd sg ἀσθενέω. The subject of this predicate is not specified, although it is likely a referent to the law.

διὰ τῆς σαρκός. Instrumental. The agent (instrument) of being weak (ἠσθένει) is "the flesh."

ὁ θεὸς. Nominative subject of κατέκρινεν.

τὸν ἑαυτοῦ υἱὸν πέμψας ἐν ὁμοιώματι σαρκὸς ἁμαρτίας καὶ περὶ ἁμαρτίας. Embedded clause within the main clause: ὁ θεὸς . . . κατέκρινεν τὴν ἁμαρτίαν ἐν τῇ σαρκί.

τὸν ἑαυτοῦ υἱὸν. Accusative direct object of πέμψας. The placement of ἑαυτοῦ between the article and noun reflects its emphasis in the word group. Also, the fronting of the accusative word group before its predicator (πέμψας) reflects its emphasis in the embedded clause.

πέμψας. Aor act ptc masc nom sg πέμπω (means). The participle modifies κατέκρινεν and functions as circumstantial in the co-text.

ἐν ὁμοιώματι. Locative (sphere or realm).

σαρκὸς. Genitive of description, modifying ὁμοιώματι. It further describes or circumscribes "likeness" as "flesh."

ἁμαρτίας. Genitive of quality, modifying σαρκὸς. The quality of "sin" is restricted to "flesh" (e.g., "sinful flesh").

καὶ. Coordinating conjunction. It connects ἐν ὁμοιώματι σαρκὸς ἁμαρτίας with περὶ ἁμαρτίας.

περὶ ἁμαρτίας. Reference.

κατέκρινεν. Aor act ind 3rd sg κατακρίνω.

τὴν ἁμαρτίαν. Accusative direct object of κατέκρινεν.

ἐν τῇ σαρκί. Locative (sphere or realm). The sphere in which God condemned sin is "the flesh."

8:4 ἵνα τὸ δικαίωμα τοῦ νόμου πληρωθῇ ἐν ἡμῖν τοῖς μὴ κατὰ σάρκα περιπατοῦσιν ἀλλὰ κατὰ πνεῦμα.

ἵνα. Introduces a purpose clause. The purpose of God condemning sin in the flesh (from previous verse) is laid out.

τὸ δικαίωμα. Nominative subject of πληρωθῇ (cf. Rom 1:32; 2:26; 5:16, 18). However, while this is the grammatical subject of the clause, it is not the agent but the Goal of the predicate πληρωθῇ; in other words, the conceptual (not grammatical) object of "fulfilling" is the "just requirement of the law."

τοῦ νόμου. Genitive of source of origin, modifying τὸ δικαίωμα. The just requirement comes from the law.

πληρωθῇ. Aor pass subj 3rd sg πληρόω. Subjunctive with ἵνα. The agent of the passive voice verb is not specified in this immediate co-text, but the previous co-text indicates that it is God.

ἐν ἡμῖν. Distributional ("among us"; cf. Porter 1994a, 156–57).

τοῖς . . . περιπατοῦσιν. Pres act ptc masc dat pl περιπατέω (substantival). Dative in apposition to ἡμῖν.

μὴ . . . ἀλλά. A point/counterpoint set that contrasts κατὰ σάρκα with κατὰ πνεῦμα.

κατὰ σάρκα. Standard. The standard, or basis, by which the Christians live is not the flesh. While σάρξ itself does not have any pejorative meaning, in this context, contrasted with πνεῦμα, it has a pejorative sense.

κατὰ πνεῦμα. Standard. The standard, or basis, by which the Christians live is the Spirit (in juxtaposition with the flesh).

8:5 οἱ γὰρ κατὰ σάρκα ὄντες τὰ τῆς σαρκὸς φρονοῦσιν, οἱ δὲ κατὰ πνεῦμα τὰ τοῦ πνεύματος.

οἱ . . . κατὰ σάρκα ὄντες. Nominative subject of φρονοῦσιν. The embedded prepositional word group κατὰ σάρκα taken as a single unit functions attributively in the nominal word group.

οἱ . . . ὄντες. Ptc masc nom pl εἰμί (substantival).

κατὰ σάρκα. Standard.

γάρ. Postpositive explanatory conjunction that marks the continuation of the explanation from 8:2 and 8:3.

τὰ τῆς σαρκὸς. The article functions as a nominalizer, changing the genitive phrase τῆς σαρκὸς into the accusative direct object of φρονοῦσιν ("the [things] of the flesh").

τῆς σαρκὸς. Possessive genitive. It refers to things that belong to the flesh.

φρονοῦσιν. Pres act ind 3rd pl φρονέω.

οἱ . . . κατὰ πνεῦμα. The article functions as a nominalizer, changing the prepositional word group κατὰ πνεῦμα into the nominative subject of an elided φρονοῦσιν ("those according to the Spirit").

κατὰ πνεῦμα. Standard.

δὲ. Adversative conjunction (mild).

τὰ τοῦ πνεύματος. The article functions as a nominalizer, changing the genitive word group τοῦ πνεύματος into the accusative direct object of the elided φρονοῦσιν from the previous clause ("the [things] of the Spirit"). Parallel to τὰ τῆς σαρκὸς above.

τοῦ πνεύματος. Possessive genitive. It refers to the things belonging to the Spirit.

8:6 τὸ γὰρ φρόνημα τῆς σαρκὸς θάνατος, τὸ δὲ φρόνημα τοῦ πνεύματος ζωὴ καὶ εἰρήνη·

τὸ . . . φρόνημα. Nominative subject of verbless clause. A "to be" verb can be supplied in an English translation. The nominal form of φρονέω (see the previous verse) is used here to reflect cohesion between these verses.

γὰρ. Explanatory conjunction. It introduces a continued explanation of Paul's line of argument in this co-text.

τῆς σαρκὸς. Genitive of source or origin, modifying τὸ . . . φρόνημα. The "way of thinking" comes from the flesh.

θάνατος. Predicate nominative.

τὸ . . . φρόνημα. Nominative subject of verbless clause. A "to be" verb can be supplied in an English translation.

δὲ. Adversative conjunction (mild). It connects the clause before and after it.

τοῦ πνεύματος. Genitive of source or origin, modifying τὸ . . . φρόνημα. The "way of thinking" comes from the Spirit here.

ζωὴ. Predicate nominative.

καὶ. Coordinating conjunction. It connects ζωὴ with εἰρήνη.

εἰρήνη. Predicate nominative.

8:7 διότι τὸ φρόνημα τῆς σαρκὸς ἔχθρα εἰς θεόν, τῷ γὰρ νόμῳ τοῦ θεοῦ οὐχ ὑποτάσσεται, οὐδὲ γὰρ δύναται·

διότι. Causal conjunction. The cause of death from the way of thinking of the flesh (or fleshly way of thinking) is that it is hostile towards God.

τὸ φρόνημα. Nominative subject of verbless clause. The repetition of τὸ φρόνημα τῆς σαρκὸς reflects cohesion with the previous co-text (but τὸ φρόνημα τοῦ πνεύματος is not repeated in this verse), signalling focus on this word group.

τῆς σαρκὸς. Genitive of source or origin, modifying τὸ φρόνημα. The "way of thinking" comes from the flesh.

ἔχθρα. Predicate nominative.

εἰς θεόν. Directional (movement toward). The hostility is directed towards God.

τῷ . . . νόμῳ. Dative indirect object of ὑποτάσσεται. The fronting of the prepositional word group in the clause reflects prominence of the word group in the clause.

γὰρ. Postpositive explanatory conjunction that introduces a further explanation of why the fleshly way of thinking is hostile to God.

τοῦ θεοῦ. Genitive of source of origin, modifying τῷ . . . νόμῳ.

οὐχ. Negative particle normally used with indicative verbs. Here it negates ὑποτάσσεται.

ὑποτάσσεται. Pres mid ind 3rd sg ὑποτάσσω. The implied subject is τὸ φρόνημα τῆς σαρκὸς from the previous clause.

οὐδὲ. Negative particle normally used with indicative verbs. Here it negates δύναται.

γὰρ. Postpositive explanatory conjunction that introduces a further explanation of why the fleshly way of thinking does not submit to the law of God.

δύναται. Pres mid ind 3rd sg δύναμαι. The middle voice-form reflects indirect, internal causality—despite the so-called deponent verb (see "Deponency" in the Series Introduction and Introduction).

8:8 οἱ δὲ ἐν σαρκὶ ὄντες θεῷ ἀρέσαι οὐ δύνανται.

οἱ . . . ἐν σαρκὶ ὄντες. Nominative subject of δύνανται. The embedded prepositional word group as a single unit functions attributively in the nominal word group.

οἱ . . . ὄντες. Ptc masc nom pl εἰμί (substantival).

ἐν σαρκὶ. Locative (sphere or realm).

δὲ. Adversative conjunction (mild).

θεῷ. Dative complement of ἀρέσαι.

ἀρέσαι. Aor act inf ἀρέσκω (complementary). The infinitive is a complement of δύνανται, fronted before its head term for prominence.

οὐ. Negative particle normally used with indicative verbs. Here it negates δύνανται.

δύνανται. Pres mid ind 3rd pl δύναμαι.

8:9 Ὑμεῖς δὲ οὐκ ἐστὲ ἐν σαρκὶ ἀλλ᾽ ἐν πνεύματι, εἴπερ πνεῦμα θεοῦ οἰκεῖ ἐν ὑμῖν. εἰ δέ τις πνεῦμα Χριστοῦ οὐκ ἔχει, οὗτος οὐκ ἔστιν αὐτοῦ.

Ὑμεῖς. Nominative subject of ἐστὲ. The use of this personal pronoun here is emphatic. It also begins the apodosis, which is fronted before the protasis to emphasize the apodosis.

δὲ. Adversative conjunction (mild).

οὐκ … ἀλλ᾽. A point/counterpoint set that establishes a contrast between ἐν σαρκὶ and ἐν πνεύματι.

ἐστὲ. Unaugmented ind 2nd pl εἰμί.

ἐν σαρκὶ. Locative (sphere or realm).

ἐν πνεύματι. Locative (sphere or realm).

εἴπερ. Introduces the protasis of a first-class conditional. εἴπερ is an intensive form of εἰ (cf. Porter 1994a, 209). It occurs only in Paul in the New Testament (Rom 3:30; 8:17; 1 Cor 8:5; 15:15; 2 Thess 1:6). The placement of the apodosis before the protasis puts the apodosis in a prominent position (cf. Porter 2009, 71–73; Yoon 2019, 132).

πνεῦμα. Nominative subject of οἰκεῖ.

θεοῦ. Possessive genitive, modifying πνεῦμα.

οἰκεῖ. Pres act ind 3rd sg οἰκέω.

ἐν ὑμῖν. Locative (sphere or realm).

εἰ. Introduces the protasis of a first-class conditional (the second conditional structure in this verse). The order of the protasis before the apodosis is unmarked and thus not prominent.

δέ. Adversative conjunction (mild).

τις. Nominative subject of ἔχει.

πνεῦμα. Accusative direct object of ἔχει.

Χριστοῦ. Possessive genitive, modifying πνεῦμα.

οὐκ. Negative particle normally used with indicative verbs. Here it negates ἔχει.

ἔχει. Pres act ind 3rd sg ἔχω.

οὗτος. Nominative subject of ἔστιν. The demonstrative pronoun refers anaphorically to τις.

οὐκ. Negative particle normally used with indicative verbs. Here it negates ἔστιν.

ἔστιν. Unaugmented ind 3rd sg εἰμί.

αὐτοῦ. Possessive genitive. The personal pronoun refers anaphorically to Christ (matching the gender of the referent).

8:10 εἰ δὲ Χριστὸς ἐν ὑμῖν, τὸ μὲν σῶμα νεκρὸν διὰ ἁμαρτίαν τὸ δὲ πνεῦμα ζωὴ διὰ δικαιοσύνην.

εἰ. Introduces the protasis of a first-class conditional.

δὲ. Adversative conjunction (mild).

Χριστὸς. Nominative subject of verbless clause. A "to be" verb can be supplied in an English translation.

ἐν ὑμῖν. Locative (sphere or realm).

τὸ . . . σῶμα. Nominative subject of verbless clause. It introduces the apodosis of the conditional structure, which consists of two primary clauses (τὸ μὲν σῶμα νεκρὸν διὰ ἁμαρτίαν and τὸ δὲ πνεῦμα ζωὴ διὰ δικαιοσύνην) that are in contrastive relationship to each other.

μὲν . . . δὲ. A point/counterpoint set that establishes the contrast between the body being dead and the Spirit giving life.

νεκρὸν. Predicate adjective.

διὰ ἁμαρτίαν. Causal. The cause of the body being dead is "sin."

τὸ . . . πνεῦμα. Nominative subject of verbless clause.

ζωὴ. Predicate nominative.

διὰ δικαιοσύνην. Causal. The cause of the Spirit giving life is "righteousness."

8:11 εἰ δὲ τὸ πνεῦμα τοῦ ἐγείραντος τὸν Ἰησοῦν ἐκ νεκρῶν οἰκεῖ ἐν ὑμῖν, ὁ ἐγείρας Χριστὸν ἐκ νεκρῶν ζῳοποιήσει καὶ τὰ θνητὰ σώματα ὑμῶν διὰ τοῦ ἐνοικοῦντος αὐτοῦ πνεύματος ἐν ὑμῖν.

εἰ. Introduces the protasis of a first-class conditional.

δὲ. Adversative conjunction (mild). The mild contrast is with the previous conditional structure.

τὸ πνεῦμα. Nominative subject of οἰκεῖ.

τοῦ ἐγείραντος. Aor act ptc masc gen sg ἐγείρω (substantival). Genitive of description, modifying τὸ πνεῦμα. It describes the Spirit as "one who raised Jesus from the dead."

τὸν Ἰησοῦν. Accusative direct object of ἐγείραντος.

ἐκ νεκρῶν. Locative (movement out of/separation). The prepositional word group modifies ἐγείραντος.

οἰκεῖ. Pres act ind 3rd sg οἰκέω.

ἐν ὑμῖν. Locative (sphere or realm). The sphere or realm where the Spirit lives is "in you."

ὁ ἐγείρας. Aor act ptc masc nom sg ἐγείρω (substantival). Nominative subject of ζῳοποιήσει. This begins the apodosis.

Χριστὸν. Accusative direct object of ἐγείρας. The switch from "Jesus" to "Christ" here is not significant and probably just for stylistic variation (cf. Dunn, 1:445–46).

ἐκ νεκρῶν. Locative (movement out of/separation). The prepositional word group modifies ἐγείρας.

ζῳοποιήσει. Fut act ind 3rd sg ζῳοποιέω. The future form grammaticalizes the semantic feature of expectation; the one who raised Jesus is expected to give life.

καὶ. Adverbial use (adjunctive). It modifies ζῳοποιήσει.

τὰ θνητὰ σώματα. Accusative object of ζῳοποιήσει. The adjective θνητός occurs only in Paul in the New Testament (Rom 6:12; 8:11; 1 Cor 15:53, 54; 2 Cor 4:11; 5:4) and reflects that which is subject to death.

ὑμῶν. Possessive genitive, modifying τὰ θνητὰ σώματα.

διὰ τοῦ . . . πνεύματος. Instrumental. The means by which God (the one who raised Christ) gives life to mortal bodies is his indwelling Spirit. There are two textual variants, διά + genitive (διὰ τοῦ ἐνοικοῦντος αὐτοῦ πνεύματος; "through his indwelling Spirit"; ℵ A C Pᶜ) and διά + accusative (διὰ τὸ ἐνοικοῦν αὐτοῦ πνεῦμα; "on account of his indwelling Spirit"; B D F G), but the manuscript tradition favors the genitive reading (cf. Metzger, 456).

ἐνοικοῦντος. Pres act ptc neut gen sg ἐνοικέω (attributive). The participle modifies τοῦ . . . πνεύματος (first attributive position). A cognate of οἰκέω is used here, prefixed by ἐν-, to emphasize the sphere in which the Spirit dwells.

αὐτοῦ. Possessive genitive, modifying τοῦ . . . πνεύματος. The personal pronoun refers anaphorically to τοῦ ἐγείραντος at the beginning of the verse.

ἐν ὑμῖν. Locative (sphere or realm). It is parallel to the same word group as above. The figurative place of the indwelling Spirit is "in you."

8:12 Ἄρα οὖν, ἀδελφοί, ὀφειλέται ἐσμὲν οὐ τῇ σαρκὶ τοῦ κατὰ σάρκα ζῆν,

Ἄρα οὖν. A combination of two inferential conjunctions (see 5:18). The inference is from the previous co-text regarding the Spirit giving life to our mortal bodies.

ἀδελφοί. Nominative of address (so-called vocative).

ὀφειλέται. Predicate nominative. Its position as object before the predicate signifies its prominence.

ἐσμὲν. Unaugmented ind 1st pl εἰμί.

οὐ. Negative particle. It negates τῇ σαρκὶ.

τῇ σαρκὶ. Dative of disadvantage or dative indirect object of ὀφειλέται ἐσμὲν.

τοῦ ... ζῆν. Pres act inf ζάω (epexegetical to ὀφειλέται ἐσμὲν οὐ τῇ σαρκὶ; cf. Porter 1994a, 198). The infinitive clarifies the statement "we are not debtors to the flesh" as meaning "to live according to the flesh." The articular infinitive with an embedded prepositional word group (τοῦ κατὰ σάρκα ζῆν) stands as a single unit.

κατὰ σάρκα. Standard. The standard or basis by which they were not to live is "according to the flesh." As an embedded word group between the article and infinitive, its function is attributive.

8:13 εἰ γὰρ κατὰ σάρκα ζῆτε, μέλλετε ἀποθνῄσκειν· εἰ δὲ πνεύματι τὰς πράξεις τοῦ σώματος θανατοῦτε, ζήσεσθε.

εἰ. Introduces the protasis of a first-class conditional, the first of two in this verse.

γὰρ. Postpositive explanatory conjunction. It introduces an explanation of the previous statement of living according to the flesh.

κατὰ σάρκα. Standard or basis. The concept of the standard for living (according to the flesh) is continued in this co-text.

ζῆτε. Pres act ind 2nd pl ζάω.

μέλλετε. Pres act ind 2nd pl μέλλω. This verb begins the apodosis of the first conditional structure in this verse. It functions as the head term of a catenative construction (μέλλετε ἀποθνῄσκειν). This construction indicates that the fleshly life is headed towards death (cf. Porter 2015, 163). See below on ζήσεσθε to compare the semantics of expectation here.

ἀποθνῄσκειν. Pres act inf ἀποθνῄσκω (complementary). The infinitive is a complement of μέλλετε in catenative structure.

εἰ. Introduces the protasis of a first-class conditional, the second of two in this verse.

δὲ. Adversative conjunction (mild). It contrasts the previous conditional structure with the subsequent one in this verse.

πνεύματι. Dative of instrument. The instrument (or means) by which one puts to death the acts of the body is the "Spirit." Its placement at the beginning of the clause (εἰ ... πνεύματι τὰς πράξεις τοῦ σώματος θανατοῦτε) signifies clausal prominence.

τὰς πράξεις. Accusative direct object of θανατοῦτε. Its placement before the predicate, as object, signifies prominence in the clause, although since πνεύματι occurs first in the clause it has greater prominence.

τοῦ σώματος. Genitive of source or origin, modifying τὰς πράξεις.

θανατοῦτε. Pres act ind 2nd pl θανατόω.

ζήσεσθε. Fut mid ind 2nd pl ζάω. This is the apodosis of the second conditional structure. While the previous parallel conditional structure contains a catenative construction (with μέλλω) as its apodosis, the apodosis here contains a future form predicate. Both predicate structures convey semantics of expectation, but the future form is more direct. In other words, the future form conveys a more direct sense of expectation, while the catenative construction with μέλλω conveys expectation in light of its connected circumstances (cf. LN 67.62).

8:14 ὅσοι γὰρ πνεύματι θεοῦ ἄγονται, οὗτοι υἱοὶ θεοῦ εἰσιν.

ὅσοι γὰρ πνεύματι θεοῦ ἄγονται, οὗτοι υἱοὶ θεοῦ εἰσιν. Although this verse is not formally a conditional statement, it reflects a condition conceptually, with the hypothetical (protasis-like) statement, ὅσοι γὰρ πνεύματι θεοῦ ἄγονται, and the apodosis-like statement, οὗτοι υἱοὶ θεοῦ εἰσιν.

ὅσοι. Nominative subject of ἄγονται. ὅσοι is quantitative correlative relative pronoun.

γὰρ. Postpositive explanatory conjunction that introduces a further explanation of the previous statement that those who put to death the acts of the body by the Spirit will live.

πνεύματι. Dative of instrument. The instrument by which they are led (to put to death bodily deeds, inferred from the previous verse) is the Spirit of God.

θεοῦ. Possessive genitive, modifying πνεύματι.

ἄγονται. Pres pass ind 3rd pl ἄγω. Passive voice indicates external agency. Here, the agent of the predicate is πνεύματι θεοῦ. As such, the Goal of the predicate is ὅσοι (see Introduction).

οὗτοι. Nominative subject of εἰσιν. This demonstrative pronoun refers anaphorically to ὅσοι πνεύματι θεοῦ ἄγονται.

υἱοί. Predicate nominative. While usually translated as "sons," this should not be interpreted as a gender-exclusive term.

θεοῦ. Possessive genitive, modifying υἱοί.

εἰσιν. Unaugmented ind 3rd pl εἰμί.

8:15 οὐ γὰρ ἐλάβετε πνεῦμα δουλείας πάλιν εἰς φόβον ἀλλ᾿ ἐλάβετε πνεῦμα υἱοθεσίας ἐν ᾧ κράζομεν· αββα ὁ πατήρ.

οὐ . . . ἀλλ᾿. A point/counterpoint set that establishes the contrast between two clauses.

γὰρ. Explanatory conjunction. This is the third consecutive occurrence of the explanatory conjunction, which serves to continue the line of argument in the previous co-text.

ἐλάβετε. Aor act ind 2nd pl λαμβάνω. Perfective aspect reflects supportive background material to the mainline (which is reflected by use of the imperfective aspect in expositional texts; see Introduction for mainline and supportive material).

πνεῦμα. Accusative direct object of ἐλάβετε.

δουλείας. Genitive of source or origin, modifying πνεῦμα ("the spirit that comes from slavery").

πάλιν. Adverb (temporal). It modifies εἰς φόβον.

εἰς φόβον. Result (telic). The result of receiving a spirit of slavery is "fear."

ἐλάβετε. Aor act ind 2nd pl λαμβάνω. Repetition of the same lexeme in the two connecting clauses reflects lexical cohesion.

πνεῦμα. Accusative direct object of ἐλάβετε.

υἱοθεσίας. Genitive of source or origin, modifying πνεῦμα ("the spirit that comes from adoption"). Coined from classical Greek, this is a compound word consisting of υἱός and τίθημι (Sanday and Headlam, 203). It occurs in the NT only in the Pauline epistles (Rom 8:23; 9:4; Gal 4:5; Eph 1:5). Some see this imagery of adoptive sonship as based on Old Testament notions of sonship (cf. Scott), while others see no need for any Jewish or Greco-Roman context for understanding sonship in this letter (cf. Blackwell, 144). But Greco-Roman background seems to elucidate the notion of sonship and adoption here. In Greco-Roman culture, the eldest son would receive the inheritance of the family once the *paterfamilias* died. In some cases, this inheritance was bestowed upon someone outside the line of patrilineage through adoption, sometimes including slaves. Paul relates this aspect of Greco-Roman culture, which the Roman readers would be familiar with, to the relationship of God the Father to the Roman believers (Porter 2015, 164–65).

ἐν ᾧ. Instrumental. The relative pronoun refers anaphorically to πνεῦμα υἱοθεσίας, which is the instrument by which "we cry."

κράζομεν. Pres act ind 1st pl κράζω.

αββα. Nominative of address (so-called vocative). αββα is a transliteration of the Aramaic אַבָּא. Only other occurrences in the New Testament are in Paul (Rom 9:27; Gal 4:6). The meaning of this word is generally misunderstood. A widely held, popularized view is that it is equivalent to the English "daddy," an address from a young child to his/ her father reflecting a child-like faith (Jeremias, 11–65). While having a child-like faith appears in other parts of Scripture and is an essential part of the Christian life, the meaning of αββα itself does not reflect that meaning. The evidence suggests that it is a general term used of a child of any age to a father, indicating a certain amount of intimacy, affection, and respect (cf. Barr 1988; Porter 2015, 165; Ong). The more important point here is the transition from slave (πνεῦμα δουλείας) to son (πνεῦμα υἱοθεσίας).

ὁ πατήρ. Nominative of address (so-called vocative). It functions as appositional to αββα.

8:16 αὐτὸ τὸ πνεῦμα συμμαρτυρεῖ τῷ πνεύματι ἡμῶν ὅτι ἐσμὲν τέκνα θεοῦ.

αὐτὸ τὸ πνεῦμα. Nominative subject of συμμαρτυρεῖ. The intensive pronoun modifies τὸ πνεῦμα in attributive structure ("the Spirit himself").

συμμαρτυρεῖ. Pres act ind 3rd sg συμμαρτυρέω. There are a number of occurrences of predicates with the συν- prefix in this and the next verse. Here, the Spirit testifies *with* our spirit. In the next verse, we are co-heirs *with* Christ, suffer *with* Christ, and are glorified *with* Christ.

τῷ πνεύματι. Dative of association. With the predicate (συμμαρτυρεῖ) having the συν- prefix, its function is focal with respect to accompaniment ("with").

ἡμῶν. Possessive genitive, modifying τῷ πνεύματι.

ὅτι. Introduces the clausal complement (indirect discourse) of συμμαρτυρεῖ. The content of what the Spirit with our spirit testifies is stated.

ἐσμὲν. Unaugmented ind 1st pl εἰμί.

τέκνα. Predicate nominative. The language here shifts from "son" (υἱός θεοῦ and υἱοθεσία) to "child" (τέκνον), to focus on the personal nature of the relationship that God has with those he has adopted (cf. Porter 2015, 165–66).

θεοῦ. Possessive genitive, modifying τέκνα.

8:17 εἰ δὲ τέκνα, καὶ κληρονόμοι· κληρονόμοι μὲν θεοῦ, συγκληρονόμοι δὲ Χριστοῦ, εἴπερ συμπάσχομεν ἵνα καὶ συνδοξασθῶμεν.

εἰ δὲ τέκνα, καὶ κληρονόμοι. The first conditional clause in this verse. The conditional structure is verbless in both the protasis (εἰ δὲ τέκνα) and the apodosis (καὶ κληρονόμοι).

εἰ. Introduces the protasis of a first-class conditional.

δὲ. Adversative conjunction (mild).

τέκνα. Nominative absolute. The single lexeme in the nominative case functions as its own clause.

καί. Adverbial use (adjunctive). It modifies κληρονόμοι and begins the apodosis.

κληρονόμοι. Nominative absolute. The single lexeme in the nominative case (here with an adverbial adjunct) functions as its own clause.

κληρονόμοι μὲν θεοῦ, συγκληρονόμοι δὲ Χριστοῦ εἴπερ συμπάσχομεν. The second conditional clause in this verse. The apodosis is placed before the protasis, making the apodosis prominent. It also contains two clauses (in a μὲν . . . δὲ construction) as in 8:10.

κληρονόμοι. Nominative absolute. The single lexeme in the nominative case (here with a genitive modifier) functions as its own clause.

μὲν . . . δὲ. A point/counterpoint set that marks the comparison between being an heir of God (κληρονόμοι μὲν θεοῦ) and being co-heirs with Christ (συγκληρονόμοι δὲ Χριστοῦ).

θεοῦ. Possessive genitive, modifying κληρονόμοι.

συγκληρονόμοι. Predicate nominative. συγκληρονόμοι is a substantival adjective (cf. Eph 3:6).

δὲ. Adversative conjunction (mild). Together with μὲν in contrastive relationship.

Χριστοῦ. Possessive genitive, modifying συγκληρονόμοι.

εἴπερ. Introduces the protasis of a first-class conditional (see 8:9). εἴπερ is an intensive form of εἰ; hence, it is marked/emphatic (cf. Porter 1994a, 209).

συμπάσχομεν. Pres act ind 1st pl συμπάσχω (cf. 1 Cor 12:26).

ἵνα. Introduces a purpose clause. The purpose of suffering together is being glorified together.

καί. Adverbial use (adjunctive). It modifies συνδοξασθῶμεν.

συνδοξασθῶμεν. Aor pass subj 1st pl συνδοξάζω. Subjunctive with ἵνα. συνδοξάζω is a NT *hapax legomenon*. The passive voice reflects external causality. The agent is not specified in this co-text, although it is probably God who does the glorifying. Subjunctive mood form projects the glorification as a result of suffering together.

Romans 8:18–30

[18]For I consider that the sufferings of the present time [are] not worthy of the anticipated glory to be revealed to us. [19]For the deep longing of creation expects the revelation of the sons of God. [20]For the creation was subjected to futility, not willingly but on account of him who subjected [it], upon hope [21]that the creation itself will also be liberated from the slavery of corruption unto the freedom of glory of the children of God. [22]For we know that all creation is groaning together and is suffering great pain up to the present time. [23]And not only [that], but we ourselves

having the firstfruits of the Spirit, even we ourselves groan within ourselves, eagerly expecting adoptive sonship, the redemption of our body. [24]For in this hope we have been saved; and hope that sees is not hope; for who hopes in what he sees? [25]But if we hope in what we do not see, through perseverance we eagerly expect [it]. [26]But likewise, the Spirit also helps in our weaknesses. For what we should pray as it is necessary, we do not know, but the Spirit himself intercedes with groanings without words. [27]And the one who searches the hearts knows what the mind of the Spirit [is] because according to God, he intercedes for the saints. [28]And we know that for those who love God, all things work together for good, for those who are called according to [his] purpose. [29]Because whom he foreknew, he also predestined similar forms of the image of his Son, in order that he is the firstborn among many brothers [and sisters]. [30]And whom he predestined, these he also called; and whom he called, these he also justified; and whom he justified, these he also glorified.

Concluding the sub-peak of the body of the letter in 8:17 (see notes above 8:1), this section (8:18–30) turns to the themes of suffering and glorification in, along with an outline of the scheme of, the Christian life. There is a distinct sense that Paul comes full circle with this section, as he returns to the opening of the letter body when he used creation and fall language to describe the sinful human condition. In this section, however, because of the work of Christ in justification, reconciliation, and the Spirit, Paul speaks of the renewal of creation and the glory that redeemed humanity can anticipate enjoying.

8:18 Λογίζομαι γὰρ ὅτι οὐκ ἄξια τὰ παθήματα τοῦ νῦν καιροῦ πρὸς τὴν μέλλουσαν δόξαν ἀποκαλυφθῆναι εἰς ἡμᾶς.

Λογίζομαι. Pres mid ind 1st sg λογίζομαι.

γὰρ. Postpositive conjunction that is used here to introduce a further explanation of the previous statement regarding suffering.

ὅτι. Introduces a clausal complement (indirect discourse) of Λογίζομαι.

οὐκ. Negative particle normally used with indicative verbs. Here it negates ἄξια.

ἄξια. Predicate adjective.

τὰ παθήματα. Nominative subject of verbless clause.

τοῦ ... καιροῦ. Genitive or source or origin, modifying τὰ παθήματα.

νῦν. Adverb (temporal). It functions adjectivally, modifying τοῦ καιροῦ.

πρὸς τὴν ... δόξαν. Locative (movement toward). The prepositional word group has the sense of "face-to-face competition," as "the

sufferings of this present age not standing up to the scrutiny of the glory
to be revealed" (Porter 1994a, 173).

μέλλουσαν. Pres act ptc fem acc sg μέλλω (attributive). The participle modifies τὴν . . . δόξαν (first attributive position).

ἀποκαλυφθῆναι. Aor pass inf ἀποκαλύπτω (complementary). The
infinitive is a complement of μέλλουσαν in a catenative structure.

εἰς ἡμᾶς. Locative (towards).

**8:19 ἡ γὰρ ἀποκαραδοκία τῆς κτίσεως τὴν ἀποκάλυψιν τῶν υἱῶν τοῦ
θεοῦ ἀπεκδέχεται.**

ἡ . . . ἀποκαραδοκία. Nominative subject of ἀπεκδέχεται. The lexeme
ἀποκαραδοκία is a "highly expressive word," reflecting a metaphor of
straining forward (Sanday and Headlam, 206). It is found in Phil 1:20
(the only other occurrence in the NT).

γὰρ. Postpositive explanatory conjunction that introduces the explanation of Paul's claim in the previous verse.

τῆς κτίσεως. Genitive of source or origin, modifying ἡ . . .
ἀποκαραδοκία. "Creation" is personified here by ascribing personal
attributes of deep longing and expectation to it (cf. Porter 2015, 167).

τὴν ἀποκάλυψιν. Accusative direct object of ἀπεκδέχεται. Its position before the predicate indicates clausal prominence; hence, emphasis
on this word group in the clause.

τῶν υἱῶν. Genitive of description, modifying τὴν ἀποκάλυψιν. It further describes or circumscribes "revelation" as "the sons of God." Some
may wish to label this as an objective genitive, if ἀποκάλυψιν were to
become a verb (i.e., to reveal the sons of God). Reference to "sons of
God" here reflects lexical cohesion with the occurrences of this word
group in the previous co-text.

τοῦ θεοῦ. Possessive genitive, modifying τῶν υἱῶν.

ἀπεκδέχεται. Pres mid ind 3rd sg ἀπεκδέχομαι. According to LN,
ἀποκαραδοκία and ἀπεκδέχομαι are found in the same semantic sub-
domain (25D: "Hope, Look Forward To"), reflecting synonymity. The
use of these synonyms, then, as subject and predicate of this clause indicates not only lexical cohesion through reiteration but also prominence
through proximate repetition.

**8:20 τῇ γὰρ ματαιότητι ἡ κτίσις ὑπετάγη, οὐχ ἑκοῦσα ἀλλὰ διὰ τὸν
ὑποτάξαντα, ἐφ᾽ ἐλπίδι**

τῇ . . . ματαιότητι. Dative indirect object of ὑπετάγη. Its placement
before the subject and predicate reflects clausal prominence.

γὰρ. Postpositive explanatory conjunction. It introduces a further explanation for the previous statement regarding the creation.

ἡ κτίσις. Nominative subject of ὑπετάγη.

ὑπετάγη. Aor pass ind 3rd sg ὑποτάσσω. Passive voice indicates external causality. The agent is "he who subjected it," i.e., God. Some commentators refer to this as a "divine passive," although this may be theologizing a grammatical category (e.g., Sanday and Headlam, 208; Leenhardt, 220; Murray, 1:303; Althaus, 93; Black, 122; Schlier, 260; Cranfield, 1:414; Wilckens, 2:153; Käsemann 1980, 235; Bruce, 172–73; Ziesler, 220; Stuhlmacher, 134; Moo, 316; Schreiner, 436; cf. Porter 2015, 168). The perfective aspect (aorist tense-form) depicts the "subjecting" as a whole, complete action.

οὐχ . . . ἀλλὰ. A point/counterpoint set that establishes a contrast between ἑκοῦσα and διὰ τὸν ὑποτάξαντα.

ἑκοῦσα. Adjective used adverbially to indicate manner ("willingly"; see Robertson, 549–50).

διὰ τὸν ὑποτάξαντα. Causal. The cause, or agent, of the creation being put under subjection to futility is τὸν ὑποτάξαντα.

τὸν ὑποτάξαντα. Aor act ptc masc acc sg ὑποτάσσω (substantival). The referent is God, but the use of a substantival participle, instead of a direct reference to God, focuses on the identity of God as the one who caused the subjection. The same lexeme is used as above, reflecting lexical cohesion of the same referent.

ἐφ' ἐλπίδι. Locative. God subjected the creation "upon" the hope that . . . (the thought continues in the next verse).

8:21 ὅτι καὶ αὐτὴ ἡ κτίσις ἐλευθερωθήσεται ἀπὸ τῆς δουλείας τῆς φθορᾶς εἰς τὴν ἐλευθερίαν τῆς δόξης τῶν τέκνων τοῦ θεοῦ.

ὅτι. Introduces a clause that is epexegetical to ἐλπίδι.

καὶ. Adverbial use (adjunctive). It modifies the clause αὐτὴ ἡ κτίσις ἐλευθερωθήσεται.

αὐτὴ ἡ κτίσις. Nominative subject of ἐλευθερωθήσεται. αὐτὴ is intensive personal pronoun.

ἐλευθερωθήσεται. Fut pass ind 3rd sg ἐλευθερόω. The future form conveys the semantic feature of expectation; "freeing" is not depicted as having taken place already but as expected to take place. Passive voice indicates external causality; again, the cause or agent in this co-text is God. In other words, God is the one who both subjects the creation and frees the creation. The occurrences of ὑποτάσσω, ἐλευθερόω, and δουλεία in this and the previous verse reflects lexical cohesion through synonymity and antonymity, as they are found within the same semantic domain, "Control, Rule" (LN Domain 37).

ἀπὸ τῆς δουλείας. Locative (movement away from/separation). The movement of freedom is away from "the slavery of corruption."

τῆς φθορᾶς. Genitive of quality, modifying τῆς δουλείας. The quality of "corrupt" is attributed to "slavery." The use of the genitive, instead of a modifying adjective, relates the quality of slavery as "corruption" in nominal form.

εἰς τὴν ἐλευθερίαν. Goal. The goal of setting the creation free from slavery is "freedom of the glory of the children of God."

τῆς δόξης. Genitive of description, modifying τὴν ἐλευθερίαν. It further describes or circumscribes "freedom" as "glory."

τῶν τέκνων. Possessive genitive, modifying τῆς δόξης. The glory is that which the children of God possess (and by extension, enjoy; cf. Porter 2015, 168).

τοῦ θεοῦ. Possessive genitive, modifying τῶν τέκνων.

ἀπὸ τῆς δουλείας τῆς φθορᾶς / εἰς τὴν ἐλευθερίαν τῆς δόξης τῶν τέκνων τοῦ θεοῦ. The two prepositional word groups are syntactically parallel but semantically contrastive to each other in a number of ways. First is the contrast between ἀπὸ and εἰς, the former signifying movement away from and the latter signifying movement towards or into, both prepositions. Second is the contrast of the prepositional modifier, τῆς δουλείας and τὴν ἐλευθερίαν, which are antonymous to each other. Third are the genitive modifiers for τῆς δουλείας and τὴν ἐλευθερίαν (τῆς φθορᾶς and τῆς δόξης, respectively), which can also be seen to be in contrastive relationship to each other.

8:22 οἴδαμεν γὰρ ὅτι πᾶσα ἡ κτίσις συστενάζει καὶ συνωδίνει ἄχρι τοῦ νῦν·

οἴδαμεν. Prf act ind 1st pl οἶδα. The stative aspect of this verb reflects them being in a state of knowing. Paul wants to make sure at this point that his readers know about the creation to which he refers in his argument. He includes himself with his readers by using the first-person plural.

γὰρ. Postpositive explanatory conjunction. It continues the discussion from the previous co-text on the creation.

ὅτι. Introduces the clausal complement (indirect discourse) of οἴδαμεν.

πᾶσα ἡ κτίσις. Nominative subject of συστενάζει and συνωδίνει.

συστενάζει καὶ συνωδίνει. The use of the συν- prefix for both predicates "emphasizes the sense of all of creation being interwoven and jointly suffering together" (Porter 2015, 169).

συστενάζει. Pres act ind 3rd sg συστενάζω. A NT *hapax legomenon*.

καὶ. Coordinating conjunction. Connects the two predicates συστενάζει and συνωδίνει.

συνωδίνει. Pres act ind 3rd sg συνωδίνω. A NT *hapax legomenon*.

ἄχρι τοῦ νῦν. Temporal (cf. Porter 1994a, 178). ἄχρι ("until") is a temporal conjunction, which here serves as an improper preposition. The article functions as a nominalizer, changing the adverb νῦν into the object of the preposition ἄχρι.

8:23 οὐ μόνον δέ, ἀλλὰ καὶ αὐτοὶ τὴν ἀπαρχὴν τοῦ πνεύματος ἔχοντες, ἡμεῖς καὶ αὐτοὶ ἐν ἑαυτοῖς στενάζομεν υἱοθεσίαν ἀπεκδεχόμενοι, τὴν ἀπολύτρωσιν τοῦ σώματος ἡμῶν.

οὐ μόνον . . . ἀλλὰ καὶ. A point/counterpoint set ("not only . . . but also") that supplements Paul's assertion from the previous verse about the groaning of creation by the assertion about the groaning of the believers.

δέ. Adversative conjunction (mild).

αὐτοὶ. Nominative subject of ἔχοντες. The intensive pronoun refers cataphorically to ἡμεῖς and is emphatic.

τὴν ἀπαρχὴν. Accusative direct object of ἔχοντες. This word "entails the notion of the small portion of a forthcoming harvest that was given as a pledge to God as an indication of what was to come (see Exod 23:19)" (Porter 2015, 169).

τοῦ πνεύματος. Genitive of source or origin, modifying τὴν ἀπαρχὴν.

ἔχοντες. Pres act ptc masc nom pl ἔχω (concessive). The participle functions as circumstantial in this co-text and modifies στενάζομεν.

ἡμεῖς . . . αὐτοὶ. Nominative subject of στενάζομεν. The intensive pronoun modifies ἡμεῖς.

καὶ. Adverbial use (ascensive). It modifies ἡμεῖς . . . αὐτοὶ.

ἐν ἑαυτοῖς. Locative (sphere or realm). The groaning occurs "within ourselves." Its position before the predicate indicates clausal prominence.

στενάζομεν. Pres act ind 1st pl στενάζω.

υἱοθεσίαν. Accusative direct object of ἀπεκδεχόμενοι. Its position before the predicate indicates clausal prominence as well.

ἀπεκδεχόμενοι. Pres mid ptc masc nom pl ἀπεκδέχομαι (temporal). It functions in this co-text as circumstantial, modifying στενάζομεν.

τὴν ἀπολύτρωσιν. Accusative in apposition to υἱοθεσίαν.

τοῦ σώματος. Genitive of description, modifying τὴν ἀπολύτρωσιν. It further describes or circumscribes "redemption" with "of our bodies." Some may wish to label this as an objective genitive, if ἀπολύτρωσιν were to become a verb (i.e., to redeem our bodies).

ἡμῶν. Possessive genitive, modifying τοῦ σώματος.

8:24 τῇ γὰρ ἐλπίδι ἐσώθημεν· ἐλπὶς δὲ βλεπομένη οὐκ ἔστιν ἐλπίς· ὃ γὰρ βλέπει τίς ἐλπίζει;

τῇ . . . ἐλπίδι. Dative of sphere. While it is also possible that τῇ . . . ἐλπίδι is a dative of instrument—so "hope" is the instrument or means by which they are saved—it seems more likely that hope is the sphere or realm in which salvation is found. In other words, referring to the previous verse in which they eagerly expect or await adoptive sonship, it is in this realm of hope that salvation (another way of viewing adoptive sonship) is obtained. This lexeme is in the same semantic domain as the previous lexeme ἀπεκδέχομαι (LN Domain 25D: "Hope, Look Forward To") and so reflects lexical cohesion through synonymity. The articular dative also particularizes this "hope" to the previously referenced "eagerly expecting" adoptive sonship, which the translation above ("this hope") attempts to reflect. Its position before the subject and predicate indicates clausal prominence.

γὰρ. Postpositive explanatory conjunction. It introduces a further explanation of the groaning and eager expectation from the previous verse.

ἐσώθημεν. Aor pass ind 1st pl σῴζω. Passive voice indicates external agency, which is not specified in the co-text but refers to God. The grammatical subject (first-person plural, "we") is the Goal.

ἐλπὶς . . . βλεπομένη. Nominative subject of ἔστιν.

βλεπομένη. Pres mid ptc fem nom sg βλέπω (attributive). The participle modifies ἐλπὶς (fourth attributive position). Although the voice-form could also be passive, the meaning of the middle voice fits in this context better. Passive voice would mean that the object of hope is seen, but not hope itself. But the middle voice would mean that hope itself is involved in seeing its object, through personification of hope. In other words, Paul is saying that hope that sees the thing that it hopes in is not hope at all.

δὲ. Adversative conjunction (mild).

οὐκ. Negative particle normally used with indicative verbs. Here it negates ἔστιν.

ἔστιν. Unaugmented ind 3rd sg εἰμί.

ἐλπίς. Predicate nominative.

ὃ. The relative pronoun introduces a headless relative clause (ὃ . . . βλέπει) that serves as the direct object of ἐλπίζει. Within its clause, ὃ is the accusative direct object of βλέπει. The fronting of the relative clause before the subject and predicate indicates clausal prominence.

γὰρ. Postpositive explanatory conjunction that introduces a clause that further explains the previous statement that hope that sees is not really hope.

βλέπει. Pres act ind 3rd sg βλέπω.

τίς. Nominative subject of ἐλπίζει.

ἐλπίζει. Pres act ind 3rd sg ἐλπίζω. A few manuscripts (ℵ* A) have ὑπομένει here, but the majority of manuscripts (𝔓⁴⁶ ℵ² B C D F G) contain ἐλπίζει. Given the strength of the external evidence, and the likelihood that ἐλπίζω is collocated with βλέπω in the immediate co-text (both before and after), it is likely that ἐλπίζει is the original reading (cf. Metzger, 457).

8:25 εἰ δὲ ὃ οὐ βλέπομεν ἐλπίζομεν, δι' ὑπομονῆς ἀπεκδεχόμεθα.

εἰ. Introduces the protasis of a first-class conditional.

δὲ. Adversative conjunction (mild).

ὃ. The relative pronoun introduces a headless relative clause (ὃ οὐ βλέπομεν) that serves as the direct object of ἐλπίζομεν. Within the relative clause, ὃ is the accusative direct object of βλέπομεν. The fronting of the relative clause before the predicate indicates clausal prominence.

οὐ. Negative particle normally used with indicative verbs. Here it negates βλέπομεν.

βλέπομεν. Pres act ind 1st pl βλέπω.

ἐλπίζομεν. Pres act ind 1st pl ἐλπίζω.

δι' ὑπομονῆς. Instrumental. The instrument or means by which they "eagerly expect" is "through perseverance." This begins the apodosis. The fronting of the prepositional word group before the predicate indicates clausal prominence.

ἀπεκδεχόμεθα. Pres mid ind 1st pl ἀπεκδέχομαι. The middle voice indicates indirect, internal causality; the subject is involved in the eager expectation (regardless of the so-called deponent verb; see "Deponency" in the Series Introduction and Introduction).

8:26 Ὡσαύτως δὲ καὶ τὸ πνεῦμα συναντιλαμβάνεται τῇ ἀσθενείᾳ ἡμῶν· τὸ γὰρ τί προσευξώμεθα καθὸ δεῖ οὐκ οἴδαμεν, ἀλλ' αὐτὸ τὸ πνεῦμα ὑπερεντυγχάνει στεναγμοῖς ἀλαλήτοις·

Ὡσαύτως . . . καὶ. A combination of the adverb Ὡσαύτως, which serves as a marker of similarity or identity ("likewise"), and the adjunctive καὶ ("also"). Ὡσαύτως is a compound of ὡς and αὕτως.

δὲ. Adversative conjunction (mild).

τὸ πνεῦμα. Nominative subject of συναντιλαμβάνομαι.

συναντιλαμβάνεται. Pres mid ind 3rd sg συναντιλαμβάνομαι. The two prefixes (συν- "with" and αντι- "in place of") here help reflect the sense of coming alongside the object and putting oneself in the object's place. The middle voice indicates indirect, internal causality. This verb occurs only here in Paul (cf. Luke 10:40).

τῇ ἀσθενείᾳ. Dative of sphere. The sphere in which the Spirit helps is "our weaknesses."

ἡμῶν. Genitive or source or origin, modifying τῇ ἀσθενείᾳ.

τὸ. The article functions as a nominalizer, changing the clause τί προσευξώμεθα καθὸ δεῖ into the accusative direct object of οἴδαμεν. The nominalized accusative phrase is fronted before the predicate for clausal prominence.

γὰρ. Postpositive explanatory conjunction. It introduces an explanation of how the Spirit helps us in our weakness.

τί. Accusative direct object of προσευξώμεθα.

προσευξώμεθα. Aor mid subj 1st pl προσεύξωμαι (deliberative).

καθὸ. Adverb, marker of similarity. It only occurs here and in 2 Cor 8:12 in Paul.

δεῖ. Pres act ind 3rd sg δεῖ. It is not a part of a catenative construction here, as it usually is, but has an implied infinitive of προσεύξωμαι from the co-text.

οὐκ . . . ἀλλ'. A point/counterpoint set that establishes the contrast between knowing what we should be necessary to pray for and the interceding of the Spirit with groanings without words.

οἴδαμεν. Prf act ind 1st pl οἶδα. The stative aspect reflects being in a state of knowing—or in this case with the negation, not knowing.

αὐτὸ τὸ πνεῦμα. Nominative subject of ὑπερεντυγχάνει. The intensive pronoun emphasizes that it is the Spirit himself who intercedes.

ὑπερεντυγχάνει. Pres act ind 3rd sg ὑπερεντυγχάνω. A NT *hapax legomenon*. The same root, without the prefix ὑπερ-, occurs in the next verse. The occurrence of this lexeme with the prefix ὑπερ- indicates an intensive intercession here, especially in relation to the next verse.

στεναγμοῖς ἀλαλήτοις. Dative of manner. The manner in which the Spirit intercedes is (with) "groanings without words." It is uncertain precisely what these "groanings without words" or "inarticulate groanings" are. Some have suggested these refer to speaking in tongues, but since the Spirit is the subject of this action, not a person who is praying, it is unlikely that speaking in tongues is in view. It is probably a reference to the Spirit's identification with the agony of the earthly life in anticipation of glorification (see Porter 2015, 171; cf. also Jewett, 523–24).

8:27 ὁ δὲ ἐραυνῶν τὰς καρδίας οἶδεν τί τὸ φρόνημα τοῦ πνεύματος, ὅτι κατὰ θεὸν ἐντυγχάνει ὑπὲρ ἁγίων.

ὁ . . . ἐραυνῶν. Pres act ptc masc nom sg ἐραυνάω (substantival). Nominative subject of οἶδεν. This is presumably a reference to God.

δὲ. Adversative conjunction (mild). It continues the discourse.

τὰς καρδίας. Accusative direct object of ἐραυνῶν.

οἶδεν. Prf act ind 3rd sg οἶδα. It is consistent with the use of the stative aspect for "know" in this co-text.

τί. Predicate nominative. This interrogative pronoun introduces an indirect question (τί τὸ φρόνημα τοῦ πνεύματος) that serves as the direct object of οἶδεν.

τὸ φρόνημα. Nominative subject of an implied ἐστιν in the verbless complement (τί τὸ φρόνημα τοῦ πνεύματος).

τοῦ πνεύματος. Possessive genitive, modifying τὸ φρόνημα.

ὅτι. Introduces a causal clause. The cause or reason for God (the one who searches hearts) knowing the mind of the Spirit is introduced.

κατὰ θεὸν. Standard. The standard for interceding on behalf of the saints is "according to God," or according to the will of God (cf. NASB; NIV; NKJV; NRSV).

ἐντυγχάνει. Pres act ind 3rd sg ἐντυγχάνω. The same lexeme without the first of the two prefixes in the previous verse is used here; thus, less intensive than ὑπερεντυγχάνω. The implicit subject of this predicate is the Spirit (from the immediate and previous co-text).

ὑπὲρ ἁγίων. Beneficial. The beneficiaries of the intercession are "the saints" (cf. Porter 1994a, 176). The genitive adjective functions as a substantive here.

8:28 Οἴδαμεν δὲ ὅτι τοῖς ἀγαπῶσιν τὸν θεὸν πάντα συνεργεῖ εἰς ἀγαθόν, τοῖς κατὰ πρόθεσιν κλητοῖς οὖσιν.

Οἴδαμεν. Prf act ind 1st pl οἶδα. The stative aspect depicts the state of knowing or assumed knowledge.

δὲ. Adversative conjunction (mild). It is used to continue the line of thought.

ὅτι. Introduces the clausal complement (indirect discourse) of Οἴδαμεν.

τοῖς ἀγαπῶσιν. Pres act masc ptc dat pl ἀγαπάω (substantival). Dative of advantage. The clause "all things work together for good" is directed towards τοῖς ἀγαπῶσιν τὸν θεὸν for their advantage or benefit.

τὸν θεὸν. Accusative direct object of ἀγαπῶσιν.

πάντα. Nominative subject of συνεργεῖ. Although this form is identical to the neuter accusative plural (so "he works all things for good"), without another explicit subject in this clause, it is preferable to interpret this lexeme as nominative neuter plural.

συνεργεῖ. Pres act ind 3rd sg συνεργέω. Neuter plural subjects typically take singular verbs (BDF §133). A number of predicates with the συν- prefix occur in this co-text (συστενάζει and συνωδίνει in 8:22; συναντιλαμβάνεται in 8:26), reflecting the unified experiences of creation and God's intervention in it. Some manuscripts ($\mathfrak{P}^{46}$ A B) include ὁ θεὸς after συνεργεῖ (ostensibly to disambiguate the function of πάντα), but the shorter reading, which is supported by the majority of the manuscripts (ℵ C D F G), is more likely to be original (see Porter 2015, 171–72; Metzger, 458; cf. also Cranfield, 1:425–28).

εἰς ἀγαθόν. Purpose.

τοῖς . . . οὖσιν. Ptc masc dat pl εἰμί (substantival). Dative in apposition to τοῖς ἀγαπῶσιν. "Those who love God" are further described as "those who are called according to [his] purpose." The use of this "to be" participle highlights their "being" as called.

κατὰ πρόθεσιν. Standard. The standard or basis by which they are called is "according to [his] purpose."

κλητοῖς. Attributive adjective, modifying τοῖς . . . οὖσιν.

8:29 ὅτι οὓς προέγνω, καὶ προώρισεν συμμόρφους τῆς εἰκόνος τοῦ υἱοῦ αὐτοῦ, εἰς τὸ εἶναι αὐτὸν πρωτότοκον ἐν πολλοῖς ἀδελφοῖς·

ὅτι. Introduces a causal clause. Paul offers now a causal explanation of the previous statement that all things work together for the good for those who love God, those who have been called according to his purpose.

οὕς. The relative pronoun introduces a headless relative clause (οὓς προέγνω) that serves as the direct object of προώρισεν in a double accusative object-complement construction. Within its clause, οὕς is the accusative direct object of προέγνω. The relative pronoun anaphorically refers to "those who love God" and "those who are called according to his purpose." The fronting of the object before the predicate emphasizes the object in the clause.

προέγνω. Aor act ind 3rd sg προγινώσκω. The subject is not identified here, but the co-text indicates it is God who "foreknew." The perfective aspect (aorist tense-form) of προέγνω and προώρισεν reflects not only the process depicted as a whole but important background information to the previous statement that "all things work together for good."

καὶ. Adverbial use (adjunctive). It modifies προώρισεν.

προώρισεν. Aor act ind 3rd sg προορίζω. Although this word is frequently translated as "predestined" (as in our translation above), there is unfortunately much theological freight carried with this word, even if a general sense of predestination applies here. However, the semantic core of this lexeme is "circumscribed beforehand," referring to the idea of setting a limit (ὁρίζω) beforehand (προ), reflecting the prefix and root (see Porter 2015, 172).

συμμόρφους. Accusative complement to the headless relative clause οὓς προέγνω in a double accusative object-complement construction. The lexeme σύμμορφος (with prefix συν and root μόρφος) refers to "having a similar form" or "sharers of the same form" (Porter 2015, 173).

τῆς εἰκόνος. Appositional genitive. It is used to restate or restrict συμμόρφους as τῆς εἰκόνος.

τοῦ υἱοῦ. Genitive of source or origin, modifying τῆς εἰκόνος. The image comes from "his Son."

αὐτοῦ. Possessive genitive, modifying τοῦ υἱοῦ.

εἶναι. Inf εἰμί. Used with εἰς τό to denote purpose.

αὐτὸν. Accusative subject of the infinitive εἶναι. The personal pronoun refers anaphorically to τοῦ υἱοῦ αὐτοῦ.

πρωτότοκον. Predicate adjective. There has been much discussion on the meaning of this word (cf. Col 1:15, 18), but it invokes the language of adoption, sonship, and inheritance that occur in the previous co-text. The Son of God being the "firstborn" means that those who love God and are called according to his purpose become adopted brothers and sisters along with him (see Aasgaard, 137–50).

ἐν πολλοῖς ἀδελφοῖς. Distributional ("among many brothers [and sisters]").

8:30 οὓς δὲ προώρισεν, τούτους καὶ ἐκάλεσεν· καὶ οὓς ἐκάλεσεν, τούτους καὶ ἐδικαίωσεν· οὓς δὲ ἐδικαίωσεν, τούτους καὶ ἐδόξασεν.

The consistent use of the perfective aspect (aorist) in this verse continues background information (begun in 8:29), providing support to the previous statement that all things work together for good (8:28). The use of the aorist tense-forms does not indicate any temporal progression of the processes identified (contra Bruce, 168), as they reflect the process as an undifferentiated whole—even if the processes are logically in order.

οὓς. The relative pronoun introduces the headless relative clause (οὓς . . . προώρισεν) that serves as the direct object of ἐκάλεσεν, in apposition to τούτους (see note on 7:15 for the so-called left-dislocation). Within its clause, οὓς is the accusative direct object of προώρισεν. The consistent fronting of the accusative object before its predicate (two more times below) reflects emphasis of the object in each of its clauses.

δέ. Adversative conjunction (mild). It is used to continue the line of thought.

προώρισεν. Aor act ind 3rd sg προορίζω. For discussion on the meaning of this lexeme, see προώρισεν in 8:29.

τούτους. Accusative direct object of ἐκάλεσεν, appositional to οὓς . . . προώρισεν.

καί. Adverbial use (adjunctive). It modifies ἐκάλεσεν.

ἐκάλεσεν. Aor act ind 3rd sg καλέω. The use of the same lexical root (verbal cognate of κλητός in 8:28) provides a repetitive link (cohesion) to the statement in 8:28.

καί. Coordinating conjunction. It connects οὓς δὲ προώρισεν, τούτους καὶ ἐκάλεσεν with οὓς ἐκάλεσεν, τούτους καὶ ἐδικαίωσεν.

οὕς. The relative pronoun introduces the headless relative clause (οὓς ἐκάλεσεν) that serves as the direct object of ἐδικαίωσεν, in apposition to τούτους. Within its clause, οὕς is the accusative direct object of ἐκάλεσεν.

ἐκάλεσεν. Aor act ind 3rd sg καλέω.

τούτους. Accusative direct object of ἐδικαίωσεν, appositional to οὓς ἐκάλεσεν.

καί. Adverbial use (adjunctive). It modifies ἐδικαίωσεν.

ἐδικαίωσεν. Aor act ind 3rd sg δικαιόω.

οὕς. The relative pronoun introduces the headless relative clause (οὓς . . . ἐδικαίωσεν) that serves as the direct object of ἐδόξασεν, in apposition to τούτους. Within its clause, οὕς is the accusative direct object of ἐδικαίωσεν.

δέ. Adversative conjunction (mild). While the previous statements of predestination leading to calling and calling leading to justification are connected by καί, the statements of calling leading to justification and justification leading to glorification are connected by δέ. The switch from the connective conjunction to the mild adversative serves to distinguish the process of glorifying from the other processes of predestining, calling, and justifying. Thus, Paul wants to especially highlight the culmination of glorification in this series of processes.

ἐδικαίωσεν. Aor act ind 3rd sg δικαιόω.

τούτους. Accusative direct object of ἐδόξασεν, appositional to οὓς . . . ἐδικαίωσεν.

καί. Adverbial use (adjunctive). It modifies ἐδόξασεν.

ἐδόξασεν. Aor act ind 3rd sg δοξάζω. The use of this lexeme reaches back to Paul's mention of the anticipated δόξα (nominal cognate of δοξάζω) in 8:28. At the beginning of this sub-section (8:18–30), Paul began with the statement that the sufferings of the present time are not worth the anticipated glory. In this verse, Paul outlines the processes by which this anticipated glory is received.

Romans 8:31–39

[31]What, then, shall we say to these things? If God [is] for us, who [is] against us? [32]He who indeed did not spare his own Son but gave him up for us all, how will he not also with him give graciously everything to us? [33]Who will accuse the elect of God? God [is] the justifier. [34]Who [is] the condemner? Christ Jesus [is] the one who died but indeed was raised, who is also at the right hand of God, who also intercedes for us. [35]Who will separate us from the love of Christ? Tribulation, or distress, or persecution, or famine, or nakedness, or danger, or sword? [36]Just as it is written, "On account of you, we are being killed the entire day; we are reckoned as sheep of slaughter." [37]But in all these things, we hyper-conquer through him who loved us. [38]For I stand convinced that neither death, nor life, nor angels, nor rulers, nor present things, nor coming things, nor powers, [39]nor height, nor depth, nor any other created thing will be able to separate us from the love of God that is in Christ Jesus our Lord.

Paul brings the fourth section of the body of the letter of Romans (1:18–8:30) to a close with a doxology. Since Paul has traced the course of his letter from human fallenness through justification, reconciliation, the Christian life, and life in the Spirit, he ends upon a note of exaltation at the end of the figurative and spiritual process. He uses a doxology for this purpose, before his retrogression regarding Israel. This section utilizes a number of different poetic elements. These elements include elevated language, parallelism, and repetition, all to create the effect of exalting God, who is responsible for this possible transformation of humankind.

8:31 Τί οὖν ἐροῦμεν πρὸς ταῦτα; εἰ ὁ θεὸς ὑπὲρ ἡμῶν, τίς καθ᾽ ἡμῶν;

Τί οὖν ἐροῦμεν. A rhetorical question that has been used by Paul throughout this letter to transition to a related but new logical progression (4:1; 6:1; 7:7; 8:31; 9:14, 30).

Τί. Accusative direct object of ἐροῦμεν.

οὖν. Postpositive inferential conjunction. From what has been stated thus far, he poses a potential interlocutionary inference.

ἐροῦμεν. Fut act ind 1st pl λέγω.

πρὸς ταῦτα. Directional (movement toward). This preposition is commonly used with verbs of speaking (Porter 1994a, 173).

εἰ. Introduces the protasis of a first-class conditional.

ὁ θεὸς. Nominative subject of verbless clause.

ὑπὲρ ἡμῶν. Beneficial. The benefit to us is God. The idea of benefit is easily extracted from the basic semantic meaning of ὑπὲρ being "above" or "over" (Porter 1994a, 176). In essence, this statement (ὁ θεὸς ὑπὲρ ἡμῶν) means that God is over us for our benefit. Also, Paul here moves from third person ("those who love God") to first person ("us"), identifying the descriptions in the previous co-text to himself and the Roman believers.

τίς. Nominative subject of verbless clause. It begins the apodosis.

καθ' ἡμῶν. Positional (down from). The preposition has the metaphoric sense of "against." The contrast of κατά (down from) with ὑπέρ (above) is evident directionally.

8:32 ὅς γε τοῦ ἰδίου υἱοῦ οὐκ ἐφείσατο ἀλλὰ ὑπὲρ ἡμῶν πάντων παρέδωκεν αὐτόν, πῶς οὐχὶ καὶ σὺν αὐτῷ τὰ πάντα ἡμῖν χαρίσεται;

This verse reflects a conditional-like structure, with a protasis-like clause ὅς γε τοῦ ἰδίου υἱοῦ οὐκ ἐφείσατο ἀλλὰ ὑπὲρ ἡμῶν πάντων παρέδωκεν αὐτόν and an apodosis-like clause πῶς οὐχὶ καὶ σὺν αὐτῷ τὰ πάντα ἡμῖν χαρίσεται, posed as a question. This verse also begins a series of four rhetorical questions (Paul returning to diatribe for a moment), the first beginning with πῶς and the rest beginning with τίς, which continue Paul's line of argument in this section. These questions are reminiscent of earlier Greek rhetorical devices (cf. Daube) but also anachronistically are thought to reflect later rabbinic writings (Porter 2015, 175).

ὅς. Nominative subject of ἐφείσατο. The relative pronoun refers anaphorically to God.

γε. Emphatic particle. It is found only here in Paul.

τοῦ ἰδίου υἱοῦ. Genitive direct object of ἐφείσατο. A number of verbs take the object in the genitive case (Porter 1994a, 96–97; BDF §169–78), including φείδομαι (cf. Acts 20:29; Rom 11:21; 1 Cor 7:28; 2 Cor 1:23; 2 Pet 2:4, 5). The language of sonship found in the previous co-text continues here. The fronting of the genitive object before the predicate reflects clausal prominence.

οὐκ ... ἀλλά. A point/counterpoint set that establishes a strong contrast between τοῦ ἰδίου υἱοῦ ... ἐφείσατο and ὑπὲρ ἡμῶν πάντων παρέδωκεν αὐτόν.

ἐφείσατο. Aor mid ind 3rd sg φείδομαι. On the voice, see "Deponency" in the Series Introduction and Introduction.

ὑπὲρ ἡμῶν πάντων. Beneficial. The beneficiaries of giving him up is "us all." The pronominal referent to "us all" does not refer to all of humanity but anaphorically to "us" and "those who love God" in the previous co-text. The fronting of the prepositional word group before the predicate reflects clausal prominence.

παρέδωκεν. Aor act ind 3rd sg παραδίδωμι.

αὐτόν. Accusative direct object of παρέδωκεν. The personal pronoun refers anaphorically to "his own Son."

πῶς. Adverb (interrogative). It modifies χαρίσεται, functioning to establish manner.

οὐχὶ. Negative particle (emphatic) that introduces a question that expects an affirmative answer.

καί. Adverbial use (adjunctive). It modifies χαρίσεται.

σὺν αὐτῷ. Accompaniment. The prepositional word group is fronted before the predicate, indicating clausal prominence.

τὰ πάντα. Accusative direct object of χαρίσεται. The fronting of the object before the predicate indicates clausal prominence.

ἡμῖν. Dative indirect object of χαρίσεται.

χαρίσεται. Fut mid ind 3rd sg χαρίζομαι. It is found only here in Romans.

8:33 τίς ἐγκαλέσει κατὰ ἐκλεκτῶν θεοῦ; θεὸς ὁ δικαιῶν·

τίς. Nominative subject of ἐγκαλέσει.

ἐγκαλέσει. Fut act ind 3rd sg ἐγκαλέω. The prefix ἐν- is attached to καλέω, with the etymological sense of "calling in" to account, i.e., "accuse" or "bring a charge against." Future form grammaticalizes the semantic feature of expectation ("who is expected to accuse").

κατὰ ἐκλεκτῶν. Positional (down from). κατά has the metaphoric sense of "against." The lexeme ἐκλεκτός is a derivative of ἐκλογή and ἐκλέγομαι, referring to a "choice" among several options. The use of this lexeme is a cohesive reference (summary) to those described in 8:29–30 (those who are eventually glorified). It occurs in the Pauline corpus here and in Rom 16:13; Col 3:12; 1 Tim 5:21; 2 Tim 2:10; and Titus 1:1.

θεοῦ. Possessive genitive, modifying ἐκλεκτῶν. Some may wish to label this a subjective genitive, if ἐκλεκτῶν were a verb (i.e., God elects).

θεός. Nominative subject of verbless clause. It begins the answer to the rhetorical question just posed.

ὁ δικαιῶν. Pres act ptc masc nom sg δικαιόω (substantival). The participle functions in the clause as the predicate nominative.

8:34 τίς ὁ κατακρινῶν; Χριστὸς [Ἰησοῦς] ὁ ἀποθανών, μᾶλλον δὲ ἐγερθείς, ὃς καί ἐστιν ἐν δεξιᾷ τοῦ θεοῦ, ὃς καὶ ἐντυγχάνει ὑπὲρ ἡμῶν.

τίς. Predicate nominative of verbless clause.

ὁ κατακρινῶν. Fut act ptc masc nom sg κατακρίνω (substantival). The participle functions as the nominative subject of the clause.

Χριστὸς [Ἰησοῦς]. Nominative subject of verbless clause. It begins the answer to the rhetorical question. The early manuscript evidence is divided for Χριστὸς Ἰησοῦς (‭א‬ A C) and Χριστὸς (B D), but there is little difference in meaning between the two (cf. Metzger, 458).

ὁ ἀποθανών... δὲ ἐγερθείς. Predicate nominative consisting of two substantival participles connected by an adversative conjunction and governed by a single article ("the one who died but was raised"). This is an example of the Granville Sharp rule, where the single article indicates that both substantives have the same referent.

ἀποθανών. Aor act ptc masc nom sg ἀποθνήσκω (substantival).

ἐγερθείς. Aor pass ptc masc nom sg ἐγείρω (substantival).

μᾶλλον. Comparative of the adverb μάλα. Here it functions as emphatic ("indeed"). It modifies ἐγερθείς (see 5:9, 10, 15, and 17, which all occur with πολλῷ).

ὅς. Nominative subject of ἐστιν. The relative pronoun refers to Χριστὸς [Ἰησοῦς].

καί. Adverbial use (adjunctive). It modifies ἐστιν.

ἐστιν. Unaugmented ind 3rd sg εἰμί.

ἐν δεξιᾷ. Locative.

τοῦ θεοῦ. Possessive genitive, modifying δεξιᾷ.

ὅς. Nominative subject of ἐντυγχάνει. The relative pronoun refers to Χριστὸς [Ἰησοῦς].

καί. Adverbial use (adjunctive). Modifies ἐντυγχάνει.

ἐντυγχάνει. Pres act ind 3rd sg ἐντυγχάνω (see 8:27 on ἐντυγχάνει).

ὑπὲρ ἡμῶν. Beneficial (see 8:27 on ὑπὲρ ἁγίων, 8:31 on ὑπὲρ ἡμῶν, and 8:32 on ὑπὲρ ἡμῶν πάντων).

8:35 τίς ἡμᾶς χωρίσει ἀπὸ τῆς ἀγάπης τοῦ Χριστοῦ; θλῖψις ἢ στενοχωρία ἢ διωγμὸς ἢ λιμὸς ἢ γυμνότης ἢ κίνδυνος ἢ μάχαιρα;

This final rhetorical question occurs in two parts: first, with the general question, and second, with the suggestions of possible answers to the general question.

τίς. Nominative subject of χωρίσει.

ἡμᾶς. Accusative direct object of χωρίσει.

χωρίσει. Fut act ind 3rd sg χωρίζω.

ἀπὸ τῆς ἀγάπης. Locative (movement away from/separation).

τοῦ Χριστοῦ. Genitive of source or origin, modifying τῆς ἀγάπης. Some may wish to label this as a subjective genitive, if τῆς ἀγάπης were to become a verb (i.e., Christ loves).

θλῖψις... στενοχωρία... διωγμὸς... λιμὸς... γυμνότης... κίνδυνος... μάχαιρα. A series of nominative absolutes in apposition to τίς.

ἤ . . . ἤ . . . ἤ . . . ἤ . . . ἤ . . . ἤ. A series of disjunctive conjunctions that connect the seven nominatives in this list.

8:36 καθὼς γέγραπται ὅτι ἕνεκεν σοῦ θανατούμεθα ὅλην τὴν ἡμέραν, ἐλογίσθημεν ὡς πρόβατα σφαγῆς.

καθὼς γέγραπται. A standard Pauline formula for introducing a scriptural quotation (see note on 1:17).

καθὼς. Comparative conjunction. It compares the previous statement with the following Scripture quotation.

γέγραπται. Prf pass ind 3rd sg γράφω. The stative aspect reflects the state of what is written. The scriptural quotation is from Ps 44:22 (LXX 43:23).

ὅτι. Introduces the clausal complement (direct discourse) of γέγραπται.

ἕνεκεν σοῦ. Cause or reason. ἕνεκεν is an improper preposition (see Porter 1994a, 179–80, for a list of the so-called improper prepositions). The fronting of the prepositional word group indicates clausal prominence.

θανατούμεθα. Pres pass ind 1st pl θανατόω. While the form is identical to the middle voice ("we die"), the passive voice ("we are being put to death") is preferable for the following reasons: (1) in the original quotation, Ps 44:22, the Greek is translated from the passive verb הֹרַגְנוּ; (2) middle voice would indicate internal agency; and (3) the comparison to sheep would reflect a passive sense, as sheep are depicted here as dying by external agency rather than internal.

ὅλην τὴν ἡμέραν. Accusative indicating the extent of time.

ἐλογίσθημεν. Aor pass ind 1st pl λογίζομαι. Passive voice indicates external causality; the agent is not specified in this co-text.

ὡς. Comparative conjunction. The comparison is between "we are considered" and "sheep of slaughter."

πρόβατα. Nominative complement to the implied subject of ἐλογίσθημεν in a double nominative subject-complement construction.

σφαγῆς. Genitive of quality, modifying πρόβατα. The quality of "slaughter" is applied to "sheep."

8:37 ἀλλ᾽ ἐν τούτοις πᾶσιν ὑπερνικῶμεν διὰ τοῦ ἀγαπήσαντος ἡμᾶς.

ἀλλ᾽. Adversative conjunction (strong). In strong contrast to his previous statement (the quotation from Psalms) that they are dying every day, Paul asserts the following.

ἐν τούτοις πᾶσιν. Locative (sphere or realm). The sphere is "all these things," which is a pronominal reference to items in the previous co-text, such as tribulation, distress, persecution, famine, nakedness, danger, sword, and dying. The fronting of the prepositional word group indicates clausal prominence.

ὑπερνικῶμεν. Pres act ind 1st pl ὑπερνικάω. A NT *hapax legomenon* with prefixed form (cf. 3:4; 12:21).

διὰ τοῦ ἀγαπήσαντος. Instrumental. The instrument or agent through whom we "hyper-conquer" is "the one who loves us."

ἀγαπήσαντος. Aor act ptc masc gen sg ἀγαπάω (substantival). On the function of this participle, see διὰ τοῦ ἀγαπήσαντος above.

ἡμᾶς. Accusative direct object of ἀγαπήσαντος.

8:38 πέπεισμαι γὰρ ὅτι οὔτε θάνατος οὔτε ζωὴ οὔτε ἄγγελοι οὔτε ἀρχαὶ οὔτε ἐνεστῶτα οὔτε μέλλοντα οὔτε δυνάμεις

πέπεισμαι. Prf pass ind 1st sg πείθω. The stative aspect reflects a state of being persuaded and is frontgrounded in the co-text, hence prominent in the immediate discourse. It is translated as "stand convinced" above to reflect the stative aspect of the verb.

γὰρ. Postpositive conjunction that introduces the explanation of the previous statements that "we hyper-conquer."

ὅτι. Introduces the clausal complement (indirect discourse) of πέπεισμαι.

οὔτε . . . οὔτε . . . οὔτε . . . οὔτε . . . οὔτε . . . οὔτε . . . οὔτε. Negative correlatives ("neither . . . nor . . . nor . . . nor . . . nor . . . nor . . . nor") that negate individual items listed in this verse.

θάνατος. Nominative subject of δυνήσεται in 8:39.

ζωὴ. Nominative subject of δυνήσεται in 8:39.

ἄγγελοι. Nominative subject of δυνήσεται in 8:39.

ἀρχαὶ. Nominative subject of δυνήσεται in 8:39.

ἐνεστῶτα. Prf act ptc neut nom pl ἐνίστημι (substantival). Nominative subject of δυνήσεται in 8:39. The stative aspect depicts the process of "be present" as a state or condition, i.e., the present state of affairs (although the translation above is simply "present things"). It also reflects front-ground material in the co-text to make it prominent.

μέλλοντα. Pres act ptc neut nom pl μέλλω (substantival). Nominative subject of δυνήσεται in 8:39.

δυνάμεις. Nominative subject of δυνήσεται in 8:39.

8:39 οὔτε ὕψωμα οὔτε βάθος οὔτε τις κτίσις ἑτέρα δυνήσεται ἡμᾶς χωρίσαι ἀπὸ τῆς ἀγάπης τοῦ θεοῦ τῆς ἐν Χριστῷ Ἰησοῦ τῷ κυρίῳ ἡμῶν.

οὔτε . . . οὔτε . . . οὔτε. Negative correlatives that negate the final three items in the list that starts in the previous verse.

ὕψωμα. Nominative subject of δυνήσεται.

βάθος. Nominative subject of δυνήσεται.

τις κτίσις ἑτέρα. Nominative subject of δυνήσεται. τις is an adjectival use of the indefinite pronoun.

δυνήσεται. Fut mid ind 3rd sg δύναμαι.

ἡμᾶς. Accusative direct object of χωρίσαι.

χωρίσαι. Aor act inf χωρίζω (complementary). The infinitive is a complement of δυνήσεται in a catenative structure. The only other occurrence of this verb in Romans is in 8:35.

ἀπὸ τῆς ἀγάπης. Locative (movement away from/separation).

τοῦ θεοῦ. Genitive of source or origin, modifying τῆς ἀγάπης.

τῆς ἐν Χριστῷ Ἰησοῦ. The article functions as an adjectivizer, changing the prepositional word group ἐν Χριστῷ Ἰησοῦ into an attributive modifier of ἀγάπης.

ἐν Χριστῷ Ἰησοῦ. Locative (sphere or realm; see notes on ἐν Χριστῷ Ἰησοῦ in 3:24; 6:11, 23; 8:1, 2).

τῷ κυρίῳ. Dative in apposition to Χριστῷ Ἰησοῦ.

ἡμῶν. Possessive genitive, modifying τῷ κυρίῳ.

Romans 9:1–13

[1]I speak truth in Christ, I do not lie, as my conscience testifies to me in the Holy Spirit, [2]that pain in me is great, and grief [is] unrelenting in my heart. [3]For I pray that I myself were cursed away from Christ for my brothers [and sisters], my kinsmen according to the flesh, [4]who are Israelites, from whom [are] the adoptive sonship and the glory and the covenants and the giving of the law and the divine service and the promises, [5]from whom [are] the fathers, and out of whom [is] Christ, with respect to the flesh, the one being God over all, blessed forever, amen. [6]But it [is] not such that the word of God has failed. For not all who come from Israel [are] these Israel; [7]and nor—just because they are offspring of Abraham—[are] all children, but "through Isaac it will be called to you offspring." [8]In other words, [it is] not the children of the flesh, these [are not] the children of God, but the children of the promise will be reckoned as offspring. [9]For this word of promise [is]: "At this time, I will come, and there will be to Sarah a son." [10]And not only this, but [there is] also Rebekah, having conceived from one, Isaac our father. [11]For while they had not yet been born nor had they done anything good or evil, in order that the purpose of God according to election might remain, [12]not by works but by him who calls, it was told to her, "The older will serve the younger," [13]just as it stands written, "Jacob I loved, but Esau I hated."

Romans 9–11 is divided into four sections. Romans 9:1–13 addresses the place of Israel in God's economy, Rom 9:14–29 the question of God's justice and mercy, Rom 9:30–10:21 the destiny of Israel, and Rom 11:1–32 the matter of Israel's final salvation.

9:1 Ἀλήθειαν λέγω ἐν Χριστῷ, οὐ ψεύδομαι, συμμαρτυρούσης μοι τῆς συνειδήσεώς μου ἐν πνεύματι ἁγίῳ,

Ἀλήθειαν. Accusative direct object of λέγω. The fronting of the object in the clause reflects clausal prominence. In other words, Paul emphasizes that truth is what he is speaking. The use of asyndeton, i.e., the lack of the cohesive tie at the beginning of this verse (such as γάρ or δέ), reflects a new sub-section and topic of discourse.

λέγω. Pres act ind 1st sg λέγω.

ἐν Χριστῷ. Locative (sphere or realm). See notes on this prepositional word group in 3:24; 6:11; 8:1, 2, 39.

οὐ. Negative particle normally used with indicative verbs. Here it negates ψεύδομαι.

ψεύδομαι. Pres mid ind 1st sg ψεύδομαι.

συμμαρτυρούσης. Pres act ptc fem gen sg συμμαρτυρέω (genitive absolute, manner).

μοι. Dative indirect object of συμμαρτυρούσης.

τῆς συνειδήσεώς. Genitive subject of συμμαρτυρούσης. The use of this lexeme, "conscience," as opposed to simply referring to himself with a personal pronoun, personifies a separate witness to what he is about to state (cf. Sanday and Headlam, 227). The additional accent on the ultima is a result of the following word being enclitic (see note on πνεύματί in 1:9).

μου. Possessive genitive, modifying τῆς συνειδήσεώς.

ἐν πνεύματι ἁγίῳ. Locative (sphere or realm). It is parallel to ἐν Χριστῷ.

9:2 ὅτι λύπη μοί ἐστιν μεγάλη καὶ ἀδιάλειπτος ὀδύνη τῇ καρδίᾳ μου.

ὅτι λύπη μοί ἐστιν μεγάλη καὶ ἀδιάλειπτος ὀδύνη τῇ καρδίᾳ μου. Despite most English translations reflecting this as one clause (e.g., "I have great sorrow and unceasing anguish in my heart" [NIV 2011; cf NASB; NKJV; NRSV; ESV], which has as its subject "I"), this verse likely consists of two clauses, λύπη μοί ἐστιν μεγάλη and ἀδιάλειπτος ὀδύνη τῇ καρδίᾳ μου, the latter being a verbless clause (ἐστιν as elided from the previous clause). The reason for preferring this interpretation is due to the parallel constituents of the two clauses joined by καί: (1) the nominative subject (λύπη and ὀδύνη), (2) the two adjectives (μεγάλη and ἀδιάλειπτος), and (3) the two modifying datives (μοί and τῇ καρδίᾳ μου). The function of the adjective ἀδιάλειπτος is discussed below.

ὅτι. Introduces a clausal complement (indirect discourse) of λέγω in the preceding verse.

λύπη. Nominative subject of ἐστιν.

μοί. Locative dative.

ἐστιν. Unaugmented ind 3rd sg εἰμί.

μεγάλη. Predicate adjective.

καὶ. Coordinating conjunction that connects two clauses.

ἀδιάλειπτος. Predicate adjective. While it can also function as an attributive adjective, modifying ὀδύνη, within the co-text, it is more likely parallel to the predicate adjective μεγάλη with an elided ἐστιν.

ὀδύνη. Nominative subject of verbless clause.

τῇ καρδίᾳ μου. Locative dative. It is parallel to μοί in the previous clause. The use of "my heart" reflects the depth of unceasing grief in Paul.

9:3 ηὐχόμην γὰρ ἀνάθεμα εἶναι αὐτὸς ἐγὼ ἀπὸ τοῦ Χριστοῦ ὑπὲρ τῶν ἀδελφῶν μου τῶν συγγενῶν μου κατὰ σάρκα,

ηὐχόμην. Impf mid ind 1st sg εὔχομαι. While most English translations render this lexeme as "wish," it has the sense of "pray" or "petition," which conveys a stronger force for what Paul states here (cf. Acts 26:29; 27:29; 2 Cor 13:7, 9; James 5:16; 3 John 2).

γὰρ. Postpositive explanatory conjunction that introduces the explanation of Paul's deep pain and grief.

ἀνάθεμα. Predicate nominative of εἶναι. While the accusative form is equivalent, εἰμί takes objects in nominative form, and it occurs before the linking verb. ἀνάθεμα occurs in Paul in 1 Cor 12:3; 16:22; Gal 1:8, 9.

εἶναι. Inf εἰμί (complementary). The infinitive is a complement of ηὐχόμην in a catenative structure.

αὐτὸς ἐγὼ. Nominative subject of εἶναι. αὐτὸς is intensive pronoun ("I myself") that puts emphasis on the referent (Paul).

ἀπὸ τοῦ Χριστοῦ. Locative (movement away from/separation).

ὑπὲρ τῶν ἀδελφῶν. Beneficial. The benefit is not stated yet, but Paul would pray for a curse to be on him for the *benefit* of his brothers and sisters.

μου. Possessive genitive or genitive of association, modifying τῶν ἀδελφῶν.

τῶν συγγενῶν. Genitive in apposition to τῶν ἀδελφῶν.

μου. Possessive genitive or genitive of association, modifying τῶν συγγενῶν.

κατὰ σάρκα. Standard. The standard by which they are kinsmen to Paul is "the flesh," i.e., by ethnic association.

9:4 οἵτινές εἰσιν Ἰσραηλῖται, ὧν ἡ υἱοθεσία καὶ ἡ δόξα καὶ αἱ διαθῆκαι καὶ ἡ νομοθεσία καὶ ἡ λατρεία καὶ αἱ ἐπαγγελίαι,

οἵτινές. Nominative subject of εἰσιν. οἵτινές is an indefinite relative pronoun.

εἰσιν. Unaugmented ind 3rd pl εἰμί.

Ἰσραηλῖται. Predicate nominative.

ὧν. Possessive genitive. The relative pronoun refers anaphorically to Ἰσραηλῖται. The items of possession are listed subsequently.

ἡ υἱοθεσία καὶ ἡ δόξα καὶ αἱ διαθῆκαι καὶ ἡ νομοθεσία καὶ ἡ λατρεία καὶ αἱ ἐπαγγελίαι. Compound nominative subject of verbless subordinate clause.

9:5 ὧν οἱ πατέρες καὶ ἐξ ὧν ὁ Χριστὸς τὸ κατὰ σάρκα, ὁ ὢν ἐπὶ πάντων θεὸς εὐλογητὸς εἰς τοὺς αἰῶνας, ἀμήν.

There are three possible ways to punctuate this verse:

(1) ὧν οἱ πατέρες καὶ ἐξ ὧν ὁ Χριστὸς τὸ κατὰ σάρκα. ὁ ὢν ἐπὶ πάντων θεὸς εὐλογητὸς εἰς τοὺς αἰῶνας, ἀμήν.
(2) ὧν οἱ πατέρες καὶ ἐξ ὧν ὁ Χριστὸς τὸ κατὰ σάρκα, ὁ ὢν ἐπὶ πάντων, θεὸς εὐλογητὸς εἰς τοὺς αἰῶνας, ἀμήν.
(3) ὧν οἱ πατέρες καὶ ἐξ ὧν ὁ Χριστὸς τὸ κατὰ σάρκα, ὁ ὢν ἐπὶ πάντων θεὸς εὐλογητὸς εἰς τοὺς αἰῶνας, ἀμήν.

The NA[28], UBS[5], and the THGNT all use the punctuations in option 3.

ὧν. Possessive genitive. The relative pronoun refers anaphorically to Ἰσραηλῖται from the previous verse. The item of possession is listed subsequently.

οἱ πατέρες. Nominative subject of verbless clause.

καὶ. Coordinating conjunction. It connects the two clauses ὧν οἱ πατέρες and ἐξ ὧν ὁ Χριστὸς τὸ κατὰ σάρκα.

ἐξ ὧν. Source or origin. In a sense, the origin of Christ (the fleshly Christ) is the Israelites. The relative pronoun is appositional to the prior ὧν.

ὁ Χριστὸς. Nominative subject of verbless clause.

τὸ κατὰ σάρκα. The article functions as a nominalizer, changing the prepositional word group κατὰ σάρκα into a substantival entity. The neuter article, τὸ, may be nominative and thus in apposition to ὁ Χριστὸς, or, more likely, it is accusative and thus an accusative of respect. In other words, Christ (the Anointed One, the Messiah) with respect to his fleshly or earthly condition comes from the Israelite line. The neuter article is typically used when modifying abstract items such as a prepositional word group (cf. Porter 1994a, 108).

κατὰ σάρκα. Standard. The standard of Christ coming from the Israelites is "the flesh." The use of this prepositional word group underlines the humanness of Christ (cf. 9:3; see Harris 1992, 155; Porter 2015, 182).

ὁ ὤν. Ptc masc nom sg εἰμί (adjectival or substantival). The function of this participle depends on the punctuation.

(1) Those who think that a full stop comes after σάρκα understand the remainder of the verse as an independent doxology to God: "God who is over all [be] blessed forever" (cf. RSV, NEB, GNB, CEV). In that case, the participle modifies θεὸς (ὁ ὤν . . . θεὸς), standing in the first attributive position.

(2) Those who place commas after σάρκα and after πάντων regard ὁ ὤν as a substantival participle that functions as the nominative in apposition to ὁ Χριστὸς and θεὸς εὐλογητὸς as nominative in apposition to ὁ ὤν: "from whom [is] Christ according to the flesh, the one who is over all, God blessed forever" (KJV, NASB, JB, NRSV, ESV, NET).

(3) The NA[28] punctuation presumes that ὁ ὤν is a substantival participle that functions as the nominative in apposition to ὁ Χριστὸς and that θεὸς εὐλογητὸς is the predicate nominative.

ἐπὶ πάντων. Positional (over, upon).

θεὸς. (1) If a full stop comes after σάρκα, θεὸς is the nominative subject of a verbless clause (doxology): "God who is over all [be] blessed forever." (2) If commas are placed after σάρκα and after πάντων (the second option), θεὸς is the nominative in apposition to ὁ ὤν: "from whom [is] Christ according to the flesh, the one who is over all, God blessed forever" (KJV, NASB, JB, NRSV, ESV, NET). (3) The NA[28] punctuation presumes that θεὸς is the predicate nominative.

εὐλογητὸς εἰς τοὺς αἰῶνας, ἀμήν. Interpretation of this doxology (including the previous clause ὁ ὤν ἐπὶ πάντων θεὸς) is a subject of scholarly debate and can be viewed in two major ways: (1) the doxology is attributed to Christ and Christ is seen as "the God over all things," or (2) the doxology is attributed to God, and "God over all things" stands apart from "Christ." It seems preferable, however, given the syntax and lexicogrammar here, that "one being God over all things" is taken as epexegetical to "Christ," and that the doxology is attributed to Christ (cf. Beet, 267–72; Vaughan, 175; Sanday and Headlam, 233–38; Cranfield, 2:464–70; Wilckens, 2:189; Ziesler, 238–39; Käsemann 1980,

259–60; Harris 1992, 143–72; Fee, 239, 272–277; Carraway; Porter 2015, 182–84).

εὐλογητὸς. Attributive adjective, modifying θεὸς in fourth attributive position (cf. Wallace 1996, 310–11; Porter 1994a, 116–17).

εἰς τοὺς αἰῶνας. Goal or state ("forever").

ἀμήν. Asseverative particle (see 1:25).

9:6 Οὐχ οἷον δὲ ὅτι ἐκπέπτωκεν ὁ λόγος τοῦ θεοῦ. οὐ γὰρ πάντες οἱ ἐξ Ἰσραὴλ οὗτοι Ἰσραήλ·

Οὐχ. Negative particle that negates οἷον.

οἷον. Nominative subject of verbless clause. οἷον is neuter relative pronoun, qualitative correlative (see Porter 1994a, 134).

δὲ. Adversative conjunction (mild). It marks a transition from what Paul has thus stated regarding the privileges of Israel to clarify that not all who descend from Israel are Israel.

ὅτι. Introduces a clause that is epexegetical to Οὐχ οἷον (cf. Robertson, 1034).

ἐκπέπτωκεν. Prf act ind 3rd sg ἐκπίπτω. The stative aspect depicts a state of failing. In other words, God's word is not in a state of failure or fallenness. The use of the stative aspect also reflects prominence in the discourse.

ὁ λόγος. Nominative subject of ἐκπέπτωκεν.

τοῦ θεοῦ. Genitive of source or origin, modifying ὁ λόγος.

οὐ γὰρ πάντες οἱ ἐξ Ἰσραὴλ οὗτοι Ἰσραήλ. One suggested interpretation (Wengst, 287–302) is that this clause is a (rhetorical) question, in line with Paul's use of diatribe elsewhere in this letter (such as in Romans 6). This would require the next clause, connected by οὐδέ, to also be a rhetorical question. While this interpretation is possible syntactically, it seems unlikely, as the negative particle οὐ would require a positive answer, yes, to the question, are all who come from Israel, Israel? (Yes, they are.) However, this seems contrary to the point that Paul makes in this co-text, especially in v. 9, when he distinguishes between physical and spiritual offspring.

οὐ. The first element of the compound point/counterpoint set (οὐ . . . οὐδ' . . . ἀλλ') that is completed in the next verse (see οὐδ' . . . ἀλλ' in 9:7). The negative particle negates the entire clause πάντες οἱ ἐξ Ἰσραὴλ οὗτοι Ἰσραήλ.

γὰρ. Postpositive explanatory conjunction that introduces the explanation why God's word is not in a state of failure.

πάντες οἱ ἐξ Ἰσραὴλ. Nominative subject of verbless clause. If πάντες is viewed as substantival, the article functions as an adjectivizer, changing the prepositional word group ἐξ Ἰσραὴλ into an attributive modifier of πάντες. If πάντες is viewed as adjectival, the article functions as a nominalizer, changing the prepositional word group ἐξ Ἰσραὴλ into the nominative subject of an implied εἰσιν. While the latter interpretation seems likely, since πάντες is an adjective, both convey the same sense of "all who are of Israel."

ἐξ Ἰσραὴλ. Source or origin.

οὗτοι. Nominative subject of verbless clause. The demonstrative pronoun is epexegetical to πάντες οἱ ἐξ Ἰσραὴλ and is emphatic.

Ἰσραήλ. Predicate nominative.

9:7 οὐδ᾿ ὅτι εἰσὶν σπέρμα Ἀβραὰμ πάντες τέκνα, ἀλλ᾿ ἐν Ἰσαὰκ κληθήσεταί σοι σπέρμα.

οὐδ᾿ . . . ἀλλ᾿. The second and third elements of the point/counterpoint set that started in the previous verse, which establishes a contrast between ὅτι εἰσὶν σπέρμα Ἀβραὰμ πάντες τέκνα and ἐν Ἰσαὰκ κληθήσεταί σοι σπέρμα. οὐδ᾿ is a compound of οὐ and δέ.

ὅτι εἰσὶν σπέρμα Ἀβραὰμ. This clause is secondary (subordinate) to, or perhaps better considered embedded within, οὐδ᾿ . . . πάντες τέκνα. Thus, a rough translation might be: "and nor—because they are offspring of Abraham—[are] all children."

ὅτι. Introduces a causal clause.

εἰσὶν. Unaugmented ind 3rd pl εἰμί. The subject is implied anaphorically (probably πάντες οἱ ἐξ Ἰσραὴλ).

σπέρμα. Predicate nominative.

Ἀβραὰμ. Possessive genitive, modifying σπέρμα.

πάντες. Nominative subject of verbless clause. The repetition of πάντες (see πάντες οἱ ἐξ Ἰσραὴλ in v. 6) reflects lexical cohesion in these verses.

τέκνα. Predicate nominative.

ἐν Ἰσαὰκ. Instrumental. The rest of this verse is a quotation of LXX Gen 21:12 (cf. also Heb 11:18).

κληθήσεταί. Fut pass ind 3rd sg καλέω. Passive voice reflects external causality, although the agent is unspecified in this co-text.

σοι. Dative of advantage of κληθήσεταί.

σπέρμα. Nominative subject of κληθήσεταί. Although the grammatical subject, the passive voice reflects "offspring" to be the Goal of "call."

9:8 τοῦτ᾽ ἔστιν, οὐ τὰ τέκνα τῆς σαρκὸς ταῦτα τέκνα τοῦ θεοῦ ἀλλὰ τὰ τέκνα τῆς ἐπαγγελίας λογίζεται εἰς σπέρμα.

τοῦτ᾽ ἔστιν. Explanatory formula (lit. "this is") that means something like "in other words" (Porter 2015, 185).

τοῦτ᾽. Nominative subject of ἔστιν.

ἔστιν. Unaugmented ind 3rd sg εἰμί.

οὐ… ἀλλὰ. A point/counterpoint set that establishes a contrast between between τὰ τέκνα τῆς σαρκὸς and τὰ τέκνα τῆς ἐπαγγελίας.

τὰ τέκνα. Predicate nominative of verbless clause, resumed by ταῦτα.

τῆς σαρκὸς. Genitive of quality, modifying τὰ τέκνα ("fleshly children").

ταῦτα. Nominative subject of verbless clause. The pronominal substantive is an anaphoric referent to τὰ τέκνα τῆς σαρκὸς.

τέκνα. Predicate nominative of verbless clause.

τοῦ θεοῦ. Genitive of source or origin, modifying τέκνα.

τὰ τέκνα. Nominative subject of λογίζεται.

τῆς ἐπαγγελίας. Genitive of source or origin, modifying τὰ τέκνα.

λογίζεται. Pres pass ind 3rd sg λογίζομαι.

εἰς σπέρμα. Goal or state. The directional nature of εἰς (into) signifies that the children of the promise were considered (or reckoned) to be "into" the category of "offspring," with "offspring" as the goal of their considering (or reckoning).

9:9 ἐπαγγελίας γὰρ ὁ λόγος οὗτος· κατὰ τὸν καιρὸν τοῦτον ἐλεύσομαι καὶ ἔσται τῇ Σάρρᾳ υἱός.

ἐπαγγελίας … ὁ λόγος οὗτος. The syntax of this clause is difficult to interpret. It can be taken one of three ways:

(1) ἐπαγγελίας ὁ λόγος (nominative subject) οὗτος (predicate nominative), so "the word of promise is this."

(2) ἐπαγγελίας ὁ λόγος (predicate nominative) οὗτος (nominative subject), so "this is the word of promise."

(3) ἐπαγγελίας ὁ λόγος (nominative absolute) οὗτος (pronominal adjective), so "this word of promise."

Options (1) and (2) are related, assuming an implied "to be" verb connecting the two substantives. Although Wallace (1996, 44) states that the pronoun will always have priority in being the subject, thus possibly option (2), his examples are of pronouns that also occur before a "to be" verb, and the basis of his conclusion is unclear. Option (3) is considered "awkward" in English (as a translation) but is a valid interpretation if modern punctuations (both in Greek editions and English translations) are disregarded. This assumes a "to be" verb to be placed after the nominative absolute, before the Scripture reference (see below on κατὰ τὸν καιρὸν τοῦτον). Thus, an English translation can be something like: "For this word of promise is . . ." While this handbook prefers option (3), any of these options are syntactically valid and the differences are semantically minor.

ἐπαγγελίας. Genitive of description or definition, modifying ὁ λόγος οὗτος. It further circumscribes the "word" as "of promise." The fronting of the genitive before the head term (ὁ λόγος) indicates prominence at the word group level; Paul wishes to emphasize the notion of promise from the previous verse.

γὰρ. Postpositive explanatory conjunction that introduces a clause that is used to explain further Paul's statement that the children of the promise are reckoned as offspring.

ὁ λόγος οὗτος. Nominative absolute. The demonstrative pronoun οὗτος functions as a pronominal adjective in attributive structure, modifying ὁ λόγος.

κατὰ τὸν καιρὸν τοῦτον. Temporal. The word group simply means "at this time," not "opportune tune" or the like (cf. Barr 1969, 21–49; Porter 2015, 185). This begins a mixed quotation from LXX Gen 18:10, 14.

ἐλεύσομαι. Fut mid ind 1st sg ἔρχομαι. The subject, unspecified in the co-text, but evident in the context, is God.

καὶ. Coordinating conjunction that connects ἐλεύσομαι and ἔσται.

ἔσται. Fut 3rd sg εἰμί.

τῇ Σάρρᾳ. Dative of advantage. The advantage to "Sarah" is "a son."

υἱός. Nominative subject of ἔσται.

9:10 Οὐ μόνον δέ, ἀλλὰ καὶ Ῥεβέκκα ἐξ ἑνὸς κοίτην ἔχουσα, Ἰσαὰκ τοῦ πατρὸς ἡμῶν·

Οὐ μόνον . . . ἀλλὰ καί. A point/counterpoint set ("not only . . . but also") that supplements the reference to Sarah's son with the reference to Rebekah's children.

δέ. Adversative conjunction (mild). Postpositive usually occurs as the second item, but here, οὐ μόνον is considered to be a single item, so δέ occurs third.

Ῥεβέκκα. Nominative subject of ἔχουσα.

ἐξ ἑνός. Instrumental (agentive). The one (ἑνός) is a reference to Isaac, who is the instrument or agent by which Rebekah had conceived.

κοίτην. Accusative direct object of ἔχουσα.

ἔχουσα. Pres act ptc fem nom sg ἔχω (attributive). The participle functions attributively and modifies Ῥεβέκκα.

Ἰσαάκ. Genitive in apposition to ἑνὸς. Ἰσαάκ is a proper noun.

τοῦ πατρὸς. Genitive in apposition to Ἰσαάκ.

ἡμῶν. Possessive genitive, modifying τοῦ πατρὸς.

9:11 μήπω γὰρ γεννηθέντων μηδὲ πραξάντων τι ἀγαθὸν ἢ φαῦλον, ἵνα ἡ κατ' ἐκλογὴν πρόθεσις τοῦ θεοῦ μένῃ,

μήπω. Adverb (temporal). It modifies γεννηθέντων. It occurs only here in Paul (cf. Heb 9:8).

γὰρ. Postpositive explanatory conjunction. The explanation of Rebekah's conception from the previous verse continues.

γεννηθέντων. Aor pas ptc masc gen pl γεννάω (genitive absolute, temporal). The implied subject (plural) of this genitive absolute is Isaac and Rebekah's children.

μηδὲ. Negative disjunctive particle. It negates πραξάντων.

πραξάντων. Aor act ptc masc gen pl πράσσω (genitive absolute, temporal). The implied subject (plural) of this genitive absolute is again Isaac and Rebekah's children.

τι ἀγαθὸν ἢ φαῦλον. Accusative direct objects of πραξάντων. The indefinite pronoun (τι) is modified by two attributive adjectives (ἀγαθὸν and φαῦλον) connected by a disjunctive conjunction (ἢ).

ἵνα. Introduces a purpose clause. The purpose of Rebekah being told that the older will serve the younger (see next verse) is "the purpose of God according to election."

ἡ . . . πρόθεσις. Nominative subject of μένῃ (cf. the use of the same lexeme in Rom 8:28).

κατ' ἐκλογὴν. Standard. The standard or basis of "the purpose of God" is "election." The embedded prepositional word group between the article and substantive has attributive function, reflecting strict modification of the substantive (i.e., "the according-to-election purpose of God").

τοῦ θεοῦ. Genitive of source of origin, modifying ἡ . . . πρόθεσις.

μένῃ. Pres act subj 3rd sg μένω. Subjunctive with ἵνα.

9:12 οὐκ ἐξ ἔργων ἀλλ' ἐκ τοῦ καλοῦντος, ἐρρέθη αὐτῇ ὅτι ὁ μείζων δουλεύσει τῷ ἐλάσσονι,

οὐκ . . . ἀλλ'. A point/counterpoint set that establishes a contrast between ἐξ ἔργων and ἐκ τοῦ καλοῦντος.

ἐξ ἔργων. Instrumental or causal. The instrument or cause of ἐρρέθη αὐτῇ is "not works."

ἐκ τοῦ καλοῦντος. Instrumental or causal. The instrument or cause of ἐρρέθη αὐτῇ is "the one who calls."

τοῦ καλοῦντος. Pres act ptc masc gen sg καλέω (substantival). The participle refers to God.

ἐρρέθη. Aor pass ind 3rd sg λέγω. The passive voice reflects external causality; here the agent is not specified, although inferring from the co-text, it is τοῦ καλοῦντος, i.e., God.

αὐτῇ. Dative indirect object of ἐρρέθη. The personal pronoun is an anaphoric reference to Rebekah from 9:10.

ὅτι. Introduces the clausal complement (direct discourse) of ἐρρέθη. The following is a quotation from LXX Gen 25:23.

ὁ μείζων. Nominative subject of δουλεύσει. The article indicates that the adjective (a comparative of μέγας) functions as a substantive. This lexeme occurs only here in Romans (cf. 1 Cor 12:31; 13:13; 14:5).

δουλεύσει. Fut act ind 3rd sg δουλεύω. Future form reflects the semantic feature of expectation; it was expected that the older would serve the younger.

τῷ ἐλάσσονι. Dative direct object of δουλεύσει. The article indicates that the adjective (used as a comparative of μικρός) functions as a substantive. This lexeme occurs only here in Romans (cf. 1 Tim 5:9).

9:13 καθὼς γέγραπται· τὸν Ἰακὼβ ἠγάπησα, τὸν δὲ Ἡσαῦ ἐμίσησα.

καθὼς γέγραπται. A common Pauline formula to indicate an OT reference (see note on 1:17). It introduces a quotation from LXX Mal 1:2–3, although the word order is changed here from ἠγάπησα τὸν Ἰακὼβ.

καθὼς. Comparative conjunction. The comparison is between what Paul has just stated regarding the older serving the younger and the following Scripture quotation.

γέγραπται. Prf pass ind 3rd sg γράφω.

τὸν Ἰακὼβ. Accusative direct object of ἠγάπησα. The fronting of the object before the subject—especially in light of the LXX word order—indicates clausal prominence.

ἠγάπησα. Aor act ind 1st sg ἀγαπάω.

τὸν . . . Ἡσαῦ. Accusative direct object of ἐμίσησα. The fronting of the object before the subject indicates clausal prominence.

δὲ. Adversative conjunction (mild). It contrasts τὸν Ἰακὼβ ἠγάπησα with τὸν Ἡσαῦ ἐμίσησα.

ἐμίσησα. Aor act ind 1st sg μισέω.

Romans 9:14–29

[14]What shall we say, then? [Is there] injustice with God? Indeed not.
[15]For to Moses he says, "I will have mercy on whom I might have
mercy, and I will have compassion on whom I might have compassion." [16]So then, it [is] not of the one who wills nor of the one who runs
but of the God who shows mercy. [17]For the Scripture says to Pharaoh,
"For this very purpose I raised you up, in order that I might show my
power in you and in order that my name might be proclaimed in all
the earth." [18]So then, he has mercy on whom he wills, and he hardens
whom he wills. [19]You will say to me, then, "Why, then, does he still find
fault? For who has stood against his will?" [20]However, oh human, who
are you who answers back to God? Will that which is molded say to the
molder, "Why did you make me this way?" [21]Or does not the potter of
the clay have authority to make from the same lump a vessel, one unto
honor but another unto dishonor? [22]And what if God, wanting to show
wrath and make known his power, put up with in great patience vessels
of wrath prepared for destruction, [23]also in order to make known the
riches of his glory for vessels of mercy, which he prepared beforehand
for glory [24]—us, whom he also called not only from the Jews but also
from the Gentiles? [25]Just as he also says in Hosea, "I will call those
not my people, my people, and those not beloved, beloved." [26]"And
it will be in the place where it was said to them, 'You [are] not my
people,' there they will be called sons of the living God." [27]And Isaiah
cries out on behalf of Israel, "Even though the number of the sons of
Israel should be like the sand of the sea, the remnant will be saved."
[28]For the Lord, carrying [it] out and cutting [it] short, will accomplish
[his] word upon the earth. [29]And just as Isaiah spoke in advance, "If
the Lord of armies had not left us offspring, we would have been like
Sodom and would have become like Gomorrah."

In this next sub-section within Romans 9–11, Paul reintroduces his
interlocutor and applies diatribe again. The major issue in this sub-
section is with the potential misunderstanding that God might be
unjust. Paul's argument is largely supported by Scripture from Malachi,
Exodus, Isaiah, and Hosea (see below).

9:14 Τί οὖν ἐροῦμεν; μὴ ἀδικία παρὰ τῷ θεῷ; μὴ γένοιτο.

Τί οὖν ἐροῦμεν. A rhetorical question that has been used by Paul
throughout this letter to transition to a related but new logical progression (cf. Rom 4:1; 6:1; 7:7; 8:31; 9:14, 30).

Τί. Accusative direct object of ἐροῦμεν.

οὖν. Postpositive inferential conjunction. From what has been stated thus far, he poses a potential interlocutionary inference.

ἐροῦμεν. Fut act ind 1st pl λέγω.

μὴ. Negative particle that introduces a question that expects a negative answer.

ἀδικία. Nominative subject of verbless clause.

παρὰ τῷ θεῷ. Association. The prepositional word group has the sense of "alongside" or "with" God.

μὴ γένοιτο. A common emphatic negation for Paul after posing a question, usually rhetorical (see 3:4).

μὴ. Negative particle normally used with non-indicative verbs. Here it negates γένοιτο.

γένοιτο. Aor mid opt 3rd sg γίνομαι.

9:15 τῷ Μωϋσεῖ γὰρ λέγει· ἐλεήσω ὃν ἂν ἐλεῶ καὶ οἰκτιρήσω ὃν ἂν οἰκτίρω.

τῷ Μωϋσεῖ. Dative indirect object of λέγει. Fronting of the dative construction before the predicate indicates clausal prominence.

γὰρ. Postpositive explanatory conjunction that introduces Paul's explanation of why God is not unjust.

λέγει. Pres act ind 3rd sg λέγω. The implied subject of the verb is probably "God" from the previous co-text. It introduces a quotation from LXX Exod 33:19.

ἐλεήσω. Fut act ind 1st sg ἐλεέω. The future form conveys the semantic feature of expectation.

ὃν. The relative pronoun introduces a headless relative clause (ὃν ἂν ἐλεῶ) that functions as the direct object of ἐλεήσω. Within its clause, ὃν is the accusative direct object of ἐλεῶ.

ἂν. Conditional particle (cf. Porter 1994a, 206). It signifies a conditional generality. Here, then, God is saying (to Moses) that the one who receives mercy is based on a condition. Although the condition is not explicitly stated, it is likely God's purpose according to election (ἡ κατ᾽ ἐκλογὴν πρόθεσις). For both clauses with the future form (ἐλεήσω/οἰκτιρήσω), conditional particle (ἂν), and the subjunctive mood form (ἐλεῶ/οἰκτίρω), the meaning is that where God's showing mercy and compassion is a projected possibility, the showing of that mercy and compassion is to be expected. In other words, where a generality exists with showing mercy and compassion, the fulfillment of that is expected.

ἐλεῶ. Pres act subj 1st sg ἐλεέω. Subjunctive with ἂν.

καὶ. Coordinating conjunction that connects the two clauses ἐλεήσω ὃν ἂν ἐλεῶ and οἰκτιρήσω ὃν ἂν οἰκτίρω.

οἰκτιρήσω. Fut act ind 1st sg οἰκτίρω. A NT *hapax legomenon* (but see LXX Exod 33:19; Jer 13:14; 21:17).

ὃν. The relative pronoun introduces a headless relative clause (ὃν ἂν οἰκτίρω) that serves as the direct object of οἰκτιρήσω. Within its clause, ὃν is the accusative direct object of οἰκτίρω.

ἂν. Conditional particle. It signifies a conditional generality. Again, the condition for who receives compassion is God's purpose according to election (see above).

οἰκτίρω. Pres act subj 1st sg οἰκτίρω. Subjunctive with ἄν.

9:16 ἄρα οὖν οὐ τοῦ θέλοντος οὐδὲ τοῦ τρέχοντος ἀλλὰ τοῦ ἐλεῶντος θεοῦ.

Ἄρα οὖν. A combination of two inferential conjunctions; together it is emphatic (see 5:18). The inference of God's basis for bestowing mercy and compassion is from the previous quotation of LXX Exod 33:19.

οὐ . . . οὐδὲ . . . ἀλλὰ. A compound point/counterpoint set ("Neither . . . nor . . . but"). The negative particles negate the substantive participles τοῦ θέλοντος and τοῦ τρέχοντος, while the adversative conjunction ἀλλὰ replaces them with τοῦ ἐλεῶντος θεοῦ.

τοῦ θέλοντος. Pres act ptc masc gen sg θέλω (substantival). Genitive of origin or source, although there is no head term in this co-text. The inference is God's mercy and compassion; hence, the source of God's mercy and compassion is *not* the one who wills.

τοῦ τρέχοντος. Pres act ptc masc gen sg τρέχω (substantival). Genitive of origin or source. The source of God's mercy and compassion is *not* the one who runs.

τοῦ . . . θεοῦ. Genitive of origin or source. The source of God's mercy and compassion is the God who gives mercy.

ἐλεῶντος. Pres act ptc masc gen sg ἐλεάω (attributive). The participle modifies τοῦ . . . θεοῦ (first attributive position).

9:17 λέγει γὰρ ἡ γραφὴ τῷ Φαραὼ ὅτι εἰς αὐτὸ τοῦτο ἐξήγειρά σε ὅπως ἐνδείξωμαι ἐν σοὶ τὴν δύναμίν μου καὶ ὅπως διαγγελῇ τὸ ὄνομά μου ἐν πάσῃ τῇ γῇ.

λέγει. Pres act ind 3rd sg λέγω.

γὰρ. Postpositive explanatory conjunction. Paul continues his explanation regarding God's prerogative in showing mercy and compassion.

ἡ γραφὴ. Nominative subject of λέγει.

τῷ Φαραώ. Dative indirect object of λέγει.

ὅτι. Introduces the clausal complement (direct discourse) of λέγει.

εἰς αὐτὸ τοῦτο. Purpose. The use of the intensive pronoun and demonstrative pronoun ("for this very purpose") is emphatic (cf. Rom 13:6; 2 Cor 5:5; 7:11; Gal 2:10; Eph 6:22; Phil 1:6; Col 4:8; 2 Pet 1:5). The fronting of the prepositional word group before the predicate reflects clausal prominence.

ἐξήγειρά. Aor act ind 1st sg ἐξεγείρω. The additional accent on the ultima is a result of the following word being enclitic (see note on πνεύματί in 1:9).

σε. Accusative direct object of ἐξήγειρά.

ὅπως. Introduces a purpose clause.

ἐνδείξωμαι. Aor mid subj 1st sg ἐνδείκνυμι. Subjunctive with ὅπως.

ἐν σοί. Instrumental. Pharaoh is the instrument whereby God would display his power.

τὴν δύναμίν. Accusative direct object of ἐνδείξωμαι. The additional accent on the ultima is a result of the following word being enclitic (see note on πνεύματί in 1:9).

μου. Genitive of source or origin, modifying τὴν δύναμίν.

καὶ. Coordinating conjunction. It connects the two clauses ὅπως ἐνδείξωμαι ἐν σοὶ τὴν δύναμίν μου and ὅπως διαγγελῇ τὸ ὄνομά μου ἐν πάσῃ τῇ γῇ.

ὅπως. Introduces a second purpose clause.

διαγγελῇ. Aor pass subj 3rd sg διαγγέλλω. Subjunctive with ὅπως. Passive voice reflects external causality, the agent being unspecified here. The grammatical subject, "my name," is the Goal of the proclaiming.

τὸ ὄνομά. Nominative subject of διαγγελῇ. But with the passive voice, τὸ ὄνομά is the Goal of "proclaim." In other words, the object of proclaiming is God's name. The additional accent on the ultima is a result of the following word being enclitic (see note on πνεύματί in 1:9).

μου. Possessive genitive, modifying τὸ ὄνομά.

ἐν πάσῃ τῇ γῇ. Distributional. Metaphoric extension of the locative sense, where the proclamation of God's name is "distributed" among "all the earth."

9:18 ἄρα οὖν ὃν θέλει ἐλεεῖ, ὃν δὲ θέλει σκληρύνει.

ἄρα οὖν. A combination of two inferential conjunctions (see 9:16). The inference is from the previous co-text regarding God's basis for bestowing mercy and compassion.

ὅν. Introduces a headless relative clause (ὅν θέλει) that serves as the direct object of ἐλεεῖ. Within its clause, ὅν is the accusative direct object of θέλει.

θέλει. Pres act ind 3rd sg θέλω.

ἐλεεῖ. Pres act ind 3rd sg ἐλεέω.

ὅν. Introduces a headless relative clause (ὅν . . . θέλει) that serves as the direct object of σκληρύνει. Within its clause, ὅν is the accusative direct object of θέλει.

δὲ. Adversative conjunction (mild). The mild contrast is between the two clauses.

θέλει. Pres act ind 3rd sg θέλω.

σκληρύνει. Pres act ind 3rd sg σκληρύνω. It occurs only here in Paul.

9:19 Ἐρεῖς μοι οὖν· τί [οὖν] ἔτι μέμφεται; τῷ γὰρ βουλήματι αὐτοῦ τίς ἀνθέστηκεν;

Ἐρεῖς. Fut act ind 2nd sg λέγω. The second-person singular reflects Paul's hypothetical conversation partner, whether a Roman Jew or Gentile.

μοι. Dative indirect object of Ἐρεῖς.

οὖν. Postpositive inferential conjunction. The inference from the previous statements regarding God's prerogative in having mercy and hardening is stated here.

τί. Adverbial use of the interrogative pronoun ("why?").

[οὖν]. Transitional inferential conjunction. The major witnesses are divided on whether this word should be included in the text (with ουν: 𝔓⁴⁶, B, D, F, G; without ουν: ℵ, A, K, L, P).

ἔτι. Adverb (temporal). It modifies μέμφεται.

μέμφεται. Pres mid ind 3rd sg μέμφομαι. It occurs only here in Paul.

τῷ . . . βουλήματι. Dative direct object of ἀνθέστηκεν. The fronting of the direct object before the subject and the predicate indicates clausal prominence. In other words, the emphasis is on God's will, which they stand against.

γὰρ. Postpositive explanatory conjunction, introducing an explanation of the previous question of why he finds fault, since no one can resist his will (through use of a rhetorical question).

αὐτοῦ. Possessive genitive, modifying τῷ . . . βουλήματι.

τίς. Nominative subject of ἀνθέστηκεν.

ἀνθέστηκεν. Prf act ind 3rd sg ἀνθίστημι. The stative aspect of this lexeme reflects being in a state of standing against God; it also reflects discourse prominence as a marked tense-form. This lexeme depicts a sense of diametric opposition, especially with the prefix ἀντι- attached to it. It occurs only here in Paul.

9:20 ὦ ἄνθρωπε, μενοῦνγε σὺ τίς εἶ ὁ ἀνταποκρινόμενος τῷ θεῷ; μὴ ἐρεῖ τὸ πλάσμα τῷ πλάσαντι· τί με ἐποίησας οὕτως;

ὦ. Interjection.

ἄνθρωπε. Nominative of address (so-called vocative). The use of this address highlights the humanness of Paul's hypothetical conversation partner.

μενοῦνγε. Emphatic compound conjunction of contradiction consisting of three particles: μέν, οὖν, and γέ (Porter 1994a, 213; Porter 2015, 189; cf. Moule, 163–64; Thrall, 34–36). It occurs only in Paul (cf. Rom 10:18; Phil 3:8).

σὺ. Nominative subject of εἶ.

τίς. Predicate nominative.

εἶ. Unaugmented ind 2nd sg εἰμί.

ὁ ἀνταποκρινόμενος. Pres mid ptc masc nom sg ἀνταποκρίνομαι (substantival). It functions as a nominative in apposition to σύ. The double prefixed form of the predicate implies answering in a confrontational manner. This verb occurs only here in Paul.

τῷ θεῷ. Dative indirect object of ἀνταποκρινόμενος.

μὴ. Negative particle that introduces a question that expects a negative answer.

ἐρεῖ. Fut act ind 3rd sg λέγω.

τὸ πλάσμα. Nominative subject of ἐρεῖ.

τῷ πλάσαντι. Aor act ptc masc dat sg πλάσσω (substantival). Dative indirect object of ἐρεῖ. There is a clear play on the lexeme πλάσμα/πλάσσω here, referring here to God as "the one who molds" and the human as "that which is molded" (cf. 1 Tim 2:13).

τί. Adverbial use of the interrogative pronoun ("why?").

με. Accusative direct object of ἐποίησας.

ἐποίησας. Aor act ind 2nd sg ποιέω.

οὕτως. Adverb (manner). It modifies ἐποίησας.

9:21 ἢ οὐκ ἔχει ἐξουσίαν ὁ κεραμεὺς τοῦ πηλοῦ ἐκ τοῦ αὐτοῦ φυράματος ποιῆσαι ὃ μὲν εἰς τιμὴν σκεῦος ὃ δὲ εἰς ἀτιμίαν;

ἢ. Disjunctive conjunction. It functions adversatively, contrasting the statements before and after it.

οὐκ. Negative particle that introduces a question that expects an affirmative answer.

ἔχει. Pres act ind 3rd sg ἔχω.

ἐξουσίαν. Accusative direct object of ἔχει. The fronting of the accusative object before the head term (nominative subject) indicates clausal prominence.

ὁ κεραμεὺς. Nominative subject of ἔχει.

τοῦ πηλοῦ. Possessive genitive. While most English translations supply "over the clay" here in reference to the potter's authority, the syntax here indicates that the genitive modifies ὁ κεραμεὺς, most likely with a possessive function ("the potter of the clay").

ἐκ τοῦ αὐτοῦ φυράματος. Source or origin. The source or origin of the making is "the same lump." The intensive pronoun αὐτοῦ functions as an identifying adjective ("the same").

ποιῆσαι. Aor act inf ποιέω (epexegetical to ἐξουσίαν).

ὃ. Accusative direct object of ποιῆσαι. The relative pronoun introduces an internally headed relative clause because its antecedent (σκεῦος) is incorporated into the relative clause.

μὲν . . . δὲ. A point/counterpoint set that is used for contrast between ὃ . . . εἰς τιμὴν σκεῦος and ὃ . . . εἰς ἀτιμίαν.

εἰς τιμὴν. Purpose. The purpose of making the vessel, here, is for "honor."

σκεῦος. Accusative direct object of ποιῆσαι.

ὃ. Accusative direct object of ποιῆσαι. The antecedent of the relative pronoun is σκεῦος.

εἰς ἀτιμίαν. Purpose. The purpose of making the vessel, here, is for "dishonor."

9:22 εἰ δὲ θέλων ὁ θεὸς ἐνδείξασθαι τὴν ὀργὴν καὶ γνωρίσαι τὸ δυνατὸν αὐτοῦ ἤνεγκεν ἐν πολλῇ μακροθυμίᾳ σκεύη ὀργῆς κατηρτισμένα εἰς ἀπώλειαν,

This verse and the next two (9:22–24) comprise a single, albeit lengthy, question (as opposed to the UBS⁵ and NA²⁸ editions, which include only Rom 9:22–23 in the question) utilizing a conditional structure.

εἰ. Introduces the protasis of a first-class conditional. This conditional clause has no apodosis.

δὲ. Adversative conjunction (mild). The line of questioning continues, with a mild adversative here.

θέλων. Pres act ptc masc nom sg θέλω (causal). The participle functions as circumstantial and modifies the main predicate ἤνεγκεν.

ὁ θεὸς. Nominative subject of ἤνεγκεν.

ἐνδείξασθαι. Aor mid inf ἐνδείκνυμι (complementary). The infinitive is a complement of θέλων.

τὴν ὀργὴν. Accusative direct object of ἐνδείξασθαι.

καὶ. Coordinating conjunction that connects two infinitival clauses, ἐνδείξασθαι τὴν ὀργὴν and γνωρίσαι τὸ δυνατὸν αὐτοῦ.

γνωρίσαι. Aor act inf γνωρίζω (complementary). The infinitive is a complement of θέλων, parallel to ἐνδείξασθαι.

τὸ δυνατὸν. Accusative direct object of γνωρίσαι. τὸ δυνατὸν is a substantival adjective.

αὐτοῦ. Genitive of source or origin, modifying τὸ δυνατὸν. The use of the personal pronoun here, but omitted in the parallel construction ἐνδείξασθαι τὴν ὀργὴν, reflects *his* power but wrath in general.

ἤνεγκεν. Aor act ind 3rd sg φέρω. This is the main predicate in this verse.

ἐν πολλῇ μακροθυμίᾳ. Manner. The manner in which God bore, or put up with, vessels of wrath is "great patience."

σκεύη. Accusative direct object of ἤνεγκεν.

ὀργῆς. Genitive of description or definition, modifying σκεύη. "Vessels" is further described or circumscribed as "of wrath."

κατηρτισμένα. Prf pass ptc neut acc pl καταρτίζω (attributive). This adjectival participle modifies σκεύη (fourth attributive position). The stative aspect of this participle reflects a state of preparation that the vessels of wrath are in. The passive voice indicates external causality. The agent is not specified here, but in the context of God being the potter having authority over the clay, it seems to indicate that he is the one preparing vessels of wrath for destruction, albeit "in great patience" (Porter 2015, 190–91).

εἰς ἀπώλειαν. Purpose. The purpose of "being prepared" is "destruction."

9:23 καὶ ἵνα γνωρίσῃ τὸν πλοῦτον τῆς δόξης αὐτοῦ ἐπὶ σκεύη ἐλέους ἃ προητοίμασεν εἰς δόξαν;

καὶ. Adverbial use (adjunctive). It modifies the entire clause that follows.

ἵνα. Introduces a purpose clause.

γνωρίσῃ. Aor act subj 3rd sg γνωρίζω. Subjunctive with ἵνα.

τὸν πλοῦτον. Accusative direct object of γνωρίσῃ.

τῆς δόξης. Partitive genitive, modifying τὸν πλοῦτον.

αὐτοῦ. Possessive genitive, modifying τῆς δόξης.

ἐπὶ σκεύη. Directional. The riches of his glory are directed to "vessels of mercy."

ἐλέους. Genitive of description or definition, modifying σκεύη. "Vessels" is further described or circumscribed as "of mercy."

ἅ. Accusative direct object of γνωρίσῃ. The antecedent of the relative pronoun is σκεύη ἐλέους.

προητοίμασεν. Aor act ind 3rd sg προετοιμάζω. This verb only occurs here and in Eph 2:10 in the NT.

εἰς δόξαν. Purpose. The purpose of "preparing beforehand" is "glory." The absence of an article or a possessive pronoun for δόξαν indicates reference to a general glory (not necessarily to "his glory" in this verse).

9:24 Οὓς καὶ ἐκάλεσεν ἡμᾶς οὐ μόνον ἐξ Ἰουδαίων ἀλλὰ καὶ ἐξ ἐθνῶν,

Οὓς. Accusative direct object of ἐκάλεσεν. The relative pronoun introduces an internally headed relative clause because its cataphoric referent (ἡμᾶς) is incorporated into the relative clause, hence matching the masculine plural. Although the punctuation in NA[28] and UBS[5] makes this a relative clause starting a new paragraph, it is better to take it with verses 22–23, as most English translations do. The change from neuter ἅ to masculine Οὓς reflects the real gender (Robertson, 713).

καὶ. Adverbial use (adjunctive). It modifies ἐκάλεσεν.

ἐκάλεσεν. Aor act ind 3rd sg καλέω.

ἡμᾶς. The incorporation of the antecedent into the relative clause gives the impression that this is the accusative direct object of ἐκάλεσεν, but in a reconstructed word order (ἡμᾶς οὓς καὶ ἐκάλεσεν), ἡμᾶς functions as the accusative in apposition to the relative pronoun ἅ in the previous verse: ". . . which he prepared beforehand for glory—us, whom he also called . . ."

οὐ μόνον . . . ἀλλὰ καὶ. A point/counterpoint set ("not only . . . but also") that supplements ἐξ Ἰουδαίων with ἐξ ἐθνῶν.

ἐξ Ἰουδαίων. Origin or source.

ἐξ ἐθνῶν. Origin or source.

9:25 ὡς καὶ ἐν τῷ Ὡσηὲ λέγει· καλέσω τὸν οὐ λαόν μου λαόν μου καὶ τὴν οὐκ ἠγαπημένην ἠγαπημένην·

ὡς. Comparative conjunction. It compares the previous statement with the following Hosea passage.

καὶ. Adverbial use (adjunctive). It modifies the prepositional word group ἐν τῷ Ὡσηὲ λέγει.

ἐν τῷ Ὡσηὲ. Locative.

λέγει. Pres act ind 3rd sg λέγω. The loose quotation that follows is from LXX Hos 2:23.

καλέσω. Fut act ind 1st sg καλέω. The verb has two sets of double accusative object-complement constructions, each one introduced by an accusative article, τὸν and τὴν.

τὸν. Accusative singular article with direct objects of καλέσω in the first double accusative object-complement construction. The article modifies both objects, one negative and the other positive.

οὐ λαόν. Accusative direct object of καλέσω in the first double accusative object-complement construction. The noun is negated ("those who [were] not my people").

μου. Possessive genitive, modifying οὐ λαόν.

λαόν. Complement to οὐ λαόν in the first double accusative object-complement construction. This noun is not negated ("those who [were] my people").

μου. Possessive genitive, modifying λαόν.

καί. Coordinating conjunction that connects the two double accusative object-complement constructions.

τὴν. Accusative singular article with direct objects of καλέσω in the second double accusative object-complement construction. As in the first, the article modifies both objects, one negative and the other positive.

οὐκ ἠγαπημένην. Prf pass ptc fem acc sg ἀγαπάω (substantival). Accusative direct object of καλέσω in the second double accusative object-complement construction. The substantival participle is negated ("those not beloved"). The stative aspect (also below) reflects a state of being loved.

ἠγαπημένην. Prf pass ptc fem acc sg ἀγαπάω (substantival). Complement to οὐκ ἠγαπημένην in the second double accusative object-complement construction. This substantival participle is not negated ("those beloved").

9:26 καὶ ἔσται ἐν τῷ τόπῳ οὗ ἐρρέθη αὐτοῖς· οὐ λαός μου ὑμεῖς, ἐκεῖ κληθήσονται υἱοὶ θεοῦ ζῶντος.

καί. Coordinating conjunction that connects the previous statement with the following. It marks the beginning of the quotation of Hos 1:10, here quoted verbatim from LXX Hos 2:1.

ἔσται. Fut 3rd sg εἰμί.

ἐν τῷ τόπῳ. Locative.

οὗ. The genitive relative pronoun sometimes serves, as it does here, as an adverb of place (cf. 5:20).

ἐρρέθη. Aor pass ind 3rd sg λέγω. Passive voice indicates external causality. The agent is not specified here, but contextually implies God who is speaking.

αὐτοῖς. Dative indirect object of ἐρρέθη.

οὐ. Negative particle that negates λαός μου.

λαός. Predicate nominative.

μου. Possessive genitive, modifying λαός.

ὑμεῖς. Nominative subject of verbless clause.

ἐκεῖ. Adverb of place. It modifies κληθήσονται.

κληθήσονται. Fut pass ind 3rd pl καλέω. Passive voice indicates external causality. The implied agent is God (see ἐρρέθη above).

υἱοί. Nominative complement to the implied third-person plural subject of κληθήσονται in a double nominative subject-complement construction. With the predicate in passive voice, the grammatical subject is the Goal of κληθήσονται.

θεοῦ ζῶντος. Possessive genitive, or genitive of source or origin, modifying υἱοί.

ζῶντος. Pres act ptc masc gen sg ζάω (attributive). The participle modifies θεοῦ (fourth attributive position).

9:27 Ἠσαΐας δὲ κράζει ὑπὲρ τοῦ Ἰσραήλ· ἐὰν ᾖ ὁ ἀριθμὸς τῶν υἱῶν Ἰσραὴλ ὡς ἡ ἄμμος τῆς θαλάσσης, τὸ ὑπόλειμμα σωθήσεται·

Ἠσαΐας. Nominative subject of κράζει.

δὲ. Adversative conjunction (mild).

κράζει. Pres act ind 3rd sg κράζω.

ὑπὲρ τοῦ Ἰσραήλ. Beneficial. Isaiah crying out is for the benefit of Israel. Some translations (e.g., NASB, NIV, NKJV, NRSV) render this as "concerning Israel," but the function of the preposition here has a stronger sense of benefit, with the core meaning of the preposition as "above" or "over" (Robertson, 631; Porter 1994a, 176).

ἐὰν. Introduces the protasis of a third-class conditional. The paraphrased reference from LXX Isa 10:22–23 begins here.

ᾖ. Subj 3rd sg εἰμί. Subjunctive with ἐὰν

ὁ ἀριθμὸς. Nominative subject of ᾖ.

τῶν υἱῶν. Partitive genitive, modifying ὁ ἀριθμὸς.

Ἰσραὴλ. Genitive of source or origin, modifying τῶν υἱῶν. Ἰσραὴλ is a proper noun.

ὡς. Comparative conjunction. The comparison is made between "the number of the sons of Israel" and "the sand of the sea."

ἡ ἄμμος. Predicate nominative.

τῆς θαλάσσης. Genitive of source or origin, modifying ἡ ἄμμος.

τὸ ὑπόλειμμα. Nominative subject of σωθήσεται. A NT *hapax legomenon* (although an unprefixed form is found in 11:5). With the passive voice predicate, it is the Goal of σωθήσεται. The apodosis of the third-class conditional structure begins here.

σωθήσεται. Fut pass ind 3rd sg σῴζω. Passive voice indicates external causality. The implied agent is God.

9:28 λόγον γὰρ συντελῶν καὶ συντέμνων ποιήσει κύριος ἐπὶ τῆς γῆς.

λόγον. Accusative direct object of ποιήσει. The fronting of the accusative object reflects clausal prominence. This verse continues a paraphrased reference from LXX Isa 10:23.

γὰρ. Postpositive explanatory conjunction that introduces Paul's explanation of the previous statement that the remnant will be saved.

συντελῶν καὶ συντέμνων. Although it may seem redundant, the two participles modifying ποιήσει are present for the sake of emphasis.

συντελῶν. Pres act ptc masc nom sg συντελέω (manner). The participle modifies ποιήσει.

καὶ. Coordinating conjunction. Connects the two participles συντελῶν and συντέμνων.

συντέμνων. Pres act ptc masc nom sg συντέμνω (manner). The participle modifies ποιήσει.

ποιήσει. Fut act ind 3rd sg ποιέω.

κύριος. Nominative subject of ποιήσει.

ἐπὶ γῆς. Locative. The place where God will accomplish his word is "upon earth."

9:29 καὶ καθὼς προείρηκεν Ἠσαΐας· εἰ μὴ κύριος σαβαὼθ ἐγκατέλιπεν ἡμῖν σπέρμα, ὡς Σόδομα ἂν ἐγενήθημεν καὶ ὡς Γόμορρα ἂν ὡμοιώθημεν

καὶ. Coordinating conjunction that adds the reference from LXX Isa 1:9 to the previous scriptural quotations.

καθὼς. Comparative conjunction. The comparison is with what Isaiah states in the following.

προείρηκεν. Prf act ind 3rd sg προλέγω. The stative aspect reflects a state of speaking in advance and thus is prominent in the discourse.

Ἠσαΐας. Nominative subject of προείρηκεν.

εἰ μὴ. A combination of the conditional conjunction and the negative particle (usually translated "except" or "if not") that introduces the protasis of a second-class conditional (the so-called contrary-to-fact conditional; it reflects the writer's belief that this conditional does not reflect reality). See note on εἰ μή in 7:7.

κύριος. Nominative subject of ἐγκατέλιπεν.

σαβαώθ. Possessive genitive, modifying κύριος. σαβαώθ is a transliteration from Hebrew, "meaning armies and used with κύριος Lord" (LN 12.8).

ἐγκατέλιπεν. Aor act ind 3rd sg ἐγκαταλείπω.

ἡμῖν. Dative indirect object of ἐγκαταλείπω.

σπέρμα. Accusative direct object of ἐγκαταλείπω. It probably functions as a cohesive substitutionary reference to τὸ ὑπόλειμμα in 9:27 (cf. Porter 2015, 192).

ὡς. Comparative conjunction that marks the beginning of the apodosis. Comparison is to Sodom.

Σόδομα. Predicate nominative.

ἄν. Conditional particle. It signifies a conditional generality.

ἐγενήθημεν. Aor pass ind 1st pl γίνομαι. Passive voice indicates external causality. The agent is unspecified, but likely implies God is the one who makes them like Sodom.

καί. Coordinating conjunction that connects the two clauses, ὡς Σόδομα ἂν ἐγενήθημεν and ὡς Γόμορρα ἂν ὡμοιώθημεν.

ὡς. Comparative conjunction. Comparison is to Gomorrah.

Γόμορρα. Predicate nominative.

ἄν. Conditional particle. It signifies a conditional generality.

ὡμοιώθημεν. Aor pass ind 1st pl ὁμοιόω. Passive voice indicates external causality. The agent is unspecified, but likely implies that God is the one who makes them like Gomorrah. This is the only occurrence of this verb in Romans.

Romans 9:30–33

[30]What shall we say, then? That Gentiles who did not pursue righteousness obtained righteousness, but a righteousness which is by faith. [31]But Israel, pursuing a law of righteousness, did not attain law. [32]Why? Because [it was] not by faith but as by works; they stumbled upon the stone of stumbling, [33]just as it is written, "Behold, I lay in Zion a stone of stumbling and a rock of offense, and the one who believes in him will not be put to shame."

This brief sub-section continues Paul's interlocutory dialogue and his appeals to Scripture as in the previous sub-section.

9:30 Τί οὖν ἐροῦμεν; ὅτι ἔθνη τὰ μὴ διώκοντα δικαιοσύνην κατέλαβεν δικαιοσύνην, δικαιοσύνην δὲ τὴν ἐκ πίστεως,

Τί οὖν ἐροῦμεν. A rhetorical question that has been used by Paul throughout this letter to transition to a related but new logical progression (4:1; 6:1; 7:7; 8:31; 9:14, 30). It marks Paul's return to his diatribal, interlocutory style.

Τί. Accusative direct object of ἐροῦμεν.

οὖν. Postpositive inferential conjunction. From what has been stated thus far, he poses a potential interlocutionary inference.

ἐροῦμεν. Fut ind 1st pl λέγω.

ὅτι. Introduces a clausal complement (indirect discourse) of an implied repetition of ἐροῦμεν ("[Shall we say] that Gentiles . . ").

ἔθνη. Nominative subject of κατέλαβεν.

τὰ μὴ διώκοντα. Pres act ptc neut nom pl διώκω (attributive). The negated adjectival participle modifies ἔθνη (third attributive position).

δικαιοσύνην. Accusative direct object of διώκοντα.

κατέλαβεν. Aor act ind 3rd sg καταλαμβάνω.

δικαιοσύνην. Accusative direct object of κατέλαβεν.

δικαιοσύνην. Accusative in apposition to the previous instance of the same lexeme. The repetition of δικαιοσύνην in this verse reflects lexical cohesion and thematic prominence.

δὲ. Adversative conjunction (mild). The mild contrast is between "righteousness" in general and "righteousness that is by faith."

τὴν ἐκ πίστεως. The article functions as a nominalizer, changing the prepositional word group ἐκ πίστεως into an attributive modifier of δικαιοσύνην (third attributive position).

ἐκ πίστεως. Instrumental.

9:31 Ἰσραὴλ δὲ διώκων νόμον δικαιοσύνης εἰς νόμον οὐκ ἔφθασεν.

Ἰσραὴλ. Nominative subject of ἔφθασεν.

δὲ. Adversative conjunction (mild). It continues the discourse and contrasts the statement about Gentiles with the following statement about Israel.

διώκων. Pres act ptc masc nom sg διώκω (concessive). If functions as circumstantial in the co-text and modifies ἔφθασεν.

νόμον. Accusative direct object of διώκων. The anarthrous substantive refers to an unspecified (general) law of righteousness.

δικαιοσύνης. Genitive of description or definition, modifying νόμον. "Law" is further described or circumscribed as "of righteousness."

εἰς νόμον. Goal or state. The goal of attainment is "law" (anarthrous, referring to the law qualitatively). The fronting of the prepositional word group before the predicate indicates clausal prominence; i.e., Paul emphasizes "law" in this phrase.

οὐκ. Negative particle normally used with indicative verbs. Here it negates ἔφθασεν.

ἔφθασεν. Aor act ind 3rd sg φθάνω. By placing the main predicate at the end of the clause, Paul wants to identify the situation or circumstance first, that they sought after a law of righteousness.

9:32 διὰ τί; ὅτι οὐκ ἐκ πίστεως ἀλλ᾽ ὡς ἐξ ἔργων· προσέκοψαν τῷ λίθῳ τοῦ προσκόμματος,

διὰ τί. Causal. With the interrogative pronoun, the prepositional word group means "why" or "because of what."

ὅτι. Introduces a causal clause that begins the answer to the posed question.

οὐκ . . . ἀλλ᾽. A point/counterpoint set that contrasts ἐκ πίστεως with ὡς ἐξ ἔργων.

ἐκ πίστεως. Instrumental. The elided, but implied, predicate is ἔφθασεν from the previous co-text. In other words, they attained it "not by faith."

ὡς. Comparative conjunction. It compares the implied predicate ἔφθασεν with ἐξ ἔργων. It is parallel to οὐκ above.

ἐξ ἔργων. Instrumental.

προσέκοψαν. Aor act ind 3rd pl προσκόπτω. The subject is not specified but co-textually is Israel.

τῷ λίθῳ. Dative direct object of προσέκοψαν.

τοῦ προσκόμματος. Genitive of quality, modifying τῷ λίθῳ. The repetition of προσκόπτω (but in nominal form) reflects prominence through lexical cohesion here.

9:33 καθὼς γέγραπται· ἰδοὺ τίθημι ἐν Σιὼν λίθον προσκόμματος καὶ πέτραν σκανδάλου, καὶ ὁ πιστεύων ἐπ᾽ αὐτῷ οὐ καταισχυνθήσεται.

καθὼς γέγραπται. A common Pauline formula to indicate an OT quotation (see note on 1:17). It introduces a combination of LXX Isa 28:16 and 8:14.

καθώς. Comparative conjunction. The comparison is to the previous statement.

γέγραπται. Prf pass ind 3rd sg γράφω.

ἰδού. A fixed form imperative (Porter 2015, 194), a marker of attention (LN 91.13). This is its only occurrence in Romans (cf. 1 Cor 15:51;
2 Cor 5:17; 6:2, 9; 7:11; 12:14; Gal 1:20).

τίθημι. Pres act ind 1st sg τίθημι. The implied subject is God.

ἐν Σιών. Locative.

λίθον. Accusative direct object of τίθημι.

προσκόμματος. Genitive of quality, modifying λίθον (see 9:32 on
τοῦ προσκόμματος).

καί. Coordinating conjunction that connects λίθον προσκόμματος
with πέτραν σκανδάλου.

πέτραν. Accusative direct object of τίθημι.

σκανδάλου. Genitive of quality, modifying πέτραν.

καί. Coordinating conjunction that connects the two clauses before
and after it.

ὁ πιστεύων. Pres act ptc masc nom sg πιστεύω (substantival). Nominative subject of καταισχυνθήσεται. As the grammatical subject of a
passive voice predicate, it is the Goal.

ἐπ' αὐτῷ. Locative (sphere or realm). The sphere or realm of belief is
"him" (contextually referring to Jesus).

οὐ. Negative particle normally used with indicative verbs. Here it
negates καταισχυνθήσεται.

καταισχυνθήσεται. Fut pass ind 3rd sg καταισχύνω. Passive voice
indicates external causality. The agent (cause) is unspecified here and
thus is probably a generality.

Romans 10:1–13

[1]Brothers [and sisters], the desire of my heart and the prayer to God on
their behalf [is] for [their] salvation. [2]For I testify about them that they
have zeal for God but not according to knowledge. [3]For being ignorant
of the righteousness of God and seeking to establish their own [righ-
teousness], they were not subjected to the righteousness of God. [4]For the
end of law [is] Christ for righteousness to everyone who believes. [5]For
Moses writes about the righteousness that comes from the law, that the
person who does them lives in them. [6]But the righteousness that comes
from faith thus says, "Do not say in your heart, 'Who will ascend into
heaven?' (that is, to bring Christ down), [7]or, 'Who will descend into the
abyss?' (that is, to lead Christ up from the dead)." [8]But what does it say?
"The word is near you, in your mouth and in your heart." That is the
word of faith which we proclaim. [9]Because if you would confess in your
mouth Jesus is Lord and would believe in your heart that God raised
him from the dead, you will be saved. [10]For with the heart one believes,

leading to righteousness, and with the mouth one confesses, leading to salvation. [11]For the Scripture says, "Everyone who believes upon him will not be put to shame." [12]For there is no distinction between Jew and Gentile, for [he is] the same Lord of all, giving abundantly to all who call upon him. [13]For "everyone who calls upon the name of the Lord will be saved."

This next sub-section continues Paul's discourse on Israel, his kinsmen. Paul briefly pauses his interlocutory style (except for in 10:8), and liberally uses γάρ (nine times in this sub-section) to further his explanation of the salvation of his fellow Israelite people.

10:1 Ἀδελφοί, ἡ μὲν εὐδοκία τῆς ἐμῆς καρδίας καὶ ἡ δέησις πρὸς τὸν θεὸν ὑπὲρ αὐτῶν εἰς σωτηρίαν.

Ἀδελφοί. Nominative of address (so-called vocative). Ἀδελφοί is an address commonly used by Paul to communicate equal status in God's family.

ἡ . . . εὐδοκία. Nominative subject of verbless clause.

μὲν. The first element of a point/counterpoint set. The correlative δέ is missing.

τῆς ἐμῆς καρδίας. Genitive of source or origin, modifying ἡ . . . εὐδοκία. ἐμῆς is a possessive adjective, which is embedded between the genitive article and noun in an attributive structure to highlight its attributive relationship to the noun.

καὶ. Coordinating conjunction. It connects ἡ εὐδοκία with ἡ δέησις.

ἡ δέησις. Nominative subject of verbless clause. It is parallel with ἡ εὐδοκία.

πρὸς τὸν θεὸν. Directional (movement toward). The prayer is directed to God.

ὑπὲρ αὐτῶν. Beneficial. The beneficiaries of Paul's prayer to God is "them," i.e., Israel.

εἰς σωτηρίαν. Purpose. The purpose of Paul's desire and prayer is "salvation." The prepositional word group modifies αὐτῶν.

10:2 μαρτυρῶ γὰρ αὐτοῖς ὅτι ζῆλον θεοῦ ἔχουσιν ἀλλ' οὐ κατ' ἐπίγνωσιν·

μαρτυρῶ. Pres act ind 1st sg μαρτυρέω.

γὰρ. Postpositive explanatory conjunction. Paul explains his desire and prayer for Israel to be saved.

αὐτοῖς. Dative of respect of μαρτυρῶ.

ὅτι. Introduces a clausal complement (indirect discourse) of μαρτυρῶ.

ζῆλον. Accusative direct object of ἔχουσιν.

θεοῦ. Genitive of description of definition, modifying ζῆλον. "Zeal" is further described or circumscribed as "of God." Some may wish to interpret this as an objective genitive, with God as the object of zeal.

ἔχουσιν. Pres act ind 3rd pl ἔχω.

ἀλλ'. Adversative conjunction (strong).

οὐ. Negative particle that negates κατ' ἐπίγνωσιν.

κατ' ἐπίγνωσιν. Standard. The standard by which Israel has the zeal of God is not knowledge (cf. Rom 1:28). The prefixed form of ἐπίγνωσιν highlights "knowledge" that is *upon* an object; in this context, the object is "God."

10:3 ἀγνοοῦντες γὰρ τὴν τοῦ θεοῦ δικαιοσύνην καὶ τὴν ἰδίαν [δικαι-οσύνην] ζητοῦντες στῆσαι, τῇ δικαιοσύνῃ τοῦ θεοῦ οὐχ ὑπετάγησαν.

This verse consists of two secondary (subordinate) clauses, marked by nominative participles, before the primary (main) clause. The fronting of supporting material before the main predicate (both secondary clauses and the prepositional word group) in this verse reflects clause complex (or sentence) prominence. Furthermore, there is a micro-chiastic structure (cf. Porter and Reed) in this verse with the two participial clauses:

A—ἀγνοοῦντες
B—τὴν τοῦ θεοῦ δικαιοσύνην
B'—τὴν ἰδίαν [δικαιοσύνην]
A'—ζητοῦντες στῆσαι

The focal points of this structure are the middle elements (B and B'). Paul focuses on the contrast between the righteousness of God and their own righteousness.

ἀγνοοῦντες. Pres act ptc masc nom pl ἀγνοέω (causal). The participle functions as circumstantial and modifies ὑπετάγησαν.

γὰρ. Postpositive explanatory conjunction. Paul further explains what he means by his prior statement that the Israelites have a zeal not based on knowledge.

τὴν . . . δικαιοσύνην. Accusative direct object of ἀγνοοῦντες.

τοῦ θεοῦ. Possessive genitive, or possibly genitive of source or origin, modifying τὴν . . . δικαιοσύνην. The placement of the genitive between the article and substantive gives it an attributive function (i.e., "the of-God righteousness" or "the from-God righteousness").

καί. Coordinating conjunction. It connects the two participial clauses before and after it.

τὴν ἰδίαν [δικαιοσύνην]. Accusative direct object of ζητοῦντες. See above on the micro-chiastic structure here. Of the earliest manuscripts, 𝔓⁴⁶ and א contain δικαιοσύνην, while A, B, and D do not. It is likely that a scribe inserted this lexeme for purposes of clarification and parallelism with the previous clause (cf. Porter 2015, 195–96). In the shorter text, ἰδίαν functions as a substantival adjective. In the longer text, ἰδίαν functions as a regular adjective (first attributive position).

ζητοῦντες. Pres act ptc masc nom pl ζητέω (causal). The participle functions as circumstantial and modifies ὑπετάγησαν. It is parallel to ἀγνοοῦντες.

στῆσαι. Aor act inf ἵστημι (complementary). The statement would stand alone without στῆσαι, but in using it to complement ζητοῦντες, Paul identifies not only them seeking their own righteousness but seeking *to establish* their own righteousness.

τῇ δικαιοσύνῃ. Dative complement of ὑπετάγησαν. The primary clause of this verse begins here. The fronting of τῇ δικαιοσύνῃ reflects clausal prominence.

τοῦ θεοῦ. Possessive genitive, or possibly genitive of source or origin, modifying τῇ δικαιοσύνῃ.

οὐχ. Negative particle normally used with indicative verbs. Here it negates ὑπετάγησαν.

ὑπετάγησαν. Aor pass ind 3rd pl ὑποτάσσω. The use of the passive voice-form here indicates that the grammatical subject, "they" (i.e., Israel, from 9:31), is the Goal of the "subjecting." The agent, however, is unspecified.

10:4 τέλος γὰρ νόμου Χριστὸς εἰς δικαιοσύνην παντὶ τῷ πιστεύοντι.

τέλος. Nominative subject of verbless clause. The meaning of τέλος is debated: it can either mean (1) end, as in termination of law, or (2) goal, as in purpose of law. While the goal or purpose of the law is indeed Christ, in the sense that he is the fulfillment of it, it makes better sense in this co-text to interpret this as "end" or "termination" of law, where Paul has been arguing for the ineffectiveness of the law to attain righteousness.

γάρ. Postpositive explanatory conjunction that introduces an explanation of righteousness.

νόμου. Partitive genitive, modifying τέλος.

Χριστός. Predicate nominative of verbless clause.

εἰς δικαιοσύνην. Purpose. The purpose of the end of the law being Christ is "righteousness." The repetition of δικαιοσύνη in this co-text reflects lexical cohesion.

παντὶ τῷ πιστεύοντι. Dative of advantage. See notes on παντὶ τῷ πιστεύοντι in 1:16.

πιστεύοντι. Pres act ptc masc dat sg πιστεύω (attributive).

10:5 Μωϋσῆς γὰρ γράφει τὴν δικαιοσύνην τὴν ἐκ [τοῦ] νόμου ὅτι ὁ ποιήσας αὐτὰ ἄνθρωπος ζήσεται ἐν αὐτοῖς.

Μωϋσῆς. Nominative subject of γράφει. Μωϋσῆς is a proper noun.

γὰρ. Postpositive explanatory conjunction that continues the explanation regarding righteousness.

γράφει. Pres act ind 3rd sg γράφω.

τὴν δικαιοσύνην. Accusative of respect.

τὴν ἐκ [τοῦ] νόμου. The article functions as an adjectivizer, changing the prepositional word group into an attributive modifier of τὴν δικαιοσύνην.

ἐκ [τοῦ] νόμου. Instrumental. The instrument, or cause, of righteousness that Moses refers to here is the law. The article τοῦ does not appear in the best early manuscripts.

ὅτι. Introduces the clausal complement (indirect discourse) of γράφει. While some may view this as a purpose or casual conjunction (i.e., "because"), it is more likely that Paul is referencing Lev 18:5 here (see Porter 2015, 197).

ὁ . . . ἄνθρωπος. Nominative subject of ζήσεται.

ποιήσας. Aor act ptc masc nom sg ποιέω (attributive). The participle functions in attributive structure (along with αὐτὰ), modifying ὁ ἄνθρωπος.

αὐτὰ. Accusative direct object of ποιήσας.

ζήσεται. Fut mid ind 3rd sg ζάω. The middle voice indicates indirect, internal causality. In other words, it is not simply that the subject lives in them but that the subject is directly involved in, perhaps even responsible for, the living.

ἐν αὐτοῖς. Locative (sphere or realm). The sphere or realm that they will live is "in them," an anaphoric reference to αὐτὰ, i.e., the righteousness found in the law. The use of the plural pronoun is probably due to the reference of Lev 18:5, although the clause itself is not a direct quotation of it.

10:6 ἡ δὲ ἐκ πίστεως δικαιοσύνη οὕτως λέγει· μὴ εἴπῃς ἐν τῇ καρδίᾳ σου· τίς ἀναβήσεται εἰς τὸν οὐρανόν; τοῦτ᾽ ἔστιν Χριστὸν καταγαγεῖν·

ἡ . . . δικαιοσύνη. Nominative subject of λέγει. "Righteousness" is personified here by relating a speaking verb to it.

δέ. Adversative conjunction (mild). The mild contrast is between the righteousness that comes from the law (10:5) and the righteousness that comes from faith.

ἐκ πίστεως. Instrumental. The instrument, or cause, of righteousness is "faith." Occurring between the article and substantive, it functions in attributive structure as a modifier (i.e., "the by-faith righteousness").

οὕτως. Adverb (manner). It modifies λέγει.

λέγει. Pres act ind 3rd sg λέγω.

μή. Negative particle used with aorist subjunctive to convey a prohibition. This begins a reference to LXX Deut 9:4.

εἴπῃς. Aor act subj 2nd sg λέγω (prohibitive subjunctive). The use of the aorist in this prohibition depicts the verbal process as an undifferentiated whole; thus, it is a general prohibition from saying this in their hearts.

ἐν τῇ καρδίᾳ. Locative.

σου. Possessive genitive, modifying τῇ καρδίᾳ.

τίς. Nominative subject of ἀναβήσεται. This begins a reference to LXX Deut 30:12.

ἀναβήσεται. Fut mid ind 3rd sg ἀναβαίνω. The middle voice indicates indirect, internal causality. In contrast to an active voice-form, the middle reflects the ascending as being internal but direct agency is unspecified (see Introduction).

εἰς τὸν οὐρανόν. Directional, but also entailing by extension the senses of goal/state and purpose (telic).

τοῦτ' ἔστιν. Explanatory formula (see 9:8).

τοῦτ'. Nominative subject of ἔστιν.

ἔστιν. Unaugmented ind 3rd sg εἰμί.

Χριστὸν. Accusative direct object of καταγαγεῖν. The fronting of the accusative object before the infinitive indicates clausal prominence.

καταγαγεῖν. Aor act inf κατάγω (purpose). Complementary infinitive is typically used with "helper verbs," which ἔστιν is not in this verse (it is a part of the phrase τοῦτ' ἔστιν). In fact, this infinitive continues the thought of the quoted text, indicating the purpose of ascending into heaven.

10:7 ἤ· τίς καταβήσεται εἰς τὴν ἄβυσσον; τοῦτ' ἔστιν Χριστὸν ἐκ νεκρῶν ἀναγαγεῖν.

ἤ. Disjunctive conjunction.

τίς. Nominative subject of καταβήσεται.

καταβήσεται. Fut mid ind 3rd sg καταβαίνω. The middle voice indicates indirect, internal causality and is parallel to ἀναβήσεται in the previous verse.

εἰς τὴν ἄβυσσον. Directional, but also entailing the senses of goal/ state and purpose (telic).

τοῦτ᾽ ἔστιν. Explanatory formula (see 9:8).

τοῦτ᾽. Nominative subject of ἔστιν.

ἔστιν. Unaugmented ind 3rd sg εἰμί.

Χριστὸν. Accusative direct object of καταγαγεῖν. The fronting of the accusative object before the infinitive indicates clausal prominence.

ἐκ νεκρῶν. Locative (movement out of/separation). The fronting of the prepositional word group before the infinitive indicates clausal prominence as well.

ἀναγαγεῖν. Aor act inf ἀνάγω (purpose).

10:8 ἀλλὰ τί λέγει; ἐγγύς σου τὸ ῥῆμά ἐστιν ἐν τῷ στόματί σου καὶ ἐν τῇ καρδίᾳ σου, τοῦτ᾽ ἔστιν τὸ ῥῆμα τῆς πίστεως ὃ κηρύσσομεν.

ἀλλὰ. Adversative conjunction (strong). The strong contrast is between what they should not say and what is to be said.

τί. Accusative direct object of λέγει.

λέγει. Pres act ind 3rd sg λέγω.

ἐγγύς σου. Locative. ἐγγύς is an improper preposition (cf. Porter 1994a, 179). This begins a reference to LXX Deut 30:14.

τὸ ῥῆμά. Nominative subject of ἐστιν (for the meaning of ῥῆμα, see 10:17 on διὰ ῥήματος).

ἐστιν. Unaugmented ind 3rd sg εἰμί. It equates ἐγγύς σου with τὸ ῥῆμά.

ἐν τῷ στόματί. Locative.

σου. Possessive genitive, modifying τῷ στόματί.

καὶ. Coordinating conjunction. It connects ἐν τῷ στόματί σου with ἐν τῇ καρδίᾳ σου.

ἐν τῇ καρδίᾳ. Locative.

σου. Possessive genitive, modifying τῇ καρδίᾳ.

τοῦτ᾽ ἔστιν. Explanatory formula (see 9:8).

τὸ ῥῆμα. Predicate nominative.

τῆς πίστεως. Genitive of description or definition, modifying τὸ ῥῆμα. It further describes or circumscribes "the word" as "of faith." Alternatively, it could function as a genitive of source or origin ("the word that comes from faith").

ὃ. Accusative direct object of κηρύσσομεν. The relative pronoun refers anaphorically to τὸ ῥῆμα τῆς πίστεως.

κηρύσσομεν. Pres act ind 1st pl κηρύσσω.

10:9 ὅτι ἐὰν ὁμολογήσῃς ἐν τῷ στόματί σου κύριον Ἰησοῦν καὶ πιστεύσῃς ἐν τῇ καρδίᾳ σου ὅτι ὁ θεὸς αὐτὸν ἤγειρεν ἐκ νεκρῶν, σωθήσῃ·

ὅτι. Introduces a causal clause ("because"; cf. RSV; ESV) that explains the reason for Paul's previous statement about the word of faith or a clause that is epexegetical τὸ ῥῆμα τῆς πίστεως from the previous verse ("that"; cf. KJV; NASB; NIV).

ἐὰν. Introduces the protasis of a third-class conditional. The protasis consists of two clauses joined by καί.

ὁμολογήσῃς. Aor act subj 2nd sg ὁμολογέω. Subjunctive with ἐάν. The subjunctive is used in the third-class conditional to reflect probability.

ἐν τῷ στόματί. Locative. Although the instrumental sense might be valid, the locative sense seems preferable: the confessing is simply located in the mouth, in contrast with the traditional understanding of the mouth being an *instrument* of confession (i.e., a verbal confession is required with the instrumental sense).

σου. Possessive genitive, modifying τῷ στόματί. The use of the singular pronoun reflects individual confession.

κύριον Ἰησοῦν. Accusative direct object of ὁμολογήσῃς. While κύριον Ἰησοῦν can be interpreted as a proper noun ("Lord Jesus"), since both words are in the accusative, it is likely that it is a verbless clause ("Jesus is Lord") in the accusative (the entire clause being the object of ὁμολογήσῃς), with the proper noun, "Jesus," being the subject and "Lord" as object (see Porter 2015, 198–99; cf. Fantin). It can also be that κύριον Ἰησοῦν represents a double accusative object-complement construction, in which Ἰησοῦν serves as the accusative direct object of ὁμολογήσῃς, while κύριον serves as its complement (i.e., "if you confess with your mouth Jesus as Lord").

καὶ. Coordinating conjunction. It connects the two clauses in the protasis.

πιστεύσῃς. Aor act subj 2nd sg πιστεύω. Subjunctive with ἐάν. It is parallel to ὁμολογήσῃς and is the second part of the protasis.

ἐν τῇ καρδίᾳ. Locative. As with the above prepositional word group, ἐν τῷ στόματί, the locative sense is preferred over the instrumental: the believing is located in the heart.

σου. Possessive genitive, modifying τῇ καρδίᾳ.

ὅτι. Introduces a clausal complement (indirect discourse) of πιστεύσῃς. It begins a secondary (subordinate) clause, ὁ θεὸς αὐτὸν ἤγειρεν ἐκ νεκρῶν.

ὁ θεὸς. Nominative subject of ἤγειρεν.

αὐτὸν. Accusative direct object of ἤγειρεν. The personal pronoun refers anaphorically to Jesus.

ἤγειρεν. Aor act ind 3rd sg ἐγείρω.

ἐκ νεκρῶν. Locative (movement out of/separation).

σωθήσῃ. Fut pass ind 2nd sg σῴζω. The apodosis of the third-class conditional consists of this lexeme alone.

10:10 καρδίᾳ γὰρ πιστεύεται εἰς δικαιοσύνην, στόματι δὲ ὁμολογεῖται εἰς σωτηρίαν.

καρδίᾳ. Instrumental dative. The instrument by which one believes is the heart.

γὰρ. Postpositive explanatory conjunction. Paul further explains the previous statement of confessing with one's mouth and believing in one's heart.

πιστεύεται. Pres mid ind 3rd sg πιστεύω. We interpret the middle/passive form as middle. The middle voice grammaticalizes indirect, internal causality. The agent or cause is unspecified. However, the shift from the 2nd person in the previous verse to 3rd person here reflects a shift from a more direct address to Paul's audience ("you [pl.]") about confessing and believing to a general statement ("he/she") about believing and confessing (here; also note the reversal of order of the two processes). Alternatively, this could also be interpreted as a passive voice use of the verb (the so-called "impersonal passive" [BDF §130.3]).

εἰς δικαιοσύνην. Result. The result of believing with the heart is "righteousness."

στόματι. Instrumental dative.

δὲ. Adversative conjunction (mild). While connecting the two clauses, the adversative feature reflects the (mild) contrast between believing and confessing.

ὁμολογεῖται. Pres mid ind 3rd sg ὁμολογέω. Again, the middle voice grammaticalizes indirect, internal causality, with agency or causality unspecified.

εἰς σωτηρίαν. Result. The result of confessing with the mouth is "salvation."

10:11 λέγει γὰρ ἡ γραφή· πᾶς ὁ πιστεύων ἐπ᾽ αὐτῷ οὐ καταισχυνθήσεται.

λέγει. Pres act ind 3rd sg λέγω.

γὰρ. Postpositive explanatory conjunction. Paul continues his explanation about believing (and, by extension, confessing).

ἡ γραφή. Nominative subject of λέγει.

πᾶς ὁ πιστεύων. Nominative subject of καταισχυνθήσεται. This begins a reference to LXX Isa 28:16 (which is also referenced in 9:33).

πιστεύων. Pres act ptc masc nom sg πιστεύω (substantival).

ἐπ᾽ αὐτῷ. Locative (upon or onto). The believing is "upon him." This preposition is often used with verbs of believing, hoping, and trusting to express state of being, action, or result (BDAG, 364.6.b). The referent of the personal pronoun is Jesus from the previous co-text.

οὐ. Negative particle normally used with indicative verbs. Here it negates καταισχυνθήσεται.

καταισχυνθήσεται. Fut pass ind 3rd sg καταισχύνω. Passive voice indicates external causality, although the agent is not specified.

10:12 οὐ γάρ ἐστιν διαστολὴ Ἰουδαίου τε καὶ Ἕλληνος, ὁ γὰρ αὐτὸς κύριος πάντων, πλουτῶν εἰς πάντας τοὺς ἐπικαλουμένους αὐτόν·

οὐ. Negative particle normally used with indicative verbs. Here it negates ἐστιν.

γάρ. Postpositive explanatory conjunction that introduces an explanation of the previous statement regarding "everyone who believes."

ἐστιν. Unaugmented ind 3rd sg εἰμί.

διαστολὴ. Nominative subject of ἐστιν.

Ἰουδαίου τε καὶ Ἕλληνος. Genitives of comparison (cf. Porter 1994a, 95–96). The comparison is drawn between Jews and Gentiles.

τε καὶ. Enclitic particle τε joined with conjunction καί. The use is emphatic (see 1:12, 14, 27). That the emphatic particle is associated with Ἰουδαίου is consistent and appropriate in this co-text (Romans 9–11), where Paul wishes that Israel, his own people, would be saved.

ὁ … αὐτὸς κύριος πάντων. The syntax here is ambiguous; it can mean "the same Lord [is] of all" or "the same one [is] Lord of all." However, Paul is known to use independent nominative word groups as a single clause (e.g., 2 Cor 5:17—καινὴ κτίσις) to make emphatic statements, so it is likely that this is an independent nominative word group functioning as a single clause, i.e., "[he is] the same Lord of all."

ὁ … αὐτὸς κύριος. Nominative absolute or predicate nominative of subjectless clause.

πάντων. Possessive genitive, modifying ὁ … αὐτὸς κύριος.

γὰρ. Postpositive explanatory conjunction that introduces an explanation of the previous statement that there is no distinction between Jew and Greek.

πλουτῶν. Pres act ptc masc nom sg πλουτέω (attributive). The participle functions as an attributive modifier of κύριος (fourth attributive position).

εἰς πάντας τοὺς ἐπικαλουμένους. Directional (movement toward). The figurative direction of πλουτῶν is "all who call."

ἐπικαλουμένους. Pres mid ptc masc acc pl ἐπικαλέω (substantival).

αὐτόν. Accusative direct object of ἐπικαλουμένους. The personal pronoun refers anaphorically to κύριος.

10:13 πᾶς γὰρ ὃς ἂν ἐπικαλέσηται τὸ ὄνομα κυρίου σωθήσεται.

πᾶς. Nominative subject of σωθήσεται. This adjective is used here as a substantive ("everyone").

γὰρ. Postpositive explanatory conjunction that introduces an explanation of Paul's argument that all belong to Jesus. This verse is a quotation from LXX Joel 2:32 (cf. also Acts 2:21).

ὃς. Nominative subject of ἐπικαλέσηται. The relative pronoun followed by the particle ἂν introduces an indefinite relative clause, which is roughly equivalent to a third-class conditional (cf. Wallace 1996, 478). The relative pronoun refers anaphorically to πᾶς.

ἂν. Conditional particle. It signifies a conditional generality. The condition here is calling on the name of the Lord.

ἐπικαλέσηται. Aor mid subj 3rd sg ἐπικαλέω. Subjunctive with ἂν. Middle voice indicates indirect, internal causality.

τὸ ὄνομα. Accusative direct object of ἐπικαλέσηται.

κυρίου. Genitive of source or origin, modifying τὸ ὄνομα.

σωθήσεται. Fut pass ind 3rd sg σῴζω. Passive voice indicates external causality. The agent is not specified in this co-text (cf. 9:27).

Romans 10:14–21

[14]Therefore, how might they call upon him whom they have not believed? And how might they believe whom they have not heard? And how might they hear apart from the one preaching? [15]And how might they preach unless they are sent? As it is written, "How beautiful [are] the feet of those who proclaim the good news regarding [the] good things." [16]But not all obey the good news. For Isaiah says, "Lord, who believed our report?" [17]So faith [is] from a report, and the report [is] through the word of Christ. [18]But I say, it is not that they did not hear, is it? To the contrary. "Their voice went out into all the earth and their words into the ends of the world." [19]But I say, Israel did not know, did they? First, Moses says, "I will make you jealous of a not-people; of an ignorant people, I will anger you." [20]And Isaiah dares and says, "I was found among those who are not seeking me; I manifested myself to those who are not asking for me." [21]But to Israel he says, "For the entire day, I stretched out my hands towards a people rebellious and contrary."

Paul begins this sub-section by returning to his diatribal and interlocutory method with a series of rapid-fire questions. He proposes four "how" questions using πῶς (the fourth appearing in 10:15), resulting from his previous statement that those who call on him will be saved.

10:14 Πῶς οὖν ἐπικαλέσωνται εἰς ὃν οὐκ ἐπίστευσαν; πῶς δὲ πιστεύσωσιν οὗ οὐκ ἤκουσαν; πῶς δὲ ἀκούσωσιν χωρὶς κηρύσσοντος;

Πῶς. Adverb (interrogative). It modifies ἐπικαλέσωνται, functioning to establish manner.

οὖν. Postpositive inferential conjunction, functioning adversatively. The inference is from the previous statement that all who call on the name of the Lord will be saved. The adversative function here contrasts the calling on the name of the Lord with the question of how they are supposed to do this.

ἐπικαλέσωνται. Aor mid subj 3rd pl ἐπικαλέω (deliberative subjunctive). The use of the perfective aspect (aorist tense-form) depicts the process as a whole. The middle voice indicates indirect, internal causality. The subjunctive mood grammaticalizes projection; the process of "calling" is viewed in terms of its potential realization.

εἰς ὃν οὐκ ἐπίστευσαν. Goal or state. The goal of "calling" is "him whom they have not believed."

ὃν. Introduces a headless relative clause (ὃν οὐκ ἐπίστευσαν) that serves as the object of the preposition εἰς. Within its clause, ὃν is the accusative direct object of ἐπίστευσαν.

οὐκ. Negative particle normally used with indicative verbs. Here it negates ἐπίστευσαν.

ἐπίστευσαν. Aor act ind 3rd pl πιστεύω. It occurs as a part of the prepositional word group (εἰς ὃν οὐκ ἐπίστευσαν).

πῶς. Adverb (interrogative). It modifies πιστεύσωσιν, functioning to establish manner.

δὲ. Adversative conjunction (mild). In this co-text, it carries more of a connective sense, albeit with a mild adversative force.

πιστεύσωσιν. Aor act subj 3rd pl πιστεύω (deliberative subjunctive). As parallel to ἐπικαλέσωνται above, the switch from the middle voice to the active voice here is noteworthy. The switch to the active voice-form reflects a switch to direct causality; the believing is directly caused by the subject. Again, the subjunctive mood grammaticalizes projection, the process viewed in terms of its potential realization.

οὗ. Genitive relative pronoun. οὗ introduces a headless relative clause (οὗ οὐκ ἤκουσαν) that functions as the direct object of πιστεύσωσιν.

Within its clause, οὗ is the genitive direct object of ἤκουσαν (since ἀκούω takes its object in the genitive).

οὐκ. Negative particle normally used with indicative verbs. Negates ἤκουσαν.

ἤκουσαν. Aor act ind 3rd pl ἀκούω.

πῶς. Adverb (interrogative). It modifies ἀκούσωσιν, functioning to establish manner.

δὲ. Adversative conjunction (mild). In this co-text, it carries more of a connective sense, albeit with a mild adversative force.

ἀκούσωσιν. Aor act subj 3rd pl ἀκούω (deliberative subjunctive). As with ἐπικαλέσωνται and πιστεύσωσιν above, the subjunctive mood grammaticalizes projection, the process viewed in terms of its potential realization.

χωρὶς κηρύσσοντος. Separation. χωρὶς is an improper preposition.

κηρύσσοντος. Pres act ptc masc gen sg κηρύσσω (substantival), functioning as the object of the preposition. The imperfective aspect (present tense-form) of the participle depicts the process as in progress. The contrast between the perfective aspect used of the main verbs in this verse and the imperfective aspect of the participle here should be noted; Paul is depicting the process of "preaching" or "proclaiming" (even if substantival) as unfolding, in contrast to the processes of "calling," "believing," and "hearing" depicted as an undifferentiated whole.

10:15 πῶς δὲ κηρύξωσιν ἐὰν μὴ ἀποσταλῶσιν; καθὼς γέγραπται· ὡς ὡραῖοι οἱ πόδες τῶν εὐαγγελιζομένων [τὰ] ἀγαθά.

πῶς. Adverb (interrogative). It modifies κηρύξωσιν, functioning to establish manner. The final "how" question of four total (cf. 10:14) differs in its syntax from the previous questions, in that in addition to the question, it contains a conditional clause and a scriptural reference (LXX Isa 52:7).

δὲ. Adversative conjunction (mild). In this co-text, as in the previous verse, the conjunction carries more of a connective sense, albeit with a mild adversative force.

κηρύξωσιν. Aor act subj 3rd pl κηρύσσω (deliberative subjunctive). The consistent use of the subjunctive mood form in the "how" questions in this co-text reflects the process as projection, in terms of its potential realization.

ἐὰν. Introduces the protasis of a third-class (general probable) conditional. The apodosis (πῶς δὲ κηρύξωσιν) appears before the protasis (ἐὰν μὴ ἀποσταλῶσιν) here, reflecting prominence of the apodosis.

μὴ. Negative particle normally used with non-indicative verbs. Here it negates ἀποσταλῶσιν. The combination ἐὰν μὴ has the idea of "unless."

ἀποσταλῶσιν. Aor pass subj 3rd pl ἀποστέλλω. Subjunctive with ἐάν. Passive voice indicates external causality; the agent here is unspecified, so it probably is a reference to a general "sending."

καθὼς γέγραπται. A standard Pauline formula for introducing a scriptural quotation (see note on 1:17).

καθὼς. Comparative conjunction. It compares the previous statement with the following scriptural reference, indicated by γέγραπται.

γέγραπται. Prf pass ind 3rd sg γράφω.

ὡς. Comparative conjunction. The comparison is between ὡραῖοι and οἱ πόδες.

ὡραῖοι. Predicate adjective.

οἱ πόδες. Nominative absolute or nominative subject of verbless clause.

τῶν εὐαγγελιζομένων. Pres mid ptc masc gen pl εὐαγγελίζω (substantival). Genitive of source or origin, modifying οἱ πόδες. The middle voice reflects indirect, internal causality.

[τὰ] ἀγαθά. Accusative direct object of εὐαγγελιζομένων. The earliest manuscript traditions are divided on the presence of the article here (without article: ℵ² A B C D*; with article: 𝔓⁴⁶ ℵ* D¹), although the semantic significance of the article is minimal.

10:16 Ἀλλ᾽ οὐ πάντες ὑπήκουσαν τῷ εὐαγγελίῳ. Ἡσαΐας γὰρ λέγει· κύριε, τίς ἐπίστευσεν τῇ ἀκοῇ ἡμῶν;

Ἀλλ᾽. Adversative conjunction (strong). It indicates a strong contrast to the previous statement.

οὐ. Negative particle that negates πάντες. οὐ πάντες is an instance of litotes ("not all" = "only a few").

πάντες. Nominative subject of ὑπήκουσαν.

ὑπήκουσαν. Aor act ind 3rd pl ὑπακούω. The metaphoric picture from the prefixed form of this verb is to "listen under" someone. In other words, the picture is of people obeying or submitting to the gospel.

τῷ εὐαγγελίῳ. Dative direct object of ὑπήκουσαν.

Ἡσαΐας. Nominative subject of λέγει. The Isaiah reference is from LXX Isa 53:1.

γὰρ. Postpositive explanatory conjunction that introduces an explanation of the previous statement that not all have obeyed the gospel is supported with the following Isaiah reference.

λέγει. Pres act ind 3rd sg λέγω.

κύριε. Nominative of address (so-called vocative). This lexeme does not occur in the referenced Isaiah passage.

τίς. Nominative subject of ἐπίστευσεν.

ἐπίστευσεν. Aor act ind 3rd sg πιστεύω.

τῇ ἀκοῇ. Dative direct object of ἐπίστευσεν. This lexeme refers to that which is heard, i.e., "report" or "news," or the act of hearing itself.

ἡμῶν. Genitive of source or origin, modifying τῇ ἀκοῇ. The report comes from "us."

10:17 ἄρα ἡ πίστις ἐξ ἀκοῆς, ἡ δὲ ἀκοὴ διὰ ῥήματος Χριστοῦ.

ἄρα. Inferential conjunction.

ἡ πίστις. Nominative subject of verbless clause. It is parallel to ἡ . . . ἀκοὴ in the next clause.

ἐξ ἀκοῆς. Locative (origin or source). The origin or source of "faith" is "hearing" or "report."

ἡ . . . ἀκοὴ. Nominative subject of verbless clause.

δὲ. Adversative conjunction (mild). The mild contrast is between faith and report.

διὰ ῥήματος. Instrumental. The "word of Christ" is the instrument, agent, or means of "report." The lexeme ῥῆμα refers to a statement or a word in the sense of a "minimal unit of discourse" (LN 33.9; see also Porter 2015, 198 n. 40).

Χριστοῦ. Genitive of source or origin, modifying ῥήματος. The origin or source of the "word" is Christ. Some may wish to see this as an objective genitive, if ῥήματος were to become a verb such as "to say" or "to speak."

ἐξ ἀκοῆς . . . διὰ ῥήματος Χριστοῦ. The contrast between the two prepositions used here in parallel structures is significant. Faith is "from" or "out of" hearing a report of good news, while hearing this report is "through" the word of Christ. The former signifies a figurative location, i.e., origin or source, while the latter signifies instrumentality or agency.

10:18 ἀλλὰ λέγω, μὴ οὐκ ἤκουσαν; μενοῦνγε· εἰς πᾶσαν τὴν γῆν ἐξῆλ-θεν ὁ φθόγγος αὐτῶν καὶ εἰς τὰ πέρατα τῆς οἰκουμένης τὰ ῥήματα αὐτῶν.

ἀλλὰ. Adversative conjunction (strong). In strong contrast with the previous statement about faith and hearing of a report of good news, Paul poses the following question.

λέγω. Pres act ind 1st sg λέγω. The use of λέγω instead of ἐρωτάω (or another related word) to indicate a posed question is not uncommon in the NT.

μὴ οὐκ. The combination of two negative particles indicates emphatic negation. The use of μὴ in the first position negates the entire clause, indicating an expectation of a negative answer. οὐκ directly negates ἤκουσαν in the second position.

ἤκουσαν. Aor act ind 3rd pl ἀκούω.

μενοῦνγε. Emphatic compound conjunction (consisting of μέν, οὖν, and γέ) of contradiction (see note on 9:20). It fulfills the expectation of the negative answer from the posed question.

εἰς πᾶσαν τὴν γῆν. Directional. This begins a direct quotation from LXX Ps 19:4. The fronting of the prepositional word group at the beginning of the clause indicates clausal prominence.

ἐξῆλθεν. Aor act ind 3rd sg ἐξέρχομαι.

ὁ φθόγγος. Nominative subject of ἐξῆλθεν.

αὐτῶν. Possessive genitive, modifying ὁ φθόγγος.

καὶ. Coordinating conjunction. It connects the two clauses.

εἰς τὰ πέρατα. Directional (movement toward). This begins a direct quotation from LXX Ps 19:4. The fronting of the prepositional word group at the beginning of the clause indicates clausal prominence.

τῆς οἰκουμένης. Partitive genitive, modifying τὰ πέρατα.

τὰ ῥήματα. Nominative subject of verbless clause (ἐξῆλθεν is implied from the previous clause).

αὐτῶν. Possessive genitive, modifying τὰ ῥήματα.

10:19 ἀλλὰ λέγω, μὴ Ἰσραὴλ οὐκ ἔγνω; πρῶτος Μωϋσῆς λέγει· ἐγὼ παραζηλώσω ὑμᾶς ἐπ' οὐκ ἔθνει, ἐπ' ἔθνει ἀσυνέτῳ παροργιῶ ὑμᾶς.

ἀλλὰ. Adversative conjunction (strong).

λέγω. Pres act ind 1st sg λέγω (see the note on λέγω in 10:18).

μὴ. Negative particle that indicates that Paul expects a negative answer, parallel to the above question in 10:19.

Ἰσραὴλ. Nominative subject of ἔγνω.

οὐκ. Negative particle normally used with indicative verbs. Here it negates ἔγνω.

ἔγνω. Aor act ind 3rd sg γινώσκω.

πρῶτος. Adverb (ordinal). It modifies the clause Μωϋσῆς λέγει.

Μωϋσῆς. Nominative subject of λέγει. The Moses reference is from LXX Deut 32:21.

λέγει. Pres act ind 3rd sg λέγω.

ἐγώ. Nominative subject of παραζηλώσω. The use of the personal pronoun is emphatic.

παραζηλώσω. Fut act ind 1st sg παραζηλόω. The prefixed form of the verb intensifies the root meaning.

ὑμᾶς. Accusative direct object of παραζηλώσω. This word is αὐτοὺς in the LXX Deut 32:21 quotation.

ἐπ᾽ οὐκ ἔθνει. Locative (movement upon). The jealousy is figuratively placed upon "not-people" ("of" is used in the above translation for English purposes). Normally in the NT, ἔθνος refers to Gentiles, so οὐκ ἔθνει might be confused as "not-Gentiles," but its semantic core refers to a people-group (i.e., nation) in general. In this co-text (and the LXX Deut 32:21 co-text), ἔθνος refers to God's people or God's nation, so here it refers to not-God's-people or not-God's-nation. The parallel prepositional word group (ἐπ᾽ ἔθνει ἀσυνέτῳ) clarifies the meaning in this co-text. Some may argue that λαός refers to God's people and ἔθνος to other nations, but this is an instance of illegitimate identity transfer (see e.g., LXX Gen 12:2; Matt 4:16; Mark 7:6; 1 Pet 2:9; cf. Barr 1961, 234–35; Yoon 2021, 283).

ἐπ᾽ ἔθνει ἀσυνέτῳ. Locative (movement upon). The micro-chiasm used here, with the prepositional word groups in the middle, reflects an emphasis on the middle elements. The chiastic structure can be seen as:

A—παραζηλώσω ὑμᾶς
B—ἐπ᾽ οὐκ ἔθνει
B′—ἐπ᾽ ἔθνει ἀσυνέτῳ
A′—παροργιῶ ὑμᾶς

παροργιῶ. Fut act ind 1st sg παροργίζω. A NT *hapax legomenon*.

ὑμᾶς. Accusative direct object of παροργιῶ. This word is αὐτοὺς in the LXX Deut 32:21 quotation.

10:20 Ἠσαΐας δὲ ἀποτολμᾷ καὶ λέγει· εὑρέθην [ἐν] τοῖς ἐμὲ μὴ ζητοῦσιν, ἐμφανὴς ἐγενόμην τοῖς ἐμὲ μὴ ἐπερωτῶσιν.

Ἠσαΐας. Nominative subject of ἀποτολμᾷ and λέγει. The reference is from LXX Isa 65:11, although Paul reverses the clause order and verb choices.

δὲ. Adversative conjunction (mild). The mild contrast is between this Isaiah reference and the previous Moses reference.

ἀποτολμᾷ. Pres act ind 3rd sg ἀποτολμάω. A NT *hapax legomenon*.

καὶ. Coordinating conjunction. It connects the two verbs, ἀποτολμᾷ and λέγει.

λέγει. Pres act ind 3rd sg λέγω.

εὑρέθην. Aor pass ind 1st sg εὑρίσκω.

[ἐν] τοῖς . . . μὴ ζητοῦσιν. Distributional ("among those who are not seeking"). The earliest manuscripts are divided on the presence of the preposition ἐν (without: ℵ A C D¹; with: 𝔓⁴⁶ B D*).

ζητοῦσιν. Pres act ptc masc dat pl ζητέω (substantival).

ἐμὲ. Accusative direct object of ζητοῦσιν.

ἐμφανὴς. Predicate adjective. This lexeme occurs only here in Paul.

ἐγενόμην. Aor mid ind 1st sg γίνομαι. The middle voice indicates indirect, internal causality. In other words, God makes himself manifest.

τοῖς ... μὴ ἐπερωτῶσιν. Dative of advantage.

ἐπερωτῶσιν. Pres act ptc masc dat pl ἐπερωτάω (substantival).

ἐμὲ. Accusative direct object of ἐπερωτῶσιν.

10:21 πρὸς δὲ τὸν Ἰσραὴλ λέγει· ὅλην τὴν ἡμέραν ἐξεπέτασα τὰς χεῖράς μου πρὸς λαὸν ἀπειθοῦντα καὶ ἀντιλέγοντα.

πρὸς ... τὸν Ἰσραὴλ. Directional (movement toward). The preposition πρός is commonly used with verbs of speaking. The fronting of the prepositional word group indicates clausal prominence; Israel is emphasized probably since the previous statement was in reference to Gentiles.

δὲ. Adversative conjunction (mild). Similar to the above usage, Paul continues the mild contrasts between several OT statements from Moses and Isaiah.

λέγει. Pres act ind 3rd sg λέγω. In this co-text, this lexeme is Paul's preferred method of quoting or referencing Scripture. In contrast to his typical use of γέγραπται for invoking Scripture (usually in contexts where he invokes the Law), his use of λέγει in this co-text highlights the OT figures, as well as God himself, speaking directly to Paul's present-day audience.

ὅλην τὴν ἡμέραν. Accusative indicating extent of time. The direct quotation from LXX Isa 65:2 begins here.

ἐξεπέτασα. Aor act ind 1st sg ἐκπετάννυμι. The unspecified agent is God.

τὰς χεῖράς. Accusative direct object of ἐξεπέτασα.

μου. Possessive genitive, modifying τὰς χεῖράς.

πρὸς λαὸν. Directional (movement toward). The apparent switch from ἔθνος to λαός is probably due to the different OT references (here LXX Isa 65:2; previously LXX Deut 32:21).

ἀπειθοῦντα. Pres act ptc masc acc sg ἀπειθέω (attributive). The participle modifies λαὸν (fourth attributive position). This lexeme (ἀπειθέω) is a negated form of πείθομαι and refers to "not-obey" or "without-obey."

καὶ. Coordinating conjunction. It connects the two attributive participles.

ἀντιλέγοντα. Pres act ptc masc acc sg ἀντιλέγω (attributive). The participle modifies λαὸν (fourth attributive position). This lexeme contains the prefix ἀντι- attached to the root λέγω, having the meaning of "being contrary," "objecting," or "opposing."

Romans 11:1–10

¹I say, therefore, God has not rejected his people, has he? Indeed not; for I myself am also an Israelite, from the offspring of Abraham, of the tribe of Benjamin. ²God has not rejected his people, whom he foreknew. Or do you not know what the Scripture says in Elijah, as he pleads to God against Israel? ³"Lord, your prophets they killed and your altars they demolished, and I alone am left, and they are seeking my life." ⁴But what does the oracle say to him? "I kept for myself seven thousand men who did not bow their knee to Baal." ⁵In this way, therefore, also in the present time, there is a remnant on the basis of gracious election. ⁶But if by grace, [it is] no longer from works, because grace is no longer grace. ⁷What then? What Israel sought, this they did not obtain, but the elect obtained it; but the rest were hardened. ⁸As it is written, "God gave them a spirit of numbness, eyes that do not see and ears that do not hear, until this very day." ⁹And David says, "Their table should be turned into a snare, a trap, a cause of stumbling, and a retributive payment to them. ¹⁰Their eyes should become darkened to not see, and you should constantly thoroughly bend their backs."

This next sub-section continues Paul's discussion regarding the people of Israel. Paul continues his use of diatribe, question and answer, and reference to Scripture for progressing his argument that God has not rejected Israel. From his previous argumentation, it may be possible that his interlocutors may have concluded that God had indeed rejected Israel.

11:1 Λέγω οὖν, μὴ ἀπώσατο ὁ θεὸς τὸν λαὸν αὐτοῦ; μὴ γένοιτο· καὶ γὰρ ἐγὼ Ἰσραηλίτης εἰμί, ἐκ σπέρματος Ἀβραάμ, φυλῆς Βενιαμίν.

Λέγω. Pres act ind 1st sg λέγω. The switch from λέγει in the previous co-text to λέγω is noteworthy. The previous OT figures have spoken; now Paul speaks.

οὖν. Postpositive inferential conjunction. The inference is drawn from the previous co-text, regarding the negative light in which Paul has described Israel.

μὴ. Negative particle introducing a question that expects a negative answer.

ἀπώσατο. Aor mid ind 3rd sg ἀπωθέω. The middle voice-form reflects indirect, internal causality (so-called deponent verb; see "Deponency" in the Series Introduction). There are five other occurrences of this lexeme in the NT (Acts 7:27, 39; 13:46; Rom 11:2; and 1 Tim 1:19).

ὁ θεός. Nominative subject of ἀπώσατο.

τὸν λαόν. Accusative direct object of ἀπώσατο. The repetition of λαός from the previous verse (10:21) reflects lexical cohesion. Its repetition seems to indicate that this same rebellious and contrary people are still "his people."

αὐτοῦ. Possessive genitive, modifying τὸν λαὸν.

μὴ γένοιτο. A commonly used emphatic negation of Paul, after a question, usually rhetorical (see 3:4).

μὴ. Negative particle normally used with non-indicative verbs. Here it negates γένοιτο.

γένοιτο. Aor mid opt 3rd sg γίνομαι.

καὶ. Adverbial use (adjunctive). It modifies the clause ἐγὼ Ἰσραηλίτης εἰμί.

γὰρ. Postpositive explanatory conjunction. Paul explains why God has not rejected his people, using the example of himself.

ἐγώ. Nominative subject of εἰμί. The use of the personal pronoun is emphatic.

Ἰσραηλίτης. Predicate nominative.

εἰμί. Unaugmented ind 1st sg εἰμί.

ἐκ σπέρματος Ἀβραάμ. Locative (source or origin).

φυλῆς Βενιαμίν. Genitive in apposition to σπέρματος Ἀβραάμ.

11:2 οὐκ ἀπώσατο ὁ θεὸς τὸν λαὸν αὐτοῦ ὃν προέγνω. ἢ οὐκ οἴδατε ἐν Ἠλίᾳ τί λέγει ἡ γραφή, ὡς ἐντυγχάνει τῷ θεῷ κατὰ τοῦ Ἰσραήλ;

οὐκ. Negative particle normally used with indicative verbs. Here it negates ἀπώσατο.

ἀπώσατο. Aor mid ind 3rd sg ἀπωθέομαι (see note in 11:1). The repetition and fronting of this predicate create cohesion and prominence regarding rejection.

ὁ θεὸς. Nominative subject of ἀπώσατο.

τὸν λαὸν. Accusative direct object of ἀπώσατο (see note on τὸν λαὸν in 11:1).

αὐτοῦ. Possessive genitive, modifying τὸν λαὸν.

ὅν. Accusative direct object of προέγνω. The relative pronoun refers to τὸν λαὸν αὐτοῦ.

προέγνω. Aor act ind 3rd sg προγινώσκω.

ἤ. Disjunctive particle.

οὐκ. Negative particle introducing a question that expects a positive answer.

οἴδατε. Prf act ind 2nd pl οἶδα. The stative aspect (perfect tense-form) reflects their state of knowledge.

ἐν Ἠλίᾳ. Locative. The place where Scripture says is "in" Elijah, or rather the OT reference to Elijah. The fronting of the prepositional word group in this (secondary or subordinate) clause (ἐν Ἠλίᾳ τί λέγει ἡ γραφή) indicates clausal prominence. It also begins the content of what they should know.

τί. Accusative direct object of λέγει.

λέγει. Pres act ind 3rd sg λέγω.

ἡ γραφή. Nominative subject of λέγει.

ὡς. Comparative conjunction. The comparison is between what Paul has just stated regarding God not rejecting his people and what Elijah (in Scripture) states regarding his people, Israel.

ἐντυγχάνει. Pres act ind 3rd sg ἐντυγχάνω (cf. 8:27, 34).

τῷ θεῷ. Dative of destination.

κατὰ τοῦ Ἰσραήλ. Positional (away from, i.e., against).

11:3 κύριε, τοὺς προφήτας σου ἀπέκτειναν, τὰ θυσιαστήριά σου κατέσκαψαν, κἀγὼ ὑπελείφθην μόνος καὶ ζητοῦσιν τὴν ψυχήν μου.

This verse is a loose quotation of Elijah from LXX 1 Kgs 19:10, 14.

κύριε. Nominative of address (so-called vocative).

τοὺς προφήτας. Accusative direct object of ἀπέκτειναν. The fronting of the accusative before the predicate indicates clausal prominence.

σου. Possessive genitive, modifying τοὺς προφήτας.

ἀπέκτειναν. Aor act ind 3rd pl ἀποκτείνω.

τὰ θυσιαστήριά. Accusative direct object of κατέσκαψαν. The fronting of the accusative before the predicate indicates clausal prominence. θυσιαστήριά, which has an acute accent on the antepenult, acquired an additional accent, the acute, on the ultima from the enclitic σου.

σου. Possessive genitive, modifying τὰ θυσιαστήριά.

κατέσκαψαν. Aor act ind 3rd pl κατασκάπτω.

κἀγὼ. Formed by crasis from καί and ἐγώ. καὶ is a coordinating conjunction; ἐγώ is the nominative subject of ὑπελείφθην. The use of this compound word is emphatic.

ὑπελείφθην. Aor pass ind 1st sg ὑπολείπω. A NT *hapax legomenon*. Passive voice indicates external causality; the agent is not specified in this co-text. The cause of Elijah being left alone is external to him. Also, in the perfective aspect, his being left alone is depicted as a complete process.

μόνος. Adjective modifying ἐγώ ("I alone").

καὶ. Coordinating conjunction. Connects the two clauses.

ζητοῦσιν. Pres act ind 3rd pl ζητέω. The switch of aspect from perfective (ὑπελείφθην) to imperfective (ζητοῦσιν) is significant here. Elijah depicts his being left alone as complete but his being sought as in progress; thus, his being sought is emphasized.

τὴν ψυχήν. Accusative direct object of ζητοῦσιν.

μου. Possessive genitive, modifying τὴν ψυχήν.

11:4 ἀλλὰ τί λέγει αὐτῷ ὁ χρηματισμός; κατέλιπον ἐμαυτῷ ἑπτακισχιλίους ἄνδρας, οἵτινες οὐκ ἔκαμψαν γόνυ τῇ Βάαλ.

ἀλλὰ. Adversative conjunction (strong).

τί. Accusative direct object of λέγει.

λέγει. Pres act ind 3rd sg λέγω.

αὐτῷ. Dative indirect object of λέγει. The personal pronoun refers to Elijah.

ὁ χρηματισμός. Nominative subject of λέγει. A NT *hapax legomenon*. The choice of this lexeme, instead of other potentially expected choices such as θεός or γραφή, may be because Paul wants to highlight both the divine and revelatory nature of what is said.

κατέλιπον. Aor act ind 1st sg καταλείπω. The verb begins a loose quotation of LXX 1 Kgs 19:18.

ἐμαυτῷ. Dative indirect object of κατέλιπον.

ἑπτακισχιλίους ἄνδρας. Accusative direct object of κατέλιπον.

οἵτινες. Nominative subject of ἔκαμψαν. The relative pronoun refers anaphorically to ἑπτακισχιλίους ἄνδρας.

οὐκ. Negative particle normally used with indicative verbs. Here it negates ἔκαμψαν.

ἔκαμψαν. Aor act ind 3rd pl κάμπτω.

γόνυ. Accusative direct object of ἔκαμψαν.

τῇ Βάαλ. Dative indirect object of ἔκαμψαν.

11:5 οὕτως οὖν καὶ ἐν τῷ νῦν καιρῷ λεῖμμα κατ᾽ ἐκλογὴν χάριτος γέγονεν·

οὕτως. Inferential adverb. It introduces an inference from God's response to the Elijah references in the previous co-text.

οὖν. Postpositive inferential conjunction. The inference, along with the occurrence of οὕτως, is from the previous statement regarding the seven thousand men who were left behind by God.

καὶ. Adverbial use (adjunctive). It modifies ἐν τῷ νῦν καιρῷ.

ἐν τῷ νῦν καιρῷ. Temporal. The adverb νῦν has an attributive function ("in the present time").

λεῖμμα. Nominative subject of γέγονεν. A NT *hapax legomenon*.

κατ' ἐκλογὴν. Standard. The standard by which they are a remnant is according to "election."

χάριτος. Genitive of quality or description, modifying ἐκλογὴν. Election is described or qualified as gracious (cf. NASB).

γέγονεν. Prf act ind 3rd sg γίνομαι. The stative aspect depicts their state of being a remnant.

11:6 εἰ δὲ χάριτι, οὐκέτι ἐξ ἔργων, ἐπεὶ ἡ χάρις οὐκέτι γίνεται χάρις.

εἰ. Introduces the protasis of a first-class conditional.

δὲ. Adversative conjunction (mild). The mild contrast is between Paul's assertion that the remnant was chosen by grace (gracious election) and the following conditional statement.

χάριτι. Dative of instrument. The instrument (or means, cause, agent, or manner) by which they were chosen is grace. The dative stands alone as its own clause.

οὐκέτι. Adverb (temporal). It modifies ἐξ ἔργων and begins the apodosis.

ἐξ ἔργων. Instrumental (causal, agentive). The use of the preposition for instrumentality intensifies it more than simply use of the dative χάριτι.

ἐπεὶ. Causal conjunction. The cause, or reason, why election is based on grace and not by works is provided in the following clause.

ἡ χάρις. Nominative subject of γίνεται. The articular substantive specifies the previously referred to grace which would be based on works.

οὐκέτι. Adverb (temporal). It modifies γίνεται.

γίνεται. Pres mid ind 3rd sg γίνομαι.

χάρις. Predicate nominative. The anarthrous substantive here refers to the general notion of grace.

11:7 Τί οὖν; ὃ ἐπιζητεῖ Ἰσραήλ, τοῦτο οὐκ ἐπέτυχεν, ἡ δὲ ἐκλογὴ ἐπέτυχεν· οἱ δὲ λοιποὶ ἐπωρώθησαν,

Τί οὖν. The opening question of the verse that is syntactically separate from the following verb. Paul usually adds ἐροῦμεν with this question (cf. 4:1; 6:1; 7:7; 8:31; 9:14, 30; but see 3:9, 6:15 without the predicate). Four clauses answer this question in this verse.

Τί. Nominative absolute. The nominative singular neuter and accusative singular neuter forms are identical for this interrogative pronoun, but as a single lexeme clause (plus conjunction), it may be preferable to interpret this as a nominative absolute.

οὖν. Postpositive inferential conjunction. The inference is from the previous co-text regarding gracious election.

ὅ. The relative pronoun introduces a headless relative clause (ὅ ἐπιζητεῖ Ἰσραήλ), which functions in apposition to τοῦτο. Within its clause, ὅ is the accusative direct object of ἐπιζητεῖ.

ἐπιζητεῖ. Pres act ind 3rd sg ἐπιζητέω. The prefix ἐπι- directionalizes their seeking, i.e., "seeking upon."

Ἰσραήλ. Nominative subject of ἐπιζητεῖ. The use of the proper noun here, as a cohesive substitution for "his people" (τὸν λαὸν αὐτοῦ; Rom 11:1, 2), specifies the previous referent.

τοῦτο. Accusative direct object of ἐπέτυχεν. The demonstrative pronoun is appositional to the headless relative clause (ὅ ἐπιζητεῖ Ἰσραήλ).

οὐκ. Negative particle normally used with indicative verbs. Here it negates ἐπέτυχεν.

ἐπέτυχεν. Aor act ind 3rd sg ἐπιτυγχάνω.

ἡ . . . ἐκλογὴ. Nominative subject of ἐπέτυχεν. The use of this lexeme reflects lexical cohesion with the same lexeme in 11:5.

δὲ. Adversative conjunction (mild).

ἐπέτυχεν. Aor act ind 3rd sg ἐπιτυγχάνω.

οἱ . . . λοιποί. Nominative subject of ἐπωρώθησαν. It is parallel to ἡ ἐκλογὴ.

δὲ. Adversative conjunction (mild).

ἐπωρώθησαν. Aor pass ind 3rd pl πωρόω. Passive voice indicates external causality, but the agent is not specified here. However, in the next verse, the agent is clarified as God who hardened them.

11:8 καθὼς γέγραπται· ἔδωκεν αὐτοῖς ὁ θεὸς πνεῦμα κατανύξεως, ὀφθαλμοὺς τοῦ μὴ βλέπειν καὶ ὦτα τοῦ μὴ ἀκούειν, ἕως τῆς σήμερον ἡμέρας.

καθὼς γέγραπται. A standard Pauline formula for introducing a scriptural quotation (see note on 1:17). The Scripture reference is from LXX Deut 29:4 and LXX Isa 29:10.

καθὼς. Comparative conjunction.

γέγραπται. Prf pass ind 3rd sg γράφω.

ἔδωκεν. Aor act ind 3rd sg δίδωμι.

αὐτοῖς. Dative indirect object of ἔδωκεν.

ὁ θεὸς. Nominative subject of ἔδωκεν.

πνεῦμα. Accusative direct object of ἔδωκεν.

κατανύξεως. Genitive of definition or description, modifying πνεῦμα. "Spirit" is further described or circumscribed as "numbness" or "stupor." This lexeme refers to "a state of not being able to think satisfactorily because of complete bewilderment and stupor" (LN 30.19).

ὀφθαλμοὺς. Accusative in apposition to πνεῦμα κατανύξεως.

τοῦ μὴ βλέπειν. Pres act inf βλέπω. The article functions as an attributive modifier, transforming the infinitive to a genitive of definition or description that modifies ὀφθαλμοὺς. "Eyes" are further described or circumscribed as not seeing. Alternatively, the infinitive indicates the result or purpose of ἔδωκεν: "God gave them eyes not to see" (cf. Zerwick §384).

καὶ. Coordinating conjunction. It connects the appositional accusatives ὀφθαλμοὺς and ὦτα.

ὦτα. Accusative in apposition to πνεῦμα κατανύξεως. It is parallel to ὀφθαλμοὺς.

τοῦ μὴ ἀκούειν. Pres act inf ἀκούω. The article functions as an attributive modifier, transforming the infinitive to a genitive of definition or description that modifies ὦτα. "Ears" are further described or circumscribed as not hearing. Alternatively, the infinitive indicates the result or purpose of ἔδωκεν: "God gave them ears not to hear" (cf. Zerwick §384).

ἕως τῆς σήμερον ἡμέρας. Temporal. ἕως is an improper preposition (cf. Porter 1994a, 180). σήμερον is an adverb of time in the first attributive position; this use is emphatic ("this very day"; cf. 2 Cor 3:14, 15). This is the only occurrence of σήμερον in Romans.

11:9 καὶ Δαυὶδ λέγει· γενηθήτω ἡ τράπεζα αὐτῶν εἰς παγίδα καὶ εἰς θήραν καὶ εἰς σκάνδαλον καὶ εἰς ἀνταπόδομα αὐτοῖς,

καὶ. Coordinating conjunction. It is used to connect the two OT references.

Δαυὶδ. Nominative subject of λέγει. Δαυὶδ is a proper noun.

λέγει. Pres act ind 3rd sg λέγω. As in the previous co-text, the use of an OT figure + λέγει has been an alternative way that Paul uses to introduce a scriptural reference (here LXX Ps 68:23–24, with v. 24 extending to the next verse, 11:10).

γενηθήτω. Aor pass impv 3rd sg γίνομαι. The use of the passive imperative indicates external agency, which is not specified. Along with the preposition εἰς here, the meaning of this lexeme is "be turned into."

ἡ τράπεζα. Nominative subject of γενηθήτω. As the subject of a passive voice verb, it is the Goal; the agent is unspecified. The lexeme normally refers to a physical table, but here it is a conceptual metaphor referring to what is on the table, i.e., a feast or meal, usually implying a bountiful one (cf. Sanday and Headlam, 315; LN 23.26).

αὐτῶν. Possessive genitive, modifying ἡ τράπεζα.

εἰς παγίδα... εἰς θήραν... εἰς σκάνδαλον... εἰς ἀνταπόδομα.
Goal or state. The goals of "becoming" (γενηθήτω) are listed.

καὶ... καὶ... καὶ. Coordinating conjunctions that connect the four prepositional word groups.

αὐτοῖς. Dative of disadvantage.

11:10 σκοτισθήτωσαν οἱ ὀφθαλμοὶ αὐτῶν τοῦ μὴ βλέπειν καὶ τὸν νῶτον αὐτῶν διὰ παντὸς σύγκαμψον.

σκοτισθήτωσαν. Aor pass impv 3rd pl σκοτίζω. The use of the passive imperative indicates external agency, which is not specified. This introduces a verbatim quotation of LXX Ps 68:24 (MT 69:23).

οἱ ὀφθαλμοί. Nominative subject of σκοτισθήτωσαν. As the grammatical subject of the passive verb, it is the Goal.

αὐτῶν. Possessive genitive, modifying οἱ ὀφθαλμοί.

τοῦ μὴ βλέπειν. Pres act inf βλέπω (purpose).

καὶ. Coordinating conjunction. It connects the two clauses represented by the two predicates σκοτισθήτωσαν and σύγκαμψον.

τὸν νῶτον. Accusative direct object of σύγκαμψον.

αὐτῶν. Possessive genitive, modifying τὸν νῶτον.

διὰ παντός. Temporal. This word group (lit. "through all") is a common idiom to mean "constantly," "always," or "continually" (cf. Matt 18:10; Mark 5:5; Luke 24:53; Acts 2:25; 10:2; 24:16; 2 Thess 3:16; Heb 2:15; 9:6; 13:15).

σύγκαμψον. Aor act impv 2nd sg συγκάμπτω. The implied subject is God co-textually. The switch from a passive imperative (σκοτισθήτωσαν) to an active one (σύγκαμψον) with God as the implied subject makes this imperative more direct.

Romans 11:11–24

[11]I therefore say, they did not stumble so that they might fall, did they? Indeed not. But because of their trespass, salvation [came] to the Gentiles in order to make them jealous. [12]But if their trespass [is] riches for the world and their failure [is] riches for Gentiles, how much more [is] their fullness? [13]But to you I speak, to Gentiles; inasmuch, then, I am an apostle to the Gentiles, I magnify my ministry, [14]if somehow I might make jealous my own flesh and save some of them. [15]For if their rejection [is] reconciliation of the world, what [might] their acceptance [be], if not life from the dead? [16]And if the firstfruit [is] holy, [so] also [is] the lump of dough; and if the root is holy, [so] also [are] the branches. [17]But if some of the branches were broken off, and you, being a wild olive

plant, were grafted in among them and became a joint sharer of the rich root of the olive tree, [18]you should not boast against the branches. But if you do boast against [them], you do not bear the root, but the root [bears] you. [19]You will say, therefore, "Branches were cut off so that I myself might be engrafted." [20]Indeed, by unbelief they were broken off, but by faith you stand. Do not think highly but fear. [21]For if God did not spare the natural branches, neither will he spare you. [22]See, then, the kindness and severity of God; severity upon those who fell, but upon you, God's kindness, if you should continue in the kindness, otherwise you also will be cut off. [23]And also those ones, if they do not continue in unbelief, will be grafted in; for God is able to engraft them again. [24]For if you were cut off from a natural wild olive plant and were engrafted, contrary to nature, into a domesticated plant, how much more will these who are natural be engrafted into their own olive plant?

Paul introduces this sub-section with the same words (Λέγω οὖν) as he did in the previous sub-section, both using μή to ask a question expecting a negative answer, and both answering with μὴ γένοιτο. He also continues his diatribe and interlocutory method of argumentation.

11:11 Λέγω οὖν, μὴ ἔπταισαν ἵνα πέσωσιν; μὴ γένοιτο· ἀλλὰ τῷ αὐτῶν παραπτώματι ἡ σωτηρία τοῖς ἔθνεσιν εἰς τὸ παραζηλῶσαι αὐτούς.

Λέγω. Pres act ind 1st sg λέγω. On the use of λέγω in this co-text, see 11:1.

οὖν. Postpositive inferential conjunction. The inference is drawn from the previous OT references, continuing Paul's line of thought.

μὴ. Negative particle introducing a question that expects a negative answer.

ἔπταισαν. Aor act ind 3rd pl πταίω.

ἵνα. Introduces a purpose clause. The purpose of stumbling is posited to be "to fall/fail."

πέσωσιν. Aor act subj 3rd pl πίπτω. Subjunctive with ἵνα.

μὴ γένοιτο. A commonly used emphatic negation of Paul, usually after a rhetorical question (see 3:4; this is the final occurrence in this letter).

μὴ. Negative particle normally used with non-indicative verbs. Here it negates γένοιτο.

γένοιτο. Aor mid opt 3rd sg γίνομαι.

ἀλλὰ. Adversative conjunction (strong). It marks a strong contrast between Paul's rhetorical question and the following statement.

τῷ . . . παραπτώματι. Dative of instrument. The instrument, cause, or reason by which salvation has come is "their trespass." The singular here views their trespass as a single unit, rather than as individual instances of trespasses.

αὐτῶν. Possessive genitive, modifying τῷ . . . παραπτώματι. Frequent use of the personal pronoun (3rd plural) in this co-text refers anaphorically to Israel.

ἡ σωτηρία. Nominative subject of verbless clause.

τοῖς ἔθνεσιν. Dative of advantage. The advantage of salvation is to "the Gentiles."

εἰς τὸ παραζηλῶσαι. Aor act inf παραζηλόω. Used with εἰς τὸ to denote purpose. Salvation is given to the Gentiles for the purpose of making Israel jealous.

αὐτούς. Accusative direct object of παραζηλῶσαι.

11:12 εἰ δὲ τὸ παράπτωμα αὐτῶν πλοῦτος κόσμου καὶ τὸ ἥττημα αὐτῶν πλοῦτος ἐθνῶν, πόσῳ μᾶλλον τὸ πλήρωμα αὐτῶν.

εἰ. Introduces the protasis of a first-class conditional. There are two clauses in the protasis connected by καὶ.

δὲ. Adversative conjunction (mild).

τὸ παράπτωμα. Nominative subject of verbless clause. As in 11:11, the use of this lexeme in the singular depicts "trespass" as a whole, as a single unit.

αὐτῶν. Possessive genitive or possibly genitive of source or origin, modifying τὸ παράπτωμα.

πλοῦτος. Predicate nominative.

κόσμου. Genitive of value or price modifying πλοῦτος.

καὶ. Coordinating conjunction. It connects the two clauses in the protasis.

τὸ ἥττημα. Nominative subject of verbless clause.

αὐτῶν. Possessive genitive or possibly genitive of source or origin, modifying τὸ ἥττημα.

πλοῦτος. Predicate nominative.

ἐθνῶν. Genitive of value or price modifying πλοῦτος.

πόσῳ μᾶλλον. Dative of advantage + the comparative of the adverb μάλα. πόσῳ μᾶλλον is a variation of πολλῷ μᾶλλον (see 5:9, 10, 15, 17) and means "how much more." This is not an uncommon phrase found in the apodosis of first-class conditionals (Matt 7:11; 10:25; Luke 11:13; 12:28; Heb 9:13–14; cf. Luke 12:24).

τὸ πλήρωμα. Nominative subject of verbless clause.

αὐτῶν. Possessive genitive or possibly genitive of source or origin, modifying τὸ πλήρωμα. The continued use of this personal pronoun referring to Israel ends here in the immediate co-text.

11:13 Ὑμῖν δὲ λέγω τοῖς ἔθνεσιν· ἐφ᾽ ὅσον μὲν οὖν εἰμι ἐγὼ ἐθνῶν ἀπόστολος, τὴν διακονίαν μου δοξάζω,

Ὑμῖν. Dative indirect object of λέγω. The personal pronoun refers cataphorically to τοῖς ἔθνεσιν. The fronting of the personal pronoun before the predicate indicates clausal prominence (emphasis at the clause level).

δὲ. Adversative conjunction (mild).

λέγω. Pres act ind 1st sg λέγω.

τοῖς ἔθνεσιν. Dative in apposition to Ὑμῖν.

ἐφ᾽ ὅσον. Directional (movement upon). ἐφ᾽ ὅσον (lit. "upon which") is usually translated "inasmuch" (cf. NASB, NIV, NKJV, NRSV; see also Rom 7:1).

μὲν. The first element of a point/counterpoint set. It is used to compare the clauses εἰμι ἐγὼ ἐθνῶν ἀπόστολος and τὴν διακονίαν μου δοξάζω. The usual δέ in this point/counterpoint construction is not used here, probably due to the use of ἐφ᾽ ὅσον.

οὖν. Inferential conjunction. As a postpositive, it occurs as the fourth element in this clause (rare).

εἰμι. Unaugmented ind 1st sg εἰμί.

ἐγὼ. Nominative subject of εἰμι. The use of the personal pronoun is emphatic.

ἐθνῶν. Genitive of description or definition, modifying ἀπόστολος. It further describes or circumscribes "apostle" to "Gentiles." The fronting of the genitive before the head term indicates word group prominence, emphasizing "Gentiles" above "apostle."

ἀπόστολος. Predicate nominative.

τὴν διακονίαν. Accusative direct object of δοξάζω. It introduces the apodosis of a conditional structure that continues in the next verse. As the apodosis occurs before the protasis here, it is prominent at the clause complex level (see also 11:14 on εἴ). This also begins the counterpoint from μέν. The fronting of the accusative object in the clause indicates clausal prominence. In other words, through both fronting of the accusative and fronting of the apodosis, Paul emphasizes his ministry in this co-text.

μου. Possessive genitive, modifying τὴν διακονίαν.

δοξάζω. Pres act ind 1st sg δοξάζω.

11:14 εἴ πως παραζηλώσω μου τὴν σάρκα καὶ σώσω τινὰς ἐξ αὐτῶν.

εἴ. Introduces the protasis of a first-class conditional. This begins the protasis, but the apodosis is in the previous verse (τὴν διακονίαν μου δοξάζω). As the order of the default clause order of conditionals is reversed, the apodosis is emphatic here.

πως. Adverb (manner). It is used to denote "how" Paul might make his people jealous. The interrogative particle modifies παραζηλώσω.

παραζηλώσω. Aor act subj 1st sg παραζηλόω. This form is identical to fut act ind 1st sg. The subjunctive mood form is related to the future form, both sharing similar morphological features (the sigma and connecting vowels, as evinced here; cf. Porter 1994a, 43–45). It, however, seems preferable to interpret this as an aorist subjunctive, since the semantic feature of projection (subjunctive) is more likely rather than the semantic feature of expectation, since Paul is indicating the possibility of making his people jealous instead of indicating the expectation of making them jealous.

μου. Possessive genitive, modifying τὴν σάρκα. The fronting of the genitive before the head term reflects word group prominence for μου (rare construction). That they belong to Paul is emphasized here.

τὴν σάρκα. Accusative direct object of παραζηλώσω. σάρξ is a lexical metaphor to refer to Paul's compatriots, the Jewish people. The use of this metaphor highlights his physical identity with them.

καὶ. Coordinating conjunction. It connects the two clauses παραζηλώσω μου τὴν σάρκα and σώσω τινὰς ἐξ αὐτῶν, with εἴ governing the entire clause complex.

σώσω. Aor act subj 1st sg σῴζω. Its form is identical to fut act ind 1st sg. As with παραζηλώσω, it is more likely an aorist subjunctive for the same reasons (see above on παραζηλώσω).

τινὰς. Accusative direct object of σώσω.

ἐξ αὐτῶν. Locative (movement out of).

11:15 εἰ γὰρ ἡ ἀποβολὴ αὐτῶν καταλλαγὴ κόσμου, τίς ἡ πρόσλημψις εἰ μὴ ζωὴ ἐκ νεκρῶν;

εἰ. Introduces the protasis of a first-class conditional.

γὰρ. Postpositive explanatory conjunction. It continues the explanation from the previous co-text.

ἡ ἀποβολὴ. Nominative subject of verbless clause. This lexeme only occurs in the NT here in Paul and in Acts 27:22.

αὐτῶν. Possessive genitive, modifying ἡ ἀποβολὴ. The personal pronoun is used again to refer to Israel.

καταλλαγὴ. Predicate nominative. Anarthrous substantives reflect quality of the substantive, rather than particularity.

κόσμου. Possessive genitive, modifying καταλλαγὴ. Some may wish to label this as an objective genitive, if καταλλαγὴ were to become a verb ("to reconcile").

τίς. Predicate nominative. The interrogative pronoun begins the apodosis of the conditional structure.

ἡ πρόσλημψις. Nominative subject of verbless clause.

εἰ μὴ. A combination of the conditional conjunction and the negative particle (usually "except" or "if not") that introduces a second-class (verbless) conditional, sharing the apodosis from the previous conditional clause.

ζωὴ. Nominative subject of verbless clause. Anarthrous noun reflects the quality of the noun rather than its particularity.

ἐκ νεκρῶν. Locative (movement out of/separation).

11:16 εἰ δὲ ἡ ἀπαρχὴ ἁγία, καὶ τὸ φύραμα· καὶ εἰ ἡ ῥίζα ἁγία, καὶ οἱ κλάδοι.

εἰ. Introduces the protasis of a first-class conditional in a string of conditionals in this co-text.

δὲ. Adversative conjunction (mild). It is used to continue the argument from the previous co-text by appealing to illustrations.

ἡ ἀπαρχὴ. Nominative subject of verbless clause. Verbless clauses reflect simple statements to make simple assertions (cf. Yoon 2019, 106–8).

ἁγία. Predicate adjective.

καὶ. Adverbial use (adjunctive). It modifies τὸ φύραμα and begins the apodosis (καὶ τὸ φύραμα).

τὸ φύραμα. Nominative absolute.

καὶ. Coordinating conjunction. It connects the two conditional structures.

εἰ. Introduces the protasis of the second first-class conditional in this verse.

ἡ ῥίζα. Nominative subject of verbless clause.

ἁγία. Predicate adjective.

καὶ. Adverbial use (adjunctive). It modifies οἱ κλάδοι and begins the apodosis (καὶ οἱ κλάδοι).

οἱ κλάδοι. Nominative absolute.

11:17 Εἰ δέ τινες τῶν κλάδων ἐξεκλάσθησαν, σὺ δὲ ἀγριέλαιος ὢν ἐνεκεντρίσθης ἐν αὐτοῖς καὶ συγκοινωνὸς τῆς ῥίζης τῆς πιότητος τῆς ἐλαίας ἐγένου,

Εἰ. Introduces the compound protasis of a first-class conditional that extends to the next verse. There are three protases in this conditional structure.

δέ. Adversative conjunction (mild). It is used to connect the previous conditional statements. This begins the first of the three protases.

τινες. Nominative subject of ἐξεκλάσθησαν.

τῶν κλάδων. Partitive genitive, modifying τινες.

ἐξεκλάσθησαν. Aor pass ind 3rd pl ἐκκλάω. Passive voice indicates external agency (not specified in the co-text).

σὺ. Nominative subject of ἐνεκεντρίσθης and ἐγένου. The personal pronoun refers anaphorically to τοῖς ἔθνεσιν (11:13). The switch from the plural to the singular personal pronoun here (cf. ὑμῖν in 11:13) reflects Paul's dialogue with a hypothetical Gentile, to whom he speaks. This begins the second of the three protases.

δὲ. Adversative conjunction (mild).

ἀγριέλαιος. Predicate nominative of ὤν.

ὤν. Ptc masc nom sg εἰμί (concessive). The participle functions as circumstantial, modifying ἐνεκεντρίσθης.

ἐνεκεντρίσθης. Aor pass ind 2nd sg ἐγκεντρίζω. See comment on σὺ above for the use of second-person singular.

ἐν αὐτοῖς. Distributional ("among them").

καὶ. Coordinating conjunction. It joins the two clauses represented by the main verbs ἐνεκεντρίσθης and ἐγένου.

συγκοινωνὸς. Predicate nominative of ἐγένου. The fronting of the predicate nominative before the predicate indicates clausal prominence.

τῆς ῥίζης. Genitive of description or definition, modifying συγκοινωνὸς. It further describes or circumscribes "joint sharer" as "of root."

τῆς πιότητος. Genitive of quality, modifying τῆς ῥίζης ("rich root").

τῆς ἐλαίας. Genitive of source or origin, modifying τῆς πιότητος.

ἐγένου. Aor mid ind 2nd sg γίνομαι. See comment on σὺ above for the use of the second-person singular.

11:18 μὴ κατακαυχῶ τῶν κλάδων· εἰ δὲ κατακαυχᾶσαι οὐ σὺ τὴν ῥίζαν βαστάζεις ἀλλ᾽ ἡ ῥίζα σέ.

μὴ. Negative particle used with aorist subjunctive to convey a prohibition. This begins the apodosis from the compound protasis.

κατακαυχῶ. Pres mid impv 2nd sg κατακαυχάομαι (prohibitive subjunctive). The prefixed verb (κατα-; cf. 2:17) adds a directional sense of the root, e.g., "boast down upon" or "boast against."

τῶν κλάδων. Genitive object of κατακαυχῶ. The object of "boasting against" is "branches." The genitive is probably related to the κατα- prefix as a complement.

εἰ. Introduces the protasis of a first-class conditional. Paul utilizes another first-class conditional structure to continue his argument regarding boasting.

δέ. Adversative conjunction (mild).

κατακαυχᾶσαι. Pres mid ind 2nd sg κατακαυχάομαι. See above for the prefixed form of the verb.

οὐ . . . ἀλλ'. A point/counterpoint set that establishes a contrast between σὺ τὴν ῥίζαν βαστάζεις and ἡ ῥίζα σέ.

σύ. Nominative subject of βαστάζεις. The singular personal pronoun is maintained to represent the hypothetical Gentile.

τὴν ῥίζαν. Accusative direct object of βαστάζεις. The fronting of the accusative before the verb indicates clausal prominence.

βαστάζεις. Pres act ind 2nd sg βαστάζω.

ἡ ῥίζα. Nominative subject of verbless clause (the implied verb is βαστάζει).

σέ. Accusative direct object of verbless clause. For an explanation of the use of the singular personal pronoun, see the notes on 11:17.

11:19 ἐρεῖς οὖν· ἐξεκλάσθησαν κλάδοι ἵνα ἐγὼ ἐγκεντρισθῶ.

ἐρεῖς. Fut act ind 2nd sg λέγω. The semantic feature of expectation for the future form is felicitous here, as Paul anticipates or expects a response from his interlocutor.

οὖν. Postpositive inferential conjunction. The inference is from Paul's previous analogy of branches and roots.

ἐξεκλάσθησαν. Aor pass ind 3rd pl ἐκκλάω. Passive voice indicates external agency; in this co-text, however, the agent is not specified.

κλάδοι. Nominative subject of ἐξεκλάσθησαν. As the grammatical subject of a passive voice predicate, it is the Goal.

ἵνα. Introduces a purpose clause.

ἐγώ. Nominative subject of ἐγκεντρισθῶ. The use of the personal pronoun here is emphatic. The singular pronoun is continued to be used to represent the hypothetical Gentile.

ἐγκεντρισθῶ. Aor pass subj 1st sg ἐγκεντρίζω. Subjunctive with ἵνα. Passive voice indicates external agency, but as in the above predicate (ἐξεκλάσθησαν), the agent is not specified. The focus of this verse, then, by using the passive voice-form, is not on the agent—i.e., the one responsible for the breaking off and grafting in—but on the ones who are broken off and grafted in.

11:20 καλῶς· τῇ ἀπιστίᾳ ἐξεκλάσθησαν, σὺ δὲ τῇ πίστει ἕστηκας. μὴ ὑψηλὰ φρόνει ἀλλὰ φοβοῦ·

καλῶς. Adverb, used here as an exclamation of assent, although usually it functions as an adjunctive adverb (BDAG, 506.4.c; Porter 2015,

213–14; cf. Mark 12:32). It is used to cast agreement on the previously supposed response by the interlocutor.

τῇ ἀπιστίᾳ. Dative of instrument. The fronting of the dative before the predicate indicates clausal prominence. In other words, Paul focuses on how they were broken off: by unbelief.

ἐξεκλάσθησαν. Aor pass ind 3rd pl ἐκκλάω. The passive voice is used frequently in this co-text, putting the focus on the Goal rather than the agent.

σὺ. Nominative subject of ἕστηκας. The singular personal pronoun is continued to be used to represent the hypothetical Gentile.

δὲ. Adversative conjunction (mild). The mild contrast is between Israel who was broken off and Gentiles who remain standing.

τῇ πίστει. Dative of instrument. It is parallel to τῇ ἀπιστίᾳ. The fronting of the dative before the predicate indicates clausal prominence.

ἕστηκας. Prf act ind 2nd sg ἵστημι. The stative aspect (perfect tense-form) depicts the standing as a (complex) state or condition. Stative aspect also reflects discourse prominence (emphasis at the discourse level).

μὴ ὑψηλὰ φρόνει. Lit. "do not think high things." An idiom that refers to considering oneself highly (cf. 12:3).

μὴ . . . ἀλλὰ. A point/counterpoint set that establishes a strong contrast between the prohibition against thinking highly and the command to fear. The negative particle negates φρόνει (negated imperative as a prohibition), with the accusative embedded between the particle and the predicate.

ὑψηλὰ. Accusative direct object of φρόνει. The fronting of the accusative object before the predicate indicates clausal prominence (emphasis at the clause level).

φρόνει. Pres act impv 2nd sg φρονέω. The present imperative indicates an in-progress, specific process, i.e., "do not be thinking highly."

φοβοῦ. Pres mid impv 2nd sg φοβέω. As in the parallel predicate, the present imperative indicates an in-progress, specific process, i.e., "be fearing."

11:21 εἰ γὰρ ὁ θεὸς τῶν κατὰ φύσιν κλάδων οὐκ ἐφείσατο, [μή πως] οὐδὲ σοῦ φείσεται.

εἰ. Introduces the protasis of a first-class conditional.

γὰρ. Postpositive explanatory conjunction. Paul provides further explanation regarding the analogy of branches.

ὁ θεὸς. Nominative subject of ἐφείσατο.

τῶν … κλάδων. Genitive direct object of ἐφείσατο. The predicate φείδομαι often takes a genitive as its object (cf. Acts 20:29; Rom 8:32; 1 Cor 7:28; 2 Cor 1:23; 2 Pet 2:4, 5).

κατὰ φύσιν. Standard. The standard of the branches is "nature" ("the branches according to nature" or "natural branches"). The placement of the prepositional word group between the article and the substantive indicates that it functions attributively (lit. "the 'according-to-nature' branches").

οὐκ. Negative particle normally used with indicative verbs. Here it negates ἐφείσατο.

ἐφείσατο. Aor mid ind 3rd sg φείδομαι. Middle voice indicates indirect, internal agency. As a so-called deponent verb (see "Deponency" in the Series Introduction and Introduction), the meaning of the lexeme here ("to spare or refrain") by definition indirectly involves the subject in the process.

[μή πως]. Negated adverb, modifying the entire clause. This begins the apodosis. This word group is a textual variant, found in the earliest manuscript, 𝔓⁴⁶, but omitted in the major codices, such as ℵ, A, B, and C. It may have been omitted because it could seem redundant with οὐδέ. But with it, the negation is emphatic.

οὐδέ. Negative particle functioning as an adverb. οὐδέ is a combination of οὐ and δέ. If μή πως is included in the original reading, then οὐδέ would be emphatic.

σοῦ. Genitive direct object of φείσεται (cf. τῶν … κλάδων above).

φείσεται. Fut mid ind 3rd sg φείδομαι. The future form, grammaticalizing expectation, is appropriate, as if the conditional (God did not spare the natural branches) is true, then he can be expected to not spare "you" either.

11:22 ἴδε οὖν χρηστότητα καὶ ἀποτομίαν θεοῦ· ἐπὶ μὲν τοὺς πεσόντας ἀποτομία, ἐπὶ δὲ σὲ χρηστότης θεοῦ, ἐὰν ἐπιμένῃς τῇ χρηστότητι, ἐπεὶ καὶ σὺ ἐκκοπήσῃ.

ἴδε. Aor act impv 2nd sg ὁράω. The use of the perfective imperative reflects a general command, viewing the process as a whole. The use of the second-person singular reflects Paul continuing to dialogue with the hypothetical Gentile.

οὖν. Postpositive inferential conjunction. The following inference is from the previous co-text regarding God's potential sparing of branches.

χρηστότητα. Accusative direct object of ἴδε.

καὶ. Coordinating conjunction. It connects the two accusative objects χρηστότητα and ἀποτομίαν.

ἀποτομίαν. Accusative direct object of ἴδε. The lexeme occurs only in this verse (2x) in the NT and LXX.

θεοῦ. Genitive of source or origin, modifying both χρηστότητα and ἀποτομίαν.

ἐπὶ ... τοὺς πεσόντας. Directional (movement upon). This begins the compound apodosis of a third-class conditional, with the protasis occurring after it. The placement of the apodosis before the protasis indicates prominence at the clause-complex level.

πεσόντας. Aor act ptc masc acc pl πίπτω (substantival).

μὲν ... δὲ. A point/counterpoint set that establishes the contrast between "those who fell" and "you."

ἀποτομία. Nominative absolute.

ἐπὶ ... σὲ. Directional (movement upon). This begins the second apodosis of the third-class conditional.

χρηστότης. Nominative absolute.

θεοῦ. Genitive of source or origin, modifying χρηστότης.

ἐάν. Introduces the protasis of a third-class conditional. The use of the third-class conditional here, as opposed to the string of first-class conditionals in the previous co-text, reflects Paul's hopeful projection that his readers would remain in God's kindness.

ἐπιμένῃς. Pres act subj 2nd sg ἐπιμένω. Subjunctive with ἐάν.

τῇ χρηστότητι. Dative of sphere.

ἐπεὶ. Causal conjunction. The causality is implied, that if they do *not* continue in God's kindness, they would be cut off.

καὶ. Adverbial use (adjunctive). It modifies ἐκκοπήσῃ.

σὺ. Nominative subject of ἐκκοπήσῃ. The use of the personal pronoun is emphatic.

ἐκκοπήσῃ. Fut pass ind 2nd sg ἐκκόπτω. The future form grammaticalizes expectation; they are expected to be cut off. Passive voice indicates external causality; agent is not specified in this co-text. Passive voice is often used to highlight other elements of the clause than the agent, namely the grammatical subject or Goal (here, "you").

11:23 κἀκεῖνοι δέ, ἐὰν μὴ ἐπιμένωσιν τῇ ἀπιστίᾳ, ἐγκεντρισθήσονται· δυνατὸς γάρ ἐστιν ὁ θεὸς πάλιν ἐγκεντρίσαι αὐτούς.

κἀκεῖνοι. A compound of καί + ἐκεῖνοι formed by crasis (BDAG, 500.1.b). καί is adverbial (adjunctive); ἐκεῖνοι is the nominative subject of ἐγκεντρισθήσονται. The demonstrative pronoun refers anaphorically to τοὺς πεσόντας and is fronted before the conditional conjunction for prominence at the clause-complex level. The protasis is embedded between the subject and the verb of the apodosis (e.g., apodosis: κἀκεῖνοι δέ . . . ἐγκεντρισθήσονται; protasis: ἐὰν μὴ ἐπιμένωσιν τῇ ἀπιστίᾳ).

δέ. Adversative conjunction (mild).

ἐὰν. Introduces the protasis of a third-class conditional.

μὴ. Negative particle normally used with non-indicative verbs. Here it negates ἐπιμένωσιν.

ἐπιμένωσιν. Pres act subj 3rd pl ἐπιμένω. Subjunctive with ἐάν.

τῇ ἀπιστίᾳ. Dative of sphere. The sphere of continuing is "unbelief."

ἐγκεντρισθήσονται. Fut pass ind 3rd pl ἐγκεντρίζω. The future form reflects expectation, i.e., "they are expected to be engrafted."

δυνατὸς. Predicate adjective.

γάρ. Postpositive explanatory conjunction. It introduces a clause that explains how those who do not continue in disbelief can be engrafted again.

ἐστιν. Unaugmented ind 3rd sg εἰμί.

ὁ θεὸς. Nominative subject of ἐστιν.

πάλιν. Adverb (temporal). It modifies ἐγκεντρίσαι.

ἐγκεντρίσαι. Aor act inf ἐγκεντρίζω (epexegetical to δυνατὸς).

αὐτούς. Accusative direct object of ἐγκεντρίσαι. The personal pronoun continues to refer anaphorically to τοὺς πεσόντας from the co-text.

11:24 εἰ γὰρ σὺ ἐκ τῆς κατὰ φύσιν ἐξεκόπης ἀγριελαίου καὶ παρὰ φύσιν ἐνεκεντρίσθης εἰς καλλιέλαιον, πόσῳ μᾶλλον οὗτοι οἱ κατὰ φύσιν ἐγκεντρισθήσονται τῇ ἰδίᾳ ἐλαίᾳ.

εἰ. Introduces the protasis of a first-class conditional, which consists of two clauses joined by καί.

γὰρ. Postpositive explanatory conjunction. Paul continues his explanation of the branches and engrafting analogy here.

σὺ. Nominative subject of ἐξεκόπης and ἐνεκεντρίσθης. The second-person singular maintains Paul's dialogue with the hypothetical Gentile.

ἐκ τῆς . . . ἀγριελαίου. Locative (movement away from). Embedded between ἐκ τῆς . . . ἀγριελαίου are two elements, an embedded prepositional word group (κατὰ φύσιν) and a finite verb (ἐξεκόπης). Lit. "out of the 'according-to-nature'-'you-were-cut-off' olive plant."

κατὰ φύσιν. Standard (see a note on this prepositional word group in 11:21).

ἐξεκόπης. Aor pass ind 2nd sg ἐκκόπτω. Passive voice indicates external agency; the agent is not specified in the immediate co-text but implied to be God.

καὶ. Coordinating conjunction. It connects the two clauses that form the protasis.

παρὰ φύσιν. Locative. The locative sense is figurative, in the sense of replacing the thing it is alongside and usurping its place (cf. παρὰ τὸν κτίσαντα in 1:25; see Porter 1994a, 166–67).

ἐνεκεντρίσθης. Aor pass ind 2nd sg ἐγκεντρίζω. It is parallel to ἐξεκόπης above.

εἰς καλλιέλαιον. Directional (movement toward or into).

πόσῳ μᾶλλον. Dative of advantage + the comparative of the adverb μάλα (see 11:12). It marks the beginning of the apodosis.

οὗτοι. Nominative subject of ἐγκεντρισθήσονται.

οἱ κατὰ φύσιν. The article functions as an adjectivizer, changing the prepositional word group κατὰ φύσιν into an attributive modifier (third attributive position) of οὗτοι (Porter 1994a, 116–17; Wallace 1996, 307).

κατὰ φύσιν. Standard.

ἐγκεντρισθήσονται. Fut pass ind 3rd pl ἐγκεντρίζω. Passive voice indicates external agency, but the agent is not specified here, which is consistent with the use of the passive voice in this co-text (see 11:19 on ἐγκεντρισθῶ).

τῇ ἰδίᾳ ἐλαίᾳ. Locative dative.

Romans 11:25-36

²⁵For I do not want you to be ignorant, brothers [and sisters], of this mystery—in order that you may not be in your own estimations wise—that a hardening in part for Israel has occurred, until which the fullness of the Gentiles might enter, ²⁶and in this way all Israel will be saved, just as it is written, "The rescuer will come out of Zion; he will stray away ungodliness from Jacob. ²⁷And this [is] the covenant from me to them, when I take away their sins." ²⁸According to the good news, [they are] enemies because of you; but according to election, [they are] beloved through the fathers. ²⁹For irrevocable [are] the gracious gifts and calling of God. ³⁰For just as you were at one time disobedient to God but now you were shown mercy because of the disobedience of these, ³¹so also these now have been disobedient with respect to your mercy, in order that now they may also be shown mercy. ³²For God locked up all in disobedience, in order that he would have mercy on all. ³³Oh, the depth of the abundance and wisdom and knowledge of God; how unsearchable [are] his judgments and unfathomable his ways. ³⁴For "who knows the mind of the Lord?" Or "who can become his counselor?" ³⁵Or "who gave in advance to him and will be repaid by him?" ³⁶For from him and through him and for him [are] all things. To him [be] the glory forever, amen.

To end this major section (Romans 9–11), Paul shifts from a predominantly diatribe and interlocutory approach (except for in 11:34–35), but he maintains the use of Scripture and explains the "mystery" surrounding the fate of the people of Israel. Paul begins this sub-section with a disclosure formula (see below) to draw attention to what his readers should know.

11:25 Οὐ γὰρ θέλω ὑμᾶς ἀγνοεῖν, ἀδελφοί, τὸ μυστήριον τοῦτο, ἵνα μὴ ἦτε [παρ'] ἑαυτοῖς φρόνιμοι, ὅτι πώρωσις ἀπὸ μέρους τῷ Ἰσραὴλ γέγονεν ἄχρι οὗ τὸ πλήρωμα τῶν ἐθνῶν εἰσέλθῃ

Οὐ . . . θέλω ὑμᾶς ἀγνοεῖν. A disclosure formula (a verb of "desire" + a verb of "knowing"; cf. comments on 1:13; Porter and Pitts 2013), but with a double negative (οὐ + α-prefixed verb). Together, Οὐ . . . θέλω . . . ἀγνοεῖν is an instance of litotes.

Οὐ. Negative particle normally used with indicative verbs. Here it negates θέλω.

γὰρ. Postpositive explanatory conjunction. Moving from Paul's analogy of the branches and root, he now explains the implications of this analogy.

θέλω. Pres act ind 1st sg θέλω.

ὑμᾶς. Accusative subject of ἀγνοεῖν. The switch from the 2nd singular to the 2nd plural here is probably used to differentiate his address of the hypothetical Gentile from the previous co-text to those of the Gentiles who are believers (i.e., ἀδελφοί).

ἀγνοεῖν. Pres act inf ἀγνοέω (complementary). The infinitive complements θέλω in a catenative structure.

ἀδελφοί. Nominative of address (so-called vocative).

τὸ μυστήριον τοῦτο. Accusative direct object of ἀγνοεῖν. The demonstrative pronoun is cataphoric; explanation of this mystery is stated subsequently. This is the first time Paul uses the lexeme μυστήριον in this letter.

ἵνα. Introduces a purpose clause. The purpose of Paul's desire for Gentiles to know this mystery is explained.

μὴ. Negative particle normally used with non-indicative verbs. Here it negates ἦτε.

ἦτε. Subj 2nd pl εἰμί. Subjunctive with ἵνα.

[παρ'] ἑαυτοῖς. Positional (alongside). ἑαυτοῖς is a reflexive pronoun. Manuscript evidence is divided on the textual variant of παρ'. Of the earliest papyri and codices, ℵ, C, and D contain παρ', 𝔓⁴⁶, F, and G omit it, and A and B contain ἐν in its place. Regardless of the textual options here, the function of the dative as a case of relation is evident here, i.e., to not be wise *with respect to* yourselves.

φρόνιμοι. Predicate adjective.

ὅτι. Introduces a clause that is epexegetical to τὸ μυστήριον τοῦτο.

πώρωσις. Nominative subject of γέγονεν.

ἀπὸ μέρους. Locative (movement away from). The prepositional word group refers to a hardening or stubbornness from (out of) a part (of the group, i.e., Israel).

τῷ Ἰσραὴλ. Dative of disadvantage. A hardening in part has occurred to/for/with Israel.

γέγονεν. Prf act ind 3rd sg γίνομαι. The stative aspect depicts the "becoming" as a complex state or condition.

ἄχρι οὗ. Temporal. ἄχρι is an improper preposition (Porter 1994a, 178; cf. 1:13; 5:13; 8:22). The relative pronoun οὗ functions as a marker of situation or set of circumstances (BDAG 732.2) and refers cataphorically to the next clause.

τὸ πλήρωμα. Nominative subject of εἰσέλθῃ.

τῶν ἐθνῶν. Genitive of description or definition, modifying τῶν ἐθνῶν. "Fullness" is further described or circumscribed as "of the Gentiles."

εἰσέλθῃ. Aor act subj 3rd sg εἰσέρχομαι. Subjunctive in indefinite temporal clause. It depicts projection, i.e., that Paul projects the coming fullness of the Gentiles.

11:26 καὶ οὕτως πᾶς Ἰσραὴλ σωθήσεται, καθὼς γέγραπται· ἥξει ἐκ Σιὼν ὁ ῥυόμενος, ἀποστρέψει ἀσεβείας ἀπὸ Ἰακώβ.

καὶ. Coordinating conjunction. It connects the following clause with the previous.

οὕτως. Adverb (manner). It introduces the comparison between the fullness of the Gentiles and all Israel being saved.

πᾶς Ἰσραὴλ. Nominative subject of σωθήσεται. As the grammatical subject of passive voice verb, it is the Goal of the process.

σωθήσεται. Fut pass ind 3rd sg σῴζω. The semantics of the future form as grammaticalizing expectation is evident here.

καθὼς γέγραπται. A standard Pauline formula for introducing a scriptural quotation (see note on 1:17). It introduces here the loose quotation from LXX Isa 59:20 and continues to LXX Isa 59:21 in the next verse.

καθὼς. Comparative conjunction. The comparison is with the previous clause (οὕτως πᾶς Ἰσραὴλ σωθήσεται) and the following OT quotation.

γέγραπται. Prf pass ind 3rd sg γράφω.

ἥξει. Fut act ind 3rd sg ἥκω.

ἐκ Σιών. Locative ("out of/from Zion").

ὁ ῥυόμενος. Pres mid ptc masc nom sg ῥύομαι (substantival). Nominative subject of ἥξει.

ἀποστρέψει. Fut act ind 3rd sg ἀποστρέφω.

ἀσεβείας. Accusative direct object of ἀποστρέψει.

ἀπὸ Ἰακώβ. Locative ("out of/from Jacob"). It is parallel to ἐκ Σιών. The use of a different preposition here, however, is likely due to ἀπό having a sense of movement away from and implying the semantics of separation, while ἐκ is more semantically restricted and referring to "withinness" (cf. Porter 1994a, 146; Robertson, 577–78).

11:27 καὶ αὕτη αὐτοῖς ἡ παρ' ἐμοῦ διαθήκη, ὅταν ἀφέλωμαι τὰς ἁμαρτίας αὐτῶν.

καὶ. Coordinating conjunction. It connects the following clause with the previous. This verse continues the loose OT quotation from the previous verse (specifically LXX Isa 59:21 here).

αὕτη. Nominative subject of verbless clause. The demonstrative pronoun refers to the previous statement that "the rescuer . . . will stray away ungodliness from Jacob" (11:26). αὕτη agrees in gender and number with διαθήκη.

αὐτοῖς. Dative of advantage.

ἡ . . . διαθήκη. Predicate nominative.

παρ' ἐμοῦ. Directional (movement away from, in the sense of "from"). The placement of the prepositional word group between the article and the substantive reflects its attributive function (i.e., "the from-me covenant"), focusing on the directionality from the object of the preposition, "me."

ὅταν. Temporal conjunction.

ἀφέλωμαι. Aor mid subj 1st sg ἀφαιρέω. Subjunctive in indefinite temporal clause. This is the only use of this verb in Paul (cf. Heb 10:4). Middle voice indicates indirect, internal agency. The subjunctive mood form reflects the act of forgiving as projected, i.e., probable action.

τὰς ἁμαρτίας. Accusative direct object of ἀφέλωμαι.

αὐτῶν. Possessive genitive or genitive of source or origin, modifying τὰς ἁμαρτίας.

11:28 κατὰ μὲν τὸ εὐαγγέλιον ἐχθροὶ δι' ὑμᾶς, κατὰ δὲ τὴν ἐκλογὴν ἀγαπητοὶ διὰ τοὺς πατέρας·

κατὰ . . . τὸ εὐαγγέλιον. Standard. The standard or basis by which Israel is considered an enemy is "the good news" or "gospel."

μὲν ... δὲ. A point/counterpoint set that establishes the contrast between the two clauses (i.e., "on one hand ... but on the other hand").

ἐχθροί. Nominative absolute or predicate nominative in a verbless clause.

δι' ὑμᾶς. Causal. The cause of Israel being an enemy is "you" (i.e., Gentiles and their inclusion).

κατὰ ... τὴν ἐκλογὴν. Standard. The standard or basis by which Israel is considered a beloved is "election."

ἀγαπητοί. Predicate adjective.

διὰ τοὺς πατέρας. Causal. The cause of Israel being beloved is "the fathers" (i.e., their heritage).

11:29 ἀμεταμέλητα γὰρ τὰ χαρίσματα καὶ ἡ κλῆσις τοῦ θεοῦ.

ἀμεταμέλητα. Predicate adjective.

γὰρ. Postpositive explanatory conjunction. It introduces a clause that explains the previous statement regarding Israel being enemies on one hand and beloved on the other.

τὰ χαρίσματα καὶ ἡ κλῆσις. Compound nominative subject of verbless clause.

τοῦ θεοῦ. Genitive of source or origin, modifying τὰ χαρίσματα καὶ ἡ κλῆσις.

11:30 ὥσπερ γὰρ ὑμεῖς ποτε ἠπειθήσατε τῷ θεῷ, νῦν δὲ ἠλεήθητε τῇ τούτων ἀπειθείᾳ,

ὥσπερ. The first element of the point/counterpoint set ("just as ... so also") that is completed in 11:31 with οὕτως καὶ.

γὰρ. Postpositive explanatory conjunction. It is used to continue the argument from previous co-text.

ὑμεῖς. Nominative subject of ἠπειθήσατε. The personal pronoun maintains the anaphoric referent to ἀδελφοί (see 11:25).

ποτε. Temporal particle.

ἠπειθήσατε. Aor act ind 2nd pl ἀπειθέω.

τῷ θεῷ. Dative direct object of ἠπειθήσατε.

νῦν. Adverb (temporal). It modifies ἠλεήθητε.

δὲ. Adversative conjunction (mild).

ἠλεήθητε. Aor pass ind 2nd pl ἐλεέω. Passive voice indicates external agency, which is not specified but implied to be God.

τῇ ... ἀπειθείᾳ. Dative of cause. "Their disobedience" was the cause or reason why which they received mercy.

τούτων. Possessive genitive or genitive of source or origin, modifying τὰς ἁμαρτίας.

11:31 οὕτως καὶ οὗτοι νῦν ἠπείθησαν τῷ ὑμετέρῳ ἐλέει, ἵνα καὶ αὐτοὶ [νῦν] ἐλεηθῶσιν.

οὕτως καὶ. The second element of the point/counterpoint set ("just as . . . so also") that completes the comparison begun in 11:30 with ὥσπερ.

οὗτοι. Nominative subject of ἠπείθησαν. The use of demonstrative pronoun is emphatic and refers anaphorically to Israel (11:26).

νῦν. Adverb (temporal). It modifies ἠπείθησαν.

ἠπείθησαν. Aor act ind 3rd pl ἀπειθέω.

τῷ ὑμετέρῳ ἐλέει. Dative of respect. They were disobedient with respect to "your mercy," i.e., the mercy that the Gentiles received.

ἵνα. Introduces a purpose clause. The purpose of Israel's disobedience is indicated here.

καὶ. Adverbial use (adjunctive). It modifies the clause.

αὐτοὶ. Nominative subject of ἐλεηθῶσιν. The personal pronoun in emphatic and refers anaphorically to οὗτοι in the immediate co-text (i.e., Israel).

[νῦν]. Adverb (temporal). Most of the early manuscripts contain this word, and only one early papyrus, 𝔓⁴⁶, omits it. The occurrence of νῦν in the previous clause may be the reason for this textual variant.

ἐλεηθῶσιν. Aor pass subj 3rd pl ἐλεέω. Subjunctive with ἵνα. Passive voice indicates external agency. The agent is not specified in the co-text, but it is implied to be God.

11:32 συνέκλεισεν γὰρ ὁ θεὸς τοὺς πάντας εἰς ἀπείθειαν, ἵνα τοὺς πάντας ἐλεήσῃ.

συνέκλεισεν. Aor act ind 3rd sg συγκλείω. This lexeme refers to being locked up, closed up, or shut in, as in imprisoned or in the context of a woman's womb, often metaphorically (e.g., LXX Gen 16:2; LXX Josh 6:1; LXX 1 Sam 1:6; LXX Mal 1:10; Luke 5:6, where συγκλείω is used as a metaphor for catching fish; and Gal 3:22–23).

γὰρ. Postpositive explanatory conjunction. It continues Paul's argument in this co-text.

ὁ θεὸς. Nominative subject of συνέκλεισεν.

τοὺς πάντας. Accusative direct object of συνέκλεισεν. The substantive adjective "all" is used here in the sense of all groups being addressed by Paul, both Jews and Gentiles, rather than everyone in an individualistic sense (cf. Porter 2015, 221–22).

εἰς ἀπείθειαν. Movement (towards or into). It refers to God's locking up all "towards" disobedience.

ἵνα. Introduces a purpose clause. The purpose of God locking up all to disobedience is introduced.

τοὺς πάντας. Accusative direct object of ἐλεήσῃ. Again, "all" is a reference to all groups of people (i.e., Jews and Gentiles) and not every single person (see above). In other words, all groups of people have the opportunity to be shown mercy.

ἐλεήσῃ. Aor act subj 3rd sg ἐλεέω. Subjunctive with ἵνα.

11:33 Ὦ βάθος πλούτου καὶ σοφίας καὶ γνώσεως θεοῦ· ὡς ἀνεξεραύνητα τὰ κρίματα αὐτοῦ καὶ ἀνεξιχνίαστοι αἱ ὁδοὶ αὐτοῦ.

Ὦ. Interjection. Without a formal conjunction (instead, an asyndeton), it reflects Paul's eruption of this built-up doxology.

βάθος. Nominative absolute.

πλούτου καὶ σοφίας καὶ γνώσεως. Three partitive genitives, modifying βάθος. The noun σοφία occurs only here in Romans, but frequently in some of other letters in the Pauline corpus (1 Cor 1:17, 19, 20, 21, 22, 24, 30; 2:1, 4, 5, 6, 7, 13; 3:19; 12:8; 2 Cor 1:12; Eph 1:8, 17; 3:10; Col 1:9, 28; 2:3, 23; 3:16; 4:5). This may indicate that wisdom is not so much a major topic in Romans but that it may be in others of his letters.

θεοῦ. Genitive of source or origin, modifying all three head terms (πλούτου, σοφίας, and γνώσεως).

ὡς. Comparative conjunction. The comparison is with the depths of the abundance, wisdom, and knowledge of God with the following statement.

ἀνεξεραύνητα. Predicate adjective. The repetition of the double prefix, ἀ(ν) + ἐκ ("not-from-"), of the two predicates here emphasizes the semantics of the negation (so-called alpha privative) and prepositional prefix for each lexeme.

τὰ κρίματα. Nominative subject of verbless clause.

αὐτοῦ. Possessive genitive, modifying τὰ κρίματα.

καὶ. Connects the two parallel clauses.

ἀνεξιχνίαστοι. Predicate adjective. The repetition of the double prefix, ἀ(ν) + ἐκ ("not-from-"), of the two predicates here emphasizes the semantics of the negation (so-called alpha privative) and prepositional prefix for each lexeme.

αἱ ὁδοὶ. Nominative subject of verbless clause.

αὐτοῦ. Possessive genitive, modifying αἱ ὁδοί.

11:34 τίς γὰρ ἔγνω νοῦν κυρίου; ἢ τίς σύμβουλος αὐτοῦ ἐγένετο;

τίς. Nominative subject of ἔγνω. It begins a quotation of LXX Isa 40:13.
γὰρ. Postpositive explanatory conjunction. It introduces a clause that further explains his praise of God in the previous co-text.
ἔγνω. Aor act ind 3rd sg γινώσκω.
νοῦν. Accusative direct object of ἔγνω.
κυρίου. Possessive genitive, modifying νοῦν.
ἢ. Disjunctive conjunction. It joins the two questions before and after it in an adversative, comparative sense.
τίς. Predicate nominative of ἐγένετο.
σύμβουλος. Nominative subject of ἐγένετο.
αὐτοῦ. Possessive genitive, modifying σύμβουλος. The personal pronoun refers anaphorically to κυρίου.
ἐγένετο. Aor mid ind 3rd sg γίνομαι. Middle voice indicates indirect, internal causality. As a so-called deponent verb (see "Deponency" in the Series Introduction), the lexical meaning of the verb indicates indirect subject involvement or participation of the verbal process.

11:35 ἢ τίς προέδωκεν αὐτῷ, καὶ ἀνταποδοθήσεται αὐτῷ;

ἢ. Disjunctive conjunction. It joins the two questions before and after it in an adversative, comparative sense (see 11:34).
τίς. Nominative subject of προέδωκεν and ἀνταποδοθήσεται. The interrogative pronoun appears to begin a reference to LXX Job 35:7, although paraphrased by Paul.
προέδωκεν. Aor act ind 3rd sg προδίδωμι.
αὐτῷ. Dative indirect object of προέδωκεν. The personal pronoun reference is anaphoric, going back to κυρίου in 11:34.
καὶ. Coordinating conjunction. It connects the previous clause with the following clause. Some English translations (NIV, NASB, ESV) supply "that" instead of the customary "and" here, but the connective sense is appropriate (cf. NKJV).
ἀνταποδοθήσεται. Ful pass ind 3rd sg ἀνταποδίδωμι. It maintains τίς as its grammatical subject. This lexeme is double prefixed (ἀντι- + ἀπο-) and means "to pay something back to someone as the result of an incurred obligation" (LN 57.154). The future form grammaticalizing expectation is clear here: "[who] can expect to be repaid?" The passive voice indicates external agency, identified by the dative αὐτῷ that follows.
αὐτῷ. Dative of instrument or agency. The agent of the passive form of ἀνταποδίδωμι, "repay," is "him." The personal pronoun continues the anaphoric reference to κυρίου in 11:34.

11:36 ὅτι ἐξ αὐτοῦ καὶ δι᾽ αὐτοῦ καὶ εἰς αὐτὸν τὰ πάντα· αὐτῷ ἡ δόξα εἰς τοὺς αἰῶνας, ἀμήν.

ὅτι. Introduces a causal clause. It is used to indicate that what he has said thus far is true for the following cause or reason.

ἐξ αὐτοῦ. Locative (movement out of), in the sense of source or origin. The personal pronoun continues to refer anaphorically to κυρίου in 11:34. This prepositional word group is used to indicate that "all things" originate from him, that the Lord is the source. The fronting of this and the following two prepositional word groups reflect clausal prominence.

καὶ. Coordinating conjunction. It connects the prepositional word groups.

δι᾽ αὐτοῦ. Instrumental. Along with ἐξ αὐτοῦ, this preposition is used to indicate instrumentality; however, the focus of δι᾽ αὐτοῦ is not on *source* (as in ἐξ αὐτοῦ; "out of him") but on *means* ("through him"). In other words, ἐξ αὐτοῦ reflects the origin of all things being the Lord and δι᾽ αὐτοῦ reflects the sustenance of all things being the Lord.

καὶ. Coordinating conjunction. It connects the prepositional word groups.

εἰς αὐτὸν. Purpose. Whereas the first two prepositions reflect instrumentality, this one reflects purpose or telicity. In other words, the purpose of all things is God.

τὰ πάντα. Nominative subject of verbless clause. The substantival adjective probably refers to the totality of all things.

αὐτῷ. Dative of advantage. Its fronting before the nominative absolute indicates clausal prominence, i.e., the Lord (the pronominal referent) is emphatic.

ἡ δόξα. Nominative absolute. This lexeme has a semantic core meaning of "opinion or thought," and so the implication is that a right and high opinion/ thought is directed towards God (Porter 2015, 226).

εἰς τοὺς αἰῶνας. Goal or state. The usual translation of "forever" may not fully capture the semantics of this prepositional word group, as "forever" may indicate temporality. But here, the prepositional word group signifies the goal of "glory" to the Lord: "into the ages."

ἀμήν. Asseverative particle (see 1:25).

Romans 12:1–2

¹I urge you, therefore, brothers [and sisters], through the compassions of God to present your bodies as a sacrifice, living, holy, [and] acceptable to God, [which is] your reasonable worship. ²And do not conform to

the scheme of this present age, but be transformed by the renewing of your mind, so that you may discern what the will of God [is], good and pleasing and complete.

Romans 12:1–15:33 is commonly seen as the paraenesis (or exhortation) section of this letter (although 15:14–33 is less exhortatory and more a reflection of Paul's own ministry). As our view is the five-part Pauline letter structure, consisting of (1) opening, (2) greeting, (3) body, (4) paraenesis, and (5) closing, this section marks the fourth major part. We identify seven sections of the paraenesis, based on ideational or topical cohesion within the sections (see the outline in the beginning of the handbook). The first section (12:1–2) within the paraenesis is a general, overarching exhortation.

12:1 Παρακαλῶ οὖν ὑμᾶς, ἀδελφοί, διὰ τῶν οἰκτιρμῶν τοῦ θεοῦ παραστῆσαι τὰ σώματα ὑμῶν θυσίαν ζῶσαν ἁγίαν εὐάρεστον τῷ θεῷ, τὴν λογικὴν λατρείαν ὑμῶν·

Παρακαλῶ. Pres act ind 1st sg παρακαλέω. The use of this lexeme is often for an exhortation formula, usually accompanied by an infinitive complement (here, παραστῆσαι; for non-formulaic uses, see 12:8).

οὖν. Postpositive inferential conjunction. This conjunction is sometimes used to mark a major transition in a text, determined by co-textual factors. The inference is especially in light of Paul's doxology (11:33–36) and can also include not only what he has stated in Romans 9–11 but also in the entire body of the letter.

ὑμᾶς. Accusative direct object of παρακαλῶ. The use of the plural personal pronoun refers generally to his audience, believing Jews and Gentiles (cf. note on ὑμᾶς in 11:25).

ἀδελφοί. Nominative of address (so-called vocative). The use of this lexeme ("brothers [and sisters]") here focuses on Paul's interpersonal relationship with his Roman audience as equal members of God's family.

διὰ τῶν οἰκτιρμῶν. Instrumental. οἰκτιρμός is mostly unique to Paul in the NT (Rom 12:1; 2 Cor 1:3; Phil 2:1; Col 3:12; cf. Heb 10:28), although the concept of compassion or mercy is prevalent throughout the NT. There is an interpretive question as to whether this prepositional word group modifies παρακαλῶ or παραστῆσαι. It may be best to see this prepositional word group as modifying παρακαλῶ for at least three reasons: (1) the finite verb is the head term of the predicate-infinitive construction, (2) the prepositional word group is more likely to modify an element that precedes it rather than an element that follows it, and (3) the instrumental function of the prepositional word group seems to relate better to "urging" rather than to "offering." In light of these factors, it seems that Paul urges them by means of God's compassions, which he has explained in the previous co-text, with the offering of bodies explained through appositional accusatives and their modifiers (see below).

τοῦ θεοῦ. Genitive of source or origin, modifying τῶν οἰκτιρμῶν.

παραστῆσαι. Aor act inf παρίστημι (indirect discourse). The infinitive functions as a complement of παρακαλῶ in an exhortation formula (see above on Παρακαλῶ; cf. 6:13–23).

τὰ σώματα. Accusative direct object of παραστῆσαι in a double accusative object-complement construction. The use of this lexeme, referring to one's complete self (cf. Gundry, 34–36), is notable, as it introduces how Paul outlines in the rest of the paraenesis the ways in which the Christian is to behave regarding their physical bodies and presence in the world.

ὑμῶν. Possessive genitive, modifying τὰ σώματα.

θυσίαν ζῶσαν ἁγίαν εὐάρεστον τῷ θεῷ. This phrase is usually translated "a living sacrifice, holy and acceptable to God" (cf. NIV, NRSV, NKJV, ESV). This translation, however, misses the tripartite attributions of the head term θυσίαν. In other words, there are three descriptors that modify "sacrifice," ζῶσαν, ἁγίαν, and εὐάρεστον, which stand in the fourth attributive position. A more accurate English translation would read something like: "a sacrifice: living, holy, and pleasing to God."

θυσίαν ζῶσαν ἁγίαν εὐάρεστον. Accusative complement to τὰ σώματα in a double accusative object-complement construction.

ζῶσαν. Pres act ptc fem acc sg ζάω (attributive). The participle modifies θυσίαν (fourth attributive position).

τῷ θεῷ. Dative complement of εὐάρεστον.

τὴν λογικὴν λατρείαν. Accusative in apposition to the entire infinitival clause παραστῆσαι τὰ σώματα ὑμῶν θυσίαν ζῶσαν ἁγίαν εὐάρεστον τῷ θεῷ (cf. Robertson, 1205; Moule, 35–36; BDF §480.6). λατρεία is understood to refer to either "worship" or "service," but there is no need to definably distinguish the two. The use of θυσίαν would conjure up the OT sacrificial system, which was both a service and act of worship for old covenant believers. The adjective λογική (first attributive position) occurs only here and in 1 Pet 2:2 in the NT. There are a variety of ways in which this lexeme is understood: "reasonable," "logical," or "spiritual" (cf. Hultgren, 440). Of these options, there does not seem to be a definable difference between "reasonable" and "logical" if we understand these words to refer to an expected and natural outcome based on previous circumstances.

ὑμῶν. Genitive of source or origin, modifying τὴν λογικὴν λατρείαν.

12:2 καὶ μὴ συσχηματίζεσθε τῷ αἰῶνι τούτῳ, ἀλλὰ μεταμορφοῦσθε τῇ ἀνακαινώσει τοῦ νοὸς εἰς τὸ δοκιμάζειν ὑμᾶς τί τὸ θέλημα τοῦ θεοῦ, τὸ ἀγαθὸν καὶ εὐάρεστον καὶ τέλειον.

καὶ. Coordinating conjunction. It connects the previous clause to the following.

μὴ . . . ἀλλὰ. A point/counterpoint set that establishes a strong contrast between the prohibition (μὴ συσχηματίζεσθε τῷ αἰῶνι τούτῳ) and the following command (μεταμορφοῦσθε τῇ ἀνακαινώσει τοῦ νοὸς). The negative particle μὴ negates συσχηματίζεσθε to make it a prohibition (cf. Huffman).

συσχηματίζεσθε. Pres mid impv 2nd pl συσχηματίζω. This lexeme (only occurring here and in 1 Pet 1:14 in the NT) refers to conforming to a pattern or "scheme," having a picture of being fashioned or shaped by something. The form can be either middle or passive voice, with little semantic difference between the two.

τῷ αἰῶνι τούτῳ. Dative of association or dative or rule. The prohibition against conforming to a pattern or scheme is associated with (or with respect to) "this present age." The demonstrative pronoun functions attributively and is used temporally (i.e., "this present").

μεταμορφοῦσθε. Pres mid impv 2nd pl μεταμορφόω. This lexeme, with the prefix μετα-, indicates a complete change of form (cf. Porter 2015, 232). As with the parallel συσχηματίζεσθε above, the form can be either middle or passive voice, with little semantic difference between the two.

τῇ ἀνακαινώσει. Dative of instrument. The instrument by which the "transforming" is to take place is "the renewing of the mind."

τοῦ νοὸς. Genitive of description or definition, modifying τῇ ἀνακαινώσει. "Renewing" is further described or circumscribed as "the mind." Some may wish to label this as an objective genitive, if τῇ ἀνακαινώσει were to become a verb "to renew."

δοκιμάζειν. Pres act inf δοκιμάζω. Used with εἰς τὸ to denote purpose. The purpose of the transformation (by renewing the mind) is to discern.

ὑμᾶς. Accusative subject of the infinitive δοκιμάζειν.

τί. Predicate nominative. τί is an interrogative pronoun.

τὸ θέλημα. Nominative subject of verbless clause.

τοῦ θεοῦ. Possessive genitive or genitive of source or origin, modifying τὸ θέλημα ("the will that belongs to or originates from God").

τὸ ἀγαθὸν καὶ εὐάρεστον καὶ τέλειον. Nominatives in apposition to τὸ θέλημα τοῦ θεοῦ linked by coordinating conjunctions. ἀγαθὸν, εὐάρεστον, and τέλειον are substantival adjectives. This construction reflects Granville

Sharp's rule that a single article governing two or more singular substantives linked by καί indicates that all are related or further describe the first (cf. Wallace 1983, 62; Porter 1994a, 110). This tripartite apposition of τὸ θέλημα τοῦ θεοῦ is parallel to the tripartite description of the body sacrifice in the previous verse (ζῶσαν ἁγίαν εὐάρεστον; with εὐάρεστον repeated here).

Romans 12:3–8

³For I say, by the grace that was given to me, to everyone who is among you, to not really think more than what is necessary to think but to think for the purpose of sober thinking, as God assigned to each a measure of faith. ⁴For just as in one body we have many members, but all the members do not have the same function, ⁵in the same way, we, who are many, are one body in Christ, and each one members of one another, ⁶and having different gifts according to the grace given to us, if prophecy, according to the proportion of faith, ⁷if service, in the service, if one who teaches, in the teaching, ⁸if one who exhorts, in the exhortation; the one who gives, in sincerity; the one who leads, in zeal; the one who shows mercy, in cheerfulness.

The second section of the paraenesis contains exhortations regarding proper behavior in the Christian community, focusing on the metaphor of the human body as the community and each person as a member of that body. The beginning of this section, λέγω γὰρ, is similar to λέγω οὖν in 11:1, 11, which mark a shift in Paul's argument.

12:3 Λέγω γὰρ διὰ τῆς χάριτος τῆς δοθείσης μοι παντὶ τῷ ὄντι ἐν ὑμῖν μὴ ὑπερφρονεῖν παρ' ὃ δεῖ φρονεῖν ἀλλὰ φρονεῖν εἰς τὸ σωφρονεῖν, ἑκάστῳ ὡς ὁ θεὸς ἐμέρισεν μέτρον πίστεως.

Λέγω. Pres act ind 1st sg λέγω.

γὰρ. Postpositive explanatory conjunction. It is used here to indicate a transition from the general introduction of the paraenesis to the next sub-section.

διὰ τῆς χάριτος. Instrumental. The instrument, or means, by which Paul "speaks" is "the grace that was given to me."

τῆς δοθείσης. Aor pass ptc fem gen sg δίδωμι (attributive). The participle modifies τῆς χάριτος (second attributive position).

μοι. Dative indirect object of δοθείσης.

παντὶ τῷ ὄντι. Dative indirect object of λέγω. The adjective παντὶ functions substantivally, as the head term of the participial phrase τῷ ὄντι. See notes on παντὶ τῷ πιστεύοντι 1:16 for a similar construction.

ὄντι. Ptc masc dat sg εἰμί (attributive).

ἐν ὑμῖν. Distributional ("among you"). The phrasing of the dative word group παντὶ τῷ ὄντι with the prepositional word group ἐν ὑμῖν might seem redundant and awkward, but it seems to emphasize both the individual and communal nature of Paul's address to them. παντὶ τῷ ὄντι (singular) refers to the individual aspect, while ὑμῖν (plural) refers to the communal aspect (the Christian community in Rome).

μὴ ... ἀλλὰ. A point/counterpoint set that establishes the strong contrast between the prohibition (μὴ ὑπερφρονεῖν) and the following command (φρονεῖν). The negative particle negates ὑπερφρονεῖν.

ὑπερφρονεῖν. Pres act inf ὑπερφρονέω (indirect discourse). The infinitive expresses the content of λέγω and functions as a prohibition with μή. The lexeme contains the prefix ὑπερ- which intensifies the root φρονέω, resulting in the meaning "really think" or "super-think." The repetition of φρον- words reflects lexical cohesion and highlights "thinking" as a major issue in this verse.

παρ᾽ ὃ δεῖ φρονεῖν. Replacement (figurative extension of locative to refer to something that is "alongside" another to replace it in some way; cf. Porter 1994a, 167; LN 89.132). Thus, the prohibition is to "not really think in place of what is necessary to think," i.e., not to think something else than what should actually be thought.

ὃ. The relative pronoun introduces a headless relative clause (ὃ δεῖ φρονεῖν) that serves as the object of the preposition. Within its clause, ὃ is the accusative direct object of φρονεῖν.

δεῖ. Unaugmented ind 3rd sg δεῖ.

φρονεῖν. Pres act inf φρονέω (complementary). The infinitive completes the catenative structure with δεῖ.

φρονεῖν. Pres act inf φρονέω (indirect discourse). The infinitive expresses the content of λέγω and functions as a command. It is parallel to μὴ ὑπερφρονεῖν.

σωφρονεῖν. Pres act inf σωφρονέω. Used with εἰς τὸ to denote purpose or result. The purpose or result (the distinction is immaterial here) of thinking, in general, is to "think soberly," "think soundly," or "think properly." The "think" word used here is a compound word consisting of σῶς ("sound," "whole," "safe") + φρονέω. σῶς is not a lexeme found in the NT but in Homer, Herodotus, and Thucydides (Liddell and Scott, 39344).

ἑκάστῳ. Dative indirect object of σωφρονεῖν. The sober thinking is directed towards "each" person.

ὡς. Comparative conjunction. The comparison is between the command to think soberly and the statement that God has assigned to each one a measure of faith.

ὁ θεὸς. Nominative subject of ἐμέρισεν.

ἐμέρισεν. Aor act ind 3rd sg μερίζω.

μέτρον. Accusative direct object of ἐμέρισεν.

πίστεως. Partitive genitive, modifying μέτρον.

12:4 καθάπερ γὰρ ἐν ἑνὶ σώματι πολλὰ μέλη ἔχομεν, τὰ δὲ μέλη πάντα οὐ τὴν αὐτὴν ἔχει πρᾶξιν,

καθάπερ. Comparative conjunction. It compares the following clause complex (in 12:4) with the subsequent one (in 12:5); the comparison is completed by οὕτως (12:5).

γὰρ. Postpositive explanatory conjunction. A further explanation is introduced of how Paul's audience ought to think of themselves from the previous verse.

ἐν ἑνὶ σώματι. Locative. The fronting of the prepositional word group before the predicate and accusative object indicates clausal prominence.

πολλὰ μέλη. Accusative direct object of ἔχομεν. The fronting of the adjective (πολλά) before the head term (μέλη) reflects prominence at the word group level. In other words, in the word group "many members," Paul emphasizes "many." In addition, the fronting of the accusative object before the predicate (ἔχομεν) indicates clausal prominence, although the prepositional word group ἐν ἑνὶ σώματι as the first element is more prominent.

ἔχομεν. Pres act ind 1st pl ἔχω.

τὰ . . . μέλη πάντα. Nominative subject of ἔχει.

δὲ. Adversative conjunction (mild). It connects the two clauses that make up the first part of the comparison.

οὐ. Negative particle normally used with indicative verbs. Here it negates ἔχει.

τὴν αὐτὴν . . . πρᾶξιν. Accusative direct object of ἔχει. The intensive pronoun functions as an identifying adjective ("the same"), and is fronted in the clause, apart from its head term πρᾶξιν, for clausal prominence (i.e., just as there are *many* members, not all have the *same* function).

ἔχει. Pres act ind 3rd sg ἔχω. The predicate is placed between the pronoun and substantive to create a discontinuous structure (Porter 2015, 235).

12:5 οὕτως οἱ πολλοὶ ἓν σῶμά ἐσμεν ἐν Χριστῷ, τὸ δὲ καθ᾽ εἷς ἀλλήλων μέλη.

οὕτως. Inferential particle. It completes the comparison that began in 12:4.

οἱ πολλοί. Nominative in apposition to the implied subject of ἐσμεν ("we, who are many").

ἓν σῶμά. Predicate nominative. Its pre-verbal position indicates clausal prominence.

ἐσμεν. Unaugmented ind 1st pl εἰμί.

ἐν Χριστῷ. Locative (sphere or realm; see notes in 3:24; 6:11). It refers to the "sphere of the power and control of Christ" (Porter 2015, 235).

τὸ . . . καθ' εἷς. The article functions as a nominalizer, making the prepositional word group into the nominative subject of a verbless clause (lit. "the-according-to-one" = "each one" or "individually").

καθ' εἷς. Standard. The use of a nominative cardinal number in the prepositional word group is non-standard, but it reflects an idiomatic expression (Sanday and Headlam, 355; cf. Mark 14:19; John 8:9). As an idiom, καθ' εἷς appears as one word in LXX 3 Macc 5:34, with a governing article there as well.

δέ. Adversative conjunction (mild). It is parallel to the use of δὲ in the previous clause complex containing the initial comparison (12:4).

ἀλλήλων. Partitive genitive, modifying μέλη. The fronting of the genitive modifier before the head term reflects prominence at the word group level. In other words, "one another" is emphasized over "member."

μέλη. Predicate nominative.

12:6 ἔχοντες δὲ χαρίσματα κατὰ τὴν χάριν τὴν δοθεῖσαν ἡμῖν διάφορα, εἴτε προφητείαν κατὰ τὴν ἀναλογίαν τῆς πίστεως,

This verse begins a list of "grace gifts" (i.e., gifts given graciously by God) through verse 8. The structure of this list of gifts, however, is varied. Of the seven gifts, the first two are expressed by anarthrous nouns, but the rest are expressed by articular participles. Additionally, the first four are introduced with εἴτε, while the rest omit any conjunction (see notes below on the relevant entries).

ἔχοντες. Pres act ptc masc nom pl ἔχω (independent or adverbial indicating means or manner). The participle can be seen as an independent predicate, or more likely a modifier of ἐσμεν in the previous verse, which describes being one body yet many members of one another.

δέ. Adversative conjunction (mild).

χαρίσματα . . . διάφορα. Accusative direct object of ἔχοντες. The structure of this clause, having the attributive adjective διάφορα placed at the end of the clause and having the prepositional word group embedded between it and the head term (χαρίσματα), draws attention to the diversity of the gifts.

κατὰ τὴν χάριν. Standard. The standard, or basis, of having gifts is (God's) grace.

τὴν δοθεῖσαν. Aor pass ptc fem acc sg δίδωμι (attributive). The participle modifies τὴν χάριν in attributive structure (second attributive position). Passive voice reflects external agency. Although not specified in the immediate co-text, the implication is that God is the one who gives these gifts.

ἡμῖν. Dative indirect object of δοθεῖσαν.

εἴτε. Connective conjunction, used to reflect conditionality (from εἰ) in this list of gifts.

προφητείαν. Accusative in apposition to χαρίσματα . . . διάφορα.

κατὰ τὴν ἀναλογίαν. Standard. The standard, or basis, of prophetic action is "proportion of faith." Only occurrence of ἀναλογία in the NT is here (cf. μέτρον in 12:3). This lexeme refers to an amount in relation to the whole or sum, so "proportion" or "measure" of faith that a person has. Considering this, it appears that there were various abilities or qualities of prophecy, depending on the proportion or measure of faith one was given.

τῆς πίστεως. Partitive genitive, modifying τὴν ἀναλογίαν.

12:7 εἴτε διακονίαν ἐν τῇ διακονίᾳ, εἴτε ὁ διδάσκων ἐν τῇ διδασκαλίᾳ,

εἴτε. Connective conjunction, used to reflect conditionality (from εἰ) in this list of gifts.

διακονίαν. Accusative in apposition to προφητείαν (and the prior χαρίσματα . . . διάφορα; cf. 12:6 on προφητείαν). While this lexeme came to have a more circumscribed meaning in the organization of the early church, referring to the office of deacon, here it simply refers to acts of service, providing for physical needs for one another.

ἐν τῇ διακονίᾳ. Locative (sphere or realm). While this clause may seem unnecessarily redundant, it is not uncommon for Paul to repeat lexemes in the same co-text for emphasis, and the point that Paul makes here is that if service is one gift that has been given by God (of course, it is), then it must be demonstrated in the sphere or realm of service, through actual acts of service and not just as an abstract notion.

εἴτε. Connective conjunction, used to reflect conditionality (from εἰ) in this list of gifts.

ὁ διδάσκων. Pres act ptc masc nom sg διδάσκω (substantival). The switch from the appositional accusatives to a nominative absolute here, and following, may signal a switch from the gift itself to the one who possesses and uses the gift.

ἐν τῇ διδασκαλίᾳ. Locative (sphere or realm). As with the above use of the prepositional word group repeating the same lexeme, Paul simply states that one who teaches must actually realize the gift through acts of teaching.

12:8 εἴτε ὁ παρακαλῶν ἐν τῇ παρακλήσει· ὁ μεταδιδοὺς ἐν ἁπλότητι, ὁ προϊστάμενος ἐν σπουδῇ, ὁ ἐλεῶν ἐν ἱλαρότητι.

εἴτε. Connective conjunction, used to reflect conditionality (from εἰ) in this list of gifts.

ὁ παρακαλῶν. Pres act ptc masc nom sg παρακαλέω (substantival). Nominative absolute.

ἐν τῇ παρακλήσει. Locative (figurative, sphere or realm). As with the above uses of the prepositional word group repeating the same lexeme, Paul simply states that one who encourages must actually realize the gift through acts of encouragement.

ὁ μεταδιδοὺς. Pres act ptc masc nom sg μεταδίδωμι (substantival). Nominative absolute. This begins the listing of gifts without the conjunctive εἴτε, probably due to stylistic variation. The lexeme with the prefix μετα- adds the meaning "with" to the root, i.e., to "give with" or to "share."

ἐν ἁπλότητι. Instrumental (or manner). Here, the prepositional word group does not contain a repetition of the head term but uses a different lexeme to expand on the manner in which the gift is to be used. The one who gives does so by sincerity or singlemindedness.

ὁ προϊστάμενος. Pres mid ptc masc nom sg προΐστημι (substantival). Nominative absolute. The word picture reflected in the lexeme, which contains the prefix προ-, is one who takes up a position at the forefront, or to "stand before" others to lead them.

ἐν σπουδῇ. Instrumental (or manner). The one who leads must do so by zeal or eagerness.

ὁ ἐλεῶν. Pres act ptc masc nom sg ἐλεάω (substantival). Nominative absolute.

ἐν ἱλαρότητι. Instrumental (or manner). The one who shows mercy must do so by cheerfulness or gladness. While there may be an etymological connection between ἱλαρότης and the English word "hilarious," one should be careful not to equate or relate the two meanings, since the meaning of the English word is much more circumscribed than that of the Greek.

Romans 12:9–21

[9]Love [is] unhypocritical. Abhor evil, cling onto good, [10]through brotherly love, [be] devoted to one another; through honor, be at the forefront of

one another; ¹¹do not be lacking in diligence, be zealous in spirit, be a slave to the Lord, ¹²rejoice in hope, endure in trial, continue in prayer, ¹³share in the needs of the saints, pursue hospitality. ¹⁴Bless those who pursue you, bless and do not curse. ¹⁵Rejoice with rejoicers, weep with weepers. ¹⁶Think the same towards each other, do not think highly [of yourself], but associate with the humble. Do not become wise in the presence of each other. ¹⁷Pay back evil for evil to no one; presume good in the presence of all people; ¹⁸if possible, what [can be done] from you, foster peace with all people. ¹⁹Exact revenge not for yourselves, beloved, but give place to anger, for it is written, "Retribution [is] mine, I will repay," says the Lord. ²⁰But "if your enemy is hungry, feed him; if he is thirsty, give him a drink." For by doing this, you will heap coals of fire upon his head. ²¹Do not be conquered by the bad but conquer the bad with the good.

Whereas the previous paraenetic section focuses on grace gifts, this third section provides exhortations of a broader scope related to standards for Christian behavior. The beginning of this section contains many short and pithy exhortations, verbless clauses and non-finite verbal clauses, that function as commanding or directive, based on their co-textual usages and location in the paraenetic section of the letter.

12:9 Ἡ ἀγάπη ἀνυπόκριτος. ἀποστυγοῦντες τὸ πονηρόν, κολλώμενοι τῷ ἀγαθῷ,

Ἡ ἀγάπη. Nominative absolute or nominative subject of verbless clause.

ἀνυπόκριτος. Predicate adjective. While some translations render this lexeme as "genuine" or "sincere," the precise meaning is reflected in the alpha-privative with the root "hypocrite." The metaphor of an ὑπόκριτος is that of an ancient actor, who wore masks to represent the character they were playing. The idea behind this lexeme is one who is without hypocrisy, or multi-faced-ness.

ἀποστυγοῦντες. Pres act ptc masc nom pl ἀποστυγέω (imperatival). The participle functions as commanding in this co-text. A NT *hapax legomenon*. This and the next participle (κολλώμενοι) function as secondary (subordinate) to the primary clause (Ἡ ἀγάπη ἀνυπόκριτος) and provides supportive material to it. In other words, after the statement that "love is unhypocritical," two supportive participial commands are provided: "abhor evil" and "be joined to good."

τὸ πονηρόν. Accusative direct object of ἀποστυγοῦντες.

κολλώμενοι. Pres mid ptc masc nom pl κολλάω (imperatival). Like ἀποστυγοῦντες, this participle functions as commanding and provides supportive material to the main clause (see above on ἀποστυγοῦντες). Although the form can be either middle or passive, it seems that as a commanding participle the middle voice is intended here. The middle voice reflects indirect, internal causality, as reflected in the lexical meaning of κολλάω, "to join," "to hold on," or "to cling on." Alternatively, the passive voice would result in a translation such as "let yourself be joined to good."

τῷ ἀγαθῷ. Dative direct object of κολλάω. This verb often takes the dative as its object (cf. Matt 19:5; Luke 15:15; Acts 5:13; 8:29; 9:26; 17:34; 1 Cor 6:16, 17). The use of the dative instead of the accusative may be due to the focus on directionality.

12:10 τῇ φιλαδελφίᾳ εἰς ἀλλήλους φιλόστοργοι, τῇ τιμῇ ἀλλήλους προηγούμενοι,

τῇ φιλαδελφίᾳ. Dative of manner or means. The manner or means by which they are to be devoted is "brotherly love." The dative is fronted in the clause for prominence (emphasis).

εἰς ἀλλήλους. Directional (movement toward).

φιλόστοργοι. Nominative absolute. It functions as commanding, as parallel to the participles in this co-text. A substantival adjective is probably used instead of a commanding participle to focus on the quality of devotion, even if it has a commanding function in this co-text. This lexeme is a compound of φίλος and στοργή, but combined it means "devoted" or "loving." A NT *hapax legomenon* (cf. 4 Macc 15:13).

τῇ τιμῇ. Dative of manner or means. The manner or means by which they were to lead the way is "honor." The fronting of the dative in the clause reflects prominence (emphasis).

ἀλλήλους. Accusative direct object of προηγούμενοι.

προηγούμενοι. Pres mid ptc masc nom pl προηγέομαι (imperatival). The participle functions as a command in this co-text. This lexeme contains the root ἡγέομαι ("lead" or "govern") and the prefix προ- ("before"), which means to "lead before" or "be at the forefront." A NT *hapax legomenon*.

12:11 τῇ σπουδῇ μὴ ὀκνηροί, τῷ πνεύματι ζέοντες, τῷ κυρίῳ δουλεύοντες,

τῇ σπουδῇ. Dative of respect. With respect to "diligence" or "effort," they were not to be characterized by lacking. The fronting of the dative, a pattern in this co-text, indicates clausal prominence.

μὴ. While this negation is normally used of verbs, and usually non-indicative verbs, here it is used to negate a predicate adjective. The use of μὴ instead of οὐ reflects a negation of the notional or ideal instead of the actual or concrete.

ὀκνηροί. Nominative absolute. As with φιλόστοργοι (12:10), the use of a substantival adjective instead of a commanding participle here probably focuses on the quality of lacking, even if co-textually it has a commanding function.

τῷ πνεύματι. Dative of sphere. They were to be zealous in the sphere of the Spirit. The fronting of the dative indicates clausal prominence.

ζέοντες. Pres act ptc masc nom pl ζέω (imperatival). The participle functions as a command in this co-text.

τῷ κυρίῳ. Dative direct object of δουλεύοντες. The dative case is probably used to focus on the directionality of the "serving" or "being a slave" to the Lord. The fronting of the dative, a consistent pattern in this co-text, indicates clausal prominence.

δουλεύοντες. Pres act ptc masc nom pl δουλεύω (imperatival). The participle functions as a command in this co-text. The word is some-times translated as "serving," but it does not refer to simply serving; the lexeme is used to describe serving as a slave or being a slave.

12:12 τῇ ἐλπίδι χαίροντες, τῇ θλίψει ὑπομένοντες, τῇ προσευχῇ προσκαρτεροῦντες,

τῇ ἐλπίδι. Dative of sphere. The rejoicing was to be done in the sphere of "hope." Hope is not simply a wish, but an expectation of the future sal-vation that believers in Christ have. The fronting of the dative indicates clausal prominence.

χαίροντες. Pres act ptc masc nom pl χαίρω (imperatival). The parti-ciple functions as commanding in this co-text.

τῇ θλίψει. Dative of sphere. The sphere in which they were to endure is "tribulation." The fronting of the dative indicates clausal prominence.

ὑπομένοντες. Pres act ptc masc nom pl ὑπομένω (imperatival). The participle functions as commanding in this co-text. The lexeme does not mean to literally "remain under," as when simply combining the mean-ings of the root (μένω) and prefix (ὑπο-), but it does create a picture of a person remaining in place under pressure or opposition, i.e., "persevere" or "endure."

τῇ προσευχῇ. Dative of sphere. The sphere in which they were to "continue" is "prayer." The fronting of the dative indicates clausal prominence.

προσκαρτεροῦντες. Pres act ptc masc nom pl προσκαρτερέω (imperatival). The participle functions as commanding in this co-text.

12:13 ταῖς χρείαις τῶν ἁγίων κοινωνοῦντες, τὴν φιλοξενίαν διώκοντες.

ταῖς χρείαις. Dative of sphere. The sharing is to be in the sphere of "the needs of the saints."

τῶν ἁγίων. Genitive of source or origin, modifying ταῖς χρείαις. The "needs" come from "the saints."

κοινωνοῦντες. Pres act ptc masc nom pl κοινωνέω (imperatival). The participle functions as commanding in this co-text. This lexeme, widely translated as "fellowship," simply refers to the sharing or joining together with others.

τὴν φιλοξενίαν. Accusative direct object of διώκοντες. The only other occurrence of this lexeme in the NT is Heb 13:2.

διώκοντες. Pres act ptc masc nom pl διώκω (imperatival). The participle functions as commanding in this co-text.

12:14 εὐλογεῖτε τοὺς διώκοντας [ὑμᾶς], εὐλογεῖτε καὶ μὴ καταρᾶσθε.

εὐλογεῖτε. Pres act impv 2nd pl εὐλογέω. The transition from the string of participles in the previous co-text to the imperative mood form here probably signals a more explicit command and a transition from commands on proper conduct internally, within the body of believers, to commands on proper conduct externally, towards those outside of the body (cf. Porter 2015, 239). After the use of the imperative mood form here, infinitives and participles are used to support the general, umbrella commands to bless and not curse those who persecute them.

τοὺς διώκοντας. Pres act ptc masc acc pl διώκω (substantival). Accusative direct object of εὐλογεῖτε. There is lexical cohesion between this verse and the previous with the repetition of διώκω. In the previous verse, it is used in a positive sense, pursuing hospitality; here it is used in a negative sense, pursuing to harm in some way.

[ὑμᾶς]. Accusative direct object of διώκοντας. The early manuscript tradition is divided on this textual variant (with: ℵ A D; without: 𝔓⁴⁶ B). The decision is given a C rating by Metzger (466), due to its split manuscript evidence and the difficulty in deciding whether it was deleted to extend the range of the exhortation or added it in light of parallel sayings in Matt 5:44 and Luke 6:28. Either way, the meaning of the command is not affected overall by this textual variant.

εὐλογεῖτε. Pres act impv 2nd pl εὐλογέω. The repetition of the imperative "bless" creates lexical cohesion for emphasis.

καὶ. Coordinating conjunction. It connects the imperative with the prohibition.

μή. Negative particle normally used with non-indicative verbs. Here it negates καταρᾶσθε.

καταρᾶσθε. Pres mid impv 2nd pl καταράομαι. With μή, it functions as a prohibition and iterates the converse of the imperative εὐλογεῖτε with καί. This is the only occurrence of this verb in Paul (cf. Matt 25:41; Mark 11:21; Luke 6:28; Jas 3:9).

12:15 χαίρειν μετὰ χαιρόντων, κλαίειν μετὰ κλαιόντων.

χαίρειν. Pres act inf χαίρω (imperatival). The infinitive functions as commanding in this co-text. The infinitive is used here, instead of the imperative or participle, as a syntactically subordinate command under the general commands in 12:14 to bless and not curse (see note on εὐλογεῖτε in 12:14).

μετὰ χαιρόντων. Accompaniment. Sometimes μετά depicts accompaniment with dissimilarly viewed items (in contrast with σύν, which may depict similar items). In that case, in the co-text of commands to "outsiders" in this sub-section, the dissimilar use of μετά is appropriate.

χαιρόντων. Pres act ptc masc gen pl χαίρω (substantival).

κλαίειν. Pres act inf κλαίω (imperatival). The infinitive functions as a command, parallel to χαίρειν above.

μετὰ κλαιόντων. Accompaniment (see μετὰ χαιρόντων above).

κλαιόντων. Pres act ptc masc gen pl κλαίω (substantival).

12:16 τὸ αὐτὸ εἰς ἀλλήλους φρονοῦντες, μὴ τὰ ὑψηλὰ φρονοῦντες ἀλλὰ τοῖς ταπεινοῖς συναπαγόμενοι. μὴ γίνεσθε φρόνιμοι παρ' ἑαυτοῖς.

τὸ αὐτὸ. Accusative direct object of φρονοῦντες. The intensive pronoun functions as an identifying adjective ("the same").

εἰς ἀλλήλους. Directional (movement toward).

φρονοῦντες. Pres act ptc masc nom pl φρονέω (imperatival). The participle functions as commanding in this co-text, as syntactically subordinate to the general, umbrella commands to bless and not curse (see note on εὐλογεῖτε in 12:14).

μὴ ... ἀλλὰ. A point/counterpoint set that establishes the strong contrast between the prohibition and the subsequent command, continuing the function of the participle as command or prohibition. The negative particle, placed first in the clause, negates the participial clause with φρονοῦντες ("do not think highly (of yourselves)") and is contrastive by means of ἀλλὰ with the following participial clause.

τὰ ὑψηλὰ. Accusative direct object of φρονοῦντες.

φρονοῦντες. Pres act ptc masc nom pl φρονέω (imperatival). The participle functions as commanding in this co-text, as syntactically subordinate to the general, umbrella commands to bless and not curse (see note on εὐλογεῖτε in 12:14).

τοῖς ταπεινοῖς. Dative of association. They were to associate with the humble.

συναπαγόμενοι. Pres mid ptc masc nom pl συναπάγω (imperatival). The participle functions as commanding in this co-text, as syntactically subordinate to the general, umbrella commands to bless and not curse (see note on εὐλογεῖτε in 12:14). There is a question on whether this is a middle or passive voice-form, as the forms are identical in the present tense-form. As a so-called deponent verb, there is no active voice-form. The semantic difference between the middle and passive voices is minimal, however (whether "associate with" or "be associated with").

μὴ. Negative particle normally used with non-indicative verbs. Here it negates γίνεσθε.

γίνεσθε. Pres mid impv 2nd pl γίνομαι. The switch to another imperative (or prohibition with μή) distinguishes this command from the previous string of infinitival and participial commands, under the general command to bless and not curse (12:14). This begins a new set of commands, followed by participles, in 12:17–20, to elaborate on how they are to not become wise in their own eyes.

φρόνιμοι. Predicate adjective. This lexeme reflects "wisdom" in the sense of wise thinking. It has the same root as φρονέω, creating lexical cohesion and focusing on the right and wrong ways of thinking.

παρ' ἑαυτοῖς. Positional (alongside); lit. "alongside yourselves" = "in the presence of each other."

12:17 μηδενὶ κακὸν ἀντὶ κακοῦ ἀποδιδόντες, προνοούμενοι καλὰ ἐνώπιον πάντων ἀνθρώπων·

μηδενὶ. Dative indirect object of ἀποδιδόντες.

κακὸν. Accusative direct object of ἀποδιδόντες.

ἀντὶ κακοῦ. Substitutionary ("[one type of] evil against [another type of] evil").

ἀποδιδόντες. Pres act ptc masc nom pl ἀποδίδωμι (imperatival). A return to the use of a participle to function as commanding here reflects syntactical subordination to the imperative, or prohibition, at the end of the previous verse (μὴ γίνεσθε). In other words, one way to not be wise in one's own estimation is identified with participial commands.

προνοούμενοι. Pres mid ptc masc nom pl προνοέω (imperatival). Parallel to ἀποδιδόντες, this participle functions as commanding.

καλά. Accusative direct object of προνοούμενοι.

ἐνώπιον πάντων ἀνθρώπων. Positional ("before/in the presence of . . . all people"). ἐνώπιον is an improper preposition (cf. Porter 1994a, 179).

12:18 εἰ δυνατὸν τὸ ἐξ ὑμῶν, μετὰ πάντων ἀνθρώπων εἰρηνεύοντες·

εἰ. Introduces the protasis of a first-class conditional.

δυνατὸν. Nominative subject of verbless clause.

τὸ ἐξ ὑμῶν. The article functions as a nominalizer, changing the prepositional word group ἐξ ὑμῶν into an accusative of manner. The manner in which the condition is presented as "possible" is "that which is out of you" or "what [can be done] from you."

ἐξ ὑμῶν. Instrumental. "You" is the instrument by which it may be possible to do the following (contained in the apodosis).

μετὰ πάντων ἀνθρώπων. Accompaniment (for an explanation on its function, see 12:15 on μετὰ χαιρόντων). The apodosis begins here. The fronting of the prepositional word group indicates clausal prominence.

εἰρηνεύοντες. Pres act ptc masc nom pl εἰρηνεύω (imperatival). The participle functions as commanding in this co-text.

12:19 μὴ ἑαυτοὺς ἐκδικοῦντες, ἀγαπητοί, ἀλλὰ δότε τόπον τῇ ὀργῇ, γέγραπται γάρ· ἐμοὶ ἐκδίκησις, ἐγὼ ἀνταποδώσω, λέγει κύριος.

μὴ . . . ἀλλὰ. A point/counterpoint set that establishes a contrast between the command to exact revenge or justice not for themselves and the command to give room for (God's) wrath. As with the negation in 12:16 (μὴ τὰ ὑψηλὰ), the placement of the negative particle μή before the reflexive pronoun ἑαυτοὺς negates it directly (i.e., "avenge not yourselves").

ἑαυτοὺς. Accusative direct object of ἐκδικοῦντες.

ἐκδικοῦντες. Pres act ptc masc nom pl ἐκδικέω (imperatival). The participle functions as commanding, among the string of participial commands in this co-text. The δικ- root with the ἐκ- prefix creates a word picture of seeking justice, rightness, or appropriateness out of something. Here, the justice they are seeking is presumably for themselves.

ἀγαπητοί. Nominative of address (so-called vocative). The use of this lexeme to refer to his audience as "loved ones" or "beloved" draws attention to the affective involvement between Paul and the Romans.

δότε. Aor act impv 2nd pl δίδωμι. The imperative is used here, instead of the commonly used participle in this co-text, to reflect a more direct command and to highlight it above the others. While previous imperatives in this section are seen as general umbrella commands, it is contrasting parallel to the previous command to seek justice not for themselves and is thus used as a highlighting or emphatic device.

τόπον. Accusative direct object of δότε.

τῇ ὀργῇ. Dative indirect object of δότε. While the source of wrath is not stated directly here (i.e., God), the focus is more on the action of leaving room for wrath to take place naturally, rather than for one to take action for themselves.

γέγραπται. Prf pass ind 3rd sg γράφω. This is the usual formula for Paul to introduce a scriptural reference (here, LXX Lev 19:18).

γάρ. Postpositive explanatory conjunction. An explanation of why one should leave room for wrath instead of seeking it for themselves is provided.

ἐμοί. Dative of possession. The dative is used than the more common genitive for possession to focus on the directionality of ἐκδίκησις.

ἐκδίκησις. Nominative absolute.

ἐγώ. Nominative subject of ἀνταποδώσω. The use of the personal pronoun here emphasizes the subject of the clause.

ἀνταποδώσω. Fut act ind 1st sg ἀνταποδίδωμι. The future form grammaticalizes the semantic feature of expectation. The double pre-fixed form (ἀντι- + ἀπο-) here contributes to the root word δίδωμι and means "to repay in kind."

λέγει. Pres act ind 3rd sg λέγω.

κύριος. Nominative subject of λέγει.

12:20 ἀλλ' ἐὰν πεινᾷ ὁ ἐχθρός σου, ψώμιζε αὐτόν· ἐὰν διψᾷ, πότιζε αὐτόν· τοῦτο γὰρ ποιῶν ἄνθρακας πυρὸς σωρεύσεις ἐπὶ τὴν κεφαλὴν αὐτοῦ.

ἀλλ'. Adversative conjunction (strong). It contrasts the previous statement of exacting vengeance for oneself and allowing room for God to repay with the following. The rest of this verse is a quotation of LXX Prov 25:21–22.

ἐάν. Introduces the protasis of a third-class conditional.

πεινᾷ. Pres act subj 3rd sg πεινάω. Subjunctive with ἐάν.

ὁ ἐχθρός. Nominative subject of πεινᾷ.

σου. Possessive genitive, modifying ὁ ἐχθρός.

ψώμιζε. Pres act impv 2nd sg ψωμίζω. The apodosis begins here.

αὐτόν. Accusative direct object of ψώμιζε. The personal pronoun refers anaphorically to ὁ ἐχθρός σου.

ἐάν. Introduces the protasis of another third-class conditional.

διψᾷ. Pres act subj 3rd sg διψάω. Subjunctive with ἐάν.

πότιζε. Pres act impv 2nd sg ποτίζω. The apodosis begins here.

αὐτόν. Accusative direct object of πότιζε. The personal pronoun refers anaphorically to ὁ ἐχθρός σου.

τοῦτο. Accusative direct object of ποιῶν. The demonstrative pronoun refers to both conditions stated previously. The fronting of the object before its predicate reflects clausal prominence.

γὰρ. Postpositive explanatory conjunction. It introduces an explanation for the two conditional statements.

ποιῶν. Pres act ptc masc nom sg ποιέω (means). The participle functions as circumstantial in the co-text and modifies σωρεύσεις.

ἄνθρακας. Accusative direct object of σωρεύσεις. A NT *hapax legomenon.*

πυρὸς. Genitive of description, modifying ἄνθρακας. "Coals" is further described as "of fire."

σωρεύσεις. Fut act ind 2nd sg σωρεύω. Future form grammaticalizes the semantic feature of expectation.

ἐπὶ κεφαλὴν. Directional (movement upon).

αὐτοῦ. Possessive genitive, modifying κεφαλὴν.

12:21 μὴ νικῶ ὑπὸ τοῦ κακοῦ ἀλλὰ νίκα ἐν τῷ ἀγαθῷ τὸ κακόν.

μὴ . . . ἀλλὰ. A point/counterpoint set that establishes a contrast between being conquered by the bad and conquering the bad with the good. The negative particle negates νικῶ.

νικῶ. Pres pass impv 2nd sg νικάω. With μή, it functions as a prohibition. Paul returns to the imperative mood form in this verse to conclude this section with a final general, summative command (or prohibition). The only other occurrence of this lexeme in Romans is in 3:4.

ὑπὸ τοῦ κακοῦ. Instrumental/agency. The agent of "conquer" is "the bad." The lexeme κακός, usually translated "evil" in this verse (cf. NIV, NASB, NKJV, NRSV), is a semantically broad, general word used to refer to something bad or negative.

νίκα. Pres act impv 2nd sg νικάω.

ἐν τῷ ἀγαθῷ. Instrumental. The instrument, or manner, by which one is to conquer bad is "good." The fronting of the prepositional word group before the object reflects clausal prominence.

τὸ κακόν. Accusative direct object of νίκα.

Romans 13:1–7

¹Every person must be subjected to the superior authorities. For [there] is no authority except through God, and those who are [authority] have

been appointed by God. ²As a result, he who opposes the authority
stands against the order of God, and those who have stood against will
receive judgment against themselves. ³For the rulers are not a fear for
good work but for bad. Do you want not to fear the authority? Do good,
and you will receive praise from it. ⁴For it is God's servant to you for
good. But if you might do something bad, be afraid. For not in vain does
it bear the sword; for God's servant is a punisher for wrath towards
the one who practices bad. ⁵Therefore, it is a necessity to be obedient,
not only because of wrath but also because of conscience. ⁶For this is
why you also fulfill your tributes; for they are public servants of God
devoted for this very purpose. ⁷Give to all what is owed; to whom [is
owed] tribute, tribute; to whom [is owed] tax, tax; to whom [is owed]
fear, fear; to whom [is owed] honor, honor.

This fourth section of the paraenesis focuses on one exhortative topic
of submitting to authorities, in comparison with the previous section
composed of shorter commands regarding general Christian behavior.

**13:1 Πᾶσα ψυχὴ ἐξουσίαις ὑπερεχούσαις ὑποτασσέσθω. οὐ γὰρ ἔστιν
ἐξουσία εἰ μὴ ὑπὸ θεοῦ, αἱ δὲ οὖσαι ὑπὸ θεοῦ τεταγμέναι εἰσίν.**

Πᾶσα ψυχὴ. Nominative subject of ὑποτασσέσθω. ψυχὴ is usually
translated as "soul," but here is used refer to "every individual as animated
by life" (Porter 2015, 244).
ἐξουσίαις. Dative indirect object of ὑποτασσέσθω.
ὑπερεχούσαις. Pres act ptc fem dat pl ὑπερέχω (attributive). The participle modifies ἐξουσίαις (fourth attributive position). This word is usually translated as "governing" in a political sense (cf. NIV, NASB, NKJV,
NRSV, ESV). But the lexeme, which occurs four times in Paul (here; Phil
2:3; 3:8; 4:7; cf. 1 Pet 2:13), is used by Paul to refer to qualitative superiority rather than positional authority. In 1 Pet 2:13, the interpretation of
ὑπερέχοντι as qualitatively superior fits the context as well. Thus, Paul is
not commanding every person to submit or be obedient to "governing
authorities" but to those authorities who are "superior." Contextually, it
refers to those who are upright (cf. Porter 2015, 244).
ὑποτασσέσθω. Pres pass impv 3rd sg ὑποτάσσω. The middle and
passive voice-forms are identical, but the passive is preferred (i.e., "allow
themselves to be subjected").
οὐ γὰρ ἔστιν ἐξουσία εἰ μὴ ὑπὸ θεοῦ. This clause-complex is a
second-class conditional (the so-called contrary-to-fact conditional; it
reflects the writer's belief that this conditional does not reflect reality).

The apodosis occurs before the protasis, reflecting prominence at the clause-complex level and emphasizing the apodosis over the protasis.

οὐ. Negative particle normally used with indicative verbs. Here it negates ἔστιν. The apodosis begins here.

γὰρ. Postpositive explanatory conjunction. It further explains the command to be obedient or submit.

ἔστιν. Unaugmented ind 3rd sg εἰμί.

ἐξουσία. Predicate nominative of ἔστιν.

εἰ μὴ. A combination of the conditional conjunction and the negative particle (usually translated as "except" or "if not") that introduces the protasis of a second-class conditional (see note on εἰ μή in 7:7).

ὑπὸ θεοῦ. Instrumental. The instrument, or means, of the protasis (being an authority) is God.

αἱ . . . οὖσαι. Ptc fem nom pl εἰμί (substantival). Nominative subject of τεταγμέναι εἰσίν. The use of εἰμί as a substantive in this co-text (the previous clause being οὐ γὰρ ἔστιν ἐξουσία) along with a following periphrastic structure (τεταγμέναι εἰσίν) highlights the *existence* of these (superior) authorities. The feminine gender is used to relate it to ἐξουσία.

δὲ. Adversative conjunction (mild).

ὑπὸ θεοῦ. Instrumental. "God" is the agent of the passive voice predicate (τεταγμέναι εἰσίν). The fronting of the prepositional word group before the predicate indicates clausal prominence.

τεταγμέναι. Prf pass ptc fem nom pl τάσσω (perfect periphrastic). The participle is a complement of εἰσίν in a periphrastic structure, but it occurs before the head term, making it prominent. The perfect tense form (stative aspect) depicts the process of "appointing" as a state or condition and adds to the prominence of this lexeme in this co-text.

εἰσίν. Unaugmented ind 3rd pl εἰμί. It is the head term of the periphrastic structure.

13:2 ὥστε ὁ ἀντιτασσόμενος τῇ ἐξουσίᾳ τῇ τοῦ θεοῦ διαταγῇ ἀνθέστηκεν, οἱ δὲ ἀνθεστηκότες ἑαυτοῖς κρίμα λήμψονται.

ὥστε. Introduces a result clause that explains the consequences of Paul's claims in the previous verse.

ὁ ἀντιτασσόμενος. Pres mid ptc masc nom sg ἀντιτάσσω (substantival). Nominative subject of ἀνθέστηκεν. A form of this lexeme, without the prefix ἀντι-, is used in the previous verse.

τῇ ἐξουσίᾳ. Dative direct object of ἀντιτασσόμενος. This verb takes its object in the dative (cf. BDAG, 90).

τῇ ... διαταγῇ. Dative direct object of ἀνθέστηκεν. This verb also takes its object in the dative (cf. BDAG, 80.1.b). The fronting of the noun indicates clausal prominence, and the micro-chiasm in this clause (A predicate—B dative object—B′ dative object—A′ predicate) highlights the dative objects (B and B′).

τοῦ θεοῦ. Genitive of source or origin, modifying τῇ ... διαταγῇ.

ἀνθέστηκεν. Prf act ind 3rd sg ἀνθίστημι. The use of another pre-fixed word (with ἀντι-) creates semantic cohesion and highlights the meaning of the prefix ("against") in this co-text.

οἱ ... ἀνθεστηκότες. Prf act ptc masc nom pl ἀνθίστημι (substantival). Nominative subject of λήμψονται. It turns the previous predicate of "standing against" into a substantive "ones who stand against," creating lexical continuity and cohesion. The perfect tense form (stative aspect) reflects the process as a state or condition, i.e., "ones who are in a state of standing against."

δὲ. Adversative conjunction (mild).

ἑαυτοῖς. Dative indirect object of λήμψονται or dative of disadvantage. The reflexive pronoun refers anaphorically to οἱ ... ἀνθεστηκότες.

κρίμα. Accusative direct object of λήμψονται. The accusative object occurring before the predicate indicates clausal prominence.

λήμψονται. Fut mid ind 3rd pl λαμβάνω. Future form reflects semantics of expectation.

13:3 οἱ γὰρ ἄρχοντες οὐκ εἰσὶν φόβος τῷ ἀγαθῷ ἔργῳ ἀλλὰ τῷ κακῷ. θέλεις δὲ μὴ φοβεῖσθαι τὴν ἐξουσίαν· τὸ ἀγαθὸν ποίει, καὶ ἕξεις ἔπαινον ἐξ αὐτῆς·

οἱ ... ἄρχοντες. Nominative subject of εἰσὶν. It serves as a lexical substitute for ἐξουσία in 13:1–2. The switch of lexemes here may reflect a switch from "authority" as an abstract notion to a more concrete reference to the people in positions of authority, i.e., "rulers."

γὰρ. Postpositive explanatory conjunction. It introduces a further explanation about submitting to and resisting authorities.

οὐκ ... ἀλλά. A point/counterpoint set that establishes a contrast between good conduct and bad conduct. The negative particle negates εἰσὶν.

εἰσὶν. Unaugmented ind 3rd pl εἰμί.

φόβος. Predicate nominative.

τῷ ἀγαθῷ ἔργῳ. Dative of respect. The fear is with respect to "good work."

τῷ κακῷ. Dative of respect. It is parallel to τῷ ἀγαθῷ ἔργῳ, with the dative substantive elided.

θέλεις. Pres act ind 2nd sg θέλω. The use of the singular here prob-ably indicates that Paul is not addressing everyone in the Roman audi-ence here but a hypothetical person to whom this statement may apply (cf. the use of the second-person singular throughout Romans 2 to address a hypothetical person).

δὲ. Adversative conjunction (mild).

μὴ. Negative particle normally used with non-indicative verbs. Here it negates φοβεῖσθαι.

φοβεῖσθαι. Pres mid inf φοβέομαι (complementary). The infinitive is a complement of θέλεις in a catenative construction.

τὴν ἐξουσίαν. Accusative direct object of φοβεῖσθαι. Return to the use of ἐξουσία reflects a return to an abstraction of authority instead of the more concrete reference to people in authority.

τὸ ἀγαθὸν. Accusative direct object of ποίει. The fronting of the accusative object before the predicate reflects clausal prominence.

ποίει. Pres act impv 2nd sg ποιέω. The use of the second-person sin-gular is consistent with addressing a hypothetical addressee (see com-ment on θέλεις above).

καὶ. Coordinating conjunction. Connects the two clauses.

ἕξεις. Fut act ind 2nd sg ἔχω. Future form grammaticalizes the semantics of expectation.

ἔπαινον. Accusative direct object of ἕξεις. The lexeme in this co-text refers to approval or commendation.

ἐξ αὐτῆς. Instrumental. The personal pronoun refers anaphorically to ἐξουσίαν in the previous clause.

13:4 θεοῦ γὰρ διάκονός ἐστιν σοὶ εἰς τὸ ἀγαθόν. ἐὰν δὲ τὸ κακὸν ποιῇς, φοβοῦ· οὐ γὰρ εἰκῇ τὴν μάχαιραν φορεῖ· θεοῦ γὰρ διάκονός ἐστιν ἔκδικος εἰς ὀργὴν τῷ τὸ κακὸν πράσσοντι.

θεοῦ. Possessive genitive, modifying διάκονός. The occurrence of the genitive before the head term reflects prominence within the word group (θεοῦ διάκονός); "God" is emphasized over "servant."

γὰρ. Postpositive explanatory conjunction. A further explanation of Paul's command to submit to superior authorities is given.

διάκονός. Predicate nominative. The additional accent on the ultima is a result of the following word being enclitic (see note on πνεύματί in 1:9).

ἐστιν. Unaugmented ind 3rd sg εἰμί. The third singular person refers to αὐτῆς in the previous verse.

σοὶ. Dative of possession. The second-person singular continues the discourse with the hypothetical addressee.

εἰς τὸ ἀγαθόν. Purpose. The purpose of the person in authority being God's servant is doing good. This is the third time this lexeme (ἀγαθός) is used in 13:3–4. The first (13:3) describes good conduct, the second (13:3) commands doing good, and third (here) defines the purpose of ensuring good is being done.

ἐὰν. Introduces the protasis of a third-class conditional.

δὲ. Adversative conjunction (mild).

τὸ κακὸν. Accusative direct object of ποιῇς. The adjective is used as a substantive. The fronting of the accusative before the main predicate indicates clausal prominence, emphasis on the object.

ποιῇς. Pres act subj 2nd sg ποιέω. Subjunctive with ἐάν.

φοβοῦ. Pres mid impv 2nd sg φοβέω. This lexeme makes up the entire apodosis of the third-class conditional clause. Considering the protasis to be true, that they are doing bad, they are commanded to fear as a result.

οὐ. Negative particle that negates εἰκῇ.

γὰρ. Postpositive explanatory conjunction. It introduces a sentence that further explains the previous conditional statement regarding doing bad and fearing as a result.

εἰκῇ. Adverb (manner; Porter 1994a, 125). It modifies τὴν μάχαιραν φορεῖ. There are only five other occurrences of this adverb in the NT, all found in the Pauline corpus (1 Cor 15:2; Gal 3:4 (2x); 4:11; Col 2:18; cf. LXX Prov 28:25).

τὴν μάχαιραν. Accusative direct object of φορεῖ. Metonymy for power or authority (cf. Sanday and Headlam, 367).

φορεῖ. Pres act ind 3rd sg φορέω.

θεοῦ γὰρ διάκονός ἐστιν. This clause is repeated in this verse for cohesion and prominence. Clausal repetition functions as a cohesive tie but also serves to emphasize the identity (ἐστιν) of authority as God's servant. While in most English translations this second clause is usually translated as "he is God's servant" (or the like; NIV, NKJV, NRSV, NASB), paralleling the first occurrence, the following nominative ἔκδικος is likely a predicate nominative (see below). Thus, we prefer a translation such as "God's servant is a punisher."

θεοῦ. Possessive genitive, modifying διάκονός. The occurrence of the genitive before the head term reflects prominence within the word group (θεοῦ διάκονός); "God" is emphasized over "servant."

γὰρ. Postpositive explanatory conjunction. A further explanation of Paul's command to submit to superior authorities is given.

διάκονός. Nominative subject of ἐστιν. The additional accent on the ultima is a result of the following word being enclitic (see note on πνεύματί in 1:9).

ἐστιν. Unaugmented ind 3rd sg εἰμί.

ἔκδικος. Predicate nominative. While some may wish to categorize this as a nominative in apposition to θεοῦ . . . διάκονός, the natural syntax seems to indicate that ἐστιν equates the two nominatives before and after it. The nominal form of ἐκδικέω, both having the εκ- prefix with the δικ- root, has the sense of just or proper punishment.

εἰς ὀργὴν. Purpose. The purpose of God's servant being a punisher is to exercise wrath or anger against wrongdoing.

τῷ . . . πράσσοντι. Pres act ptc masc dat sg πράσσω (substantival). Dative of disadvantage.

τὸ κακὸν. Accusative direct object of πράσσοντι. It is embedded between the dative article and participle to reflect prominence of the accusative object. The adjective is used as a substantive.

13:5 διὸ ἀνάγκη ὑποτάσσεσθαι, οὐ μόνον διὰ τὴν ὀργὴν ἀλλὰ καὶ διὰ τὴν συνείδησιν.

διὸ. Inferential conjunction. An inference is drawn from the previous co-text regarding obedience to the superior authorities.

ἀνάγκη. Predicate nominative of an implied ἐστιν.

ὑποτάσσεσθαι. Pres pass inf ὑποτασσω. The infinitive functions as the subject of an implied ἐστιν (lit. "to be subjected [is] a necessity"). On the omission of ἐστιν in this verse, see BDF (§127.2).

οὐ μόνον . . . ἀλλὰ καὶ. A point/counterpoint set ("not only . . . but also") that supplements the "necessity to submit" and contrasts the two διά prepositional word groups (cf. Rom 1:32; 5:3, 11; 8:23; 9:10, 24).

διὰ τὴν ὀργὴν. Causal. The cause, or reason, of being subjected (ὑποτάσσεσθαι) is "wrath."

διὰ τὴν συνείδησιν. Causal. The cause, or reason, of being subjected (ὑποτάσσεσθαι) is "conscience."

13:6 διὰ τοῦτο γὰρ καὶ φόρους τελεῖτε· λειτουργοὶ γὰρ θεοῦ εἰσιν εἰς αὐτὸ τοῦτο προσκαρτεροῦντες.

διὰ τοῦτο. Causal. The demonstrative pronoun refers anaphorically to the previous statement regarding the necessity to be obedient not only because of wrath but also conscience.

γὰρ. Postpositive explanatory conjunction. It introduces a clause that explains the previous statement on obedience.

καὶ. Adverbial use (adjunctive).

φόρους. Accusative direct object of τελεῖτε. φόρος refers to "a payment made by the people of one nation to another, with the implication that this is a symbol of submission and dependence" (LN 57.182; cf. Sanday and Headlam, 369; Porter 2015, 248–49).

τελεῖτε. Pres act ind 2nd pl τελέω. The core meaning of this lexeme has to do with completion or fulfillment, but collocated with a "tax/tribute" word, it means to "pay" the tax/tribute (LN 57.178). The verb form can be either an indicative or imperative. The imperative makes sense if there was a problem among Roman Christians who did not pay their taxes. But this is highly speculative, so the indicative makes the best sense here (Moo, 804; Morris, 465 n. 40; Porter 2015, 248).

λειτουργοὶ. Predicate nominative. The lexeme λειτουργός refers to a liturgist, a participant of cultic practice, or a public servant, who were compensated for their service. Paul's argument is that since they occupy their time and devote themselves to their civic duties, they deserve due compensation.

γὰρ. Postpositive explanatory conjunction. It introduces a clause that explains why they fulfill (or pay) taxes.

θεοῦ. Possessive genitive, modifying λειτουργοὶ.

εἰσιν. Unaugmented ind 3rd pl εἰμί.

εἰς αὐτὸ τοῦτο. Purpose. The use of the intensive pronoun and demonstrative pronoun ("for this very purpose") is emphatic (cf. Rom 9:17; 2 Cor 5:5; 7:11; Gal 2:10; Eph 6:22; Phil 1:6; Col 4:8; 2 Pet 1:5).

προσκαρτεροῦντες. Pres act ptc masc nom pl προσκαρτερέω (manner). The participle functions as circumstantial and modifies λειτουργοὶ θεοῦ.

13:7 ἀπόδοτε πᾶσιν τὰς ὀφειλάς, τῷ τὸν φόρον τὸν φόρον, τῷ τὸ τέλος τὸ τέλος, τῷ τὸν φόβον τὸν φόβον, τῷ τὴν τιμὴν τὴν τιμήν.

ἀπόδοτε. Aor act impv 2nd pl ἀποδίδωμι. This lexeme, with the prefix ἀπό-, has a reciprocal sense (i.e., "give back").

πᾶσιν. Dative indirect object of ἀπόδοτε.

τὰς ὀφειλάς. Accusative direct object of ἀπόδοτε. Paul lists four examples of giving back "what is owed": tributes, taxes, fear, and honor. Each of the four examples is a restatement in the singular of a specific instance of what is indicated by the plural initial statement.

τῷ. Dative indirect object of ἀπόδοτε, appositional to πᾶσιν. The article functions pronominally ("to whom"; cf. Porter 1994a, 104, 108, 112), probably a specification of those referred to by πᾶσιν. It begins the first of four parallel phrases consisting of a dative word group indicating with the accusative what is owed and a repeated accusative of the object owed.

τὸν φόρον. Accusative in apposition to τὰς ὀφειλάς. See note in 13:6 for the meaning of φόρος.

τὸν φόρον. Accusative direct object of ἀπόδοτε.

τῷ. Dative indirect object of ἀπόδοτε, appositional to πᾶσιν. The article functions pronominally (see above on τῷ).

τὸ τέλος. Accusative in apposition to τὰς ὀφειλάς. τέλος generally refers to "end," "perfect," "complete," or "goal" (cf. 10:4), but it is modulated in this co-text to refer to taxes that a government may impose on its people (Sanday and Headlam, 369; Moo, 805 n. 83; Porter 2015, 249; cf. Matt 17:25; 1 Macc 5:31).

τὸ τέλος. Accusative direct object of ἀπόδοτε.

τῷ. Dative indirect object of ἀπόδοτε, appositional to πᾶσιν. The article functions pronominally (see above on τῷ).

τὸν φόβον. Accusative in apposition to τὰς ὀφειλάς.

τὸν φόβον. Accusative direct object of ἀπόδοτε.

τῷ. Dative indirect object of ἀπόδοτε. The article functions pronominally (see above on τῷ).

τὴν τιμήν. Accusative in apposition to τὰς ὀφειλάς.

τὴν τιμήν. Accusative direct object of ἀπόδοτε.

Romans 13:8–10

[8]Owe nothing to anyone, except to love one another. For the one who loves another has fulfilled the law. [9]For example, that "You shall not commit adultery, you shall not murder, you shall not steal, you shall not covet"—also if there is any other commandment—is summarized in this statement, "You shall love your neighbor as yourself." [10]Love does not accomplish bad to a neighbor; therefore, love [is] a fulfillment of law.

This next paraenetic section addresses the exhortation to love one another by referring to Scripture.

13:8 Μηδενὶ μηδὲν ὀφείλετε εἰ μὴ τὸ ἀλλήλους ἀγαπᾶν· ὁ γὰρ ἀγαπῶν τὸν ἕτερον νόμον πεπλήρωκεν.

Μηδενὶ. Dative indirect object of ὀφείλετε. Μηδενὶ is a negated indefinite pronoun. This begins the apodosis of a second-class conditional (see below).

μηδὲν. Accusative direct object of ὀφείλετε. μηδὲν is a negated indefinite pronoun. The use of two negated pronouns function as emphatic. Also, the fronting of both the dative and accusative in the clause reflects further prominence of these items, i.e., nothing at all, to anyone at all, is to be owed.

ὀφείλετε. Pres act impv 2nd pl ὀφείλω. The repeated lexeme from previous verse creates lexical cohesion for thematic continuity (owing, obligation).

εἰ μὴ. A combination of the conditional conjunction and the negative particle that introduces the protasis of a second-class conditional (see note on εἰ μή in 7:7). This word group is typically translated as "except" or "unless." The condition of not owing love to one another is presented by Paul as contrary to reality (they in fact do owe loving one another).

τὸ . . . ἀγαπᾶν. Pres act inf ἀγαπάω. The articular infinitive functions as the direct object of an implied ὀφείλετε from the apodosis.

ἀλλήλους. Accusative direct object of ἀγαπᾶν. The embedding of the object between the article and predicate reflects clausal prominence of the object.

ὁ . . . ἀγαπῶν τὸν ἕτερον νόμον πεπλήρωκεν. This clause can be read in two ways: (1) "the one who loves another has fulfilled the law" or (2) "the one who loves has fulfilled another law." While both options are syntactically possible, it is best to take the first option for co-textual reasons. Paul refers to the Ten Commandments in the next verse, indicating that he is not referring to "another law" but to "the law."

ὁ . . . ἀγαπῶν. Pres act ptc masc nom sg ἀγαπάω (substantival). Nominative subject of πεπλήρωκεν.

γὰρ. Postpositive explanatory conjunction.

τὸν ἕτερον. Accusative direct object of ἀγαπῶν.

νόμον. Accusative object of πεπλήρωκεν. Having no article, it refers to the law qualitatively rather than particularly or categorically.

πεπλήρωκεν. Prf act ind 3rd sg πληρόω. The perfect tense-form (stative aspect) reflects the fulfilling as a state or condition and is prominent at the discourse level.

13:9 τὸ γὰρ οὐ μοιχεύσεις, οὐ φονεύσεις, οὐ κλέψεις, οὐκ ἐπιθυμήσεις, καὶ εἴ τις ἑτέρα ἐντολή, ἐν τῷ λόγῳ τούτῳ ἀνακεφαλαιοῦται [ἐν τῷ]· ἀγαπήσεις τὸν πλησίον σου ὡς σεαυτόν.

τὸ. The article functions as a nominalizer, changing the four commands (οὐ μοιχεύσεις, οὐ φονεύσεις, οὐ κλέψεις, οὐκ ἐπιθυμήσεις) into a compound nominative subject of ἀνακεφαλαιοῦται. The singular article here (translated as "that" for smooth English) treats the four commands as a single item (cf. Porter 1994a, 108–109).

γὰρ. Postpositive explanatory conjunction. It introduces a clause that explains Paul's previous statement regarding the obligation to love one another. Taken with the neuter article τό, it has the semantic effect of "for example" (Porter 2015, 252).

οὐ. Negative particle normally used with indicative verbs. Here it negates μοιχεύσεις and begins the reference to LXX Exod 20:12–17.

μοιχεύσεις. Fut act ind 2nd sg μοιχεύω. While the future form maintains the semantics of expectation, it is used in a commanding sense here; there is an expectation to not commit adultery.

οὐ. Negative particle normally used with indicative verbs. Here it negates φονεύσεις.

φονεύσεις. Fut act ind 2nd sg φονεύω (see above on μοιχεύσεις).

οὐ. Negative particle normally used with indicative verbs. Here it negates κλέψεις.

κλέψεις. Fut act ind 2nd sg κλέπτω (see above on μοιχεύσεις).

οὐκ. Negative particle normally used with indicative verbs. Here it negates ἐπιθυμήσεις.

ἐπιθυμήσεις. Fut act ind 2nd sg ἐπιθυμέω (see above on μοιχεύσεις).

καὶ. Adverbial use (adjunctive). It modifies the conditional clause as a parenthetical statement.

εἴ. Introduces the protasis of a first-class conditional that functions syntactically as parenthetical (indicated in the above translation with em-dashes).

τις ἑτέρα ἐντολή. Predicate nominative or independent nominative of verbless clause. τις is an indefinite pronoun that generalizes ἑτέρα ἐντολή ("any other commandment").

ἐν τῷ λόγῳ τούτῳ. Locative. The prepositional word group begins the apodosis of the first-class condition and resumption of the main clause. Its fronting before the predicate indicates clausal prominence. The demonstrative pronoun refers cataphorically to the OT reference.

ἀνακεφαλαιοῦται. Pres pass ind 3rd sg ἀνακεφαλαιόω.

[ἐν τῷ]. Locative. The earliest manuscripts are divided on this reading (without: 𝔓⁴⁶ᵛⁱᵈ B; with: ℵ A D). It is likely that later scribes omitted this phrase, due to its redundancy with ἐν τῷ λόγῳ τούτῳ. With this reading, however, the prepositional word group parallels both the previous prepositional word group (ἐν τῷ λόγῳ τούτῳ) and the articular nominalizer found at the beginning of the LXX Exod 20:12–17 quotation.

ἀγαπήσεις. Fut act ind 2nd sg ἀγαπάω. It begins the reference from LXX Lev 19:18.

τὸν πλησίον. Accusative direct object of ἀγαπήσεις. The word itself is an improper preposition (with genitive; Porter 1994a, 180) and generally means "a position quite close to another position, with the possible implication of being contiguous—quite near, nearby" (LN 83.27; cf. John 4:5; LXX Ezek 40:9; 41:17). But with the article usually, it is often used as a lexical metaphor referring to a "neighbor."

σου. Possessive genitive, modifying τὸν πλησίον.

ὡς. Introduces an elliptical comparative clause: ὡς [ἀγαπᾷς] σεαυτόν = as [you love] yourself.

σεαυτόν. Accusative direct object of an implied ἀγαπᾷς.

13:10 ἡ ἀγάπη τῷ πλησίον κακὸν οὐκ ἐργάζεται· πλήρωμα οὖν νόμου ἡ ἀγάπη.

ἡ ἀγάπη. Nominative subject of ἐργάζεται.

τῷ πλησίον. Dative indirect object of ἐργάζεται ("to a neighbor") or dative of disadvantage ("against a neighbor"). For the meaning of πλησίον, see note in 13:9.

κακὸν. Accusative direct object of ἐργάζεται. Without the article, the substantival adjective focuses on the quality of "bad," rather than its particularity.

οὐκ. Negative particle normally used with indicative verbs. Here it negates ἐργάζεται.

ἐργάζεται. Pres mid ind 3rd sg ἐργάζομαι.

πλήρωμα. Predicate nominative. The fronting of the predicate nominative indicates clausal prominence.

οὖν. Postpositive inferential conjunction. An inference is made from the previous statement that love does not do bad to one's neighbor.

νόμου. Genitive of description or definition, modifying πλήρωμα. "Fulfillment" is further described or circumscribed as "law." Some may wish to label this as an objective genitive, if πλήρωμα is taken as a verb, "to fulfill the law."

ἡ ἀγάπη. Nominative subject of verbless clause.

Romans 13:11–14

[11]And know this, with respect to the time, that an hour [is present] already for you to be raised from your sleep. For our salvation [is] nearer now than when we believed. [12]The night has advanced, and the day stands near. Therefore, we should put away works of darkness, and clothe [ourselves] in weapons of light. [13]As in the day, we should walk properly, not in partying and drunkenness, not in sex and sensuality, not in strife and jealousy. [14]Instead, clothe [yourselves] with the Lord Jesus Christ and do not make [for yourselves] fleshly provision for lust.

This next paraenetic section identifies proper Christian behavior in light of Christ's return. This section utilizes participles, subjunctives, and imperatives in commanding/exhortative senses.

13:11 Καὶ τοῦτο εἰδότες τὸν καιρόν, ὅτι ὥρα ἤδη ὑμᾶς ἐξ ὕπνου ἐγερθῆναι, νῦν γὰρ ἐγγύτερον ἡμῶν ἡ σωτηρία ἢ ὅτε ἐπιστεύσαμεν.

Καὶ. Coordinating conjunction. It connects the previous statement with the following one.

τοῦτο. Accusative direct object of εἰδότες. Some other interpretations include an accusative direct object of an implied ποιεῖτε (see Robertson, 1134; Jewett, 818; cf. NASB; NET; LEB) or of an implied λέγω (see BDF §480.5). Wallace (1996, 335) argues that the phrase Καὶ τοῦτο is adverbial with no antecedent for τοῦτο ("and especially").

εἰδότες. Prf act ptc masc nom pl οἶδα (imperatival). The participle functions as commanding in this co-text (without a head predicate). However, if τοῦτο functions as accusative direct object of an implied ποιεῖτε or λέγω (see the previous entry), εἰδότες would be an adverbial participle expressing cause: "And [do] this because you know the time." The perfect tense-form (stative aspect) depicts the process as a state or condition of "knowing," and reflects discourse prominence.

τὸν καιρόν. Accusative of respect. Alternatively, this could be accusative direct object of εἰδότες.

ὅτι. Introduces the clausal complement (indirect discourse) of εἰδότες.

ὥρα. Nominative subject of verbless clause.

ἤδη. Adverb (temporal). It modifies an implied "to be" verb in the clause (here, "is present").

ὑμᾶς. Accusative subject of the infinitive ἐγερθῆναι.

ἐξ ὕπνου. Locative (movement out of).

ἐγερθῆναι. Aor pass inf ἐγείρω (epexegetical to ὥρα).

νῦν. Adverb (temporal).

γὰρ. Postpositive explanatory conjunction. It introduces a further explanation of being raised from sleep.

ἐγγύτερον. Predicate adjective. ἐγγύτερον is formed by ἐγγύς + the comparative adjective ending τερον ("nearer"; cf. Porter 1994a, 179). A NT *hapax legomenon*.

ἡμῶν. Possessive genitive, modifying ἡ σωτηρία. Its placement before the head term reflects prominence within the word group.

ἡ σωτηρία. Nominative subject of verbless clause.

ἤ. Comparative conjunction. It completes the comparison initiated by ἐγγύτερον.

ὅτε. Introduces a temporal clause. ὅτε ("when") is used in comparison with νῦν ("now").

ἐπιστεύσαμεν. Aor act ind 1st pl πιστεύω. The use of the aorist tense-form (perfective aspect) itself does not indicate past time but depicts the process of believing as an undifferentiated whole, complete. Past time is indicated by use of ὅτε.

13:12 ἡ νὺξ προέκοψεν, ἡ δὲ ἡμέρα ἤγγικεν. ἀποθώμεθα οὖν τὰ ἔργα τοῦ σκότους, ἐνδυσώμεθα [δὲ] τὰ ὅπλα τοῦ φωτός.

ἡ νὺξ. Nominative subject of προέκοψεν.

προέκοψεν. Aor act ind 3rd sg προκόπτω.

ἡ . . . ἡμέρα. Nominative subject of ἤγγικεν.

δὲ. Adversative conjunction (mild). It provides a mild contrast between the night and the day.

ἤγγικεν. Prf act ind 3rd sg ἐγγίζω. The perfect tense-form (stative aspect) depicts the process as in a state or condition of being near and reflects discourse prominence, especially in comparison to the parallel predicate προέκοψεν in the aorist form.

ἀποθώμεθα. Aor mid subj 1st pl ἀποτίθημι (hortatory subjunctive).

οὖν. Postpositive inferential conjunction, introducing two commands as a result of the previous statements regarding night and day.

τὰ ἔργα. Accusative direct object of ἀποθώμεθα.

τοῦ σκότους. Genitive of source or origin, modifying τὰ ἔργα. The genitive construction here probably does not have a qualitative function (i.e., "dark works") but refers to "inconsequential activities done during the period of 'darkness'" (Porter 2015, 255), i.e., works originating in the darkness.

ἐνδυσώμεθα. Aor mid subj 1st pl ἐνδύω (hortatory subjunctive). The middle voice-form indicates indirect, internal causality, having a reflexive function here, i.e., "clothe yourselves."

[δὲ]. Adversative conjunction (mild). It provides a mild disjunction to the two hortatory subjunctives. The earliest manuscripts are divided on the wording here (ενδυσωμεθα δε: A B C* D*; ενδυσωμεθα: 𝔓⁴⁶ᶜ ℵ*; και ενδυσωμεθα ℵ² C³ D¹). It appears a later scribe inserted δε so that it would be parallel to the previous clause complex ἡ νὺξ προέκοψεν, ἡ δὲ ἡμέρα ἤγγικεν.

τὰ ὅπλα. Accusative direct object of ἐνδυσώμεθα.

τοῦ φωτός. Genitive of description or definition, modifying τὰ ὅπλα. "Weapons" are defined or circumscribed as "of light."

13:13 ὡς ἐν ἡμέρᾳ εὐσχημόνως περιπατήσωμεν, μὴ κώμοις καὶ μέθαις, μὴ κοίταις καὶ ἀσελγείαις, μὴ ἔριδι καὶ ζήλῳ,

ὡς. Comparative conjunction. It makes a comparison to walking properly.

ἐν ἡμέρᾳ. Temporal.

εὐσχημόνως. Adverb (manner). It modifies περιπατήσωμεν.

περιπατήσωμεν. Aor act subj 1st pl περιπατέω (hortatory subjunctive).

μὴ . . . μὴ . . . μὴ. Three negative particles that negate three groups of datives, each containing two semantically similar substantives, which form the first element of the composite point/counterpoint set that continues with ἀλλ᾽ in the next verse.

κώμοις καὶ μέθαις. Two datives of manner creating a hendiadys. The lexeme κῶμος is defined as "drinking parties involving unrestrained indulgence in alcoholic beverages and accompanying immoral behavior" (LN 88.287).

κοίταις καὶ ἀσελγείαις. Two datives of manner creating a hendiadys. The lexeme κοίτη is where the English word "coitus" originates and retains its meaning of sexual intercourse. In this co-text, it is used pejoratively, referring to a particular lifestyle of sex that does not reflect proper living.

ἔριδι καὶ ζήλῳ. Two datives of manner creating a hendiadys.

13:14 ἀλλ᾽ ἐνδύσασθε τὸν κύριον Ἰησοῦν Χριστὸν καὶ τῆς σαρκὸς πρόνοιαν μὴ ποιεῖσθε εἰς ἐπιθυμίας.

ἀλλ᾽. Adversative conjunction introducing the point clause that forms the second element of a point/counterpoint set that began in the preceding verse.

ἐνδύσασθε. Aor mid impv 2nd pl ἐνδύω. The same command was given by Paul in 13:12, except in the subjunctive form; here, a more direct command is given by use of the imperative form. As in 13:12, the middle voice-form reflects indirect, internal causality and is used reflexively here.

τὸν κύριον. Accusative direct object of ἐνδύσασθε.

Ἰησοῦν Χριστὸν. Accusative in apposition to τὸν κύριον.

καὶ. Coordinating conjunction. It connects the two commands.

τῆς σαρκὸς. Genitive of quality, modifying πρόνοιαν ("fleshly provision"). The genitive is fronted before the head term for prominence in the word group.

πρόνοιαν. Accusative direct object of ποιεῖσθε.

μὴ. Negative particle normally used with non-indicative verbs. Here it negates ποιεῖσθε.

ποιεῖσθε. Pres mid impv 2nd pl ποιέω. The middle voice-form is consistently used in this co-text reflexively ("make for yourselves").

εἰς ἐπιθυμίας. Purpose. The purpose of making provision of the flesh is "passion" or "lust."

Romans 14:1–12

¹Now accept the one who is weak in faith not in disputations of opinions. ²One believes in eating everything, but the weak eats vegetables. ³The one who eats must not look down on the one who does not eat, and the one who does not eat must not judge the one who eats, for God accepts him. ⁴Who are you, who judges another's servant? To his own lord, he stands or falls; but he will be upheld, for the Lord is able to uphold him. ⁵One considers a day more than [another] day, but another one considers every day [alike]. Each one in his own mind should be completely convinced. ⁶The one who holds the day holds to the Lord; and the one who eats, eats to the Lord, for he gives thanks to God. And the one who does not eat, does not eat to the Lord and gives thanks to God. ⁷For none of us lives for himself and none dies for himself. ⁸For if we live, to the Lord we live; if we die, to the Lord we die. Therefore, if we live [or] if we die, we are the Lord's. ⁹Because for this Christ died and came back to life, so that he would be Lord of both the dead and the living. ¹⁰But with respect to what do you judge your brother [or sister]? Or with respect to what do you look down on your brother [or sister]? For we all will stand before the judgment seat of God. ¹¹For it is written, "I live," says the Lord, "to me every knee will bow, and every tongue will strongly confess to God." ¹²Therefore, each of us will give an account to God concerning himself.

This paraenetic section (and the next several) deals with a major topic of accepting those who were "weak" in faith. Paul identifies two hypothetical people, the so-called "weak" and the so-called "strong." Paul also returns, in this section, to the use of several rhetorical questions to underscore his point.

14:1 Τὸν δὲ ἀσθενοῦντα τῇ πίστει προσλαμβάνεσθε, μὴ εἰς διακρίσεις διαλογισμῶν.

Τὸν ... ἀσθενοῦντα. Pres act ptc masc acc sg ἀσθενέω (substantival). Accusative direct object of προσλαμβάνεσθε.

δὲ. Adversative conjunction (mild). It serves as a transition from the previous sub-section on proper living, in day/light, to a new sub-section on the strong and weak in faith.

τῇ πίστει. Dative of sphere.

προσλαμβάνεσθε. Pres mid impv 2nd pl προσλαμβάνω. The middle voice-form here reflects indirect, internal causality. In contrast to the active voice-form, which reflects direct causality, the middle voice-form reflects indirect causality, although agency is internal to the grammatical subject. The prefix προσ- probably reinforces the sense of the root λαμβάνω.

μὴ. Negative particle that negates εἰς διακρίσεις.

εἰς διακρίσεις. Purpose. The purpose for receiving the one who is weak in faith is not so that they can dispute with them. διάκρισις is commonly translated as "judgment" or "discernment," but the co-text modulates its meaning to "disputation" here (cf. NKJV).

διαλογισμῶν. Genitive of definition or description, modifying διακρίσεις. "Disputations" are further described or circumscribed as "debatable things." As with διάκρισις, the meaning of διαλογισμός is modulated in this co-text from the more common translation "opinion" or "thought" to "debatable things."

14:2 ὃς μὲν πιστεύει φαγεῖν πάντα, ὁ δὲ ἀσθενῶν λάχανα ἐσθίει.

ὅς. Nominative subject of πιστεύει. The headless relative pronoun functions as the subject of the clause.

μὲν... δὲ. A point/counterpoint set that establishes the contrast between one who believes in eating everything and a weak person who eats only vegetables.

πιστεύει. Pres act ind 3rd sg πιστεύω.

φαγεῖν. Aor act inf ἐσθίω (indirect discourse). The infinitive expresses the content of πιστεύει.

πάντα. Accusative direct object of φαγεῖν.

ὁ... ἀσθενῶν. Pres act ptc masc nom sg ἀσθενέω (substantival). Nominative subject of ἐσθίει.

λάχανα. Accusative direct object of ἐσθίει. The fronting of the accusative before the predicate, especially compared to the previous clause, where the accusative comes after the predicate, reflects clausal prominence.

ἐσθίει. Pres act ind 3rd sg ἐσθίω. The use of ἐσθίει here, instead of πιστεύει φαγεῖν in the previous clause, focuses more on the weak's actions of eating than on his/her beliefs about eating.

14:3 ὁ ἐσθίων τὸν μὴ ἐσθίοντα μὴ ἐξουθενείτω, ὁ δὲ μὴ ἐσθίων τὸν ἐσθίοντα μὴ κρινέτω, ὁ θεὸς γὰρ αὐτὸν προσελάβετο.

ὁ ἐσθίων. Pres act ptc masc nom sg ἐσθίω (substantival). Nominative subject of ἐξουθενείτω.

τὸν μὴ ἐσθίοντα. Pres act ptc masc acc sg ἐσθίω (substantival). Accusative direct object of ἐξουθενείτω.

μὴ. Negative particle normally used with non-indicative verbs. Here it negates ἐξουθενείτω.

ἐξουθενείτω. Pres act impv 3rd sg ἐσθίω. The third-person imperative conveys the full force of the imperative as a command.

ὁ... μὴ ἐσθίων. Pres act ptc masc nom sg ἐσθίω (substantival). Nominative subject of κρινέτω.

δὲ. Adversative conjunction (mild). It connects (with mild adversative) the two commands.

τὸν ἐσθίοντα. Pres act ptc masc acc sg ἐσθίω (substantival). Accusative direct object of κρινέτω.

μὴ. Negative particle normally used with non-indicative verbs. Here it negates κρινέτω.

κρινέτω. Pres act impv 3rd sg κρίνω. The third-person imperative conveys the full force of the imperative as a command. The switch from ἐξουθενείτω to κρινέτω in the parallel clauses is notable.

ὁ θεὸς. Nominative subject of προσελάβετο.

γὰρ. Postpositive explanatory conjunction. It introduces a clause that explains why "the one who does not eat" should not judge "the one who eats." It appears in third place in this clause, which is uncommon, probably to emphasize ὁ θεὸς.

αὐτὸν. Accusative direct object of προσελάβετο. The referent of the personal pronoun is ambiguous but probably refers anaphorically to τὸν ἐσθίοντα. Given that the next verse poses the question of who judges another's servant, using the same lexeme (κρίνω) as applied to "the one who eats," this interpretation seems to make the most sense.

προσελάβετο. Aor mid ind 3rd sg προσλαμβάνω. The middle voice, as in 14:1 with the same lexeme, reflects indirect, internal causality.

14:4 σὺ τίς εἶ ὁ κρίνων ἀλλότριον οἰκέτην; τῷ ἰδίῳ κυρίῳ στήκει ἢ πίπτει· σταθήσεται δέ, δυνατεῖ γὰρ ὁ κύριος στῆσαι αὐτόν.

σὺ. Nominative subject of εἶ. The second singular person is used to address a hypothetical person to whom this might apply (cf. Romans 2, 13:3–4).

τίς. Predicate nominative.

εἶ. Unaugmented ind 2nd sg εἰμί.

ὁ κρίνων. Pres act ptc masc nom sg κρίνω (substantival). Nominative in apposition to σὺ.

ἀλλότριον οἰκέτην. Accusative direct object of κρίνων. ἀλλότριον is an adjective in attributive structure. οἰκέτης refers to a household servant.

τῷ ἰδίῳ κυρίῳ. Dative of respect. The fronting of the dative in the clause indicates clausal prominence. κύριος here, especially with the attributive adjective ἰδίῳ, draws from a secular analogy to a master or paterfamilias of a household in which the servant lives.

στήκει. Pres act ind 3rd sg στήκω.

ἤ. Disjunctive conjunction. It functions adversatively, contrasting στήκει and πίπτει.

πίπτει. Pres act ind 3rd sg πίπτω.

σταθήσεται. Fut pass ind 3rd sg ἵστημι. Future form reflects that the servant is expected to be upheld. The passive voice-form indicates external causality; the next clause identifies God as the agent who upholds the servant.

δέ. Adversative conjunction (mild).

δυνατεῖ. Pres act ind 3rd sg δυνατέω.

γὰρ. Postpositive explanatory conjunction. The cause for being upheld is the Lord's ability to uphold his servant.

ὁ κύριος. Nominative subject of δυνατεῖ. The articular κύριος here probably particularizes "lord" in the previous clause to "the Lord."

στῆσαι. Aor act inf ἵστημι (complementary). The infinitive is a complement of δυνατεῖ.

αὐτόν. Accusative direct object of στῆσαι. The personal pronoun refers anaphorically to οἰκέτην.

14:5Ὃς μὲν [γὰρ] κρίνει ἡμέραν παρ᾽ ἡμέραν, ὃς δὲ κρίνει πᾶσαν ἡμέραν· ἕκαστος ἐν τῷ ἰδίῳ νοῒ πληροφορείσθω.

Ὅς. Nominative subject of κρίνει. The headless relative pronoun functions as the subject of the clause (cf. 14:2).

μὲν ... δὲ. A point/counterpoint set that establishes the contrast between one who distinguishes one day above another and one who regards every day as the same.

[γὰρ]. Postpositive explanatory conjunction. Paul continues his explanation between the two differing views from the previous co-text. The textual evidence is somewhat divided in the early manuscripts (with: ℵ* A P; without: 𝔓⁴⁶ ℵᶜ B D F G).

κρίνει. Pres act ind 3rd sg κρίνω.

ἡμέραν. Accusative direct object of κρίνει.

παρ᾽ ἡμέραν. Replacement. This is a figurative extension of the locative function, referring to something that is "alongside" another to replace it in some way (cf. Porter 1994a, 167; LN 89.132; see note on παρ᾽ ὃ δεῖ φρονεῖν in 12:3). In other words, the preposition means one day "in place of" another, or "more than" another (cf. BDF §236.3).

ὃς. Nominative subject of κρίνει. The headless relative pronoun functions as the subject of the clause.

κρίνει. Pres act ind 3rd sg κρίνω.

πᾶσαν ἡμέραν. Accusative direct object of κρίνει.

ἕκαστος. Nominative subject of πληροφορείσθω.

ἐν ἰδίῳ νοΐ. Locative.

πληροφορείσθω. Pres pass impv 3rd sg πληροφορέω. The third-person imperative retains its full commanding force. In its middle and passive voice-forms (which are identical), πληροφορέω means "to be completely convinced" (cf. LN 31.45). The distinction between middle and passive voice here is semantically minimal ("completely convince yourself" or "be completely convinced"; cf. 4:21).

14:6 ὁ φρονῶν τὴν ἡμέραν κυρίῳ φρονεῖ· καὶ ὁ ἐσθίων κυρίῳ ἐσθίει, εὐχαριστεῖ γὰρ τῷ θεῷ· καὶ ὁ μὴ ἐσθίων κυρίῳ οὐκ ἐσθίει καὶ εὐχαριστεῖ τῷ θεῷ.

ὁ φρονῶν. Pres act ptc masc nom sg φρονέω (substantival). Nominative subject of φρονεῖ.

τὴν ἡμέραν. Accusative direct object of φρονῶν.

κυρίῳ. Dative indirect object of φρονεῖ.

φρονεῖ. Pres act ind 3rd sg φρονέω.

καὶ. Coordinating conjunction. Connects the two clauses before and after it.

ὁ ἐσθίων. Pres act ptc masc nom sg ἐσθίω (substantival). Nominative subject of ἐσθίει.

κυρίῳ. Dative indirect object of ἐσθίει.

ἐσθίει. Pres act ind 3rd sg ἐσθίω.

εὐχαριστεῖ. Pres act ind 3rd sg εὐχαριστέω.

γὰρ. Postpositive explanatory conjunction. It introduces an explanation for the one who observes days and eats to the Lord.

τῷ θεῷ. Dative direct object of εὐχαριστεῖ.

καὶ. Coordinating conjunction. Connects the previous clause with the following clause.

ὁ μὴ ἐσθίων. Pres act ptc masc nom sg ἐσθίω (substantival). Nominative subject of ἐσθίει.

κυρίῳ. Dative indirect object of ἐσθίει.

οὐκ. Negative particle normally used with indicative verbs. Here it negates ἐσθίει.

ἐσθίει. Pres act ind 3rd sg ἐσθίω.

καὶ. Coordinating conjunction. It connects the two clauses before and after it.

εὐχαριστεῖ. Pres act ind 3rd sg εὐχαριστέω.

τῷ θεῷ. Dative direct object of εὐχαριστεῖ.

14:7 οὐδεὶς γὰρ ἡμῶν ἑαυτῷ ζῇ καὶ οὐδεὶς ἑαυτῷ ἀποθνῄσκει·

οὐδεὶς. Nominative subject of ζῇ. The negated indefinite pronoun is used in this form in Romans only in this verse.

γὰρ. Postpositive explanatory conjunction. It introduces an explanation for the previous statement that eating and not eating is done with thanks to God.

ἡμῶν. Partitive genitive, modifying οὐδεὶς.

ἑαυτῷ. Dative of advantage. The fronted dative before the predicate reflects clausal prominence.

ζῇ. Pres act ind 3rd sg ζάω.

καὶ. Coordinating conjunction. It connects the two clauses before and after it.

οὐδεὶς. Nominative subject of ἀποθνῄσκει.

ἑαυτῷ. Dative of disadvantage. The fronted dative before the predicate reflects clausal prominence.

ἀποθνῄσκει. Pres act ind 3rd sg ἀποθνῄσκω.

14:8 ἐάν τε γὰρ ζῶμεν, τῷ κυρίῳ ζῶμεν, ἐάν τε ἀποθνῄσκωμεν, τῷ κυρίῳ ἀποθνῄσκομεν. ἐάν τε οὖν ζῶμεν ἐάν τε ἀποθνῄσκωμεν, τοῦ κυρίου ἐσμέν.

ἐάν. Introduces the protasis of the first third-class conditional in this verse.

τε. Enclitic, emphatic conjunction. This is the only occurrences of ἐάν τε (4x in this verse) in the NT (cf. εἴτε in Rom 12:6–8).

γὰρ. Postpositive explanatory conjunction. It introduces an explanation of living and dying to oneself from the previous verse. It comes in a third position in the clause, probably due to the emphatic τε with ἐάν.

ζῶμεν. Pres act subj 1st pl ζάω. Subjunctive with ἐάν.

τῷ κυρίῳ. Dative of advantage. It begins the apodosis of the first third-class conditional. The fronting of the dative before the predicate indicates clausal prominence.

ζῶμεν. Pres act ind 1st pl ζάω. The indicative and subjunctive forms are equivalent for ζάω; the imperative is preferred, however, due to co-textual reasons, as the next third-class conditional contains an indicative in the apodosis.

ἐάν. Introduces the protasis of the second third-class conditional in this verse.

τε. Enclitic, emphatic conjunction.

ἀποθνῄσκωμεν. Pres act subj 1st pl ἀποθνῄσκω. Subjunctive with ἐάν.

τῷ κυρίῳ. Dative of advantage. It begins the apodosis of the second third-class conditional. The fronting of the dative before the predicate indicates clausal prominence.

ἀποθνῄσκομεν. Pres act ind 1st pl ἀποθνῄσκω.

ἐάν. Introduces the protasis of the third third-class conditional in this verse, with a shared apodosis (τοῦ κυρίου ἐσμέν) with the fourth conditional.

τε. Enclictic, emphatic conjunction.

οὖν. Postpositive inferential conjunction, drawing a conclusion from the two previous conditionals. It comes in a third position in the clause, probably due to the emphatic τε with ἐάν.

ζῶμεν. Pres act subj 1st pl ζάω. Subjunctive with ἐάν.

ἐάν. Introduces the protasis of the fourth third-class conditional in this verse, with a shared apodosis (τοῦ κυρίου ἐσμέν) with the third conditional.

τε. Enclictic, emphatic conjunction.

ἀποθνῄσκωμεν. Pres act subj 1st pl ἀποθνῄσκω. Subjunctive with ἐάν.

τοῦ κυρίου. Possessive genitive. The fronting of the genitive before the predicate indicates clausal prominence. The switch from the dative form of κύριος to the genitive here is notable. The genitive is probably used to grammaticalize possession instead of advantage; i.e., "we are of God" rather than "we are to God."

ἐσμέν. Unaugmented ind 1st pl εἰμί.

14:9 εἰς τοῦτο γὰρ Χριστὸς ἀπέθανεν καὶ ἔζησεν, ἵνα καὶ νεκρῶν καὶ ζώντων κυριεύσῃ.

εἰς τοῦτο. Purpose. The demonstrative pronoun is cataphoric, referring to the clause introduced by ἵνα. It may seem redundant to have both purpose markers here, but they are used to emphasize the purpose of Christ dying and living.

γὰρ. Postpositive explanatory conjunction. It introduces an explanation of the previous statement regarding death, life, and belonging to God.

Χριστὸς. Nominative subject of the compound predicates ἀπέθανεν καὶ ἔζησεν.

ἀπέθανεν. Aor act ind 3rd sg ἀποθνῄσκω.

καὶ. Coordinating conjunction. It connects the compound predicate.

ἔζησεν. Aor act ind 3rd sg ζάω.

ἵνα. Introduces a purpose clause. A purpose marker is reiterated for emphasis.

καὶ . . . καὶ. Correlative conjunctions: "both . . . and" (cf. Culy, Parsons, and Stigall, 363).

νεκρῶν. Genitive direct object of κυριεύσῃ. νεκρῶν is a substantival adjective.

ζώντων. Pres act ptc masc gen pl ζάω (substantival). Genitive direct object of κυριεύσῃ. The use of the participle here, instead of a noun in the parallel genitive νεκρῶν, focuses on the verbal character of the participle.

κυριεύσῃ. Aor act subj 3rd sg κυριεύω. Subjunctive with ἵνα.

14:10 Σὺ δὲ τί κρίνεις τὸν ἀδελφόν σου; ἢ καὶ σὺ τί ἐξουθενεῖς τὸν ἀδελφόν σου; πάντες γὰρ παραστησόμεθα τῷ βήματι τοῦ θεοῦ,

Σὺ. Nominative subject of κρίνεις. The use of the personal pronoun is emphatic. The singular person is used to address the hypothetical interlocutor (cf. 14:4, which has a similar construction as well).

δὲ. Adversative conjunction (mild).

τί. Accusative of respect of κρίνεις. The interrogative pronoun is used to question the hypothetical locutor's judgment of his brother or sister (i.e., "with respect to what" or commonly "why"; Porter 2015, 262).

κρίνεις. Pres act ind 2nd sg κρίνω.

τὸν ἀδελφόν. Accusative direct object of κρίνεις.

σου. Possessive genitive, modifying τὸν ἀδελφόν.

ἢ. Disjunctive conjunction. It functions adversatively, contrasting the questions before and after it.

καὶ. Adverbial use (adjunctive). It modifies the entire clause.

σὺ. Nominative subject of ἐξουθενεῖς (see above).

τί. Accusative of respect of ἐξουθενεῖς (see above).

ἐξουθενεῖς. Pres act ind 2nd sg ἐξουθενέω.

τὸν ἀδελφόν. Accusative direct object of ἐξουθενέω.

σου. Possessive genitive, modifying τὸν ἀδελφόν.

πάντες. Nominative in attributive structure to the implied first-person plural referent of παραστησόμεθα ("we all").

γὰρ. Postpositive inferential conjunction. It introduces an inference of Paul's two posed questions.

παραστησόμεθα. Fut mid ind 1st pl παρίστημι. The future form grammaticalizes the semantics of expectation; i.e., they can expect to stand before . . .

τῷ βήματι. Dative of location.

τοῦ θεοῦ. Possessive genitive, modifying τῷ βήματι.

14:11 γέγραπται γάρ· ζῶ ἐγώ, λέγει κύριος, ὅτι ἐμοὶ κάμψει πᾶν γόνυ καὶ πᾶσα γλῶσσα ἐξομολογήσεται τῷ θεῷ.

γέγραπται. Prf pass ind 3rd sg γράφω. The common Pauline Scripture invocation. The OT reference is from a part of LXX Isa 49:18 (ζῶ ἐγώ, λέγει κύριος) and a part of LXX Isa 45:23 (ὅτι . . . θεῷ), in which the word order of πᾶσα γλῶσσα ἐξομολογήσεται is switched from ἐξομολογήσεται πᾶσα γλῶσσα (cf. Phil 2:10–11).

γάρ. Inferential conjunction. It is used with γέγραπται often to draw a scriptural inference from the previous statement, here regarding standing before the judgment seat of God.

ζῶ. Pres act ind 1st sg ζάω. Most English translations have "As I live" here (NIV, NASB, NKJV, NRSV), but it is more a declarative statement than a comparative statement.

ἐγώ. Nominative subject of ζῶ. The use of the personal pronoun is emphatic.

λέγει. Pres act ind 3rd sg λέγω.

κύριος. Nominative subject of λέγει.

ὅτι. Introduces a clausal complement (direct discourse) of λέγει. In this case, the use of λέγει κύριος can doubly apply to both the clause before it and the clause complex after it.

ἐμοὶ κάμψει πᾶν γόνυ καὶ πᾶσα γλῶσσα ἐξομολογήσεται τῷ θεῷ. The two clauses form a micro-chiasm here (cf. Porter and Reed), with the following constituents:

A—ἐμοὶ
B—κάμψει
C—πᾶν γόνυ
C′—πᾶσα γλῶσσα
B′—ἐξομολογήσεται
A′—τῷ θεῷ

In such a structure, the middle constituents, C and C′, are the focus: "every knee" and "every tongue."

ἐμοὶ. Dative indirect object of κάμψει.

κάμψει. Fut act ind 3rd sg κάμπτω.

πᾶν γόνυ. Nominative subject of κάμψει.

καὶ. Coordinating conjunction. It connects the two clauses before and after it.

πᾶσα γλῶσσα. Nominative subject of ἐξομολογήσεται.

ἐξομολογήσεται. Fut mid ind 3rd sg ἐξομολογέω. The prefix ἐκ/ἐξ-intensifies the root ὁμολογέω: "to strongly confess."

τῷ θεῷ. Dative indirect object of ἐξομολογήσεται.

14:12 ἄρα [οὖν] ἕκαστος ἡμῶν περὶ ἑαυτοῦ λόγον δώσει [τῷ θεῷ].

ἄρα [οὖν]. A combination of two inferential conjunctions for emphasis (see Rom 5:18; 7:3, 15; 8:12; 9:16, 18). The inference is from the previous co-text regarding every knee bowing and every tongue confessing. The early manuscript evidence is slightly favorable towards including οὖν (with: ℵ A C D¹; without: B D*).

ἕκαστος. Nominative subject of δώσει.

ἡμῶν. Partitive genitive, modifying ἕκαστος. The plural pronoun indicates that all will be accounted for, including Paul, the Roman Christians, and all others.

περὶ ἑαυτοῦ. Reference. The singular reflexive pronoun indicates that, while everyone (ἕκαστος ἡμῶν) will give an account, each person will give his/her own account, with the implication that one is not responsible for others' accounts.

λόγον. Accusative direct object of δώσει. The lexeme has a broad semantic range but is modulated in this co-text to refer to an "account" (LN 57.228).

δώσει. Fut act ind 3rd sg δίδωμι. Consistent use of the future form here and in 14:10b–11 maintains the semantics of expectation in this co-text.

[τῷ θεῷ]. Dative indirect object of δώσει. The early manuscript evidence is in favor of including τῷ θεῷ (with: ℵ A C D; without: B).

Romans 14:13–23

¹³Therefore, we must no longer judge one another, but judge this instead: not to place a stumbling block to a brother [or sister] or a cause of scandal. ¹⁴I know and stand persuaded in the Lord Jesus that nothing [is] unclean by itself, except to the one who considers something to be unclean; to that one, [it is] unclean. ¹⁵For if through food your brother [or sister] is grieved, you no longer behave according to love. Do not by your food destroy the one for whom Christ died. ¹⁶Therefore, your good thing must not be blasphemed. ¹⁷For the kingdom of God is not food or drink but righteousness, peace, and joy in the Holy Spirit. ¹⁸For the one who in this [way] serves Christ [is] pleasing to God and approved by people. ¹⁹Therefore, we pursue the things of peace and the things of building up of one another. ²⁰Do not on account of food completely destroy the work of God. All things [are] clean, but it is bad for the person who eats by a stumbling block. ²¹[It is] good not to eat meat nor drink wine nor [anything] by which your brother [or sister] stumbles. ²²You—the faith which you have—have [it] according to yourself before God. Blessed [is] the one who does not judge himself by what he approves. ²³But the one who doubts, if he eats, stands condemned, because [it is] not of faith. And everything which [is] not of faith is sin.

The section in the paraenesis continues Paul's exhortations regarding how the so-called strong should interact with the so-called weak. While the previous section focused on a specific example of how the strong were to accept the weak, regarding eating foods that were involved in idol worship, this section turns to general principles involving potentially divisive behavior and attitudes.

14:13 Μηκέτι οὖν ἀλλήλους κρίνωμεν· ἀλλὰ τοῦτο κρίνατε μᾶλλον, τὸ μὴ τιθέναι πρόσκομμα τῷ ἀδελφῷ ἢ σκάνδαλον.

Μηκέτι . . . ἀλλὰ. A point/counterpoint set that establishes a contrast between the two halves of this verse. Μηκέτι is a temporal adverb that modifies κρίνωμεν. Μηκέτι is used with the subjunctive mood form (οὐκέτι is used with the indicative).

οὖν. Postpositive inferential conjunction, functioning as summarizing the previous statements regarding judgment towards one another in the previous co-text.

ἀλλήλους. Accusative direct object of κρίνωμεν.

κρίνωμεν. Pres act subj 1st pl κρίνω (hortatory subjunctive). Subjunctive functions as a command but maintains the semantics of projection of the subjunctive.

τοῦτο. Accusative direct object of κρίνατε. The demonstrative pronoun is cataphoric, referring to the clause introduced by τὸ μὴ τιθέναι. The fronted object before the predicate indicates clausal prominence.

κρίνατε. Aor act impv 2nd pl κρίνω. The switch from the hortatory subjunctive to the imperative here is to provide a more direct command.

μᾶλλον. Comparative of the adverb μάλα. Here it functions as contrastive: "instead" or "rather" (LN 89.126). It modifies κρίνατε.

τὸ μὴ τιθέναι. Pres act inf τίθημι (appositional). The negated articular infinitive stands in apposition to the demonstrative pronoun τοῦτο (cf. Robertson, 1059; Wallace 1996, 607).

πρόσκομμα. Accusative direct object of τιθέναι.

τῷ ἀδελφῷ. Dative indirect object of τιθέναι.

ἢ. Disjunctive conjunction. It adversatively joins the two accusative objects of τιθέναι ("or").

σκάνδαλον. Accusative direct object of τιθέναι.

14:14 οἶδα καὶ πέπεισμαι ἐν κυρίῳ Ἰησοῦ ὅτι οὐδὲν κοινὸν δι' ἑαυτοῦ, εἰ μὴ τῷ λογιζομένῳ τι κοινὸν εἶναι, ἐκείνῳ κοινόν.

οἶδα. Prf act ind 1st sg οἶδα. The perfect tense-form (stative aspect) depicts the process of knowing as a state or condition.

καί. Coordinating conjunction. It connects the two compound predicates οἶδα and πέπεισμαι.

πέπεισμαι. Prf pass ind 1st sg πείθω. The perfect tense-form (stative aspect) depicts the process of being convinced as a state or condition.

ἐν κυρίῳ. Locative (sphere or realm). Paul's state of knowledge and persuasion is in the sphere of the Lord. The anarthrous κυρίῳ should not be taken as an indefinite reference to "a lord" but as an individual use.

Ἰησοῦ. Dative in apposition to κυρίῳ.

ὅτι. Introduces the clausal complement (indirect discourse) of οἶδα καὶ πέπεισμαι.

οὐδὲν. Nominative subject of verbless clause. It begins the apodosis of the second-class conditional (see εἰ μὴ below).

κοινὸν. Predicate adjective.

δι' ἑαυτοῦ. Instrumental. There is a minor textual variant here, which NA²⁸ mentions (but not UBS⁵ nor THGNT), between αυτου (e.g., A C* D F G L P) and εαυτου (e.g., ℵ B C²). The evidence seems strong for εαυτου, for both external and internal reasons. If αυτου, the pronominal referent would be Jesus, which would not make sense. Alternatively, αυτου can have a rough breathing mark at the beginning (αὑτοῦ), which is a contraction for εαυτου.

εἰ μὴ. A combination of the conditional conjunction and the negative particle (usually translated "except" or "if not") that introduces the protasis of a second-class conditional (the so-called contrary-to-fact conditional; it reflects the writer's belief that this conditional does not reflect reality); see note on εἰ μή in 7:7. In other words, the condition that anything is unclean is depicted by Paul as being contrary to reality (i.e., nothing is unclean of itself).

τῷ λογιζομένῳ. Pres mid ptc masc dat sg λογίζομαι (substantival). Dative of respect (i.e., something is unclean with respect to the one who thinks it is). The fronting of the dative participle reflects clausal prominence.

τι. Accusative subject of εἶναι. The indefinite pronoun refers to "something" that one might think is unclean.

κοινὸν. Predicate accusative. It is joined with τι by the infinitive εἶναι.

εἶναι. Inf εἰμί (indirect discourse). The infinitive expresses the content of λογιζομένῳ.

ἐκείνῳ. Dative of respect. The demonstrative pronoun refers anaphorically to τῷ λογιζομένῳ. The fronted dative, as with τῷ λογιζομένῳ, reflects clausal prominence.

κοινόν. Predicate adjective of an implied ἐστιν.

14:15 εἰ γὰρ διὰ βρῶμα ὁ ἀδελφός σου λυπεῖται, οὐκέτι κατὰ ἀγάπην περιπατεῖς· μὴ τῷ βρώματί σου ἐκεῖνον ἀπόλλυε ὑπὲρ οὗ Χριστὸς ἀπέθανεν.

εἰ. Introduces the protasis of a first-class conditional.

γὰρ. Postpositive explanatory conjunction. It is used to continue the explanation about proper attitudes towards differing views on eating.

διὰ βρῶμα. Instrumental. The fronting of the prepositional word group indicates clausal prominence, consistent with the subject matter of food (and by implication observance of certain days earlier in the chapter). "Food" is a lexical metaphor here, representing the potentially controversial issues that food might bring.

ὁ ἀδελφός. Nominative subject of λυπεῖται.

σου. Possessive genitive, modifying ὁ ἀδελφός.

λυπεῖται. Pres pass ind 3rd sg λυπέω. The passive voice indicates external causality, which is indicated by διὰ βρῶμα. As the grammatical subject of a passive voice verb, ὁ ἀδελφός is the Goal (or recipient) of "grieving."

οὐκέτι. Negative temporal adverb. It modifies περιπατεῖς and begins the apodosis of the first-class conditional.

κατὰ ἀγάπην. Standard. The standard by which they (no longer) walk is "love."

περιπατεῖς. Pres act ind 2nd sg περιπατέω.

μὴ. Negative particle normally used with non-indicative verbs. Here it negates ἀπόλλυε.

τῷ βρώματί. Dative of instrument. The fronting of the dative, especially regarding "food," reflects clausal prominence.

σου. Possessive genitive, modifying τῷ βρώματί. It refers to "your" views on "food."

ἐκεῖνον. Accusative direct object of ἀπόλλυε. The demonstrative pronoun refers anaphorically to ὁ ἀδελφός.

ἀπόλλυε. Pres act impv 2nd sg ἀπόλλυμι. Based on the first-class conditional, Paul follows with a prohibition.

ὑπὲρ οὗ. Substitutionary. οὗ refers anaphorically to ἐκεῖνον, which refers to ὁ ἀδελφός.

Χριστὸς. Nominative subject of ἀπέθανεν.

ἀπέθανεν. Aor act ind 3rd sg ἀποθνήσκω.

14:16 μὴ βλασφημείσθω οὖν ὑμῶν τὸ ἀγαθόν.

μὴ. Negative particle normally used with non-indicative verbs. Here it negates βλασφημείσθω.

βλασφημείσθω. Pres pass impv 3rd sg βλασφημέω. The force of the imperative (or prohibition with μή) is maintained in the third person—but most English translations direct the imperative to a second-person ("do not let"; cf. NIV, NASB, NKJV, NRSV, ESV). However, the prohibition is not directed to the reader but to a third person, "him/her," an anaphoric referent to ὁ ἀδελφός from the previous co-text. The passive voice makes the grammatical subject ("your good thing") the Goal; the agent is not specified here but refers co-textually to other people.

οὖν. Postpositive inferential conjunction, functioning as a summary of the previous command.

ὑμῶν. Possessive genitive, modifying τὸ ἀγαθόν. The fronting of the genitive reflects prominence in the word group.

τὸ ἀγαθόν. Nominative subject of βλασφημείσθω. This lexeme has a broad semantic range, here modulated to refer to what the reader thinks is "good" regarding food issues.

14:17 οὐ γάρ ἐστιν ἡ βασιλεία τοῦ θεοῦ βρῶσις καὶ πόσις ἀλλὰ δικαιοσύνη καὶ εἰρήνη καὶ χαρὰ ἐν πνεύματι ἁγίῳ·

οὐ . . . ἀλλὰ. A point/counterpoint set that establishes the contrast between the the incorrect and correct understandings of the kingdom of God. The negative particle negates ἐστιν.

γάρ. Postpositive explanatory conjunction. It is used in this co-text to explain the broader principle about food.

ἐστιν. Unaugmented ind 3rd sg εἰμί.

ἡ βασιλεία. Nominative subject of ἐστιν.

τοῦ θεοῦ. Possessive genitive, modifying ἡ βασιλεία.

βρῶσις καὶ πόσις. Compound predicate nominatives.

δικαιοσύνη καὶ εἰρήνη καὶ χαρὰ. Compound nominative absolutes. They can also be seen as compound predicate nominatives of an implied ἐστιν, parallel to the previous clause contrasted by ἀλλά.

ἐν πνεύματι ἁγίῳ. Locative (sphere or realm). The prepositional word group can either modify all three substantives or just the final one. Given that all three substantives are anarthrous, it is likely that ἐν πνεύματι ἁγίῳ applies to all three. Righteousness, peace, and joy are in the sphere or realm of the Holy Spirit.

14:18 ὁ γὰρ ἐν τούτῳ δουλεύων τῷ Χριστῷ εὐάρεστος τῷ θεῷ καὶ δόκιμος τοῖς ἀνθρώποις.

ὁ . . . δουλεύων. Pres act ptc masc nom sg δουλεύω (substantival). Nominative subject of verbless clause.

γὰρ. Postpositive inferential conjunction. An inference is drawn from the previous co-text regarding not allowing one's brother or sister be blasphemed (or insulted) due to issues of food and other contentious issues.

ἐν τούτῳ. Manner ("in this way"). The demonstrative pronoun refers anaphorically to what has been stated about the kingdom of God.

τῷ Χριστῷ. Dative direct object of δουλεύων.

εὐάρεστος. Predicate adjective.

τῷ θεῷ. Dative complement of εὐάρεστος.

καὶ. Coordinating conjunction. It connects the two predicate nominatives and their dative modifiers.

δόκιμος. Predicate adjective.

τοῖς ἀνθρώποις. Dative of agency.

14:19 Ἄρα οὖν τὰ τῆς εἰρήνης διώκωμεν καὶ τὰ τῆς οἰκοδομῆς τῆς εἰς ἀλλήλους.

Ἄρα οὖν. A combination of two inferential conjunctions for emphasis (see 14:12). The inference is from the previous co-text regarding what is pleasing to God and acceptable to others.

τὰ τῆς εἰρήνης. The article functions as a nominalizer, changing the genitive to an accusative direct object of διώκωμεν. The accusative is fronted for clausal prominence.

τῆς εἰρήνης. Genitive of quality. The quality of peace (i.e., "peaceful things") is represented by the genitive.

διώκωμεν. Pres act subj 1st pl διώκω. However, despite the NA[28] and UBS[5] having the subjunctive form in their texts, the earliest manuscript evidence seems to favor the indicative reading (διώκομεν: ℵ A B; διώκωμεν: C D; cf. NASB). In this case, the reading should be διώκομεν, not διώκωμεν (see translation above). Paul is not exhorting his readers to pursue but is stating the logical outcome (ἄρα οὖν) of his previous statements regarding Christians showing appropriate respect for one another in spite of differing views of food and other issues.

καὶ. Coordinating conjunction. Connects the compound accusatives.

τὰ τῆς οἰκοδομῆς. The article functions as a nominalizer, changing the genitive to an accusative direct object of διώκωμεν. τὰ τῆς οἰκοδομῆς creates a compound accusative direct object with τὰ τῆς εἰρήνης, with τὰ τῆς εἰρήνης fronted in the clause.

τῆς οἰκοδομῆς. Genitive of quality. The quality of building up or edifying (i.e., "edifying things") is represented by the genitive.

τῆς εἰς ἀλλήλους. The article functions as a nominalizer, changing the prepositional word group εἰς ἀλλήλους to a genitive of description of τῆς οἰκοδομῆς. "Building up" is further described as "of one another." Some may wish to label this as an objective genitive if οἰκοδομῆς is changed to a verb, "to build up one another."

εἰς ἀλλήλους. Purpose. The purpose of building up is for "one another."

14:20 μὴ ἕνεκεν βρώματος κατάλυε τὸ ἔργον τοῦ θεοῦ. πάντα μὲν καθαρά, ἀλλὰ κακὸν τῷ ἀνθρώπῳ τῷ διὰ προσκόμματος ἐσθίοντι.

μὴ. Negative particle normally used with non-indicative verbs. It negates κατάλυε to make it a prohibition.

ἕνεκεν βρώματος. Cause or reason (cf. 8:36). ἕνεκεν is an improper preposition (cf. Porter 1994a, 179). The fronting of the prepositional word group indicates clausal prominence.

κατάλυε. Pres act impv 2nd sg καταλύω. The prefixed verb (κατα-) intensifies the root meaning of λύω ("completely destroy"). Prohibition with μή in the present tense-form does not indicate ceasing an activity that one was already participating in (i.e., "stop completely destroying"), but rather indicates an in-progress cessation of activity (lit. "do not be completely destroying"; see Huffman, 74–75).

τὸ ἔργον. Accusative direct object of κατάλυε.

τοῦ θεοῦ. Possessive genitive, modifying τὸ ἔργον.

πάντα. Nominative subject of verbless clause. πάντα is a substantival adjective.

μὲν . . . ἀλλὰ. A point/counterpoint set that establishes the contrast between the two statements. This is an unusual point/counterpoint set because μέν typically goes with δέ. The use of ἀλλά instead of δέ indicates a strong adversative contrast between the point and counterpoint.

καθαρά. Predicate adjective.

κακὸν. Predicate adjective. It is parallel to καθαρά in sharing the head term πάντα.

τῷ ἀνθρώπῳ. Dative of disadvantage.

τῷ . . . ἐσθίοντι. Pres act ptc masc dat sg ἐσθίω (attributive). The participle modifies τῷ ἀνθρώπῳ in attributive structure (second attributive position).

διὰ προσκόμματος. Instrumental. The prepositional word group modifies τῷ . . . ἐσθίοντι and is embedded between the article and participle. The instrument or cause for stumbling is the person's eating.

14:21 καλὸν τὸ μὴ φαγεῖν κρέα μηδὲ πιεῖν οἶνον μηδὲ ἐν ᾧ ὁ ἀδελφός σου προσκόπτει.

καλὸν. Predicate adjective.

τὸ μὴ φαγεῖν . . . μηδὲ πιεῖν. The article functions as a nominalizer, changing the negated infinitives into a compound nominative subject of verbless clause.

φαγεῖν. Aor act inf ἐσθίω.

πιεῖν. Aor act inf πίνω.

κρέα. Accusative direct object of φαγεῖν.

οἶνον. Accusative direct object of πιεῖν.

μηδὲ. Negative disjunctive particle that negates ἐν ᾧ.

ἐν ᾧ. Instrumental. The dative relative pronoun is headless and serves as the object of the preposition ἐν.

ὁ ἀδελφός. Nominative subject of προσκόπτει.

σου. Possessive genitive, modifying ὁ ἀδελφός.

προσκόπτει. Pres act ind 3rd sg προσκόπτω.

14:22 σὺ πίστιν [ἣν] ἔχεις κατὰ σεαυτὸν ἔχε ἐνώπιον τοῦ θεοῦ. μακάριος ὁ μὴ κρίνων ἑαυτὸν ἐν ᾧ δοκιμάζει·

σύ. Nominative subject of ἔχε. The use of the personal pronoun is emphatic.

πίστιν. Accusative direct object of ἔχε. The fronting of the accusative object in the clause reflects clausal prominence.

[ἣν]. Accusative direct object of ἔχεις. The relative pronoun refers anaphorically to πίστιν. The earliest manuscripts strongly favor including the relative pronoun (with: ℵ A B C; without: D). It may have been omitted by a later scribe due to its potentially awkward syntax in the clause.

ἔχεις. Pres act ind 2nd sg ἔχω. It is the predicate within the relative clause (ἣν ἔχεις).

κατὰ σεαυτόν. Standard. The fronting of the prepositional word group before the predicate that it modifies (ἔχε) reflects clausal prominence.

ἔχε. Pres act impv 2nd sg ἔχω.

ἐνώπιον τοῦ θεοῦ. Locative ("in the presence of God"). ἐνώπιον is an improper preposition (cf. Porter 1994a, 179–80).

μακάριος. Predicate adjective.

ὁ μὴ κρίνων. Pres act ptc masc nom sg κρίνω (substantival). Nominative subject of verbless clause.

ἑαυτόν. Accusative direct object of κρίνων.

ἐν ᾧ. Instrumental. The dative relative pronoun is headless and serves as the object of the preposition ἐν.

δοκιμάζει. Pres act ind 3rd sg δοκιμάζω.

14:23 ὁ δὲ διακρινόμενος ἐὰν φάγῃ κατακέκριται, ὅτι οὐκ ἐκ πίστεως· πᾶν δὲ ὃ οὐκ ἐκ πίστεως ἁμαρτία ἐστίν.

ὁ . . . διακρινόμενος. Pres mid ptc masc nom sg διακρίνω (substantival). Nominative subject of κατακέκριται. The subject of the predicate in the apodosis (ὁ δὲ διακρινόμενος . . . κατακέκριται) is fronted in the conditional structure for emphasis (prominence in the clause complex).

δὲ. Adversative conjunction (mild).

ἐὰν. Introduces the protasis of a third-class conditional. The protasis is embedded in the apodosis to emphasize the apodosis (see ὁ . . . διακρινόμενος above).

φάγῃ. Aor act subj 3rd sg ἐσθίω. Subjunctive with ἐὰν.

κατακέκριται. Prf pass ind 3rd sg κατακρίνω. It continues the apodosis of the third-class conditional. The perfect tense-form (stative aspect) depicts a state or condition of being condemned ("stands condemned").

ὅτι. Introduces a causal clause that explains the reason for which one stands condemned.

οὐκ. Negative particle normally used with indicative verbs. Here it negates ἐκ πίστεως.

ἐκ πίστεως. Instrumental. The instrument (or cause or agent) is "not faith."

πᾶν. Nominative subject of ἐστίν. πᾶν is a substantival adjective.

δὲ. Adversative conjunction (mild).

ὃ. Nominative subject of a verbless clause. The antecedent of the relative pronoun is πᾶν.

οὐκ. Negative particle normally used with indicative verbs. Here it negates ἐκ πίστεως.

ἐκ πίστεως. Instrumental. The instrument (or cause or agent) is "not faith."

ἁμαρτία. Predicate nominative.

ἐστίν. Unaugmented ind 3rd sg εἰμί.

Romans 15:1-6

¹But we who are the capable ought to bear the weaknesses of the incapable and not to please ourselves. ²Each of us must please [our] neighbor for the good toward building up. ³For also Christ did not please himself, but just as it is written, "The reproaches of those who reproach you

fall upon me." ⁴For whatever was written beforehand was written for our very own instruction, so that through patience and through the encouragement from the Scriptures we might have hope. ⁵And may the God of patience and encouragement give you [the ability] to think the same way among one another according to Christ Jesus, ⁶so that in one accord, with one mouth, you may glorify the God and Father of our Lord Jesus Christ.

This paraenetic section continues Paul's exhortations regarding the so-called weak and the strong. Paul, for the first time in this discussion, identifies himself with the strong, or "the capable."

15:1 Ὀφείλομεν δὲ ἡμεῖς οἱ δυνατοὶ τὰ ἀσθενήματα τῶν ἀδυνάτων βαστάζειν καὶ μὴ ἑαυτοῖς ἀρέσκειν.

Ὀφείλομεν. Pres act ind 1st pl ὀφείλω.

δὲ. Adversative conjunction (mild).

ἡμεῖς. Nominative subject of Ὀφείλομεν. The use of the personal pronoun is emphatic.

οἱ δυνατοὶ. Nominative in apposition to ἡμεῖς. The substantival adjective, usually translated "the strong," refers to those who are "capable" of, in this instance, eating freely.

τὰ ἀσθενήματα. Accusative direct object of βαστάζειν.

τῶν ἀδυνάτων. Possessive genitive, modifying οἱ δυνατοὶ. The substantival adjective, which is a genitive negated (so-called alpha privative) form of οἱ δυνατοὶ but usually translated "the weak," refers to those who are "incapable" of, in this instance, eating freely.

βαστάζειν. Pres act inf βαστάζω (complementary). The infinitive is a complement of Ὀφείλομεν.

καὶ. Coordinating conjunction. It connects two infinitival clauses.

μὴ. Negative particle normally used with non-indicative verbs. Here it negates ἀρέσκειν.

ἑαυτοῖς. Dative direct object of ἀρέσκειν.

ἀρέσκειν. Pres act inf ἀρέσκω (complementary). The infinitive is a complement of Ὀφείλομεν.

15:2 ἕκαστος ἡμῶν τῷ πλησίον ἀρεσκέτω εἰς τὸ ἀγαθὸν πρὸς οἰκοδομήν·

ἕκαστος. Nominative subject of ἀρεσκέτω. ἕκαστος is a substantival indefinite adjective.

ἡμῶν. Partitive genitive, modifying ἕκαστος. The first-person plural refers ostensibly to the Roman Christians, including Paul himself.

τῷ πλησίον. Dative complement of ἀρεσκέτω. For the meaning of this lexeme, see note in 13:9.

ἀρεσκέτω. Pres act impv 3rd sg ἀρέσκω.

εἰς τὸ ἀγαθὸν. Purpose. The purpose of pleasing one's neighbor is for "good."

πρὸς οἰκοδομήν. Directional (movement toward). The direction of pleasing one's neighbor is "towards" building up.

15:3 καὶ γὰρ ὁ Χριστὸς οὐχ ἑαυτῷ ἤρεσεν, ἀλλὰ καθὼς γέγραπται· οἱ ὀνειδισμοὶ τῶν ὀνειδιζόντων σε ἐπέπεσαν ἐπ᾽ ἐμέ.

καὶ. Adverbial use (adjunctive). It modifies ὁ Χριστὸς.

γὰρ. Postpositive explanatory conjunction. It continues the discussion about pleasing others, introducing the example of Christ.

ὁ Χριστὸς. Nominative subject of ἤρεσεν.

οὐχ . . . ἀλλὰ. A point/counterpoint set that establishes a contrast between the statement that Christ did not please himself and the introductory scriptural formula that follows. The negative particle negates ἤρεσεν.

ἑαυτῷ. Dative direct object of ἤρεσεν.

ἤρεσεν. Aor act ind 3rd sg ἀρέσκω.

καθὼς γέγραπται. A standard Pauline formula for introducing a scriptural quotation (see note on 1:17). The OT reference, quoted verbatim, is to LXX Ps 68:10b (69:9b in English versions).

καθὼς. Comparative conjunction. It is often used with γέγραπται to compare the immediate statement with a scriptural reference.

γέγραπται. Prf pass ind 3rd sg γράφω.

οἱ ὀνειδισμοὶ. Nominative subject of ἐπέπεσαν.

τῶν ὀνειδιζόντων. Pres act ptc masc gen pl ὀνειδίζω (substantival). Genitive of source or origin, modifying οἱ ὀνειδισμοὶ. The use of a cognate of the head term is emphatic.

σε. Accusative direct object of ὀνειδιζόντων.

ἐπέπεσαν. Aor act ind 3rd pl ἐπιπίπτω. The use of a prefixed form (ἐπι-) of πίπτω, with the preposition ἐπι, emphasizes the meaning of ἐπι.

ἐπ᾽ ἐμέ. Directional (movement upon).

15:4 ὅσα γὰρ προεγράφη, εἰς τὴν ἡμετέραν διδασκαλίαν ἐγράφη, ἵνα διὰ τῆς ὑπομονῆς καὶ διὰ τῆς παρακλήσεως τῶν γραφῶν τὴν ἐλπίδα ἔχωμεν.

ὅσα. The quantitative correlative relative pronoun introduces a headless relative clause (ὅσα γὰρ προεγράφη) that functions, in its entirety, as the subject of ἐγράφη. Within its clause, ὅσα is the nominative subject of προεγράφη.

γὰρ. Postpositive explanatory conjunction. It introduces an explanation of the previous OT reference.

προεγράφη. Aor pass ind 3rd sg προγράφω. The prefix προ- adds to the meaning of the root word: "written beforehand." The passive voice indicates external causation, which is not directly identified in this co-text. Paul simply wants to identify writings (beforehand) without concern for the agent.

εἰς τὴν ἡμετέραν διδασκαλίαν. Purpose. The purpose of what was written beforehand is "for our very own instruction." The possessive adjective ἡμετέραν carries semantic weight (first attributive position).

ἐγράφη. Aor pass ind 3rd sg γράφω. On the use of the passive voice, see προεγράφη above. Rather than use the perfect tense-form that Paul is accustomed to using (γέγραπται; see 15:7), he uses the aorist to depict perfective aspect, viewing the process of writing as a general, complete, and whole process. As such, no specific Scripture is referenced here (cf. Rom 4:23; 1 Cor 9:10; 10:11).

ἵνα. Introduces a purpose clause.

διὰ τῆς ὑπομονῆς. Instrumental.

καὶ. Coordinating conjunction. It connects the two prepositional word groups.

διὰ τῆς παρακλήσεως. Instrumental.

τῶν γραφῶν. Genitive of source of origin, modifying τῆς παρακλήσεως. The source of "encouragement" is "the Scriptures." The genitive only modifies the second prepositional word group.

τὴν ἐλπίδα. Accusative direct object of ἔχωμεν.

ἔχωμεν. Pres act subj 1st pl ἔχω. Subjunctive with ἵνα.

15:5 ὁ δὲ θεὸς τῆς ὑπομονῆς καὶ τῆς παρακλήσεως δῴη ὑμῖν τὸ αὐτὸ φρονεῖν ἐν ἀλλήλοις κατὰ Χριστὸν Ἰησοῦν,

ὁ . . . θεός. Nominative subject of δῴη.

δὲ. Adversative conjunction (mild).

τῆς ὑπομονῆς. Genitive of quality or description, modifying ὁ . . . θεός. "God" has the quality of, or is described in terms of, "patience."

καὶ. Coordinating conjunction. It connects two genitive word groups.

τῆς παρακλήσεως. Genitive of quality or description, modifying ὁ . . . θεός. "God" has the quality of, or is described in terms of, "encouragement."

δῴη. Aor act opt 3rd sg δίδωμι. The optative mood form grammaticalizes the semantic feature of projection with contingency and functions as volitive (commanding or wishing).

ὑμῖν. Dative indirect object of δῴη.

τὸ αὐτὸ. Accusative direct object of φρονεῖν. The intensive pronoun functions as an identifying adjective ("the same").

φρονεῖν. Pres act inf φρονέω. The infinitival clause, τὸ αὐτὸ φρονεῖν ἐν ἀλλήλοις κατὰ Χριστὸν Ἰησοῦν, functions as the direct object of δῴη.

ἐν ἀλλήλοις. Distributional ("among one another").

κατὰ Χριστὸν Ἰησοῦν. Standard. "Christ Jesus" is the standard or basis by which they are to think the same among each other.

15:6 ἵνα ὁμοθυμαδὸν ἐν ἑνὶ στόματι δοξάζητε τὸν θεὸν καὶ πατέρα τοῦ κυρίου ἡμῶν Ἰησοῦ Χριστοῦ.

ἵνα. Introduces a purpose clause. The purpose of thinking the same way among each other is introduced.

ὁμοθυμαδὸν. Adverb (manner). It modifies δοξάζητε. This is the only occurrence of this word in Paul. The fronted adverb is prominent in the clause.

ἐν ἑνὶ στόματι. Instrumental. The instrument or means by which they were to glorify God is "with one mouth." The fronted prepositional word group is prominent in the clause (as second fronted element).

δοξάζητε. Pres act subj 2nd pl δοξάζω. Subjunctive with ἵνα.

τὸν θεὸν καὶ πατέρα. Accusative direct object of δοξάζητε. Granville Sharp's rule applies here. When a single article governs two or more substantives connected by καί, the substantives have the same referent.

τοῦ κυρίου. Genitive of source or origin, modifying πατέρα.

ἡμῶν. Possessive genitive, modifying τοῦ κυρίου.

Ἰησοῦ Χριστοῦ. Genitive in apposition to τοῦ κυρίου ἡμῶν.

Romans 15:7–13

[7]Therefore, welcome one another, just as Christ also welcomed you for the glory of God. [8]For I say, Christ was made to become a servant of circumcision on behalf of the truth of God, in order to confirm the promises of the fathers, [9]and in order that the Gentiles might glorify God for mercy, just as it is written, "Because of this, I will strongly confess to you among the Gentiles and to your name I will sing." [10]Likewise, it says, "Rejoice, Gentiles, with his people." [11]Likewise, "Praise the Lord, all the Gentiles, and all the people should pile on praise to him." [12]Likewise, Isaiah says, "It will be the root of Jesse and the one who arises to rule the Gentiles; in him Gentiles will hope." [13]Now may the God of hope fulfill you of all joy and peace while believing, in order that you abound in hope in the power of the Holy Spirit.

This is the final section of Paul's discourse on the so-called weak and the strong. He concludes this subject by appealing to several Scriptures and pronouncing a blessing upon his readers.

15:7 Διὸ προσλαμβάνεσθε ἀλλήλους, καθὼς καὶ ὁ Χριστὸς προσελάβετο ὑμᾶς εἰς δόξαν τοῦ θεοῦ.

Διὸ. Inferential conjunction. It introduces an inference from the previous sub-section regarding pleasing and living in harmony with each other.

προσλαμβάνεσθε. Pres mid impv 2nd pl προσλαμβάνω. See note on this lexeme in 14:1.

ἀλλήλους. Accusative direct object of προσλαμβάνεσθε.

καθὼς. Comparative conjunction. It is used to draw comparison to Christ.

καὶ. Adverbial use (adjunctive). It modifies προσελάβετο.

ὁ Χριστὸς. Nominative subject of προσελάβετο.

προσελάβετο. Aor mid ind 3rd sg προσλαμβάνω.

ὑμᾶς. Accusative direct object of προσελάβετο. There is a textual variant here; the early manuscript evidence is divided (υμας: ℵ A C D¹; ημας: B D*). Metzger (473) gives it an A rating due to superior and more diversified support for and use of ὑμᾶς in the co-text.

εἰς δόξαν. Purpose.

τοῦ θεοῦ. Possessive genitive, modifying δόξαν.

15:8 λέγω γὰρ Χριστὸν διάκονον γεγενῆσθαι περιτομῆς ὑπὲρ ἀληθείας θεοῦ, εἰς τὸ βεβαιῶσαι τὰς ἐπαγγελίας τῶν πατέρων,

λέγω. Pres act ind 1st sg λέγω.

γὰρ. Postpositive explanatory conjunction. It is used to further explain how Christ received them.

Χριστὸν. Accusative subject of γεγενῆσθαι.

διάκονον. Predicate accusative.

γεγενῆσθαι. Prf pass inf γίνομαι (indirect discourse). The infinitive expresses the content λέγω. The passive voice indicates external agency or causality, which is not specified in this co-text. The perfect tense-form (stative aspect) reflects a state or condition of becoming. Together, the stative aspect and passive voice results in a translation such as "Christ was made to become a servant" (woodenly).

περιτομῆς. Possessive genitive, modifying διάκονον. "Servant" is depicted as belonging to "the circumcision." Some may label this as an objective genitive, if διάκονον is changed into a verb, "to serve." περιτομῆς is a personification for those who are circumcised.

ὑπὲρ ἀληθείας. Beneficial. Christ became a servant of circumcision for the benefit of the truth of God; in other words, to confirm God's truth.

θεοῦ. Genitive of source or origin, modifying ἀληθείας.

βεβαιῶσαι. Aor act inf βεβαιόω. Used with εἰς τό to denote purpose. The purpose of Christ becoming a servant is stated with the infinitive and following complements.

τὰς ἐπαγγελίας. Accusative direct object of βεβαιῶσαι.

τῶν πατέρων. Possessive genitive, modifying τὰς ἐπαγγελίας.

15:9 τὰ δὲ ἔθνη ὑπὲρ ἐλέους δοξάσαι τὸν θεόν, καθὼς γέγραπται· διὰ τοῦτο ἐξομολογήσομαί σοι ἐν ἔθνεσιν καὶ τῷ ὀνόματί σου ψαλῶ.

τὰ . . . ἔθνη. Accusative subject of δοξάσαι.

δὲ. Adversative conjunction (mild). It connects the previous infinitival clause with the following infinitival clause.

ὑπὲρ ἐλέους. Beneficial. Parallel to ὑπὲρ ἀληθείας in 15:8, it reflects that Christ became a servant of circumcision for the benefit of "mercy." In other words, "the inclusion of the Gentiles was especially glorifying to God because it benefited his mercy by showing its extent" (Porter 2015, 273).

δοξάσαι. Aor act inf δοξάζω (purpose). It is parallel to βεβαιῶσαι in 15:8 (but without εἰς τό).

τὸν θεόν. Accusative direct object of δοξάσαι.

καθὼς γέγραπται. A standard Pauline formula for introducing a scriptural quotation (see note on 1:17). The quotation is from LXX Ps 17:50 (cf. LXX 2 Sam 22:50, which essentially has the same wording).

καθὼς. Comparative conjunction, often used in conjunction with γέγραπται to invoke a scriptural reference as a comparison to what has been stated.

γέγραπται. Prf pass ind 3rd sg γράφω.

διὰ τοῦτο. Causal. The demonstrative pronoun—which begins the Psalm quotation, so the referent is different in that co-text—may be used by Paul in this co-text to refer anaphorically to the previous statement about Gentiles glorifying God.

ἐξομολογήσομαί. Fut mid ind 1st sg ἐξομολογέω. The prefix ἐκ/ἐξ intensifies the root ὁμολογέω; i.e., "to confess strongly" (cf. 14:11).

σοι. Dative indirect object of ἐξομολογήσομαί.

ἐν ἔθνεσιν. Distributional ("among the Gentiles").

καὶ. Coordinating conjunction. It connects the two clauses before and after it. A micro-chiasm (predicate-adjunct/adjunct-predicate) connected by καί emphasizes the middle elements, the adjuncts ("to you" and "to your name").

τῷ ὀνόματί. Dative indirect object of ψαλῶ.
σου. Possessive genitive, modifying τῷ ὀνόματί.
ψαλῶ. Fut act ind 1st sg ψάλλω.

15:10 καὶ πάλιν λέγει· εὐφράνθητε, ἔθνη, μετὰ τοῦ λαοῦ αὐτοῦ.

καὶ πάλιν. Lit. "and again," or more idiomatically, "likewise." This is a common formula to add an additional scriptural reference to a previous reference (cf. Brookins and Longenecker, 89).
λέγει. Pres act ind 3rd sg λέγω. It is used to cite Scripture more explicitly. Here, a portion of LXX Deut 32:43 is quoted verbatim.
εὐφράνθητε. Aor pass impv 2nd pl εὐφραίνω. The passive voice of εὐφραίνω means "to be made glad," which is translated in English as "to rejoice."
ἔθνη. Nominative of address (so-called vocative).
μετὰ τοῦ λαοῦ. Accompaniment. Some may argue that λαός refers to God's people and ἔθνος to other nations, but this interpretation across the board is an instance of illegitimate identity transfer (see, e.g., LXX Gen 12:2; Matt 4:16; Mark 7:6; 1 Pet 2:9; cf. Rom 10:19; Barr 1961, 234–35; Yoon 2021, 283). In this co-text, however, it seems that this distinction between λαός and ἔθνος is modulated through the use of μετὰ τοῦ λαοῦ αὐτοῦ in distinction to ἔθνη.
αὐτοῦ. Possessive genitive, modifying τοῦ λαοῦ.

15:11 καὶ πάλιν· αἰνεῖτε, πάντα τὰ ἔθνη, τὸν κύριον καὶ ἐπαινεσάτω-σαν αὐτὸν πάντες οἱ λαοί.

καὶ πάλιν. Lit. "and again," or more idiomatically, "likewise" (see 15:10). The scriptural reference is to LXX Ps 116:1 (117:1 in English versions).
αἰνεῖτε. Pres act impv 2nd pl αἰνέω.
πάντα τὰ ἔθνη. Nominative of address (so-called vocative).
τὸν κύριον. Accusative direct object of αἰνεῖτε.
καὶ. Coordinating conjunction. It connects the two clauses before and after it.
ἐπαινεσάτωσαν. Aor act impv 3rd pl ἐπαινέω. The prefixed form (with ἐπι-) of αἰνεῖτε from the previous clause is intensive (i.e., "they should pile on praise").
αὐτὸν. Accusative direct object of ἐπαινεσάτωσαν. The personal pronoun refers anaphorically to τὸν κύριον.
πάντες οἱ λαοί. Nominative subject of ἐπαινεσάτωσαν (see 15:10 on μετὰ τοῦ λαοῦ).

15:12 καὶ πάλιν Ἠσαΐας λέγει· ἔσται ἡ ῥίζα τοῦ Ἰεσσαὶ καὶ ὁ ἀνιστάμενος ἄρχειν ἐθνῶν, ἐπ᾽ αὐτῷ ἔθνη ἐλπιοῦσιν.

καὶ πάλιν. Lit. "and again," or more idiomatically, "likewise" (see 15:10, 11). It introduces the third and final scriptural reference in this series (15:10–12).

Ἠσαΐας. Nominative subject of λέγει.

λέγει. Pres act ind 3rd sg. The final scriptural reference comes from a portion of LXX Isa 11:10.

ἔσται. Fut 3rd sg εἰμί.

ἡ ῥίζα. Nominative subject of ἔσται.

τοῦ Ἰεσσαὶ. Genitive of source or origin, modifying ἡ ῥίζα.

καὶ. Coordinating conjunction. It connects the two compound nominative subjects. These are probably two descriptions of the same person connected by καί, although it is also possible that these are two different figures, given the different genders (Porter 2015, 274). However, the singular verb (ἔσται) and the singular pronominal referent (ἐπ᾽ αὐτῷ) may be a clue that these are one and the same.

ὁ ἀνιστάμενος. Pres mid ptc masc nom sg ἀνίστημι (substantival). Nominative subject of ἔσται.

ἄρχειν. Pres act inf ἄρχω (purpose). The purpose of ἀνιστάμενος is "to rule." ἄρχειν also modifies ἀνιστάμενος. This is the only occurrence of this lexeme in Romans (cf. 2 Cor 3:1; 1 Pet 4:17; and throughout the Gospels and Acts, usually in middle voice-form).

ἐθνῶν. Genitive direct object of ἄρχειν (cf. Mark 10:42 for use of the genitive object for ἄρχω).

ἐπ᾽ αὐτῷ. Locative (sphere or realm). Gentiles hope in the sphere of realm of "him." The personal pronoun refers to the compound subject (ἡ ῥίζα τοῦ Ἰεσσαὶ καὶ ὁ ἀνιστάμενος ἄρχειν ἐθνῶν). The fronting of the prepositional word group reflets clausal prominence.

ἔθνη. Nominative subject of ἐλπιοῦσιν.

ἐλπιοῦσιν. Fut act ind 3rd pl ἐλπίζω.

15:13 Ὁ δὲ θεὸς τῆς ἐλπίδος πληρώσαι ὑμᾶς πάσης χαρᾶς καὶ εἰρήνης ἐν τῷ πιστεύειν, εἰς τὸ περισσεύειν ὑμᾶς ἐν τῇ ἐλπίδι ἐν δυνάμει πνεύματος ἁγίου.

Ὁ ... θεὸς. Nominative subject of πληρώσαι.

δὲ. Adversative conjunction (mild).

τῆς ἐλπίδος. Genitive of quality or description, modifying Ὁ ... θεὸς. "God" is further described by "hope." Repetition of "hope" (cognate of ἐλπίζω) from the previous verse reflects lexical cohesion.

πληρῶσαι. Aor act opt 3rd sg πληρόω. The optative mood form grammaticalizes the semantic feature of projection with contingency and functions as volitive (commanding or wishing; cf. 15:5).

ὑμᾶς. Accusative direct object of πληρῶσαι.

πάσης χαρᾶς. Genitive of quality, modifying ὑμᾶς. The quality or characteristic of ὑμᾶς (who is fulfilled) is "of all joy" or all-joyful. While most English translations have "with all joy" (cf. NIV; NASB; NKJV; NRSV; ESV), the genitive is used here to reflect the characteristic or attribute of the one who is fulfilled.

καὶ. Coordinating conjunction. It connects the two genitives of πληρῶσαι.

εἰρήνης. Genitive of quality, modifying ὑμᾶς. It is parallel to πάσης χαρᾶς (see entry above).

πιστεύειν. Pres act inf πιστεύω. Used with ἐν τῷ to denote contemporaneous time.

περισσεύειν. Pres act inf περισσεύω. Used with εἰς τό to denote purpose.

ὑμᾶς. Accusative subject of περισσεύειν.

ἐν τῇ ἐλπίδι. Locative (sphere or realm).

ἐν δυνάμει. Instrumental.

πνεύματος ἁγίου. Genitive of source or origin, modifying δυνάμει.

Romans 15:14–21

[14]But I myself indeed stand persuaded, my brothers [and sisters], concerning you, that also you yourselves are full of goodness, being full of all knowledge, being able also to instruct each other. [15]But more daringly I write to you in part so as to remind you through the grace which was given to me by God [16]for me to be a servant of Christ Jesus to the Gentiles, serving as priest the gospel of God, in order that the offering of the Gentiles might become acceptable, having been sanctified by the Holy Spirit. [17]Therefore, I have [grounds for] boasting in Christ Jesus, with respect to the things that are directed towards God. [18]For I will not dare to speak about any of the things which Christ did not accomplish through me in the obedience of the Gentiles, in word and in deed, [19]in the power of signs and wonders, in the power of the Spirit of God. Thus, from Jerusalem and in a circle as far as Illyricum, I have fulfilled the gospel of Christ, [20]and in the same way, being ambitious to preach the gospel not where Christ has been named, in order that I might not build upon another foundation. [21]But just as it is written, "Those to whom it is not announced concerning him will see, and those who do not hear will understand."

This section, and the next, complete the paraenetic section of the letter, or more accurately serves as a transition between the paraenesis and the closing of the letter, as it does not contain exhortative material as in the previous sections. In this section, Paul outlines the nature of his ministry and the reasons why he writes to the Romans.

15:14 Πέπεισμαι δέ, ἀδελφοί μου, καὶ αὐτὸς ἐγὼ περὶ ὑμῶν ὅτι καὶ αὐτοὶ μεστοί ἐστε ἀγαθωσύνης, πεπληρωμένοι πάσης [τῆς] γνώσεως, δυνάμενοι καὶ ἀλλήλους νουθετεῖν.

Πέπεισμαι. Prf pass ind 1st sg πείθω. The perfect tense-form (stative aspect) reflects Paul's state or condition of being persuaded. The passive voice reflects external causality or agency, which is not specified in this co-text.

δέ. Adversative conjunction (mild). This and the next sub-section is a sort of an aside from Paul's paraenesis section.

ἀδελφοί. Nominative of address (so-called vocative).

μου. Possessive genitive, modifying ἀδελφοί. The addition of this personal pronoun emphasizes his interpersonal connection to his "brothers [and sisters]."

καὶ. Adverbial use (ascensive). It modifies αὐτὸς ἐγὼ.

αὐτὸς ἐγὼ. Nominative subject of Πέπεισμαι. The intensive pronoun, along with the personal pronoun, are both emphatic.

περὶ ὑμῶν. Reference.

ὅτι. Introduces the clausal complement (indirect discourse) of Πέπεισμαι.

καὶ. Adverbial use (adjunctive). It modifies αὐτοὶ.

αὐτοὶ. Nominative subject of ἐστε. The intensive pronoun modifies the implied second-person plural subject of ἐστε ("you yourselves").

μεστοί. Predicate adjective.

ἐστε. Unaugmented ind 2nd pl εἰμί.

ἀγαθωσύνης. Genitive of description, modifying μεστοί. "Full" is further described or circumscribed as "of goodness." Some may wish to label this as an objective genitive, if μεστοί is changed into a verb, "to fill."

πεπληρωμένοι. Prf pass ptc masc nom pl πληρόω (manner). The participle functions as circumstantial and modifies μεστοί ἐστε ἀγαθωσύνης.

πάσης [τῆς] γνώσεως. Genitive of quality. It further qualifies "being filled" as "of all knowledge." The article is a minor textual variant, with the early manuscripts slightly in favor of omitting the article (with: ℵ B; without: 𝔓⁴⁶ A C D). Co-textually, the anarthrous genitive noun makes better sense, referring to the quality of knowledge rather than a particular or categorical reference to it.

δυνάμενοι. Pres mid ptc masc nom pl δύναμαι (manner). The participle functions as circumstantial and modifies μεστοί ἐστε ἀγαθωσύνης along with πεπληρωμένοι.

καὶ. Adverbial use (adjunctive). It modifies δυνάμενοι.

ἀλλήλους. Accusative direct object of νουθετεῖν.

νουθετεῖν. Pres act inf νουθετέω (complement). Complements δυνάμενοι.

15:15 τολμηρότερον δὲ ἔγραψα ὑμῖν ἀπὸ μέρους ὡς ἐπαναμιμνῄσκων ὑμᾶς διὰ τὴν χάριν τὴν δοθεῖσάν μοι ὑπὸ τοῦ θεοῦ

τολμηρότερον. Adverb. τολμηρότερον is a comparative of τολμη-ρῶς. A NT *hapax legomenon*.

δὲ. Adversative conjunction (mild).

ἔγραψα. Aor act ind 1st sg γράφω.

ὑμῖν. Dative indirect object of ἔγραψα.

ἀπὸ μέρους. Locative (movement away from). Paul writes from (out of) a part. The idiom can be translated as "in part" or "partial" (cf. 11:25).

ὡς. Comparative conjunction used here to indicate purpose ("so as to . . .").

ἐπαναμιμνῄσκων. Pres act ptc masc nom sg ἐπαναμιμνῄσκω (purpose). The doubly prefixed verb (ἐπ + ἀνα + μιμνήσκω/-ομαι) retains each of the prefix's meanings and results in an emphatic verb of remembering.

ὑμᾶς. Accusative direct object of ἐπαναμιμνῄσκων.

διὰ τὴν χάριν. Causal. The cause for the reminder is "the grace."

τὴν δοθεῖσάν. Aor pass ptc fem acc sg δίδωμι (attributive). The participle modifies τὴν χάριν in attributive structure (second attributive position). Passive voice indicates external agency, identified as God by the prepositional word group ὑπὸ τοῦ θεοῦ. δοθεῖσάν, which has a circumflex accent on the penult, acquired an additional accent, the acute, on the ultima from the enclitic μοι.

μοι. Dative indirect object of δοθεῖσάν.

ὑπὸ τοῦ θεοῦ. Instrumental (agency).

15:16 εἰς τὸ εἶναί με λειτουργὸν Χριστοῦ Ἰησοῦ εἰς τὰ ἔθνη, ἱερουργοῦντα τὸ εὐαγγέλιον τοῦ θεοῦ, ἵνα γένηται ἡ προσφορὰ τῶν ἐθνῶν εὐπρόσδεκτος, ἡγιασμένη ἐν πνεύματι ἁγίῳ.

εἶναί. Inf εἰμί. Used with εἰς τό to denote purpose. εἶναί, which has a circumflex accent on the penult, acquired an additional accent, the acute, on the ultima from the enclitic με.

με. Accusative subject of εἶναί.

λειτουργὸν. Predicate accusative. The lexeme λειτουργός refers to a liturgist, a participant of cultic practice, or a public servant, who were compensated for their service (cf. 13:6).

Χριστοῦ Ἰησοῦ. Possessive genitive, modifying λειτουργὸν.

εἰς τὰ ἔθνη. Goal. The goal of Paul being a servant is "for the Gentiles."

ἱερουργοῦντα. Pres act ptc masc acc sg ἱερουργέω (manner). The participle functions as circumstantial and modifies εἶναί.

τὸ εὐαγγέλιον. Accusative direct object of ἱερουργοῦντα.

τοῦ θεοῦ. Genitive of definition or description, modifying τὸ εὐαγγέλιον. The "gospel" is further defined as or circumscribed to "God."

ἵνα. Introduces a purpose clause.

γένηται. Aor mid subj 3rd sg γίνομαι. Subjunctive with ἵνα.

ἡ προσφορὰ. Nominative subject of γένηται.

τῶν ἐθνῶν. Genitive of definition or description, modifying ἡ προσφορά. "Offering" is further described or circumscribed as "of the Gentiles." Some may wish to label this an objective genitive, if προσφορὰ were to become a verb, "to offer" (cf. NIV: "the Gentiles might become an offering").

εὐπρόσδεκτος. Predicate adjective.

ἡγιασμένη. Prf pass ptc fem nom sg ἁγιάζω (manner). It functions to indicate how the Gentiles become acceptable to God and modifies εὐπρόσδεκτος in an adverbial structure. The perfect tense-form (stative aspect) reflects a state or condition of being sanctified. The passive voice reflects external agency, here identified as the Holy Spirit. Only occurrence of this lexeme in Romans.

ἐν πνεύματι ἁγίῳ. Instrumental. The instrument or means by which they are in a state of being sanctified is the Holy Spirit.

15:17 ἔχω οὖν [τὴν] καύχησιν ἐν Χριστῷ Ἰησοῦ τὰ πρὸς τὸν θεόν·

ἔχω. Pres act ind 1st sg ἔχω.

οὖν. Postpositive inferential conjunction, introducing an inference from the previous statement regarding Paul's service to Christ for the Gentiles.

[τὴν] καύχησιν. Accusative direct object of ἔχω. The article is a textual variant, with three readings in the earliest manuscripts: εχω ουν (א A), ην εχω (𝔓⁴⁶), and εχω ουν την (B C D). The witnesses are divided (Metzger does not comment on this variant), but it appears that support for ἔχω οὖν without the article is preferred, based on the fact that "boasting" is probably depicted as qualitative and not particular.

ἐν Χριστῷ Ἰησοῦ. Locative (sphere or realm). Paul's boasting is "in" the sphere of Christ Jesus.

τὰ πρὸς τὸν θεόν. The article functions as a nominalizer, changing the prepositional word group into an accusative of respect (cf. Heb 2:17 and 5:1 for a similar construction).

πρὸς τὸν θεόν. Directional (movement toward).

15:18 οὐ γὰρ τολμήσω τι λαλεῖν ὧν οὐ κατειργάσατο Χριστὸς δι' ἐμοῦ εἰς ὑπακοὴν ἐθνῶν, λόγῳ καὶ ἔργῳ,

οὐ. Negative particle normally used with indicative verbs. Here it negates τολμήσω.

γὰρ. Postpositive explanatory conjunction. It is used to further explain Paul's boasting.

τολμήσω. Fut act ind 1st sg τολμάω. The future form reflects the semantics of expectation; Paul does not expect to dare to speak.

τι. Accusative direct object of λαλεῖν. The fronting of the accusative object before its predicate indicates clausal prominence.

λαλεῖν. Pres act inf λαλέω (complementary). The infinitive is a complement of τολμήσω.

ὧν. Partitive genitive, modifying τι ("any of the things which"). The headless relative pronoun introduces the relative clause (ὧν οὐ κατειργάσατο Χριστὸς δι' ἐμοῦ εἰς ὑπακοὴν ἐθνῶν).

οὐ. Negative particle normally used with indicative verbs. Here it negates κατειργάσατο. Most English translations (e.g., NIV, NASB, NRSV, ESV; cf. NKJV) translate this clause as "except what Christ has accomplished," turning this into a positive statement, but this does not account for the double negatives in this and the head clause. Paul is stating that he will not dare to speak of any of the things that Christ has not done through him; in order words, he will only speak of the things that Christ has done through him. The double negative statement is a litotes as an understatement or a mitigated statement.

κατειργάσατο. Aor mid ind 3rd sg κατεργάζομαι.

Χριστὸς. Nominative subject of κατειργάσατο.

δι' ἐμοῦ. Instrumental.

εἰς ὑπακοὴν. Purpose.

ἐθνῶν. Genitive of source or origin, modifying ὑπακοὴν ("obedience that comes from Gentiles").

λόγῳ. Dative of sphere. The sphere of the Gentiles' obedience is "in word."

καὶ. Coordinating conjunction. It connects the two dative substantives.

ἔργῳ. Dative of sphere. The sphere of the Gentiles' obedience is "in deed."

15:19 ἐν δυνάμει σημείων καὶ τεράτων, ἐν δυνάμει πνεύματος [θεοῦ]· ὥστε με ἀπὸ Ἰερουσαλὴμ καὶ κύκλῳ μέχρι τοῦ Ἰλλυρικοῦ πεπληρωκέναι τὸ εὐαγγέλιον τοῦ Χριστοῦ,

ἐν δυνάμει. Instrumental.

σημείων καὶ τεράτων. Genitives of description or definition, modifying δυνάμει. They further describe or circumscribe "power" as "of signs and wonders."

ἐν δυνάμει. Instrumental.

πνεύματος. Genitive of description or definition, modifying δυνάμει. It further describes or circumscribes "power" as "of the Spirit." Alternatively, it can be considered a genitive of source or origin ("power that comes from the Spirit").

[θεοῦ]. Genitive of description or definition, modifying πνεύματος. "Spirit" is further described or circumscribed as "of God." The earliest manuscripts are divided on this textual variant (omitted: B; with θεου: 𝔓⁴⁶ ℵ D¹; with αγιου A D*·²), with slightly stronger attestation for the θεοῦ reading.

ὥστε. Introduces a result clause. As a result of what Christ has accomplished through Paul by the various means listed, Paul states the following.

με. Accusative subject of the infinitive πεπληρωκέναι.

ἀπὸ Ἰερουσαλὴμ. Locative.

καὶ. Coordinating conjunction. It connects the two prepositional word groups.

κύκλῳ. Adverb (spatial), modifying the prepositional word group μέχρι τοῦ Ἰλλυρικοῦ. It refers to "a position completely encircling an area or object—around, in a circle" (LN 83.19).

μέχρι τοῦ Ἰλλυρικοῦ. Extent ("until Illyricum"). μέχρι is an improper preposition (cf. Porter 1994a, 179).

πεπληρωκέναι. Prf act inf πληρόω. Used with ὥστε to indicate result.

τὸ εὐαγγέλιον. Accusative direct object of πεπληρωκέναι.

τοῦ Χριστοῦ. Possessive genitive, modifying τὸ εὐαγγέλιον.

15:20 οὕτως δὲ φιλοτιμούμενον εὐαγγελίζεσθαι οὐχ ὅπου ὠνομάσθη Χριστός, ἵνα μὴ ἐπ᾽ ἀλλότριον θεμέλιον οἰκοδομῶ,

οὕτως. Adverb (manner). It modifies φιλοτιμούμενον.

δὲ. Adversative conjunction (mild).

φιλοτιμούμενον. Pres mid ptc masc acc sg φιλοτιμέομαι (means). The participle functions as circumstantial and modifies πεπληρωκέναι in 15:19.

εὐαγγελίζεσθαι. Pres mid inf εὐαγγελίζω (complementary). The infinitive is a complement of φιλοτιμούμενον. The middle voice reflects indirect, internal causality.

οὐχ. Negative particle that negates ὅπου.

ὅπου. Particle marking a position in place ("where"; BDAG 717.1).

ὠνομάσθη. Aor pass ind 3rd sg ὀνομάζω.

Χριστός. Nominative subject of ὠνομάσθη.

ἵνα. Introduces a purpose clause. The purpose of Paul's ambition to preach where Christ has not been named follows.

μὴ. Negative particle normally used with non-indicative verbs. Here it negates οἰκοδομῶ.

ἐπ᾽ ἀλλότριον θεμέλιον. Directional (movement upon). The fronting of the prepositional word group before the predicate indicates clausal prominence.

οἰκοδομῶ. Pres act subj 1st sg οἰκοδομέω. Subjunctive with ἵνα.

15:21 ἀλλὰ καθὼς γέγραπται· οἷς οὐκ ἀνηγγέλη περὶ αὐτοῦ ὄψονται, καὶ οἳ οὐκ ἀκηκόασιν συνήσουσιν.

ἀλλὰ. Adversative conjunction (strong). A strong contrast is made between (not) building upon another foundation and what is written in Scripture.

καθὼς γέγραπται. A standard Pauline formula for introducing a scriptural quotation (see note on 1:17).

καθὼς. Comparative conjunction. It is often used with γέγραπται to compare the immediate statement with a Scripture reference.

γέγραπται. Prf pass ind 3rd sg γράφω. Paul's usual marker of a Scripture reference, here from LXX Isa 52:15b, quoted verbatim.

οἷς. The relative pronoun introduces a headless relative clause (οἷς οὐκ ἀνηγγέλη περὶ αὐτοῦ) which functions as the subject of ὄψονται. Within its clause, οἷς is the dative indirect object of ἀνηγγέλη.

οὐκ. Negative particle normally used with indicative verbs. Here it negates ἀνηγγέλη.

ἀνηγγέλη. Aor pass ind 3rd sg ἀναγγέλλω. The passive voice indicates external agency, which is not specified in this co-text; however, to these who have not been given the announcement, Paul wishes to go (cf. 15:20).

περὶ αὐτοῦ. Reference. The personal pronoun has no direct referent in the immediate co-text but refers to Christ (cf. 15:18–20).

ὄψονται. Fut mid ind 3rd pl ὁράω. The middle voice reflects indirect, internal causality.

καὶ. Coordinating conjunction. It connects the two clause complexes before and after it.

οἵ. The relative pronoun introduces a headless relative clause (οἳ οὐκ ἀκηκόασιν) which functions as the subject of συνήσουσιν. Within its clause, οἳ is the nominative subject of ἀκηκόασιν.

οὐκ. Negative particle normally used with indicative verbs. Negates ἀκηκόασιν.

ἀκηκόασιν. Prf act ind 3rd pl ἀκούω. The perfect tense-form (stative aspect) reflects those who are in a state or condition of not hearing.

συνήσουσιν. Fut act ind 3rd pl συνίημι.

Romans 15:22–33

²²Therefore, also I was hindered many times from coming to you, ²³and now, no longer having a place in these regions, but having the desire to come to you for many years, ²⁴as I might proceed to Spain. For I hope, while passing through, to see you and to be sent on ahead by you there, if first I might be enjoyed by you for a little while. ²⁵But now I proceed to Jerusalem, serving the saints. ²⁶For Macedonia and Achaia were pleased to make a certain contribution to the poor among the saints who are in Jerusalem. ²⁷For they were pleased and are their debtors. For if the Gentiles shared in their spiritual things, they ought also to serve them in the material things. ²⁸Therefore, after completing this and sealing this fruit to you, I will leave to Spain through you. ²⁹But I know that when I come to you, I will come in the fullness of the blessing of Christ. ³⁰But I urge you, brothers [and sisters], through our Lord Jesus Christ and through the love of the Spirit, to struggle together with me in the prayers for me to God, ³¹that I may be rescued from those who disbelieve in Judea, and that my service which is in Jerusalem may be pleasing to the saints, ³²so that, when I come in joy to you through the will of God, I might have complete restful refreshment with you. ³³The God of peace [be] with all of you. Amen.

This section, like the previous one, serves as a transition between the paraenesis and the closing of the letter. While the previous section outlines the nature of Paul's ministry, this section outlines Paul's desire and plans for travel, including his desire to come to Rome on his way to Spain.

15:22 Διὸ καὶ ἐνεκοπτόμην τὰ πολλὰ τοῦ ἐλθεῖν πρὸς ὑμᾶς·

Διὸ. Inferential conjunction. It introduces an inference from the previous sub-section regarding Paul's mission.

καὶ. Adverbial use (adjunctive). It modifies ἐνεκοπτόμην.

ἐνεκοπτόμην. Impf pass ind 1st sg ἐγκόπτω. The imperfect tense form (imperfective aspect) is used to depict Paul being "hindered" as a process in development but depicting the process remotely, used here in a past tense context (although the tense form itself does not grammaticalize tense, the context modulates it). The passive voice reflects external agency, not specified in this co-text.

τὰ πολλά. Adverbial accusative of time (cf. Robertson, 470).

τοῦ ἐλθεῖν. Aor act inf ἔρχομαι (substantival). The genitive article is a nominalizer, changing the infinitive into a genitive of description (how Paul was hindered is further described as "from coming").

πρὸς ὑμᾶς. Directional (movement toward).

15:23 νυνὶ δὲ μηκέτι τόπον ἔχων ἐν τοῖς κλίμασι τούτοις, ἐπιποθίαν δὲ ἔχων τοῦ ἐλθεῖν πρὸς ὑμᾶς ἀπὸ πολλῶν ἐτῶν,

νυνὶ. Adverb (temporal). It modifies ἔχων.

δὲ. Adversative conjunction (mild).

μηκέτι. Adverb (extent of time). It modifies ἔχων.

τόπον. Accusative direct object of ἔχων.

ἔχων. Pres act ptc masc nom sg ἔχω (causal). The participle functions as circumstantial, modifying ἐνεκοπτόμην in 15:22. This verse consists of two circumstantial participial clauses (both with ἔχων) that are subordinate to the main clause in 15:22.

ἐν τοῖς κλίμασι τούτοις. Locative.

ἐπιποθίαν. Accusative direct object of ἔχων (second occurrence).

δὲ. Adversative conjunction (mild).

ἔχων. Pres act ptc masc nom sg ἔχω (causal). The participle functions as circumstantial (along with the first occurrence of ἔχων), modifying ἐνεκοπτόμην in 15:22.

τοῦ ἐλθεῖν. Aor act inf ἔρχομαι (epexegetical to ἐπιποθίαν). The infinitive explains what Paul's desire is ("to come to you").

πρὸς ὑμᾶς. Directional (movement toward).

ἀπὸ πολλῶν ἐτῶν. Temporal.

15:24 ὡς ἂν πορεύωμαι εἰς τὴν Σπανίαν· ἐλπίζω γὰρ διαπορευόμενος θεάσασθαι ὑμᾶς καὶ ὑφ' ὑμῶν προπεμφθῆναι ἐκεῖ ἐὰν ὑμῶν πρῶτον ἀπὸ μέρους ἐμπλησθῶ.

ὡς. Temporal conjunction ("as" or "while").

ἂν. Conditional particle (usually left untranslated). While not directly in a conditional structure, it adds conditionality to Paul's statement of proceeding to Spain.

πορεύωμαι. Pres mid subj 1st sg πορεύομαι. Subjunctive in an indefinite temporal clause. Subjunctive mood adds to the tentativeness or projection of this statement.

εἰς τὴν Σπανίαν. Directional (movement toward or into).

ἐλπίζω. Pres act ind 1st sg ἐλπίζω. It introduces the apodosis of a third-class conditional, fronted in the conditional structure for prominence (emphasis).

γὰρ. Postpositive explanatory conjunction. It introduces a further explanation of Paul's wish to see the Roman Christians.

διαπορευόμενος. Pres mid ptc masc nom sg διαπορεύομαι (temporal). The participle functions as circumstantial, modifying ἐλπίζω. The prefixed form (with δια-) has the same root as πορεύωμαι above.

θεάσασθαι. Aor mid inf θεάομαι (complementary). The infinitive is a complement of ἐλπίζω.

ὑμᾶς. Accusative direct object of θεάσασθαι.

καὶ. Coordinating conjunction. It connects the two infinitival clauses that complement ἐλπίζω.

ὑφ' ὑμῶν. Instrumental.

προπεμφθῆναι. Aor pass inf προπέμπω (complementary). The infinitive is a complement of ἐλπίζω. The passive voice indicates external agency, indicated by ὑφ' ὑμῶν.

ἐκεῖ. Adverb (locative).

ἐὰν. Introduces the protasis of a third-class conditional. It is placed in the second position to emphasize the apodosis. The use of the third-class conditional is consistent with the conditional particle ἄν above.

ὑμῶν. Genitive complement of ἐμπλησθῶ (BDAG, 324.3).

πρῶτον. Adverb (ordinal). It modifies ἐμπλησθῶ.

ἀπὸ μέρους. Locative (movement away from). Paul hopes to enjoy their company from (out of) a part. The idiom can be translated as "in part," or modulated in this co-text to "for a little while."

ἐμπλησθῶ. Aor pass subj 1st sg ἐμπίπλημι. Subjunctive with ἐάν. Subjunctive mood is consistent in this co-text to reflect tentativeness or projection. The passive voice indicates external causality, here reflected by ὑμῶν (i.e., Paul's enjoyment was caused by "you"; cf. BDAG 324.3, which has "your company").

15:25 Νυνὶ δὲ πορεύομαι εἰς Ἰερουσαλὴμ διακονῶν τοῖς ἁγίοις.

Νυνὶ. Adverb (temporal; cf. 15:23). It modifies πορεύομαι.

δὲ. Adversative conjunction (mild).

πορεύομαι. Pres mid ind 1st sg πορεύομαι.

εἰς Ἰερουσαλήμ. Directional (movement toward or into).

διακονῶν. Pres act ptc masc nom sg διακονέω (purpose). The participle functions as circumstantial, modifying πορεύομαι. Only occurrence
of this lexeme in Paul.
τοῖς ἁγίοις. Dative direct object of διακονῶν.

**15:26 εὐδόκησαν γὰρ Μακεδονία καὶ Ἀχαΐα κοινωνίαν τινὰ ποιήσα-
σθαι εἰς τοὺς πτωχοὺς τῶν ἁγίων τῶν ἐν Ἰερουσαλήμ.**

εὐδόκησαν. Aor act ind 3rd pl εὐδοκέω.
γὰρ. Postpositive explanatory conjunction. It introduces an explanation for Paul's travel to Jerusalem, in spite of his desire to go to Spain.
Μακεδονία καὶ Ἀχαΐα. Compound nominative subjects of
εὐδόκησαν.
κοινωνίαν τινὰ. Accusative direct object of ποιήσασθαι. The indefinite pronoun functions as an attributive adjective, referring to "a certain
contribution." κοινωνία is usually translated "fellowship," but generally
refers to a commonly held element or something shared. It is a lexical
metaphor, modulated in this co-text to refer to a "contribution," probably financial or material. The accusative object is fronted before the
predicate ποιήσασθαι for clausal prominence.
ποιήσασθαι. Aor mid inf ποιέω (complementary). The infinitive is a
complement of εὐδόκησαν.
εἰς τοὺς πτωχοὺς. Directional (movement toward or into).
τῶν ἁγίων. Partitive genitive, modifying τοὺς πτωχοὺς.
τῶν ἐν Ἰερουσαλήμ. The article functions as an adjectivizer, changing the prepositional word group into an attributive modifier of τῶν
ἁγίων.
ἐν Ἰερουσαλήμ. Locative.

**15:27 εὐδόκησαν γὰρ καὶ ὀφειλέται εἰσὶν αὐτῶν· εἰ γὰρ τοῖς πνευμα-
τικοῖς αὐτῶν ἐκοινώνησαν τὰ ἔθνη, ὀφείλουσιν καὶ ἐν τοῖς σαρκικοῖς
λειτουργῆσαι αὐτοῖς.**

εὐδόκησαν. Aor act ind 3rd pl εὐδοκέω.
γὰρ. Postpositive explanatory conjunction, used to continue the
explanation of those in Macedonia and Achaia being pleased to make a
contribution to those in Jerusalem.
καὶ. Coordinating conjunction. It connects the two clauses before
and after it.
ὀφειλέται. Predicate nominative.
εἰσὶν. Unaugmented ind 3rd pl εἰμί.
αὐτῶν. Possessive genitive, modifying ὀφειλέται.

εἰ. Introduces the protasis of a first-class conditional.

γὰρ. Postpositive explanatory conjunction, used to continue the explanation of their contribution.

τοῖς πνευματικοῖς. Dative of means. They shared by means of their spiritual things. It can also be classified as a dative complement of ἐκοινώνησαν (cf. κοινωνέω τινί; BDAG, 552.1.b.α).

αὐτῶν. Possessive genitive, modifying τοῖς πνευματικοῖς.

ἐκοινώνησαν. Aor act ind 3rd pl κοινωνέω. See note on κοινωνίαν (its nominal cognate) in 15:26. Repetition of a κοινων- word creates lexical cohesion.

τὰ ἔθνη. Nominative subject of ἐκοινώνησαν.

ὀφείλουσιν. Pres act ind 3rd pl ὀφείλω. It begins the apodosis of the first-class conditional. Repetition of an ὀφείλ- word in this verse creates lexical cohesion.

καί. Adverbial use (adjunctive). It modifies ὀφείλουσιν.

ἐν τοῖς σαρκικοῖς. Locative. It is parallel to τοῖς πνευματικοῖς in the conditional structure (similar to being a dative complement of λειτουργῆσαι), but the use of the preposition ἐν constrains its meaning to a locative function. σαρκικός is another lexical metaphor (lit. "fleshly"), along with κοινονία, to refer to the material or financial contribution.

λειτουργῆσαι. Aor act inf λειτουργέω (complementary). The infinitive is a complement of ὀφείλουσιν. See note on λειτουργὸν (its nominal cognate) in 15:16.

αὐτοῖς. Dative direct object of λειτουργῆσαι.

15:28 τοῦτο οὖν ἐπιτελέσας καὶ σφραγισάμενος αὐτοῖς τὸν καρπὸν τοῦτον, ἀπελεύσομαι δι᾽ ὑμῶν εἰς Σπανίαν·

τοῦτο. Accusative direct object of ἐπιτελέσας. The demonstrative pronoun refers cataphorically to the next participial clause (σφραγισάμενος αὐτοῖς τὸν καρπὸν τοῦτον).

οὖν. Postpositive inferential conjunction, drawing a summary of his statements in 15:24–27 regarding his plans to go first to Jerusalem, then to stop by Rome on his way to Spain.

ἐπιτελέσας. Aor act ptc masc nom sg ἐπιτελέω (temporal). The participle functions as circumstantial, modifying ἀπελεύσομαι.

καί. Coordinating conjunction. It connects the two participial clauses before and after it.

σφραγισάμενος. Aor mid ptc masc nom sg σφραγίζω (temporal). The participle functions as circumstantial, modifying ἀπελεύσομαι. The middle voice indicates indirect, internal agency (cf. NASB: "have put my seal").

αὐτοῖς. Dative indirect object of σφραγισάμενος.

τὸν καρπὸν τοῦτον. Accusative direct object of σφραγισάμενος. καρπός is another lexical metaphor for the contribution to Jerusalem (also, κοινωνία and σαρκικός) mentioned in 15:26–27.

ἀπελεύσομαι. Fut mid ind 1st sg ἀπέρχομαι.

δι᾽ ὑμῶν. Locative ("through you").

εἰς Σπανίαν. Directional (movement toward or into).

15:29 οἶδα δὲ ὅτι ἐρχόμενος πρὸς ὑμᾶς ἐν πληρώματι εὐλογίας Χριστοῦ ἐλεύσομαι.

οἶδα. Prf act ind 1st sg οἶδα. The perfect tense-form (stative aspect) depicts Paul being in a state or condition of knowing and reflects discourse prominence.

δὲ. Adversative conjunction (mild).

ὅτι. Introduces the clausal complement (indirect discourse) of οἶδα.

ἐρχόμενος. Pres mid ptc masc nom sg ἔρχομαι (temporal). The participle functions as circumstantial and is subordinate to ἐλεύσομαι.

πρὸς ὑμᾶς. Directional (movement toward).

ἐν πληρώματι. Manner.

εὐλογίας. Genitive of description or definition, modifying πληρώματι, used to further describe or circumscribe "fullness" as "of blessing."

Χριστοῦ. Genitive of source or origin, modifying εὐλογίας.

ἐλεύσομαι. Fut mid ind 1st sg ἔρχομαι.

15:30 Παρακαλῶ δὲ ὑμᾶς [, ἀδελφοί,] διὰ τοῦ κυρίου ἡμῶν Ἰησοῦ Χριστοῦ καὶ διὰ τῆς ἀγάπης τοῦ πνεύματος συναγωνίσασθαί μοι ἐν ταῖς προσευχαῖς ὑπὲρ ἐμοῦ πρὸς τὸν θεόν,

Παρακαλῶ. Pres act ind 1st sg παρακαλέω. This lexeme, with δέ, is used in this co-text to draw the sub-section regarding his travels and his desire to visit Rome, along with the entire paraenetic section, to a close.

δὲ. Adversative conjunction (mild).

ὑμᾶς. Accusative direct object of παρακαλῶ.

[ἀδελφοί]. Nominative of address (so-called vocative). Two early manuscripts omit this word ($\mathfrak{P}^{46}$ B), while the vast majority of the manuscripts include it (e.g., ℵ A C D). The textual variant is not too significant, but it appears that inclusion of the address is preferred based on the strength of the manuscripts and the appropriateness of its use in the co-text.

διὰ τοῦ κυρίου. Instrumental. The instrument or means by which Paul urges them is "through our Lord Jesus Christ." The compound instrumental διά depicts the urgency by which Paul urges or encourages his audience.

ἡμῶν. Possessive genitive, modifying τοῦ κυρίου.

Ἰησοῦ Χριστοῦ. Genitive in apposition to τοῦ κυρίου ἡμῶν.

καὶ. Coordinating conjunction. It connects the two prepositional word groups.

διὰ τῆς ἀγάπης. Instrumental (see above on διὰ τοῦ κυρίου).

τοῦ πνεύματος. Possessive genitive, or possibly genitive of source or origin, modifying τῆς ἀγάπης.

συναγωνίσασθαί. Aor mid inf συναγωνίζομαι (complementary). The infinitive is a complement of Παρακαλῶ.

μοι. Dative of association.

ἐν ταῖς προσευχαῖς. Locative (sphere or realm). The struggle is in the sphere or realm of "prayer." Alternatively, it can be seen as instrumental, with prayer as the instrument by which they struggle together.

ὑπὲρ ἐμοῦ. Beneficial.

πρὸς τὸν θεόν. Directional (movement toward).

15:31 ἵνα ῥυσθῶ ἀπὸ τῶν ἀπειθούντων ἐν τῇ Ἰουδαίᾳ καὶ ἡ διακονία μου ἡ εἰς Ἰερουσαλὴμ εὐπρόσδεκτος τοῖς ἁγίοις γένηται,

ἵνα. Introduces a purpose clause that explains the purpose of praying for him. The purpose is twofold, linked by καί.

ῥυσθῶ. Aor pass subj 1st sg ῥύομαι. Subjunctive with ἵνα. Passive voice indicates external agency, which is not specified here.

ἀπὸ τῶν ἀπειθούντων. Locative (movement away from).

ἀπειθούντων. Pres act ptc masc gen pl ἀπειθέω (substantival). Lit. "those who are unpersuaded" = "those who disbelieve" (cf. Rom 2:8).

ἐν τῇ Ἰουδαίᾳ. Locative.

καὶ. Coordinating conjunction. It connects the two subordinate clauses under ἵνα.

ἡ διακονία. Nominative subject of γένηται.

μου. Possessive genitive, modifying ἡ διακονία.

ἡ εἰς Ἰερουσαλὴμ. The article functions as an adjectivizer, changing the prepositional word group into an attributive modifier of ἡ διακονία.

εἰς Ἰερουσαλὴμ. Directional (movement toward or into).

εὐπρόσδεκτος. Predicate adjective. This lexeme appears in Romans only in this chapter (as an adjective, Rom 15:16; cf. 2 Cor 6:2; 8:12; 1 Pet 2:5; but twice as a verb, Rom 15:26, 27).

τοῖς ἁγίοις. Dative complement of εὐπρόσδεκτος.
γένηται. Aor mid subj 3rd sg γίνομαι. Subjunctive with ἵνα.

15:32 ἵνα ἐν χαρᾷ ἐλθὼν πρὸς ὑμᾶς διὰ θελήματος θεοῦ συναναπαύσωμαι ὑμῖν.

ἵνα. Introduces a purpose or result clause that indicates the potential or expected purpose or result of the above-mentioned prayers for him.
ἐν χαρᾷ. Manner.
ἐλθὼν. Aor act ptc masc nom sg ἔρχομαι (temporal). The participle functions as circumstantial and modifies συναναπαύσωμαι.
πρὸς ὑμᾶς. Directional (movement toward).
διὰ θελήματος. Instrumental. Syntactically, this prepositional word group can either be attached to the previous predicate (ἐλθὼν) or the following predicate (συναναπαύσωμαι), but it is likely that the prepositional word group is attached to ἐλθὼν for semantic reasons. The "will of God" is probably the instrument by which Paul comes to them, given the previous co-text, not the instrument by whom Paul is refreshed (although this may be true nonetheless).
θεοῦ. Possessive genitive or genitive of source or origin, modifying θελήματος.
συναναπαύσωμαι. Aor mid subj 1st sg συναναπαύομαι. Subjunctive with ἵνα. The doubly prefixed word (συν- + ἀνα- + παύομαι) is defined as "to experience restorative rest together with someone else" (LN 23.86). A NT *hapax legomenon* (cf. LXX Isa 11:6).
ὑμῖν. Dative of association (cf. LXX Isa 11:6).

15:33 Ὁ δὲ θεὸς τῆς εἰρήνης μετὰ πάντων ὑμῶν, ἀμήν.

Ὁ ... θεὸς. Nominative absolute.
δὲ. Adversative conjunction (mild).
τῆς εἰρήνης. Genitive of description or definition, modifying Ὁ ... θεὸς. It describes or circumscribes "God" as "of peace" (cf. 16:20; Phil 4:9; 1 Thess 5:23; Heb 13:20).
μετὰ πάντων ὑμῶν. Accompaniment.
ἀμήν. Asseverative particle (see 1:25).

Romans 16:1–2

[1]I commend to you Phoebe, our sister, who is also a deaconess of the church which is in Cenchrea, [2]so that you may welcome her in the Lord worthily of the saints, and stand with her in whatever matter she may

have need of you. For she herself also has become a helper of many and of me myself.

This section begins the letter closing and identifies the sender and likely carrier for the letter, Phoebe. This is the only time where Paul sends recommendation of someone with his letter. In addition, the closing of this letter is the longest of his other letters, containing some elements that are not typically found in his letters. Here the letter closing includes a personal commendation, personal greetings, closing comments, and the doxological conclusion (Weima).

16:1 Συνίστημι δὲ ὑμῖν Φοίβην τὴν ἀδελφὴν ἡμῶν, οὖσαν [καὶ] διάκονον τῆς ἐκκλησίας τῆς ἐν Κεγχρεαῖς,

Συνίστημι. Pres act ind 1st sg συνίστημι. This lexeme is used only two other times in Romans (3:5; 5:8), but here its use is modulated as: "to indicate approval of a person or event, with the implication that others adopt the same attitude" (LN 33.344). συνίστημι is commonly used in letters of recommendation to commend or recommend a person (usually the carrier of the letter) to the addressee (cf. Yoon 2016, 67–68).

δὲ. Adversative conjunction (mild).

ὑμῖν. Dative indirect object of Συνίστημι.

Φοίβην. Accusative direct object of Συνίστημι.

τὴν ἀδελφὴν. Accusative in apposition to Φοίβην. It is used to further describe Phoebe as a member of the Christian community or family. Paul uses the feminine form of this lexeme in only three other places (1 Cor 7:15; 9:5; Phlm 2).

ἡμῶν. Possessive genitive, modifying τὴν ἀδελφὴν.

οὖσαν. Ptc fem acc sg εἰμί (attributive). The adjectival participle modifies Φοίβην (and through apposition ἀδελφὴν) in attributive structure (fourth attributive position).

[καὶ]. Adjectival use (adjunctive). Modifies διάκονον. The word καὶ is found in 𝔓⁴⁶ and B, but not in ℵ A and D, among the earliest manuscripts.

διάκονον. Predicate accusative. There is disagreement as to whether διάκονος (here to be taken as grammatically feminine) refers generally to "servant" or to the office of "deacon(ess)." There are three other times this substantive is used in this letter (13:4 [2x] and 15:8), referring to "superior authorities" or Christ Jesus as "servant." However, in this co-text, the sense seems to be modulated to refer to the function of a "deacon(ess)" for three main reasons. First, it is used in an ecclesial context, where Phoebe is a διάκονος of the church in Cenchrea. Second, the genitive instead of a dative or a preposition is used to modify διάκονος, functioning as possessive (in the sense of "belonging to"). The semantics of the genitive as a case of restriction shows that Phoebe being a διάκονος is restricted to "the church." Third, by the time Paul writes the Letter to the Romans, there seem to have been established leadership positions in the church (cf. Porter 2015, 290–91). Thus, διάκονος probably refers to a leadership position (deaconess) in the church at Cenchrea.

τῆς ἐκκλησίας. Possessive genitive, modifying διάκονον.

τῆς ἐν Κεγχρεαῖς. The article functions as an adjectivizer, changing the prepositional word group into an attributive modifier of τῆς ἐκκλησίας.

ἐν Κεγχρεαῖς. Locative (cf. Acts 18:18 for the church at Cenchrea).

16:2 ἵνα αὐτὴν προσδέξησθε ἐν κυρίῳ ἀξίως τῶν ἁγίων καὶ παραστῆτε αὐτῇ ἐν ᾧ ἂν ὑμῶν χρῄζῃ πράγματι· καὶ γὰρ αὐτὴ προστάτις πολλῶν ἐγενήθη καὶ ἐμοῦ αὐτοῦ.

ἵνα. Introduces a purpose clause that explains the purpose of Paul's recommendation of Phoebe.

αὐτὴν. Accusative direct object of προσδέξησθε. The personal pronoun refers anaphorically to Phoebe (16:1).

προσδέξησθε. Aor mid subj 2nd pl προσδέχομαι. Subjunctive with ἵνα.

ἐν κυρίῳ. Locative (sphere or realm; see notes in 3:24; 6:11 for ἐν Χριστῷ).

ἀξίως. Adverb (manner). It modifies προσδέξησθε.

τῶν ἁγίων. Genitive complement of ἀξίως.

καὶ. Coordinating conjunction. It connects the two clauses under ἵνα.

παραστῆτε. Aor act subj 2nd pl παρίστημι. Subjunctive with ἵνα.

αὐτῇ. Dative indirect object of παραστῆτε.

ἐν ᾧ. Sphere or reference. This phrase, ἐν ᾧ ἂν ὑμῶν χρῄζῃ πράγματι, is an internally headed relative clause because the antecedent of the relative pronoun (πράγματι) is incorporated into the relative clause. When this happens, "the article going with the noun must be omitted and the noun itself then attracted to the case of the relative" (BDF §294.5). The headless relative pronoun serves as the object of the preposition.

ἂν. Conditional particle. It signifies a conditional generality. The condition is that Phoebe may or may not be in need of them.

ὑμῶν. Genitive object of χρῄζῃ. χρῄζω often takes the genitive as its object (cf. Matt 6:32; Luke 11:8; 12:30; 2 Cor 3:1). Not to be confused with the so-called objective genitive.

χρήζῃ. Pres act subj 3rd sg χρήζω. The third-person singular refers to Phoebe.

πράγματι. Dative of respect. Her need may be with respect to a "matter."

καὶ. Adverbial use (adjunctive). It modifies ἐγενήθη.

γὰρ. Postpositive explanatory conjunction. It is used to explain why they should welcome her.

αὐτὴ. Nominative subject of ἐγενήθη.

προστάτις. Predicate nominative.

πολλῶν. Possessive genitive, modifying προστάτις. Some may wish to label this as an objective genitive, if προστάτις is changed to a verb (i.e., "to help").

ἐγενήθη. Aor mid ind 3rd sg γίνομαι. On the middle voice, see "Deponency" in the Series Introduction and Introduction.

καὶ. Coordinating conjunction. It connects the two genitive word groups which modify προστάτις.

ἐμοῦ αὐτοῦ. Possessive genitive, modifying προστάτις. αὐτοῦ functions as an intensive pronoun ("of me myself").

Romans 16:3–16

³Greet Prisca and Aquila, my fellow workers in Christ Jesus, ⁴who risked their necks on behalf of my life, to whom not only I give thanks but also all the churches of the Gentiles. ⁵Also [greet] the church based at their home. Greet Epaenetus, my beloved, who is the firstfruit of Asia into Christ. ⁶Greet Mary, who has worked very hard for you. ⁷Greet Andronicus and Junia, my kinsmen and my fellow prisoners, who are well-known among the apostles, who also were in Christ before me. ⁸Greet Ampliatus, my beloved in the Lord. ⁹Greet Urbanus, our fellow worker in Christ, and Stachys, my beloved. ¹⁰Greet Apelles, who is approved in Christ. Greet the [household] of Aristobulus. ¹¹Greet Herodion, my kinsman. Greet the [household] of Narcissus who are in the Lord. ¹²Greet Tryphena and Tryphosa, workers in the Lord. Greet Persis the beloved, who works very hard in the Lord. ¹³Greet Rufus, the elect in the Lord, and his mother and mine. ¹⁴Greet Asyncritus, Phlegon, Hermes, Patrobas, Hermas, and the brothers with them. ¹⁵Greet Philologus and Julia, Nereus and his sister, and Olympas, and all the saints who are with them. ¹⁶Greet each other with a holy kiss. All the churches of Christ greet you.

This section of the letter closing consists of the various greetings that Paul sends to the people in Rome. This is the longest greeting in the letter closing in any of the Paul's letters.

16:3 Ἀσπάσασθε Πρίσκαν καὶ Ἀκύλαν τοὺς συνεργούς μου ἐν Χριστῷ Ἰησοῦ,

Ἀσπάσασθε. Aor mid impv 2nd pl ἀσπάζομαι. The aorist imperative depicts the command as perfective (whole, complete action), not as a punctiliar, one-time, command.

Πρίσκαν καὶ Ἀκύλαν. Compound accusative direct objects of Ἀσπάσασθε. Πρίσκα is the diminutive form of Πρίσκιλλα (cf. Acts 18:2).

τοὺς συνεργούς. Accusative in apposition to Πρίσκαν καὶ Ἀκύλαν.

μου. Possessive genitive, modifying τοὺς συνεργούς.

ἐν Χριστῷ Ἰησοῦ. Locative (sphere or realm; see notes on ἐν Χριστῷ Ἰησοῦ in 3:24; 6:11).

16:4 οἵτινες ὑπὲρ τῆς ψυχῆς μου τὸν ἑαυτῶν τράχηλον ὑπέθηκαν, οἷς οὐκ ἐγὼ μόνος εὐχαριστῶ ἀλλὰ καὶ πᾶσαι αἱ ἐκκλησίαι τῶν ἐθνῶν,

οἵτινες. Nominative subject of ὑπέθηκαν. The relative pronoun refers anaphorically to Prisca and Aquila and introduces the first of two relative clauses.

ὑπὲρ τῆς ψυχῆς. Beneficial.

μου. Possessive genitive, modifying τῆς ψυχῆς.

τὸν . . . τράχηλον. Accusative direct object of ὑπέθηκαν.

ἑαυτῶν. Possessive genitive, modifying τὸν . . . τράχηλον. ἑαυτῶν is a reflexive pronoun.

ὑπέθηκαν. Aor act ind 3rd pl ὑποτίθημι.

οἷς. Dative direct object of εὐχαριστῶ. The relative pronoun refers anaphorically to Prisca and Aquila and introduces the second relative clause.

οὐκ . . . μόνος . . . ἀλλὰ καί. A point/counterpoint set ("not only . . . but also") that supplements Paul's thanks with the thanks of all the churches of the Gentiles.

ἐγώ. Nominative subject of εὐχαριστῶ. The use of the personal pronoun is emphatic.

εὐχαριστῶ. Pres act ind 1st sg εὐχαριστέω.

πᾶσαι αἱ ἐκκλησίαι. Nominative subject of verbless clause (with an implied active third-person plural form of εὐχαριστέω).

τῶν ἐθνῶν. Possessive genitive, modifying αἱ ἐκκλησίαι.

16:5 καὶ τὴν κατ᾽ οἶκον αὐτῶν ἐκκλησίαν. ἀσπάσασθε Ἐπαίνετον τὸν ἀγαπητόν μου, ὅς ἐστιν ἀπαρχὴ τῆς Ἀσίας εἰς Χριστόν.

καί. Adverbial use (adjunctive). It modifies an implied ἀσπάσασθε from 16:3.

τὴν . . . ἐκκλησίαν. Accusative direct object of an implied ἀσπάσασθε from 16:3.

κατ᾽ οἶκον. Positional (location). The embedding of the prepositional word group between the article and the modified substantive (ἐκκλησίαν) indicates prominence of this prepositional word group.

αὐτῶν. Possessive genitive, modifying οἶκον. The personal pronoun refers anaphorically to Prisca and Aquila.

ἀσπάσασθε. Aor mid impv 2nd pl ἀσπάζομαι (see note in 16:3).

Ἐπαίνετον. Accusative direct object of ἀσπάσασθε.

τὸν ἀγαπητόν. Accusative in apposition to Ἐπαίνετον.

μου. Possessive genitive, modifying τὸν ἀγαπητόν.

ὅς. Nominative subject of ἐστιν. The relative pronoun refers anaphorically to Ἐπαίνετον.

ἐστιν. Unaugmented ind 3rd sg εἰμί.

ἀπαρχὴ. Predicate nominative. The lexeme is a metaphor for "first convert" here.

τῆς Ἀσίας. Genitive of source or origin, modifying ἀπαρχὴ.

εἰς Χριστόν. Goal.

16:6 ἀσπάσασθε Μαρίαν, ἥτις πολλὰ ἐκοπίασεν εἰς ὑμᾶς.

ἀσπάσασθε. Aor mid impv 2nd pl ἀσπάζομαι (see note in 16:3).

Μαρίαν. Accusative direct object of ἀσπάσασθε.

ἥτις. Nominative subject of ἐκοπίασεν. The relative pronoun introduces a relative clause and is an anaphoric referent to Μαρίαν.

πολλὰ. Accusative direct object of ἐκοπίασεν. The adjective functions adverbially: lit. "has labored much" = "has worked very hard."

ἐκοπίασεν. Aor act ind 3rd sg κοπιάω.

εἰς ὑμᾶς. Goal. The goal of Mary's work is "you."

16:7 ἀσπάσασθε Ἀνδρόνικον καὶ Ἰουνίαν τοὺς συγγενεῖς μου καὶ συναιχμαλώτους μου, οἵτινές εἰσιν ἐπίσημοι ἐν τοῖς ἀποστόλοις, οἳ καὶ πρὸ ἐμοῦ γέγοναν ἐν Χριστῷ.

ἀσπάσασθε. Aor mid impv 2nd pl ἀσπάζομαι (see note in 16:3).

Ἀνδρόνικον καὶ Ἰουνίαν. Accusative direct objects of ἀσπάσασθε.

Ἰουνίαν. There has been debate as to whether the nominative form is Ἰσυνιᾶς (a man) or Ἰουνία (a woman), since the accusative form is identical to both. The difficulty lies in that this name appears nowhere else in the NT. It appears, however, that the evidence favors a feminine reading for at least a couple of reasons: (1) while most of the earliest manuscripts contain Ἰουνίαν here (unaccented), 𝔓⁴⁶ contains its alternate form Ἰουλίαν (Julia; cf. Rom 16:15), which is clearly feminine; (2) the witnesses of Origen (c. 184–253 AD) and Chrystosom (c. 347–407 AD), among a vast majority of early church witnesses, attest to a feminine reading (the equivalent of "Junia"). Furthermore, it is likely, although not definite, that Andronicus and Junia were a married couple (see note on τοὺς συγγενεῖς below) by the way Paul uses four descriptors for this pair (my kinsmen, my fellow prisoners, outstanding among the apostles, and in Christ before him).

τοὺς συγγενεῖς. Accusative in apposition to Ἀνδρόνικον καὶ Ἰουνίαν. This lexeme appears three other times in Romans (9:3; 16:11, 21) and has the core meaning of "one with the same genesis," i.e., a relative or kinsman. In 9:3, it is modulated with the prepositional word group κατὰ σάρκα to refer to Paul's fellow Jews. Andronicus and Junia were Paul's kinsmen or compatriots; they were also perhaps a married couple.

μου. Possessive genitive, modifying τοὺς συγγενεῖς.

καὶ. Coordinating conjunction. It connects the two accusatives. Both accusatives are applied to Andronicus and Junia; however, the first appears with the article and the second without. Granville Sharp's rule regarding the scope of the article would not apply here, since they are plural substantives. However, the reason why the first appears with an article and the second without is probably due to the function of the article itself as a particularizer. In other words, Andronicus and Junia were particular kinsmen of Paul, while they were fellow prisoners with Paul in a general, non-particular sense.

συναιχμαλώτους. Accusative in apposition to Ἀνδρόνικον καὶ Ἰουνίαν.

μου. Possessive genitive, modifying συναιχμαλώτους.

οἵτινές. Nominative subject of εἰσιν. The relative pronoun refers anaphorically to Ἀνδρόνικον καὶ Ἰουνίαν.

εἰσιν. Unaugmented ind 3rd pl εἰμί.

ἐπίσημοι. Predicate adjective. This lexeme occurs only here and in Matt 27:16 in the NT and is defined as "pertaining to being well known or outstanding, either because of positive or negative characteristics—'outstanding, famous, notorious, infamous'" (LN 28.31). It refers to notoriety, whether positive or negative (negative in Matt 27:16, positive here; cf. Porter 2015, 296), not simply being well-known.

ἐν τοῖς ἀποστόλοις. Distributional ("among the apostles"). While some may wish to interpret this preposition as functioning as directional ("to the apostles"), the fundamental sense of ἐν meaning "in" or "in the realm of" points to a distributional or locative function (cf. Bauckham, 165–80; Belleville; Epp, 69–78). This likely indicates that Andronicus and Junia were themselves two apostles.

οἵ. Nominative subject of γέγοναν. The relative pronoun refers anaphorically to Ἀνδρόνικον καὶ Ἰουνίαν.

καὶ. Adverbial use (adjunctive). It modifies γέγοναν.

πρὸ ἐμοῦ. Temporal (antecedent).

γέγοναν. Prf act ind 3rd pl γίνομαι. The perfect tense-form (stative aspect) reflects that they were in a state of being "in Christ."

ἐν Χριστῷ. Locative (sphere or realm; see notes on ἐν Χριστῷ Ἰησοῦ in 3:24; 6:11).

16:8 ἀσπάσασθε Ἀμπλιᾶτον τὸν ἀγαπητόν μου ἐν κυρίῳ.

ἀσπάσασθε. Aor mid impv 2nd pl ἀσπάζομαι (see note in 16:3).

Ἀμπλιᾶτον. Accusative direct object of ἀσπάσασθε.

τὸν ἀγαπητόν. Accusative in apposition to Ἀμπλιᾶτον.

μου. Possessive genitive, modifying τὸν ἀγαπητόν.

ἐν κυρίῳ. Locative (sphere or realm; see notes on ἐν Χριστῷ Ἰησοῦ in 3:24; 6:11).

16:9 ἀσπάσασθε Οὐρβανὸν τὸν συνεργὸν ἡμῶν ἐν Χριστῷ καὶ Στάχυν τὸν ἀγαπητόν μου.

ἀσπάσασθε. Aor mid impv 2nd pl ἀσπάζομαι. See note in 16:3.

Οὐρβανὸν. Accusative direct object of ἀσπάσασθε.

τὸν συνεργὸν. Accusative in apposition to Οὐρβανὸν.

ἡμῶν. Possessive genitive, modifying τὸν συνεργὸν.

ἐν Χριστῷ. Locative (sphere or realm; see notes on ἐν Χριστῷ Ἰησοῦ in 3:24; 6:11).

καὶ. Coordinating conjunction. It connects Οὐρβανὸν with Στάχυν.

Στάχυν. Accusative direct object of ἀσπάσασθε.

τὸν ἀγαπητόν. Accusative in apposition to Στάχυν.

μου. Possessive genitive, modifying τὸν ἀγαπητόν. The use of the singular pronoun here versus the plural (ἡμῶν) for Urbanus reflects Paul's differentiation between personal and communal identifications in this list.

16:10 ἀσπάσασθε Ἀπελλῆν τὸν δόκιμον ἐν Χριστῷ. ἀσπάσασθε τοὺς ἐκ τῶν Ἀριστοβούλου.

ἀσπάσασθε. Aor mid impv 2nd pl ἀσπάζομαι (see note in 16:3).

Ἀπελλῆν. Accusative direct object of ἀσπάσασθε.

τὸν δόκιμον. Accusative in apposition to Ἀπελλῆν.

ἐν Χριστῷ. Locative (sphere or realm; see notes on ἐν Χριστῷ Ἰησοῦ in 3:24; 6:11).

ἀσπάσασθε. Aor mid impv 2nd pl ἀσπάζομαι (see note in 16:3).

τοὺς ἐκ τῶν Ἀριστοβούλου. The article functions as a nominalizer, changing the prepositional word group into the accusative direct object of ἀσπάσασθε.

ἐκ τῶν Ἀριστοβούλου. Locative (movement out of; i.e., source or origin). It is used metaphorically here to refer to those who originate from Aristobulus, i.e., his household family (Porter 2015, 297).

16:11 ἀσπάσασθε Ἡρῳδίωνα τὸν συγγενῆ μου. ἀσπάσασθε τοὺς ἐκ τῶν Ναρκίσσου τοὺς ὄντας ἐν κυρίῳ.

ἀσπάσασθε. Aor mid impv 2nd pl ἀσπάζομαι (see note in 16:3).

Ἡρῳδίωνα. Accusative direct object of ἀσπάσασθε.

τὸν συγγενῆ. Accusative in apposition to Ἡρῳδίωνα. It is likely used to refer to Paul's relative (see note on τοὺς συγγενεῖς in 16:7 for the meaning of this lexeme).

μου. Possessive genitive, modifying τὸν συγγενῆ.

ἀσπάσασθε. Aor mid impv 2nd pl ἀσπάζομαι (see note in 16:3).

τοὺς ἐκ τῶν Ναρκίσσου. The article functions as a nominalizer, changing the prepositional word group into the accusative direct object of ἀσπάσασθε.

ἐκ τῶν Ναρκίσσου. Locative (movement out of; i.e., source or origin). See similar note in 16:10.

τοὺς ὄντας. Ptc masc acc pl εἰμί (attributive). The participle modifies τοὺς ἐκ τῶν Ναρκίσσου in attributive structure (second attributive position).

ἐν κυρίῳ. Locative (sphere or realm; see notes on ἐν Χριστῷ Ἰησοῦ in 3:24; 6:11). The use of this prepositional word group to modify Narcissus' household implies that there were some in his family who were not "in Christ" and that the greeting was limited to those who were "in Christ" (cf. 16:10).

16:12 ἀσπάσασθε Τρύφαιναν καὶ Τρυφῶσαν τὰς κοπιώσας ἐν κυρίῳ. ἀσπάσασθε Περσίδα τὴν ἀγαπητήν, ἥτις πολλὰ ἐκοπίασεν ἐν κυρίῳ.

ἀσπάσασθε. Aor mid impv 2nd pl ἀσπάζομαι (see note in 16:3).

Τρύφαιναν καὶ Τρυφῶσαν. Compound accusative direct objects of ἀσπάσασθε.

τὰς κοπιώσας. Pres act ptc fem acc pl κοπιάω (substantival). Accusative in apposition to Τρύφαιναν καὶ Τρυφῶσαν.

ἐν κυρίῳ. Locative (sphere or realm; see notes on ἐν Χριστῷ Ἰησοῦ in 3:24; 6:11).

ἀσπάσασθε. Aor mid impv 2nd pl ἀσπάζομαι (see note in 16:3).
Περσίδα. Accusative direct object of ἀσπάσασθε.
τὴν ἀγαπητήν. Accusative in apposition to Περσίδα.
ἥτις. Nominative subject of ἐκοπίασεν. The relative pronoun introduces a relative clause and is an anaphoric referent to Μαρίαν.
πολλά. Accusative direct object of ἐκοπίασεν. The adjective functions adverbially: lit. "has labored much" = "has worked very hard."
ἐκοπίασεν. Aor act ind 3rd sg κοπιάω.
ἐν κυρίῳ. Locative (sphere or realm; see notes on ἐν Χριστῷ Ἰησοῦ
in 3:24; 6:11).

**16:13 ἀσπάσασθε Ῥοῦφον τὸν ἐκλεκτὸν ἐν κυρίῳ καὶ τὴν μητέρα
αὐτοῦ καὶ ἐμοῦ.**

ἀσπάσασθε. Aor mid impv 2nd pl ἀσπάζομαι (see note in 16:3).
Ῥοῦφον. Accusative direct object of ἀσπάσασθε.
τὸν ἐκλεκτὸν. Accusative in apposition to Ῥοῦφον.
ἐν κυρίῳ. Locative (sphere or realm; see notes in on ἐν Χριστῷ Ἰησοῦ
in 3:24; 6:11).
καὶ. Coordinating conjunction. It connects Ῥοῦφον with τὴν μητέρα.
τὴν μητέρα. Accusative direct object of ἀσπάσασθε.
αὐτοῦ. Possessive genitive, modifying τὴν μητέρα. It shares its
head term with ἐμοῦ.
καὶ. Coordinating conjunction. It connects two genitives.
ἐμοῦ. Possessive genitive, modifying τὴν μητέρα. It shares its head
term with αὐτοῦ.

**16:14 ἀσπάσασθε Ἀσύγκριτον, Φλέγοντα, Ἑρμῆν, Πατροβᾶν, Ἑρμᾶν
καὶ τοὺς σὺν αὐτοῖς ἀδελφούς.**

ἀσπάσασθε. Aor mid impv 2nd pl ἀσπάζομαι (see note in 16:3).
Ἀσύγκριτον Φλέγοντα Ἑρμῆν Πατροβᾶν Ἑρμᾶν. Compound accusative direct objects of ἀσπάσασθε.
καὶ. Coordinating conjunction. It connects the compound direct
objects with τοὺς ... ἀδελφούς.
τοὺς ... ἀδελφούς. Accusative direct object of ἀσπάσασθε.
σὺν αὐτοῖς. Accompaniment. The embedded prepositional word
group functions as an attributive modifier (first attributive position) of
τοὺς ἀδελφούς.

16:15 ἀσπάσασθε Φιλόλογον καὶ Ἰουλίαν, Νηρέα καὶ τὴν ἀδελφὴν αὐτοῦ, καὶ Ὀλυμπᾶν καὶ τοὺς σὺν αὐτοῖς πάντας ἁγίους.

ἀσπάσασθε. Aor mid impv 2nd pl ἀσπάζομαι (see note in 16:3).
Φιλόλογον καὶ Ἰουλίαν. Compound accusative direct objects of ἀσπάσασθε. The pairing of this and the next two names with καί reflects some sort of grouping of this list, probably related to familial ties. Here, it is likely that Philologus and Julia are a married couple.
Νηρέα καὶ τὴν ἀδελφὴν. Compound accusative direct objects of ἀσπάσασθε.
αὐτοῦ. Possessive genitive, modifying τὴν ἀδελφὴν.
καὶ. Coordinating conjunction. It connects the compound direct objects.
Ὀλυμπᾶν. Accusative direct object of ἀσπάσασθε.
καὶ. Coordinating conjunction. It connects the compound direct objects.
τοὺς . . . πάντας ἁγίους. Accusative direct object of ἀσπάσασθε. πάντας is in an attributive structure (first attributive position) with τοὺς . . . ἁγίους to reflect completeness of the attributed entities (i.e., the entirety of the saints with them; Porter 1994a, 120).
σὺν αὐτοῖς. Accompaniment. The embedded prepositional word group functions as an attributive modifier (first attributive position) of τοὺς . . . πάντας ἁγίους.

16:16 ἀσπάσασθε ἀλλήλους ἐν φιλήματι ἁγίῳ. ἀσπάζονται ὑμᾶς αἱ ἐκκλησίαι πᾶσαι τοῦ Χριστοῦ.

ἀσπάσασθε. Aor mid impv 2nd pl ἀσπάζομαι (see note in 16:3).
ἀλλήλους. Accusative direct object of ἀσπάσασθε.
ἐν φιλήματι ἁγίῳ. Instrumental.
ἀσπάζονται. Pres mid ind 3rd pl ἀσπάζομαι.
ὑμᾶς. Accusative direct object of ἀσπάζονται.
αἱ ἐκκλησίαι πᾶσαι. Nominative subject of ἀσπάζονται.
τοῦ Χριστοῦ. Possessive genitive, modifying αἱ ἐκκλησίαι πᾶσαι.

Romans 16:17–20

[17]I urge you, brothers [and sisters], to watch for those who cause divisions and scandals other than the teaching which you learned, and turn away from them. [18]For such people do not serve our Lord Christ but their own stomach, and through smooth talk and flattery they deceive the hearts of the guileless. [19]For your obedience is known among everyone; therefore,

upon you I rejoice, but I want you to be wise unto good but innocent unto evil. ²⁰The God of peace will crush Satan under your feet in quickness. The grace of our Lord Jesus [be] with you.

In this section of the letter closing, Paul offers a final exhortation, reasons to obey his exhortation, a peace statement, and a grace statement.

16:17 Παρακαλῶ δὲ ὑμᾶς, ἀδελφοί, σκοπεῖν τοὺς τὰς διχοστασίας καὶ τὰ σκάνδαλα παρὰ τὴν διδαχὴν ἣν ὑμεῖς ἐμάθετε ποιοῦντας, καὶ ἐκκλίνετε ἀπ᾽ αὐτῶν·

Παρακαλῶ. Pres act ind 1st sg παρακαλέω.
δὲ. Adversative conjunction (mild).
ὑμᾶς. Accusative direct object of Παρακαλῶ.
ἀδελφοί. Nominative of address (so-called vocative).
σκοπεῖν. Pres act inf σκοπέω (indirect discourse). The infinitive expresses the content Παρακαλῶ.
τοὺς . . . ποιοῦντας. Pres act ptc masc acc pl ποιέω (substantival). Accusative direct object of σκοπεῖν. The article and substantive are divided by a rather long, embedded accusative object and a relative clause (τὰς διχοστασίας καὶ τὰ σκάνδαλα παρὰ τὴν διδαχὴν ἣν ὑμεῖς ἐμάθετε), to highlight the compound accusative direct objects.
τὰς διχοστασίας. Accusative direct object of ποιοῦντας.
καὶ. Coordinating conjunction. It connects the two accusative objects.
τὰ σκάνδαλα. Accusative direct object of ποιοῦντας.
παρὰ διδαχὴν. Replacement. παρά generally has the meaning of "alongside" or "beside" and here metaphorically is a replacement of (i.e., putting to the side) "teaching" they had learned (cf. 1:25; 12:3; LN 89.132; Porter 1994a, 167).
ἣν. Accusative direct object of ἐμάθετε. The relative pronoun refers anaphorically to διδαχὴν.
ὑμεῖς. Nominative subject of ἐμάθετε. The use of personal pronoun is emphatic.
ἐμάθετε. Aor act ind 2nd pl μανθάνω. The use of the aorist tense form (perfective aspect) is appropriate for depicting background information within the relative clause.
καὶ. Coordinating conjunction. It connects the infinitival clause (σκοπεῖν . . .) with the imperatival clause (ἐκκλίνετε ἀπ᾽ αὐτῶν).
ἐκκλίνετε. Pres act impv 2nd pl ἐκκλίνω. The command marks a shift from the use of an infinitive to express the content of a παρακαλῶ formula to the use of a more direct imperative.

ἀπ’ αὐτῶν. Locative (movement away from). The personal pronoun refers anaphorically to τοὺς . . . ποιοῦντας.

16:18 οἱ γὰρ τοιοῦτοι τῷ κυρίῳ ἡμῶν Χριστῷ οὐ δουλεύουσιν ἀλλὰ τῇ ἑαυτῶν κοιλίᾳ, καὶ διὰ τῆς χρηστολογίας καὶ εὐλογίας ἐξαπατῶσιν τὰς καρδίας τῶν ἀκάκων.

οἱ . . . τοιοῦτοι. Nominative subject of δουλεύουσιν. The use of the articular demonstrative pronoun (cf. 1 Cor 7:28; 2 Cor 2:7; 10:11; Titus 3:11) may indicate that Paul had specific troublemakers in mind.
γὰρ. Postpositive explanatory conjunction. It introduces an explanation for Paul's twofold command in the previous verse.
τῷ κυρίῳ. Dative direct object of δουλεύουσιν.
ἡμῶν. Possessive genitive, modifying τῷ κυρίῳ.
Χριστῷ. Dative in apposition to τῷ κυρίῳ.
οὐ . . . ἀλλὰ. A point/counterpoint set that establishes a contrast between serving the Lord and serving one's own stomach. The negative particle negates δουλεύουσιν.
δουλεύουσιν. Pres act ind 3rd pl δουλεύω.
τῇ . . . κοιλίᾳ. Dative direct object of an implied δουλεύουσιν from the previous clause. The embedded genitive plural ἑαυτῶν indicates that κοιλίᾳ is a distributive singular.
ἑαυτῶν. Possessive genitive, modifying τῇ . . . κοιλίᾳ. ἑαυτῶν is a reflexive pronoun.
καὶ. Coordinating conjunction. It connects the two clause complexes containing the predicates δουλεύουσιν and ἐξαπατῶσιν.
διὰ τῆς χρηστολογίας καὶ εὐλογίας. Instrumental. The fronting of the prepositional word group before the predicate reflects clausal prominence. It contains compound objects of the preposition connected by καί.
ἐξαπατῶσιν. Pres act ind 3rd pl ἐξαπατάω.
τὰς καρδίας. Accusative direct object of ἐξαπατῶσιν.
τῶν ἀκάκων. Possessive genitive, modifying τὰς καρδίας (lit. "the hearts of the un-bad" = "the hearts of the guileless"). This is the only occurrence of this lexeme in Paul (cf. Heb 7:26).

16:19 ἡ γὰρ ὑμῶν ὑπακοὴ εἰς πάντας ἀφίκετο· ἐφ’ ὑμῖν οὖν χαίρω, θέλω δὲ ὑμᾶς σοφοὺς εἶναι εἰς τὸ ἀγαθόν, ἀκεραίους δὲ εἰς τὸ κακόν.

ἡ . . . ὑπακοὴ. Nominative subject of ἀφίκετο.
γὰρ. Postpositive explanatory conjunction. It is used to explain further their obedience in comparison to the troublemakers from the previous verse.

ὑμῶν. Possessive genitive, modifying ἡ . . . ὑπακοή.

εἰς πάντας. Distributional ("among everyone").

ἀφίκετο. Aor mid ind 3rd sg ἀφικνέομαι. The middle voice (so-called deponent verb; see "Deponency" in the Series Introduction) indicates indirect, internal agency. In other words, "your obedience" is the subject of what is known or has reached Paul's audience (internal causality), but cause (or agent) of knowing/reaching is unspecified (indirect causality). A NT *hapax legomenon*.

ἐφ' ὑμῖν. Locative ("upon you"). Paul's rejoicing is figuratively located or placed upon them.

οὖν. Postpositive inferential conjunction. An inference is drawn from the previous statement that their obedience is known among everyone, that Paul rejoices.

χαίρω. Pres act ind 1st sg χαίρω.

θέλω. Pres act ind 1st sg θέλω.

δὲ. Adversative conjunction (mild).

ὑμᾶς. Accusative subject of εἶναι.

σοφοὺς. Predicate accusative.

εἶναι. Inf εἰμί (complementary). The infinitive is a complement of θέλω in a catenative construction.

εἰς τὸ ἀγαθόν. Directional (movement toward or into). Being wise is directed towards "the good."

ἀκεραίους. Predicate accusative.

δὲ. Adversative conjunction (mild). It contrasts the two predicate accusatives.

εἰς τὸ κακόν. Directional (movement toward or into). Being innocent is directed towards "the evil."

16:20 ὁ δὲ θεὸς τῆς εἰρήνης συντρίψει τὸν σατανᾶν ὑπὸ τοὺς πόδας ὑμῶν ἐν τάχει. Ἡ χάρις τοῦ κυρίου ἡμῶν Ἰησοῦ μεθ' ὑμῶν.

ὁ . . . θεὸς. Nominative subject of συντρίψει.

δὲ. Adversative conjunction (mild).

τῆς εἰρήνης. Genitive of description or definition, modifying ὁ . . . θεὸς. It describes or circumscribes "God" as "of peace" (cf. 15:33; Phil 4:9; 1 Thess 5:23; Heb 13:20).

συντρίψει. Fut act ind 3rd sg συντρίβω. The future form indicates expectation.

τὸν σατανᾶν. Accusative direct object of συντρίψει. This is the only reference to Satan in Romans (it is unlikely that this lexeme refers to Paul's opponents; cf. Jewett, 994).

ὑπὸ τοὺς πόδας. Locative (beneath).

ὑμῶν. Possessive genitive, modifying τοὺς πόδας.
ἐν τάχει. Temporal.
Ἡ χάρις. Nominative absolute.
τοῦ κυρίου. Genitive of source or origin, modifying Ἡ χάρις.
ἡμῶν. Possessive genitive, modifying τοῦ κυρίου.
Ἰησοῦ. Genitive in apposition to τοῦ κυρίου ἡμῶν.
μεθ' ὑμῶν. Accompaniment.

Romans 16:21–23/24

²¹Timothy, my co-worker, greets you, and [so do] Lucius and Jason and
Sosipater, my kinsmen. ²²I, Tertius, the one who wrote this letter in the
Lord, greet you. ²³Gaius, the host of me and the whole church, greets you.
Erastus, the manager of the city, greets you, and Quartus, the brother.

This section of the letter closing contains greetings from several people
to the Roman recipients of this letter. Among them, Tertius, who physically wrote this letter as Paul's amanuensis, is identified.

16:21 Ἀσπάζεται ὑμᾶς Τιμόθεος ὁ συνεργός μου καὶ Λούκιος καὶ
Ἰάσων καὶ Σωσίπατρος οἱ συγγενεῖς μου.

Ἀσπάζεται. Pres mid ind 3rd sg ἀσπάζομαι (cf. the use of the aorist tense-form in 16:3). By use of the present tense-form (imperfective
aspect), Paul draws added attention to Timothy's greeting in this co-text.
ὑμᾶς. Accusative direct object of Ἀσπάζεται.
Τιμόθεος. Nominative subject of Ἀσπάζεται. This is the first of several compound subjects.
ὁ συνεργός. Nominative in apposition to Τιμόθεος.
μου. Possessive genitive, modifying ὁ συνεργός.
καὶ Λούκιος καὶ Ἰάσων καὶ Σωσίπατρος. Compound nominative
subjects of Ἀσπάζεται, along with Τιμόθεος.
οἱ συγγενεῖς. Nominative in apposition to the compound subjects
Λούκιος καὶ Ἰάσων καὶ Σωσίπατρος (see comments on this lexeme in
16:7).
μου. Possessive genitive, modifying οἱ συγγενεῖς.

16:22 ἀσπάζομαι ὑμᾶς ἐγὼ Τέρτιος ὁ γράψας τὴν ἐπιστολὴν ἐν κυρίῳ.

ἀσπάζομαι. Pres mid ind 1st sg ἀσπάζομαι.
ὑμᾶς. Accusative direct object of ἀσπάζομαι.
ἐγὼ. Nominative subject of ἀσπάζομαι. The use of the personal pronoun is emphatic.

Τέρτιος. Nominative in apposition to ἐγώ. This nominative has the epexegetical function because it is used to clarify the referent of ἐγώ, as it would be confused with Paul here. Tertius only appears here in the NT.

ὁ γράψας. Aor act ptc masc nom sg γράφω (substantival). Nominative in apposition to Τέρτιος.

τὴν ἐπιστολὴν. Accusative direct object of γράψας.

ἐν κυρίῳ. Locative (sphere or realm; see notes on ἐν Χριστῷ Ἰησοῦ in 3:24; 6:11). This prepositional word group can modify either ἀσπάζομαι or γράψας (i.e., he either greets them in the Lord or writes in the Lord). Based on the co-text, it probably modifies γράψας, being closer in proximity to this prepositional word group—contrary to most English translations (e.g., NIV, NASB, NKJV, NRSV, ESV; cf. the word order in the greetings of 16:3, 5, 8, 10, 12, 13). As Paul's scribe, he recognizes the gravity of his role in writing this letter.

16:23 ἀσπάζεται ὑμᾶς Γάϊος ὁ ξένος μου καὶ ὅλης τῆς ἐκκλησίας. ἀσπάζεται ὑμᾶς Ἔραστος ὁ οἰκονόμος τῆς πόλεως καὶ Κούαρτος ὁ ἀδελφός.

ἀσπάζεται. Pres mid ind 3rd sg ἀσπάζομαι.

ὑμᾶς. Accusative direct object of ἀσπάζεται.

Γάϊος. Nominative subject of ἀσπάζεται.

ὁ ξένος. Nominative in apposition to Γάϊος. This lexeme usually refers to a stranger or foreigner in the NT, but here it is modulated (with ὅλης τῆς ἐκκλησίας) to refer to a host of someone who is not of their own household (cf. LN 34.60). This is the only occurrence of this lexeme in Romans (cf. Eph 2:12, 19 in Paul).

μου. Possessive genitive, modifying ὁ ξένος.

καὶ. Coordinating conjunction. It connects the two genitive modifiers.

ὅλης τῆς ἐκκλησίας. Possessive genitive, modifying ὁ ξένος. It is parallel to μου. ὅλης functions as an attribute ("the whole church") although it stands in a predicate position (cf. BDAG, 704.1.b.α).

ἀσπάζεται. Pres mid ind 3rd sg ἀσπάζομαι.

ὑμᾶς. Accusative direct object of ἀσπάζεται.

Ἔραστος ... καὶ Κούαρτος. Compound nominative subjects of ἀσπάζεται. When the verb precedes its two (or more) subjects, as here, it is in singular, agreeing with the first (BDF §135).

ὁ οἰκονόμος. Nominative in apposition to Ἔραστος.

τῆς πόλεως. Genitive of definition, modifying ὁ οἰκονόμος. It further defines or circumscribes "manager" to "the city." Some may label this as an objective genitive, if οἰκονόμος were to become a verb ("to manage"). With τῆς πόλεως, οἰκονόμος refers to the city treasurer (LN 57.231).

ὁ ἀδελφός. Nominative in apposition to Κούαρτος.

16:24

This verse is omitted in NA[28] and UBS[5], as with most English translations (except NASB in italics and NKJV, and a footnote in NIV). It appears in later manuscripts (notably D F G L), but none of the major manuscripts (א A B C) contain it (cf. Hurtado; Longenecker, 32–34).

Romans 16:25–27

[25]Now to him who is able to establish you according to my gospel and the preaching of Jesus Christ, according to the mystery which has been silent for long ages, [26]but now manifested and made known through the writings of the prophets according to the commandment of the eternal God for obedience of faith among all the Gentiles, [27]to the only wise God, through Jesus Christ, to whom [be] the glory forever. Amen.

This section, the concluding doxology to the letter, consists of a subjectless (cf. ἡ δόξα in 16:27) and verbless clause complex with several embedded participial clauses (16:25b–26) and a secondary relative clause (16:27a).

16:25 Τῷ δὲ δυναμένῳ ὑμᾶς στηρίξαι κατὰ τὸ εὐαγγέλιόν μου καὶ τὸ κήρυγμα Ἰησοῦ Χριστοῦ, κατὰ ἀποκάλυψιν μυστηρίου χρόνοις αἰωνίοις σεσιγημένου,

Τῷ . . . δυναμένῳ. Pres mid ptc masc dat sg δύναμαι (substantival). Dative indirect object of verbless clause.

δὲ. Adversative conjunction (mild).

ὑμᾶς. Accusative direct object of στηρίξαι.

στηρίξαι. Aor act inf στηρίζω (complementary). The infinitive is a complement of δυναμένῳ.

κατὰ τὸ εὐαγγέλιόν . . . καὶ τὸ κήρυγμα. Standard.

μου. Possessive genitive, modifying τὸ εὐαγγέλιόν.

Ἰησοῦ Χριστοῦ. Genitive of definition or description, modifying τὸ κήρυγμα. It further describes or circumscribes "preaching" to "Jesus Christ." Some may label this as an objective genitive, if κήρυγμα were to become a verb (to preach).

κατὰ ἀποκάλυψιν. Standard. It is parallel to κατὰ τὸ εὐαγγέλιόν . . . καὶ τὸ κήρυγμα above.

μυστηρίου. Genitive of definition or description, modifying ἀποκάλυψιν. It further describes or circumscribes "revelation" to "mystery." Some may label this as an objective genitive, if ἀποκάλυψιν is changed to a verb (to reveal).

χρόνοις αἰωνίοις. Dative of time. The fronting of the dative before the predicate σεσιγημένου indicates clausal prominence.

σεσιγημένου. Prf mid ptc neut gen sg σιγάω (attributive). The participle modifies μυστηρίου (fourth attributive position). The perfect tense-form (stative aspect) depicts the process as being in a state of silence.

16:26 φανερωθέντος δὲ νῦν διά τε γραφῶν προφητικῶν κατ' ἐπιταγὴν τοῦ αἰωνίου θεοῦ εἰς ὑπακοὴν πίστεως εἰς πάντα τὰ ἔθνη γνωρισθέντος,

This clause contains two genitive participles, one beginning the verse and the other ending the verse, both parallel to σεσιγημένου and in attributive structure modifying μυστηρίου.

φανερωθέντος. Aor pass ptc neut gen sg φανερόω (attributive). This participle modifies μυστηρίου (16:25) and is parallel to σεσιγημένου (16:25).

δὲ. Adversative conjunction (mild).

νῦν. Adverb (temporal).

διά ... γραφῶν προφητικῶν. Instrumental.

τε. Enclitic, emphatic conjunction.

κατ' ἐπιταγὴν. Standard.

τοῦ αἰωνίου θεοῦ. Genitive of source or origin, modifying ἐπιταγὴν.

εἰς ὑπακοὴν. Purpose.

πίστεως. Genitive of quality, modifying ὑπακοὴν. "Obedience" is qualified as "of faith."

εἰς πάντα τὰ ἔθνη. Distributional. The fronting of the prepositional word group before the predicate γνωρισθέντος reflects clausal prominence.

γνωρισθέντος. Aor pass ptc neut gen sg γνωρίζω (attributive). This is the third attributive participle that modifies μυστηρίου (16:25).

16:27 μόνῳ σοφῷ θεῷ, διὰ Ἰησοῦ Χριστοῦ, ᾧ ἡ δόξα εἰς τοὺς αἰῶνας, ἀμήν.

μόνῳ σοφῷ θεῷ. Dative in apposition to Τῷ ... δυναμένῳ in 16:25.

διὰ Ἰησοῦ Χριστοῦ. Instrumental.

ᾧ. Dative in apposition to μόνῳ σοφῷ θεῷ, which also functions as its antecedent.

ἡ δόξα. Nominative absolute.

εἰς τοὺς αἰῶνας. Goal.

ἀμήν. Asseverative particle (see 1:25).

GLOSSARY

Actor—The logical subject of the clause, as opposed to the grammatical subject. The Actor is the participant in the clause performing the verbal process, the grammatical subject in an active voice clause, or the grammatical object in a passive voice clause.

Adjectivizer—An article that transforms a non-adjective into an adjectival modifier. Thus, in the phrase τὸν διὰ Ἰησοῦ Χριστοῦ (Phil 1:11), the article τὸν transforms the prepositional phrase διὰ Ἰησοῦ Χριστοῦ into an attributive modifier of καρπὸν.

Adjunctive—Providing something additional and supplemental. The term is used in relation to Greek conjunctions, especially καί when it signifies "also."

Agent/Agency—The individual or thing that is responsible for the verbal process. In active voice clauses, the grammatical subject is the agent, while in passive voice clauses, the agent can be unspecified, or specified through the use of prepositions such as διά, ὑπό, or even ἐν.

Aktionsart—The kind or objective quality of the verbal action, e.g., punctiliar, durative, iterative, inceptive, etc.

Alliteration—The repetition of similar sounds in a stream of lexemes.

Anacoluthon—A logical and syntactical break in the flow of a sentence, in which a different idea and corresponding syntax begin without completing what came before.

Anaphoric—Referring back to a word or phrase that is coreferential. In the sentence "Ben went on a drive, and he liked it," the pronoun *he* refers, anaphorically, to *Ben*.

Anarthrous—Not modified by an article.

Antecedent—A word to which another word later in the discourse refers. A relative pronoun's antecedent is the preceding word about which the relative clause will provide further information.

Antepenult—The third-to-last syllable in a word, followed by the penult (second-to-last syllable) and ultima (last syllable).

Apodosis—The second element, providing the "then" clause after the protasis in a conditional sentence.

Apposition—A semantic relationship by which an item (such as a word, word group, or clause) further defines or elaborates another. Appositions can be found in any of the cases, as well as infinitives.

Articular—Modified by an article.

Ascensive—Rising or intensifying. The term is often applied to conjunctions, especially καί when it signifies "even."

Aspect—The writer's depiction of an action or process as either: perfective (process depicted as a complete and undifferentiated whole; e.g., "I helped"), imperfective (process depicted as in progress; e.g., "I help" or "I am helping"), or stative (process depicted as a state or condition; e.g., "I had helped").

Asseverative—An item that affirms or declares positively or earnestly; similar to emphatic.

Asyndeton—The absence of conjunctions connecting one clause to the next, effecting a faster sense of pace or intensity of tone. This is the default mode of connecting sentences in the FG.

Attraction—Rather than taking on the case required by its function within its clause, a relative pronoun occasionally reflects or "attracts" to the case of the antecedent.

Background—Material in the word group, clause, or discourse that is least prominent and serve to provide background or supportive information.

Cataphoric—Referring forward to a word or phrase that is coreferential. In the clauses "I saw her; Jane was running," the pronoun *her* refers, cataphorically, to *Jane*.

Causative—An action or circumstance is produced or initiated by the action of the verbal element.

Clausal complement—A clause that serves as direct object. Frequently this involves the use of ὅτι after verbs of speech; e.g., in the sentence καὶ πᾶσα γλῶσσα ἐξομολογήσηται ὅτι κύριος Ἰησοῦς Χριστὸς εἰς δόξαν θεοῦ πατρός ("and every tongue should confess that Jesus Christ is Lord, to the glory of God the Father") in Phil 2:11, the ὅτι clause serves as the clausal complement of ἐξομολογήσηται.

Collocate/Collocation—A regular or standard combination of words that appear together often. For example, in English, "toasted bread" and "grilled steak" are collocations.

Complement—A clause, phrase, or word required to complete a given expression. This is especially common in double accusative constructions; e.g., in the sentence "Emmet calls turtles frogs," *turtles* is the object and *frogs* is the complement. Without the complement, the expression is incomplete.

Concessive—An element introducing an idea, action, or circumstance that runs counter to the main clause. Concessive clauses are typically introduced with "although" or "even though."

Constructio ad sensum—A construction that does not correspond to the expected number or gender dictated by normal syntax, because it is responding to something inherent in the *sense* of that word rather than the word itself as a morphosyntactical entity; e.g., "The crowd is hungry and *are* getting restless." The plural *are* results from conceiving the singular crowd in terms of the multiple individuals making up the crowd.

Copula—The linking verb in an equative or copular clause, connecting a subject and predicate. In the copular clause Ὅσοι οὖν τέλειοι ("Therefore, as many as [are] mature"), the implied copula is ἐσμέν or εἰσίν.

Crasis—The formation of a single word from two words by contraction, e.g., κἀγώ for καὶ ἐγώ.

Development—The use of δέ that signals an advance in an argument or narrative but does not convey the overt continuity or discontinuity of a conjunction or adversative.

Deponency—When verbs with middle, passive, or middle/passive morphology were ascribed active meanings, they were labeled "deponent." This view has faced important challenges. Thus, the BHGNT acknowledges that middle morphology involves nuances associated with middle voice that should be taken into consideration. See Series Introduction for more.

Direct discourse—A record of the speech or thought of a character, introduced by an untranslated ὅτι and placed in quotation marks.

Double accusative construction—Some verbs can take two accusatives. In a person-thing double accusative, verbs of teaching, reminding, clothing, or asking can take an accusative direct object (the person) and an object-complement (the thing). In an object-complement double accusative, verbs of making, sending, calling, and reckoning take both an object and the object's complement in the accusative. In the clause οὐδένα γὰρ ἔχω ἰσόψυχον ("For I have no one like-minded"), οὐδένα is the direct object and ἰσόψυχον is the complement.

Elide/elision—The omission of a letter in a word or of an entire word. In the former case, the closing vowel in certain prepositions or conjunctions may be omitted, as in the α in ἀλλ᾽ ὁ θεὸς (Phil 2:27). In the latter case, an entire word is omitted and must be supplied by reference to context. In Phil 2:15, a repetition of the verb φαίνω in the clause φαίνεσθε ὡς φωστῆρες [φαίνονται] ἐν κόσμῳ ("you shine like luminaries [shine] in the world") is elided, leaving only φωστῆρες ἐν κόσμῳ.

Emphasis—Important information placed in a marked position for greater prominence.

Enclitic—A word that donates its accent to the word directly preceding it, as in πάντοτέ ἐστιν.

Epexegetical—An additional word or group of words that offer greater clarity. Infinitives can function in this way—clarifying or completing words like those relating to duty, ability, expectation, or necessity (e.g., "I hope *to eat*"). Similarly, an epexegetical use of clauses beginning with ἵνα or ὅτι function to clarify or complete an idea. When a head noun is ambiguous, an epexegetical genitive can be used to offer a particular example that clarifies the noun it modifies and may, therefore, be introduced in translation by "namely" or "which is."

Equative verb/clause—Equative clauses link subjects and predicates in constructions of the type "this is that." The verbs that do the linking (typically εἰμί, γίνομαι, or ὑπάρχω) are equative verbs. The sentence ὧν τὸ τέλος [ἐστίν] ἀπώλεια ("whose end [is] destruction") is an equative clause, and the implied ἐστὶν is the equative verb.

External evidence—A term from textual criticism, referring to the evidence of manuscripts and versions (e.g., the text-type or antiquity of particular witnesses to a reading) rather than on considerations relating to the content of the text at hand (e.g., the author's style or theology).

First-class conditional—Stipulates the truth of the protasis (by means of εἰ with an indicative verb) for the sake of argument. The apodosis takes any mood and any tense.

Focal/focus—The key piece of information in a clause, frequently highlighted by placement in a marked position.

Foreground—Material in the word group, clause, or discourse that is prominent and serve to provide mainline or emphatic information.

Frontground—Material in the word group, clause, or discourse that is most prominent and serve to provide heightened emphasis, functioning as attention grabbers.

Fronting/fronted—When an element occurs earlier in the clause or sentence than might be expected in default or standard word order. One example may be when the prepositional word group occurs before the main predicate.

Genitive absolute—A dependent clause consisting of a genitive substantive and an anarthrous genitive participle, which is, most of the time, independent of the verb in the main clause. The participle is usually temporal but can perform any of the adverbial functions of participles.

Genitive of . . .—*quality* attributes a quality to the head term; *description* describes the head term in a very general manner and is typically used when another, more specified category cannot be determined, the "catch all" category; *definition* further defines the head term by restricting its meaning to the genitive; *partitive* (specifies the whole of which the head noun is a part); *possession/ownership/origin/source* reveals some sort of dependent or derivative status for the head term; *object* identifies certain verbs which use genitives for their objects (e.g., Rom 7:1); *comparison* usually comes after a comparative adjective and is introduced with "than" (e.g., "greater *than cats*").

Goal—The logical object of the clause, as opposed to the grammatical object. The Goal is the one receiving the verbal process, the grammatical object in an active voice clause, or the grammatical subject in a passive voice clause (cf. the definition of Actor above).

Grammaticalize—To express semantic information by means of a particular structure (usually the form of an individual word) in a language. For example, the aorist tense-form grammaticalizes perfective verbal aspect.

Hapax legomenon—The only instance of a word recorded in a designated body of literature (in this case, the New Testament).

Head-term—The syntactically dominant or governing term in a construction or word group. Usually the head term is the noun in a nominal word group or the verb in a verbal group. The head term has the same function as the entire construction in which it exists.

Headless relative clause—A relative clause without an antecedent, e.g., "Among you stands [one] *whom you do not know*."

Hendiadys—Two words linked by καί and expressing one idea.

Imperfective (aspect)—The meaning of the present or imperfect tense-forms when used by a writer or speaker to depict an action or process as in progress. See, by contrast, *perfective aspect* and *stative aspect*.

Indeclinable—Having no inflected forms; e.g., apart from a preceding article it is impossible to know whether Ναθαναήλ is nominative, genitive, etc.

Indirect discourse—A record of the content of speech or thought introduced by ὅτι. If someone utters the sentence "I'd like to hold the baby," the indirect discourse would report the content of that utterance but not the utterance itself: "Someone said *he would like to hold the baby*."

Intermediate agent—The personal or impersonal agent by means of whom/which an action took place, though he/she/it is not the ultimate cause or initiator of the action. The intermediate agent is introduced with διά + the agent in genitive case.

Intransitive—A verb that does not take a direct object. Some verbs allow but do not require a direct object and can, therefore, function transitively or intransitively.

Lectio difficilior—A text-critical principle that states that the more difficult reading is more likely to be original.

Left-dislocation—A sentence-structuring device in which the new topic of the discourse is put at the beginning of the sentence and then picked up again with a resumptive pronoun in the main clause; e.g., "*The parents with the new baby*, they need more sleep."

Litotes—Making a statement by negating the opposite idea: "no small feat" = "quite an accomplishment." This kind of understatement typically serves as a means of emphasis.

Marked/unmarked—Labels given to various constructions and morphological items to imply their relative semantic weight. The unmarked structure is often more frequently found, more diverse in form, more regular in structure, of less formal substance, less emphatic, and of minimum essential meaning. The marked structure is often less frequent in appearance, more stable in form, more regular in structure, or of greater formal substance, more emphatic, and of greater significance in meaning.

Metonymy/metonym—Substituting a word or description closely associated with something for the name/term of the thing itself. "Lend me your *ear*" is metonymy for "Lend me your [auditory] attention." In the expression "the enemies of the cross of Christ" (a wooden rendering of Phil 3:18), "the cross" (τοῦ σταυροῦ) is a metonym for the death of Christ.

Nominal clause—A group of words containing a verb and functioning as a noun.

Nominalizer—An article that converts a word, phrase, or clause (frequently adjectives and participial constructions) into substantives.

Penult—The second-to-last syllable in a word, preceded by antepenult (third-to-last syllable) and followed by ultima (last syllable).

Perfective (aspect)—The function of the aorist tense-form when used by a writer or speaker to depict a verbal process summarily as a complete whole, without respect to its progress or completion. See, for contrast, *imperfective aspect* and *stative aspect*.

Periphrastic construction—The combination of an anarthrous participle and a verb of being functioning together like a finite verb.

Pleonasm/pleonastic—The use of additional words beyond what is strictly necessary.

Point/counterpoint set—One statement is negated (usually by οὐ or μή) to reject a possible misconception or to establish a key point of contrast and is followed by a positive statement beginning with and emphasized by an introductory ἀλλά.

Postpositive—Not occurring first in a clause. Postpositive conjunctions include γάρ, οὖν, and δέ.

Predicate nominative/accusative/adjective—The anarthrous element in an equative clause sharing the same case as the subject that it identifies, renames, or describes. In the sentence "Teddie is tough," *tough* is the predicate adjective and would occur in the nominative case.

Prominence—The state of being more emphasized or highlighted than other elements. In Greek this is regularly achieved by means of paradigmatic and syntagmatic structures.

Protasis—The "if" clause in a conditional sentence.

Right-dislocation—A structuring device in which grammatically dispensable information is placed outside of the main clause, thus providing post hoc elaboration of something within the main clause; e.g., "They went outside, Zoe and Lee."

Second-class conditional—The "contrary-to-fact conditional," in which the protasis assumes the falsity of a premise for the sake of argument (by means of εἰ and a secondary tense-form indicative, typically aorist or imperfect). The apodosis typically has ἄν and an indicative secondary tense.

Semitism—Semitic style, idiom, or sentence structure that is not normally found in composition by native speakers/writers of Greek.

Stative (aspect)—The meaning of the perfect and pluperfect tense-forms used by a writer or speaker to depict a verbal process as in a complex state or condition without reference to unfolding action or process.

Substantive—A word which is used like a noun in the clause, such as a participle, infinitive, adjective, and nouns.

Synecdoche—A figure of speech in which one term is used in place of another with which it is associated, specifically involving a part-whole relationship. In the sentence, "Do you have your own *wheels*?" the word "wheels" stands for the entire "vehicle" of which it is a part.

Third-class conditional—Conveys a logical connection, a hypothetical, or a projected eventuality. The protasis uses ἐάν and a subjunctive verb (any tense). The apodosis is in any tense and any mood. A "present general" condition is formed when the apodosis contains a present indicative verb.

Ultima—The final syllable in a word, preceded by penult (second-to-last syllable) and antepenult (third-to-last syllable).

Ultimate agent—The person ultimately authorizing/initiating and, therefore, bearing final responsibility for an action without necessarily carrying out that action him- or herself. The ultimate agent is conveyed by means of the genitive with ὑπό, ἀπό, or παρά.

Unmarked—See *marked/unmarked* above.

Word group—A group of words that form a single unit, such as a prepositional word group (e.g., διὰ Ἰησοῦ Χριστοῦ) or a nominal word group (e.g., υἱὸς τοῦ Θεοῦ).

WORKS CITED

Aasgaard, Reidar. *'My Beloved Brothers and Sisters!'*: *Christian Sibling-ship in Paul*. JSNTSup 265. London: T&T Clark, 2004.

Adams, Sean A. "Paul's Letter Opening and Greek Epistolography: A Matter of Relationship." Pages 33–56 in *Paul and the Ancient Letter Form*. Pauline Studies 6. Edited by Stanley E. Porter and Sean A. Adams. Leiden: Brill, 2010.

Althaus, Paul. *Der Brief an die Römer*. NTD. Gottingen: Vandenhoeck & Ruprecht, 1970.

Arzt-Grabner, Peter. "Paul's Letter Thanksgiving." Pages 129–58 in *Paul and the Ancient Letter Form*. Pauline Studies 6. Edited by Stanley E. Porter and Sean A. Adams. Leiden: Brill, 2010.

Bakker, Egbert J. "Voice, Aspect and Aktionsart: Middle and Passive in Ancient Greek." Pages 23–47 in *Voice: Form and Function*. Typological Studies in Language 27. Edited by B. A. Fox and P. J. Hopper. Philadelphia: John Benjamins, 1994.

Banks, Robert. *Paul's Idea of Community*. Rev. ed. Peabody, MA: Hendrickson, 1994.

Barclay, John M.G. *Paul and the Gift*. Grand Rapids: Eerdmans, 2016.

Barr, James. *The Semantics of Biblical Language*. Oxford: Oxford University Press, 1961.

———. *Biblical Words for Time*. SBT 33. 2nd ed. London: SCM Press, 1969.

———. "'Abbā Isn't 'Daddy.'" *Journal of Theological Studies* 39 (1988): 28–47.

Bauckham, Richard. *Gospel Women: Studies of the Named Women of the Gospels*. Grand Rapids: Eerdmans, 2002.

Beet, Joseph Agar. *Commentary on St. Paul's Epistle to the Romans*. 7th ed. London: Hodder & Stoughton, 1890.

Belleville, Linda L. "Ἰουνιαν ἐπίσημοι ἐν τοῖς ἀποστόλοις: A Re-Examination of Romans 16.7 in Light of Primary Source Materials." *New Testament Studies* 51 (2005): 231–49.

Bird, Michael F., and Preston M. Sprinkle, eds. *The Faith of Jesus Christ: The Pistis Christou Debate.* Peabody, MA: Hendrickson, 2009.

Black, Matthew. *Romans.* NCB. Grand Rapids: Eerdmans, 1973.

Blackwell, Ben C. *Christosis: Pauline Soteriology in Light of Deification in Irenaeus and Cyril of Alexandria.* WUNT 2:314. Tübingen: Mohr Siebeck, 2011.

Blass, F., A. Debrunner, and R.W. Funk. *A Greek Grammar of the New Testament and Other Early Christian Literature.* 11th ed. Chicago: University of Chicago Press, 1961.

Breytenbach, Cilliers. "'Charis' and 'Eleos' in Paul's Letter to the Romans." Pages 247–77 in *The Letter to the Romans.* BETL 226. Edited by Udo Schnelle. Leuven: Peeters, 2009.

Brookins, Timothy A., and Bruce W. Longenecker. *1 Corinthians 1–9: A Handbook on the Greek Text.* BHGNT. Waco, TX: Baylor University Press 2016.

Bruce, F. F. *Romans.* TNTC. Rev. ed. Grand Rapids: Eerdmans, 1985.

Burk, Denny. "The Righteousness of God (Dikaiosune Theou) and Verbal Genitives: A Grammatical Clarification." *Journal for the Study of the New Testament* 34 (2012): 346–60.

Campbell, Constantine R. *Basics of Verbal Aspect in Biblical Greek.* Grand Rapids: Zondervan, 2008.

Campbell, Douglas A. *The Rhetoric of Righteousness in Romans 3.21–26.* JSNTSup 65. Sheffield: JSOT Press, 1992.

Caragounis, Chrys C. "Rom. 5.15–16 in the Context of 5.12–21: Contrast or Comparison." *New Testament Studies* 31 (1985): 142–48.

———. *The Development of Greek and the New Testament: Morphology, Syntax, Phonology, and Textual Transmission.* Grand Rapids: Baker Academic, 2006.

Carraway, George. *Christ Is God over All: Romans 9:5 in the Context of Romans 9–11.* LNTS 489. London: Bloomsbury, 2013.

Cirafesi, Wally V. "'To Fall Short' or 'To Lack'? Reconsidering the Meaning and Translation of ὙΣΤΕΡΕΩ in Romans 3:23." *Expository Times* 123 (2012): 429–34.

Collins, Raymond F. "A Significant Decade: The Trajectory of the Hellenistic Epistolary Thanksgiving." Pages 159–84 in *Paul and the Ancient Letter Form.* Pauline Studies 6. Edited by Stanley E. Porter and Sean A. Adams. Leiden: Brill, 2010.

Colwell, E. C. "A Definite Rule for the Use of the Article in the Greek NT." *Journal of Biblical Literature* 52 (1933): 12–21.

Conrad, Carl W. "New Observations on Voice in the Ancient Greek Verb. November 19, 2002." Online: http://artsci.wustl.edu/~cwconrad/docs/NewObsAncGrkVc.pdf. Accessed June 8, 2009.

Cousar, Charles B. *A Theology of the Cross: The Death of Jesus in the Pauline Letters*. Philadelphia: Fortress, 1990.

Cranfield, C. E. B. *A Critical and Exegetical Commentary on the Epistle to the Romans*. 2 vols. ICC. Edinburgh: T&T Clark, 1975/79.

Crook, Zeba "The Divine Benefactions of Paul the Client." *Journal of Greco-Roman Christianity and Judaism* 2 (2001–2005): 9–26.

Culy, Martin M. "The Clue is in the Case: Distinguishing Adjectival and Adverbial Participles." *Perspectives in Religious Studies* (2003): 441–53.

———. *I, II, III John: A Handbook on the Greek Text*. BHGNT. Waco, TX: Baylor University Press, 2004.

———. "Double Case Constructions in Koine Greek." *Journal of Greco-Roman Christianity and Judaism* 6 (2009): 82–106.

Culy, Martin M., Mikeal C. Parsons, and Joshua J. Stigall. *Luke: A Handbook on the Greek Text*. BHGNT. Waco, TX: Baylor University Press, 2010.

Daube, David. "Rabbinic Methods of Interpretation and Hellenistic Rhetoric." *Hebrew Union College Annual* 22 (1949): 239–64.

Decker, Rodney J. *Temporal Deixis of the Greek Verb in the Gospel of Mark with Reference to Verbal Aspect*. Studies in Biblical Greek 10. New York: Peter Lang, 2001.

Dunn, James D.G. *Romans*. 2 vols. WBC 38. Dallas: Word, 1988.

Ehrenberg, Victor, and A. H. M. Jones. *Documents Illustrating the Reigns of Augustus and Tiberius*. 2nd ed. Oxford: Clarendon, 1955.

Enderlein, Stephen E. "The Faithfulness of the Second Adam in Romans 3:21–26: A Response to Porter and Cirafesi." *Journal for the Study of Paul and His Letters* 3 (2013): 11–24.

Engberg-Pedersen, Troels. "Gift-Giving and God's Charis: Bourdieu, Seneca and Paul in Romans 1–8." Pages 95–111 in *The Letter to the Romans*. BETL 226. Edited by Udo Schnelle. Leuven: Peeters, 2009.

Epp, Eldon Jay. *Junia: The First Woman Apostle*. Minneapolis: Fortress, 2005.

Exler, Francis Xavier. *The Form of the Ancient Greek Letter*. Washington, DC: Catholic University Press, 1923.

Fanning, Buist M. *Verbal Aspect in New Testament Greek*. Oxford: Clarendon, 1990.

Fantin, Joseph D. *The Lord of the Entire World: Lord Jesus, a Challenge to Lord Caesar?* New Testament Monographs 31. Sheffield: Sheffield Phoenix, 2011.

Fee, Gordon D. *Pauline Christology: An Exegetical-Theological Study.* Peabody, MA: Hendrickson, 2007.

Fitzmyer, Joseph A. *Romans.* Anchor Bible 33. New York: Doubleday, 1993.

Gathercole, Simon J. *Where Is Boasting? Early Jewish Soteriology and Paul's Response in Romans 1–5.* Grand Rapids: Eerdmans, 2002.

Gundry, Robert H. *Soma in Biblical Theology with Emphasis on Pauline Anthropology.* SNTSMS 29. Cambridge: Cambridge University Press, 1976.

Halliday, M. A. K. *Explorations in the Functions of Language.* EILS. London: Arnold, 1973.

———. *Language as Social Semiotic: The Social Interpretation of Language and Meaning.* London: Edward Arnold, 1978.

———. *Halliday's Introduction to Functional Grammar.* London: Arnold, 1st ed., 1985; 2nd ed., 1994; 3rd ed., 2004; 4th ed., 2014.

Halliday, M. A. K., and Ruqaiya Hasan. *Cohesion in English.* London: Longman, 1976.

———. *Language, Context, and Text: Aspects of Language in a Social Semiotic Perspective.* Geelong, Victoria, Australia: Deakin University Press, 1985.

Harris, Murray J. *Jesus as God: The New Testament Use of Theos in Reference to Jesus.* Grand Rapids: Baker, 1992.

———. *Prepositions and Theology in the Greek New Testament: An Essential Reference Resource for Exegesis.* Grand Rapids: Zondervan, 2012.

Hays, Richard B. "Psalm 143 as Testimony to the Righteousness of God." Pages 50–60 in *The Conversion of the Imagination: Paul as Interpreter of Israel's Scripture.* Grand Rapids: Eerdmans, 2005.

Huffman, Douglas S. *Verbal Aspect and the Prohibitions in the Greek New Testament.* SBG 16. New York: Peter Lang, 2014.

Hultgren, Arland J. *Paul's Letter to the Romans: A Commentary.* Grand Rapids: Eerdmans, 2011.

Hurtado, Larry W. "The Doxology at the End of Romans." Pages 185–99 in *New Testament Textual Criticism: Its Significance for Exegesis (Essays in Honour of Bruce M. Metzger).* Edited by Eldon Jay Epp and Gordon D. Fee. Oxford: Clarendon, 1981.

Jeremias, Joachim. *The Prayers of Jesus.* SBT Second Series 6. Translated by John Bowden, Christoph Burchard, and John Reumann. London: SCM Press, 1967.

Jewett, Robert. *Romans: A Commentary.* Hermeneia. Minneapolis: Fortress, 2007.

Käsemann, Ernst. *New Testament Questions of Today.* Translated by W. J. Montague. Philadelphia: Fortress, 1969.

———. *Commentary on Romans*. Translated and edited by Geoffrey W. Bromiley. Grand Rapids: Eerdmans, 1980.

Kirk, J. R. Daniel. *Unlocking Romans: Resurrection and the Justification of God*. Grand Rapids: Eerdmans, 2008.

Lee, Jae Hyun. *Paul's Gospel in Romans: A Discourse Analysis of Rom 1:16–8:39*. Linguistic Biblical Studies 3. Leiden: Brill, 2010.

Leenhardt, Franz J. *The Epistle to the Romans: A Commentary*. Translated by Harold Knight. New York: World, 1961.

Liddell, H. G., and R. Scott. *A Greek-English Lexicon*. 9th ed. with revised supplement. Oxford: Clarendon, 1999.

Longenecker, Richard N. *Introducing Romans: Critical Issues in Paul's Most Famous Letter*. Grand Rapids: Eerdmans, 2011.

Louw, Johannes P., and Eugene A. Nida. *Greek-English Lexicon of the New Testament: Based on Semantic Domains*. 2 vols. New York: United Bible Societies, 1988.

Lyons, John. *Semantics*. 2 vols. Cambridge: Cambridge University Press, 1977.

McGaughy, Lane C. *A Descriptive Analysis of EINAI as a Linking Verb in NT Greek*. SBLDS 6. Missoula, MT: Scholars, 1972.

Marshall, I. Howard. "The Meaning of 'Reconciliation.'" Pages 117–32 in *Unity and Diversity in New Testament Theology: Essays in Honor of George E. Ladd*. Edited by Robert A. Guelich. Grand Rapids: Eerdmans, 1978.

Martin, Troy W. "Investigating the Pauline Letter Body: Issues, Methods, and Approaches." Pages 183–212 in *Paul and the Ancient Letter Form*. Edited by Stanley E. Porter and Sean A. Adams. PAST 6. Leiden: Brill, 2010.

Mathewson, David L. *Voice and Mood: A Linguistic Approach*. Essentials of Biblical Greek Grammar. Grand Rapids: Baker Academic, 2021.

McKay, K. L. *A New Syntax of the Verb in New Testament Greek: An Aspectual Approach*. SBG 5. New York: Peter Lang, 1994.

Metzger, Bruce M. *A Textual Commentary on the Greek New Testament*. 2nd ed. Stuttgart: Deutsche Bibelgesellschaft, 2002.

Moffatt, James. *Grace in the New Testament*. London: Hodder & Stoughton, 1931.

Moo, Douglas J. *The Epistle to the Romans*. NICNT. Grand Rapids: Eerdmans, 1996.

Moorhouse, A. C. *Studies in the Greek Negatives*. Cardiff: University of Wales Press, 1959.

Morris, Leon. *The Epistle to the Romans*. PNTC; Grand Rapids: Eerdmans, 1988.

Moule, C. F. D. *An Idiom Book of NT Greek*. 2nd ed. Cambridge: Cambridge University Press, 1959.

Moulton, James Hope. *Prolegomena*. Vol. 1 of *A Grammar of New Testament Greek*. 3rd ed. Edinburgh: T&T Clark, 1908.

Murray, John. *The Epistle to the Romans*. 2 vols. Grand Rapids: Eerdmans, 1968.

Novenson, Matthew V. "Can the Messiahship of Jesus Be Read off Paul's Grammar? Nils Dahl's Criteria 50 Years Later." *New Testament Studies* 56 (2010): 396–412.

———. *Christ among the Messiahs: Christ Language in Paul and Messiah Language in Ancient Judaism*. New York: Oxford University Press, 2012.

O'Brien, Peter T. *Introductory Thanksgivings in the Letters of Paul*. NovTSup 49. Leiden: Brill, 1977.

Ong, Hughson T. "Has the True Meaning and Purpose of the Lord's Prayer Been Lost? A Sociolinguistic Study of the Lord's Prayer in Dialogue with Wilson-Kastner and Crossan." *McMaster Journal of Theology and Ministry* 14 (2012–13): 98–123.

Pao, David W. "Gospel within the Constraints of an Epistolary Form: Pauline Introductory Thanksgivings and Paul's Theology of Thanksgiving." Pages 101–28 in *Paul and the Ancient Letter Form*. Pauline Studies 6. Edited by Stanley E. Porter and Sean A. Adams. Leiden: Brill, 2010.

Pennington, Jonathan T. "Deponency in Koine Greek: The Grammatical Question and the Lexicographical Dilemma." *Trinity Journal* 24 (2003): 55–76.

Peters, Ronald D. *The Greek Article: A Functional Grammar of ὁ-items in the Greek New Testament with Special Emphasis on the Greek Article*. Linguistic Biblical Studies 9. Leiden: Brill, 2014.

Porter, Stanley E. *Verbal Aspect in the Greek of the New Testament, with Reference to Tense and Mood*. SBG 1. New York: Peter Lang, 1989.

———. "The Argument of Romans 5: Can a Rhetorical Question Make a Difference?" *Journal of Biblical Literature* 110 (1991): 655–77. Reprinted and revised in Stanley E. Porter, *Studies in the Greek New Testament: Theory and Practice*. Pages 213–38. SBG 6. New York: Peter Lang, 1996.

———. *Idioms of the Greek New Testament*. BLG 2. 2nd ed. Sheffield: JSOT Press, 1994a.

———. *Καταλλάσσω in Ancient Greek Literature, with Reference to the Pauline Writings*. EFN 5. Córdoba: Ediciones El Almendro, 1994b.

———. "Prominence: An Overview." Pages 45–74 in *The Linguist as Pedagogue: Trends in the Teaching and Linguistic Analysis of the Greek New Testament*. Edited by Stanley E. Porter and Matthew Brook O'Donnell. New Testament Monographs 11. Sheffield: Sheffield Phoenix, 2009.

———. *The Letter to the Romans: A Linguistic and Literary Commentary*. NTM 37. Sheffield: Sheffield Phoenix, 2015.

Porter, Stanley E., and Wally V. Cirafesi. "ὑστερέω and πίστις Χριστοῦ in Romans 3:23: A Response to Steven Enderlein." *Journal for the Study of Paul and His Letters* 3 (2013): 1–9.

Porter, Stanley E., and Matthew Brook O'Donnell. *Discourse Analysis and the Greek New Testament: Text-Generating Resources*. T&T Clark Greek Language Reference Library. London: T&T Clark, 2023.

Porter, Stanley E., and Andrew W. Pitts. "Πίστις with a Preposition and Genitive Modifier: Lexical, Semantic, and Syntactic Considerations in the πίστις Χρίστου Discussion." Pages 33–53 in *The Faith of Jesus Christ: Exegetical, Biblical, and Theological Studies*. Edited by Michael F. Bird and Preston M. Sprinkle. Peabody, MA: Hendrickson, 2009.

———. "The Disclosure Formula in the Epistolary Papyri and in the New Testament: Development, Form, Function, and Syntax." Pages 421–38 in *The Language of the New Testament: Context, History, and Development*. Linguistic Biblical Studies 6. Edited by Stanley E. Porter and Andrew W. Pitts. Leiden: Brill, 2013.

Porter, Stanley E., and Jeffrey T. Reed. "Philippians as a Macro-Chiasm and Its Exegetical Significance." *New Testament Studies* 44 (1998): 213–31.

Porter, Stanley E., Jeffrey T. Reed, and Matthew Brook O'Donnell. *Fundamentals of New Testament Greek*. Grand Rapids: Eerdmans, 2010.

Reed, Jeffrey T. "Are Paul's Thanksgivings 'Epistolary'?" *Journal for the Study of the New Testament* 61 (1996): 87–99.

———. *A Discourse Analysis of Philippians: Method and Rhetoric in the Debate over Literary Integrity*. JSNTSup 136. Sheffield: Sheffield Academic, 1997.

Robertson, A. T. *A Grammar of the GNT in the Light of Historical Research*. Nashville: Broadman, 1934.

Runge, Steven E. *Discourse Grammar of the Greek New Testament: A Practical Introduction for Teaching and Exegesis*. Peabody, MA: Hendrickson, 2010.

———. "Contrastive Substitution and the Greek Verb: Reassessing Porter's Argument." *Novum Testamentum* 56 (2014): 154–73.

Sanday, William, and A. C. Headlam. *A Critical and Exegetical Commentary on the Epistle to the Romans*. 5th ed. ICC. Edinburgh: T&T Clark, 1902.

Schlier, Heinrich. *Der Römerbrief.* HTKNT 6. Freiburg: Herder, 1977.

Schnider, Franz, and Werner Stenger. *Studien zum Neutestamentlichen Briefformular*. NTTS 11. Leiden: Brill, 1987.

Schreiner, Thomas R. *Romans*. BECNT. Grand Rapids; Baker, 1998.

Schubert, Paul. *The Form and Function of the Pauline Thanksgivings*. Berlin: Töpelmann, 1939.

Scott, James M. *Adoption as Sons of God: An Exegetical Investigation into the Background of ΥΙΟΘΕΣΙΑ in the Pauline Corpus*. WUNT 2:48. Tübingen: Mohr Siebeck, 1992.

Seifrid, Mark A. *Justification by Faith: The Origin and Development of a Central Pauline Theme*. Leiden: Brill, 1992.

Song, Changwon. *Reading Romans as a Diatribe*. Studies in Biblical Literature 59. New York: Peter Lang, 2004.

Stowers, Stanley K. *The Diatribe and Paul's Letter to the Romans*. SBLDS 57. Atlanta: Scholars, 1981.

———. *Letter Writing in Greco-Roman Antiquity*. Philadelphia: Westminster, 1986.

Stuhlmacher, Peter. *Paul's Letter to the Romans*. Translated by Scott J. Hafemann. Louisville: Westminster/John Knox, 1994. Originally *Der Brief an die Römer*. NTD 6.14. Göttingen: Vandenhoeck & Ruprecht, 1994.

Sumney, Jerry L., ed. *Reading Paul's Letter to the Romans*. Atlanta: SBL, 2012.

Taylor, Bernard A. "Deponency and Greek Lexicography." Pages 167–76 in *Biblical Greek Language and Lexicography: Essays in Honor of Frederick W. Danker*. Edited by B. A. Taylor et al. Grand Rapids: Eerdmans, 2004.

Thrall, M. E. *Greek Particles in the NT: Linguistic and Exegetical Studies*. Leiden: Brill, 1962.

Tite, Philip L. "How to Begin, and Why? Diverse Functions of the Pauline Prescript within a Greco-Roman Context." Pages 57–100 in *Paul and the Ancient Letter Form*. Pauline Studies 6. Edited by Stanley E. Porter and Sean A. Adams. Leiden: Brill, 2010.

Vaughan, C. J. *St Paul's Epistle to the Romans*. 5th ed. London: Macmillan, 1880.

Wallace, Daniel B. "The Semantic Range of the Article-Noun-Kai-Noun Plural Construction in the NT." *Grace Theological Journal* 4 (1983): 59–62.

———. *Greek Grammar Beyond the Basics: An Exegetical Syntax of the NT*. Grand Rapids: Zondervan, 1996.

Weima, Jeffrey A. D. *Neglected Endings: The Significance of the Pauline Letter*. JSNTSup 101. Sheffield: JSOT Press, 1994.

Wengst, Klaus. *"Freut euch, ihr Völker, mit Gottes Volk!": Israel und die Völker als Thema des Paulus—ein Gang durch den Römerbrief*. Stuttgart: Kohlhammer, 2008.

Westfall, Cynthia Long. *A Discourse Analysis of the Letter to the Hebrews: The Relationship between Form and Meaning*. JSNTSup 297. LNTS 11. New York: Bloomsbury/T&T Clark, 2005.

White, John L. *The Form and Function of the Body of the Greek Letter: A Study of the Letter-Body in the Non-Literary Papyri and in Paul the Apostle*. 2nd ed. SBLDS 5; Missoula, MT: Scholars, 1972.

———. *Light from Ancient Letters*. FFNT. Philadelphia: Fortress, 1986.

Wilckens, Ulrich. *Der Brief an die Römer*. 3 vols. EKK 6. Zürich: Benziger Verlag; Neukirchen-Vluyn: Neukirchener Verlag, 1978–1982.

Winer, Georg Benedict. *A Treatise on the Grammar of New Testament Greek*. 3rd ed. Translated by W. F. Moulton. Edinburgh: T&T Clark, 1882.

Wright, N. T. *Paul and the Faithfulness of God*. 2 vols. Minneapolis: Fortress, 2013.

———. "A New Perspective on Käsemann? Apocalyptic, Covenant, and the Righteousness of God." Pages 243–58 in *Studies in the Pauline Epistles: Essays in Honor of Douglas J. Moo*. Edited by Matthew S. Harmon and Jay E. Smith. Grand Rapids: Zondervan, 2014.

Yoon, David I. "Ancient Letters of Recommendation and 2 Corinthians 3.1–3: A Literary Analysis." *Journal of Greco-Roman Christianity and Judaism* 12 (2016): 45–72.

———. *A Discourse Analysis of Galatians and the New Perspective on Paul*. LBS 17. Leiden: Brill, 2019.

———. "James Barr and Erroneous Method in Biblical Theology: *Paul and the Gift* as a Test Case." Pages 278–94 in *James Barr Assessed: Evaluating His Legacy over the Last Sixty Years*. Edited by Stanley E. Porter. BINS 192. Leiden: Brill, 2021.

Zerwick, Maximilian. *Biblical Greek: Illustrated by Examples*. English Edition adapted from the Fourth Latin Edition by Joseph Smith. Rome: Pontifical Biblical Institute, 1963.

Ziesler, John. *Paul's Letter to the Romans*. Philadelphia: Trinity Press International, 1989.

AUTHOR INDEX

GRAMMAR INDEX